AIR International VOLUME ELEVEN

ILLUSTRATIONS

Photographs half-tone and (c) colour

Tone illustrations and colour (c) drawings

Line illustrations and cut-away drawings (c/a)

AIR International

Volume 11   Number 1   July 1976

Managing Editor   William Green
Editor   Gordon Swanborough
Modelling Editor   Fred J Henderson
Contributing Artists   Dennis Punnett
                       John Weal
Cover Art   W R Hardy
Contributing Photographer
                       Stephen Peltz
Editorial Representative, Washington
                       Norman Polmar
Publisher   Donald Hannah
Circulation Director   Donald Syner
Subscription Manager   Claire Sillette
Advertising/Public Relations
                       Elizabeth Baker
Advertising Manager   Jim Boyd

Editorial Offices:
The AIR INTERNATIONAL, PO Box 16,
Bromley, BR2 7RB Kent.

**Subscription, Advertising and
Circulation Offices:**
The AIR INTERNATIONAL, De Worde
House, 283 Lonsdale Road, London
SW13 9QW. Telephone 01-878 2454.
US and Canadian readers may address
subscriptions and general enquiries to
AIR INTERNATIONAL PO Box 353, White-
stone, NY 11357 for onward transmis-
sion to the UK, from where all corres-
pondence is answered and orders
despatched.

MEMBER OF THE AUDIT   ABC
BUREAU OF CIRCULATIONS

Subscription rates, inclusive of postage,
direct from the publishers, per year:
United Kingdom   £5·50
USA $17·50
Canada $17·50

Rates for other countries and for air mail
subscriptions available on request from
the Subscription Department at the
above address.

The AIR INTERNATIONAL is published
monthly by Fine Scroll Limited, distributed by Ducimus Books Ltd and
printed by William Caple & Co Ltd,
Chevron Press, Leicester, England.
Editorial contents © 1976 by Pilot Press
Limited. The views expressed by named
contributors and correspondents are their
own and do not necessarily reflect the
views of the editors. Neither the editors
nor the publishers accept responsibility
for any loss or damage, however caused,
to manuscripts or illustrations submitted
to the AIR INTERNATIONAL.

Second Class postage approved at New
York, NY. USA Mailing Agents: Air-Sea
Freight Inc, 527 Madison Avenue, New
York, NY 10022.

CONTENTS

**WRENDEZVOUS
WITH WREN**

'It's called a flying boat, my boy — you just add water'.

AIRSCENE

MILITARY AFFAIRS

ABU DHABI

It has been unofficially reported that the Abu Dhabi government has at last placed its long-awaited **repeat order for** Dassault-Breguet **Mirages,** preliminary discussions concerning which were initially held early in 1974 (see *Airscene*/April 1974). The new order reportedly covers 18-20 Mirages of an unspecified version — the original discussions allegedly concerned four two-seat Mirage IIIDADs and 14 single-seat Mirage IIIEADs and IIIRADs — and these are expected to replace the Hunter Mk 76s and 76As currently equipping one ADAF squadron and are likely to be delivered during 1977-78.

ARGENTINA

The **Army's air component,** the *Comando de Aviación Ejercito,* is continuing its limited **expansion** and modernisation programme, the latest acquisitions including five Cessna T-41 trainers and five Cessna 207 Turbo Skywagon light utility aircraft purchased under an agreement worth more than $1·5m (£830,000), including spares and support equipment.

CANADA

On 19 May, it was announced that the Canadian **government has cancelled** its $614m (£324m) fixed-price **contract for** 18 Lockheed **CP-3C** maritime patrol aircraft, which, barely a week earlier, had been announced by Lockheed as its biggest-ever international contract, with a total value (including additional spares that had not been specifically priced) of the order of $750m (£416m). The contract was contingent on completion of the financing to a total of $375m (£208m) to cover the first three years of the contract, but the consortium of 19 Canadian banks that was to have provided this financing has now refused funding owing to the unsatisfactory terms offered by the Canadian government. The Canadian cabinet has apparently voted against the use of public funds to support the contract. Delivery of the 18 CP-3Cs was scheduled between May 1979 and February 1980, and the eventual total of industrial offsets received by Canadian industry was expected to reach $686m (£381m). Various alternatives have since been discussed between Lockheed and Canadian defence officials, the options including a reduction in the number of CP-3C aircraft to be purchased initially, procurement of a simpler, less costly version of the Orion and stretching the programme over a longer period of time, although the last-mentioned option would undoubtedly increase total cost as well as delay the planned operational schedule.

DENMARK

The *Kongelige Danske Flyvevåben* began taking **delivery of** its additional batch of five two-seat **TF-35 Drakens** from Saab-Scania in May. The supplementary TF-35s, ordered by the Air Material Command on 29 November 1973, are to be operated by the training flight at Karup, the *Flyvevåben* Draken operational base. The new deliveries bring total *Flyvevåben* Draken procurement to 51 aircraft.

EIRE

The protracted evaluation by the Army Air Corps of current light training aircraft to succeed the Chipmunk in the primary training rôle and to fulfil a newly-formulated armed coastal patrol task has finally resulted in an **order** being placed **for** 10 SIAI-Marchetti **SF 260W Warriors** with deliveries commencing in September and being completed by the year's end. In announcing the purchase on 4 April, the Defence Department stressed the fact that the Warrior possessed sufficient range to permit its use for coastal patrol and fishery protection tasks when required. The refurbished CM 170-2 Magister basic trainers — the delivery of the last two of the six purchased reportedly being imminent at the time of closing for press — are currently being fitted out with new avionics by Aer Lingus, and the Air Corps is not withdrawing its three Vampire T 55s until the Magisters have attained fully operational status. The remainder of the Air Corps inventory comprises six Provost T 51s and T 53s, one Dove Srs 7 and one Dove Srs 8A, eight Aérospatiale Alouette III helicopters and eight Reims-built Cessna FR-172Hs.

FEDERAL GERMANY

According to current Defence Ministry planning, the progressive **replacement** in the *Luftwaffe* **of** the **F-104G** Starfighter force by the Panavia Tornado from 1979 onwards will **not** now be completed **before 1987,** whereas the process was earlier scheduled to be completed by the end of 1983. This suggests that the service lives of a proportion of the *Luftwaffe* F-104Gs will have to be extended by some five years longer than previously anticipated. It will be recalled that the *Luftwaffe* received only 14 of the 50 new-production F-104Gs produced by MBB in 1971-73 (the remainder going to the *Marineflieger)* and although VFW-Fokker modified 240 sets of F-104G wings to extend their fatigue lives during 1972-74, it is likely that a further modification programme will now be necessary to enable a proportion of F-104Gs to remain in the active *Luftwaffe* inventory until the late mid 'eighties. Some *Luftwaffe* F-104Gs have recently been transferred to Portugal (see news item).

The Defence Committee of the Federal German Parliament gave its approval during May to the **purchase of** 322 **Tornado** multi-rôle combat aircraft for the *Luftwaffe* (210) and the *Marineflieger* (112). This approval follows Cabinet approval given on 7 April, and the final approval of the Budget Committee was expected early in June, as this issue closed for press. Total cost of the 322 German Tornados is given as DM 15,500m (£3,357m) at end-1975 prices. The Tornado flight test programme is now proceeding at a rate somewhat higher than projected, after the earlier delays associated with late engine deliveries, and the seventh prototype entered the programme on 30 March. Based at Manching, P-07 is the second "avionics" aircraft, sharing this primary flight test rôle with P-04, also at Manching.

FINLAND

As earlier anticipated, the Finnish government has signed a **contract** worth FMk 63m (£9m) **for** the purchase of 15 **Saab Drakens** comprising the six Saab 35BS Drakens (refurbished ex-*Flygvapen* J 35Bs) which have been operated on lease for a number of years by HävLv 11 (the *Lapin Lennosto*) at Rovaniemi, six low-hour ex-*Flygvapen* J 35F Drakens, the purchase of which was authorised on 10 October 1975, and three ex-*Flygvapen* two-seat S 35C Draken trainers. Also included in the package, delivery of which will be completed by 1978, are spares and a flight simulator. The Drakens will re-equip HävLv 21 (the *Satakunnan Lennosto*) at Pori which is currently operating aged Magister armed trainers. Although *Ilmavoimat* C-in-C, Maj Gen Rauno Meriö, recently referred to a requirement for up to 40 new fighters by 1980 to replace the ageing MiG-21F fighters operated by HävLv 31 (the *Karjalan Lennosto*) at Rissala, it is understood that *Ilmavoimat* currently has no definitive plans for the re-equipment of this unit.

No decision is now expected before September concerning the selection of a new **basic trainer/light strike aircraft** for *Ilmavoimat.* At the time of closing for press, the frontrunners in the contest appear to be the Hawker Siddeley Hawk and the Saab 105S, both contending companies reportedly offering more than 100 per cent of the value of the 50-aircraft contract in industrial offsets. The Hawker Siddeley proposal includes co-production of the Hawk by Valmet and Saab-Scania is proposing that Valmet build some 50 per cent of the Saab 105S airframe as well as assembling the entire aircraft and its General Electric engines. The latter company is, of course, already well established in Finland as a result of Valmet assembly of the Saab 35XS Draken. Aérospatiale has submitted a revised version of the projected turbofan-powered development of the Magister, now known as the Fouga 90, which would offer Valmet the advantage of using much existing tooling and jigging, but is generally considered a non-starter, and somewhat improbable contenders are the Vought TA-7C Corsair and the JuRom (IAR 93) Orao. The Saab 105S is being offered at an average unit price of £1·07m as compared with approximately £1·26m for the Hawk and £1·6m for the Alpha Jet, but apart from cost, the last-mentioned type has a political problem to contend with — under Finland's 1947 Peace Treaty with the Soviet Union, the country may not purchase weapons or combat aircraft of German design or manufacture. It is known that *Ilmavoimat* would like to take delivery of the selected aircraft in 1979-80, but the general consensus is that the September selection deadline is unlikely to be met, although the field may be narrowed to two or three finalists by that time.

FRANCE

Gen Marie-Philippe Fleurot, CO of the *Forces Aériennes Stratégiques,* announced recently that the present **dispersal of** the nine four-**Mirage IVA** long-range strike aircraft *escadrons* between a similar number of bases **is to be changed** for reasons of economy. From this summer, the *escadrons* will be concentrated at fewer bases but will be immediately dispersed in an emergency and the stockpiles of atomic weapons for use by the Mirage IVAs will remain at their present locations (ie, the nine bases hitherto used). A year ago, it was announced that the Mirage IVA force was to have its "alert posture" reduced (see *Airscene*/June 1975).

The **re-equipment** of the *Armée de l'Air* **with** the Dassault-Breguet **Mirage F1C** is now **entering** its **final phase** with the re-equipment of the 12ᵉ *Escadre de Chasse* at Cambrai. All four *escadrons* of the 5ᵉ *Escadre* at Orange and the 30ᵉ *Escadre* at Reims are now operational, each *Escadre* operating 31 Mirage F1Cs (including one in reserve) with approximately 600 personnel (of which some 47 are pilots). Pilots of the 12ᵉ *Escadre* began Mirage F1C conversion in February with the 30ᵉ *Escadre,* and the first *escadron* of the former is expected to attain operational status with its new equipment before the end of this year. The 79th and subsequent Mirage F1Cs delivered to the *Armée de l'Air* have incorporated passive warning radar in the fin. Other modifications include provision for the use of combat flap settings to reduce turning radii, and the last 35 Mirage F1Cs built against the currently-envisaged total procurement are embodying fittings for quick-attachment flight refuelling probes. The *Armée de l'Air* envisages procurement of a small batch of two-seat Mirage F1Bs to follow on the completion of deliveries of the service's 116 F1Cs, these providing facilities for flight refuelling and other specialised training, including the use of Magic AAMs. The prototype Mirage F1B made its first flight at Istres on 26 May.

IRAN

At least six US aerospace **companies** are reported to be **negotiating** with the Iranian government in an **oil-for-weapons barter** deal. The initiative for the barter proposals comes from Iran — these resulting from cashflow problems following on a shortfall in oil revenues coinciding with payments falling due for the country's massive military hardware imports — and items involved are reported to be Boeing E-3A AWACS aircraft, General Dynamics F-16 fighters, McDonnell Douglas F-18L fighters, various Pratt & Whitney engines (primarily the TF30 for the Grumman F-14) and Litton Industries for avionics systems (and destroyers). Even though barter deals are currently being negotiated for the F-16 and the F-18L, it is considered unlikely that *both* types of fighter will be acquired.

On 4 May, an **order** was announced from the Iranian government **for** one Fokker F27 Mk 400M passenger-cargo aircraft and one F27 Mk 600 all-passenger aircraft for operation by Iranian Army Aviation, both aircraft to be delivered during the second half of 1977. The **two F27s** will be equipped with a double Marquardt-reeling launcher installation under the wings which will permit the reeling of targets up to 25,000 ft (7 620 m) behind the aircraft. The Iranian government has previously placed orders with Fokker-VFW for a total of 23 F27s.

It has been unofficially reported that the Iranian government has confirmed its **intention to purchase** up to 30 **Sea Harriers,** the order being contingent on agreement being reached for the purchase of up to four mini-carriers from which the Sea Harriers will operate.

JAPAN

The 11-man **F-X evaluation team** led by Gen Toshimitsu Komatsu left Japan **for the USA** on 21 May for a 50-day investigation intended to make a definitive choice between the Grumman F-14, the McDonnell Douglas F-15 and the General Dynamics F-16 to meet the Air Self-Defence Force's F-X requirement. The ASDF hopes to finalise its selection before September and an analysis of the contenders indicates that the unit cost of the competitors if imported will be approximately $24m (£13·3m) for the F-14, $17m (£9·44m) for the F-15 and $5m (£2·77m) for the F-16. If these aircraft are manufactured under licence in Japan, it is calculated that their respective unit costs will rise to $30m (£16·66m), $22m (£12·2m) and $6m (£3·3m).

The Maritime Self-Defence **Force** is becoming increasingly **concerned over** the **delays in** selecting the **P-XL** maritime patrol aircraft and the continual cost escalation that must inevitably result from these delays. The MSDF anticipates acquiring a total of 60-70 P-XLs of which 41 will be included in the next five-year defence build-up programme at a rate of eight aircraft per year, but increasing doubt is being expressed that procurement of anything like the necessary quantities of aircraft will be possible in view of continuing budgetary restrictions and escalating costs. The MSDF anticipates that a licence-built P-3C Orion will cost approximately $27m (£15m) and the Kawasaki-designed P-XL upwards of $30m (£16·6m), and whereas the service had anticipated approval of an annual budget for

procurement of some $200m (£111m), this now seems likely to be reduced to $130m-$140m (£72m-£77m) with which only four-five P-XLs may be procured each year, assuming that all other procurement is abandoned. Currently, the MSDF possesses 20 P-2H Neptunes, 61 P-2Js, 24 S-2A Trackers and 16 PS-1s. The last P-2H Neptunes and S-2A Trackers are scheduled to be retired by 1979 and 1982 respectively, and by the latter year the maritime patrol force will comprise only 70 P-2Js and approximately 30 PS-1s which the MSDF considers insufficient to meet its full maritime patrol commitments. Furthermore, the phase-out of the P-2J is currently scheduled to commence in 1981 (with completion in 1990), thus further increasing the urgency of a P-XL decision.

PAKISTAN

Following on discussions with the British Aircraft Corporation in March, the **Pakistan** government is reportedly seeking a British **loan to** permit the **purchase** of an initial batch of six SEPECAT **Jaguar International** tactical strike fighters.

PERU

The **Peruvian** government is apparently evincing **interest in** the purchase of one of the Royal Navy's three remaining capital ships, the 27,705-ton **commando ship** HMS *Bulwark,* together with a squadron of Hawker Siddeley Sea Harrier V/STOL fighters. The *Bulwark* is currently being reduced to reserve at Portsmouth (earlier plans to scrap the vessel as part of the defence cuts having been abandoned). The Navy is unlikely to be willing to relinquish the *Bulwark* before about 1980, when the first of the service's new anti-submarine cruisers, the 20,000-ton HMS *Invincible,* joins the Fleet, but it is unlikely that Hawker Siddeley could fulfil any Peruvian Sea Harrier order much before 1979-80.

PORTUGAL

The *Força Aérea Portuguesa* has recently received an infusion of **new equipment** in the form of aid **from Federal Germany,** this having included an unspecified number of ex-*Luftwaffe* Lockheed F-104G Starfighters and six Fiat G.91T trainers (one of the latter having crashed during its delivery flight). Although the majority of the North American T-6s that were employed in the COIN rôle and for training tasks by the FAP have now been supplanted by such types as Cessna FR-337s, up to 40 aircraft of this type are scheduled to

remain in the active inventory until early next year when they will be finally withdrawn. The supply of additional aircraft surplus to the requirements of the *Luftwaffe* is anticipated.

SAUDI ARABIA

Purchase of an **additional** batch of about a dozen BAC **Strikemaster Mk 80s** is being negotiated by the Royal Saudi Air Force. All Strikemasters ordered to date have now been delivered (a total of 134) but additional aircraft are in production at Warton against prospective orders and are expected to be absorbed into the RSAF contract.

SINGAPORE

The Government of **Singapore has purchased** the four BAC 167 Strikemaster Mk 81s supplied by the UK Government as assistance to South Yemen in the late 'sixties. The **ex-Southern Yemeni aircraft** are supplementing the Strikemasters of the Republic of Singapore Air Force's No 130 Squadron, 16 having originally been procured by Singapore and at least one having been lost (in a take-off accident at Tengah on 27 January).

Lockheed Air Service Singapore (LASS), which delivered the last of 32 **remanufactured** single-seat A-4S **Skyhawk** attack **aircraft** (which followed on eight A-4S Skyhawks produced at Lockheed Aircraft Service's Ontario, Calif, facility) to the Republic of Singapore Air Force in January, has received a contract to produce four two-seat TA-4S Skyhawk trainers to supplement the three delivered last year from the USA.

AIRCRAFT AND INDUSTRY

ARGENTINA

Flight **testing** is under way at Funes, Santa Fé, of a prototype ag-plane, **the RRA FAGA J-1 Martin Fierro.** Of all-metal construction and powered by a 300 hp Avco Lycoming IO-540-K1JG engine, the J-1 has been developed by Ronchetti, Razzetti Aviacion SA and is of classic agplane low-wing configuration. It has a span of 42 ft 7½ in (13,0 m), length of 22 ft 11½ in (7,0 m) and height of 13 ft 1 in (4,0 m), and carries a load of 1,872 lb (850 kg) with a cruising speed of 149 mph (240 km/h). An initial batch of five J-1s is under construction.

FEDERAL GERMANY

Sportavia in Germany is now **flight testing** an

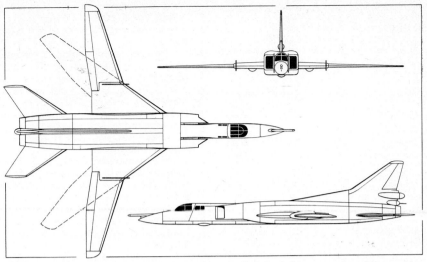

This new general arrangement drawing of the Tupolev Backfire-B shows a number of features that differ from those of previous provisional drawings, notably the shape of the trailing edge of the swivelling section of the wing, the contours of the vertical tail surfaces and the spacing of the jetpipes of the Kuznetsov two-spool turbofans. The Backfire-B's wings fully extended span approximately 115 ft (35,00 m), reducing to some 92 ft (28,00 m) fully swept. Maximum take-off weight is now estimated at 286,000 lb (129 730 kg).

uprated and improved derivative of the Fournier-designed RF6 Sportsman as the **RF6-180**; the prototype flew on 28 April and was demonstrated at the recent Hanover Air Show. Powered by a 180 hp Avco Lycoming IO-360-A1F6D, whereas the original RF6 had a 125 hp engine, the new model features a larger cabin for the four occupants (within the same overall dimensions), a steerable instead of castoring nosewheel, constant speed Hoffman propeller and other small changes.

Dornier GmbH has concluded an agreement with Pilatus Flugzeugwerke AG providing for **joint marketing** of the latter's PC-7 **Turbo-Trainer** (*AirData File*/August 1975). Type certification of the PC-7 is expected shortly, following completion of flight testing of the second prototype, and first deliveries will be possible in the autumn of 1977.

MBB has confirmed that it is planning **to launch** a new helicopter, the **BO 107** (*Airscene*/February 1975), to complement the BO 105, which is expected to remain in production for at least another 15 years. The BO 107 will be an IFR-equipped 8-seat helicopter, developed on an equal-share basis by MBB and Kawasaki, with prototype first flight expected in late 1979. MBB also plans to market a stretched version of its smaller helicopter as the BO 105S, using kits made in the US by Carson Helicopters to lengthen the cabin. This version is already being marketed in the USA by Boeing Vertol, which collaborated in its design (*Airscene*/June 1975). Development of the BO 115 anti-armour helicopter has now been cancelled by the Federal Government in favour of an armed version of the BO 105. This, the BO 105PAH, is expected to enter service around 1979, together with the observation and liaison version, the BO 105VBH.

FRANCE
Aérospatiale has obtained French civil **certification for the SA 342J** version of the Gazelle, which has an Astazou XIVH turboshaft in place of the Astazou III of the SA 341 variants. Deliveries of the SA 342J are expected to begin early in 1977, but the similarly-powered military variant, the SA 342K, is already in service, Kuwait being the initial customer. A version of the Gazelle with the Turboméca Arriel engine is being studied as the SA 343.

Dassault-Breguet has given further details of the **Mercure 200** in the form in which it provides the basis for a possible **joint development programme** with McDonnell Douglas. The new variant would use 80 per cent of the components of the Mercure 100, but would have a fuselage lengthened by 19 ft 8 in (6,0 m) to carry 160-186 passengers, CFM-56 turbofans and an improved wing. Dassault-Breguet would be the programme manager and would control the single final assembly line, at Istres, with Aérospatiale having a 35-45

per cent share in production. McDonnell Douglas would be responsible for marketing the Mercure 200, which could be certificated by the first half of 1980, by which time the first five aircraft would be flying.

The **Garrett ATF3-6** turbofan has been selected by Dassault-Breguet as the power plant **for the Falcon 20G** (*Airscene*/January 1976), which in other respects will be similar to the Falcon 20F. Use of the 5,050 lb st (2 293 kgp) turbofans will give the Falcon 20G some 30 per cent greater range and considerable improvements in take-off and climb performance. In the first instance, Dassault-Breguet will offer the new engines, complete with nacelles and thrust reversers, for retrofit on existing Falcons, with deliveries of certificated production engines becoming available at the end of 1978. New production Falcon 20Gs will be offered at a later date.

Aérospatiale has begun testing a **Starflex rotorhead on** one of the two prototypes of the **SA 365** Dauphin, the first flight having been made on 26 April. Testing is also about to begin with an SA 360 Dauphin powered by an Astazou XX in place of the usual Astazou XVIIIA, giving an increase of 300 hp.

Wassmer has entered the two-seat lightplane market with the **WA80 Piranha**, the prototype of which is now **in flight test** (having first flown last November) while a second is undergoing static testing. Like the larger WA50 Atlantic and WA51 Pacific, the WA80 is of all-plastics construction (including the mainspar). Powered by a 100 hp Rolls-Royce Continental O-200-A, the Piranha is now entering production for deliveries to start late this year.

ITALY
Rinaldo Piaggio is about to start **flight-testing,**

at Finale Ligure, a turboprop version **of** its P.166 light twin transport. Designated **P.166-DL3,** this new model has two 600 hp Avco Lycoming LTP-101 turboprops arranged as pushers, and is expected to be shown at Farnborough International '76 in September. Production at a rate of 2-4 a month is planned to start later this year.

INTERNATIONAL
Aérospatiale confirmed, in an announcement on 7 May, that the C.160 **Transall** tactical transport is to go **back into production,** with deliveries to resume in 1979. The decision is based on an assumed sale of 75 aircraft over five years and has been influenced by Aérospatiale's urgent need for additional work. The French company will provide the only final assembly line for the new Transalls, at Toulouse, and the *Armée de l'Air* will purchase 25 aircraft, of which 14 are to be delivered before 1982 and the remainder later. Among possible other customers is Egypt, which is understood to have indicated a requirement for at least 20 Transalls. Production will be shared equally between France and Germany, with MBB and VFW-Fokker sharing the German work; the Tyne engines will be built by a consortium of Rolls-Royce, MTU and SNECMA. Previous production of the Transall totalled 178 examples (plus two structural test airframes); of these, 110 were delivered to the *Luftwaffe* and 20 have subsequently been transferred to the Turkish Air Force, 50 were for the *Armée de l'Air* and four are currently on loan to Air France for the Aérospatiale operation, and nine went to the South African Air Force.

CFM International, marketing company for the GE/SNECMA **CFM-56** turbofan, has made formal proposals to Boeing for the use of this ten-tonne engine **in the E-3A AWACS** aircraft if the latter is ordered by NATO. Possible orders for up to 32 E-3As for NATO use are being considered, with a decision likely before the end of the year. The fifth CFM-56 will commence testing in July at Evendale and the sixth in September at Melun-Villaroche. The first four, meanwhile, have totalled 1,600 hrs of testing and flight trials will begin early next year in the Caravelle III No 193 (a SNECMA test-bed) and in the McDonnell Douglas YC-15.

SOVIET UNION
The USSR recently claimed two time-to-height class **records for** an aircraft referred to as **the Beriev Be-32** — apparently a derivative of the Be-30 twin-turboprop transport that has been discontinued. The Be-32 is reported to carry 18 passengers, or 4,185 lb (1 900 kg) of freight,

Hawker Siddeley has begun delivery of the final batch of Harrier GR Mk 3s on the current RAF order; the first of this batch, XZ128, is the 207th Harrier to come off the Kingston production line. As illustrated below, these new-batch Harriers are being delivered with Ferranti LRMTS (Laser Ranging and Marker Target Seeker) installation in the nose, and all RAF squadron Harriers previously delivered are to be retrofitted with this equipment at RAF Wittering in due course.

and the record performance comprised a climb to 3 000 m (9,836 ft) in 2 min 25 sec and to 6,000 m (19,672 ft) in 5 min 8 sec. Before confirmation of these records was announced by the FAI, however, they had been again broken by a DHC-5D Buffalo (*Airscene*/May).

A **marketing** campaign to sell the **Yak-40 in Canada** began during April, with a cross-country sales tour organised by Socan Aircraft Ltd — a jointly-owned subsidiary of Allarco Development Ltd and Aviaexport. Allarco is also parent company of International Jet Air. Canadian certification of the Yak-40 is expected late this year. Any examples sold in Canada will have King Gold Crown avionics and interiors installed in Canada.

SWEDEN
Saab has given **details** of its Model 108 **Transporter** light transport project and is expected to make a decision this year on whether to build a prototype, with flight testing to begin in 1978. The Transporter has a square-section fuselage, high wing, twin tail and fixed undercarriage; it is being studied in versions with four 320 hp Continental Tiara T6-320 piston engines or two 850 shp turbo-props — either PT6A-45s or Garrett TPE 331s. At a gross weight of 13,500 lb (6 120 kg), the Saab 108 is designed to carry 19 passengers or assorted freight loads over distances of up to 500 mls (800 km). Full details will appear in *AirData File* next month.

TAIWAN
The Aero Industry Development Centre at Taichung on the island of Taiwan is now well into its Northrop **F-5E Tiger II co-production programme** and, by mid-April, 33 F-5Es had been delivered against total orders for 120 (expected to eventually be increased to 180) and production tempo is now building up to four per month, current orders carrying the programme through to June 1978. The Development Centre has now completed two prototypes of the XT-CH-1B turboprop-powered two-seat basic trainer and expects to commence production of a series of 30 aircraft of this type later this year. The Development Centre is also engaged in the design of a jet trainer and a turboprop-powered replacement for the Fairchild C-119.

UNITED KINGDOM
Smiths Industries has concluded an agreement with Sundstrand Data Control Inc permitting **manufacture** of the latter's GPWS (ground proximity warning system) by Smiths **in the UK**. Initial production of the Sundstrand GPWS is now under way at Smiths Cheltenham factory, in a version designed to meet the special requirements of the CAA. More than 2,500 Sundstrand GPWS have been delivered for airline use around the world.

For the next step in development of the HS.125 biz-jet, Hawker Siddeley has selected the Garrett AiResearch TFE 731 turbofans. Installation of 3,700 lb (1 680 kg) thrust **TFE 731-3 engines** in the HS.125 Series 600 airframe, with a series of other improvements, will produce the **HS.125 Series 700,** customer deliveries of which are expected to begin in the second quarter of 1977 (see *AirData File* page 52 of this issue). Use of turbofan engines in place of the Viper turbojets that have been in use in all previous versions of the HS.125 provides a major increase in range — up to 50 per cent more — and allows the aircraft to meet the latest proposed amendments to FAR Part 36. Complete engine nacelles will be supplied to HSA by Grumman, which produces pods for TFE 731 installations in other aircraft, and a retrofit programme will be offered for these engines to be used on earlier HS.125 variants. In the longer term, Hawker Siddeley is also considering the use of the Rolls-Royce

The MiG-23B (Flogger-D) is frequently seen flying with a centreline drop tank but this photograph (courtesy Flug Revue) is the first to show this now widely-deployed tactical aircraft carrying long-range ferry tanks on non-swivelling pylons under the variable-sweep outer panels. The tanks are reportedly of 308 Imp gal (1 400 l) capacity and their application renders the use of minimum sweep mandatory.

RB.401, but with a thrust of more than 5,000 lb (2 268 kg) this engine would need to be associated with a stretched fuselage and, most probably, a new wing.

USA
General Electric's Aviation Engine Department has launched a **civil version** of its TF34 turbofan under the designation CF34, in the 7,000-8,000 lb (3 175-3 629 kg) thrust bracket. Some 400 TF34s have been delivered to date, for the Lockheed S-3A Viking and Fairchild A-10A, and these have added about 70,000 in-service flight hours to the 30,000 test hrs amassed on the TF-34. The CF-34 is aimed at the business and commercial aircraft market, one possible early application being in the Grumman GIII or GIV (see separate news item).

With two aircraft now in flight status — and a third expected to have joined flight testing by the time this column appears — the Rockwell B-1 test programme is **moving ahead** more rapidly and by 11 May, the total flight time stood at 172 hr 34 min on 35 flights. Of these, four were by the No 3 aircraft (No 2 had then still to fly, following its use for static structural airframe tests), the first on 1 April (correcting *Airscene*/June) and the fourth on 11 May, the latter lasting 6 hr 40 min. On the No 1 aircraft's 28th flight, on 7 April, the speed envelope was extended to Mach = 1·9 at 43,000 ft (13 115 m); on the 29th flight on 15 April Senator Barry Goldwater was carried as an observer and on the 30th flight (19 April), Secretary of Defense Donald H Rumsfeld was carried.

The No 1 Northrop **YF-17**, after undergoing an extensive overhaul, resumed testing at Edwards AFB on 13 May in preparation for a programme of flight **tests by NASA,** in which the aircraft's advanced characteristics, and especially its performance at high angles of attack, will be investigated.

A special **long-range** version of the **Super King Air 200** has been developed by Beech to meet the needs of the French *Institut Geographique National,* which has ordered four examples as replacements for three Hurel-Dubois HD 34s based at Creil **for photo survey work.** New features are removable wing-tip tanks with a capacity of 52·5 US gal each, cameras in the fuselage, Collins VHF and HF communications with DME and Doppler and optional larger mainwheels to permit oper-

ations at weights up to 14,000 lb (6 356 kg) — an increase of 1,500 lb (680 kg) over the standard Super King Air. The first two of these survey aircraft will be delivered next January, joining two Boeing B-17s that remain in service at Creil.

Beech Aircraft is offering **"wet wing tips" on the Baron** 58, to give an increase in fuel capacity of 28 US gal (108 l) — or 24 US gal (92 l) in the case of the Baron 58P and 58TC. The extra tankage within the outer wing gives the Barons an increased range of up to 19 per cent, for a maximum of 1,447 mls (2 328 km) in the case of the Baron 58 and 1,207 mls (1 942 km) for the Baron 58P.

Piper completed its **100,000th aeroplane** recently, an event marked by ceremonies at Lock Haven, Penn, on 7 April when the aircraft, a Cheyenne turboprop business twin, was formally dedicated. Named "Heritage of 76" to mark the year of the American Bicentennial, the Cheyenne is being used for a series of visits to Piper distributors throughout the world by the company's president, Lynn Helms, and was exhibited at the recent Hanover Air Show. At the dedication ceremony, the Cheyenne was shown alongside a Cub, the first Piper aeroplane. In its PA-18 Super Cub version, the classic high-wing model is still in production and the 99,999th Piper was, in fact, such an aircraft. Piper claims that its total production represents 10 per cent of *all* aircraft production to date and that 25 per cent of all aircraft flying today are Pipers.

Maintaining its position as industry leader in the delivery of bizjets. Gates Learjet delivered 93 of its Learjet models in the year to 30 April and followed this up with **delivery of the 600th Learjet** at the beginning of May. Of the company's fiscal year deliveries, 54 were to businesses in the USA and 39 to customers in 20 different countries. The recipient of the 600th Learjet, a Model 35, was Dart Industries (previously Rexall Drug Company) which already operates three Learjet 24s. The company has received FAA certification of the Learjet 35A and Learjet 36A, these being the first of the Century III series (*AirData File*/April 1976) so approved.

Flight **testing of the Cessna 441** prototype is expected to resume in June or July after installation of the production-standard Garrett AiResearch TPE331-8-401S engines. The prototype has been flying with TPE331-8-251 engines and had totalled nearly 200 hours when it was grounded for the engine change in May. The -401S engine is optimized for the Cessna 441 installation and is derated from 865 shp to 620 shp for constant performance at high altitudes and high ambient temperatures, and to obtain long engine life.

Beech Aircraft Corp has been named winner of the US Navy competition for the VTAM(X) multi-engine advanced trainer with the **T-44A version of the King Air 90**. An initial batch of 15 has been ordered, with options on 56 more.

In another modification programme aimed at **improving** existing ag-planes, STC Engineering Co of Oklahoma City and Reclyn Aircraft Inc of Newcastle, Oklahoma, have fitted a 350 hp Jacobs R-755 S turbo-supercharged radial engine to **a Piper PA-36-285 Pawnee Brave**, normally powered by a 285 hp Teledyne Continental flat-six. The usual 95-in (2,41-m) Hartzell propeller has been replaced by a 97-in (2,46-m) Hamilton Standard and full-span fixed leading-edge slats have been fitted. The effect of the modifications is to improve the take-off, reduce the climb speed, increase the cruise speed, reduce stalling speeds and permit operation at higher weights with greater chemical loads.

Grumman American expects to make a decision before the end of this year between two alternative enlarged **developments of the Gulfstream**, known as the GIII and GIV. The former is a three-engined aircraft, the latter four-engined, with a choice between uprated versions of the Rolls-Royce M45H and General Electric CF34 turbofans for either type. In either case, the new aircraft will use a Gulfstream II wing with a stretched fuselage providing 8 ft (2,44 m) more cabin length to accommodate 20 passengers with a crew of three. Range will be adequate for transatlantic non-stop flights in either direction.

YUGOSLAVIA
Three **prototypes and** several **pre-production** examples of the joint Yugoslav-Rumanian **Orao** (Eagle) single-seat tactical fighter and two-seat operational trainer are now reported to have joined the **flight test programme**, and the first production Orao is expected to be completed in November, by which time all nine pre-production examples should have flown. Preparations are now going ahead in Rumania (where the Orao is known as the IAR 93) for the licence manufacture of the 4,000 lb (1 814 kg) Viper 623 turbojet which powers the Orao, and a Rolls-Royce team is in Rumania to assist in setting up a Viper production facility. Efforts are already being made to solicit export orders for the Orao, the type reportedly having been offered to Egypt and Finland.

CIVIL AFFAIRS

CANADA
Deliveries of the **Shorts SD3-30** were expected to begin mid-June, when Time Air of Lethbridge was to receive the first of three; others will follow this month (July) and August. Canadian Transport Commission authority to operate the SD3-30 has been granted and the **first service** was scheduled for 1 July.

FIJI
A **new airline** offering charter flights from Fiji to the Bahamas and Europe is **named Air Hibiscus**. Reported to be negotiating to lease Boeing 707s from Tempair, the airline hopes to attract passengers from Australia.

FRANCE
The **Air France Airbus A300B-4** that has been operating between New York and the French Caribbean during the winter transport season, **returned to France** as planned on 3 May, and is now assigned to the Euro-African and Middle East networks for the summer season. Between 20 November and 2 May, this aircraft flew six days a week on the Caribbean routes, achieving a total of 141 round trips New York-Pointe a Pitre, and additional trips twice a week between Pointe a Pitre and Fort de France. Excellent regularity was achieved, despite the lack of a back-up aircraft and the minimal spares holding.

INDONESIA
Perlita, a subsidiary of the Pertamina petroleum group in Indonesia providing airline service as well as executive transportation, is likely **to be taken over** by Garuda. Initially to meet the needs of Pertamina, Perlita built up a fleet that now includes a Boeing 707, a BAC One-Eleven, four Fokker F.28s, nine F.27s and two NAMC YS-11s.

INTERNATIONAL
Scheduled supersonic revenue service across the **North Atlantic** began on 24 May when British Airways and Air France flew the first **Concorde service** into Dulles Airport, Washington — respectively from London and Paris. In a co-ordinated inaugural operation, the two Concordes arrived at Dulles within three minutes of each other (British Airways' Concorde 206, G-BOAC, being the first to touch down) and taxied together to park nose-to-nose in front of the terminal building. Both aircraft carried revenue passengers as well as airline guests and media representatives. Flight time for the British Concorde was 3 hr 53 min, less than half the normal subsonic scheduled time; the French Concorde's time was 3 hr 49 min. Each airline is now operating two services a week on the North Atlantic route, under the terms of a US Department of Transportation ruling that permits a 16-month evaluation of Concorde on routes into the USA. Last minute attempts by the anti-Concorde lobby to prevent the services to Dulles were unsuccessful, but permission for services to operate into John F Kennedy Airport, New York, is still withheld pending the resolution of legal points. British Airways' third Concorde, No 208, made its maiden flight from Filton on 18 May reaching Mach 2·05 and 63,000 ft (19 215 m) in the course of a 3½-hr flight before landing at Fairford.

ISRAEL
The Israeli government is setting up a **freight airline** that is expected to start operations in October and will specialise in carrying local produce to Europe at lower rates than charged by IATA carriers. A Boeing 747C will be leased from El Al initially, making daily flights between Israel and Europe.

YUGOSLAVIA
Inex Adria Airways took **delivery of** its first **DC-9 Srs 50** on 12 May in Long Beach and put it into service immediately following its arrival in Ljubljana a few days later. Arranged to carry 139 passengers each, the Inex Adria Srs 50 is being used on charter flights throughout Europe and the Mediterranean.

SPAIN
Aviaco has taken **delivery** in Madrid **of** the first of four extended-range **DC-9 Srs 30CF** convertible freighters it has on order. The first Srs 30 DC-9s to be fitted with 16,000 lb (7 258 kg) thrust JT8D-17 engines, the Aviaco aircraft have extra fuel to provide a range of 1,880 mls (3 025 km), some 20 per cent more than the standard Srs 30, and operate at higher gross weights than previously certificated.

SUDAN
A major expansion of agriculture and **aerial spraying in the Sudan** has brought additional business to a number of British companies. ADS (Aerial) Ltd, at Southend, is acting, through its managing director LC "Ladi" Marmol, as consultant to the new Sudanese company Crop Protection (Sudan) Ltd and during May was taking delivery of 15 Rockwell Thrush Commander 600s for assembly, testing and onward ferrying to the Sudan. In the long term, Sudanese pilots will fly these aircraft and a first batch of 23 students has arrived in the UK to be trained by CSE at Carlisle. Until these, and a second batch of about 30 who will arrive in October, are fully proficient, pilots are being recruited by ADS (Aerial) to fly the Thrush Commanders and other types in the Sudan. The CSE contract is a breakthrough so far as crop-spraying pilots are concerned and although the training course will not include any specific instruction in spraying or dusting techniques, it will cover take-offs and landings in tailwheel aircraft, for which purpose CSE will add a suitable type to its fleet at least temporarily.

CIVIL CONTRACTS AND SALES

Airbus A300: Pending delivery of its recently-ordered A300B-4 (this column last month) Transavia Holland has leased an A300B-2 (aircraft No 8). Delivery was made in Amsterdam on 11 May and the aircraft flew its first service for Transavia on 14 May. The definitive B-4 for Transavia will be aircraft No 25. The B-2 No 8 had previously been operated by Air Siam, and is to be delivered to Air Inter when it is returned by Transavia later next year.

Boeing 707: Saudi has two 707-320Cs on lease from MEA, with a third on option.

Boeing 720B: One of MEA's fleet is currently leased to Libyan Arab Airlines.

Boeing 727: Delta Air Lines is to acquire 13 more 727-200s, in addition to eight Advanced 727s that were previously optioned. With deliveries of the latter to be completed this year, the additional 13 aircraft will be delivered between May 1977 and November 1978 to bring the total Delta purchase of 727s to 83. □ Libyan Arab Airlines has ordered two Advanced 727s for April 1977 delivery. □ Four more Advanced 727s have been ordered by Northwest Orient, for delivery June-Dec 1977. □ Air Malta has leased one -100 from World Airways, and Yemen Airlines has leased two from the same operator.

Boeing 737: An Advanced 737-200C convertible has been ordered by Cameroon Airlines, with gravel-runway kit; delivery will be in February 1977.

Boeing 747: Northwest Orient Airlines has ordered one additional 747F, for June 1977 delivery. □ Tunis Air is leasing a 747 from MEA. □ Air Siam has leased one from KLM.

Lockheed L-1011 Tristar: Saudia has increased its total purchase of TriStars to nine by placing an order for three more L-1011-200s, to be delivered in September and December 1977 and early 1978. Saudia currently has three new L-1011s in service with a fourth due for delivery in mid-1977, and also recently purchased two from TWA. The Saudia L-1011-200s will have RB.211-524 engines, gross weight of 466,000 lb (211 564 kg) and a non-stop range of 4,630 mls (7 450 km) carrying the full load of 253 passengers.

McDonnell Douglas DC-10: Western Airlines has taken up an option on one DC-10 Series 30, its seventh. Delivery was to be made on 25 June.

THE STYLISH SABRELINER

ASK ANYONE with an interest in aviation what his or her all-time favourite aeroplane is, and "five will get you ten" that the answer will name a combat type — Spitfire, Bf 109, Corsair, Lightning, Sabre or whatever. This is hardly surprising, since combat aircraft are always at the forefront of the high-performance league, the real "adrenalin producers" whether in or out of actual combat. Often bedecked in colourful unit identification markings and personnel emblems, the latest warplanes catch the public eye at any airfield gathering, just as the passing of a Jensen Interceptor or a Lotus Elite down the high street quickens the pulse of the average Chrysler or Ford owner.

This high level of interest in the most successful of warplanes may be less than fair to the manufacturers of the not-so-glamorous "bread-and-butter" aeroplanes, both military and civil, but it was a situation that the North American Aviation company (now absorbed into Rockwell International) fully appreciated when it adopted the name Sabreliner for its utility jet transport project in 1956. The F-86 Sabre was then at the peak of its success as the first swept-wing transonic fighter to enter service on a large scale, and the choice of the name Sabreliner was a deliberate attempt to capitalize on the reputation of the F-86 whilst also indicating certain similarities — in size, weight and some aspects of performance, other than the transonic capability — between the two types. The name was to prove singularly appropriate, for the Sabreliner has gone on, in the two decades since its conception, to achieve positive success in both military and civil rôles; it remains in production today as a business jet with a respected reputation and new versions are still under active development to prolong its production life.

The origins of the Sabreliner can be traced back beyond the 20-year span, in fact, to the spring of 1952, when North American (also often known as NAA) began some design studies and marketing analyses of a small twin-jet aircraft with possible military and civil applications. Many possible configurations were studied, and trade-offs between turbojet

and turboprop engines were made, leading to the choice of a low-wing layout in which the wing — with a modest degree of sweepback — passed under rather than through the main fuselage structure. Turbojets — General Electric J85s in the first instance — were preferred to turboprops and were located at the wing/fuselage joints.

The proposal remained in this form on paper until 1956. In March of that year, the USAF had announced plans to acquire small and medium jet trainer-transports from the industry on an "off-the-shelf" basis. NAA reactivated its twin-jet programme in order to respond to the smaller of these two requirements, more complete details of which were given in August 1956 when Maj Gen David H Baker, director of procurement and production of USAF's Air Material Command, wrote to 28 aircraft manufacturers a letter expressing the Air Force's interest in the acquisition of small and medium jet trainer-transports, at an anticipated unit cost of $200,000-$400,000. Quantities of up to 1,500 of the smaller type and 300 of the larger type were mentioned, in an apparent burst of considerable over-optimism.

Accompanying the letter were two General Design Specification documents, one for a light twin-jet utility trainer (UTX) and the other for a medium-weight four-jet utility transport (UCX). Because the USAF believed that there was "a potential commercial market for these aircraft" and that "the estimated costs of development programs of this type were within the capability of industry", manufacturers were asked to design and build prototypes at no cost to the government. Full commercial certification was also to be required of any type selected to fulfil the USAF requirement.

The UTX specification corresponded most closely with the work already done by NAA, covering "the requirement of the USAF for a twin-engine utility jet transport aircraft, the primary mission of which is combat readiness training". (A secondary specified mission, never actually engaged in by the Sabreliner was to be towing low-drag aerial targets.) A six-seat aircraft was requested — two crew with dual controls and four passengers — having a range of 1,725 mls (2 774 km) cruising at Mach = 0·76 at 45,000 ft (13 725 m).

Other significant requirements of the UTX General Design Specification included a single engine ceiling of 15,000 ft (4 575 m), a critical field length of 5,000 ft (1 525 m), a landing roll at half-fuel weight of 2,500 ft (763 m), in-flight escape provisions, single-point pressure refuelling and military type instruments and avionics.

Initially, at least eight manufacturers indicated interest in the UCX and UTX requirements; in addition to NAA, both Convair and Temco (now part of LTV) were specifically considering the UTX while Lockheed, McDonnell and Fairchild were among the companies interested in the UCX. Only NAA, however, committed itself to proceed with development of a UTX prototype, announcing its intention in this respect on 27 August 1956. Wind-tunnel testing of the initial design indicated that the engine installation produced high drag, with interference between the intakes and the leading-edge slats on the wings; an engineering mock-up further revealed that engine maintenance would be difficult. Consequently, on 1 July 1957, a major redesign was initiated in which the wing was raised into the fuselage and the engines were moved back to their final position on the fuselage sides. At the same time, wing shape was altered to increase root chord and area, providing additional fuel capacity.

The redesign made it impossible to achieve the first flight target date of early-1958 and further delays were incurred by

non-availability of the 2,500-lb st (1 135 kgp) flight-rated J85 engines required for the prototype, which had acquired the designation NA-246. Rolled-out at NAA's Inglewood factory at Los Angeles as a completely-equipped airframe on 8 May 1958, the prototype did not fly until 16 September (at Palmdale Airport), by which time the USAF had already notified NAA that it had won the UTX competition. Following a series of initial flight checks flown by NAA crews, the NA-246 was turned over to the USAF at Edwards AFB for evaluation. The Air Force put over 31 hours on the UTX prototype during 27 flights, finding the NA-246 very satisfactory. Flight evaluation of the prototype was completed in December 1959.

The Sabreliner prototype was a low-wing, tricycle-geared, pressurized aircraft with swept wing and tail surfaces and two aft-mounted turbojet engines. Accommodation in the cabin, which was pressurized to give an 8,000-ft (2 440-m) equivalent at the aircraft cruising altitude of 45,000 ft (13 725 m), consisted of four passenger seats, two on either side of an aisleway. The seats on each side faced one another, having space for a small table between them. At the rear of the pressure cabin was a toilet area, while aft of the pressure bulkhead were located the heating and ventilating equipment, batteries, and hydraulic system.

In the small but compact cockpit, everything was laid out within the pilot's reach so that the Sabreliner could be operated entirely from the left seat. Flight instruments and controls were duplicated at the right seat for pilot training. Good visibility was provided, with a number of transparencies at the sides and top of the cockpit, in addition to the V-shaped windshield. Communication and navigation equipment, including glide path and localizer, VHF radio, dual VOR, marker beacon, flight director system, interphone and ADF, was installed within the pressurized section just forward of the cockpit. Glide slope and weather radar antennae were located within a small plastic nose cone.

The Sabreliner wing was similar, but hardly identical, to those of the earlier Sabre and F-100 Super Sabre fighters.

(Above left) The prototype NA-265 Sabreliner, N4060K, in its civilian colours and (below) in USAF markings, keeping company with a Sabre and a Super Sabre in front of the NAA buildings at Inglewood on the edge of Los Angeles International Airport.

Quarter-chord sweepback was 28·5 deg, and the NACA 64-series wing section had an average thickness of 10 per cent. Aerodynamically-actuated leading edge slats were fitted to the wings, which were "wet" (ie, contained integral fuel tanks) from tip to tip. Actuation of the aerodynamically-balanced controls was accomplished via a simple unpowered mechanical control system.

Military production begins

Shortly after the successful conclusion of the UTX prototype flight evaluation, NAA received a letter contract for an initial batch of aircraft and the production programme was activated on 2 January 1959 under NAA General Order No NA-265*. This initial contract called for construction of seven flight test examples that were to be used concurrently for various tests by NAA, the USAF and the FAA. Given the designation T-39A (in the Trainer category) by the USAF, these aircraft were to differ somewhat from the UTX prototype, most notably in the employment of Pratt & Whitney J60-P-3 engines of 3,000 lb st (1 362 kgp) in place of the J85s installed in the NA-246. Engineering and tooling for production began as soon as the contract was received and actual assembly of the first T-39A commenced late in the summer of 1959.

At about the same time, USAF Tactical Air Command (TAC) was developing the supersonic, all-weather, nuclear-weapon-delivering F-105D Thunderchief fighter-bomber, and had established the need for an economical means of training F-105D pilots in the utilization of the highly-sophisticated, Autonetics-developed North American Search and Ranging Radar (NASARR) system of that aircraft. The T-39 airframe appeared to be quite suitable for adoption in this way as a radar trainer for the F-105D and North American was given the go-ahead to produce such a version in November 1959; as the Air Force was anxious to obtain these trainers as quickly as possible, priority was given to this version (designated T-39B) over the T-39A. Consequently, the sixth flight test T-39A, which was then under construction, was converted to T-39B configuration while on the line and the seventh aircraft was built from the ground up as a T-39B. By this time, North American had received a production contract for 35 T-39As, the first four of which were also to be built as T-39Bs.

The first T-39A was completed in May 1960, making its first flight on 30 June. It was soon followed by the other four flight test T-39As and the extensive NAA/USAF/FAA test programme commenced. Performance of the T-39A Sabreliner was judged to be very similar to that of its namesake, the F-86 Sabre, except, of course, for the lower maximum Mach number. Flight testing was completed in March of 1961, followed by provisional FAA certification about a month later and full commercial certification of the T-39A on 23 March 1962. Operational T-39A deliveries to the USAF began on 4 June 1961 and production of the "A" model continued until the last of 143 examples was delivered in the autumn of 1963.

The great majority of T-39As, despite the "trainer" designation, served as utility transports. Assigned to virtually all major USAF commands (SAC, TAC, ADC, USAFE, PACAF, etc), their primary function has been the rapid transportation of military personnel and high-priority cargo. In addition, the T-39A has been used for a variety of special projects. Those T-39As that were delivered to the Air Training Command for use in a training rôle were assigned to the Instrument Pilot Instructor School at Randolph AFB. These were employed in an eight-week Instrument Pilot Instructor Course and were used to check out instructor pilots who, in turn, provided T-39 training through the USAF.

In June 1967, the Air Force took delivery of the first of

Successive batches of military and civil Sabreliners have been built under different General Order or Charge numbers. A complete listing of these numbers is given on page 38.

USAF T-39As have been the subject of various modification programmes, examples being (above) the T-39F conversion to a "Wild Weasel" systems trainer and (below) this NT-39A used as an infra-red systems test-bed by the Armament Development & Test Centre at Eglin AFB.

US Navy variants of the Sabreliner have included (above) this Series 40 used by VRC-50 as a VT-39E until redesignated CT-39E in 1968 and (below) another of the CT-39Es, displaying both a civil registration and Navy serial number.

several T-39As that had been modified by North American for increased passenger accommodation. Incorporating improvements resulting from continued development of the Sabreliner, these modified aircraft had strengthened landing gears to allow greater take-off weight; cabin environment was also improved and up to seven passengers can be carried in these aircraft. While the Sabreliners continue to be utilized primarily as high-speed transports, they are no longer assigned to the major commands. As a result of a policy change effected in 1975, all USAF transport aircraft have been placed under the direct operational control of the Military Airlift Command (MAC) and the controlling organisation for T-39A Sabreliners is now MAC's 89th Military Airlift Wing, which maintains squadrons and detachments equipped with T-39As at several Air Force Bases around the world.

The early variants

As already explained, the T-39B emerged with a higher production priority than the T-39A, and was the first Sabreliner model to go into operational service with the

USAF. First flight of the No 1 T-39B (ie, the sixth of the original batch of flight test aircraft), was made in November 1960 and the first delivery was made two months later.

Although the T-39B's exterior was little different from that of the A model (the larger nose radome area being the most obvious external difference), the cabin arrangement was considerably altered. The baggage compartment was converted into an avionic equipment bay to accommodate the training radar and other units that were relocated from the nose section, the nose being occupied by the R-14 NASARR — North American Search and Ranging Radar — antenna dish. Consoles for the radar and navigation systems (including APN-131 Doppler) were provided in the cabin for three student F-105D pilots.

All operational T-39Bs were originally assigned to the 4520th Combat Crew Training Wing (CCTW) at Nellis AFB, the Air Force's F-105 training organisation. Later in the 'sixties, the F-105 training mission was transferred to the 4519th CCTS (later 419th TFTS — Tactical Fighter Training Squadron) at McConnell AFB, and the T-39Bs moved to the latter base. With the assignment of most F-105s to the Air National Guard (ANG) in the early 'seventies, the Kansas Air Guard took over F-105 pilot training and, along with the training mission, the 127th TFTS (Kansas ANG) received the T-39Bs, these aircraft being the only Sabreliners so far assigned to the Air National Guard.

During the period of T-39B development, the USAF was also considering a similar radar trainer for the F-101B Voodoo interceptor radar system. North American received a USAF Request For Proposal, and proceeded to construct an interior mock-up of the proposed configuration. The designation T-39C was assigned to the project, but a reduction in the scope of the F-101B programme led to cancellation of the T-39C before any hardware was produced. Externally, the T-39C would have been identical to the T-39B.

The final USAF Sabreliner designation to date is T-39F,

Rockwell Sabre 75A cutaway drawing key

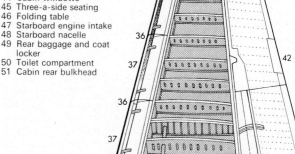

28 Forward baggage and coat locker
29 Passenger door
30 Buffet and bar locker
31 Fuselage top longeron
32 Cabin roof structure
33 Fuselage main frames
34 Starboard escape hatch
35 Starboard integral wing fuel tank, capacity 452 US gal (1 710 l)
36 Leading edge slat segments
37 Leading edge de-icing
38 Starboard wingtip
39 Navigation light
40 Static dischargers
41 Starboard aileron
42 Aileron trim tab
43 Starboard flap
44 Cabin windows
45 Three-a-side seating
46 Folding table
47 Starboard engine intake
48 Starboard nacelle
49 Rear baggage and coat locker
50 Toilet compartment
51 Cabin rear bulkhead

52 Air system intake
53 Fuselage bladder fuel tank, capacity 199 US gal (753 l)
54 Air trunking
55 Air cycling and air conditioning plant
56 Auxiliary power unit
57 Fuel dump pipe
58 Fin root fairing
59 Fin spar fixing

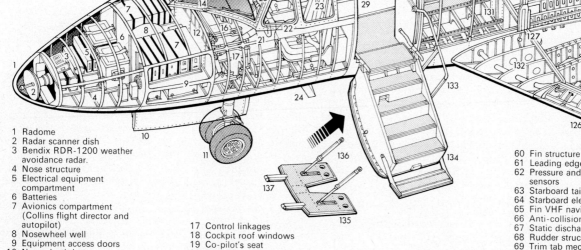

1 Radome
2 Radar scanner dish
3 Bendix RDR-1200 weather avoidance radar.
4 Nose structure
5 Electrical equipment compartment
6 Batteries
7 Avionics compartment (Collins flight director and autopilot)
8 Nosewheel well
9 Equipment access doors
10 Nosewheel door
11 Twin steerable nosewheels, Goodrich Type VII
12 Fuselage front bulkhead
13 Windscreen panels
14 Windscreen wipers
15 Instrument panel shroud
16 Back of instrument panel

17 Control linkages
18 Cockpit roof windows
19 Co-pilot's seat
20 Throttles
21 Control column
22 Opening side window
23 Pilot's seat
24 Lower VHF aerial
25 Flight deck bulkhead
26 Electrical equipment rack
27 Upper VHF aerial

60 Fin structure
61 Leading edge de-icing
62 Pressure and temperature sensors
63 Starboard tailplane
64 Starboard elevator
65 Fin VHF navigation aerial
66 Anti-collision light
67 Static dischargers
68 Rudder structure
69 Trim tab mechanism
70 Rudder trim tab
71 Tailcone
72 Fuel jettison
73 Port elevator
74 Elevator hinge connection
75 Port all-moving tailplane structure
76 Leading edge de-icing

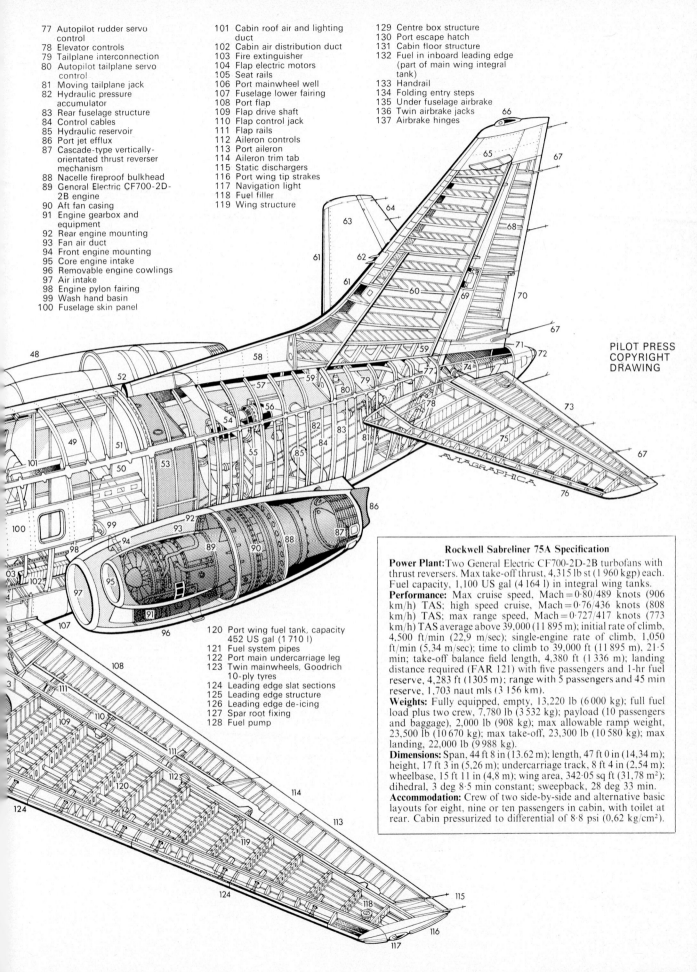

77 Autopilot rudder servo control
78 Elevator controls
79 Tailplane interconnection
80 Autopilot tailplane servo control
81 Moving tailplane jack
82 Hydraulic pressure accumulator
83 Rear fuselage structure
84 Control cables
85 Hydraulic reservoir
86 Port jet efflux
87 Cascade-type vertically-orientated thrust reverser mechanism
88 Nacelle fireproof bulkhead
89 General Electric CF700-2D-2B engine
90 Aft fan casing
91 Engine gearbox and equipment
92 Rear engine mounting
93 Fan air duct
94 Front engine mounting
95 Core engine intake
96 Removable engine cowlings
97 Air intake
98 Engine pylon fairing
99 Wash hand basin
100 Fuselage skin panel

101 Cabin roof air and lighting duct
102 Cabin air distribution duct
103 Fire extinguisher
104 Flap electric motors
105 Seat rails
106 Port mainwheel well
107 Fuselage lower fairing
108 Port flap
109 Flap drive shaft
110 Flap control jack
111 Flap rails
112 Aileron controls
113 Port aileron
114 Aileron trim tab
115 Static dischargers
116 Port wing tip strakes
117 Navigation light
118 Fuel filler
119 Wing structure

129 Centre box structure
130 Port escape hatch
131 Cabin floor structure
132 Fuel in inboard leading edge (part of main wing integral tank)
133 Handrail
134 Folding entry steps
135 Under fuselage airbrake
136 Twin airbrake jacks
137 Airbrake hinges

120 Port wing fuel tank, capacity 452 US gal (1 710 l)
121 Fuel system pipes
122 Port main undercarriage leg
123 Twin mainwheels, Goodrich 10-ply tyres
124 Leading edge slat sections
125 Leading edge structure
126 Leading edge de-icing
127 Spar root fixing
128 Fuel pump

PILOT PRESS
COPYRIGHT
DRAWING

Rockwell Sabreliner 75A Specification

Power Plant: Two General Electric CF700-2D-2B turbofans with thrust reversers. Max take-off thrust, 4,315 lb st (1 960 kgp) each. Fuel capacity, 1,100 US gal (4 164 l) in integral wing tanks.

Performance: Max cruise speed, Mach = 0·80/489 knots (906 km/h) TAS; high speed cruise, Mach = 0·76/436 knots (808 km/h) TAS; max range speed, Mach = 0·727/417 knots (773 km/h) TAS average above 39,000 (11 895 m); initial rate of climb, 4,500 ft/min (22,9 m/sec); single-engine rate of climb, 1,050 ft/min (5,34 m/sec); time to climb to 39,000 ft (11 895 m), 21·5 min; take-off balance field length, 4,380 ft (1 336 m); landing distance required (FAR 121) with five passengers and 1-hr fuel reserve, 4,283 ft (1305 m); range with 5 passengers and 45 min reserve, 1,703 naut mls (3 156 km).

Weights: Fully equipped, empty, 13,220 lb (6 000 kg); full fuel load plus two crew, 7,780 lb (3 532 kg); payload (10 passengers and baggage), 2,000 lb (908 kg); max allowable ramp weight, 23,500 lb (10 670 kg); max take-off, 23,300 lb (10 580 kg); max landing, 22,000 lb (9 988 kg).

Dimensions: Span, 44 ft 8 in (13.62 m); length, 47 ft 0 in (14,34 m); height, 17 ft 3 in (5,26 m); undercarriage track, 8 ft 4 in (2,54 m); wheelbase, 15 ft 11 in (4,8 m); wing area, 342·05 sq ft (31,78 m²); dihedral, 3 deg 8·5 min constant; sweepback, 28 deg 33 min.

Accommodation: Crew of two side-by-side and alternative basic layouts for eight, nine or ten passengers in cabin, with toilet at rear. Cabin pressurized to differential of 8·8 psi (0,62 kg/cm²).

applicable to three T-39As converted under a programme begun early in 1968. These were special-purpose trainers, engineered and modified by NAA to carry the installation of the ECM system carried by F-105G "Wild Weasel" Thunderchiefs. This ECM system was developed to locate, deceive, jam, evade and (in conjunction with Shrike and ARM missiles) destroy the radar sites used in North Vietnam to direct SAM's and anti-aircraft fire. The T-39F cabin was configured with three "Wild Weasel" system consoles, one each for a trainee pilot, a trainee EWO (Electronic Warfare Officer), and an instructor, to permit the airborne training of "Wild Weasel" crews in the use of the fighter-borne radar homing and warning system. These three T-39Fs, affectionately known as "Teeny

Side view profiles depict (1) the prototype NA-265; (2) a standard production T-39A; (3) a USAF T-39B — the T-39D was similar; (4) the T-39F "Wild Weasel" trainer; (5) Sabreliner 40, with extra window; (6) the Sabreliner 50 Autonetics test-bed; (7) Sabreliner 60, with lengthened fuselage and (8) Sabre 75 (previously Sabreliner 75).

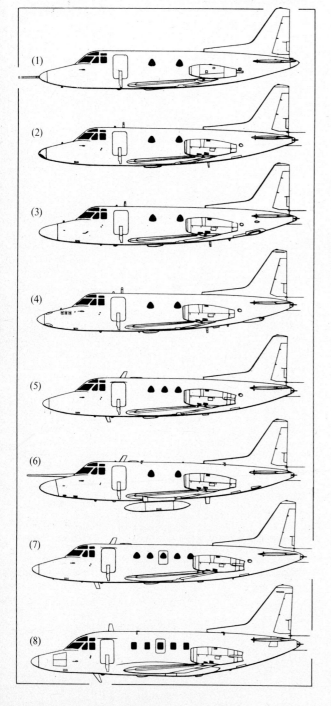

(1)
(2)
(3)
(4)
(5)
(6)
(7)
(8)

North American T-39A Sabreliner Specification
Power Plant: Two Pratt & Whitney J60-P-3 turbojets, each rated at 3,000 lb st (1 360 kgp) for take-off. Fuel capacity, 840 US gal (3 180 l) in integral wing tanks.
Performance: Max cruising speed, 502 mph (808 km/h); long-range cruise, 475 mph (764 km/h) at 44,000 ft (13 400 m); single-engine ceiling, 21,500 ft (6 550 m); take-off to 35 ft (10,7 m), 3,500 ft (1 167 m); landing distance from 50 ft (15,2 m), 2,650 ft (808 m); range with max fuel, 1,950 mls (3 140 km).
Weights: Basic operating, 9,257 lb (4 200 kg); max fuel load, 5,805 lb (2 633 kg); max take-off weight, 17,760 lb (8 055 kg); max landing weight, 13,000 lb (5 900 kg).
Dimensions: Span, 44 ft 5 in (13,53 m); length, 43 ft 9 in (13,33 m); height, 16 ft 0 in (4,88 m); wing area, 342·5 sq ft (31,83 m²).
Accommodation: Crew of two and 4-8 passengers in cabin.

North American Rockwell Sabreliner Srs 40
Power Plant: Two Pratt & Whitney JT12A-8 turbojets, each rated at 3,300 lb st (1 497 kgp) for take-off. Fuel capacity, 1,063 US gal (4 024 l) in integral wing tanks and rear fuselage bladder tank.
Performance: Max cruise, Mach=0·70 at 39,000 ft (11 900 m); initial rate of climb, 4,700 ft/min (2,39 m/sec); service ceiling, 45,000 ft (13 700 m); single-engine ceiling, 24,000 ft (7 300 m); take-off balanced field length, 4,280 ft (1 305 m); landing distance required, 2,935 ft (895 m); range with max fuel, 2,100 mls (3 380 km) with VFR reserves.
Weights: Basic operating, 9,895 lb (4 488 kg); max payload (including fuel), 2,609 lb (1 180 kg); max allowable ramp weight, 18,650 lb (8 460 kg); max take-off, 18,650 (8 498 kg); max landing weight, 17,500 lb (7 938 kg).
Dimensions: Span, 44 ft 5 in (13,53 m); length, 43 ft 9 in (13,33 m); height, 16 ft 0 in (4,88 m); wheelbase, 14 ft 6 in (4,42 m); undercarriage track, 7 ft 2½ in (2,20 m); wing area, 342·05 sq ft (31,78 m²).
Accommodation: Crew of two on flight deck and up to nine passengers in cabin, with toilet at rear.

Rockwell Sabreliner 60 Specification
Power Plant: Two Pratt & Whitney JT12A-8 turbojets. Max take-off thrust, 3,300 lb st (1 498 kgp). Fuel capacity, 1,063 US gal (4 024 l) in integral wing tanks.
Performance: Max cruise speed, Mach=0·80/489 knots (906 km/h) TAS; recommended cruise, Mach=0·75/430 knots (797 km/h) TAS; max range speed, Mach=0·71/407 knots (754 km/h) TAS; initial rate of climb, 4,700 ft/min (23,9 m/sec); single-engine rate of climb, 1,100 ft/min (5,6 m/sec); time to climb to 39,000 ft (11 895 m), 24·5 min; take-off balanced field length, 5,100 ft (1 555 m); landing distance required (FAR 121) with five passengers and 1-hr fuel reserve, 4,000 ft (1 220 m); range with five passengers and 45-min cruise reserve, 1,747 naut mls (3 237 km).
Weights: Fully equipped, empty, 11,250 lb (5 107 kg); full fuel load plus two crew, 7,522 lb (3 415 kg); payload (8 passengers and baggage), 1,600 lb (726 kg); max allowable ramp weight, 20,372 lb (9 250 kg); max take-off, 20,172 lb (9 158 kg); max landing, 17,500 lb (7 945 kg).
Dimensions: Span, 44 ft 8 in (13,62 m); length, 46 ft 11 in (14,31 m); height, 16 ft 0 in (4,88 m); undercarriage track, 7 ft 2½ in (2,19 m); wheelbase, 15 ft 10¾ in (4,85 m); wing area, 342·05 sq ft (31,78 m²); dihedral, 3 deg 8·5 min constant; sweep back, 28 deg 33 min.
Accommodation: Crew of two side-by-side and layouts for up to eight passengers in cabin, with toilet at rear. Cabin pressurized to differential of 8·8 psi (0,62 kg/cm²).

Weeny Weasels", were assigned to the 66th Fighter Weapons Squadron at Nellis AFB, where they served along with F-105Gs in the training of two-man "Weasel" aircrews; they are no longer in service.

Navy interest in the Sabreliner
From the early days of the T-39 programme, NAA believed that, in addition to the USAF, the Navy, the Marine Corps and even the Army would have requirements for aircraft with the Sabreliner's capabilities. Although the interest of these other services took longer to materialize than NAA had expected, it did finally develop. In mid-1961, the US Navy initiated procurement of a number of Sabreliner trainers under the designation T3J-1. These were to be based on the Air Force's T-39B (with navalized systems), except that the Magnavox

This T-39A, USAF serial 62-4465, in the markings of HQ, Air Force Systems Command — typical of the users of the Sabreliner in its rôle as a staff and utility transport.

APQ-94 intercept radar was to be installed in place of the NASARR. By the time the first of these Navy aircraft flew (in November 1962), the designation had been changed to T-39D. The first operational T-39D was delivered to Headquarters, Naval Air Training Command at NAS Pensacola in August 1963 and production continued until the last of 42 examples was completed in November 1964. Four others on order, intended to be used as ECM trainers for the US Marine

Corps, were cancelled before construction.

Most of the T-39Ds have been employed in two training rôles. They have been used to provide Navy fighter pilots and RIOs (Radar Intercept Officers) with airborne instruction in the art of radar intercept tactics and they have also served as Basic Jet Navigation trainers in the instruction of Naval Flight Officers. However, several "D" model Sabreliners have performed such other functions as flight-testing of missile seekers

T-39B, USAF serial 60-3476 — one of the six examples of this variant, with distinctive radome nose — that were delivered for use to train F-105 pilots (three at a time) in the use of the NASARR weapon system radar and Doppler navigation system.

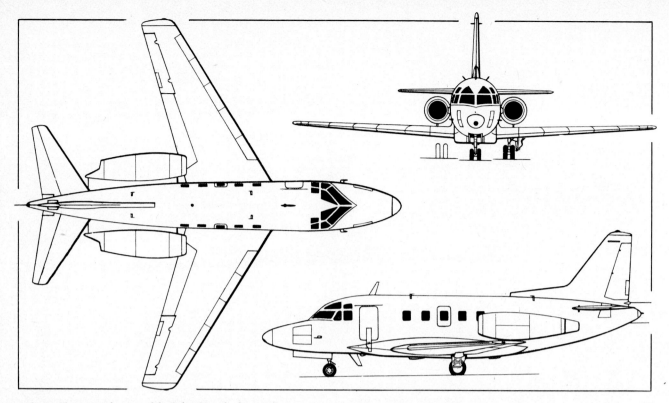

(Above) Three-view drawing of the Sabre 75A, the first production variant to switch from use of the Pratt & Whitney JT12A engine. (Below left) An early production Sabreliner 40 — the first commercial production variant.

(Above) The unique Sabreliner 50, with wing hardpoints and special nose radar, has given valuable service as an avionics test-bed. (Below) The Sabreliner 60 introduced a lengthened fuselage and additional cabin windows.

and guidance systems, or providing A-7E pilot trainees with practice in operating the Corsair's APQ-126 ground-mapping radar. In addition, some five T-39Ds have been utilized as command and staff transports, with passenger interiors. Reflecting this latter rôle, some of the aircraft used in this way were redesignated CT-39D for a brief period; the CT-39E and CT-39G versions, for use in a similar rôle, were acquired later and, being basically "off-the-shelf" purchases of commercial Sabreliners, are described under that heading below.

The commercial story

Certification of the basic Sabreliner, as already explained, was undertaken to comply with the original terms of the USAF contract and FAA approval dates from March 1962. The design conformed to CAR 46 requirements as a jet transport aircraft, meeting the special conditions of SR-422b as well as special USAF military specification requirements. The decision to proceed with commercial production of the Sabreliner was taken in 1962 and the first delivery was made in May 1963 following certification of this specific variant on 17 April.

Although the first batch of commercial Sabreliners was built on the Charge Order number NA-282, FAA documentation was facilitated by using the original NA-265 designation under which the T-39A, T-39B and T-39D had been certificated. These had been known, in FAA records, as the NA-265, NA-265-20 and NA-265-30 respectively; consequently, the new civil model was certificated as the NA-265-40 and was marketed as the Sabreliner Srs 40. Since the marketing of commercial aircraft was a relatively specialised activity in which North American had, in 1962, little experience, the company concluded a deal with the Remmert-Werner organization whereby the latter became sole distributor for the type, all aircraft being supplied "green" for finishing by R-W to customer requirements.

The Sabreliner Srs 40 was essentially the same airframe as the T-39A, but with commercially-approved engines (JT12A-6A in the first instance, with the same rating as the J60-P-3) and

continued on page 36

THE MILITARY AIRCRAFT MARKETPLACE

I BELIEVE it was Adam ("The Money Game") Smith who advised, *"When there is no game, don't play!"* He was writing, of course, of the stock market, but he might just as well have been referring to fighter design.

There are times when a preliminary design man would change places with no other mortal on this earth. On occasion the potential market is so large that it seems you will need all the floor space at St Louis *and* Seattle to satisfy the demand. You have kicked, beaten and bullied Derby into finally offering something that looks like a reasonable facsimile of an engine. Your drawing board is ten deep in directors, each of whom thought of the concept first. Lee Begin (see AIR INTERNATIONAL, January 1976) is about to be returned to the obscurity that he so richly deserves. You research whether a Lamborghini will really fit into your garage and speculate on how many cases of *Chateau Lafite* will be needed to fill your cellar. All of these things happen, but life isn't always like that!

There comes the day when good old Rolf Riccius finds he is Chief Engineer of VFW-Fokker, good old Gero Madelung finds he is Managing Director of Panavia (and a Professor too, good grief!), and good old Roy Braybrook finds the sexiest aeroplane in the world is turned down in favour of the Jaguar! The only thing you can do in that situation is to turn your back and walk away, so I crawled off to take a very long look at the military aircraft market.

Now it may be that some young designer reading this will feel that he, too, should get down to where the rubber meets the road, find out what the knuckleheads will be calling for in the next round, and plan a project accordingly. As it happens, there is no need for him to spend years risking getting trampled to death by Korean masseuses, hepatitis in the Persian Gulf, gin-poisoning in India, half-drowned in Nigeria, beaten to a pulp in Tijuana, or any of the other fun-things in the programme. To save him the trouble, I will reveal the fruits of my own excruciatingly painstaking research: DESIGN ANYTHING YOU LIKE, AS LONG AS IT IS FAST AND CHEAP!

The main fact to be grasped is that the military aircraft market is like Hampton Court maze. If you go in expecting to find some subtle solution, you will find it complicated, confusing, and ultimately defeating. On the other hand, if you accept my assurance that the affair warrants nothing more than the crudest possible analysis, then you can master the whole thing in a very short time.

The explanation behind this simplistic market assessment is that the people who *really* select military aircraft are (with obvious reservations on funding and political constraints) simply one-time fighter pilots. They are truly noteworthy for their fine physical condition, excellent co-ordination and fearless courage, but are seldom renowned for any outstanding cerebral quality. Provided they are satisfied that the iron bird will actually leave the ground and their engineering advisers are not literally tearing their hair out, then all they want to know is HOW FAST and HOW MUCH?

All fingers and thumbs

Of course, there are defence departments full of systems analysts who are all working around the clock on computer-aided fighter comparisons, but this effort is nothing more than window-dressing. In each case the CAS (whom you recognise by his well-worn killing *thumb*) has already made up his mind and is merely waiting while his staff (each of whom walks around flexing his trigger *finger*) justifies the Old Man's choice with a truck-load of computer print-out.

My assessment is borne out by the fact that the McDonnell Douglas F-4 is the *only* military jet aircraft of any great technical merit to have achieved world-wide sales. At the opposite extreme, the best-selling subsonic and supersonic fighters are probably the MiG-17 and MiG-21, both of which

Among the military aircraft discussed in this article, two of the most successful in export terms have been the Dassault-Breguet Mirage family and the McDonnell Douglas F-4 Phantom. Illustrated (above) is a Mirage 5 in the markings of the Abu Dhabi Air Force and (below) an F-4E serving with the Hellenic Air Force.

have a well-developed talent for picking up every rock on the airfield and the engine sheds its blades at the first sight of a grain of sand. If (by some miracle) FOD doesn't wreck it first, the motor has to be pulled out every 200 hours and sent back to its maker on the far side of the globe, who then can't be parted from his beloved creation for two whole years! The engineer officer complains that the whole thing is designed to be maintained by an army of professional strongmen six inches (15 cm) tall. If spares aren't ordered on 31 December, the manufacturer turns a deaf ear for a whole twelve months.

To cap it all, the thing is no good in low level flying, because it exhibits PIOs (pilot-induced oscillations) at high airspeeds and because the tailplane trim has a nasty habit of running away and creaming the aluminium into the landscape. It is just as useless in air combat at altitude, because at high AOA (angles of attack) it will suddenly pitch up, which inevitably leads to a spin and then there is nothing to do but punch out!

If our hypothetical designer gets out into the boonies and talks to the operators, he will thus learn that there is a lot more to being a fighter pilot than kicking three tyres and lighting the fire. He will also hear staff officers swearing on a wide range of holy books that they will never again, in any circumstances, allow their air force to be lumbered with half-developed scrap-iron from that particular manufacturer, nor indeed from that nation. Next year you go back, and the Old Man has pulled it off once again! More beer, more tears.

Among the multi-lingual cries of fighter pilot approbation, there will doubtless be the sound of dissent from some instant genius who has never been out among the redbacks and rattlesnakes, and who imagines that the above account is slightly exaggerated. Let me therefore assure you that there are thousands of military aircraft flying around with just those characteristics. Indeed, in most parts of the world you can find hangars full of virtually unused fighters that are simply too awful to fly! In certain countries they line up such aircraft on the airfield, just as though they were about to leap into the blue and intercept someone, but they never do. They were very fast or very cheap (occasionally both), but they are also very unusable.

have (to say the least) serious shortcomings. With any other fighter on your tail, you *never* reverse a turn, whereas with the MiG-17 behind you, if you can get him to apply ailerons under *g*, he will go out of control! The MiG-21 is full of interesting innovations, but the fatigue life of its wings is equivalent to only *two years* of normal use in the ground attack rôle!

As a result of the universally crude system of aircraft selection, the average squadron pilot spends most of his time on the ground crying into his beer and moaning about the garbage that the top brass forces him to fly. He can't reach half the switches in the cockpit, and the reflections on the windscreen make night flying an hallucinatory trauma. The salt water in the atmosphere is eating holes that you can push your fist through in the magnesium. The smallest seagull on record can fly straight through the windscreen. The intakes

It is clear that the general method of fighter selection is seriously at fault. As stated earlier, the average operator's main concern prior to purchase is with cost and speed, or rather, with in-flight performance. At present SEP (specific excess power) has taken over from Max Mach as the most important parameter (sales-wise), but there are indications that this is only a passing phase. Later models of F-16 will thus have a variable-geometry intake to enable level speed to be increased to $M = 2.0$. France has long been aiming for a Mach 3.0 interceptor and it seems likely that several types from the next fighter generation will have dash speeds of at least $M = 2.5$, with high SEP at lower Mach as a natural fall-out.

The next level of sophistication beyond the basic *how much, how fast* evaluation process is to write a list of the desired values of various parameters, summarising performance, reliability, maintainability, etc, and use this list to relate all the available aircraft to the Operational Requirement on a single sheet of paper. A tick is awarded for each parameter achieved, the ticks counted, and marks awarded to each aircraft accordingly. It may sound bizarre that contracts worth hundreds of millions are awarded on such a basis, but it happens all the time!

This evaluation process (known as a *cuadro* in Latin America) illustrates two of the main problems in fighter assessment. Firstly, how do you award bonus points for an aircraft exceeding a required value (eg, of climb rate)? Secondly, how can you be sure that a fair comparison has been achieved in regard to the less easily defined parameters?

Combat allowances

Take, for example, radius of action. This depends on many factors, of which one of the most controversial is combat fuel allowance. It is normal to demand a fuel allowance appropriate to spending several minutes in the target area at a fairly

The General Dynamics F-16 promises to repeat the success of the F-4; with only two prototypes yet flown (the second is illustrated above right) it has been selected by five air forces and more than 1,000 are on order. Considered to be "far more cost effective than a conventional main-base fighter" the Saab Viggen (below) has yet to achieve an export sale.

The McDonnell Douglas F-15, in production for the USAF and to be exported soon to Israel, has so much thrust that it "can pull 8g with external stores and simultaneously accelerate and climb", although it suffers penalties to achieve this performance.

high thrust level, to allow for several complete turns to attack the objective and evade interception. The operator may specify military power (max non-reheat thrust), but this leads to a much bigger radius penalty in (for example) a Harrier than a Mirage, since the former has a much higher non-reheat thrust. One alternative is simply to demand maximum thrust, but in the case of the F-15 or F-16 this thrust is so great that the aircraft can pull 8*g* with external stores and simultaneously accelerate and climb! The fuel (and hence radius) penalty in such cases is clearly unrealistic. In the longer term, air forces will doubtless develop combat allowances in the form of fuel provision for (say) four complete 6*g* turns carrying the specified warload, at sea level and a sustained speed of M = 0·8, but such sophistications are a long way from general use.

Comparing engineering parameters is an even worse problem. Maintenance man-hours per flying hour (MMH/FH) has unfortunately caught on in many imaginations, but is as variable as the length of a piece of string. There are at least three ways to measure this parameter: according to the number of technical staff per aircraft (giving a typical value of about 100!), or on a clock-card basis (40?), or by stop-watch timing "at the aircraft face" (20?). To make matters worse, there is no way to compare USAF, USN and RAF data. What *should* be significant is the number of technical staff per aircraft, but this differs between services according to maintenance policy (ie, the work split between squadron and depot level).

The biggest insult to anyone's intelligence is a brochure that compares the maintenance demands of British, French and American fighters, and claims that this is done on the basis of USAF manuals: there is *no way* this is possible! These manuals provide data on USAF aircraft maintenance demands for

The MiG-17 achieved the status of one of the best-ever sellers among subsonic fighters, despite some serious shortcomings. A Polish Air Force ground-attack version, the LIM-6, is illustrated.

internal planning and accounting purposes and give no clue to the needs of foreign types.

Fatigue life is another virtual non-starter, because the predicted value depends on the assumed spectrum (ie, the number of $2g$, $3g$, $4g$, etc, loads per flying hour), and on the safety factor used in assessing structural tests, which may be 4 or 5. To spell this out, if a large number of identical structures could be fatigue tested, their time-to-failure would show a considerable scatter, so in the real-life situation (where you can only afford a single test), allowance is made for this scatter by means of a safety factor, which varies between countries. Thus, if the fatigue sample fails at 20,000 equivalent flying hours, a British manufacturer would quote a safe life of 4,000 hours, whereas an American or Italian constructor would claim 5,000 hours for the same product!

The severity of the assumed fatigue spectrum also varies with nationality and with the rôle of the aircraft. For example, the Aero L 39 brochure quotes a 9,000-hour life on the basis of a fatigue spectrum taken from a certain US textbook. Without wishing to appear anti-Communist, knowledge of the loadings actually encountered in flight has come a long way since that report was prepared and it is difficult to visualise any major western constructor using such an undemanding spectrum today.

Making an accurate comparison of fatigue lives is therefore difficult. In the writer's view, the only fair approach is for the operator to demand from each manufacturer the number of $3g$, $4g$ and $5g$ loadings (ie, those responsible for most of the fatigue damage) that were actually applied to the test structure. He can then make an assessment of relative safe lives on this basis. I know of no air force that actually does this, so if Haute-Volta wants to be a world leader . . .

Beyond this level of comparison, some air forces make an attempt to carry out cost-effectiveness comparisons in the context of simple scenarios, but it is debatable how good a guide such studies provide and there is little evidence that any great significance is attached to the results.

For example, there are several countries which are threatened by a neighbour and which could provide support for their army in the border region either by a conventional aircraft operating from a rear base, or by a STOL fighter operating from small forward strips. Where forward basing is a practical proposition in terms of logistics, airfield security and camouflage, it can very easily be shown that a Viggen or Harrier is far more cost-effective than a conventional main-base fighter, using ordnance delivery rate as a measure of effectiveness. However, neither aircraft has yet been selected on such a basis.

There is evidence to suggest that cost-effectiveness studies are mistrusted by most decision-makers. For example, there can be little doubt that a comparatively small expenditure on a system to improve weapon delivery accuracy is handsomely repaid in terms of target kill probability, yet there is (as yet) no world-wide rush for better fire control equipment. Some F-5A operators are replacing its very basic reflector sight with a gyro sight (1942 all over again!), and the Israelis have specified an excellent weapon delivery system for their A-4M, but most operators seem content to sit on their money and keep missing the target!

I once attended a presentation in Zurich on the Swiss cost-effectiveness study to choose a Venom replacement. In essence it compared a fixed-price force of various alternative fighter types and ran through the first few days of a war, analysing how many aircraft would be lost due to ground fire and enemy fighters, and how many targets would be destroyed in a given period, according to aircraft weapon load and delivery accuracy. My understanding of the Swiss study is less than complete (if only because the lecturers suddenly switched from German-German to Swiss-German, which is like activating a scrambler), but I believe one point which emerged very clearly was that the A-7 could stand off outside the range of light automatic weapons and *still* hit the target more accurately than the rest. In spite of which, the results of this lengthy study were rejected and the F-5E purchased instead.

There is a certain logic behind the general unwillingness of the top brass to stick their necks out on the strength of a highly complex computer study, since there is no simple way that the results can be checked. With considerable sums of money at stake, it is perfectly natural that the decision-maker should be more concerned with not making a horribly wrong choice, rather than with achieving some theoretical optimum, which is probably little different from several other reasonably good options. In the case of a small air force, the next military aircraft may well be the *only* new type for a whole generation, hence the CAS is under tremendous pressure to make a conservative decision. In the vast majority of cases, he will select an aircraft on the basis of common sense and then let his mathematicians confirm the wisdom of his action.

Before selecting the Aermacchi MB 339 — shown below in full-scale mock-up — to replace its MB 326 trainers, the Italian Air Force evaluated nine projects and six existing types of aircraft.

Developed from the very successful Northrop F-5A Freedom Fighter, the F-5E Tiger II seems likely to go on selling well for some years to come. Illustrated is an example in the markings of the Iranian Imperial Air Force.

The limited acceptability of complex studies is well illustrated by what is loosely known as *"The Bazzocchi Paper"* in military flying training circles. Originally presented as a lecture in Rome early last year, it drew heavily on an operational analysis of training programmes, which was conducted under the direction of Gen Niccoló of the Italian Air Force and led to selection of the MB 339 to replace the MB 326. In outline, the analysis quantified learning rates for various study projects in the primary, basic and advanced phases of flying training, and derived a programme giving the minimum overall expenditure. Nine trainer projects and six existing types were compared by estimating for each one its comparative value in regard to ten characteristics (max speed, approach speed, etc), and by having experienced instructors assess the relative importance of each characteristic in twelve

different types of training mission. All the aircraft were then compared in terms of average learning rate and hence in training time, and finally in total training cost. This showed the rehashed MB 326 with Viper 600 engine to be the best buy, while a new design based on the RB.401 came in second place and a rehashed MB 326 with single Larzac 04 came third. There cannot be an operations analyst in the business who is not fascinated by, and filled with admiration for, this study.

However, consider how this sort of document is received by the potential operator. Suppose for this scenario that I am CAS of (say) the *Force Aérienne de Haute Volta*. Someone must have leaked it to AIR INTERNATIONAL that I am looking for a new trainer, because suddenly my office is jumping with eager salesmen from Aermacchi, Hawker Siddeley Aviation and Dassault-International, which may be good news down at

Matching the success of its subsonic forerunner the MiG-17, the supersonic MiG-21 has proved to be one of the best-selling fighters of the last decade. Illustrated is an example of the MiG-21MF supplied to Bangladesh shortly after that country achieved independence.

In "appalling" weather...

A Jaguar of No 14 Squadron of the Royal Air Force which put up the best individual performance in the Salmond Trophy navigation and bombing competition arrived dead overhead of target, dead on time, and scored a direct hit. The weather was officially described as "appalling".

Jaguar – the best tactical strike aircraft in existence.

Those that made the grade...

and some that didn't.

Can you identify them all? The aircraft currently used by the RAF and those which have been rejected for service.

They're all in the Royal Air Force Yearbook 1976. Plus many more fascinating features. Altogether, there are 72 pages packed with information, diagrams and full colour illustrations covering all aspects of the RAF and aviation, as it was, and today.

At only 50p you can't afford to miss the Royal Air Force Yearbook for 1976. So order your copy now from your newsagent or bookseller, or direct from RAF Yearbook, 283 Lonsdale Road, SW13 9QW, price 65p post paid.

Published by the RAF Benevolent Fund. Proceeds to the RAF Benevolent Fund and the Royal Air Forces Association.

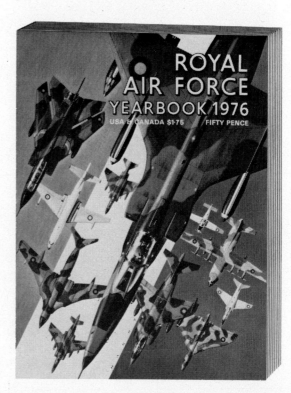

To: ROYAL AIR FORCE YEARBOOK, 283 LONSDALE ROAD, LONDON SW13 9QW.

Please send me .... copy/copies RAF YEARBOOK 1976

@ 65p ($2.00) each, post paid. Payment of .... is enclosed.

PLEASE PRINT

NAME _____

ADDRESS _____

TOWN/CITY_____

COUNTY/STATE _____

POST/ZIP CODE _____

The full export potential of the SEPECAT Jaguar has probably yet to be realised. The addition of air-to-air missiles on overwing launchers, (Matra Magics in the illustration) extends the Jaguar International's capabilities but is a feature not adopted by the RAF or Armée de l'Air.

the Hotel Intercontinental, but is a pain in the posterior for me. The guy from Aermacchi lays this Bazzocchi Paper on me. First thing, I haul my CFI out of his Cessna and ask him to run his slide-rule over the study. Like every other CFI in the world, he says, "Listen, Chief: What I do with that aluminium is like art, poetry and music. Only some dumb Italian systems analyst would try to put numbers to it!" Anyway, I'm in a good mood, so I say to Aermacchi, "Supposing for the next two minutes I believe all this stuff, if I could correct the performance and price of your paper aeroplanes using Adour and twin-Larzac engines to coincide with the data I have from these other two idiots, what would the bottom line be then?" Of course, he doesn't know, Bazzocchi doesn't know, and the only guy who could work it out is good old Col Giorgeri in Rome, and he hasn't got the competitors' data anyway! The point I am trying to make is that the most beautiful cost-effectiveness study in the world is useless saleswise, unless the foreign operator can check it out for himself and then modify it to suit his own inputs.

Summary

What does it all add up to? *Excellent in-flight performance sells. Low price sells. Advanced technology only sells when it results in excellent in-flight performance or low price. Nothing else sells aeroplanes.* Those four sentences should be tatooed on the backs of the hands of everyone in British aerospace management!

The main fault with the industry is well illustrated by the AST 396 affair. Judging from accounts leaked to the press by the RAF, this next generation aircraft was to have combined the warload-radius of a Jaguar with the airfield performance of a Harrier, and it would have been just another transonic attack aircraft, with just the same export prospects as its predecessors. In spite of this, industry spent many months running paper studies to dignify this absurdity, suggesting either that industry was too moronic to recognise an obvious non-starter, or was too gutless to tell the RAF that it didn't need another export flop. Fortunately for all concerned, the Americans saved the day by demonstrating the General Dynamics F-16 in the UK. Sanity has won: AST 396 is dead, long live 403!

British military aerospace has always been characterised by design-domination. This was all very well in the seller's market of the 1950s, but is totally out of place in today's buyer's market. We have now suffered a whole generation of military aircraft that were nothing more than a triumph of technology over marketing sense. In my view, if the present industrial reorganisation achieves nothing more than to give the salesmen an equal say with the designers on future projects, then it will have been well worthwhile. □

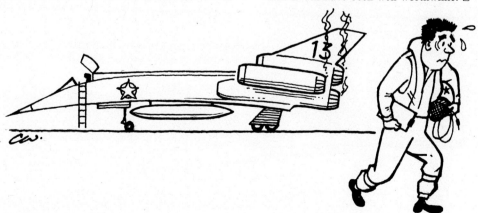

THE DHA GLIDERS

AUSTRALIA'S "WOODEN WARBIRDS"

Gp Capt Keith Isaacs AFC, RAAF (Retd) reveals the hitherto untold story of the de Havilland Australia G1 and G2 gliders of the RAAF in WW II, and how they spawned an exotic post-war gem — a suction wing glider with a Ford V-8 engine.

THE HISTORY of airpower in the Antipodes began, tentatively, in 1909 when a fragile biplane glider with a boxkite tail became the first aerodyne to fly in Australia. On 11 September 1909, the Commonwealth Government had announced a competition for "Flying Machines For Military Purposes" and one contender for the £5,000 prize was George Augustine Taylor. During September, Taylor opened an aeroplane factory — the first in Australia and, probably, the first in the southern hemisphere — at Redfern, a suburb of Sydney, New South Wales. There he constructed a glider based on the boxkite experiments of Lawrance Hargrave, a close friend and mentor for some years. Thus on 5 December 1909, Taylor became the first man in Australia to fly a heavier-than-air craft when he completed a number of flights in his glider from the sand-dunes at Narrabeen Beach, near Sydney.

Taylor's historic glider was built under the aegis of the army and, on 20 December, he was made an honorary lieutenant in the Australian Intelligence Corps. Early in 1910, Taylor designed a 20 hp engine which he planned to install in his glider to meet the requirements of the government's competition for a powered military aeroplane. The engine was not a success, however, and he abandoned the project. Nevertheless, Taylor's glider is recorded in history as the unpowered precursor of the military aeroplane in Australia.

Gliders subsequently disappeared from the Australian military scene for almost 33 years; except, perhaps, for the pseudo-glider demonstrations during the three great RAAF displays at RAAF Laverton, Victoria, on 10 November 1934, Flemington Racecourse, Victoria, on 9 April 1938, and RAAF Richmond, NSW, on 23 April 1938. Each of these pageants featured a popular event showing "a possible method of rescue of light aircraft after engine failure". In each instance a D.H.60 Gipsy Moth appeared over the spectators, simulated an engine failure and made a spot landing with a "dead stick". Mechanics immediately removed the propeller and attached 300 ft (91,5 m) of towline cable, with a special quick-release fitting, to the propeller boss. A Westland Wapiti then towed the Moth to 3,000 ft (915 m) before casting it off over the landing area; in the 1938 displays the "glider" slow-rolled during the climb to height. After release, the Moth dived for speed, made a perfect loop off the glide, executed a stall turn or two to dispose of surplus height and concluded by making another excellent spot landing. The propeller was immediately refitted and the aircraft flew off under its own power. Thus, these RAAF "Moth Gliders" — like their insect namesakes — enjoyed but a minuscule life span.

Such demonstrations were in keeping with the happy, carefree days of the inter-war air displays, but all-too-soon

(Below) The first prototype DHA G1 glider, EG-1, photographed on the tarmac outside the Special Duties and Performance Flight, RAAF Laverton, in November 1942. (Heading photo) The first of the six production DHA G2s, A57-1, in free flight near RAAF Laverton, whilst in use as a trials and pilot-conversion aircraft at the SDPF between 1943 and 1945.

these gave way to the grim reality of global conflict and, early in 1942, Japanese forces were poised around northern Australia where an invasion appeared imminent. One immediate problem facing Australia was the inability to transport, rapidly, large numbers of troops and equipment across the vast inland areas of the continent to the northern defence perimeters. Existing road and rail facilities were inadequate and the RAAF transport aircraft element was practically non-existent. In fact, a small number of civilian airliners, including Short Empire flying boats, Douglas DC-3s and de Havilland D.H.86s and D.H.89s, had been chartered and impressed to augment the RAAF's sole transport aircraft type, the Wackett-designed Tugan Gannet. In addition, a varied collection of privately owned Percival, Fairchild, Miles, Stinson, Beechcraft, Cessna, de Havilland and Lockheed light aircraft was taken over for communications duties. At the time, the demand for transport aircraft was at a premium throughout the world and the possibility of Australia obtaining such machines in a hurry was extremely remote. From this desperate situation, therefore, a need arose for production of a transport aerodyne — which could be constructed quickly and easily — for use in conjunction with the existing transport force. One answer to the problem appeared to be the military glider.

The experimental gliders

On 24 March 1942, the Aircraft Advisory Committee — which had been set up by the War Cabinet in 1941 to advise the Director-General of the Department of Aircraft Production — received a communication from the Director-General of Supply and Production, Department of Air, stating that an immediate requirement existed for 126 gliders. Accompanying the communication was an RAAF specification for an experimental seven-seat prototype glider, which was submitted to the Commonwealth Aircraft Corporation and to de Havilland Aircraft Pty Ltd (nominally known as de Havilland Australia or simply DHA). L J Wackett, as Chief Technical Adviser to the committee, considered that the project could be handled by DHA, and committee member Major A Murray Jones, General Manager of DHA, concurred with Wackett's suggestion.

The terms of reference specified that no equipment or labour — other than a chief designer and an organiser and stressing expert — would be provided by DHA. This was because of the priority allotted to contracts for the D.H.82A Tiger Moth and the DHA.84 Dragon Trainers, both of which were in full production at Mascot Aerodrome, Sydney. Furthermore, tentative plans were already in being for the construction by DHA of Australian versions of the D.H.98 Mosquito. In the event, the Sydney branch of Slazengers (Australia) Pty Ltd provided a foreman, a draughtsman, most of the labour force

and all the woodworking equipment. Perhaps the most surprising aspect of the project was the locale selected for the production of the prototype glider — the fifth floor of the Bradford Cotton Mills building at Camperdown, Sydney.

As chief designer, DHA selected Martin Warner, who was not only an engineer but a keen glider pilot and a member of the Sydney Soaring Club. Warner had already designed two attractive and efficient pod-and-boom sailplanes, the Kite I and Kite II (in no way connected with the English Slingsby designs of the same name). DHA also provided Steve Newbigin, while Gordon Andrews became the main draughtsman. As the project got under way the transport gliders became known, unofficially, as "Warner's Wooden Warbirds".

In April 1942, the RAAF authorised the construction of a second DHA G1 prototype glider, for military trials, before a production line was laid down. It is interesting to note that the RAAF referred to both aircraft as Experimental Glider 1 types, whereas DHA identified them as Experimental Glider-1 and Experimental Glider-2.

EG-1 and EG-2 were built entirely with Australian materials in accordance with the specification. Each glider was a high wing cantilever monoplane with a thick plywood covered monospar wing of 59 ft (17,9 m) span. The wing section at the root of the mainplane was NACA 23015 and changed to NACA 4415 near the wing tips. The ailerons were of a simple unbalanced type and spoilers were located on the upper surface of each wing near the maximum thickness. The box-section fuselage was plywood covered and was built up on four longerons. Seats were provided for a pilot, and six passengers in three pairs. Access doors were positioned on each side of the fuselage and a luggage locker was situated at the back of the rear seat. The windscreen and window frames of the DHA utility version of the Dragon radio and navigation trainer — equivalent to the British Dragon Mk I — were incorporated in the glider design, but the rest of the nose section was an original pattern. The tail unit was of simple construction with unbalanced elevator, "cheesecutter" longitudinal trim and a horn balanced rudder with a fixed metal trimming tab. The control surfaces were fabric covered. The undercarriage consisted of a single wheel, approximately

(Below) The second prototype DHA G1 at RAAF Laverton in 1943. The original marking EG-2 has been removed but the serial A57-1002 has yet to be applied; white and blue Pacific markings are carried. (Above right) The first production G2 being towed-off from RAAF Laverton (by a Dakota) during a display in August 1947.

De Havilland DHA G1 Specification
Performance: Towing speed, 130 mph (209 km/h); maximum speed, 185 mph (298 km/h); stalling speed, 48 mph (77 km/h).
Weights: Empty, 1,240 lb (563 kg); loaded, 2,800 lb (1 272 kg).
Dimensions: Span, 59 ft 0 in (17,99 m); length, 35 ft 0 in (10,68 m); height, 7 ft 10 in (2,39 m); wing section NACA 23015.
Accommodation: Pilot and six troops.

De Havilland DHA G2 Specification
Performance: Towing speed, 130 mph (209 km/h); max speed, 200 mph (322 km/h); stalling speed, 48 mph (77 km/h).
Weights: Empty, 1,450 lb (658 kg); loaded, 3,250 lb (1 476 kg).
Dimensions: Span, 50 ft 6 in (15,40 m); length, 33 ft 0 in (10,07 m); height, 7 ft 10 in (2,39 m); wing section NACA 23015.
Accommodation: Pilot and six troops.

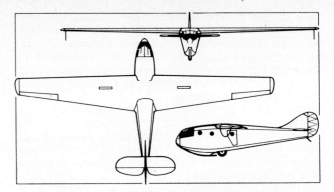

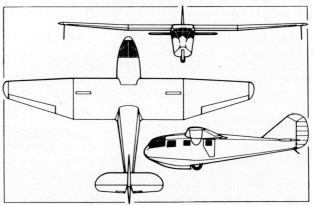

Three-view drawings depict the different wing plan forms of (above) the DHA G1 and (below) DHA G2.

beneath the aircraft's centre of gravity and braced to the mainplane spar on a tubular steel frame. The nose skid was sprung by rubber buffers and the tail skid was of laminated ash with a metal shoe sprung by coiled elastic bands.

The pilot's controls consisted of a conventional column and rudder pedals, "cheesecutter" tail trim, spoiler control lever and brake lever. The flying instruments comprised an ASI, altimeter, fore and aft level and cross level. The glider was towed from two points under the main spar and the towline — about 200 ft (61 m) of 2½ in (6,4 m) manila rope — had a 28 ft (8,5 m) bridle at the end. Maximum tow speed was 130 mph (209 km/h) which brought the gliders into the minimum tug speed range of a Supermarine Spitfire. Although the Spitfire was used for subsequent trials, the initial flying tests were made behind Wapiti and Battle aircraft; a photograph of Wapiti, A5-16 with EG-1 and EG-2 on tow appeared in "Project Skywards" (*Air International,* July 1975). The gliders had a gross weight of 2,800 lb (1 271 kg), and a tare weight of 1,240 lb (563 kg) which comprised the pilot, six passengers and 160 lb (73 kg) of luggage.

Flight testing by DHA of EG-1 began on 14 June 1942, after the glider had been assembled at RAAF Richmond. The first taxi tests were made behind a RAAF motor vehicle and a Wapiti then took over for the initial flight tests. The tests were satisfactory, although an accident occurred in the first week of July, during full load trials, when the tow rope broke on a flight behind a Battle, between Bankstown and Richmond. Warner was flying the ballast-loaded glider, and Newbigin was also aboard as an observer. Although the pilot landed successfully in a small field, the brake structure on the single landing wheel failed and the glider went through a fence with barbed-wire strands. The nose of the aircraft was considerably damaged, and Warner spent some weeks in hospital with badly lacerated shins. Meanwhile, the incomplete second prototype, EG-2, was transferred from Camperdown to a building which had previously been used as the Slingo and Williams toy factory. In early November the glider was assembled at Mascot where flight tests were made.

Prototypes enter service

In late September 1942, personnel from the Special Duties and Performance Flight, RAAF Laverton, arrived at RAAF Richmond to ferry EG-1, towed behind a Battle, to the flight's home base. On 29 September, two demonstration flights were made with EG-1 and the Battle, to enable the DHA pilot to explain the glider's capabilities to his RAAF counterpart. A further familiarisation flight of almost one hour was completed by the RAAF on 2 October.

During the morning of 5 October, the Battle took-off from RAAF Richmond with EG-1 on tow, bound for RAAF Laverton, where EG-1 was officially accepted by the RAAF on 11 October 1942 and it was later renumbered with the service prototype serial A57-1001. It was joined at RAAF Laverton on 17 November by EG-2 which eventually became A57-1002. Almost immediately the RAAF, through the Council for Scientific and Industrial Research — Division of Aeronautics

at Fishermen's Bend, Victoria, issued brief handling notes for the gliders. Part One of this report, published in November 1942, detailed the operating capabilities of A57-1001 on the ground, in towed flight, in free flight and during the landing pattern.

Part Two of the CSIR-DA report, dated April 1943, revealed that "further flying has been done on A57-1001 (EG-1), including the rate of descent in free flight and the investigation of stability on tow". This report stated that the most stable condition for towing was at 120 mph (193 km/h) with the glider below the tug; presumably, the clear vision panel above the pilot's seat had been installed since the delivery flight of A57-1001 in October 1942. The report also commented on the high accident rate with tail skids. Almost every landing resulted in a broken skid and, consequently, the tail skid was considerably strengthened. In addition, the report contained diagrams showing the estimated performances of a DAP Bristol Beaufort VIII and a Lockheed Hudson III towing one or two gliders at 10,000 ft (3 050 m), and a CAC Wirraway and a Battle each towing one glider at 10,000 ft (3 050 m).

Up to this time — April 1943 — the two gliders had been held on charge by No 1 Aircraft Depot, RAAF Laverton. During the month, however, they were transferred to SDPF, RAAF Laverton — this flight subsequently became No 1 Aircraft Performance Unit, and a detachment moved to RAAF Point Cook with the gliders. The two prototypes were used for glider trials and experiments during the 12 months that they were attached to SDPF and No 1 APU. In May 1944, A57-1001 and A57-1002 were allotted to No 5 Aircraft Depot, RAAF Cootamundra, NSW, for storage and were eventually transferred to the Department of Aircraft Production for disposal on 18 December 1947.

RAAF glider element

While the DHA G1 prototypes were undergoing initial tests in mid-1942, the RAAF glider specification had been considerably changed, necessitating a major redesign for the production models. One change involved the division of the wing into three parts for ease of transportation. A two-wheel undercarriage was also proposed, but this was rejected in favour of the original monowheel. Also, by the time production commenced on the improved DHA G2 gliders, the original requirement for a large number of these aircraft had been negated by several factors — the improved military situation, the acquisition by the RAAF of Douglas Dakotas and other transport aircraft and the availability of the Waco CG-4A glider which accommodated 15 troops. Consequently, only six DHA G2 gliders were ordered in accordance with RAAF Specification 5/42, and they were allotted the RAAF serial numbers A57-1 to A57-6. It is pertinent to record that during November 1942, DAP received an enquiry from the USAAF in connection with the supply of 20 DHA G2 gliders. Follow-up action was initiated, but an order from the USAAF did not eventuate.

The six production gliders were all built in the Slingo and Williams building and were assembled at Mascot Aerodrome for testing. Battles were flown in from No 1 Aircraft Park, RAAF Geelong, Victoria, for towing, and the tests were carried out at No 3 Communications Flight, RAAF Mascot. DHA tested the first glider on 20 March 1943, and the ailerons were found to be very heavy owing to the fitment of substitute bearings. The incorporation of a balance tab rectified this fault and, by July, all six gliders had been tested by the company.

In contrast to the DHA G1, the DHA G2 glider had a slightly larger fuselage although it still retained the DHA.84 Dragon fittings. Also, the one-piece straight wing of 59 ft (17,99 m) span on the G1 was replaced with one of 50 ft 6 in (15,40 m) span with a single box spar, a 23 ft (7,02 m) constant chord centre section and two tapering outer sections. In addition the round windows and short wingtip skids on the G1 gave way to square windows and longer wingtip skids on the G2. Most of these changes were made, under the direction of Martin Warner, by the complete fourth year University of Sydney aeronautical class of students. Professor A V Stephens, who had assisted in solving the aerodynamic problems on the prototypes, also took a close personal interest in the construction of the DHA G2s and in March 1943 he proposed fitting an experimental laminar flow wing to a DHA G2 glider for aerodynamic tests, but this project was held in abeyance.

The first production glider, A57-1, was handed over to the RAAF at DHA Mascot on 6 May 1943 and, on 11 June, it was delivered to SDPF for service trials. The glider was damaged in a landing at RAAF Laverton on 22 October and was issued to No 1 AD for repairs. On 10 January 1944, A57-1 was allotted to No 1 APU where it completed its wartime service as a trials and pilot-conversion aircraft. It was transferred to No 1 Central Recovery Depot on 20 January 1945 for storage and, as from November 1946, was kept in Category E storage at No 1 Stores Depot. But A57-1 had yet to reach the zenith of its career, and the rôle it played post-war in a major experiment is subsequently related.

The remaining five gliders, A57-2 to A57-6, were all delivered to No 2 Aircraft Depot, RAAF Richmond, from No 2 Aircraft Park, RAAF Mascot, in July 1943. On 30 August it was decided to transfer the five gliders, for temporary storage, to No 1 Air Observers School, RAAF Evans Head, NSW (where the author first saw the DHA G2 glider while on an interim posting to No 1 AOS as a staff pilot flying Avro Ansons in 1944).

The third glider, A57-3, remained in storage until March 1948 when it was transferred for overhaul from No 2 AD to DHA. It was then allotted to No 86 Wing, RAAF Richmond — comprising Nos 36, 37 and 38 Squadrons flying Dakotas — but was damaged during take-off on the delivery flight from Mascot Aerodrome on 31 May 1948. In the event, the glider continued the towed flight to Richmond and was repaired by No 2 AD before it joined the transport wing on 10 August. A57-3 is believed to have completed the occasional flight on

tow behind the Dakotas but, apparently, it was kept mainly in storage. Late in 1952, the glider was reported as being held in a serviceable condition by No 82 Wing, RAAF Amberley, Queensland — the RAAF's bomber wing comprising Nos 1 (then in Singapore), 2 and 6 Squadrons flying GAF Avro Lincoln B.Mk 30s. On 14 November 1952 A57-3 was offered for disposal and was deleted from the RAAF register.

Both A57-4 and A57-5 also remained in storage throughout the war years. Then, on 27 March 1947, A57-4 was issued to the School of Air Support, RAAF Laverton, from No 2 AD. In 1948 SAS moved to RAAF Williamtown, NSW, and was renamed the School of Land/Air Warfare. By late 1950, SCLAW had relegated A57-4 to an instructional airframe and it was eventually converted to components at the school on 7 July 1952. Like its predecessor, A57-5 was also brought out of storage in 1947 when it was issued on loan to CSIR-DA. Little is known of its history at the division but, presumably, it was used in some way with the post-war experiment conducted with A57-1. In the event A57-5 was returned to No 1 AD in late 1949 and, a year later, was converted to components.

The last glider, A57-6, was transferred from storage at No 2 AD to No 5 AD on 2 January 1944. In 1946 approval was given to convert the glider to components but, instead, it was passed to DAP for disposal on 18 December 1947.

Flying the DHA G2

As most of the RAAF gliders spent their time in storage, only a few pilots were trained for glider operations, and conversion courses were mainly conducted on A57-1 at No 1 APU. Four flights were usually sufficient to convert a normal pilot — three under instruction, and one solo. A57-1 was modified to take dual controls, although the second set comprised only a control column and rudder bar. When required, the latter installation was mounted behind the normal pilot's seat, in front of the forward row of passenger seats, where it was possible to see the instrument panel — comprising an airspeed indicator, altimeter, pitch indicator and bank indicator — over the shoulders of the first pilot.

Preparations for flight included a normal pre-flight inspection of the glider with particular attention being paid to the tow rope and release gear of the tug aircraft. On the glider the pilot checked that the tow release catches under the wing were properly closed, and that the lever for the tow rope release was in the lock position; this lever was on the left hand side of the cockpit above the cable-operated brake lever for the single landing wheel. The spoilers — which were fitted to the top surface of the wing, and were operated by a lever forward, and to the left, of the pilot's seat — were checked in the closed

Three of the DHA G2 gliders after assembly at DHA Mascot Aerodrome, awaiting delivery to No 2 AD, RAAF Richmond, in July 1943.

GLAS II cutaway drawing key

28 Ford Mercury 59A 96 bhp V-8 engine
29 Engine exhaust pipe
30 Central suction 24-in (60-cm) fan
31 Exhaust louvre doors — 2 port, 2 starboard

32 Engine coolant radiator in suction duct
33 Suction "T" duct
34 Turning vanes in suction "T" duct
35 Starboard suction duct
36 F.24 camera installation
37 Camera access door
38 Port tapered outer wing panel, 12 ft 10½ in (3,93 m) span
39 Port wing-tip skid, bungee sprung
40 Resin bonded moulded plywood tip
41 Port aileron
42 Port aileron trim tab
43 Tailwheel

44 Tailplane set at 8½ deg negative incidence
45 Port elevator
46 Port elevator trim tab
47 Original D.H.A. G2 rudder
48 Starboard elevator
49 Original D.H.A. G2 fin
50 Pitot head and incidence vane for observer's instrument panel (installed after third flight)
51 Fairing over original fuselage
52 Starboard spoiler (suction in first slot only in centre section — three slots outer section)
53 Starboard aileron trim tab
54 Starboard aileron
55 Static pressure points (150)

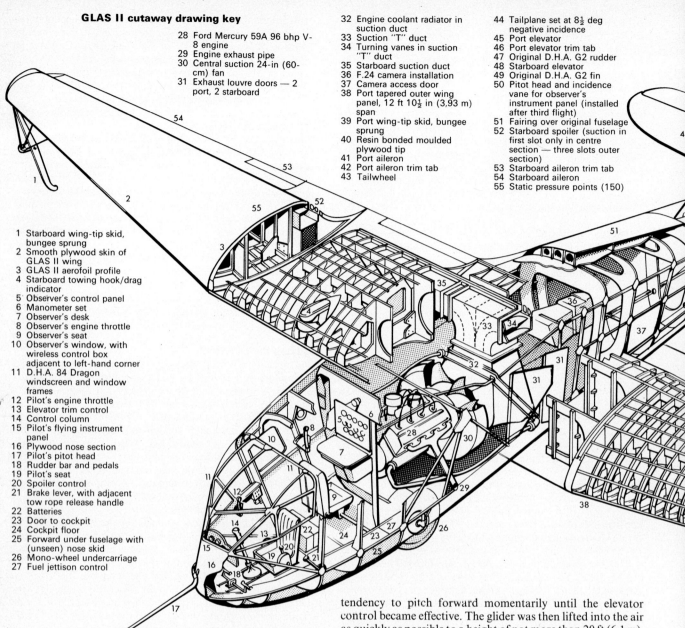

1 Starboard wing-tip skid, bungee sprung
2 Smooth plywood skin of GLAS II wing
3 GLAS II aerofoil profile
4 Starboard towing hook/drag indicator
5 Observer's control panel
6 Manometer set
7 Observer's desk
8 Observer's engine throttle
9 Observer's seat
10 Observer's window, with wireless control box adjacent to left-hand corner
11 D.H.A. 84 Dragon windscreen and window frames
12 Pilot's engine throttle
13 Elevator trim control
14 Control column
15 Pilot's flying instrument panel
16 Plywood nose section
17 Pilot's pitot head
18 Rudder bar and pedals
19 Pilot's seat
20 Spoiler control
21 Brake lever, with adjacent tow rope release handle
22 Batteries
23 Door to cockpit
24 Cockpit floor
25 Forward under fuselage with (unseen) nose skid
26 Mono-wheel undercarriage
27 Fuel jettison control

position. When checking the flying controls it was necessary to obtain full movement of the ailerons to ensure that the gap between the balance tabs and the ailerons was clear.

The glider was positioned off the runway for take-off to ensure that it would not pitch forward on its nose during the initial take-off stage; otherwise, it would stop on the nose skid and lift the tail high off the ground and, of course, the tail would be damaged when released from the tug in this condition. It was also desirable to have the wings held level before the take-off commenced. The brakes were then released by the glider pilot and take-off trim was set — longitudinal trimming was effected by a trim tab on the elevators which was operated by a lever on the right hand side of the cockpit. The tug, having been attached to the glider, would then taxi slowly forward to take up the slack in the tow rope.

For take-off the pilot of the tug applied as much power as possible while holding his aircraft on the brakes. As soon as the brakes were released full take-off power was applied. If power was not applied rapidly the glider would drag one wing on the ground for some distance before aileron control was obtained, and this could damage the wing skid. As the glider got under way the pilot would find that his aircraft had a

tendency to pitch forward momentarily until the elevator control became effective. The glider was then lifted into the air as quickly as possible to a height of not more than 20 ft (6,1 m), where the nose was eased down to allow the tug aircraft to accelerate and take-off. The pilot's notes emphasised that the glider must not be flown too high above the tail of the tug, otherwise it would "pull the towing aircraft's tail up and place the tug pilot in an extremely embarrassing position".

After take-off the tug climbed away at 115 mph (185 km/h), and the glider pilot was free to select the high or low tow positions, whereby the glider cleared the tug's slipstream by flying above or below the tail of the towing aircraft. At 400 ft (122 m), the tug usually commenced a port turn to keep the glider within gliding distance of the aerodrome. The tug normally climbed to heights between 3,000-5,000 ft (915-1 525 m), and towing speeds never exceeded 160 mph (257 km/h), the optimum speed being 130 mph (209 km/h).

To obtain free flight the glider pilot merely had to move the tow-rope release lever from the back to the forward position. The immediate result of this action, as outlined in pilot's notes was twofold:

"(a) *It releases the two ropes from under the glider's mainplanes and*
(b) *Causes a sharp 'crack' that usually brings to an abrupt halt any light conversation being held at the time by the passengers.*"

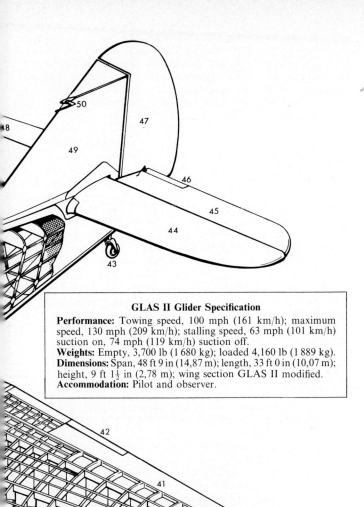

GLAS II Glider Specification

Performance: Towing speed, 100 mph (161 km/h); maximum speed, 130 mph (209 km/h); stalling speed, 63 mph (101 km/h) suction on, 74 mph (119 km/h) suction off.
Weights: Empty, 3,700 lb (1 680 kg); loaded 4,160 lb (1 889 kg).
Dimensions: Span, 48 ft 9 in (14,87 m); length, 33 ft 0 in (10,07 m); height, 9 ft 1½ in (2,78 m); wing section GLAS II modified.
Accommodation: Pilot and observer.

PILOT PRESS
COPYRIGHT
DRAWING

The glider stalled at about 48 mph (77 km/h) with the spoilers out, or in the retracted position. The stall was extremely gentle and there was no tendency of a wing to drop. The nose merely dropped slightly and, as the speed built up, control was quickly regained.

The approach to land was initiated at about 80 mph (129 km/h) with the spoilers in. The spoilers were used only when the pilot felt he was overshooting or required to lose height more rapidly. S-turns were also recommended to keep the glider on the down-wind edge of the selected landing spot. On the final approach a careful use of the spoilers enabled the pilot to reduce speed to about 55 mph (88 km/h).

The landing was made on the wheel at the slowest speed possible. If the glider landed into a wind of moderate strength, the pilot could maintain control until the glider ended its landing run. At the end of the run the glider rocked back on its tail skid, and over on to one of the wingtip skids. The glider could be brought to a halt in an emergency by applying the brake and pushing forward on the control column, which pushed the glider on to its nose skid.

The glider conversion courses all but came to an end at the conclusion of the 1939-45 War, and it appeared that the RAAF's small glider force would soon be phased out of service. In the event, at least one of the gliders was granted a new lease of life in the immediate post-war years, and it remained in flying service until 1951.

The GLAS II project
In June 1946, the inaugural meeting of the Commonwealth Advisory Aeronautical Research Council was held in London. Several proposals eventuated from this meeting including the recommendation that a Griffith-type suction wing should be tested in flight. The aims of the project were to assess the engineering problems involved in building, and flying, wings of this type, and to see how far the theoretical advantages of the suction aerofoil could be realised in practice. The task was accepted by Australia and was allocated to CSIR-DA (later the Aeronautical Research Laboratories), DAP-Beaufort Division (later the Government Aircraft Factories) and the RAAF.

Suction aerofoils had originated from a suggestion put forward in the UK in 1942 by Dr A A Griffith. He proposed a wing designed specifically for suction, and of such a shape as to have a rising velocity over a great proportion of its surface so that the major part of the boundary layer flow remained laminar. His design envisaged boundary air being sucked away towards the trailing edge of the aerofoil through suitably placed slots, the resulting sink effect giving rise to a sudden increase in pressure. Thus the adverse pressure gradient on the rear of the aerofoil, which contributed to drag, would be eliminated. In addition to the aspect of low drag, the Griffith principle permitted the design of very thick wings which, at the time, appeared to show great promise for the development of an all-wing aircraft. One outstanding design was the GLAS II*, a 31 per cent thick section that was particularly suitable for the moderate size all-wing application, in the 300-400 mph (482-643 km/h) speed range. Consequently, it was this type of wing that was selected for the Australian experiment.

The CSIR component of the GLAS II project team in Australia comprised T S Keeble, R W Cumming, and A F W Langford. A review of local resources indicated that the most expedient method of flight testing a suction wing would be to modify a DHA G2 glider by replacing the existing unswept wing with a suction aerofoil of the same plan form — a second stage of the investigation was planned to determine the effect on a swept-back wing. It was decided to accommodate the suction plant in the glider's fuselage where, unfortunately, weight and space limitations prevented the installation of a standby emergency plant. Consequently, it was necessary to provide for the possibility of suction failure. Thus, the GLAS II aerofoil was an ideal choice for the project because of its simplicity — it required suction on the upper surface only — and because the cambered aerofoil was expected to have safer characteristics in the event of suction failure.

Anticipating the requirement for a DHA G2 glider, the RAAF arranged to take A57-1 out of Category E storage at No 1 SD. On 15 January 1947, an allotment authority was issued for the aircraft to be transferred to No 1 APU. Throughout the year a limited number of flying tests were carried out with the glider at No 1 APU, RAAF Point Cook and, later, ARDU, RAAF Laverton. These flights were made with the orthodox wing to form the basis of comparison with the planned suction wing, and the glider was also used on

---

Some doubt now exists as to whether the abbreviation stood for Griffith Laminar Aerofoil Section or Glauert Lighthill Aerofoil Section.

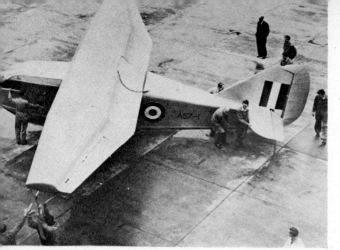

The unorthodox shape of the GLAS II suction wing aerofoil is well-shown in this view of the newly-modified A57-1 being wheeled out of the GAF hangar at Fishermen's Bend in 1948.

occasions for demonstrations at the School of Air Support, RAAF Laverton. In January 1948, A57-1 was transferred to the GAF factories at Fishermen's Bend for modifications and fitment of the new wing.

Meanwhile, preliminary design work on the suction wing at CSIR-DA had commenced in March 1947. Many details could not be settled, however, until October 1947 when the wind tunnel development of the aerofoil, in the neighbourhood of the suction slots, had brought the suction quantity and pressure to reasonable values. This arduous task, which used a ⅛th-scale model of the wing, a similar scale model of the complete glider and a quarter-scale half-wing, was carried out by Tom Keeble, Ron Cumming, and Rick Langford.

As 1948 progressed, the new wing was manufactured by GAF at Fishermen's Bend where A57-1 had been positioned early in the year. The basic design concept for the wing was originated by Nigel Joyce of CSIR-DA, and the detailed design was carried out at GAF under Gordon Appleby. GAF also appointed Paul Mardel as project engineer, and he stayed with the project throughout the construction and flight test phases.

The GLAS II wing had the same planform as the original NACA 23015 wing of the DHA G2. It was made up of a centre section of 8 ft (2,44 m) chord and 23 ft (7,02 m) span, with tapered outer panels each of 12 ft 10½ in (3,93 m) span, making a total span of 48 ft 9 in (14,88 m) as against 50 ft 6 in (15,4 m) of the original wing. The same aileron span was retained, but the conventional spoilers of the DHA G2 wing were replaced by shutters, inside the suction duct, which shut off 4 ft (1,22 m) of the front slot on each wing. The new wing was also fitted with three suction slots on the top surface at 63·4, 66·6 and 68·6 per cent of the chord from the leading edge. These slots had well rounded entries and were 0·09 in (2,3 mm), 0·05 in (1,27 mm), and 0·05 in (1,27 mm) wide, respectively, over the whole span, with tolerances of plus ·005 to 0·000 in (0,13 mm to 0,00 mm) on width. The remaining control surfaces of the DHA G2 glider were retained. The other major modification was the installation of a Ford V-8 Mercury 59A automotive engine of 96 bhp in the fuselage to drive the CSIR-DA designed centrifugal blower for the suction. The final assembly work on the glider was carried out at RAAF Laverton.

The reconstructed glider had a soundproof bulkhead dividing the fuselage into two sections with a separate access to each bay; the bulkhead was positioned approximately in line with the leading edge of the wing. The forward bay comprised the crew compartment for the pilot and observer. The pilot's controls and instruments remained standard, except for the spoiler lever. Instead of opening the surface spoilers, this lever operated a shutter which closed the exit from the slot for a distance of 4 ft (1,22 m) on each wing. This had the same effect as the spoilers and avoided the necessity of cutting into the skin to fit normal top surface flaps. Additional fittings on the starboard side of the cockpit included the engine throttle and the radio control box; a subsequent recommendation suggested that all controls should be on the port side, so that the trimmer and engine control could be operated without changing hands on the control column.

The observer sat with his back to the pilot at a desk, and his controls included the engine starting button, switches, choke, throttle, and the automatic observer camera operating button. The panel in front of the observer contained a duplicate set of flight instruments (airspeed indicator, altimeter, rate of climb, air temperature, and angle incidence), engine instruments (RPM, boost, temperature, and oil pressure gauges), and the fire warning light and extinguisher control. Three sets of indicators recorded the pressure and quantity of suction air, towline drag by direct measurement, and aerofoil pressure which showed the static pressure and, thus, the state of flow on the wing behind the slot. The observer also controlled the speed of the suction motor, but the pilot had an over-riding throttle control in case of emergency. A radio was fitted to give contact with the tug and the ground and a normal intercommunication system was installed for the pilot and observer.

The Ford Mercury car engine was housed behind the observer's compartment and was fitted with the specially designed centrifugal fan with the inlet duct coming down from the wing. The suction air passed through the radiator of the engine and provided cooling independently of aircraft speed. The suction air was discharged through two louvre doors, one on each side of the fuselage.

The next compartment contained the automatic observer, comprising a panel containing 30 standard airspeed indicators, a lighting system and an F.24 camera which was motor operated and controlled by the observer. These instruments formed, in effect, a 30 tube multi-manometer; their leads were carried forward to a connection board in the observer's compartment where they could be connected to any of the 150 pressure points fitted to the wing and suction duct.

Flight tests

After the GLAS II glider was assembled at RAAF Laverton it was allotted to ARDU where the chief test pilot, Sqdn Ldr D R Cuming, AFC, initiated the flight testing programme. Gel Cuming, as he was universally known, arranged for the glider to be tested on the ground before the first flight was made. A57-1 being tethered in the slipstream of ARDU's GAF Avro Lincoln B.Mk.30. An appreciation of the aileron handling characteristics was obtained in this way, with suction on and off, and as these tests indicated that the ailerons were positive in their action, it was decided to go ahead with the air tests.

On 26 October 1948, the GLAS II was attached to ARDU's Douglas Dakota by means of a 300-ft (92-m) nylon cable, for the first take-off. It was decided to make the flight with the glider's engine running in idle, with negligible suction, but at a speed of 60-80 mph (97-129 km/h) during the take-off, the wings started to rock laterally, the ailerons appeared to become ineffective, the port wing dropped as the glider became airborne and the wing-tip skid hit the runway. Cuming immediately released from the tug and landed straight ahead.

A second flight was attempted almost immediately, with the glider engine off, as it was thought that the lateral instability might have been caused by the transitional stage between suction-on and suction-off at low airspeed. On the second attempt, the GLAS II became airborne at 90-95 mph (145-153 km/h), but the aileron controls became slack at 150 mph (241 km/h) and were effective only when the stick was moved to the extreme of its range. The flight was continued to 10,000 ft (3050 m) and Cuming ascertained that the glider could be controlled down to 64 mph (103 km/h) with suction off.

However, when the engine was started and suction on the wing increased, a violent oscillation in the longitudinal plane began, at a frequency of about one per second, continuing until the boundary layer adhered to the wing, when the ailerons immediately stiffened and became extremely heavy to operate, becoming almost unmovable at 90 mph (145 km/h). Cuming eventually effected a reasonable landing at about 60 mph (97 km/h) with the stick hard back, the engine running and the ailerons locked solid. A somewhat relieved but very harassed pilot emerged with the comment "you'll have to do something about the b—— ailerons!".

A number of modifications were made before the next flight, involving the aileron control circuits, CG position, tailplane incidence and instrumentation, and another flight was scheduled for 3 December. Control was greatly improved although some characteristics were still unsatisfactory, and further small changes were made for the next flight, made on 7 December. Aileron control was again found to be unsatisfactory and after release at 4,000 ft (1 220 m), when suction on the wing was increased, the glider entered a spiral dive to port that was stopped only when the engine was closed down. The loss of height in the spin forced an immediate landing, which Cuming executed with considerable skill and a measure of luck on the airfield boundary; the time from casting off at 4,000 ft (1 220 m) to touch down was 1¼ minutes!

A57-1 remained grounded until early 1949 while repairs and adjustments were carried out. The starboard wingtip skid was repaired, the tailplane fittings were strengthened and the tailplane itself was braced. A swivelling pitot static system, installed after the first flight, was removed from the port wing tip and installed on top of the fin. And, once again, the aileron circuit was altered to remove excessive frictional loads and to stiffen the circuit generally.

By March 1949, two more flights had been made, but the lack of lateral stability still remained a problem. The glider was grounded again so that the wing joints could be improved and the area of the trim tabs on the elevator increased. It was also suggested that the swivelling pitot and incidence gauge should be removed from the fin to a more suitable position. Cuming recommended, at this time, that any further research gliders of the suction wing type should have a conventional three-wheel undercarriage, and a variable incidence tailplane controlled by the pilot so that he could cope with suction on and off conditions.

The test flights continued for another nine months and, in January 1950, Cuming compiled his final report on the GLAS II trials before handing over the project to another pilot. Between April and November 1949, 25 flights had been completed — making a total of 30 since October 1948 — and it was during this latter stage that an answer was found to most of the peculiarities of behaviour in the boundary layer of the GLAS II aerofoil with suction on.

Contaminated wing problem

As a result of visual and instrument observations, it was established that foreign bodies adhering to the wing, with suction on, had a marked effect on the performance of A57-1. These foreign bodies were, in fact, insects which stuck to the wing during take-off and created a contaminated, or dirty, leading edge on the GLAS II aerofoil. The presence of these foreign bodies became known to the pilot in the form of buffeting or asymmetric control loads, and the location of the insects also showed up on the observer's manometer; when the insects were small in size and number their presence was revealed only when the suction was reduced. The contaminated wing condition could be measured by the engine rpm required to stick the flow over the wing — the rpm could be as low as 1,500 before the flow would unstick but, in bad cases, full rpm of 2,850-2,900 were insufficient to stick the flow.

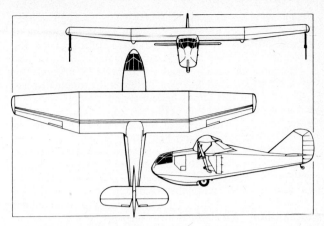

Three-view drawing of the GLAS II.

The effect of unstuck flow due to the presence of insects on the leading edge caused a loss in the lift, and increase in drag, over the section of the wing behind the insects. The aileron sections appeared less affected by the insects, and it was only on rare occasions that the flow would unstick due to insects on the leading edge. When this happened the ailerons would try to apply themselves which the pilot had to counteract by applying a considerable amount of side force.

In retrospect, it was ascertained that a badly contaminated wing was the reason Cuming almost lost control of the glider during the third test flight on 7 December 1948. The purpose of the flight had been to assess the effect of a transition on the vortex formation over the centre section of the glider — apparently, however, a considerable number of insects were collected at about 2,000 ft (610 m) on the climb away from the aerodrome. This caused a breakdown in the flow over the wing and over a portion of one aileron and, on the glide down, asymmetric control forces were required to maintain level flight. The situation was aggravated at about 800 ft (244 m) when, either, more insects were collected or one of the transition cords fell off. At this stage the spiral dive to port commenced, and application of full aileron failed to lift the wing. The only course left was to switch off the engine and carry out an emergency landing without suction — which, of course, Cuming did. As a result of these findings on the contaminated wing, plans were in hand in 1950 to modify the front slot in an endeavour to improve the flow and nullify the effect of insects on the leading edge.

By July 1951, 47 flights had been made with the GLAS II aerofoil, and most of its handling qualities were well known. A vital pre-flight requirement had been introduced whereby the

The GLAS II suction wing glider in free flight, with RAAF Point Cook in the background. This photograph was taken after the third test flight on 7 December 1948, when an additional pitot-head for the observer had been fitted to the top of the fin.

glider's wing was thoroughly cleaned before it was taken from the hangar. Prior to take-off the wing was cleaned again to remove any dust or dirt that may have collected while the glider was towed out to the starting point.

The glider was usually towed to 15,000 ft (4 575 m), and after release it settled down to a steady glide at the trimmed speed. The glider was free of any buffeting, and the only vibration was that due to the engine. All the controls worked in their normal sense, and at normal gliding speeds up to 85 mph (136 km/h) they were reasonably light and effective.

With full suction, the glider was longitudinally stable stick free, and if displaced from a trimmed speed it would return to it with practically a dead beat oscillation. When the suction was reduced the glider eventually became difficult to maintain at a steady speed — within a mile an hour or so — due to slight changes in the longitudinal trim. This appeared to be due to the formation of a fixed vortex just forward of the front slot. Further reduction of the suction after the vortex had formed produced little effect until the flow over the centre section became unsteady and broke away. This caused a further nose down change of trim and, as the suction was again decreased, this change of trim became progressively greater until the flow broke over the whole wing. The minimum steady speed achieved under these conditions was 64 mph (103 km/h) with stick full back. With suction on, the minimum speed was governed by the stall which occurred at 52-53 mph (84-85 km/h), the stick still not being fully back.

Under suction-on conditions, the aircraft was laterally unstable, and it was possible to get out of control by allowing too much skid or slip to develop. The ailerons were reasonably light and very responsive under stuck flow conditions and gliding speeds up to 80 mph (128 km/h). As speed increased the

A three-view drawing of the proposed GAD-4 suction-wing glider with sweepback which was in effect a half-scale model of a 72-passenger all-wing airliner. The glider had a span of 50 ft (15,25 m), length of 33 ft 9 in (10,30 m) and height of 12 ft (3,67 m), and a loaded weight of 3,500 lb (1 590 kg). The suction plant and air discharge fitting can be seen behind the cockpit in the plan view. The dotted cone aft of the suction plant represents the fairing that was to be installed for later tests after the temporary tailplane had been removed.

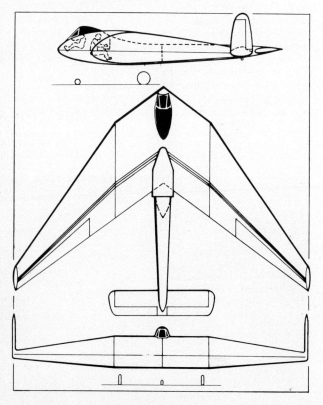

aileron forces became progressively heavier until, at 110 mph (177 km/h), they were quite high. The response, however, remained good throughout the speed range and the ailerons were still effective at the stall. As suction was decreased the ailerons became heavier and the response decreased, particularly as the flow started to break away from the centre section, and as the break away progressed out towards the ailerons. Further reduction of the suction caused the flow to break away over the whole wing, whereupon the aileron hinge moments became balanced once more, and lateral control was again achieved.

The glider was directionally stable with suction on, and satisfactory aileron turns could be made. The rudder was not very effective, and the loads were reasonably light. Under conditions of suction where the ailerons were virtually useless, the rudder had little effect, possibly due to the disturbed flow from the wing. On the occasion that the glider started to enter into a spiral dive, full opposite rudder was not sufficient to stop the nose turning. In the event, this was the wrong action to recover from the spiral and only aggravated the wing dropping tendency by increasing the slip.

The stall, suction full on, occurred at 52 mph (84 km/h) and was accompanied by a rapid dropping of the nose and buffeting over the rudder surfaces. The stall occurred first over the centre section and, as the nose dropped immediately, it was not possible to stall the whole wing. There was no warning of the stall and the flight of the glider remained smooth right up to the stall or break away at the centre section. In turns the same effect occurred, and the nose dropped out of the turn without any tendency for a wing to drop.

With suction-on, the approach speed over the last 1,500-2,000 ft (458-610 m) was 100-105 mph (161-169 km/h). This was well above the approach speed that was normally used on an orthodox glider with a stalling speed of 52 mph (84 km/h), but was necessary to ensure that the glider would still be controllable in the event of suction failure. This procedure had been justified on two occasions — once when the engine boiled and there was a chance of engine seizure, and also when the glider got out of control on the third test flight, at about 800 ft (244 m), and the engine had to be stopped to regain control. The approach path was made so that the aerodrome was always within suction-off gliding distance, even though the landing might have to take place dead across wind if the suction failed; two such landings had been made in cross winds of 15-20 mph (24-32 km/h), suction off, without difficulty. For a normal landing the speed over the fence was reduced to about 95 mph (153 km/h), and the glider was held just above the ground until a normal two point touch-down occurred. The touch-down speed was below 52 mph (84 km/h).

As from July 1951, A57-1 was kept in Category B storage at ARDU pending the results of the scientific assessments of the flying trials. Eventually the glider was grounded in December by the Director of Technical Services. It remained in Category B storage at ARDU for a year and, on 17 December 1952, A57-1 was offered for disposal.

The final report on the GLAS II project recorded that the objective of the investigation — the full-scale flight evaluation of a suction aerofoil — had been achieved. Although interest in the principle of the suction aerofoil subsequently waned as other means of achieving BLC to obtain high lift became more attractive, the GLAS II remains an important milestone in the history of Australian aeronautical research, and provided an unusual finale to the story of the little-known de Havilland Australia gliders of World War II. □

The author wishes to thank the Department of Defence — Air Office, Mr T S Keeble, BSc Be (Superintendent, Mechanical Engineering Division Department of Defence, Aeronautical Research Laboratories) and Mr S A Newbigin (Hawker de Havilland Australia Pty Ltd) for their assistance in the preparation of this article.

A Polygenetic Rumanian...

...THE STORY OF THE IAR 80

IN SOMEWHAT LESS THAN TWO YEARS' TIME, Rumania's air arm anticipates taking into its inventory a somewhat polygenetic light tactical fighter, the Orao (Eagle), which combines British engine technology with Rumanian and Yugoslavian aerodynamic and structural design. Such multi-national developments are, in this day and age, commonplace. Between the world wars, however, the licence manufacture of both engines and airframes was widespread but polygenous aircraft development such as is today accepted as logical was virtually unknown.

Yet the single-seat fighter prototype that was flown for the first time 37 years ago, in April 1939, by Capt Dumitru "Pufi" Popescu from the works airfield of the Industria Aeronautică Română (IAR) at Braşov was every bit as multi-national as the Orao which was to fly as a prototype three-and-a-half decades later. If its mixed parentage was neither admitted nor readily detectable, the IAR 80 was, nonetheless, the product of a mating of a power plant based on a French original with an airframe liberally utilising Polish structural design technology and expertise, the union of these elements having been brought to fruition with creditable results by Professors Ion Grosu and Ion Cosereanu, and Engineers Gheorghe Zotta and G Wallner.

Indeed, so elated by the results of initial flight testing were the Rumanians that they rather immodestly claimed their new 'indigenous' combat aircraft to be among the fastest in the world and within a month or two of the test programme being launched readily furnished details and a photograph of the prototype for inclusion in that year's edition of *Jane's All the World's Aircraft*. Subsequently, little more was to be heard of this Rumanian warplane, despite the fact that several hundred examples of the IAR 80 and its fighter-bomber derivative were manufactured and saw considerable operational use, and today this fighter remains one of the most obscure of World War II's combat aircraft.

When, on 22 June 1941, Rumanian forces attacked the Soviet Union in concert with the *Wehrmacht,* the Royal Air Forces of Rumania, or *Fortelor Aeriene Regal ale România* (FARR), possessed an extraordinarily heterogeneous inventory of first-line aeroplanes representing a numerically sizeable air arm, but of the 12 fighter squadrons only three — two with the Heinkel He 112B and one with Hurricanes — could be remotely considered as being mounted on combat aircraft capable of facing anything more than the most modest of opposition. The remaining nine squadrons were flying strut-braced gull-winged monoplanes, which, built under PZL licence by the IAR, were aged in concept if not manufacture, and the FARR fighter element was understandably anxious to re-equip at the earliest possible opportunity with the modern IAR 80 which was at that moment in time completing service trials.

The Industria Aeronautică Română had been founded on 1 December 1925 as a joint stock company, capital being provided by a French group comprising Blériot-SPAD and Lorraine-Dietrich, the indigenous Astra company contributing a nucleus of specialised personnel and the initial equipment, and the Rumanian state, in addition to contributing capital, providing the land at Braşov for a factory and adjacent airfield. From its inception, the IAR comprised both airframe and aero engine divisions, and although the company's fledgeling design office was to evolve several original aircraft, some of which were manufactured in limited numbers, IAR was primarily concerned with the licence production of airframes and aero engines of foreign design. In so far as fighter development was concerned, it could be alleged to have both cut its teeth and grown to maturity with Polish airframes and French engines.

The IAR association with the Polish PZL (*Panstwowe Zaklady Lotnicze,* or National Aviation Establishments) had begun in 1933 — by which time it had become obvious that neighbouring Hungary was re-arming, perhaps with the intention of recovering Transylvania from Rumania — when the P.11 gull-winged all-metal monoplane was selected as standard equipment for the fighter element of the Rumanian *Aeronautica Militara* and the decision taken to manufacture this type under licence at the IAR facility. In order to meet the most urgent need, 50 P.11b fighters were acquired direct from the parent Polish company between the autumn of 1933 and the summer of 1934, and meanwhile preparations were made at Braşov with the aid of a PZL team for licence manufacture of an improved version, the P.11f, deliveries of which to the Rumanian air arm, now redesignated FARR, actually began early in 1936.

The P.11f was of relatively advanced structural concept in

(Above) IAR 81 fighter/dive-bombers serving with the Corpul 1 Aerian operating in the vicinity of Stalingrad during September 1942. (Head of previous page) An early production IAR 80 fighter (inset) and an IAR 80 A fighter operating in the Zaporozh'ye area of the Ukraine in concert with Italian units during 1942.

its day and, basically similar to the P.11c, it was powered by the IAR-K 9 nine-cylinder radial rated at 640 hp at 13,125 ft (4 000 m). This power plant, although based on the Gnôme-Rhône 9K Mistral for which IAR had acquired a manufacturing licence, differed from its French progenitor extensively. Indeed, allegedly 580 of the 648 component parts of the engine had been modified or redesigned by IAR.

A total of 70 P.11f fighters had been built by the Braşov factory by late 1937, when this type was finally phased out in favour of the conceptually similar but refined, more powerful and more heavily armed P.24E. The newer Polish fighter had been selected as a follow-on to the P.11f in mid-1936, an IAR team spending six months at the PZL factory at Okęcie-Paluch, near Warsaw. At this time, the PZL fighter design team, headed by Wsiewolod Jakimiuk, was already investigating the design of a fighter of appreciably more advanced concept, having been influenced by trends in the USA and elsewhere towards the all-metal stressed-skin cantilever low-wing monoplane with retractable undercarriage as a fighter configuration. These studies were eventually to lead to the P.50 Jastrząb (Hawk) and the IAR team led by Prof Ion Grosu

shared Jakimiuk's conviction that the fighter of the future would standardise on this concept.

Six P.24E fighters had been built by the Okęcie-Paluch factory to Rumanian requirements as pattern aircraft, these being fitted with the IAR-K 14-II C32 14-cylinder radial based on the Gnôme-Rhône 14K Mistral-Major and providing 900 hp for take-off and 870 hp at rated altitude, and production was launched at Braşov in 1937 with deliveries to the FARR commencing in the following year against a contract for 50 aircraft. Some late production examples were to have the improved IAR-K 14-III C36 engine which afforded 930 hp at 11,810 ft (3 600 m).

A Franco-Polish-Rumanian mélange

By early 1938, when the first IAR-built P.24E fighters were delivered into the FARR inventory, the accelerated tempo of international fighter development had already rendered these gulled monoplanes with their braced wings and fixed undercarriages patently obsolescent, but the IAR design team, which had meanwhile been expanded to some 80 personnel — a quarter of these on experimental design and the remainder

The IAR 81C fighter/dive-bomber (below) differed from the IAR 81A primarily in armament, replacing the two 13,2-mm FN-Browning machine guns with 20-mm Mauser MG 151 cannon. It was finally withdrawn from production early in 1943 in favour of the Messerschmitt Bf 109G.

AIR International CLASSIFIED

ADVERTISEMENT RATES AND CONDITIONS OF ACCEPTANCE

AIR International brings a new service to its readers with the introduction of a *Classified Advertising Department,* effective June 1976. The results of a recent reader survey have clearly indicated the necessity for providing a market place for the specific sales and requirements of our readership throughout the world at all levels in industry, government agencies and civil and military aviation. We are aware, too, of the more general needs of our entire circulation and in providing a classified section where space can be bought at rates every reader can afford, we trust these needs will be catered for.

We hope you will make full and frequent use of this new service. **AIR International** offers you the largest circulation of any European-based aviation publication with an average net paid sale of 44,028 copies per month, ABC certified, and an average readership of 2·2 persons per copy. This means your advertising is seen by a total of 96,861 readers, world-wide! If you want to reach the widest possible audience, book space NOW. *AIR International Classified* can meet all your sales requirements.

Full details of rates and other conditions are given here, together with an order form for your convenience. Should you require any further information, our *Classified Advertising Department* at Barnack will be pleased to help you at all times.

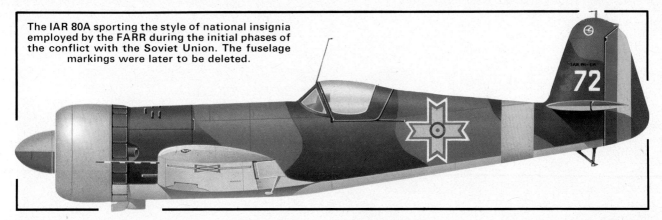

The IAR 80A sporting the style of national insignia employed by the FARR during the initial phases of the conflict with the Soviet Union. The fuselage markings were later to be deleted.

on production design — had initiated work on a more modern successor in October 1937, and the prototype of the new fighter, which had been assigned the designation IAR 80, was to be completed in the experimental shop at Braşov in December 1938.

During the course of 1938, the IAR had been nationalised and work had begun on a very substantial new factory at Braşov which was to be completed in 1939, at which time it was one of the largest aircraft plants in the world — certainly much larger than any of the US West Coast 'giants' of the time — with a total floor area of near 1·4m sq ft (130 000 m²) and a personnel strength of some 7,000. About 592,000 sq ft (55 000 m²) was devoted to airframe manufacture, 484,375 sq ft (45 000 m²) to aero engine manufacture and the remainder to aircraft equipment.

The IAR team, while setting its sights high in endeavouring to create as advanced a fighter as any known to be under development in the more technologically-advanced countries, had tempered its enthusiasm with caution in that, in designing the IAR 80, it had utilised wherever possible proven components of the P.24E. Thus, the entire circular-section semi-monocoque rear fuselage with its smooth stressed duralumin skinning, the vertical and horizontal tail surfaces and the engine bearers were essentially those of the Polish fighter. The low wing of the new fighter employed a similar structure to that of the P.24E in being built up of two I-section spars of duralumin sheet and 38 duralumin ribs, the whole being covered by smooth duralumin sheet. Both the ailerons and the hydraulically-operated flaps were of duralumin tube with fabric skinning, as were also the rudder and elevators. The forward and centre fuselage sections were built of chrome-molybdenum welded steel tubing, the rear section being, as previously mentioned, a stressed-skin duralumin semi-monocoque, and the fuel tank, which had a capacity of 88·65 Imp gal (403 l), was housed between the engine firewall and the cockpit.

Accommodated by a long-chord NACA-type cowling and driving a variable-pitch three-blade metal VDM propeller, the engine of the prototype was a similar IAR-K 14-III C36 derivative of the French Mistral-Major to that installed in late production P.24E fighters, and the hydraulically-operated wide-track main undercarriage members, which retracted inwards into wing wells, had Messier oleo legs, the fixed metal tailskid having a TU-IAR type hydro-pneumatic shock absorber. Provision was made for an armament of four 7,92-mm FN-Browning machine guns, these being mounted in the wings and firing outboard of the propeller disc, an automatic fire-extinguishing system was installed, together with a standby pilot-operated system, and the pilot was accommodated in an open cockpit aft of the wing trailing edge.

From the initiation of design in October 1937 to the commencement of flight testing in April 1939, a total of 1,250 man-weeks had been expended over a period of 18 months, but the results of initial flight trials conducted by Capt Popescu convinced IAR that it had created a fighter that compared closely with the best extant and was superior to most. Official trials proved as successful as had been factory trials, a maximum speed of 317 mph (510 km/h) being recorded at 13,125 ft (4 000 m) and an altitude of 16,405 ft (5 000 m) being attained in six minutes. Empty weight was 3,924 lb (1 780 kg) and normal loaded weight was 5,026 lb (2 280 kg). Although there was some criticism of view from the cockpit on the ground and during landing, the handling characteristics and manoeuvrability were in general commended and IAR received instructions to proceed with preparations for the series production of the fighter.

Various changes were dictated by the flight test programme and changes in FARR requirements. For example, wing area was marginally increased from 166·84 sq ft (15,50 m²) to 171·90 sq ft (15,97 m²), overall span being stretched from 32 ft 9⅔ in (10,00 m) to 34 ft 5⅓ in (10,50 m); overall length was also increased, from 26 ft 7¾ in (8,16 m) to 29 ft 2⅖ in (8,90 m), as a result of some lengthening of the engine bearers dictated by the use of the more powerful IAR-K 14-1000A and commensurate lengthening of the aft fuselage to restore the CG. The single tailplane bracing struts à la P.24E were deleted from the production model which was to feature a cantilever tailplane; the hinged flaps on the mainwheel fairings were discarded so

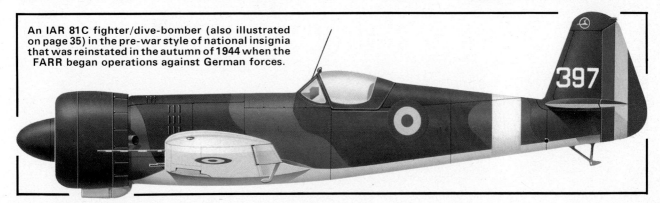

An IAR 81C fighter/dive-bomber (also illustrated on page 35) in the pre-war style of national insignia that was reinstated in the autumn of 1944 when the FARR began operations against German forces.

IAR 80B fighters preparing to scramble at a forward base during the summer of 1943. The IAR 80B was the final production variant of the initial basic model, giving place on the assembly line to the more versatile IAR 81.

that the lower half of the wheel was left exposed when retracted, and an aft-sliding blown plexiglass canopy was adopted. The IAR-K 14-1000A engine was an improved version of the IAR-K 14-III C36 which provided 1,025 hp at 6,560 ft (2 000 m).

Almost exactly one year after the début of the prototype, in the spring of 1940, the first production IAR 80 fighter was completed at Braşov, a further 2,500 man-weeks having been spent in productionising the design, and 20 aircraft had been completed by the end of the year, IAR personnel having been supplemented by a number of former PZL engineers who had succeeded in escaping from Poland. The production IAR 80 attained maximum speeds of 319 mph (514 km/h) at 13,025 ft (3 970 m) and 342 mph (550 km/h) at 22,965 ft (7 000 m), and its

maximum range was 584 miles (940 km) at 205 mph (330 km/h). An altitude of 3,280 ft (1 000 m) was attained in 1·32 min and 14,765 ft (4 500 m) in 5·67 min, maximum ceiling being 34,450 ft (10 500 m). Loaded weight had risen from that of the prototype by some 595 lb (270 kg) to 5,622 lb (2 550 kg).

At an early production stage, the FARR requested provision of heavier armament and also the further development of the basic design to fulfil the rôle of dive bomber. Thus, after the completion of the first batch of 50 IAR 80s (constructor's numbers 001-050) with a quartet of wing-mounted 7,92-mm FN-Brownings, provision was made in the outer wing for an additional FN-Browning on each side to bring total gun armament to six 7,92-mm weapons, the augmented armament being indicated by the addition of the

The plan, head-on and centre side profile below illustrate the initial production (four-gun) IAR 80, the upper side profile depicting the original IAR 80 prototype and the lower side profile showing the post-war advanced training IAR 80DC.

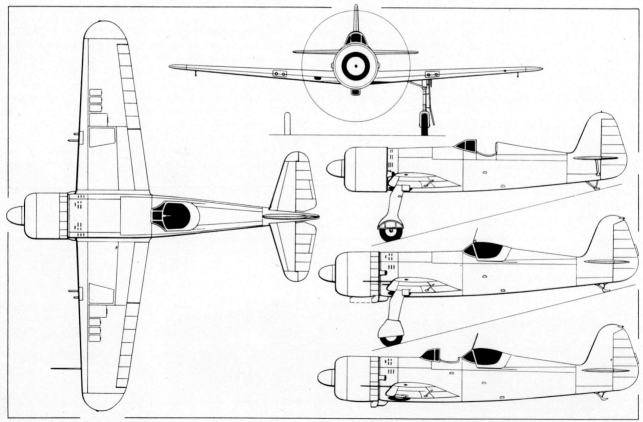

IAR 81C fighter/dive-bombers serving with the FARR after Rumanian forces had allied themselves with those of the Soviet Union in 1944. The 20-mm Mauser MG 151 cannon utilised by this model may be clearly seen protruding from the wing.

suffix letter 'A' to the designation. A total of 90 IAR 80A fighters (Nos 051-090, 106-150 and 176-180) was subsequently to be built before armament was again to be revised, two of the six 7,92-mm weapons being replaced by 13,2-mm guns to result in the IAR 80B of which 31 examples (Nos 181-211) were later built.

The dive bombing variant, to which was assigned the designation IAR 81, was essentially similar to the IAR 80A and was built on the same assembly line. Apart from some local strengthening, the only structural change was a 7·87-in (20-cm) increase in wing span. A centreline rack was provided on the fuselage for a single 551-lb (250-kg) bomb and two underwing racks were provided, each being capable of lifting two 110-lb (50-kg) bombs. The first batch of IAR 81 dive bombers (Nos 091-105) began to leave the Braşov assembly line during the autumn of 1941, and a total of 50 of this model (Nos 151-175 and 231-240) was to be built, together with 29 IAR 81As (Nos 212-230 and 291-300) which differed only in having similar wing armament to that of the IAR 80B (ie, two 13,2-mm and two 7,92-mm guns). The IAR 81As were dispersed on the line with 50 examples of the IAR 81B long-range fighter which introduced wet points in the wings for two drop tanks and supplemented the quartet of 7,92-mm machine guns with a pair of wing-mounted 20-mm Oerlikon (MG FF) or Ikaria cannon.

Production tempo was initially slow in building up but was to peak at one aircraft per day by the spring of 1942, by which time construction time had been brought down to 13,500 manhours per aircraft and some 270 IAR 80s and 81s completed. Initially, these were largely assigned by the FARR to *eskadrile* deployed in defence of the Rumanian oilfields and refineries, but by late 1942, four squadrons (*Escadrile* 11, 12, 13 and 14) assigned to the *Corpul I Aerian* which was operating as a component of the *I Fliegerkorps* of the *Luftwaffe* in the Ukraine, mainly in the Zaporozh'ye area, were flying the IAR 80 and IAR 81 primarily on close-support, fighter-bomber and tactical reconnaissance tasks. Home defence squadrons subsequently operating the IAR-built fighters subsequently included *Eskadrile* 59, 61, 62, 63, 64, 65 and 66.

The Braşov assembly line continued with the IAR 81C fighter/dive bomber which had an armament of two 20-mm Mauser MG 151 cannon and four 7,92-mm FN-Brownings, but during the course of 1942, it was decided that the IAR fighter should be phased out in favour of the Messerschmitt Bf 109G and only 167 IAR 81s were to be delivered between March 1942 and January 1943, when production of the IAR fighter series came to a halt. In the event, after assembling 30 Bf 109G-6s from imported components and sub-assemblies as

pattern aircraft, the Braşov plant was to complete only 16 additional examples of the Messerschmitt fighter before receiving, on 16 April 1944, a visit from the US 15th Air Force which brought production to a standstill, the Braşov facility being almost completely gutted as a result of a second visit three weeks later, on 6 May.

Prior to these events, some trials were conducted with one IAR 81 airframe experimentally fitted with a Junkers Jumo 211Da liquid-cooled engine and another IAR 81 had been tested with air-to-air unguided rocket missiles launched from underwing racks.

By the summer of 1943, all FARR squadrons operating IAR 80s and 81s were home based, and these were particularly active in defence of the Ploesti refineries when the US 15th Air Force launched Operation *Tidal Wave* on 1 August 1943, claiming a number of B-24 Liberators. When, a year later, on 20 August 1944, the Soviet forces launched their offensive across the Prut River, which was to result in Rumania declaring war on its erstwhile ally, Germany, the FARR still included in its first-line strength nine fighter squadrons equipped with IAR 80s or 81s and four dive bomber squadrons operating IAR 81s, but serviceability was low and had dropped to an alarming level by 21 September, when the FARR initiated operations against the German forces. By the time hostilities terminated, only four squadrons equipped with IAR fighters remained in the first-line strength (*Escadrile* 63-66).

With the declaration of a People's Republic after the abdication on 30 December 1947 of King Michael, the Rumanian air arm became the *Fortele Aeriene ale Republicii Populare România* (Air Forces of the Rumanian People's Republic), or FR-RPR, but continued to operate the IAR 80 and 81 alongside Bf 109Gs as standard operational fighter equipment until these were finally supplanted in 1949-50 by Lavochkin La-7s and Yakovlev Yak-9s. With the withdrawal of the IAR fighters from the first-line squadrons, in 1950 the *Atelierele de reparatii material volant* (ARMV) at Pipera successfully converted an IAR 80 as a tandem two-seat dual control advanced trainer, a second cockpit being inserted in the fuselage ahead of the standard cockpit at some expense to fuel capacity. Known as the IAR 80DC, the dual-control model was adopted for the training of fighter pilots and remained in service with FR-RPR schools until the end of 1952.

While the IAR 80 could never lay claim to inclusion among the *great* fighting aircraft of WW II, it was undeniably a thoroughly competent warplane that reflected only credit on its design team and one deserving of greater recognition than it has received hitherto. □

SABRELINER ———————————— *from page 14*

avionics, and substantially improved interior appointments. Subsequent to the first batch, a number of progressive product improvements have been made, including the use of 3,300 lb st (1 500 kgp) JT12A-8 engines, approved in November 1966. Goodyear Tri-metallic full-circle wheel brakes were approved in December 1966, and target-type thrust reversers were certificated in March 1968, the Sabreliner being the first biz-jet to offer this customer option. Structural testing allowed progressive increases in the max take-off and landing weights. At the same time that the -8 engines were introduced, a third cabin window was added in each side of the fuselage.

After the Sabreliner range had been extended with larger models, as noted below, a Sabre Commander version of the Srs 40 was introduced in 1971, this providing up to nine passenger seats and being the low-cost model in the range. In 1972, an increase in gross weight of 887 lb (403 kg) to 19,922 lb (9 045 kg) changed the designation to Sabre Commander 40A, the Series 40 with the same weight then becoming known as the Sabre 40A.

A single Sabreliner Srs 50 was built in 1964 for use by the Autonetics Division of North American Rockwell as an electronics test bed, delivery being made on 1 May 1964. Combining features of the civil Srs 40 and the military T-39 B/D models, the Srs 50 had a modified electrical system to

(Above left) A T-39D, the original US Navy version of the Sabreliner and (below) a CT-39G in service with the US Marine Corps. One of a dozen commercial Sabreliner 60s purchased by the Navy to date, this CT-39G is allocated to the Station Command at MCAS Cherry Point.

(Above) Since marketing of the commercial Sabreliner became the responsibility of Rockwell International's Sabreliner Division at Los Angeles, names and designations of some of the variants have changed more than once. This Sabre Commander is essentially the same as the original Sabreliner 40.

An interior view of a Sabreliner 60, showing a typical executive layout with six seats. Cabin layouts and decor are at customer option.

Sabreliner Production Numbers

NA-246	Original VTX prototype, first flown 16 September 1958. YJ85 turbojets.
NA-265	Initial T-39A production batches. 88 built: 59-2868/2872; 60-3478/3508; 61-634/685. J60-P-3 engines.
NA-270	Six T-39Bs (originally ordered as T-39As). 59-2873/2874; 60-3474/3477.
NA-271	FAA Type Certification of T-39A.
NA-276	Final procurement of T-39A. 55 built: 62-4448/4502.
NA-277	First 10 T-39Ds for US Navy: 150542/150551.
NA-282	First commercial batch of 35 Sabreliner 40s, marketed by Remmert-Werner.
NA-285	Final procurement of T-39D: 32 built and four cancelled: 150969/150992; 161336/151343; 151344/151347.
NA-287	Sabreliner Srs 50 Autonetics test-bed.
NA-290	Fourteen Sabreliner Srs 40s for Remmert-Werner.
NA-292	Sixteen Sabreliner Srs 40s for Remmert-Werner.
NA-293	Thirty-five Sabreliner Srs 40s for Remmert-Werner.
NA-297	Twenty-five Sabreliner Srs 40s for Remmert-Werner.
NA-306	FAA Type Certification of Sabreliner Srs 60.
NA-308	Production batch of 35 Sabreliner Srs 60s for Remmert-Werner.
NA-320	Eighteen Sabreliner Srs 60s for Remmert-Werner.
NA-327	Twenty-five Sabreliners plus one fatigue test specimen.
NA-336	Twenty-five Sabreliner 70s.
NA-343	Redesignation of NA-327.
NA-344	Redesignation of NA-336.
NA-345	Redesignation of NA-320.
NA-369	Sixteen Sabreliner 40s.
NA-370	Nine Sabreliner 70s and two Sabre 75A prototypes.
NA-371	Sixteen Sabreliner 60s.
NA-372	Five CT-39Gs for US Navy.
NA-373	Six Sierra TACAN sets for US Navy Sabreliners.
NA-374	Sea Sabre 75A proposal for USN/USCG.
NA-375	Twenty-five Sabre 75As.
NA-376	Conversion drawings, Sabre 75 to Sabre 75A.
NA-377	Ten Sabre 60s.
NA-378	Twenty-four Sabre 75As.
NA-386	Eighteen Sabre 60s.
NA-390 NA-391 NA-392	Manufacture of materials, detail parts and assemblies.
NA-402	Twenty-six Sabre 40As.
NA-403	Fifteen Sabre Commanders. (Numbers subsequent to 1974 not listed)

provide the additional source of electrical power required to operate the various electronic systems installed in the aircraft, and a number of unique features. These included interchangeable radomes for various microwave wavelengths; radar reflectors and a smoke generator; external stores racks to carry bombs, wing tanks or sensor pods; interchangeable escape hatches for various sensor provisions; sensors and transducers for all flight parameters and complete VHF, UHF and HF communications. An instrumentation nose boom above the radome was an obvious external distinguishing feature. The Srs 50 test-bed was used in development of automatic terrain-following systems and the Mk II navigation system for the F-111D and F-111E.

Structural development and a series of drop tests with a test specimen substantiated a gross weight of 20,000 lb (9 080 kg) for the Sabreliner, with a landing weight of 17,500 lb (7 945 kg), and permitted the introduction of a stretched version of the Srs 40 in 1966. The fuselage was lengthened by 3 ft 2 in (0,97 m) and other minor changes were made. Internal redesign allowed a toilet to be introduced in the rear of the cabin. Five windows were fitted in each side of the cabin, compared with the two or (later) three in the Srs 50, and JT12A-8 engines were used. Certification of the Srs 60 was completed on 28 April 1967, and the type went into production alongside the Srs 40 to meet the steady commercial demand that had developed for North American's business jet.

In addition, small sales continued to be made to the US Navy, which in the late 'sixties found itself with further need for jet transport aircraft to support Fleet activities world-wide by providing rapid-response airlift of high-priority passengers, ferry crews and cargo. An off-the-shelf purchase was intended, and the commercial version of the Sabreliner then in production, the NA-265-40, was selected, the initial order being placed in May 1967. Under the designation CT-39E (briefly VT-39E), a total of seven such aircraft was procured, the first being delivered on 10 July 1967. Except for having TACAN and some other Navy avionics, and less-plush interiors, these CT-39Es were identical to the commercial -40, and the last was delivered in April 1970.

Highly satisfied with its seven CT-39E aircraft, the Navy ordered more Sabreliners in September 1971. By this time, the stretched NA-265-60 model was in commercial production, so the Navy opted for the added capability of this version. The initial order was for two aircraft, which were delivered in the spring of 1972 under the designation CT-39E. Additional aircraft have since been acquired as CT-39Gs, and the first two Navy -60 models now carry the latter designation. Twelve have been delivered so far, including four for the US Marine Corps. Acquisition of small numbers of additional CT-39Gs is planned by the Navy for the next few years.

The Sabre 70 and 75 family

On 4 December 1969, by which time North American and Rockwell had merged to form the North American Rockwell Corporation, the prototype of a new Sabreliner, the Srs 70, made its first flight. Based on the Srs 60 airframe, and using the same powerplant, this model introduced a deepened fuselage with more headroom in the cabin and five square windows in each side of the fuselage, replacing the "rounded triangular" form of all previous models. Certificated on 17 June 1970, the Sabreliner 70 sold in only small numbers, the name being changed to Sabre 75 in 1971. From this point on, the name Sabre was often used in preference to Sabreliner for marketing purposes, although the Sabreliner Division of what had become Rockwell International remained responsible for production of the type, and had also by this time assumed the marketing responsibility previously granted to Remmert-Werner.

By the early 'seventies, the use of straight turbojet engines in biz-jets had become increasingly difficult to market in competition with turbofan-equipped types. A Sabreliner variant with Garrett AiResearch ATF 3 turbofans was studied as the Srs 80 but abandoned in 1972 when the company opted, instead, for the General Electric CF 700 2D-2. Still known internally as the Srs 80, this variant was marketed as the Sabre 75A, being first announced in September 1972 and flown on 18 October that year, with a second prototype joining the programme on 1 December.

The Sabre 75A is based on the Sabre 75 airframe, with the same deep fuselage, but has a number of new features, including improved cabin air conditioning, new Goodyear disc brakes and extra fuel capacity. Certification of the new model was achieved in December 1973 at a gross weight of 23,500 lb (10 670 kg), with approval for up to 10 passengers, as in the Srs 60 and 75. By the time deliveries began in March 1974, 33 orders were already in hand, including a contract from the FAA for 15 to be used for airways flight checking.

The Sabre 75A is now one of only two models of the Rockwell business jet in production, the Sabre 60 still being available but production of all the Srs 40 variants having come to an end in 1974. By the middle of 1975, nearly 500 Sabres and Sabreliners of all types had been delivered for military and civil use and the commercial models were in service in many parts of the world. Of the total, only two had been purchased for foreign military use, these being Sabre 75As delivered to Argentina in 1975, one of which was for the personal use of the Commanding General of the *Fuerza Aérea Argentina*.

Future possibilities

While refinement of the existing Sabre models continues — a typical example being the recent certification of both Srs 60 and Srs 75A to fly from gravel runways, subject to introduction of a shield on the nosewheel to deflect gravel away from the fuselage — the Sabreliner Division has turned its attention to definition of possible derivatives of the basic design for future production. One such project is based on the Sabre 60 but has Garrett AiResearch TFE 731-4 turbofans, a small increase in wing span and a new tailplane; it could be available in 1978 if an early decision is made to go ahead. Another option is based on the Sabre 75A and would have three Pratt & Whitney JT15D-4 engines, the third engine being in a modified rear fuselage; this also would have extended span and a new tailplane, and could be available in 1980.

There are also prospects for substantial additional military sales, if Rockwell succeeds in its bid to develop and sell a version of the Sabre to the US Coast Guard as a replacement

for the HU-16E Albatross in the medium-range ocean surveillance rôle. The Coast Guard decided late in 1973 to begin procurement of as many as 65 Sabre 75As, under the designation HT-39H, but the US Congress stepped in to halt the buy, objecting to the decision having been made without competitive procurement procedures having been followed.

When the Coast Guard conducted the required procurement competition in 1975, amid further controversy, Sabreliner Division offered a highly modified version of the Sabre, called the S-75C Sea Sabre, with Avco Lycoming ALF-502R turbofans, a supercritical wing and many changes in the cabin and equipment to meet the mission requirement. Selection narrowed to a choice between the Sea Sabre and the VFW-Fokker VFW 614 but contract negotiations between the USCG and the manufacturers broke down, and in 1976, a third attempt was launched by the Coast Guard to select an HU-16E replacement, with a request for proposals being issued and procurement of 41 aircraft in view.

Whatever the final outcome of the Coast Guard competition, the Sabre in one form or another obviously remains a leading contender. The swift, sleek, attractive little T-39 has assured itself a place in history — a little less glamorous, maybe, than its fighter namesake, but an aircraft that has achieved a character of its own. □

(Below) One of the first Sabreliner 75As delivered in Europe, for use as a demonstrator by Jet Aviation AG of Basle. (Above right) The flight deck of a Sabreliner 60 — a two-pilot crew is normal practice on all business jets of Sabreliner size.

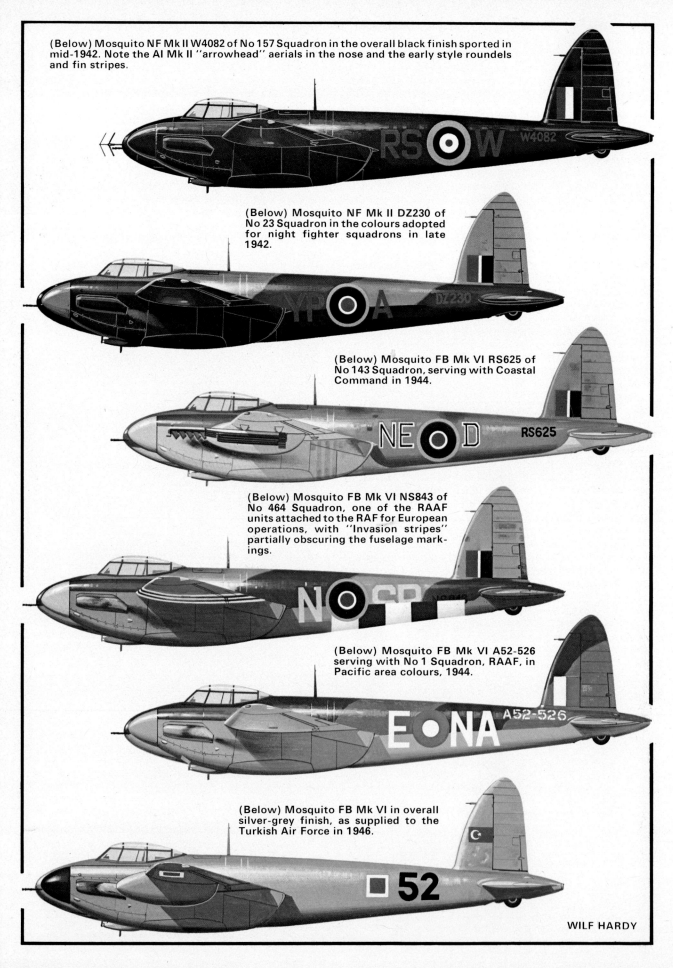

(Below) Mosquito NF Mk II W4082 of No 157 Squadron in the overall black finish sported in mid-1942. Note the AI Mk II "arrowhead" aerials in the nose and the early style roundels and fin stripes.

(Below) Mosquito NF Mk II DZ230 of No 23 Squadron in the colours adopted for night fighter squadrons in late 1942.

(Below) Mosquito FB Mk VI RS625 of No 143 Squadron, serving with Coastal Command in 1944.

(Below) Mosquito FB Mk VI NS843 of No 464 Squadron, one of the RAAF units attached to the RAF for European operations, with "Invasion stripes" partially obscuring the fuselage markings.

(Below) Mosquito FB Mk VI A52-526 serving with No 1 Squadron, RAAF, in Pacific area colours, 1944.

(Below) Mosquito FB Mk VI in overall silver-grey finish, as supplied to the Turkish Air Force in 1946.

WILF HARDY

Apertures ad nauseum

THE SOLIDITY AND SUBSTANCE suggested by a well-built aircraft model is purely illusory, but it is an illusion that every modeller worth his salt seeks to create, for, without it, no model can have serious pretensions towards realism. This not particularly profound observation is engendered by recent examination of a kit — not, we hasten to add, submitted to us for review — which, when assembled, seemed to present more gaping void than plastic surface: the cockpit area, the turbojet intakes and effluxes, the weapons bays, the air brake housings, the undercarriage wells — all provided chasms, holes, gaps; apertures that *demanded* filling if even a *reasonably* representative model was to result! We have seen some kits leaving much to be desired in respect of detail, but in this relatively enlightened modelling day and age this was ridiculous. Assembled, the kit provided no more than a simple shell of the aircraft that it purported to represent and offered a daunting task of 'filling in' that would really sort the men from the boys, yet this product is being retailed as a complete kit!

In days gone by, it was by no means unusual to be able to look into the nose intake of a model of a jet fighter and see daylight through the tail end — some of these older kits are, incidentally, still on the market — but more recent kits do usually include at least some sort of internal baffle in order to avoid this empty tube effect. The cockpit area provides the most common 'aperture' these days. All too frequently, a superb kit is marred by a naked but, we hope, ashamed cockpit interior, and then there are the wheel wells, brake housings, etc, which all look completely unrealistic when devoid of detail. If a model is to appear solid and substantial, representation of the interior of intakes and so on *must* be included.

Probably one of the most common criticisms voiced when reviewing kits is inadequacy of cockpit interior detail. The two manufacturers that err most frequently in this respect are Lesney and Frog, but, conversely, these companies have succeeded in keeping their kits within a reasonably low price range and to do so it is inevitable that something must be sacrificed. Thus, it may well be a case of 'doing it ourselves' or paying more if we expect it to be done for us. But the detailing of cockpits is not unduly difficult. It demands a certain amount of research if the modeller proposes to simulate accurately the cockpit interior of the aircraft that he is modelling rather than provide a generally representative interior, and it calls for patience if one is working to 1/72nd scale — the larger scales, such as 1/48th, 1/32nd and 1/24th almost invariably have all the main features of the cockpit interior reproduced. The prospect of starting a cockpit interior from scratch is no reason to blanch, scream *quelle horreur,* or something of the sort, and consign so demanding a kit to the spares box.

We subscribe to the view that one should attempt to model only items large enough to be appreciated with the naked eye — if you have a penchant for screwing a watchmaker's glass into your eye and reproducing the rivet heads on the instrument panel than *sua cuique voluptas* — and any reasonably competent modeller should have no difficulty in embellishing his model with a perfectly acceptable cockpit interior.

Next in importance must come undercarriage wells. These come in so many different shapes and sizes that it is not possible to be specific, although a few generalisations may prove helpful. Small wells in the undersurfaces of the wings, such as those of the Spitfire, should usually be boxed in, yet in so many kits they are just so many more apertures. Boxing in the wells is easily accomplished with strips of thin plastic card — the 0·005-in thickness will bend around a hole of only $\frac{3}{8}$ in (9,52 mm) or so without difficulty — but there is almost always in such cases a visible section of the internal stiffening of the upper wing skinning and this can be simulated with very thin strips of plastic sheet using liquid cement applied with a fine brush. These general principles apply to any of the smaller apertures, but a different approach is necessary in the case of larger openings, such as the undercarriage wells in the undersides of the engine nacelles of multi-engined WW II bombers. There may be limits imposed by lack of information, but it is possible to block off the wings on each side of the nacelle with false ribs, insert firewalls and perhaps add to the actuating gear of the undercarriage members and their doors so that there is at least a suggestion that these items could be operable — large exposed location lugs and no pretensions towards practicability hardly make for realism.

This month's colour subject
Undoubtedly one of the most successfully versatile of any of the twin-engined combat aircraft built during WW II, the Mosquito, like the Ju 88, gave the lie to the old adage "Jack-of-all-trades and master of none", for it excelled in all its widely varied rôles and in none more so than those of night fighter and fighter-bomber. Aesthetically, few if any aircraft of WW II offered the Mosquito serious competition and we doubt if many who have pursued aircraft modelling for a number of years have still to add this superlative de Havilland creation to their collection. Nevertheless, our ranks are swelling with every passing month and the Mosquito continues to hold its own as a popular modelling subject.

The earliest kit to be issued of the Mosquito was an Airfix product to 1/72nd scale and in retrospect it was certainly a somewhat crude affair, but this same company has more recently issued an entirely new kit which, accurate and well-moulded, offers alternative parts to permit completion as an NF Mk II night fighter, an FB Mk VI fighter-bomber, or a 57-mm Molins gun-toting Mk XVIII. With a total of 97 component parts and a selection of rocket and bomb armament, plus underwing slipper tanks, this Series 3 Airfix kit is to be strongly recommended. Frog's 1/72nd scale Mosquito is less accurate than that from Airfix but may be completed as either a B Mk VI bomber or as the FB Mk VI and is therefore in some respects complementary. This kit is, incidentally, in Frog's Green series. A further 1/72nd scale kit of the Mosquito, a B Mk IV, is due shortly in Lesney's 'Matchbox' three-colour orange range.

For the 1/48th scale enthusiast, there is a fine, albeit now quite old, kit from Monogram and we can see little likelihood of this being bettered for a long time to come. It embodies one very noticeable fault which must be corrected — the fin-and-rudder assembly is markedly too tall and must be reshaped but this is not a very difficult task. An abundance of alternative component parts enables this kit to be completed as an NF Mk II, a B Mk IV or an FB Mk VI. The superb quality of the mouldings and the finely engraved surface detailing of this kit certainly give no indication of its age and it is still readily obtainable.

Largest of the Mosquito kits so far — dare any manufacturer attempt to offer a 1/24th scale "Mossie"? — is Revell's 1/32nd scale version, which, with a wing span of 1 ft 8¼ in (51,40 cm), is large enough for most modellers and is a fine kit, generally quite accurate and possessing a number of very commendable features, such as well-detailed interiors to the wheel wells in the nacelles, one of which includes a Merlin engine. There are errors, particularly in the shape of the fin-and-rudder assembly and the rear portions of the engine nacelles which do not fair properly into the trailing edges of the wing, the latter calling for the use of a lot of body putty in order to rectify the shape. The surface detailing is not as good as that of the previously-mentioned Monogram kit, being mostly of raised-line type, but it is nevertheless quite well done. Unfortunately, only a B Mk IV can be assembled from this Revell kit, but conversion to a fighter or fighter-bomber variant should not present insurmountable difficulties.

Lightning and Starfighter
The latest offerings from the Lesney "Matchbox" concern to be received comprise a BAC Lightning in the Orange range carrying the UK retail price tag of 60p and a Lockheed F-104G Starfighter in the Purple range priced in the UK at 35p. Kits of the Lightning are not so thick on the ground as to preclude an addition, and this F Mk 6 offers 59 neatly-fitting component parts in light grey, white and black plastic, and an accurate outline. Some extra component parts have been included to permit conversion to Lightning F Mk 2A standard, but not all external differences have been catered for, most noticeably the shortening of the strakes on each side of the fuselage in line with the top edge of the ventral tank — these should be shortened by $\frac{7}{8}$ in (22,2 mm) at the front end to conform with those of the F Mk 2A. The wings of the F Mk 2A are

not stressed to take the overwing fuel tanks, incidentally, so those supplied with this kit are only applicable to the F Mk 6. Other stores provided are Red Top and Firestreak AAMs.

This kit marks a departure from Lesney's usual practice in so far as surface detailing is concerned, the engraved — sometimes excessively so — panel lines have given place to embossing which is rather heavy-handed but nevertheless neat. We like the realistic wheels and slender landing gear with the accompanying shaped doors. Blanking-off discs are provided for the two tail effluxes but the nose intake is decidedly see-through and calls for improvement. The cockpit area consists of a rather confined box, with seat, control column and pilot figure, again calling for improvement, but the canopy is very clear and fits snugly on the fuselage. The only direct comparison in both mark and scale is provided by the Frog/Hasegawa kit and we consider Lesney's product to be rather more accurate in outline and better detailed. The decal sheet is a good one, offering the markings of a Lightning F Mk 6 of No 74 Sqdn, RAF, Far East Air Force, at Singapore in 1970. with, as an alternative, an F Mk 2A of No 92 Sqdn, RAF, at Gutersloh, Federal Germany, in 1974, the latter sporting the dark green low-visibility finish.

The rather less expensive Lockheed F-104G Starfighter kit comprises 37 component parts moulded in white and light blue. This kit utilises an ingenious arrangement of mouldings to successfully capture the intricate fuselage contours. There are no voids in intakes or outlet but the cockpit interior is spartan in having merely a pilot figure and its seat. The wings and tailplane are praiseworthily thin and the undercarriage is suitably sturdy, but while the mainwheel doors are quite thin, those for the nosewheel are much too thick and best discarded in favour of new doors fashioned from plastic sheet. Sidewinder missiles are included for wingtip mounting, but there are no other external stores. The surface detailing is of the engraved variety but much finer than we have seen in earlier "Matchbox" kits.

The decal sheet is a very good feature of the kit and provides markings for an F-104G of JG 17 *Richthofen* in 1966, alternatives being those for a CF-104 of the Canadian No 439 Sqdn. In each case, squadron badges have been included and the register of the decals is very good. This new F-104G kit faces competition from both Airfix and Frog/Hasegawa offerings which are also good, none having a real edge on another, so a clear recommendation is not possible.

A quarter-scale 'one-ninety

Over the past couple of years or so, there has been considerable coverage of WW II types in 1/48th scale by four of the leading Japanese kit manufacturers, Fujimi, Nichimo, Otaki and Tamiya, and the latest kit to this scale to reach us — from Otaki — is a welcome addition in the shape of the Focke-Wulf Fw 190A-8. Here again we have an example of a kit, which, although very accurate and complete, is by no means complicated, being devoid of gimmickry and unnecessary operating features. Otaki's Fw 190A-8 kit possesses 51 component parts moulded in this company's usual high-quality light grey plastic, and these parts include two underwing gun pods, with separate guns, a centreline bomb rack with a

300-l drop tank and a standing figure with base, this last item being somewhat below the generally high standard that is set by the kit as a whole.

The cockpit interior is detailed, as are also the interiors of the wheel wells, and the standard of surface detailing is of the highest, the finely engraved panel lines and other features providing examples of what really can be done in this department — surely, if some manufacturers can do it, then it should be possible for others to follow suit — or is it so much more difficult or expensive than using raised lines?

Assembly is very simple as every part fits precisely, with no need whatsoever for filing or filling. The undercarriage must be carefully set in order to achieve the correct ground angle. The decal sheet provides markings for three different aircraft, two of these aircraft being illustrated as full-colour 1/48th scale side elevations on a separate insert sheet. The major scheme is for that of an aircraft of 9.*Staffel* of *Jagdgeschwader* 2, having a black stylised eagle insignia on the forward fuselage which served to obscure the untidy trail of oil stains and oxide gas left by the exhaust, this motif forming a part of the decal sheet. Unfortunately, we have no information as to the price of this kit at the time of closing for press. With now well over a score of WW II aircraft available to quarter-inch scale from the four Japanese manufacturers mentioned earlier, plus many others from Monogram, those with a penchant for this scale and a liking for the WW II period are certainly receiving excellent catering.

Some sizeable vacuforms

Apart from an occasional venture into 1/48th, vacuum-formed kits and conversions have tended to keep fairly conservatively to 1/72nd scale hitherto, but several recent samples that we have received from Horizon Conversions (PO Box, Malton, Ontario, Canada L4T 3B4) provide proof positive, if such were needed, that scale and size present no problems in this ever-expanding branch of the plastic model business. These kits are all to 1/32nd scale and form part of an extensive range, mostly being conversions applicable to available kits in this scale.

There are three different conversion kits for use with Revell's McDonnell Douglas F-4 Phantom II, one with three drop tanks (two underwing 370 US gal tanks and a centreline 600 US gal tank); one comprising only the larger tank and a third consisting of two 2,000-lb (907-kg) Mk 84 laser-guided bombs (applicable to the F-4D). Three further conversions are for WW II *Luftwaffe* aircraft, one consisting of a pair of 300 l drop tanks for use with the Bf 109F or G, the Bf 110G and the Fw 190A, another being a so-called Galland hood for a Bf 109G, and this latter may be used in conjunction with a kit for the conversion of the Bf 109G into a Czechoslovak-built Jumo-engined S 199.

One unusual conversion kit offers the central float and pylon, and the wingtip stabilising floats for the Nakajima-built A6M2-N, the float-equipped derivative of the *Zero-Sen* fighter. The A6M2-N was, of course, an adaptation of the A6M2 version of the *Zero-Sen,* whereas the only 1/32nd scale kits of the *Zero-Sen* fighter generally available — from Hasegawa and Revell — portray the shorter-span A6M5 Model 52 which featured a

substantially revised engine cowling. Thus, the conversion of either of these kits to water-based configuration will entail rather more than the mere substitution of floats for wheels! We understand that the Japanese Tomy concern has produced a 1/32nd scale kit of the A6M2 but we have not actually seen an example.

Perhaps the most interesting item in the Horizon Conversions collection are the *complete* kits for the MiG-15 and for the *Reichenberg* piloted version of the Fieseler Fi 103 (alias V-1) flying bomb. The MiG-15, considering its importance in the history of jet fighter development, has been poorly served by kit manufacturers, with only an early Airfix offering in 1/72nd scale and a nondescript version, ostensibly to 1/48th scale, produced many years ago by Hawk. We understand, however, that a new 1/48th scale kit is in the offing from Monogram and we await its début with keen interest. The vacuform of the MiG-15 from Horizon is certainly a praiseworthy effort, with well-defined, smoothly-moulded parts, which, despite the size of some of them, are completely devoid of blemishes. Surface detailing is minimal, but what there is is quite finely executed and the mouldings possess adequate strength for the modeller to score on any panelling that he may wish to add. The parts provided include the wheels, undercarriage doors, seat and a very clear cockpit transparency, while particularly noteworthy are the nose section with its bifurcated intake and the tail section with its jet efflux, both extremely well moulded. A very fine decal sheet by Micro Scale provides markings for both Soviet and North Korean aircraft, and the instruction booklet is fully comprehensive and should enable any modeller of some experience to turn out a first class miniature replica of a very famous Soviet warplane. The price at $Can 12.00 may seem rather on the high side to the average UK modeller, but it is a kit well worth having.

The Fi 103 kit provides all the parts needed for an accurate model of either the *Reichenberg III* skid-equipped trainer or the operational one-mission *Reichenberg IV*. The mouldings are sharp and accurate, and fit together well, and the kit includes drawings and full information on assembly and painting. Details of the spartan equipment of the cockpit interior are also given, and the kit includes a nice clear acetate canopy. The Fi 103 *Reichenberg* kit is priced at $Can 6.00, and the UK distributors of the Horizon kits are Modelmark Hobby Products (8 Michell Ave, Redbridge, Essex).

Addendum

We have received a letter from John Tarvin of Burnaby Hobbies of Burnaby, Canada V5J 2B7, requesting that we make it clear to readers that his company is responsible for the manufacture of the Mercury component of the Maia-Mercury composite vacuum-formed kit that we reviewed in this column in January, only the Maia component being manufactured by Contrail. We mentioned in our review that there was a disproportionate price difference between the individual components owing to the importation of the Mercury from Canada, but we should perhaps point out to readers that, owing to import duties imposed in the opposite direction, the reverse is true in Canada and the USA, where the Maia component is appreciably more expensive. □

F J HENDERSON

THE 'TURNERS AND BURNERS'

Searching for ways of improving fighter performance in the period immediately preceding the advent of the turbojet engine, the Soviet Union devoted considerable effort to the development of the Khalshchevnikov "accelerator", a device that obtained some of the advantages of jet thrust in conjunction with a conventional piston engine. Prototypes flown with this "accelerator" are described in this article, being (above and below) the Mikoyan-Gurevich I-250(N) and (left) the Sukhoi Su-5.

ACTIVITY in Soviet design bureaux and experimental establishments bordered on the frenetic at the beginning of 1944, following the arrival of intelligence reports suggesting that the operational début of the first *Luftwaffe* turbojet-driven fighter, the Messerschmitt Me 262, could be imminent and the consequent castigation by Yosif Stalin of industry leaders over their tardiness in developing comparable warplanes. Stalin was well aware that both the United Kingdom and the United States had already attained advanced stages in the production of jet fighters, yet, although Arkhip M Lyulka had developed and successfully bench-run a turbojet* during the previous year, one potentially applicable as a fighter prime mover was at least two years from production deliveries, even by the most sanguine estimates. The highest priority was suddenly assigned to the investigation of all possible interim solutions, and a range of proposals for mixed-power fighters — aircraft in which the power provided by the principal engine of conventional type was augmented by some form of less conventional auxiliary power unit — which had been considered in a desultory fashion over the previous two years immediately came under urgent scrutiny.

The application of ramjets and liquid-fuel rocket motors to existing fighters as a means of boosting performance was examined, but a more promising if longer-term scheme concerned a development known as the Khalshchevnikov "accelerator". Under development for some considerable time at the TsIAD (Central Aero Engine Institute) by a team led by Eng Khalshchevnikov, the "accelerator" comprised an engine-driven compressor which fed compressed air via a water radiator to a mixing chamber where fuel was introduced under pressure by a battery of seven injectors, the mixture

Lyulka had bench-tested the experimental VRD-2 turbojet of 1,543 lb (700 kg) thrust during 1943, and had begun work on the VRD-3 (subsequently to be known as the TR-1) which was to successfully complete official bench testing at the end of 1944 at 2,866 lb (1300 kg) thrust.

compressed air duct, the competing Mikoyan-Gurevich design featured an annular slot intake aft of the propeller spinner. The wing of the Su-5 was of two-piece single-spar construction and employed a TsAGI IV10 profile of 16·5 per cent relative thickness at the root translating to an NACA 230 profile with an 11 per cent relative thickness at the tip, gross wing area being 182·99 sq ft (17,00 m²). The Mikoyan-Gurevich team was more ambitious in that it chose a newly-developed laminar-flow section for its two-spar wing, the gross area of which was only 161·4 sq ft (15,00 m²), although overall span was marginally more at 36 ft 3 in (11,05 m) as compared with 34 ft 7¾ in (10,56 m). Both fighters featured wing wells for the inward-retracting main members of the tailwheel under-carriages, but again the Mikoyan-Gurevich team was the more adventurous in adopting levered-suspension main legs. The overall length of the dural monocoque fuselage was again marginally greater in the case of the I-250(N), this being 28 ft 8⅖ in (8,75m) whereas that of the Su-5 was 27 ft 11 in (8,51 m). The armament of both fighters comprised one 23-mm N-23 cannon with 100 rounds firing through the propeller boss and two 12,7-mm UBS machine guns with 200 rpg mounted in the engine cowling.

The prototypes of both fighters were completed virtually simultaneously, the I-250(N) flying for the first time on 3 March 1945 with A P Dyeyev at the controls and the Su-5 following it into the air during April with G Komarov in the cockpit. With a normal loaded weight of 8,112 lb (3 680 kg), the Mikoyan-Gurevich prototype clocked a maximum speed

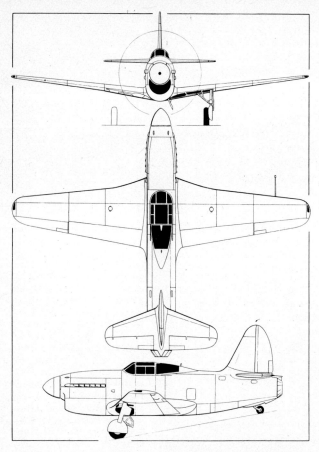

The Sukhoi Su-5, shown in the three-view above and in semi-cutaway on the right, achieved only limited success in the preliminary flight trials.

being ignited in a double-walled combustion chamber and then ejected through a variable orifice. Such was considered the potential of this "accelerator" as a means of achieving higher fighter performances that all the principal fighter design bureaux were instructed, early in 1944, to initiate design studies for fighters embodying this development. From these, the proposals submitted by the design bureaux headed by Pavel Sukhoi and by Artem Mikoyan and Mikhail Gurevich were selected for prototype construction.

In both the Sukhoi Su-5 and the Mikoyan-Gurevich I-250 (N) — the prototypes evolved to meet the mixed-power fighter requirement — the Khalshchevnikov "accelerator" was mated with the Klimov VK-107A 12-cylinder liquid-cooled vee engine rated at 1,650 hp for take-off and 1,430 hp at 14,930 ft (4 550 m), and the auxiliary unit could augment the output of the piston engine by the equivalent of 900 hp for up to 10 minutes. Both designs were relatively small all-metal stressed-skin low-wing cantilever monoplanes and both featured a large intake duct beneath the nose for the compressor, but in other respects the two fighters differed appreciably. Both fighters were somewhat corpulent owing to the considerable amount of fuselage space that had to be given over to the ducting for the "accelerator" unit, or VRDK (air turbo-compressor reaction engine), but whereas Pavel Sukhoi chose to position the pilot over the wing centre section and turbo-compressor, the Mikoyan-Gurevich team elected to place the pilot well aft, despite proximity to the combustion chamber, and utilise shorter ducting with a possible reduction in duct losses as a result.

The Su-5 employed a four-bladed constant-speed propeller of 9·51 ft (2,90 m) diameter, whereas the I-250(N) utilised a three-blader of 10·17 ft (3,10 m) diameter, and while the Sukhoi fighter tapped engine air from the downstream

Sukhoi Su-5 Drawing Key

1 Cannon port
2 Spinner
3 Four-blade controllable-pitch propeller
4 Machine gun port
5 Header tank
6 Compressor intake

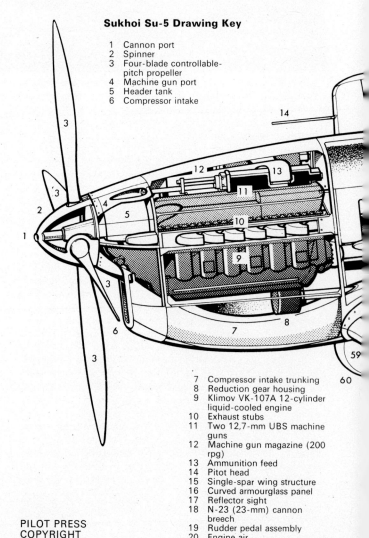

7 Compressor intake trunking
8 Reduction gear housing
9 Klimov VK-107A 12-cylinder liquid-cooled engine
10 Exhaust stubs
11 Two 12,7-mm UBS machine guns
12 Machine gun magazine (200 rpg)
13 Ammunition feed
14 Pitot head
15 Single-spar wing structure
16 Curved armourglass panel
17 Reflector sight
18 N-23 (23-mm) cannon breech
19 Rudder pedal assembly
20 Engine air
21 Compressor drive shaft

PILOT PRESS
COPYRIGHT
DRAWING

of 513 mph (825 km/h) at 25,590 ft (5 800 m) during high speed trials, this being only some 25 mph (40 km/h) lower than the maximum speed attainable at the same altitude by the Me 262 and it being calculated that the actual effect of the VRDK at that altitude was an increase in speed of 75 mph (120 km/h). The Su-5, too, quickly proved itself no sluggard, and during the same month demonstrated a level speed of 493 mph (793 km/h) at an altitude of 14,270 ft (4 350 m) as compared with an anticipated maximum speed of 477 mph (768 km/h) at that altitude, the effect of the VRDK being a 56 mph (90 km/h) boost in speed at low altitude rising to 68 mph (110 km/h) at 25,590 ft (7 800 m).

The Su-5 had empty and normal loaded weights of 6,512 lb (2 954 kg) and 8,387 lb (3 804 kg) respectively, and it was calculated that the maximum attainable speed would be 503 mph (810 km/h) at 25,590 ft (7 800 m), but in July, after the completion of the first phase of factory trials, the VK-107A engine suffered damage in flight, although Komarov succeeded in landing the prototype safely. The competitive I-250 (N) had also suffered misfortune, having crashed during the previous month, killing its pilot, Dyeyev.

Shortly before these events, German forces had finally surrendered. Soviet forces had stumbled over the first BMW 003 and Jumo 004 turbojets several months earlier, hurriedly turning these over to research centres for study, and on the basis of these, in February 1945, Yosif Stalin had ordered a crash development programme for fighter airframes capable of accommodating the newly-acquired engines. Interest in the mixed-power fighters using the Khalshchevnikov "accelerator" was thus already on the wane before either Sukhoi or Mikoyan-Gurevich prototype commenced its flight test programme, and despite the promising results turned in by both aircraft during initial factory trials, these were of no more than academic interest. Therefore, with the loss of the I-250 (N)* prototype in June and the damage suffered by the Su-5 prototype in July, the programme was abandoned. □

*Some sources have suggested that the I-250(N) actually entered production and service after the end of the war in Europe, but it did not, in fact, progress further than prototype trials.

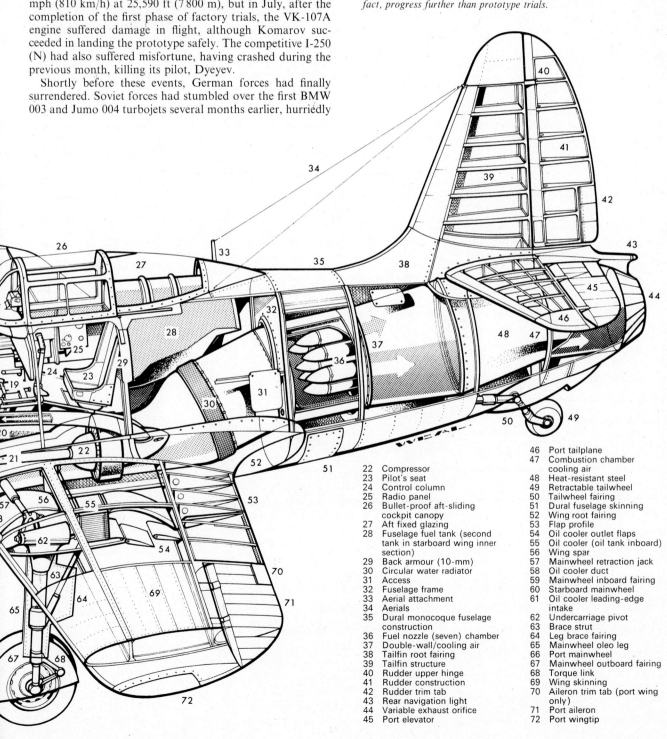

22	Compressor	46	Port tailplane
23	Pilot's seat	47	Combustion chamber cooling air
24	Control column	48	Heat-resistant steel
25	Radio panel	49	Retractable tailwheel
26	Bullet-proof aft-sliding cockpit canopy	50	Tailwheel fairing
27	Aft fixed glazing	51	Dural fuselage skinning
28	Fuselage fuel tank (second tank in starboard wing inner section)	52	Wing root fairing
		53	Flap profile
		54	Oil cooler outlet flaps
29	Back armour (10-mm)	55	Oil cooler (oil tank inboard)
30	Circular water radiator	56	Wing spar
31	Access	57	Mainwheel retraction jack
32	Fuselage frame	58	Oil cooler duct
33	Aerial attachment	59	Mainwheel inboard fairing
34	Aerials	60	Starboard mainwheel
35	Dural monocoque fuselage construction	61	Oil cooler leading-edge intake
36	Fuel nozzle (seven) chamber	62	Undercarriage pivot
37	Double-wall/cooling air	63	Brace strut
38	Tailfin root fairing	64	Leg brace fairing
39	Tailfin structure	65	Mainwheel oleo leg
40	Rudder upper hinge	66	Port mainwheel
41	Rudder construction	67	Mainwheel outboard fairing
42	Rudder trim tab	68	Torque link
43	Rear navigation light	69	Wing skinning
44	Variable exhaust orifice	70	Aileron trim tab (port wing only)
45	Port elevator	71	Port aileron
		72	Port wingtip

TALKBACK

Amendment amended

Mr Trevor M Boughton, in *Talkback*/December 1975, is correct, of course in his curt comment that my original "Project Skywards" (July 1975) story "demands" a correction. I inadvertently referred to the Commonwealth Scientific and Industrial Research Organisation (CSIRO), instead of the Council for Scientific and Industrial Research (CSIR). Perhaps I am being pedantic, but has not Mr Boughton erred also in his amendment by omitting the Division of Aeronautics after CSIR? Surely this could imply to many of your readers that the division was not in existence at the time of Project Skywards in 1943. For the record, the CSIR came into being in 1926, the CSIR Division of Aeronautics (including the Aeronautical and Engine Testing Research Laboratory at Fishermen's Bend, Victoria) during 1939-40, and the CSIRO in 1949. When the latter organisation was established, the Division of Aeronautics was disestablished, and the Aeronautical Research Laboratories were transferred to the Department of Supply and Development in 1949. Thus, the CSIR Division of Aeronautics was in operation well before 1943.

As to Mr Boughton's assertion that the Northrop Delta, VH-ADR, was not impressed but was operated on loan by the RAAF, may I present the following facts. Up to the end of the 1939-45 War, impressed aircraft, together with those on charter, were allocated RAAF serial numbers and, consequently, appeared in the Register of RAAF Aircraft. In contrast, the few aircraft acquired on loan for flying operations were not numbered, did not appear in the official list of RAAF aircraft, and retained their original registration or serial identifications. Prewar examples of aircraft used by the RAAF with civil registration were the D.H.50A VH-UAB (c/n 106) — later impressed as A10-1 during the war — and the D.H.89 Dragon Rapide VH-UVG (c/n 6314), which was rebuilt after a forced landing and became A3-2 in the late 1930s. Wartime loan aircraft included the non-flying Avro 594 Avian IV VH-UKD, the USAAF Stinson L-5 Sentinel 42-99129, three USAAF Lockheed C-60 Lodestars, 42-32173, 42-32174 and 42-32178 (with radio call-signs VH-CED, VH-CEE, and VH-CEJ), five Lockheed C-60A Lodestars, LT9-31 to 35, from the Netherlands East Indies Pool in Australia, the USAAF Consolidated (Canadian Vickers-built) OA-10A-VI Catalina 44-34054, and 24 USAAF

RAAF transport aircraft usually carried VH radio call-signs on the tail unit or fuselage, in addition to squadron codes and serials. Dakota IV A65-105, illustrated, displays the OM code letters of No 37 Squadron, and the call-sign VH-RFV.

Douglas C-47 type transports including C-49, C-50, and C-53 versions. The RAAF Form E/E88 Record Cards for the latter 34 machines specifically recorded that each aircraft was "on loan USAAF . . . or NEI", as applicable.

It is known, also, that other aircraft were used unofficially on loan — or borrowed without RAAF Headquarters authority — but these machines are not listed in RAAF records. Examples included five Royal Navy Fairey Swordfish Mk 1s, V4685, V4688-89 and V4692-93, flown at RAAF Pearce and by No 25 Squadron, the three USAAF Vultee Vigilants used by No 33 Squadron (in this instance, the identification serial A64 was tentatively allocated to the Vigilant in anticipation of the aircraft being received officially, but was not used when the order failed to materialise), and the Piper L-4 Grasshoppers operated in New Guinea by No 4 Squadron. No doubt there were many others.

Which brings us to the complex case of the Delta. On 24 July 1942 the Department of Civil Aviation released VH-ADR, on charter, to the Directorate of Air Transport, Allied Air Force, South-West Pacific Area, for US Army

Aircraft impressed by the RAAF always received serial numbers; two examples were (below) the Miles M.3D Falcon Six A37-1, ex VH-ABT (previously G-AEAG), and (above right) Stinson SR-88 Reliant A38-1, ex VH-UXL.

requirements. DAT — which was commanded by the renowned Australian navigator Group Captain Harold Charles Gatty, RAAF, co-author with Wiley Post of *Around The World In Eight Days* (1931) — did not renumber chartered aircraft as did the RAAF. The Delta was flown by USAAF personnel from Essendon, Victoria, to Geraldton, Western Australia, where it was perforce transferred to the RAAF on 3 August when the USAAF unit moved north. Because of engine malfunctions, the RAAF overhauled the Delta's 735 hp Wright Cyclone SR-1820-F2 at Daly Waters, Northern Territory, between 9-30 August. Eighteen days later, on 17 September, the RAAF returned VH-ADR to DCA at Essendon, after flying some 60 hours, thus terminating the charter originated by DAT. These facts are condensed from the DCA file for VH-ADR and disagree with Mr Boughton's statement that "the *RAAF then also chartered* the machine *once a month* for a total time of 60 hr 10 min" (my italics).

In December 1942, DCA agreed to transfer the Delta to the RAAF, but the terms of transfer are open to interpretation as the official records are somewhat contradictory. The DCA file for VH-ADR (which, admittedly, includes concurring Department of Air correspondence) repeatedly states that the aircraft was issued on loan to the RAAF. In contrast, when the RAAF's Form E/E88 was raised on 11 December an "on loan" classification was not entered on the card. It recorded merely that the Delta "was received from civil aviation" and, of course, an impressment requisition number was not registered as the aircraft was transferred from one government department to another. Bearing in mind that aircraft on loan had never been allocated RAAF serial numbers, further confusion arises from the entry against 12 January 1943 — "To be renumbered A61-1. VH-ADR to be marked on the tailplane" *(sic)*. In his letter, Mr Boughton rearranges these two sentences to read "that the *civil registration* of VH-ADR was to be carried *above* the tailplane *while the serial A61-1 was used*" (my italics). This, he added, confirmed that the Delta was to be operated on loan as VH-ADR. Notwithstanding Mr Boughton's claim, an inter-departmental memorandum on the DCA file, *dated 14 December 1942*, requested advice as to "when the aircraft was handed over so that action may be taken to strike the machine off the Civil Register". I would suggest that VH-ADR was the radio call-sign for A61-1, and was to be displayed on the tail-unit, or fuselage, in similar manner to other contemporary RAAF transport aircraft. In the event, the photograph of A61-1 accompanying my original letter shows no sign VH-ADR "above the tailplane" but, no doubt, it was applied at some time or other. The concluding entries on the E/E88 also do not refer to an original owner, and the authority to convert the aircraft to components is recorded as being the RAAF. Finally, all other RAAF records seen by the writer — including flying hour returns, equipment reports, technical service assessments, and historical sub-section records — refer to the Delta as RAAF aircraft A61-1, and not as DCA aircraft VH-ADR on loan.

To summarise: DCA records for Northrop Delta VH-ADR state that the aircraft was issued on loan to the RAAF. RAAF records state that the aircraft was received from civil aviation, and was "made use of" (Concise Oxford Dictionary definition, *inter alia*, for "impress") as A61-1. My thanks to Mr Boughton for highlighting the discrepancies in the records, and I trust that your readers have borne with me in my endeavour to substantiate the abbreviated facts in "Delta Down South" (*Talkback*/July 1975) which were based on RAAF records.

Gp Capt Keith Isaacs AFC, RAAF (Retd)
Lyneham, ACT, Australia

(Above) Aircraft on loan to the RAAF retained their original numbers and markings, such as this NEIAF Lockheed C-60A Lodestar LT9-32, 42-56034.

Aircraft on charter to the RAAF, like those impressed, were also numbered, and included (below) the Short S.23 Empire flying-boat A18-11, ex G-AEUA, from Qantas, and (above left) Douglas DC-3 A30-4, ex VH-ACB, from ANA.

The Woodbridge (Suffolk!) incident

I WAS surprised to read once again in the December 1975 issue (Capt Eric Brown's "A Fritz of All Trades") the perpetuation of the mythical location of Woodbridge in the County of Essex.

It would appear that a large number of aviation journalists are of the opinion that Woodbridge is in Essex — I have yet to read a report of the arrival of Ju 88 4R+UR which actually places the airfield in SUFFOLK. So, once and for all, can we *please* put Woodbridge 'on the map' and thus save the uninformed the trouble of searching for it in Essex?

It lies in very pleasant wooded country some 10 miles east of Ipswich and about four miles from its local town from which it acquires its name. The map reference is O S Sheet 150/340490 at Long E 1°25′ and Lat N 52°05′, which is about two miles from Bentwaters USAAF Base.

Your readers may be interested in some further information regarding the arrival of 'UR'. The date of arrival is that quoted in ROC records, which state: "13.7.44 0425 hrs. Hostile landed at Woodbridge — Junkers 88 came across coast with bomber and dropped four red flares". But, did it? I ask this because in another official record of events stemming from an apparently irrefutable source there is an entry as follows: "11.7.44 0428 hrs. Junkers 88 landed at Woodbridge — crew arrested". It should be noted that this latter source was a daily collation of events which was submitted to higher authority every 24 hours and could not therefore be incorrectly entered.

We are left with two possibilities. The unlikely event of an earlier arrival which has never been 'released' or an official delay for a period of 48 hours almost to the minute before feeding it out to the ROC and other quarters having direct interest. I'll leave this one to the historians to mull over and await the next article on Maeckle's arrival with extreme interest.

H K Ranson
Colchester, Essex

Testing the Fw 190

IT IS with some diffidence that I venture a comment on anything written by Capt Brown concerning captured enemy aircraft, but I should like to correct, if I may, the statement in his article on the Fw 190 that the AFDU trials on the Arnim Faber aircraft were carried out at Duxford.

It is true that on completion of performance tests at the RAE, which incidentally involved a total of nine flying hours, the aircraft was formally transferred to AFDU charge on 13

Arnim Faber's Fw 190A-4 as MP499, January 1943.

July 1942, but it was not so much a case of the aircraft going to the Unit as one of the Unit coming to the aircraft.

What happened was that on that day the Officer Commanding Air Fighting Development Unit, Wg Cdr Campbell-Orde, flew to Farnborough from Duxford (probably in the brand-new Spitfire F Mk IX BR980, delivered to the Unit the day before) and he then stayed at Farnborough on detachment until 2 August 1942 for the period of the tactical trials.

The day after his arrival, Campbell-Orde was joined by the Wing Commander Flying from Biggin Hill, Wg Cdr Rankin, and thereafter these two officers conducted the tactical trials interspersed with almost daily demonstrations to the many interested visitors who called at Farnborough to view the new capture. These included the AOC-in-C Fighter Command, the Controller of Research and Development at the MAP, Air Marshal Linnell, the Under-Secretary of State for Air, Capt Balfour, and several representatives of the USAAF, including Major General Spaatz. Another visitor at this time was the Rolls-Royce test pilot, Flt Lt Harker.

The biggest demonstration, however, was mounted on 22 July when to the accompaniment of a broadcast commentary by Campbell-Orde the Fw 190 was flown in mock combat with the Spitfire IX, a Typhoon and the Griffon Spitfire DP845 before assembled representatives of the aircraft industry.

Peter H Pimblett
Sale, Cheshire

The Cri-Cri in the air

AS A member of Salis Aviation and following your article on La Ferte Alais Collection by David Nicolle, I would like to correct a detail. The engine on the Cri-Cri Salmson is not a 60 hp 9A Dr but a 5AQ of 83 hp.

The aircraft was rebuilt in 1973, the previous registration being F-BFNG. The fuselage was severely damaged when the engine quit on take-off. Two friends, André Dutter and Claude Draut, and I, started the rebuild process. The fuselage was reconstructed and fairings were removed from the landing gear, giving it a spidery appearance. Test flights were made with the original engine, but RPM would not go over 1,750 and take-off was a very long affair, using all the available 700 metres of La Ferte! The engine was removed and a zero-time Salmonson 5AQ was located and installed. RPM would still not go over 2,200 (max rpm for take-off is supposed to be 2,500), and the take-off is rather slow and max speed is about 110 km/h. The aircraft is a pleasure to fly with powerful rudder and elevator, and rather heavy ailerons. Stalls are a joy, either power on or off, giving plenty of warning and the aircraft regaining straight flight very easily. Landings, either wheel type or three point, are very easy, the drag being very high.

Mr J A Marchadier
Ris Oranges, France

(Above) The Curtiss XF11C-1 prototype, with the two-row Wright engine and long-chord cowling.

(Above and below) The Curtiss BFC-2 (alias F11C-2) which had a single-row Wright Cyclone engine and short-chord cowling.

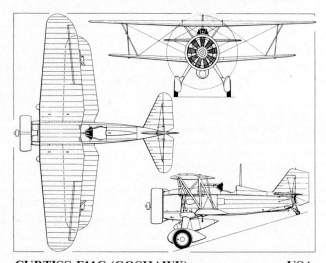

CURTISS F11C (GOSHAWK)　　　　　　USA

On 16 April 1932, the US Navy ordered two prototypes of a new shipboard fighter under the designations XF11C-1 and XF11C-2, the former with a 600 hp Wright R-1510-98 two-row radial and the latter with a 700 hp Wright R-1820-78 single-row radial. The latter was, in fact, a company demonstrator which had been flying for some time and was of mixed construction (fabric-covered wooden wings and fabric-covered metal fuselage and tail surfaces), whereas the XF11C-1, which utilised the wings of the YP-23, was of fabric-covered all-metal construction and was delivered in September 1932. The R-1820-78 Cyclone and mixed structure of the XF11C-2 found favour with the US Navy and on 18 October 1932, a production order was placed for 28 F11C-2s, deliveries of

which began in February 1933 and were completed in the following May, the fourth aircraft on the contract being completed with a manually-retractable undercarriage as the XF11C-3, subsequently being redesignated XBF2C-1 with adoption of the "bomber-fighter" category in March 1934. Simultaneously, the F11C-2s were redesignated as BFC-2s. Armament comprised two 0·3-in (7,62-mm) Browning machine guns and a single bomb of up to 500 lb (226,8 kg) or four 112-lb (50,8-kg) bombs could be carried. The BFC-2 remained in US Navy service until 1938. Max speed, 205 mph (330 km/h). Time to 5,000 ft (1 525 m), 2·6 min. Normal range, 560 mls (901 km). Empty weight, 3,037 lb (1 378 kg). Normal loaded weight, 4,120 lb (1 869 kg). Span, 31 ft 6 in (9,60 m). Length, 25 ft 0 in (7,62 m). Height, 10 ft 7¼ in (3,23 m). Wing area, 262 sq ft (24,34 m²).

CURTISS HAWK II　　　　　　　　　　USA

The Hawk II was essentially an export version of the XF11C-2 with a Wright R-1820F-3 Cyclone rated at 710 hp at 5,500 ft (1 676 m) and 94 US gal (356 l), the Hawk I differing in having only 50 US gal (236 l) of internal fuel. Only the Hawk II was exported in quantity, this having a similar mixed construction to that of the F11C-2 and normally carrying an armament of twin 0·3-in (7,62-mm) machine guns. The first customer for the Hawk II was Turkey which began to take delivery of 19 on 30 August 1932, Colombia following suit from the end of October 1932 with an initial batch of four twin-float equipped Hawk IIs, a total of 26 float fighters of this type being delivered to Colombia by the end of July 1934. Nine were delivered to Bolivia of which three had interchangeable wheel/float undercarriages; four were delivered to Chile; 50 were delivered to China; four to Cuba, two to Germany; one to Norway and 12 to Thailand. The following data should be considered as typical. Max speed, 187 mph (301 km/h) at sea level, 208 mph (335 km/h) at 6,900 ft (2 100 m). Normal range, 414 mls (666 km). Empty weight, 2,903 lb (1 317 kg). Loaded weight, 3,876

(Above) One of the Turkish Hawk IIs and (below) one of the two Hawk IIs evaluated in Germany temporarily fitted with floats.

(Above) The Curtiss XP-934 Swift prototype with Wright Cyclone engine.

(Above and below) The Curtiss XP-934 re-engined with a Curtiss Conqueror engine as the XP-31.

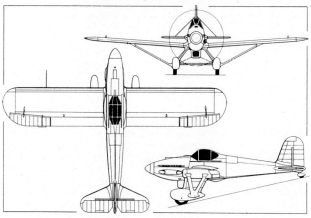

lb (1 758 kg). Span, 31 ft 6 in (9,60 m). Length, 26 ft 6 in (8,08 m). Height, 9 ft 9 in (2,97 m). Wing area, 262 sq ft (24,34 m²).

CURTISS XP-31 (XP-934)   USA

Owing much to the design of the XA-8 attack aircraft of 1931, the XP-934 Swift low-wing braced fighter monoplane with enclosed cockpit and 700 hp Wright R-1820 Cyclone air-cooled radial was flown for the first time in July 1932. Featuring retractable full-span leading-edge slats and trailing-edge flaps, the XP-934 was intended to compete with the Boeing XP-936 (see *Fighter A to Z*/March 1974), but performance proved disappointing and the prototype was therefore re-engined with a Prestone-cooled Curtiss GIV-1570 -F Conqueror geared engine of 600 hp with which it was accepted for test by the USAAC on 1 March 1933 as the XP-31. However, by this time, the Air Corps had already placed a production contract for the Boeing competitor as the P-26A. The following data relate to the Conqueror-powered XP-31. Max speed, 208 mph (335 km/h) at sea level, 202 mph (325 km/h) at 5,000 ft (1 525 m). Initial climb, 2,130 ft/min (10,82 m/sec). Range, 370 mls (595 km). Empty weight, 3,334 lb (1 512 kg). Loaded weight, 4,143 lb (1 879 kg). Span, 36 ft 0 in (10,97 m). Length, 26 ft 3 in (8,00 m). Height, 7 ft 9 in (2,36 m). Wing area, 203 sq ft (18,86 m²).

CURTISS BF2C-1 (F11C-3)   USA

The fourth production F11C-2 (Goshawk) was completed

with manually-operated retractable main undercarriage members accommodated by a deepened forward fuselage and an R-1820-80 Cyclone rated at 700 hp at 8,000 ft (2 440 m) and delivered to the US Navy on 27 May 1933 as the XF11C-3. Twenty-seven production models were ordered as F11C-3s with raised aft turtle decks, partial canopies and the metal wings that had proved satisfactory on the XF11C-1. Prior to the commencement of deliveries on 7 October 1934, the designation was changed to BF2C-1. The BF2C-1 carried an armament of two 0·3-in (7,62-mm) Brownings with 600 rpg and made provision for a single 474-lb (215-kg) bomb or up to four 116-lb (52,6-kg) bombs, and an R-1820-04 Cyclone rated at 770 hp for take-off was fitted. In the event, at cruising rpm the Cyclone set up a sympathetic vibration with the metal wing structure, the aircraft shaking dramatically in this regime, and, the problem never being satisfactorily resolved, the BF2C-1s were withdrawn within a few months. Max speed, 225 mph (362 km/h) at 8,000 ft (2 440 m). Initial climb, 2,150 ft/min (10,92 m/sec). Normal range, 570 mls (917 km). Empty weight, 3,370 lb (1 529 kg). Loaded weight, 4,555 lb (2 066 kg). Span, 31 ft 6 in (9,60 m). Length, 23 ft 0 in (7,01 m). Height, 10 ft 10 in (3,30 m). Wing area, 262 sq ft (24,34 m²).

(Above) The Curtiss XF11C-3 was a re-engined F11C-2 with retractable undercarriage.

(Above and below) The BF2C-1 (alias F11C-3) production model, with built-up rear fuselage decking.

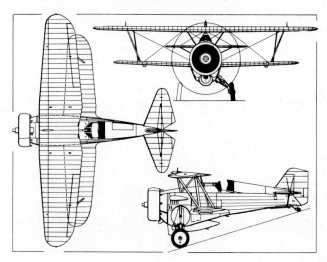

IN PRINT

"F-15 Eagle in Action"
by Lou Drendel & Capt Don Carson
"P-38 Lightning in Action"
by Gene B Stafford
Squadron/Signal Publications, Michigan,
$3·95 each
48 pp each, 11 in by 8¼ in, illustrated
TWO worthy additions to the Squadron/Signal series of "In Action" books, these titles make an interesting pair, for the F-15 and the P-38 were designed broadly to fulfil similar rôles in the US Air Force and a measure of the progress that has been made in 30 years can be gained from a comparison of the two books.

The P-38 volume gives an excellent summary of the Lightning's evolution and service record, without becoming bogged down in the minutiae of model differences. In the case of the F-15, there is little service to record as yet, since the USAF is still in process of working up its first operational unit, but this leaves space for accounts of flying the Eagle, and of the *"Streak Eagle"* flights that set eight time-to-height records in 1975. Both volumes are extensively illustrated, in keeping with the series.

"The Lockheed Aerobatic Trophy"
by Tony Lloyd
Midland Counties Publication, £1
48 pp, 8¼ in by 5¾ in, illustrated
THE Lockheed Aerobatic Trophy was presented in 1955, by the Lockheed Hydraulic Brake Co Ltd, to be competed for in aerobatic flying open to pilots of all nationalities. This small volume presents an account of each contest from 1955 to 1969 (the first year in which the UK provided the winner), with lists of all competitions and descriptions of the sequences flown. After the 1969 event, Lockheed withdrew its sponsorship, but international aerobatics competitions have survived, having been encouraged, without doubt, by the existence of this trophy.

Copies of this interesting if rather specialised little volume can be ordered direct from Midland Counties Publications (I), 17 Woodstock Close, Burbage, Hinckley, Leicestershire, LE10 2EG, price £1, post free.

"Aircraft Museums Directory"
by Gordon Riley
Battle of Britain Prints International, London
50p
32 pp, 4⅛ in by 7 in, illustrated
A SMALL but very useful booklet in a revised and enlarged second edition, detailing the many collections of historic aircraft that are

accessible to the public in the United Kingdom, with lists of the aircraft each contains and notes on opening times and prices.

"The Ships & Aircraft of the US Fleet"
(Tenth Edition)
by Samuel L Morison and John S Rowe
United States Naval Institute, Washington
and
Patrick Stephens Ltd, Cambridge, £8·50
294 pp, 10 in by 7 in, illustrated
OF PRIMARY interest to the Naval "buff" for the mass of information it contains on the ships of the US Navy, this volume should not be ignored by aviation enthusiasts. The section on aircraft occupies 42 pages and provides a useful run-down of statistics plus notes on the service status of each type still in the Navy inventory, ranging, for example, from the Grumman QF-9J Cougar: "only two remain, these at Point Mugu, California" to such types as the Lockheed S-3A Viking and Grumman F-14 Tomcat, both in the early stages of Fleet introduction when this volume went to press in mid-1975. There is also useful information on aircraft tail markings and designations and a separate section on missiles and conventional ordnance (both air and ship-launched) occupying another 25 pages.

Patrick Stephens Ltd is the sole UK, British Commonwealth and European publisher for the volume, as for other USNI publications.

"Aeroplanes in Colour"
Ian Allan, Shepperton, Middlesex, £1·95
64 pp, 7 in by 4¼ in
JUST simply a collection of colour photographs — all of which have been previously published in Ian Allan publications and many of which formed the covers, over the years of "Aircraft Illustrated". Good value but of only limited interest to the enthusiast; likely to appeal to the younger fans.

"American Fighters of World War 2"
by Alan W Hall
Patrick Stephens Ltd, Cambridge, £1·40
64 pp, 5¼ in by 8½ in, illustrated
NUMBER 14 in the Airfix Magazine Guide series, this slim volume serves as a useful primer for the modeller who is still a relative newcomer to aviation and who wants to know more about the aircraft he finds himself modelling. This is not, however, a *specific* modelling aid and does not contain information on markings and colours, beyond what can be deduced from the photographs.

"The Nuremberg Raid"
by Martin Middlebrook
Fontana Paperbacks, London, £1·50
370 pp, 5 in by 7¾ in, illustrated
FIRST paperback edition of an important work dealing with one of the major wartime operations of Bomber Command — the attack on Nuremberg on the night of 30-31 March 1944. The raid became notorious because of the high losses — more than 13 per cent of the Lancasters and Halifaxes despatched — and because of the subsequent allegations that the *Luftwaffe* had prior knowledge of Bomber Command's target that night. Mr Middlebrook provides a full account of the raid and a closely documented record of the losses. From a study of such facts as he was able to gather, he rejects the betrayal story.

"Deutsche Flugzeuge 1914-1918"
Edited by Karl R Pawlas
Karl R Pawlas, Nurnberg, W Germany
320 pp, 6 in by 8¼ in, illustrated
THE series of "Luftfahrt-Dokumente" published by Karl R Pawlas is earning a deservedly high reputation among students of German aircraft of World War II, the first 19 titles having been devoted to aircraft or projects of this period. For the 20th volume, Pawlas has assembled a comprehensive collection of photographs of the German aircraft of World War I.

There is a short introduction (in German, as are all photo captions) describing the production effort in Germany from August 1914 onwards, with an explanation of the various groups of aircraft designated as C-Type, D-Type, E-Type etc. Also reproduced are 18 pages of official contemporary three-view silhouettes, but it is the photographs, occupying more than 300 pages, that make the volume of special interest to the collector and enthusiast, whether or not he can read the language. Many of the captions quote aircraft span and length, as well as aircraft designations, purpose and date, all of which information is easily understood.

"D H Comet"
by J Graham Cowell
Airline Publications & Sales Ltd, Hounslow, Mddx, £3·95
180 pp, 5¾ in by 8¼ in, illustrated
IN THIS new publication from a company specialising in books about airliners, an attempt has been made to tell the story of the de Havilland Comet — as the world's first jet airliner, an aircraft of outstanding historic importance. There is a wealth of information contained in relatively concentrated form, including a complete production list and 56 pages of photographs. The text describing the Comet's evolution and service history is somewhat unsatisfying, however, being written in a staccato style that presents one bald fact after another in short sentences — a journalistic device more suited to a local newspaper than to the objective recording of aviation history. It also seems unfortunate that Mr Cowell felt it necessary to suggest that UFO's may somehow have been responsible for the crash of Comet I G-ALYV on 2 May 1953 near Calcutta.

Two Boeing EB-47Es — believed to be the last airworthy Stratojets in operation — are still being used in US Navy markings by McDonnell Douglas in support of Aegis missile system testing. Details of most current Navy aircraft — but not these EB-47s — are contained in the latest edition of "Ships and Aircraft of the US Fleet" noted above.

CANADA

CANADAIR LEARSTAR 600

CANADAIR LTD of Montreal has acquired worldwide exclusive rights to manufacture and market the LearStar 600, a small twin-jet transport designed by William P Lear and developed for the past two years by the latter's company, Learavia Corporation, of Stead, Nevada. Any decision to go ahead with production of the LearStar 600 will depend, however, on the results of extensive evaluation of the design and marketing studies to be conducted by James B Taylor, who has previously been responsible for developing the marketing programme for the Cessna Citation and, before that, the Fan-Jet Falcon. The deal also requires approval of the Canadian government, which currently owns Canadair but intends to transfer ownership to private interests in due course.

The LearStar 600 project grew out of earlier studies by Lear to put a supercritical wing on existing Learjet models (in the production of which, by the Gates Learjet Aircraft Division, Lear is no longer involved). These studies led to the conclusion that operators interested in the higher speeds made possible by such a wing were also likely to want greatly increased capacity, and the present project evolved as an aircraft able to carry 14 passengers in an executive layout, or up to 30 in airliner configuration, or 7,500 lb (3 405 kg) of high-priority cargo. A three-engined layout was studied, but a version with 3,700 lb st (1 680 kgp) Garrett AiResearch TFE731-3 turbofans became favoured, and then the Avco Lycoming ALF 502 was selected.

Static test airframes and one or more flying prototypes will be built by Learavia in Nevada, with the help of Canadair financing; the estimated cost to certification, including

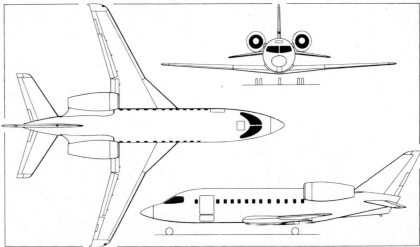

(Above) A three-view drawing and (below) artist's impression of the LearStar 600, production and marketing rights for which have been acquired by Canadair.

production tooling, is $70m (£37m), and prospective unit cost is about $3m (£1·6m). Lear claims that certification could be completed in 20 months from go-ahead of prototype construction; Canadair, more conservatively, projects initial deliveries in 1979 if the programme goes ahead.

Power Plant: Two Avco Lycoming ALF 502D turbofans each rated at 6,500 lb st (2 950 kgp) for take-off; cruising thrust, 1,050 lb (477 kg) each.

Performance: Max cruise up to Mach = 0·90; normal cruise, Mach = 0·85; max cruise altitude, 49,000 ft (14 945 m); typical ranges, 4,000 mls (6 432 km) with eight passengers at M = 0·85, 2,000 mls (3 216 km) with 7,500 lb (3 405 kg) at M = 0·75 or five 100-ml (161-km)

unrefuelled sectors with 30 passengers plus 1,000 lb (454 kg) freight at M = 0·80 at 20,000 ft (6 100 m).

Weights: Empty, 11,000 lb (4 994 kg); max fuel, 11,000 lb (4 994 kg); max payload, 7,500 lb (3 405 kg); max take-off, 26,000 lb (11 804 kg); max landing, 22,000-24,000 lb (9 988-10 896 kg).

Dimensions: Span, 53 ft 4 in (16,27 m); length, 63 ft (19,22 m); height, 18 ft 3½ in (5,58 m); sweepback, 25 deg.

Accommodation: Flight crew of two; 14 passengers and flight attendant in executive layout, 30 passengers at seat pitch of 30-in (76-cm) and a flight attendant in airline configuration. Cabin pressurized to 9 psi (0,63 kg/cm²).

JAPAN

NIPPI NP-100A

THE Nihon Hikoki Company (Nippi) has given preliminary details of a two-seat all-metal powered glider, the NP-100A, which is now undergoing certification with a view to production starting early in 1977. First flight was made at Atsugi on 25 December 1975, and a second prototype is under construction for exhibition at the Tokyo International Aerospace Show in October.

The NP-100A has side-by-side seating beneath a one-piece canopy that opens upwards and rearwards, and an unusual two-leg landing gear system with both main wheels retracting into the fuselage. The wing is a single-spar structure with FX-67K-170 section and with trailing edge flaps in two sections each side that also function as air brakes.

Most unusual feature of the NP-100A is the powerplant arrangement, a small piston engine being used to drive a ducted fan in the central fuselage, with the orifice beneath the tail boom. Intakes in the fuselage sides beneath

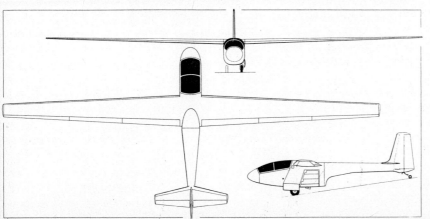

(Above) A photograph and (below) three-view drawing of the Nippi NP-100A powered glider.

the wing can be closed by Venetian-blind shutters when the engine is not in use. The prototype has a Kawasaki H-2 motorcycle engine, but the second NP-100A and production machines will have a Xenoah G-72C unit, similar to the engine now being used in the Bede BD-5D.

Production is expected to be at the rate of one a month in 1977. No price has yet been quoted by Nippi and the following data refer to the first prototype.

Power Plant: One 60 hp Kawasaki H-2kai four-cylinder motor-cycle engine driving a four-bladed wooden ducted fan of 2-ft (60-cm) diameter. Fuel capacity, 8·8 Imp gal (40 l).

Performance (engine on): Max speed, 99.5 mph (160 km/h) at sea level; econ cruising speed, 56 mph (90 km/h); stalling speed, 40 mph (65 km/h); initial rate of climb, 393 ft/min (2 m/sec); take-off to 50 ft (15,2 m), less than 1,970 ft (600 m); landing from 50 ft (15,2 m), less than 1,310 ft (400 m); range, 124 mls (200 km); endurance with max fuel, 2 hrs. Best gliding ratio, 30:1; minimum sinking speed, 157 ft/min (0,8 m/sec).

Weights: Empty, 925 lb (420 kg); max take-off, 1,320 lb (600 kg).

Dimensions: Span, 59 ft (18,0 m); length, 26 ft 3½ in (8,0 m); overall height, 7 ft 4 in (2,23 m); gross wing area, 193,75 sq ft (18,0 m²); wheelbase, (0,70 m); aspect ratio, 18:1.

UNITED KINGDOM

HAWKER SIDDELEY HS.125 SERIES 700

PRELIMINARY details have been given by Hawker Siddeley of a new version of the HS.125 executive jet, a prototype of which is to fly this month (July). With the first production aircraft to join the test programme in December, certification of this new variant, the Series 700, is expected in April 1977; deliveries, from an initial batch of 20 already in hand, will begin in the first half of 1977. The significant feature of the new model is the use of Garrett AiResearch TFE 731-3-1H turbofans, replacing the Viper turbojets used in all previous models.

Use of the turbofans gives the HS.125 Series 700 a 50 per cent increase in range over the Series 600, on the airframe of which it is based. Reduced external noise levels will allow the Series 700 to comply with the latest proposed amendments to FAR Part 36 certification requirements. There are some small external changes, including a reshaped and enlarged ventral fin with a smoother curve on the underfin, and some drag-reducing features such as fairings on the windshield wipers, flush

An artist's impression of the Hawker Siddeley HS.125 Series 700, a turbofan-engined variant of the biz-jet now under development.

or mush-head riveting techniques in place of domed rivets and aerodynamically sealed nose gear doors.

The HS.125 Series 700 also has systems improvements such as solid state AC power generation and Collins FCS 80 autopilot and flight director system, plus Collins VHF comm/nav, DME and ADF and RCA Primus 40 weather radar.

Power Plant: Two Garrett-AiResearch TFE 731-3-1H turbofans each rated at 3,700 lb st (1 680 kgp) for take-off.

Performance: High speed cruise, 506 mph (814 km/h); long-range cruise, 460 mph (740 km/h); balanced take-off field length, ISA at sea level, max weight, 6,100 ft (1 860 m); range at Mach = 0·70, six passengers and 45-min reserve, 2,660 mls (4 280 km); range at Mach = 0·75, 2,130 mls (3 427 km).

Weights: Cabin payload, 2,350 lb (1 067 kg); max take-off, 25,000 lb (11 340 kg).

Dimensions: Span, 47 ft 0 in (14,33 m); length, 50 ft 6 in (15,39 m); height, 17 ft 3 in (5,26 m); gross wing area, 353 sq ft (32,8 m²); undercarriage track, 9 ft 2 in (2,79 m); wheelbase, 20 ft 9½ in (6,34 m).

USA

McDONNELL DOUGLAS DC-9-QSF

PRELIMINARY details have been given by McDonnell Douglas of the DC-9-QSF (Quiet, Short Field) transport that it is offering for co-operative development with Japan. The requirements of All Nippon Airways, Toa Domestic Airlines and Southwest Air Lines are seen as the primary launching base for the DC-9-QSF and the proposed joint venture would give Japanese industry responsibility for production of all the QSF special features, in return for a Japanese contribution to launching costs. Current projections are for the sale of 251 QSF-type aircraft over 10 years, with the McDonnell Douglas aircraft achieving a minimum sale of 114 in competition with short-field versions of the Boeing 737, BAC One-Eleven and Fokker F28.

Basis of the DC-9-QSF proposal is a DC-9 Srs 40 airframe, with refanned 18,000 lb st (8 172 kgp) JT8D-209 engines, a modified wing and undercarriage improvements. The wing changes comprise use of a full span variable camber Krueger (VCK) flap from 64 per cent to 80 per cent of span; Moving ailerons outwards to allow for this flap extension and adding 2 ft (0,61 m) at each wing tip. Additional spoiler panels are used ahead of the trailing edge flaps.

Use of low pressure tyres (95-100 psi/6,7-7,0 kg/cm² compared with the standard 130-135 psi/9,1-9,5 kg/cm²) will bring down the LCN (load classification number) to about 40, but to meet Japanese requirements for an LCN of 20, a third main landing gear unit on the fuselage centreline is offered as an option, reducing payload by about 1,500 lb (680 kg) and taking up some rear cargo compartment volume. An alternative may be for the strengths of some Japanese runways — many of which have not been strengthened since the war — to be increased. To help reduce landing runs, the DC-9-QSF will have a new anti-skid system (already approved on the DC-9 Srs 50), nosewheel brakes and an automatic braking system which programmes the application of main wheel brakes and wing spoilers in response to wheel spin-up at touchdown.

First flight of a DC-9-QSF could be made 25 months after a go-ahead decision, with an 11-month certification period to allow entry into service 36 months after go-ahead.

Detailed data for the DC-9-QSF have not yet been given. The aircraft would have a normal seating layout for 128 passengers and would carry this load for 1,100 mls (1 770 km) from 3,935-ft (1 200-m) runways. Maximum payload of 13,500 lb (6 130 kg) could be carried for 920 mls (1 010 km) if adequate runway lengths are available.

A preliminary three-view drawing of the proposed McDonnell Douglas DC-9QSF which has a small increase in wing-span, revised flaps and ailerons and refanned JT8D engines.

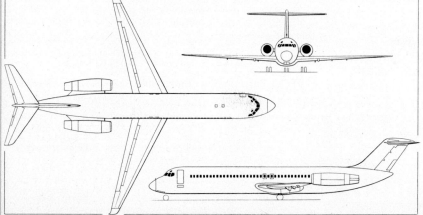

International

Volume 11   Number 2   August 1976

Managing Editor   William Green
Editor   Gordon Swanborough
Modelling Editor   Fred J Henderson
Contributing Artists   Dennis Punnett
                         John Weal
Cover Art   W R Hardy
Contributing Photographer
                         Stephen Peltz
Editorial Representative, Washington
                         Norman Polmar
Publisher   Donald Hannah
Circulation Director   Donald Syner
Financial Director   John Gold
Subscription Manager   Claire Sillette
Advertising/Public Relations
                         Elizabeth Baker
Advertising Manager   Jim Boyd

Editorial Offices:
The AIR INTERNATIONAL, PO Box 16,
Bromley, BR2 7RB Kent.

**Subscription, Advertising and
Circulation Offices:**
The AIR INTERNATIONAL, De Worde
House, 283 Lonsdale Road, London
SW13 9QW. Telephone 01-878 2454.
US and Canadian readers may address
subscriptions and general enquiries to
AIR INTERNATIONAL PO Box 353, White-
stone, NY 11357 for onward transmis-
sion to the UK, from where all corres-
pondence is answered and orders
despatched.

MEMBER OF THE AUDIT
BUREAU OF CIRCULATIONS   ABC

Subscription rates, inclusive of postage,
direct from the publishers, per year:
United Kingdom   £5·50
USA $17·50
Canada $17·50

Rates for other countries and for air mail
subscriptions available on request from
the Subscription Department at the
above address.

The AIR INTERNATIONAL is published
monthly by Fine Scroll Limited, distributed by Ducimus Books Ltd and
printed by William Caple & Co Ltd,
Chevron Press, Leicester, England.
Editorial contents © 1976 by Pilot Press
Limited. The views expressed by named
contributors and correspondents are their
own and do not necessarily reflect the
views of the editors. Neither the editors
nor the publishers accept responsibility
for any loss or damage, however caused,
to manuscripts or illustrations submitted
to the AIR INTERNATIONAL.

Second Class postage approved at New
York, NY. USA Mailing Agents: Air-Sea
Freight Inc, 527 Madison Avenue, New
York, NY 10022.

CONTENTS

**WRENDEZVOUS
WITH WREN**

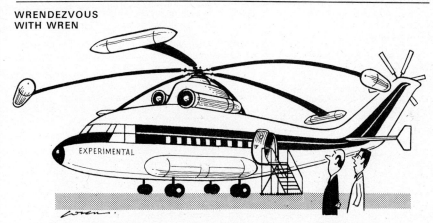

"Once we've cracked the fuel feed problem, we shall have the first long-range chopper."

AIRSCENE

MILITARY AFFAIRS

ABU DHABI

It is now known that the supplementary **order** placed on behalf of the Abu Dhabi Air Force **for Mirages** (see *Airscene*/July) comprises 18 Mirage 5s. These consist of 14 Mirage 5AD strike fighters, three Mirage 5RAD tactical reconnaissance aircraft and one Mirage 5DAD two-seat trainer. The initial batch consisted of 12 Mirage 5ADs and two Mirage 5DADs. With the commencement of deliveries of the second batch of Mirages next year, the Hunter Mk 76 and 76A aircraft currently equipping the ADAF squadron based at Sharjah will be phased out. The ADAF will provide the backbone of the Air Force of the United Arab Emirates when, as agreed by the Federal Defence Council of the UAE in May, the air components of the seven member states — Abu Dhabi, Dubai, Sharjah, Ras al Hkaimah, Ajman, Umm al Khaiwain and Fujairah — are merged under unified UAE control by the end of the year, although only Dubai possesses an air component apart from Abu Dhabi.

AUSTRALIA

In a recent press statement, Prime Minister Malcolm Fraser stated that the **replacement of the RAAF's Mirage** force is a **less urgent** problem than that of updating Australia's naval and maritime reconnaissance fleets, suggesting that reduced priority is now attached to the selection of a new fighter. Nevertheless, an RAAF evaluation team is scheduled to leave Australia this month (August) for Europe and the USA to evaluate all possible contenders for the Mirage replacement requirement. Principal RAAF interest still apparently centres on the McDonnell Douglas F-15 Eagle, although serious consideration is expected to be given to the Northrop/McDonnell Douglas F-18L alias LBD as this offers Australian industry an opportunity to participate in design and development as well as production. However, the likelihood of the purchase of two different aircraft types for the RAAF as a result of a reappraisal of future requirements has increased of late, according to reports from Canberra, one type being optimised for the air superiority mission and the other for ground attack. Among European types to be evaluated are the Tornado, the Viggen, the Jaguar International and the Mirage F1. While the RAAF is looking for an in-service date before the end of the present decade, it is being suggested that the early 'eighties (ie, 1981–82) is likely to be more realistic. Defence spending of A$12,000m (£8,330m) over the next five years has been approved, the 1976–77 defence budget to be presented this month being expected to be some A$1,900m (£1,320m).

It was announced on 1 July that the Australian Government has placed an **order** on behalf of the RAAF **for** 12 Lockheed **C-130H Hercules** transports for the re-equipment of No 36 Sqdn which is currently operating the C-130A version of the Hercules delivered 1958–59. The new Hercules are to be delivered to the RAAF during 1978 at a total programme cost of $115m (A$93·5m). The aged C-130A Hercules may be passed on to third-world countries through Australian aid programmes after the delivery of the C-130Hs.

BRAZIL

The Brazilian Air Force Academy has purchased two EMB-210 **Ipanema** Agplanes **for use as glidertugs**. To operate in full FAB livery, the Ipanemas will be stripped of spraying equipment and will be used to give air tows to the six Blanik gliders owned by the Academy.

CANADA

At the time of closing for press, a Canadian governmental **decision on** Lockheed's revised CP-3C **Orion financing** proposal was still **awaited** (see *Airscene*/July). Lockheed has proposed the stretching of the CP-3C programme by one year, delaying aircraft deliveries until 1980–81 and thus reducing funding peaks which were the primary cause of the collapse of the original agreement, and configurational changes — primarily associated with avionics — which will reduce early-year funding without impairing mission capability. The Canadian government's reaffirmation of its commitment to NATO in ASW and other areas has been interpreted as meaning that procurement of an Argus replacement will be proceeded with.

Recent **changes in** the **Maritime Command** of the CAF have included the formation of a Maritime Air Group, the disbandment of the Argus-equipped VP 449 at Greenwood and the assumption of the Argus operational training rôle by VP 404, the formation of a new reserve Tracker squadron, MR 420, at Shearwater and the expansion of the Sea King-equipped HS 50 into two new squadrons, HS 423 and HS 443.

FEDERAL GERMANY

Parliamentary **approval** was believed **imminent** at the time of closing for press **for** the first procurement stage in the ambitious **helicopter** procurement **programme** of the *Heeresflieger*, the German Army's air component. Assuming that currently proposed plans are ratified, the first stage of this programme, which covers a light liaison helicopter (VBH), will result in the placing with MBB of orders for 227 BO 105M helicopters in two batches for delivery to the *Heeresflieger* during 1979–82 as Alouette II replacements. MBB has so far delivered some 290 BO 105 helicopters with production currently running at approximately 100 per year, and the *Heeresflieger* order will necessitate more than doubling the current production tempo to approximately 4·5 helicopters per week by 1979, and particularly if the second stage of the helicopter procurement programme is resolved by the anticipated selection of an armed version of the BO 105 to meet the *Panzerabwehrhubschrauber* requirement. This will result in the purchase of a further 212 BO 105s for the *Heeresflieger* for service from 1979. Referred to as the PAH-1, the armed BO 105M will have an APX sight and carry six HOT wire-guided anti-armour missiles, uprated Allison 250 turbines and a strengthened airframe.

INTERNATIONAL

Denmark, Norway, Federal Germany and the USA have agreed in principle to participate in a **joint** Euro/NATO **basic helicopter pilot training** project at the US Army Aviation School, Fort Rucker, Alabama. The training, which began with the first European students arriving at Fort Rucker in May, follows a NATO curriculum.

ITALY

Of 125 F-104G and RF-104G **Starfighters** and 24 two-seat TF-104G Starfighters supplied to the *Aeronautica Militare*, 51 had been **lost** up to the end of April, including one F-104G converted to F-104S standards and three TF-104Gs, representing in excess of 34 per cent. In addition, 21 examples of the F-104S version of the Starfighter had been lost of approximately 170 delivered to the AMI by Aeritalia at that time against total AMI orders for 205 aircraft. Aeritalia completed the 200th F-104S in May, this being one of 40 so far on firm order for the Turkish Air Force which anticipates receiving the last of these in September. The RF-104G remains in service with the 3ª *Aerobrigata*, each of its three *Gruppi* (18°, 28° and 132°) having a nominal strength of 18 aircraft.

KENYA

In June, **agreement** was reached between US Defense Secretary Donald H Rumsfeld and the Kenyan Defence Minister, James Gichuru, **covering** the **sale** to the Kenya Air Force **of** 10 single-seat Northrop F-5E **Tiger II** fighters and two two-seat F-5F trainers, which, with associated spares and training, have a contract value of approximately $75m (£44·1m). The KAF, which is unlikely to commence taking delivery of the F-5s before late next year, currently has three-four of the six refurbished Hawker Hunters originally supplied in 1974, plus five of the six Strikemaster Mk 87s which serve in both training and light strike rôles.

MALAYSIA

The Royal Malaysian Air Force was scheduled to add the Lockheed **C-130H Hercules** to its inventory last month (July) when the first three of six transports of this type were to be **ferried** by RMAF crews from Lockheed-Georgia **to** Kuala Lumpur. The remaining three Hercules will be delivered later this year. The Hercules, which were ordered in the autumn of 1974, will operate a scheduled daily service between East and West Malaysia.

PAKISTAN

The C-in-C of the Pakistan Air Force, Air Chief Marshal Zulfikar Ali Khan, recently **visited Peking** where he was joined by a group of senior PAF officers amid speculation that an agreement was being negotiated for the acquisition of additional Chinese combat aircraft. Such procurement would seem improbable in view of current PAF interest in US aircraft reportedly centering on the Northrop F-5E Tiger II, the Vought A-7 Corsair, the McDonnell Douglas A-4 Skyhawk II and the Fairchild A-10, and their recent evaluation by a four-man PAF mission. However, the US Congress has still (at the time of closing for press) to sanction a $28m (£16m) sale of TOW missiles to Pakistan. A provision of over R7,980m (£462·6m) has been made in the national budget for defence expenditure in 1977, this showing an increase in excess of R470m (£27·25m), or 6·4 per cent, over the current year's provision.

PORTUGAL

NATO Defence Ministers meeting in Brussels in June agreed to provide Portugal with special assistance in order to modernise its armed forces and *Herr* Georg Leber, the **Federal German** Defence Minister, stated that, in addition to supplying six Fiat

G.91T trainers (see *Airscene*/July), his **government** was **making available** to the *Força Aérea Portuguesa* 14 single-seat **G.91R** light strike aircraft.

TURKEY

The Turkish **Air Force** anticipates **receiving** the **last** of the 40 Aeritalia-built F-104S **Starfighters** that it currently has on order **in September,** by which time it is likely that it will have taken up its option on a further 20 F-104S Starfighters, which, the manufacturer states, can be delivered at a rate of three per month as soon as the option is taken up. Funding for the additional 20 Starfighters is included in the 1976 budget, as is also provision for a further 40 McDonnell Douglas F-4E Phantoms, although, like the Starfighters, a firm order for the Phantoms has still to be negotiated. The Turkish Air Force has received all 40 Phantoms under the original contract (which was interrupted by the 1975 arms embargo after the delivery of 16 aircraft) and if the Turkish government takes up the letter of offer on the 40 additional Phantoms, these will be delivered at a rate of two per month from the beginning of 1978. The contract between the Turkish and Federal German governments involving 56 Alpha Jets is now believed to have been finalised with the first deliveries expected to start in 1979. The first batch of Alpha Jets will be supplied direct from Germany but the bulk will be assembled from Franco-German components by TUSAS.

UGANDA

As a result of the extraordinarily audacious Israeli commando assault on Entebbe airport on 3 July to free hostages held there by pro-Palestinian terrorists responsible for the hijacking of the Air France Airbus a week earlier, the **Uganda Air Force** reportedly **lost seven MiG-21s and four MiG-17s.** Destroyed by the Israeli commandos, these represented some **25 per cent of** the service's total **jet aircraft** inventory of L 29 Delfin and MiG-15UTI two-seaters, and MiG-17 and MiG-21 fighters.

AIRCRAFT AND INDUSTRY

CANADA

One of the two pre-production de Havilland **DASH-7** airliners has completed a **demonstration tour** in the USA, in the course of which high altitude, high temperature trials were made at Prescott, Arizona. Demonstrations were made at Aspen and Denver, Colorado — two of the points served by Rocky Mountain Airways which has ordered DASH-7s to replace its four Twin Otters — and at several airports in the Los Angeles area, including Los Angeles International, Ontario, Van Nuys and Orange County. The two DASH-7s have now accumulated some 900 hrs of flight and certification is expected early 1977. Eight companies have ordered 25 DASH-7s, although one of these, Widerøe's Flyveselskap, is reported to have postponed delivery of its aircraft because of its currently poor financial situation. De Havilland is still working on a projected DHC-7R long-endurance reconnaissance version of the airliner, primarily for coastal surveillance and in-shore patrols. With increased fuel capacity in the wing, the DHC-7R would have an endurance of about 10 hrs.

FEDERAL GERMANY

A break-through into the Chinese market appears to have been made by MBB with the **sale of four BO 105** helicopters **to the Chinese** National Machinery Import and

The South African Air Force has now received a total of seven Swearingen Merlin IVA light transports, one of which is illustrated here, and the type has entered service for communications duties with No 21 Squadron, based at Swartkops.

Export Company, which has taken an option on 16 more. To be delivered in December, the first four will be used to evaluate the performance of the BO 105 in off-shore duties along China's northern coast and in the East China Sea, for which purpose they will carry external cargo hooks and winches. The BO 105 is also being deployed, in Alaska, for the detection of incipient fires. In this rôle, they can carry four fully-equipped "smoke jumpers", who can be put down at the source of any fire that has been detected. Two BO 105s were leased for 100 days each by the government of Alaska during 1975 and because of their success in this rôle, three of the helicopters are being utilised in the same rôle in 1976.

FRANCE

An agreement was signed on 15 June between Dassault-Breguet, Aérospatiale and the French government, in respect of the **development of** the Falcon/Mystère 50, a prototype of which is scheduled to fly in November. State support for the project has thus been confirmed, covering up to 100 per cent of the Aérospatiale launching costs and 40 per cent of those of Dassault-Breguet, in respect of three development aircraft, static and fatigue test specimens, certification and production tooling. The Dassault-Breguet share of the government investment, which is repayable by means of a levy on future sales, includes a certain amount to be distributed to French equipment manufacturers. The Aérospatiale share of production represents more than 50 per cent, including the fuselage and tail unit. Dassault-Breguet builds the wings and engine nacelles and is responsible for final assembly at Merignac.

INTERNATIONAL

Up to the time this issue went to press, no final decisions about the **future transport aircraft** to be built **in Europe** were in sight, but the chances of a go-ahead for a new version of the Airbus seemed to have strengthened (see *Airscene*/June 1976). In the face of French moves to do a deal with Boeing, in which Aérospatiale would collaborate on development of the Boeing 7N7 and Boeing would join in on the Airbus A300B-10, Britain has made a move to become a partner in the Airbus consortium, to help develop and produce a B-10 variant. There are still many possible permutations, but it appears that an all-European B-10 would have substantially the same wing as at present and, if Britain comes in, Rolls-Royce RB.211 engines; this is described in general terms as the A300B-10MC (minimum change). The Franco-US deal envisages making use of a Boeing-developed wing to obtain a more significant reduction

in direct operating costs — up to 20 per cent — but this A300B-10X would be considerably more expensive to develop. All the B-10 variants make use of a shorter fuselage, to seat about 200 passengers. During June, Lufthansa made known its vigorous support for the B-10X, indicating that it could well need 25–30 such aircraft up to 1990, whereas the B-10MC would be too expensive to operate; although Lufthansa is a member of the Eurac committee that has been attempting to define the future needs of European airlines in conjunction with the Group of Seven manufacturers, it appears that its views are somewhat at variance with those of the committee as a whole.

Commenting on **discussions** that have been held **between McDonnell Douglas and French** aviation **interests,** the company's president and chief executive officer Sanford N McDonnell said there was a need for "determined efforts toward co-operation between US and overseas companies, on a partnership basis rather than through the old subcontracting relationships". Of various investigations made by the company in several countries, involving advanced derivatives of both the DC-9 and DC-10, it seemed probable that "the earliest positive decision will be taken by the French government". Of the talks held with Dassault-Breguet, Mr McDonnell said they concerned "joint engineering, marketing, manufacturing and support" of an improved Mercure (see *AirData File*/page 103); if a favourable decision was reached by the French government, participation by other companies and other countries was certainly a possibility. McDonnell Douglas was "also talking with Airbus Industrie about possible co-operation" which might benefit both the DC-10 and the A-300.

French certification has been obtained for the **Airbus A300B-4 at an increased gross weight** of 347,000 lb (157 500 kg), compared with the previous figure of 330,700 lb (150 000 kg). For operations at weights greater than 337,000 lb (153 000 kg), a reduction in max operational speed and Mach number is applicable, from 360 knots to 345 knots (666-639 km/h) and Mach 0·86 to 0·82, but there is no change in the long-range cruising speeds (300 kts/556 km/h IAS and Mach 0·78). Previously delivered A300B-4s can be modified to operate at the increased weight if required by the operators. First flight of the Airbus No 30, a B-4 for Korean Air Lines, was made on 4 June and the first B-2K for South African Airways (aircraft No 32) was expected to fly on 12 July, as this issue closed for press.

Latest variant in the Hawker Siddeley HS.125 family of business jets is the Series 700, first flown on 29 June. The revised shape of the nacelles containing the TFE 731 turbofans is clearly shown in this illustration (see accompanying news item).

JAPAN

A prototype of the Shinmeiwa **PS-1 water bomber** made its **first flight** on 17 May and was used for manufacturers trials until the end of June, when it was transferred to the Fire Protection Agency. This Agency was to use the prototype during July and August for water dropping tests. Modified from the prototype PS-1 flying boat, this water bomber carries 8 tons of water but tanks have been designed to double this capacity in any future production versions of the aircraft.

Fuji Heavy Industries expects soon to receive a contract for the first **production** batch of Rockwell **Commander 700**/FA-300 light twins, and is planning to produce about 50 in the first year. Five prototypes have been built, of which two are on test in Japan and the other three in the USA (the second and third entering the programme in July) and delivery of the first production example to Rockwell is scheduled for October, allowing the first flight to be made in January. Work is also proceeding on a prototype of the Commander 710, which will have engines of about 450 hp instead of the current 340 hp Lycomings, and on a turboprop version.

SOVIET UNION

The Soviet team at the World Aerobatic Championships, taking place at Kiev from 21 July to 2 August (after this issue went to press), is expected to fly the new **Yakovlev Yak-50 aerobatic monoplane**. Bearing a family resemblance to the Yak-18PS, from which it is derived, the Yak-50 is a smaller aeroplane, with the wing outer panels attaching directly to the fuselage without the previously-used parallel-chord centre section. The rear fuselage is now of semi-monocoque construction, and in common with other specialised aerobatic types the Yak-50 has a tailwheel undercarriage. The engine is an uprated version of the Ivchenko AI-14RF, and provisional data include a span of 26 ft 10 in (8,2 m), a gross weight (for aerobatics) of 2,015 lb (915 kg) and an initial rate of climb of 2,220 ft/min (11,3 m/sec). A single-seater, with fully enclosed cockpit, the Yak-50 is stressed for $+9g$ and $-6g$.

UNITED KINGDOM

As part of its continuing studies of **One-Eleven** derivatives, BAC has projected a **variant** of the previously-announced Srs 800 which would feature a **wider fuselage** to provide six-abreast seating, the diameter increasing from 10 ft 4 in (3,15 m) to 11 ft 11½ in (3,65 m). Fuselage length would be 132 ft 2 in (40,3 m) compared with 106 ft 10 in (32,6 m) for the present BAC One-Eleven 500. Powered by CFM-56 or JT10D "ten tonne" engines, this X-11 project

would also feature a new wing centre section, increasing the span to 106 ft 1 in (32,36 m) from 93 ft 5½ in (28,5 m). With a range of up to 2,300 mls (3 700 km), the X-11 would seat 135–152 passengers.

First flight of the Hawker Siddeley **HS.125 Srs 700** was made at Chester on 29 June, some two weeks ahead of schedule and following formal roll-out on 21 June. The aircraft, which is a conversion of a Srs 600 airframe with the Garrett AiResearch TFE 731-3-H engines, is now based at Hatfield for certification flying and will be joined there shortly by the first production Srs 700, which incorporates some new engineering features.

The **future of** the Scottish Aviation **Jet-streams** purchased by the Ministry of Defence for use as multi-engined crew trainers but not now needed in that rôle is still **uncertain**. Scottish Aviation, which has been pressing the MoD for a decision in order to have Jetstreams available for sale on the civil market at the earliest possible date, issued a statement recently in which it indicated that the MoD has not decided the future operational use of Jetstreams and that it is likely to be some months before these studies are complete. Meanwhile, the Ministry has agreed that up to eight Jetstreams could be made available should an order materialise from a specific overseas customer; but Scottish Aviation indicates that these negotiations "will be protracted". The Ministry has also suggested that eight Jetstreams could be positioned at Prestwick and a start made on refurbishing these to meet any new MoD requirements; discussions on this aspect are still continuing.

Hawker Siddeley has confirmed the receipt from Airbus Industrie of a contract for another batch of 16 sets of **wing boxes for the Airbus** A300, bringing the total to date to 84 (including two for structural test purposes). The 46th set was delivered on 23 May, by Super Guppy from Manchester Airport to Bremen, having been assembled at HSA's Chester factory; 12 more sets were scheduled for delivery this year.

First flight of the Practavia **Sprite** two-seat lightplane for home construction was made on 16 June at Sherbun-in-Elmet. This initial example was built by Peter Burril and at least one other is expected to fly this summer; many others are now under construction, according to Practavia Ltd, which sells the plans and kits. The Sprite is a semi-aerobatic low-wing monoplane designed to be powered by engines of 100–135 hp — the first example to fly has a 125 hp Lycoming. Its design was originated in 1968 by the staff of *Pilot* magazine, the detailed design

being the work of two lecturers at Lough-borough University, Lloyd Jenkinson and Peter Sharman.

USA

Possibility that **Grumman** American Aviation **might build** the Aérospatiale **Nord 262/Mohawk 298** under licence in the USA, as well as converting existing Nord 262s to the re-engined Mohawk 298 standard, is being discussed by the two companies. Such a step would replace the planned conversion of about a dozen Nord 262s to the new standard, with Pratt & Whitney PT6A-45 turboprops, by Mohawk Air Services, a subsidiary of Allegheny Airlines. Regulations that prohibit the manufacture of transport aircraft by a company also involved in airline operation cast some doubts over Allegheny's plans in this respect. FAA certification of the prototype Mohawk 298, converted for Mohawk by Frakes Aviation, was expected to be complete about the time this issue appeared in print, and Allegheny hopes to put the type into service in the final quarter of the year.

The first of two **Sikorsky S-72** RSRA rotor systems research aircraft was **rolled out** on 7 June at the company's Stratford, Conn, plant, and is expected to make its first flight, in helicopter configuration, in September. The second S-72 will follow into the air in December, and the first prototype will begin flight tests in compound helicopter configuration in March 1977. As helicopters, the S-72s are powered by two General Electric T58-GE-5 turboshaft engines and have an S-61 rotor system; in compound form, they have a 45·1-ft (13,76-m) span wing attached to the lower fuselage and a 9,275-lb st (4 210 kgp) GE TF34-GE-400A turbofan attached each side of its fuselage. As a helicopter, the S-72 has a "T-tail" with a top tailplane spanning 13·25 ft (4,04 m); as a convertiplane, it will have a 25-ft (7,63-m) span lower tailplane added and the top tailplane will be reduced to have a span of 8·58 ft (2,62 m). With a gross weight of 26,200 lb (11 900 kg), the S-72 has a number of unusual features including ejection seats for the crew of two and a rocket jettisoning system for the rotor system. After about 100 hrs of flight testing by Sikorsky, the S-72s will go to NASA's Ames Research Center where they are expected to serve for 10 years undertaking research into helicopter and compound flight characteristics with a variety of rotors.

First flight of a Boeing Advanced **727-200 with** JT8D-17R turbofans and Boeing's new reserve power system was made at Renton on 27 May. The aircraft is the first of three ordered by Hughes Airwest and was named *Spirit of Gamma* prior to its first take-off, in memory of Howard R Hughes who established three world speed records in a Northrop Gamma in 1936. Delivery is expected in mid-August following completion of FAA certification tests at Boeing Field, Seattle, with the second and third following in October and November.

The **third** Rockwell **B-1** joined the **flight test** programme on 14 June, making a 2hr 9min maiden flight from Palmdale and landing at Edwards AFB. This aircraft is prototype No 2, which has been used for eight months of structural proof load testing. At the time this aircraft flew, the two aircraft already in flight test had accumulated 185 hrs 54 min in the air, of which 6 hr 23 min was supersonic. Construction of a fourth prototype is under way and this aircraft is expected to fly early in 1979.

One of the two **Bell YAH-63** AAH prototypes was severely **damaged** on 4 June in an accident at the company's research and development facility at Arlington, Texas. Aircraft was hovering at about 20 ft (6,1 m) when control appears to have been lost and the YAH-63 dived into the ground; neither occupant was seriously injured. The accident occurred a few days before both prototypes were to have been handed over to the Army for a four-month fly-off against the **Hughes YAH-64.** The two YAH-64 prototypes were **delivered** by air from Carlsbad, Calif, to Edwards AFB on 14 June.

Interest in the Bede **BD-5J as** a low-cost **military pilot trainer** is growing, following FAA certification on 25 May of the Microturbo TRS-18 with which it is powered. In its TRS-18-046 version, the engine has a rating of 202 lb st (91,6 kgp), and delivers 119 lb (54 kg) thrust at Mach 0·5 at 19,670 ft (6 000 m) with 44,000 rpm. Ames Industrial Corp of Newton, Kansas, has acquired a licence to produce the TRS-18 in the USA and will supply engines for Bede to sell with kits of the BD-5J for amateur construction. Microturbo has ordered 20 BD-5J kits which will be assembled in France and used for engine flight development and as demonstrators. A BD-5J, on hire from Bede, was tested in France early this year, making 17 flights at the CEV, Bretigny, and Microturbo then ordered a BD-5J of its own and this example made its first flight (at Toulouse) on 22 May.

Fetsko Aviation Sales and Transportation Inc is offering a re-engined and **modified version of the** Enstrom **F-28A helicopter** as the Spitfire Mk I. Use of a 400 shp Allison 250-C 20 turboshaft derated to 240 shp, in place of the usual piston engine, gives extra space in the fuselage for baggage or fuel. Three examples have been ordered by Petroleum Helicopters Inc, with an option on three more. The empty weight of the Spitfire Mk I is 1,250 lb (567 kg) and max take-off, 2,300 lb (1 043 kg); max speed is increased to 129 mph (208 km/h), initial rate of climb to 925 ft/min (4,70 m/sec), the hovering ceiling (OGE) is 7,980 ft (2 434 m) and the endurance is 4 hr.

CIVIL AFFAIRS

BRAZIL

An agreement has been concluded between Brazil's civil aircraft certification authority, the CTA, and the American FAA providing for the latter to certificate **Brazilian aircraft for US operation** by verifying CTA data. Brazil is the 20th nation to conclude such an agreement with the USA, and the first in Latin America. The deal is expected to facilitate the sale of the EMB-110 Bandeirante to Federal Express, which is contemplating the purchase of a fleet of the type. Up to 35 EMB-110K.1 version of the Bandeirante may be acquired by Federal Express, this version being based on the FAB's EMB-110K freighter with more powerful engines, slightly lengthened fuselage and freight-loading door.

An indication of the **scale of aviation in Brazil** is given by recently-released figures collected by the *Departamento de Aviaçã Civil*, which show that the nation's four major airlines operate about 100 aircraft and employ 1,226 pilots, 498 other aircrew, 2,073 ground personnel on flight operations, 6,810 maintenance and overhaul personnel and 14,408 others. Third level and air taxi companies have 443 aircraft in service, comprising 146 single piston-engined, 216 twin piston-engined, seven twin turboprop and 11 twin-jets and 63 helicopters. There are about 4,000 general aviation aircraft in Brazil, of which 230 are ag-planes and 100 are gliders.

More details are now available of the arrangements being made to improve the **third level services** in Brazil by creating five separate regions each with its own commuter airline (*Airscene*/March 1976). The regions and their respective third-level operators are: São Paulo and Guias, VASP with Taxi Aereo Marilia (five Bandeirante); north-east area, Transbrasil with the State of Bahia (five aircraft); southern area, Varig with Top Taxi Aereo (eight Bandeirante and two light twins); northern area, TABA (five Bandeirante and four light twins); south-east area, VASP with Votec (eight Bandeirante).

INDIA

Between 1 and 5 July, a BAC **One-Eleven 475** was used for an 8,000-mile (12 870-km) demonstration **tour in India,** in the course of which it visited 15 airfields to show the high performance reliability of this 89-seat version. Starting in Delhi, the tour took the One-Eleven to some of the up-country airstrips and remote bases used by Indian Airlines and the Indian Air Force, both of which are studying possible replacements for their turboprop transports. The demonstration aircraft was one of three supplied to the Air Force of the Sultanate of Oman, on bailment to BAC for the purpose.

INTERNATIONAL

After two years of stagnation, **growth in general aviation aircraft sales** in the Common Market countries is expected to resume in 1977 and, according to a recently completed market research study by Frost & Sullivan, expenditure on such aircraft will total £1,006m ($2,060m) in the next ten years. Major growth is expected to be in business flying, and the sale of 2,435 twin-engined aircraft will account for nearly half of the projected market value of new sales. Single-engined aircraft are expected to total 13,742 and helicopters, 1,487, with an additional 191 aircraft of greater than 12,500 lb (51 100 kg) gross weight. Britain is expected to account for a major share of the new business, accounting for some 36·6 per cent of the total market value — mostly in twin-engined aircraft and helicopters.

According to a Lockheed-California market study, the **world's airlines** will **need** to spend £26,400m ($47,000m) on **new aircraft** in the next 10 years. The total is made up of £18,400m ($33,000m) needed to provide new capacity to match a projected 7·6 per cent annual growth rate and £7,800m ($14,000m) to replace older equipment. The report concludes that most of the aircraft bought in the period will be wide-body types already in production or derivatives thereof: some 1,000 long-range aircraft (over 4,000 naut mls/7 400 km), 800 medium-range (2,000–4,000 naut mls/ 3 700–7 400 km) and 400 short-range types.

JAPAN

Short-field trials were being conducted in Japan during June **with** both **a Boeing 737 and a** McDonnell Douglas **DC-9,** in the continuing search for a YS-11 replacement for the local airlines. The 737, leased by Boeing from Air New Zealand for the purpose, was demonstrated to South West Air Lines at short strips on islands in the Okinawa area, displaying take-off and landing performance in the 4,920-ft (1 500-m) class. In co-operation with McDonnell Douglas, Toa Domestic Airlines conducted a series of short-runway operations at four local airports to study the feasibility of operating the type at 4,920-ft (1 500-m) class runways. A TDA DC-9 Srs 41 was used, with automatic braking system and modified thrust reversers.

PAKISTAN

Pakistan International Airlines **and Bangladesh Biman** have concluded an agreement on commercial **collaboration.** The two airlines have agreed to provide reciprocal handling of flights and act as general sales agents for each other in their respective countries. Bangladesh Biman has inaugurated a once-

Boeing rolled out the first of its two YC-14 AMST transports at Seattle during June and the first flight was expected to be made in mid-August. The aircraft is the first to use the Boeing USB (upper surface blowing) principle to achieve good field performance.

weekly service to Karachi following conclusion of the agreement.

PARAGUAY

Three British companies — Brian Colquhoun & Ptnrs, Cable and Wireless and Coopers and Lybrand Associates — are sharing with a Paraguayan consulting engineering company in a feasibility study of **airport** and aeronautical communication **development** in the country. Eight airports are involved in the study, which will also consider the effects of replacing the DC-3 fleet operated by the domestic airline, Transporte Aereo Militar.

SAUDI ARABIA

Lockheed has won a contract, said to be valued at $625m (£340m) over 3½ years, to **develop** and install a complete **air traffic control system** in Saudi Arabia. The system is expected to be the most advanced in the Middle East.

UNITED KINGDOM

A new runway (07/25) with a length of 8,400 ft (2 560 m) has been in use at **Edinburgh** Airport since April and is already having an effect on the **pattern of traffic** at the airport, which is used primarily by domestic flights. The greater length of the new runway (previously, the longest was 13/31 at 6,000 ft/1 829 m) is attracting more international traffic and some 40,000 passengers are expected to fly on IT charters from the airport this year. Meanwhile, work is proceeding on schedule on a functional new terminal building which is being erected by the Fram Construction Division of Leonard Fairclough Ltd. With separate but inter-linked facilities for international and domestic passenger, the new terminal will initially be able to handle up to 1½-million passengers a year (about double the present total) with provision for later expansion. One portion of the domestic wing is reserved for use by British Airways Shuttle flights, now operating at a 2-hr frequency in each direction between London and Edinburgh using Trident Threes. The new terminal is expected to be open for use next Spring.

The first McDonnell Douglas **DC-9** to be **operated in Britain** will go into service on 1 September on the London-Teesside route of British Midland Airways. The aircraft is a Srs 10, originally operated by Avensa, to be leased from the manufacturers and will replace Vickers Viscounts used by BMA at present. The aircraft will operate in US registration, there being no present intention of certificating the DC-9 in the UK.

Command Airways took **delivery** of the **first** Short **SD3-30** commuter airliner on 28 June in a brief ceremony in Belfast, following FAA certification on 18 June. The company has three on order for use on its routes based on Poughkeepsie, NY; options are held on two more. Second (and only other announced) customer for the SD3-30 is Time Air of Lethbridge, Alberta, which was also expected to receive the first of three by the time this issue appeared. Shorts also announced that total **sales of the Skyvan** have reached 115, with orders for 11 placed in the last nine months. Included in the most recent orders is a batch of five Skyvans for the Mexican government, of which two are for use by the Third World University to fly personnel to locations throughout Latin and South America and the Caribbean to study and resolve local problems of agriculture, health, industry, etc, and three are for the Estado Mayor Presidencial. The Venezuelan Ministry of Communications bought two Skyvans to inaugurate an aerial postal service to isolated areas and a third for search-and-rescue operations, and the government of Mauritania acquired two for general supply duties.

USA

A **round-the-world flight in a Learjet 36,** to mark the US Bicentennial Year, was successfully completed by golfer Arnold Palmer accompanied by Gates pilots Jim Bir and Bill Purkey and observer Robert Serling. The time of 57 hr 25 min was nearly 29 hr less than the previous record for aircraft of the class.

CIVIL CONTRACTS AND SALES

Boeing 707: Compagnie Air Fret has acquired one -131C, ex-TWA. Tunis Air has leased two from British Midland until October. ☐ Saudia ordered another -320C, its fifth, for delivery in December.

Boeing 727: Pacific Southwest purchased two -100Cs from World Airways. ☐ Olympic Airways is using two leased 727s (not BAC One-Elevens as previously reported here) pending delivery of newly-ordered 737s. ☐ China Airlines is expected to add to its fleet an ex-Air Vietnam 727 confiscated by the Taiwan Government in Taipei. ☐ Tunis Air has ordered three Advanced 727s, with one for delivery in March and two in June 1977; the company already has seven -200s. ☐ Singapore International has ordered three Advanced 727s for Oct-Dec 1977 delivery, with options on six more.

Boeing 737: Frontier Airlines purchased two -200s from United, delivery in July and September. ☐ Gulf Air is reported to have decided in principle to order five -200s, for delivery July-November 1977; order has not yet been confirmed by Boeing. ☐ Britannia Airways is leasing one from NZ National Airways for summer peak. ☐ Saudia has ordered three more 737s for delivery in July and August, adding to seven in service. ☐ Yemen Airways ordered its first new -200, for delivery in November, leased 737s have been used by the airline for the past 2¼ years. ☐ Aloha Airlines bought one from Western Airlines.

EMBRAER EMB-110 Bandeirante: Additional sales of the EMB-110E executive model have been made to Brazilian companies Usina Dabarra and APRACS. ☐ Another sale is of one EMB-110S earth resources and geophysical survey version to the Rio de Janeiro-based ENCAL company.

Fairchild Swearingen Metro II: Scenic Airlines of Nevada has taken delivery of three Metro IIs, starting service on 1 June in the Grand Canyon area. ☐ Sun Aire Lines has acquired one Metro which it is operating on services from Palm Springs to San Diego and to Hollywood.

Fairey Britten-Norman Islander: Six were ordered by Aviatia Utilitara for use in the ambulance and medical supply rôle in Romania. They will be fully equipped with stretchers and other items associated with an airborne ambulance, with provision for para-dropping medical supplies, and will be used in outlying regions of the country where surface transport to villages is likely to cause delay in cases of emergency. ☐ Haiti Air Inter has taken delivery of three Islanders.

Hawker Siddeley HS.748: Varig is reported to have sold its fleet of six to PJ Bourak Indonesia Airlines. ☐ LAV Aeropostal is understood to have ordered two more 748 Srs 2As.

Lockheed L-100 Hercules: Alaska International Air is returning two of its seven Hercules to Lockheed-Georgia for conversion from Srs 20 to Srs 30 configuration. Three of the fleet will remain at the shorter Srs 20 standard.

McDonnell Douglas DC-8: Three Srs 61s purchased from Eastern Airlines were to be delivered to Capitol in June. ☐ Cargolux acquired another Srs 63F — its third — on long-term lease from Flying Tiger.

McDonnell Douglas DC-9: Garuda Indonesian Airways has six Series 30s on order for delivery this year, to increase the fleet to 18. ☐ Eastern Airlines ordered nine Series 50s, to replace nine Srs 10s at present leased from McDD. ☐ British Midland Airways is leasing one Srs 10 from McDD. ☐ SAS ordered two more Srs 41s.

McDonnell Douglas DC-10: British Caledonian has ordered two Srs 30s for 1977 delivery. The airline's first wide-body equipment, they will be powered by 51,000 lb st (23 154 kgp) General Electric GE6-50 turbofans and arranged to carry 30 first-class and 233 economy passengers. ☐ Air New Zealand has ordered one additional Srs 30, its eighth, for delivery in the last quarter of 1977. ☐ VIASA is reported to have ordered one Srs 30, its third. ☐ Air Afrique ordered its third Srs 30.

DHC-5D . . .

. . . A BEEFIER BUFFALO

AFTER a four-year gap, Buffalo STOL tactical transports are once again coming off the de Havilland Canada assembly line at Downsview, Ontario, and orders now in hand will result in a doubling of the number of Buffalo operators within the next few months. At the same time, work is now starting in Seattle on a major modification programme to turn a Buffalo into a "quiet short-haul research airplane" — this being the third significant research project for which a Buffalo airframe has been utilised in the USA — while de Havilland is actively studying further design projects that would allow it to capitalize on experience gained from the Buffalo itself and from the research programmes in which it has been involved. Thus, the Buffalo, after an admittedly slow start, is demonstrating some of the characteristics of its quadruped namesake for surviving in a harsh, if not actively hostile, environment, with a rugged ability to survive with the minimum of external encouragement and support.

The Buffalo is never more at home than when operating into and out of airstrips that are unusable by most any other type of transport. Getting an aeroplane into a 1,000-ft (305-m) grass strip somewhere out there in the jungle or dense forest or scrub may sound like no problem, but if there is 9,000 lb (4 086 kg) of cargo to be taken as well, then the Buffalo, claims de Havilland, is the only production aircraft in the world that can do it. It will haul a 7,000 lb (3 178 kg) load out of that same strip in zero wind/ISA conditions, and if the strip is just another 400 ft (122 m) longer, then the payloads jump to 12,000 lb (5 448 kg) in and 10,000 lb (4 540 kg) out.

Serious design activity on the aeroplane that was to emerge as the Buffalo began at Downsview in May 1962, when the US Army invited 25 companies to submit proposals for a new STOL transport, capable of carrying the same tactical load, in both weight and size, as the Boeing Vertol HC-1B (later CH-47A) Chinook helicopter then entering production. This implied the ability to lift a five-ton load with provision for rapid loading through a rear door and paradrop capability. Finalists in the Army competition were Fairchild, Grumman,

North American Rockwell and de Havilland, with the Canadian company being named winner of the contest before the end of 1962 and receiving a contract to build four prototypes of its DHC-5 design in March 1963. Development costs were to be shared between the US Army, the Canadian government and DHC.

The DHC-5 design, known at first as the Caribou II, was an obvious direct descendent of the smaller DHC-4 Caribou, having the same overall configuration with the exception that the tailplane was raised to the top of the fin to be clear of the airflow behind the high lift flaps. Overall dimensions were increased, but it was found possible to incorporate many Caribou components and therefore reduce the amount of new tooling needed for the Buffalo. The US Army was already a satisfied Caribou user, having started procurement in 1959 of what would prove to be an eventual total of 162, and in 1961 de Havilland Canada had modified a Caribou to serve as a test-bed for the 2,850 hp General Electric T64-GE-4 turboprop, under contract to the engine's maker.

Experience with the T64 in the Caribou test-bed, first flown on 22 September 1961, led de Havilland to adopt the GE engine for the DHC-5. Over 300 flight test hours were accumulated in the Caribou programme, testing the Hamilton

(Below) One of the four original DHC-5s built for the US Army. A subsequent change in Army fixed-wing aircraft procurement arrangements prevented further orders being placed, as explained in the text. All Buffaloes subsequent to these four had nose radar, as illustrated above.

The interior of a DHC-5A Buffalo, showing troop seating and, in the foreground, roller conveyors on the lowered rear loading ramp. The seats can be quickly folded to allow a full cargo load to be carried.

Standard 63-E-60-13 propeller as well as the engine itself. This propeller had been newly-designed for the T64, and it was found in practice that the standard 17-deg "approach fine" blade angle that had been used for CTOL aircraft was not adequate for STOL operations, and additional stops were therefore provided for an angle of +7 deg and a fully reversed angle of −27 deg. It was then found that, on power being increased with the propeller at the 7 deg angle, there was a tendency for the propeller to overspeed until the governor eventually signalled the blades to coarsen, with a resulting sudden surge of thrust. An electrical anticipator switch system was then added, with a hydraulic dump valve in the propeller which would coarsen the blades to power lever angle command before overspeeding occurred. All this work proved of particular value when the T64 was adopted in the Buffalo.

Caribou to Buffalo

The first of the four prototypes of the DHC-5 was rolled out at Downsview on 14 February 1964 with appropriate ceremony, and first flight followed on 9 April. By this time, the type was known as the Buffalo and had been assigned the US DoD designation CV-7A after briefly being the YAC-2 in the Army's own series of designations for fixed-wing cargo

aircraft. This designation was destined to change again, to C-8A, in January 1967 when the US Army was required to relinquish the operation of its fixed wing transports to the USAF. The inter-service wrangle, of which this transfer was the outcome, was to prevent the planned quantity procurement of the new de Havilland transport by the US Army, resulting in a major curtailment of prospective sales of the type, but these events were still in the future as flight testing began in earnest during the summer of 1964.

Although the wing span of the Buffalo was virtually the same as that of the Caribou, its larger fuselage and engines increased the gross weight — at the prototype stage — to 38,000 lb (17 252 kg) from the earlier aircraft's 28,500 lb (12 940 kg). Landing weight was 36,500 lb (16 570 kg) and the payload was 12,780 lb (5 802 kg). The engines of the initial quartet of Buffaloes were 2,850 eshp T64-GE-10s and the aircraft demonstrated a maximum cruising speed of 245 knots (453 km/h) and a long-range cruise of 181 knots (335 km/h) at 10,000 ft (3 050 m), with the ability to carry its max payload a distance of 550 mls (885 km).

Based, as it was, on the Caribou — and reaping the benefit of de Havilland's long experience in STOL aircraft through the earlier Beaver and Otter — the Buffalo had a similar high lift system comprising full-span double-slotted flaps, the outboard sections of which could function differentially as ailerons. Slop-lip spoilers in the wing upper surfaces forward of the inboard flap section operated (hydraulically) in conjunction with the manually-actuated ailerons to supplement the latter and could be uncoupled from the aileron circuit to operate in unison as ground spoilers, helping to shorten the landing run. No leading edge devices were used. Early figures quoted for the Buffalo showed a take-off distance of 1,265 ft (386 m) to reach 50 ft (15,2 m), and a landing distance from the

The current production model of the Buffalo is the DHC-5D, illustrated by the three-view drawing below. A DHC-5D is shown, above right, taking-off for its time-to-height record flight on 16 February 1976.

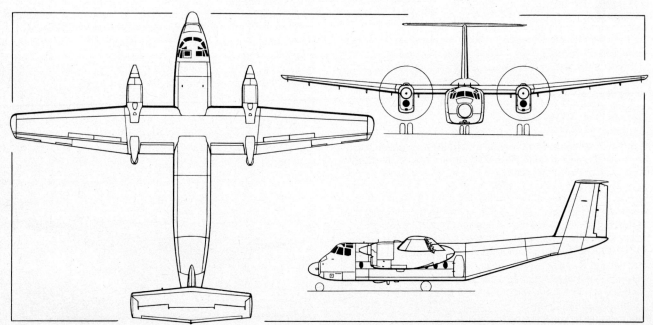

One of the first overseas customers for the Buffalo in its DHC-5A version was the Fuerza Aérea del Peru, *which acquired 16 in 1971/72. Two of the FAP aircraft are seen above on a pre-delivery check flight.*

same height of 1,170 ft (357 m); at comparable weights, the current production DHC-5D is even better.

Featuring a rear cargo loading ramp, the Buffalo offered 1,717 cu ft (48,59 m³) of cargo volume in the main cabin, with an additional 272 cu ft (7,69 m³) available for light density cargo in the aft cargo compartment up to the end of the ramp door. Loading of palletized cargo could be facilitated by an optional hydraulic winch and optional roller conveyors that stowed beneath the flush compartment floor when not in use. Anchor lines, jump lights and a pendulum ejector for extraction parachutes were developed for use with the Buffalo in due course, suiting it for aerial delivery work in either para-dropping or low-level extraction.

The four CV-7As were delivered to the US Army in 1965 but, as noted, a change in official policy made further sales to this customer impossible. The first production order, consequently, came from the Royal Canadian Air Force (now Canadian Defence Force) which acquired 15 of an improved DHC-5A model. This variant made use of the uprated T64/P2 engine, equivalent to the 3,060 shp civil-certificated CT64-820-1, and had gross and landing weights of 41,000 lb (18 614 kg) and 39,100 lb (17 750 kg) respectively. Maximum payload increased to 13,500 lb (6 129 kg) and weather radar was introduced, the small nose radome increasing overall length from 77 ft 4 in (23,59 m) to 79 ft 0 in (24,08 m) and providing the DHC-5A with a distinctive nose outline.

The CAF Buffaloes, designated CC-115, were originally based in Montreal and used for para-training, supply drops and tactical utility tasks. Later, they were divided across the country at bases such as Comox, Edmonton and Summerside, and then half of the fleet was assigned to search-and-rescue duties, undergoing a major refit during 1974 in which they received improved navigational facilities, proper crew rest facilities and suitable provision to carry SAR equipment and stretchers; at the same time, a red and white finish was applied to these aircraft, replacing an earlier tactical camouflage scheme. Nos 413 Squadron at Summerside and 442 at Comox now have three SAR Buffaloes each for overwater duties. Others are in service with the inland Transport and Rescue Squadrons — Nos 424 at Trenton and 440 at Edmonton — and these have retained a primary transport capability, although it has recently been decided by CAF that these, too, will be converted for SAR. Two of the CAF Buffaloes are

The Fôrça Aérea Brasileira *has purchased 24 DHC-5As and these Buffaloes now play an important rôle in providing transportation in the undeveloped Amazon region. Early aircraft were delivered in a camouflage finish (below), others being left in natural metal with white top (above).*

currently in the Middle East performing UN peace-keeping duties in the Golan Heights and Suez regions, and it was on such duties that another Buffalo was shot down by a Syrian SAM on 9 August 1974, killing the nine Canadian personnel on board. One other CC-115 has been assigned to the ACLS (air cushion landing system) experiment described later.

Other sales of the DHC-5A Buffalo variant were made to the air forces of Brazil and Peru. The *Fôrça Aérea Brasileira*

De Havilland DHC-5D Buffalo
Cutaway Drawing Key

1 Weather radar
2 Cabin air intake
3 Refrigeration air intake
4 Nose gear door, with taxi light
5 Rearward-retracting twin nosewheels
6 Nose gear drag strut
7 Rudder control quadrant
8 Refrigeration unit
9 Water separator
10 Cabin air duct
11 Access hatch (open)
12 Electrical equipment bay
13 Pilots' instrument panel
14 Rudder pedals
15 Pitot heads (each side)
16 VOR antenna
17 Brake air-charging access
18 Flight-deck access hatch
19 Oxygen-charging panel
20 Port avionics rack
21 Pilot's seat
22 Co-pilot's seat
23 Co-pilot's control column
24 HF antennae masts
25 Emergency escape hatch
26 Circuit breaker panels
27 Flight control cables and pulleys
28 Equipment rack/escape stair
29 Crew oxygen bottles
30 Toilet
31 Toilet compartment door
32 Washbowl
33 VHF antenna
34 Main distribution box
35 Transformer/rectifier units

36 AC distribution box (variable frequency)
37 DC distribution box
38 Side-facing troop seats (34)
39 Autopilot servo-actuator (ailerons)
40 Pressure regulator on bleed air duct
41 Fire extinguisher bottles
42 Propeller control panel
43 AC distribution box (400 Hz)
44 Jettisonable emergency doors
45 Engine bleed air-duct
46 Main spar/fuselage attachments
47 Aileron control quadrant
48 Starboard passenger door
49 Port passenger door (with footstep stowage)
50 Passenger oxygen bottles
51 Rear distribution box

52 Portable fire extinguisher
53 Loading ramp (lowered)
54 Ramp retraction shaft (port and starboard)
55 Cargo floor (in raised position)
56 Rear escape hatch in cargo floor
57 Cargo floor electric actuator
58 Autopilot servo-actuator (elevator)
59 HF coupler and receiver/transmitter
60 Autopilot actuators (rudder servo and elevator trim)
61 Cargo floor handling-rollers
62 Fin/fuselage attachment and carry-through structure
63 Fore rudder actuator
64 Trailing rudder actuator
65 Anti-collision and tail position lights
66 Fore rudder
67 Trailing rudder
68 Trailing rudder hinge

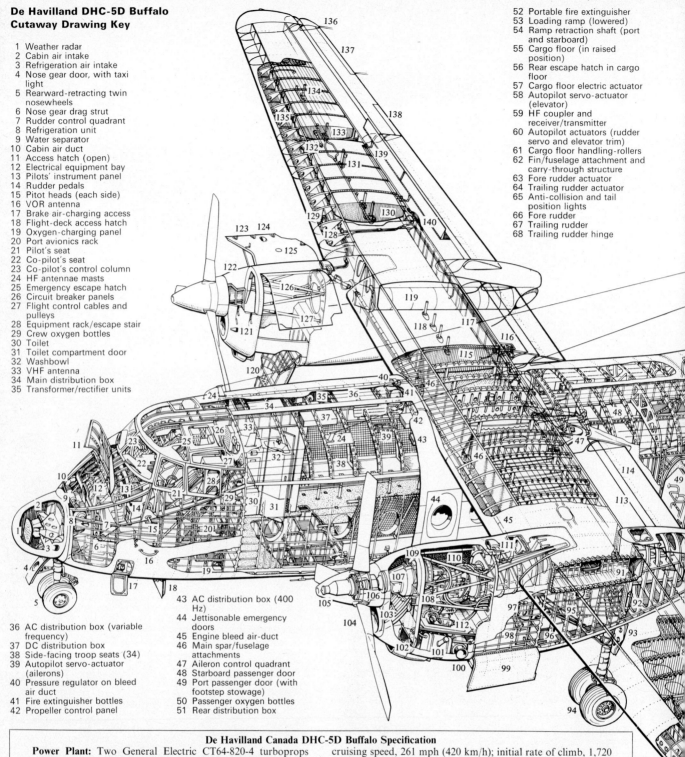

De Havilland Canada DHC-5D Buffalo Specification

Power Plant: Two General Electric CT64-820-4 turboprops rated at 3,133 shp for take-off, up to 93 deg F at sea level. Hamilton Standard 63EGO three-blade feathering and reversing propellers, diameter 14 ft 6 in (4,42 m). Fuel capacity, 1,279 US gal (4 841 l) in centre wing tanks, 828 US gal (3 133 l) in outer wing tanks; total capacity, 2,107 US gal (7 974 l).

Performance (Assault STOL mission, 41,000 lb/18 597 kg take-off weight, 39,100 lb/17 735 kg landing weight): Max cruising speed, 288 mph (463 km/h); initial rate of climb, 2,200 ft/min (11,1 m/sec); single-engine rate of climb, 650 ft/min (3,3 m/sec); service ceiling, 31,500 ft (9 600 m); single-engine ceiling, 17,800 ft (5 425 m); STOL take-off distance to 50 ft (15,2 m), 980 ft (299 m); range with max payload, 403 mls (648 km) at 10,000 ft (3 050 m); range with zero payload, 2,038 mls (3 280 km).

Performance (Transport STOL mission, 49,200 lb/22 316 kg take-off weight, 46,900 lb/21 273 kg landing weight): Max cruising speed, 261 mph (420 km/h); initial rate of climb, 1,720 ft/min (8,7 m/sec); single-engine climb, 325 ft/min (1,65 m/sec); service ceiling, 29,000 ft (8 840 m); single-engine ceiling, 13,200 ft (4 025 m); take-off distance to 50 ft (15,2 m), 2,800 ft (853 m); landing distance from 50 ft (15,2 m), 2,550 ft (777 m); range with max payload, 690 mls (1 112 km); range with zero payload, 2,038 mls (3 280 km).

Weights: Operating weight empty, 24,800 lb (11 249 kg); max fuel load, 13,696 lb (6 212 kg); max payload (assault), 12,200 lb (5 833 kg); max payload (transport), 18,000 lb (8 164 kg); max take-off (assault, 3g factor), 41,000 lb (18597 kg); max take-off (transport, 2·5g factor), 49,200 lb (22 316 kg); max landing (assault), 39,100 lb (17 750 kg); max landing (transport), 46,900 lb (21 273 kg).

Dimensions: Span 96 ft 0 in (29,26 m); length, 79 ft 0 in (24,08 m); height, 28 ft 8 in (8,73 m); wing area, 945 sq ft (87,8 m²); dihedral 5 deg constant on outer panels; wheelbase, 27 ft 9¾ in (8,48 m); undercarriage track, 30 ft 6 in (9,29 m).

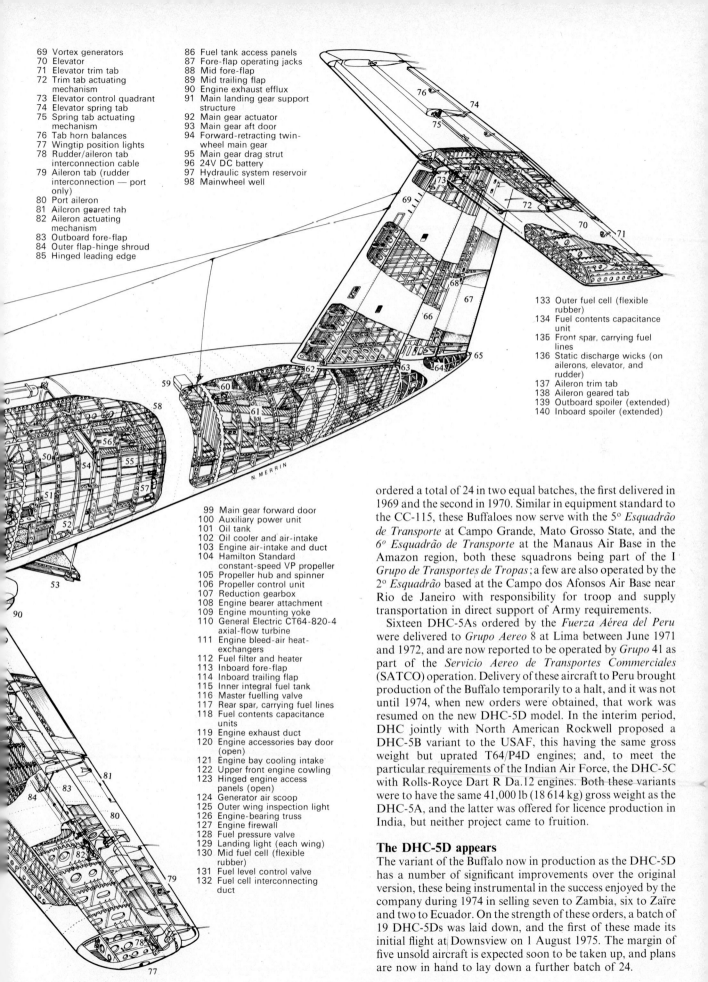

69 Vortex generators
70 Elevator
71 Elevator trim tab
72 Trim tab actuating mechanism
73 Elevator control quadrant
74 Elevator spring tab
75 Spring tab actuating mechanism
76 Tab horn balances
77 Wingtip position lights
78 Rudder/aileron tab interconnection cable
79 Aileron tab (rudder interconnection — port only)
80 Port aileron
81 Aileron geared tab
82 Aileron actuating mechanism
83 Outboard fore-flap
84 Outer flap-hinge shroud
85 Hinged leading edge

86 Fuel tank access panels
87 Fore-flap operating jacks
88 Mid fore-flap
89 Mid trailing flap
90 Engine exhaust efflux
91 Main landing gear support structure
92 Main gear actuator
93 Main gear aft door
94 Forward-retracting twin-wheel main gear
95 Main gear drag strut
96 24V DC battery
97 Hydraulic system reservoir
98 Mainwheel well

133 Outer fuel cell (flexible rubber)
134 Fuel contents capacitance unit
135 Front spar, carrying fuel lines
136 Static discharge wicks (on ailerons, elevator, and rudder)
137 Aileron trim tab
138 Aileron geared tab
139 Outboard spoiler (extended)
140 Inboard spoiler (extended)

N. MERRIN

99 Main gear forward door
100 Auxiliary power unit
101 Oil tank
102 Oil cooler and air-intake
103 Engine air-intake and duct
104 Hamilton Standard constant-speed VP propeller
105 Propeller hub and spinner
106 Propeller control unit
107 Reduction gearbox
108 Engine bearer attachment
109 Engine mounting yoke
110 General Electric CT64-820-4 axial-flow turbine
111 Engine bleed-air heat-exchangers
112 Fuel filter and heater
113 Inboard fore-flap
114 Inboard trailing flap
115 Inner integral fuel tank
116 Master fuelling valve
117 Rear spar, carrying fuel lines
118 Fuel contents capacitance units
119 Engine exhaust duct
120 Engine accessories bay door (open)
121 Engine bay cooling intake
122 Upper front engine cowling
123 Hinged engine access panels (open)
124 Generator air scoop
125 Outer wing inspection light
126 Engine-bearing truss
127 Engine firewall
128 Fuel pressure valve
129 Landing light (each wing)
130 Mid fuel cell (flexible rubber)
131 Fuel level control valve
132 Fuel cell interconnecting duct

ordered a total of 24 in two equal batches, the first delivered in 1969 and the second in 1970. Similar in equipment standard to the CC-115, these Buffaloes now serve with the 5° *Esquadrão de Transporte* at Campo Grande, Mato Grosso State, and the 6° *Esquadrão de Transporte* at the Manaus Air Base in the Amazon region, both these squadrons being part of the I *Grupo de Transportes de Tropas*; a few are also operated by the 2° *Esquadrão* based at the Campo dos Afonsos Air Base near Rio de Janeiro with responsibility for troop and supply transportation in direct support of Army requirements.

Sixteen DHC-5As ordered by the *Fuerza Aérea del Peru* were delivered to *Grupo Aereo* 8 at Lima between June 1971 and 1972, and are now reported to be operated by *Grupo* 41 as part of the *Servicio Aereo de Transportes Commerciales* (SATCO) operation. Delivery of these aircraft to Peru brought production of the Buffalo temporarily to a halt, and it was not until 1974, when new orders were obtained, that work was resumed on the new DHC-5D model. In the interim period, DHC jointly with North American Rockwell proposed a DHC-5B variant to the USAF, this having the same gross weight but uprated T64/P4D engines; and, to meet the particular requirements of the Indian Air Force, the DHC-5C with Rolls-Royce Dart R Da.12 engines. Both these variants were to have the same 41,000 lb (18 614 kg) gross weight as the DHC-5A, and the latter was offered for licence production in India, but neither project came to fruition.

The DHC-5D appears

The variant of the Buffalo now in production as the DHC-5D has a number of significant improvements over the original version, these being instrumental in the success enjoyed by the company during 1974 in selling seven to Zambia, six to Zaïre and two to Ecuador. On the strength of these orders, a batch of 19 DHC-5Ds was laid down, and the first of these made its initial flight at Downsview on 1 August 1975. The margin of five unsold aircraft is expected soon to be taken up, and plans are now in hand to lay down a further batch of 24.

The original Buffalo airframe had been designed — as required by the US Army — to have a structural load factor of +3g at the maximum weight (eventually established at 41,000 lb/18 614 kg). For pure transport-type operations, however, with an acceptable limitation on extreme manoeuvres, a factor of +2·5g was practicable, and this 20 per cent reduction permitted a directly proportional increase in gross weight, to 49,200 lb (22 337 kg). Some minor additional structural modifications were necessary, such as the thickening of the skin on the bottom of the wing, and using a solid instead of hollow front wheel axle, but these add only 300 lb (136 kg) to the aircraft's basic weight, whereas the maximum payload increases by 4,500 lb (2 043 kg).

The new Buffalo also boasts improved performance, primarily through the use of uprated engines. Feed-back from the installation of T64s in a helicopter has led to metalurgical improvements that now permit higher operating temperatures and the CT64-820-4, as the engine variant is now designated, offers 3,133 shp flat rated to 93 deg F, permitting an outstanding hot and high performance to be developed by the Buffalo. Under such conditions, the DHC-5D can carry 6,000 lb (2 724 kg) more payload than the DHC-5A. Engine design improvements have also bettered the T64's maintainability and an advanced new APU, the Solar T-26-T, also offers better

reliability and requires less maintenance. Heavier wheels and tyres are used and anti-skid brakes increase the braking capacity by 67 per cent.

Comparing the DHC-5D with the DHC-5A at the latter's max take-off weight, the new version has a 1·6 per cent better STOL take-off distance to 50 ft (15,2 m) in ISA at sea level, and 27·7 per cent better performance in ISA plus 30 deg at 5,000 ft (1 525 m). Using conventional take-off procedures, the relative improvements are 2·7 per cent and 24·2 per cent. The service ceiling in ISA plus 30 deg C is improved by 19 per cent on two engines and, in the single-engine case, by an enormous 96 per cent. Maximum cruise speed is 5·5 per cent better at 10,000 ft (3 050 m). Externally, the DHC-5D is virtually indistinguishable from the DHC-5A.

On 16 February, a new production DHC-5D set new time-to-height records, confirmed by the FAI, in the unlimited weight category for turboprop aircraft, the same records also qualifying in a new category for aircraft of 12,000-16,000 kg (26,430-35,242 lb) weight. A flight of only 17 minutes total duration took the Buffalo to 9 000 m (29,508 ft) in 8 min 3·5 sec, and new marks of 2 min 12·75 sec and 4 min 27·5 sec respectively were set at 3 000 m (9,836 ft) and 6 000 m (19,672 ft) during the climb.

Experimental Buffaloes

As previously noted, one of the CAF CC-115s was assigned for use in connection with the ACLS (air cushion landing system) developed by Bell Aerospace Company. This system is based on the ground effect principle used in hovercraft, and involves the use of a layer of air in place of a conventional wheeled undercarriage. Bell won a contract from USAF's Flight Dynamics Laboratory in November 1970 to make a full scale test of an ACLS, which was first flown on a modified Lake LA-4 amphibian, and the Canadian Department of Industry, Trade and Commerce subsequently joined with the USAF to sponsor the research, resulting in the loan of the CC-115.

The ACLS modification comprised installation of an elastic air cushion trunk under the fuselage which, when inflated, looks rather like an elongated doughnut. Compressed air is supplied to this trunk from a two-stage fan system in the fuselage, this in turn being powered by two ST6F-70 gas turbines (modified Pratt & Whitney PT6As) in pods on the sides of the fuselage. Once the cushion has inflated, air escapes from it through hundreds of small vent holes around the ground contact area, providing the lift to support the aircraft and air lubrication to keep it just clear of the surface. The trunk also has six braking pillows on the underside, which inflate when the pilot applies aircraft brakes and provide

(Above) One of the original DHC-5s of the US Army (note absence of nose radome) now in service for high-altitude photographic survey work with the Environmental Science Service Administration.

(Above) The Augmentor Wing jet STOL research aircraft based on a DHC-5 Buffalo airframe and jointly developed by de Havilland and Boeing.
(Below) The ACLS Buffalo, known as the XC-8A, is one of the original Canadian CC-115s modified to test the Bell air cushion landing system.

enough friction to stop the aircraft on hard runways in conventional distances. On low friction surfaces, propeller reversing is used for braking. Wing tip floats, plus sprung skids, are fitted to prevent the aircraft digging-in a wing when operating from water or soft land surfaces.

De Havilland made the initial modifications to the CC-115 — which has been redesignated XC-8A in its ACLS configuration — during 1972, and it was then transferred to Bell for installation of the trunk. Returned to Canada, the XC-8A made its first air cushion take-offs and landings in August 1973 and further trials have since been made by the USAF at Wright-Patterson AFB, Dayton, Ohio, including numerous taxi, obstacle and ditch crossing tests, as well as landings and take-offs.

The four original US Army Buffaloes, after being passed to the USAF, became surplus to military requirement and have found a variety of uses. One, for example, has passed into service with the US Environmental Science Service Administration (ESSA) and has been modified to carry equipment for high-altitude photographic survey work. Another has been seen operating with the National Center for Atmospheric Research (NCAR), carrying a long nose probe. The most dramatic modification of a C-8A is undoubtedly, the Augmentor Wing jet STOL research aircraft, however, this being, like the ACLS, the outcome of a programme jointly supported by the US government (through NASA) and the Canadian DITC.

De Havilland had begun theoretical studies of the augmentor wing principle in early 1960, the idea being to augment the normal lift of the wing by ducting air from a suitable turbofan engine or other source to a slot along its trailing edge. Flowing between upper and lower segments of the trailing edge flap, this air can be vectored, by operation of the flaps, to obtain powered lift, doubling the normal wing lifting capability and also contributing to thrust. Under the terms of the joint US/Canadian programme, de Havilland Canada received a contract to design the new propulsion system for the modified C-8A, in conjunction with Rolls-Royce of Canada, while Boeing received the contract to modify the airframe.

Major modifications to the Buffalo comprised a reduction of wing span to 78 ft 9 in (24,0 m) and replacement of all the original structure aft of the rear spar by the augmentor flap system; installation of full-span leading-edge slats; installation of two 9,000 lb st (4 082 kgp) Rolls-Royce Spey 801SF turbofans (in place of the T64s) to provide aircraft propulsion and a source of compressed air for the augmentor flaps. The undercarriage was modified and fixed down, extensive flight instrumentation equipment was added and many other smaller modifications made.

Rolled out at Seattle on 5 February 1972, the Augmentor Wing Buffalo made its first flight on 1 May, since which time it has been engaged in a test programme conducted by NASA at the Ames Research Center, California. It has a gross weight of 45,000 lb (20 412 kg) and at this weight with 60 deg flap and 18 deg deflection of the main hot-thrust from the engines, has a take-off distance to 35 ft (10,7 m) of 965 ft (295 m).

Use of cross-ducting of the blowing air in the wing from the two engines virtually eliminates out-of-balance trim moments in the event of engine failure, to such a degree that unless the pilot is watching the instruments, he is unlikely to notice that an engine has cut.

The powerful suction effect generated by the ejector on the upper surface of the wing affords excellent protection against premature or sudden stalling of the wing. Thus, in all configurations, the research aircraft has shown stalling angles up to 30 degrees with gentle buffet and nose-down pitching moments for recovery. Speeds as low as 40 kt (74 km/h) have been recorded during these trials and it has been demonstrated that the standard Buffalo horizontal tail is adequate to handle these very high lift conditions (in terms of pitching moment

(Above) Based on experience with the Buffalo and the augmentor wing research programme, DHC has projected this DHP-72 STOL tactical transport for future development. (Below) Boeing has received a NASA contract to produce this QSRA, based on a Buffalo airframe,

authority) because the Augmentor Wing exhibits quite low nose-down pitching moments.

The flight programme has demonstrated that the combination of vectored thrust and a powered-lift wing leads to greatly improved response and handling qualities in rough and gusty wind conditions. The aircraft has been operated successfully on several occasions in winds of 35/40 kt (65-74 km/h) gusting to 45/50 kt (83-93 km/h). During these landings, the pilot experienced wind shear resulting in 10-knot (18,5 km/h) decreases in airspeed over a period of 3 to 5 seconds, while not experiencing any appreciable change in flight path angle.

Adverse effects close to the ground (eg suck-down) have plagued many vectored thrust or powered lift concepts but tests on the Buffalo Augmentor Wing aircraft have shown very little effect due to ground proximity — in fact, the Spey-Buffalo has been flown only 2 or 3 ft (61-91 cm) above the runway at just above touch-down speeds, exhibiting if anything a slight tendency to float following the flare, an effect which can be quickly off-set by a reduction in engine power. Approach speeds are generally between 55-65 kts (102-130 km/h) depending on aircraft weight, as compared to approach speeds of 70-80 kts (130-148 km/h) for the standard DHC-5A Buffalo.

The Augmentor Wing test flight programme has also tested the new Sperry Stoland System, and numerous 'hands-off' take-offs and landings have been completed to date in both STOL and CTOL modes, including curved glide paths.

Another research programme involving the use of a C-8A Buffalo fuselage was launched earlier this year when Boeing won a NASA contract to create a quiet short-haul research

The Canadian Armed Forces purchased a total of 15 Buffaloes, with the designation CC-115, and a dozen remain in service. They originally operated as tactical transports, being used for paratroop training, supply drops and tactical utility tasks, and were camouflaged as shown (left). At least half the force is now assigned to search-and-rescue duties, bearing the white and red finish shown (right) and other CC-115s are in process of being converted.

Of the several research programmes in which Buffaloes have been involved, the flight testing of the augmentor wing principle has been one of the most significant. This aircraft (right) was modified by Boeing in close collaboration with de Havilland Canada and the test programme is being conducted by NASA at the Ames Research Center. Current production Buffaloes are being delivered to Zaïre, Zambia and Ecuador in the camouflage finish illustrated (below) on a DHC-5D used recently for an extended demonstration tour.

aeroplane (QSRA). The objectives of this programme include development of propulsive lift technology as well as establishment of short take-off and landing operating procedures. In this case, Boeing will fit a new wing using propulsive lift technology (as used by the Boeing YC-14), with four Lycoming YF102 turbofans which exhaust over the wing upper surface. Much of the jet efflux is diverted downward to improve approach and landing characteristics, and part of the air from the engines is directed through the wing and aileron surfaces to enhance aircraft performance and control at low speeds. This aircraft is also destined to undergo a flight test programme at the Ames Research Center, Moffett Field.

De Havilland Canada, meanwhile, has conducted a number of project studies making use of the augmentor wing principle and is currently promoting a STOL tactical transport designated DHP-72. This is seen by the company as the logical replacement for the Buffalo in the 'eighties, providing a maximum payload/range capability of 20,000 lb (9 080 kg) over 700 naut mls (1 295 km), with a cruising speed of about Mach = 0·80. Retaining many of the characteristics of the Buffalo, such as the T-tail and rear loading ramp, the DHP-72 has a fuselage of near-circular cross section and, like the Augmentor Wing Buffalo, two modified Speys to provide wing blowing and vectored thrust. The possibility of a joint development programme by Canada and Australia has been discussed.

Thus, while the Buffalo continues in production in its new DHC-5D version, which promises to sell in numbers matching total production of the DHC-5A model, the type has also provided the basis, through its use in diverse research programmes, for the future development of aircraft incorporating features that could keep DHC in the forefront of economic STOL state-of-the-art, where the company has been for more than 20 years. □

THE FINE ART OF DISPLAY FLYING

Wg Cdr Ian C H Dick, a member of the RAF's Red Arrows for six seasons and its leader for three, provides a "spectator's guide" to the finer points of display flying, which may often escape the layman spectator. This opening instalment is concerned primarily with solo performances; a second part to appear in the October issue will discuss formation aerobatic techniques in more detail.

ANY PILOT, given the task of providing a display for the public, should set out to "thrill the ignorant, impress the knowledgeable and frighten no one". This neatly phrased adage is easy to state as an objective, but to achieve the balance that it implies is far from easy, for what may thrill the layman does not necessarily impress the professional spectator and *vice-versa*. The immaculate inverted fly-past of a French aerobatic team, for instance, may go unnoticed by most spectators, whereas an "agricultural" bomb-burst manoeuvre by the Red Arrows will draw the breaths of any crowd; yet professionals will know that a far higher premium has been placed upon piloting skill in the execution of the former manoeuvre than in the latter and they will temper their applause accordingly. This conflict of appeal is an unfortunate aspect of display flying; it is frustrating for the pilot who wants to please everybody (including himself) and unsatisfactory for the spectator who may not appreciate all the flying that he sees.

Are you, the reader, one to be thrilled, or impressed — or both? Are the aerobatic labours of a Tiger Moth wasted on you when the sight of a Lightning rushing past at fantastic speed is not? Whatever your approach to flying displays as a spectator, I hope that in this two-part article, I may help towards a better understanding of the art of display flying. By broadening the knowledge of the uninitiated, perhaps the conflicting requirements of the spectacular and the impressive will be narrowed so that everybody experiences greater pleasure from an air display. Nevertheless, to give light and shade to a display, there will always be the need for contrast between impressive and thrilling manoeuvres. Perhaps the ideal flying display should be a combination and balance of the technically superb

and the aesthetically beautiful. Consequently, it should be the aim of every display pilot to provide a *continuous* spectacle of flying which has both artistic and technical merit.

I should explain at this point that my background and experience limit the scope of this article to a discussion of the kind of civilian and Service flying seen at the majority of air shows. I am not qualified to comment on the intricacies of competition aerobatics, which are a speciality in themselves and of considerable appeal to anybody who watches them. Likewise, I have ignored helicopter displays — the mere fact that they *fly* should be enough to impress anybody! For the purposes of this article, I have necessarily taken a simple and elementary look at the appreciation of display flying; I only hope that fellow exponents of the art will forgive me for any over-simplifications or sweeping generalizations.

What, then, are the components of a successful flying display? Clearly, the aircraft itself is a fundamental part of any display; other important facts are the presentation and content of the display and the execution of the manoeuvres comprising it. The first part of this article examines these and other aspects in the appreciation of the solo display. Part two will cover synchronised and formation aerobatic flying.

Solo display flying can apply to the whole spectrum of aircraft types from a V-Bomber to a Tipsy Nipper, and from Mach 2·0 fighters to homebuilt specials. Obviously, some aircraft lend themselves to being displayed better than others, but I would hesitate to define the ideal aircraft. Ray Hanna — former leader of the Red Arrows — when asked whether he preferred the Spitfire to the Gnat for display flying could only answer "Both". He was certainly right insofar as the Spitfire and the Gnat share two of the important qualities which, in my opinion, go to make up a good display aircraft — those of manoeuvrability and appearance.

Manoeuvrability

An aircraft that can roll quickly, turn sharply, loop tightly and pull or push lots of *g* is at an advantage over lesser aircraft. However, most are limited in the extent to which they can perform such manoeuvres. Apart from the specialist breeds of competition aerobatic aircraft, such as the Pitts biplane, aeroplanes are not designed solely for display flying. In many cases, nevertheless, the manoeuvring qualities of an aircraft (for example, modern fighters) often match those helpful to a display aircraft and it is worth considering some of the more important limiting factors in manoeuvrability so that the performance of particular aircraft types can be better appreciated.

Not unexpectedly, the better the power/weight ratio of an aircraft, the easier it is for the pilot to manoeuvre it tightly whilst maintaining speed and height. A good ratio also removes most of the common worry present in every display pilot's mind relating to the maintaining of enough speed for the next manoeuvre. The Pitts biplane, mount of Rothman's aerobatic team, is well endowed with power which enables the aircraft to enter the display area low and fast and work upwards. The pilot also has greater scope for the series of manoeuvres he can complete and this is likely to make his performance an exciting one. But spare some consideration for the Chipmunk pilot, who will not be able to emulate the Pitts completely; his display is likely to start at height and work downwards because he needs the added potential energy for his aircraft. Each manoeuvre will nibble away at his precious speed or height, and without the power to regain either he must exercise his skill to make the most of what he has in hand. Most current operational fighter aircraft have good power/weight ratios, but they frequently have other factors with which to contend when it comes to manoeuvring. In this context, the Hunter, Lightning and now the McDonnell Douglas F-15 Eagle are all examples of aircraft able to put on a good display. Military training aircraft tend to pack less of a punch and are consequently more limited in the sort of manoeuvres they can perform. The Jet Provost, a well-known sight at British displays, tends to suffer on occasions from a lack of thrust whereas the Gnat is almost ideally powered.

Another factor obviously affecting the manoeuvrability of an aircraft is its size and shape. Size is related to weight and so, not surprisingly, the bigger the aircraft, the less manoeuvrable it tends to be. The pilot of a Vulcan giving a display has no easy task to manoeuvre upwards of eighty tons of aeroplane in such a way as to provide a continuous spectacle for the crowd. The shape of an aircraft, on the other hand, probably lends more to its appearance than its manoeuvrability when it comes to display flying. Nevertheless, the aerodynamic differences between straight- and swept-wing mean differences in performance, the straight-wing aircraft being better suited to perform slow speed manoeuvres, such as stall turns, which are quite impossible in most swept-wing aircraft.

Speed has an almost mystical appeal to virtually everybody and is perhaps a prerequisite for truly spectacular and impressive display flying. However, not all aircraft are capable of breaking the sound barrier and high speed is, in any case, not always compatible with manoeuvrability and will not necessarily ensure continuity of manoeuvre. A Phantom, shrouded in ghostly condensation as it flies transonically past, has, for example, a turning radius of about five miles (8 km). Display areas are seldom that big and not all spectators are lucky enough to have binoculars, but an aircraft's high speed *does* contribute, to a certain extent, to the effectiveness of a display. At the other end of the scale, a pilot's slow speed handling of an aircraft can be equally impressive. The unique characteristics of the Harrier spring readily to mind in this case, but, more generally, slow speed handling characteristics of aircraft like the Stampe and Pitts enable them to perform impressive "flick" manoeuvres denied faster aircraft.

As a footnote to this discussion of aspects of aircraft manoeuvrability, reference needs to be made to the limitations on machine and man that are imposed either by the aircraft manufacturers or common sense. The airframe, its engines and the human body can stand only so much positive or negative *g*, which is probably the most relevant limitation on manoeuvrability. The new Acroduster (of similar design and performance to the Pitts) is stressed to $+6\,g$ and $-6\,g$ — ample for most outside manoeuvres — but heavier aircraft like the Vulcan or Nimrod are limited — not unreasonably — to much lower values. Age (of the airframe, if not the pilot!) also imposes its limitations. Do not blame the Hurricane or Spitfire pilots if they do not throw their aircraft around in the manner of 35 years ago, for the fatigue life of these aircraft has to be eked out carefully in order that they can continue to fly.

Appearance

The other important quality affecting display aircraft is appearance. The gracefulness of an aircraft can add tremendously to the aesthetic appeal of its display. Judging by the reactions I have heard at both the Farnborough and Paris air shows, Concorde epitomises this quality, and take-off, one or two flypasts and a landing are sufficient for this aircraft to thrill and impress most people. As with manoeuvrability, there are extremes of appearance which the ideal display aircraft balances and compromises. Very often, the factors which contribute to manoeuvrability detract from an aircraft's ideal appearance. In this category, shape is perhaps the most decisive factor. The angular, straight-winged outline of the Zlin or Jet Provost is not so appealing to the eye as the sleek lines of such classic swept-wing aircraft as the Hunter or Gnat. Obviously, little can be done to change the shape of an aircraft which is inherent in its design, but its lines can often be improved by an illusionary paint scheme, and this is probably the most common means of titillating an aircraft's appearance. By the clever use of a little paint, unimpressive aircraft shapes can be made to look more dramatic, the "rising sun" motif used for Stampe and Zlin aircraft being perhaps one of the best-known examples.

Probably the feature which can most enhance the appearance of an aircraft is smoke, which not only adds to the aesthetic qualities of an aircraft's performance but can also

Clever use of a little paint can make unimpressive aircraft shapes look more dramatic. This Jet Provost is in the colours of "The Poachers", the aerobatic team of the RAF College, Cranwell.

The Rothmans Aerobatic Team, mounted on Pitts biplanes, has brought display flying in the UK to a high level of achievement. In this view through a fish-eye lens, the team trails smoke as it flies formation, with the fourth aircraft inverted.

help highlight certain manoeuvres to advantage. Bill Bedford's spinning Hunter at past Farnborough shows would have provided virtually imperceptible spectacle without the benefit of smoke, used in this particular case to impress the knowledgeable with the Hunter's ability to recover from a well-established spin. However, adapting aircraft to generate smoke is a costly business which can also affect its use in other rôles, thus tending to limit such modification to specialist display aircraft.

Finally, mention must be made of noise; distasteful to many and environmentally to be discouraged but — like the whiff of kerosene — an inherent aspect of all air displays. Present fashion would seem to frown upon noise as a device to enhance the impact of a display, but I have met many people who admit to the instinctive thrill of hearing a Lightning's pair of Rolls-Royce Avons at full reheat. It is a personal preference, but I am sure that many aviation display fans cannot deny that the noise of an aircraft adds to the thrill of its flying. I even know of an aircraft company which started to investigate a noise generator for one of its aircraft types that was popular for display purposes. The company gave up when it realised that the organ pipe device it was proposing to fit would set up catastrophic sympathetic harmonics in the wings.

Thus, a number of inter-related factors all affect an aircraft's manoeuvrability and appearance, both vitally important qualities in a display aircraft. Perhaps regrettably, not everybody can fly a Pitts Special or an F-15 Eagle — probably the epitomes, in their respective classes, of extremely manoeuvrable aircraft. Nor can everybody fly such aesthetically pleasing aircraft as the Concorde or Hunter. Inevitably, a compromise must be accepted for many display aircraft and one must not forget the cost of buying or operating such aircraft — very often the ultimate limiting factor. Anyway, would not air displays be slightly boring if everybody flew the ideal aeroplane? Sure, much of the excitement and impressiveness of an air show comes from watching what a pilot can do with his particular aircraft. This is surely where a well-flown performance of a Vulcan can match or in some cases surpass that of a Hunter or Zlin. What, then, makes an aircraft's performance impressive to the spectator? Perhaps the most important point to consider is presentation.

Presentation

The presentation of a flying display is almost an art in itself. As I have already suggested, the clever presentation of a Vulcan can be as impressive in its own way as poorer presentation of a more aerobatic aircraft performing very clever manoeuvres. So what does one look for in presentation? Consideration for the audience should certainly be uppermost in the pilot's mind. Spectators should not have to strain their necks backwards to watch an aircraft over the top of a loop; everything should happen in front of the crowd and within the display area — roughly a semicircular arena based on an average crowd line of about 2,000 yds (1 830 m). The display as a whole, and individual manoeuvres, should be balanced so that they are

Display Lines

45°
plane

90°
plane

45°
plane

vertical
plane

rolling
plane

runway
display line

datum point

crowd line
(2000yd nominal length)

orientated to the centre of the crowd line or datum.

For sensible reasons, rules of presentation are imposed on all display pilots. Height limitations vary according to aircraft type, but the lowest altitude at which any aircraft is normally allowed to manoeuvre is 100 ft (30,5 m). Aircraft are neither permitted to fly supersonically at a display nor allowed to manoeuvre over the crowd, although dispensation can be given to this latter rule for specific items such as arrival or departure. The weather can also impose its limitations, and a mark of the truly professional demonstrator is his ability to present his display in widely varying conditions: display pilots in Britain become especially well practiced in this respect because they probably perform as many bad weather displays as full ones! Clearly, the height of the display area is also relevant; any manoeuvre above about 6,000 ft (1 830 m) is apt to entertain the birds rather than the crowd. The lower the top height of a display the better from the point of view of being unbaulked by the weather, and it is worth remembering that a Lightning pilot who presents a display under a low cloud base in poor visibility is working a great deal harder — and is probably worthy of more praise — than a pilot displaying a Jet Provost under the same conditions.

Possibly, the most important aspect of presentation is continuity. For any flying display to begin to be thrilling or impressive, *something* must be happening in front of the crowd *all* the time. This is where, all too often, display pilots fail in making an impression, their manoeuvres being poorly linked, with time and space wasted in repositioning or building up aircraft speed and poor use made of the display area. The display lines available to a pilot are shown in one of the accompanying diagrams.

Having performed a manoeuvre along the crowd line, pilots will often perform boring reversal manoeuvres to get back on

Despite its chunky appearance, the little Pitts biplane is highly attractive to watch, and the blue, white and gold Rothmans colours help to make it easily visible to spectators. (Above right) "Mirror flying", as demonstrated by two Zlin Z-526s, is an advanced manoeuvre for the display pilot.

Smoke can be used to add to the aesthetic qualities of an aircraft's performance and to delineate specific manoeuvres. In this picture it is being used by Bell Sioux helicopters of the Army's "Blue Eagles" aerobatic team.

to the same line, whereas the use of the 45-deg line (the most neglected one of all) can speed up the flow of manoeuvres considerably and keep the aircraft within the display area. It goes without saying that an aircraft must be visible to be impressive (although I know some experts who will disagree with me on this). A display which cannot be seen because the aircraft is hidden by clouds, trees or the head of the spectator in front is generally a waste of time, but presentation goes much further than having the display seen. Tastes vary — some people are impressed by slow, graceful manoeuvres; others by fast snappy evolutions. Contrast and balance of content are important requisites of presentation — the crowd should not have to gaze at the same piece of sky to watch loop after loop. Generally, a vertical manoeuvre should contrast with a horizontal movement; a slow roll should be balanced by a "flick" or hesitation roll. Perhaps the greatest sin that can be committed as far as presentation is concerned is to repeat a manoeuvre. To this end, most people run out of ideas, expertise and speed after about five or six minutes, which is perhaps the optimum time for any solo display.

Like most things, a flying display should have a beginning, a middle and an end. In general terms, the arrival of an aircraft should immediately attract the interest of the crowd. Punctuality is thus essential and many pilots favour a surprise arrival from behind the crowd; the now-you-see-me-now-you-don't impression that this gives is invariably a good way of drawing attention. Manoeuvres need to be presented so that their nuances and intricacies are visible to everybody. For example, there are few marks to be gained for doing a stall turn sideways to the crowd. This manoeuvre is best seen in plan form and should be presented thus. Similarly, rolls generally look better when performed along the crowd line rather than on the 90 deg or 45 deg lines. During the main part of a pilot's display, he must make varying allowances for the wind (if there is any) so that his display remains centred on datum. Slow, light aircraft are more affected by wind than faster or heavier aircraft. Thus, when there is a brisk breeze of 15 kts (28 km/h) or more, the Chipmunk pilot has a much harder job to maintain datum than a Jet Provost pilot.

In most cases, the presentation of a flying display should aim to keep the kids away from their ice creams and build towards a dramatic and adrenalin-inducing finale (hence the high speed run and vertical rolls favoured by many fast-jet display pilots to provide that final impact); suddenly, there is quiet and it is all over.

There are many finer points of detail which all contribute to the enhancement or otherwise of the presentation of a display. Whenever a pilot is flying his aircraft in front of a crowd, he is on display and should pay as much attention to detail — such

as take-off and landing — as to his main demonstration. What ignominy if, after an immaculate performance, a pilot has to overshoot his landing or bursts a tyre on touchdown and has to be pushed off the runway! A commentary can greatly help a pilot in the presentation of his display; it can explain the implications of each manoeuvre and help draw a crowd's attention to the right spot in the sky so that spectators do not miss what an aircraft may be about to do. But how many display pilots can be bothered with writing a really meaningful commentary or, better still, can afford their own commentator? This is the kind of detail which often marks the true professional.

The maxim: "A simple thing well done is worth a hundred difficult ones badly done", is particularly applicable to display flying. The third dimension adds an exciting perspective to an aircraft's ability, but a display should emphasise any unique or favourable characteristics of the aeroplane. Examples abound: the Harrier and its V/STOL capability, the Starfighter and its speed, the Eagle and its remarkable manoeuvrability, the "flicks" of a Pitts and the stalls of the Stampe. Even a Tipsy Nipper can look impressive when it almost hovers into wind. There are few aircraft so totally lacking in any characteristic that they do not lend themselves to display flying. The *pièce de résistance* for the recently-retired Varsity was to do a last-minute, near vertical approach to land from a height of about 500 ft (153 m).

To summarise, the content of a display sequence should always favour the performance characteristics of the aircraft and obviously be within its capabilities. The same is true of the pilot. The most important rule is that he flies within his capability and can *guarantee* the safe completion of any manoeuvre he undertakes. Little need be added on this subject since it is difficult for a crowd to judge, watching a flying display from the ground, whether or not the pilot is complying with this rule.

Horizontal manoeuvres

The simplest form of horizontal manoeuvre (it hardly qualifies for the name) is the fly-past. Large aircraft are flown past to show off their lines and this is best done in a slightly curving flight along the crowd line so that the spectators get the most

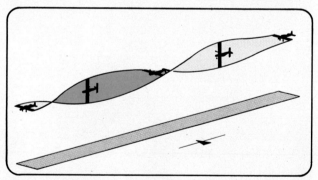

Slow Roll

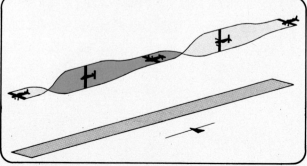

Hesitation Roll

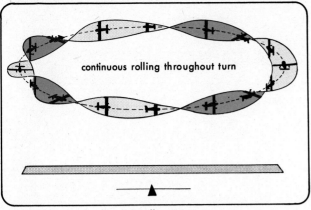

360° Rolling Turn

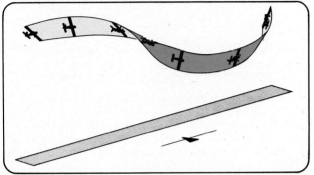

Derry Turn

pleasing view of the aircraft's shape. Concorde is invariably shown off to good effect in this way. Taken to its extreme, the ultimate form of fly-past in this case is the "knife-edge", where the aircraft flies on its side past the crowd in a most unreal manner. Not all aircraft can achieve this kind of flight, but it does show off the lines of the aircraft in an unusual way.

To contrast the speed range of modern aircraft, a fast flypast is frequently followed by a slow one by large aircraft which are otherwise limited in what they can do. This is a favourite item for the Buccaneer; a slow fly-past enables the aircraft to dangle all its accoutrements — "blown" flaps, wheels and hook — and to rotate its bomb doors (to reveal "FLY NAVY" in the case of the Royal Navy Buccaneers). The kind of elementary point to watch for if an aircraft does a fast and then slow fly-past is that, to add to the illusion of speed, the aircraft should make its fast pass down wind and *vice versa*. It is surprising how many pilots ignore this obvious, although perhaps minor, detail.

The straightforward fly-past naturally can be developed into an inverted one, which is not a common sight in solo displays because an aircraft manoeuvrable enough to do it is invariably put through sterner measures. The majority of horizontal manoeuvres involve turning or rolling of some kind or other. The reheated level turn of a Lightning shows off the planform and manoeuvrability of the aircraft to great effect. It also makes a lot of noise. In any level turns, marked changes in height should not be noticeable although the expert flyer will tilt the plane of his turn upwards very slightly so that he displaces less ground from the crowd (and so keeps his aircraft closer) and is as easily visible on the far side of the turn as when right in front. As with most manoeuvres, anything that can be flown the right way up can be flown inverted. If you discern that something has been flown inverted, immediately double your marks for technical effort; unfortunately, however, at a distance, most aircraft look the same whatever way up so marks for artistic appreciation are barely affected.

The family of rolling manoeuvres starts off with the elementary slow roll, progresses through multi-pointed hesitation rolls (four and eight points are most common) to "flick" and torque rolls which are exceedingly rapid, snappy

rolls — difficult to appreciate in detail but impressive for their disorientating spontaneity. The most obvious point about any roll in the horizontal plane is that it should be flown straight and level, which is easy or difficult to achieve depending on the inverted characteristics of a particular aeroplane. In a slow roll, invariably performed along the crowd line, the rate of roll should be constant and measured so that the roll starts at one end of the line, the inverted position is in front of datum and it finishes at the other end of the line. The same criteria apply to judging a hesitation roll, but, in this case, the rate of roll is rapid to the points of the roll, which should be distinctive and clearly held. As most rolls require the careful co-ordination of all the aircraft's controls, they are quite demanding on a pilot's ability. Any tell-tale "wobbling" at any point of a hesitation roll or "fishtailing" at the end of a slow roll are faults to be aware of. Watch also for the chap who cocks his nose up before starting his roll so as to make the inverted part and height keeping easier. In the purists' eyes, this may be a bit of a cheat, but bear in mind that some aircraft are not very prone or good at slow rolling — especially the Chipmunk as its engine cuts when inverted! One of the greatest exponents of the slow and hesitation roll I have ever watched is Renato Ferrazziutti, who spent most of his time with the *Frecce Tricolori* (the Italian Air Force's formation aerobatic team) flying the solo position and executing perfect rolls, inevitably accentuated by an immaculate straight line of white smoke.

Within the rolling class of manoeuvres, flick and torque rolls probably demand the ultimate of pilot co-ordination and skill. To most people, they are executed so quickly that it is difficult to analyse or even recognise what has happened, so perhaps the easiest way to judge a good flick is by watching how cleanly and neatly the aircraft stops and recovers. Does the pilot stop the aircraft in exactly the right attitude to lead into the next manoeuvre, or is there a touch of adjustment to pick up the correct line? Anybody who is lucky enough to watch Neil Williams (or for that matter any member of the British Aerobatic Team), will see flick and torque rolls being performed at their very best.

Finally, and getting back into the realms of more conventional aircraft, a well executed rolling, 360 deg turn (constant rate of roll, symmetrical turn, even height — difficult to do and thus a joy to watch) should receive the praise of the most blasé professional. Derry turns (rolling through the inverted position to change direction), though not so difficult, should also be judged by the same criteria and warrant equal praise when perfectly performed.

Vertical manoeuvres
By far the greatest range of manoeuvres make use of the vertical plane. I include here barrel rolls although they are rarely performed by solo aircraft, with the notable exceptions of the Spitfire and Hurricane. Also currently in vogue are undercarriage barrel rolls, which evolved from the impressive spectacle of an aircraft barrel rolling on its final approach to landing and subsequently completing the landing run. This particular roll is most impressive in such a case; anything less from a solo aircraft is likely to thrill more than impress and is often included in a sequence merely as something different to do. Generally speaking, barrel rolls should start and finish at the same height, the shape of the roll should be symmetrical (difficult to judge) and the rate of roll constant. However, because barrel rolls are more applicable to formation aerobatics, it is more appropriate to examine the appreciation of them in the second part of the article.

The looping manoeuvre provides the backbone of most aerobatic flying displays. There are many variations of the basic loop — shape and size can be altered to achieve many effects — and it can also be usefully used to position the aircraft within the display area, particularly from the extremes of the display lines. Most looping manoeuvres should be

Not the most handsome of aircraft at the best of times, the Phantom with "everything down" can nevertheless startle and impress crowds with its impression of sheer power—enhanced by the use of afterburners.

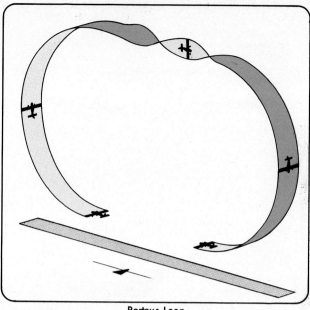

Porteus Loop

performed through the true vertical with wings level and steady. A bent loop is not readily discernible when flown along the crowd line but is clearly seen when flown on the 45-deg or, particularly, the 90-deg line. Naturally, any crosswind has to be taken into account to ensure that the loop remains straight and the ability of the pilot to achieve this is a measure of his expertise. The shape of a loop is unlikely to attract much attention unless registered with smoke, but the kind of shapes that normally result are shown in accompanying diagrams.

The Cuban-8 and Horizontal-8 shapes are achieved by rolling the aircraft crisply and neatly in the positions shown in the diagrams. I hope that by now it goes without saying that these manoeuvres should be balanced and symmetrical and with their centres in front of datum. The rolling part of the manoeuvre can be varied, and the later a pilot completes his rolls in a Cuban-8 the more impressive they tend to be. The tighter a loop the more impressive it is. A tight loop is quicker, takes up less room in the limited display area and is more readily visible to the crowd. This last requisite is most important if an additional manoeuvre is added at the top of the loop, such as a "Porteus" or 'roll-off-the-top"; the latter, as it happens, being a particularly unimpressive spectacle when demonstrated by an aircraft like the Gnat but has been

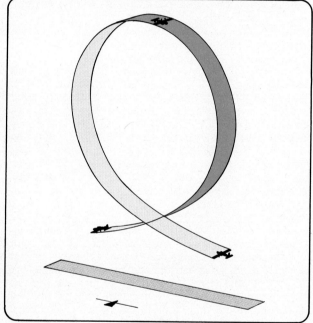

Basic Loop

Cuban 8

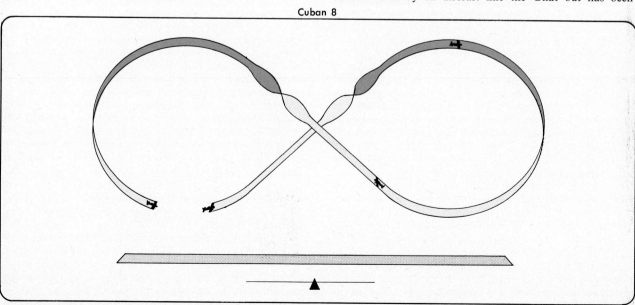

Those that made the grade...

and some that didn't.

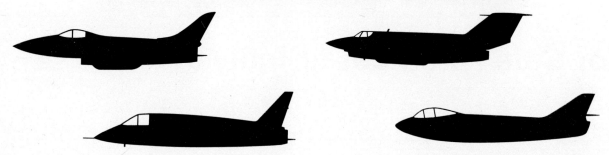

Can you identify them all? The aircraft currently used by the RAF and those which have been rejected for service.

They're all in the Royal Air Force Yearbook 1976. Plus many more fascinating features. Altogether, there are 72 pages packed with information, diagrams and full colour illustrations covering all aspects of the RAF and aviation, as it was, and today.

At only 50p you can't afford to miss the Royal Air Force Yearbook for 1976. So order your copy now from your newsagent or bookseller, or direct from RAF Yearbook, 283 Lonsdale Road, SW13 9QW, price 65p post paid.

Published by the RAF Benevolent Fund. Proceeds to the RAF Benevolent Fund and the Royal Air Forces Association.

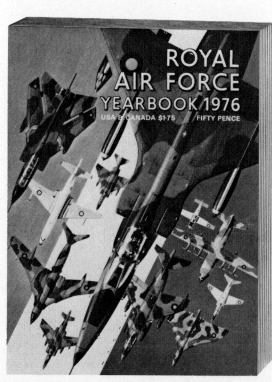

COPIES AVAILABLE AT AIR INTERNATIONAL STAND SF32
FARNBOROUGH AIR SHOW SEPTEMBER 5-12

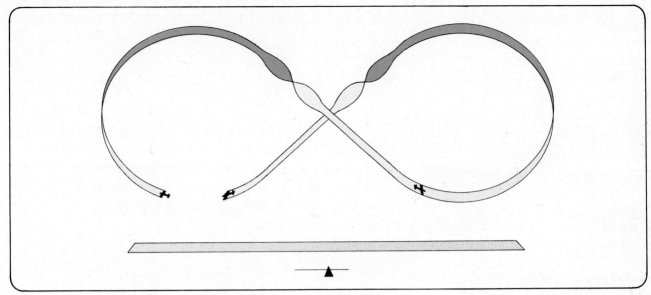

Horizontal 8

effectively used by light aircraft such as the Auster. Loops should also be flown slightly more off crowd than rolls so that necks are not strained when the aircraft passes the apex.

Most stalling manoeuvres need to make use of the vertical plane. In this category are included stall turns, hammer-head stalls, tail slides and spins. Most aerobatic display pilots normally include some kind of stalling manoeuvre in their sequence, mainly because it is difficult to control an aircraft precisely that is at very slow speed or stalled, and therefore the pilot increases his sense of achievement when he successfully completes such a manoeuvre. Additionally, it is impressive and thrilling to see an aircraft, usually needing forward speed in order to remain airborne, hang in the air at zero speed. The anticipation of what is going to happen next is the kind of suspense that reflects good showmanship in a flying display. It is difficult to generalise, however, on the finer points to look for in stall manoeuvres. Certainly, it is cheating to do them in anything more or less than the vertical. The sense of an aircraft poised in suspended animation is an important impression to gain from these manoeuvres. A stall turn which looks more like a messy wing-over fails to impress just as much as the unfortunate pilot who "falls-out" of a tail slide. Recovery to a precise attitude and line is an important point to watch for with all stall manoeuvres. When watching the more advanced stall manoeuvres or spins, perhaps safe recovery is the best criterion by which to judge them. One is almost getting into the realms of surrealist art in which you know what you like but are not quite sure why.

Not many aircraft are capable of performing vertical rolls within the airspace of a confined display area. For the lucky ones that can, eg, Pitts and Stampe, remember that the pilot has not got the same references as he has for horizontal rolls. Consequently, these manoeuvres are that much harder to perform and so more impressive in their execution. Whatever form of roll is used in the vertical plane, whether it be slow, hesitation, flick or torque, its appreciation is covered by the points already discussed for horizontal rolls. Additionally, however, one is looking for a perfectly straight, vertical axis during the roll or rolls and a neat and tidy recovery at the top of the manoeuvre in readiness for whatever is going to be performed on the way down.

As already mentioned, this is the kind of manoeuvre that can be used by the fast-jet pilot for an impressive departure. By disappearing vertically in a series of rolls, he is sure of a neat, definite and spectacular finale to his display — and his ensuing slow speed recovery will be well out of sight! □

Stall Turn

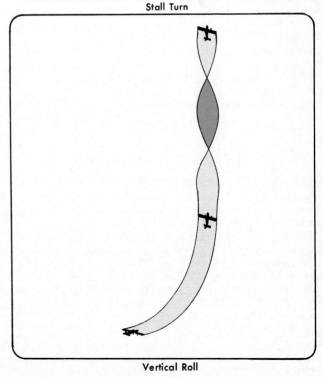

Vertical Roll

THE QUEST FOR ALTITUDE

THE APPEARANCE over England during September 1942 of the very high-flying Junkers Ju 86R, although not entirely unexpected, caused considerable consternation in Fighter Command, for these pressurized reconnaissance-bombers were to all intents and purposes beyond interception. Flying at altitudes varying from about 35,000 ft (10 675 m) to above 41,000 ft (12 505 m), they operated singly and in a somewhat desultory manner, ranging across Southern England to take photographs and dropping bombs here and there as they went. Attempts at interception were made by Spitfire Vbs and IXs, but even if their pilots could endure the effects of extreme altitudes on oxygen alone, these aircraft proved too sensitive to serve as effective gun platforms — although a specially-stripped Spitfire V flown by Flg Off G W H Reynolds did succeed in shooting down an example of the earlier Ju 86P over the Mediterranean on 24 August 1942 after a long and lonely chase to 42,000 ft (12 810 m) and a second successful interception was made subsequently by the same pilot, who was awarded the DFC for his endeavours. Pressurized Spitfire VIs, just then entering service in the UK, had no greater success against the Junkers intruders and the Spitfire VII, with its greatly improved two-stage two-speed engine, was not yet ready.

The Ju 86R operations proved of little value to the *Luftwaffe* and were soon discontinued, but this was not to be known in Britain when the type first traced a contrail across the skies above the Home Counties on 5 September 1942, and just two days later, on 7 September, the Directorate of Technical Development, Ministry of Aircraft Production, requested de Havilland to produce, with utmost urgency, a high altitude version of the Mosquito fighter. A month earlier, the company had completed and flown a new bomber prototype with a pressure cabin and two-stage Merlin 61 engines, serial number MP469*, and in response to the DTD request, this aircraft was converted to a high altitude fighter in only seven days. A standard Mk II fighter nose was fitted, with four 0·303-in (7,7-

---

The serial number was apparently allocated erroneously, duplicating the number of a production Airspeed Oxford II. As a bomber, this prototype had no distinguishing mark number.

General Aircraft GAL 46 Cutaway Drawing Key

1 Armoured nose cap
2 Nosewheel well
3 Nosewheel leg pivot
4 Nosewheel door
5 Nosewheel oleo
6 Twin nosewheels
7 Retraction mechanism
8 Armoured forward bulkhead
9 Cannon ports
10 Ventral bomb-sighting panel
11 Rudder pedal assembly
12 Pilot's seat
13 Control column

PILOT PRESS
COPYRIGHT
DRAWING

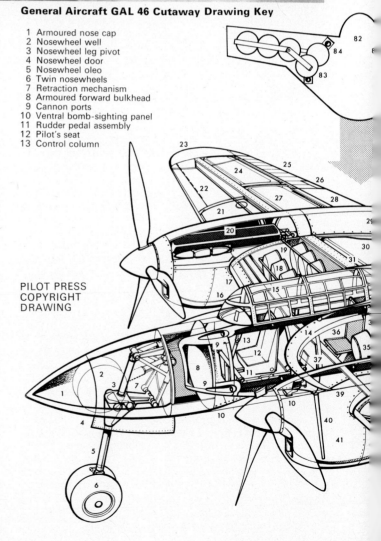

mm) machine guns, together with four-bladed propellers, small diameter wheels and extended wing tips; outer wing tanks, armour protection and some items of equipment were removed and when weighed before first flight on 14 September it was found to be 2,300 lb (1 044 kg) lighter than the standard Mk II fighter at 16,200 lb (7 355 kg). On the third flight next day an altitude of 43,500 ft (13 268 m) was reached.

Attached to a special High Altitude Flight at Northolt, MP469 waited in vain for an opportunity to intercept a Ju 86P for several weeks, and was then further modified as the prototype NF Mk XV night fighter, with AI Mk VIII radar in the nose and the machine guns carried in a tray under the fuselage; four other NF Mk XVs were produced and served in 1943 with No 85 Squadron, flights to about 44,000 ft (13 420 m) becoming commonplace.

Had high altitude attacks on the UK continued during 1942, there is little doubt that the Mosquito could have become an effective antidote, but its development, as described, was a piece of improvisation *par excellence,* and it is pertinent to ask why Fighter Command was not better prepared in 1942 to meet this particular threat. The fact is that the need for a high altitude fighter *had* been recognised, that work was under way on such a type (as well as on the pressure cabin equipped Spitfire variants already mentioned) and that the whole field of pressure cabin development was receiving special attention in Britain. However, the progress of the war in 1940-42 had required priority to be given to other aspects of fighter (and bomber) development and work on the new high altitude interceptor had progressed only relatively slowly. In these circumstances, the *Luftwaffe* had, quite simply, "stolen a

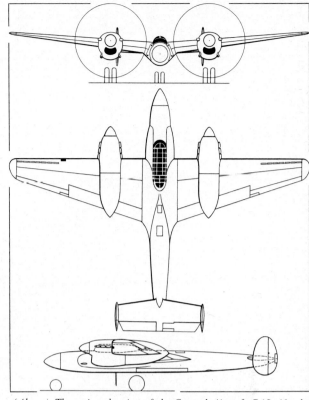

(Above) Three-view drawing of the General Aircraft GAL 46, also depicted below left. (Heading photo, opposite) A production Westland Welkin F Mk I in the final overall blue finish.

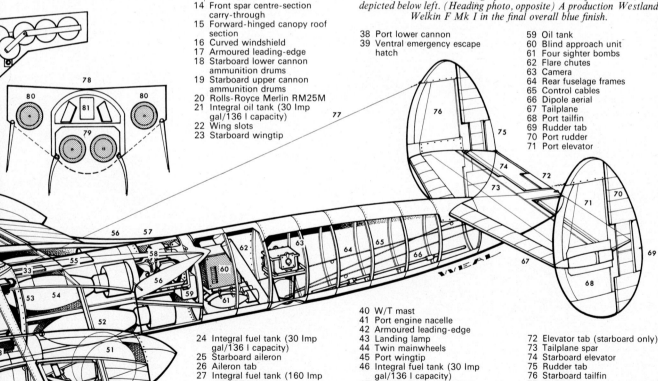

14 Front spar centre-section carry-through
15 Forward-hinged canopy roof section
16 Curved windshield
17 Armoured leading-edge
18 Starboard lower cannon ammunition drums
19 Starboard upper cannon ammunition drums
20 Rolls-Royce Merlin RM25M
21 Integral oil tank (30 Imp gal/136 l capacity)
22 Wing slots
23 Starboard wingtip

38 Port lower cannon
39 Ventral emergency escape hatch
40 W/T mast
41 Port engine nacelle
42 Armoured leading-edge
43 Landing lamp
44 Twin mainwheels
45 Port wingtip
46 Integral fuel tank (30 Imp gal/136 l capacity)
47 Integral fuel tank (160 Imp gal/727 l capacity)
48 Port aileron
49 Aileron tab
50 Flap
51 Port main undercarriage well
52 Fuselage bomb-bay (two 500-lb/227-kg bombs)
53 Rear bulkhead
54 Port wingroot bomb-bay (one 500-lb/227-kg bomb)
55 Bomb loading hatch
56 Wingroot fairings
57 Access panel
58 Cabin supercharging unit

59 Oil tank
60 Blind approach unit
61 Four sighter bombs
62 Flare chutes
63 Camera
64 Rear fuselage frames
65 Control cables
66 Dipole aerial
67 Tailplane
68 Port tailfin
69 Rudder tab
70 Port rudder
71 Port elevator
72 Elevator tab (starboard only)
73 Tailplane spar
74 Starboard elevator
75 Rudder tab
76 Starboard tailfin
77 Aerial
78 Bomb-bay cross-section showing
79 Fuselage bomb stowage
80 Wingroot bomb stowage
81 Radio installation (with empty ammunition drums to sides)
82 Drum-feed cross-section showing
83 Lower cannon with balanced swinging arm for loading
84 Upper cannon with drum rails

24 Integral fuel tank (30 Imp gal/136 l capacity)
25 Starboard aileron
26 Aileron tab
27 Integral fuel tank (160 Imp gal/727 l capacity)
28 Flap
29 Starboard main undercarriage well
30 Removable fuel tank (110 Imp gal/500 l capacity)
31 Main spar
32 Canopy fixed aft section
33 Radio installation (and empty magazine stowage)
34 Port upper cannon
35 Ammunition drums
36 Loader/bombardier's (folding) seat
37 Bomb-sight

march" on the RAF by getting a pressure-cabin bomber into service — albeit on a somewhat tentative basis — well over a year before an effective counter-weapon was expected to be ready.

That counter-weapon, the RAF's newest fighter in 1942, was to be the Westland Welkin, the prototype of which made

GAL 46 to the Director of Technical Development at the Air Ministry, where the brochure arrived "out of the blue", the Air Ministry apparently having given little or no consideration to the use of pressure cabins up to that time. The Stratospheric Fighter was an ingenious design with a long slim fuselage, thick-section wing, large engine nacelles containing the two Rolls-Royce Merlin RM12SM engines, a twin tail unit and a tricycle undercarriage (GAL also having been the pioneers of British tricycle aircraft with a modified Monospar and the GAL 42 Cygnet lightplane). A crew of two was carried under a long glasshouse canopy which could only have produced major problems so far as pressurization was concerned, a differential of 5·0 psi (0,35 kg/cm^2) being planned to give an equivalent altitude of 15,000 ft (4 575 m) at 35,000 ft (10 675 m). As in the GAL 41, a separate engine in the fuselage drove a compressor to pressurize the cabin, and the Merlins were also intended to take some air from the cabin, thus being partially supercharged.

Of composite metal and wood construction, the GAL 46

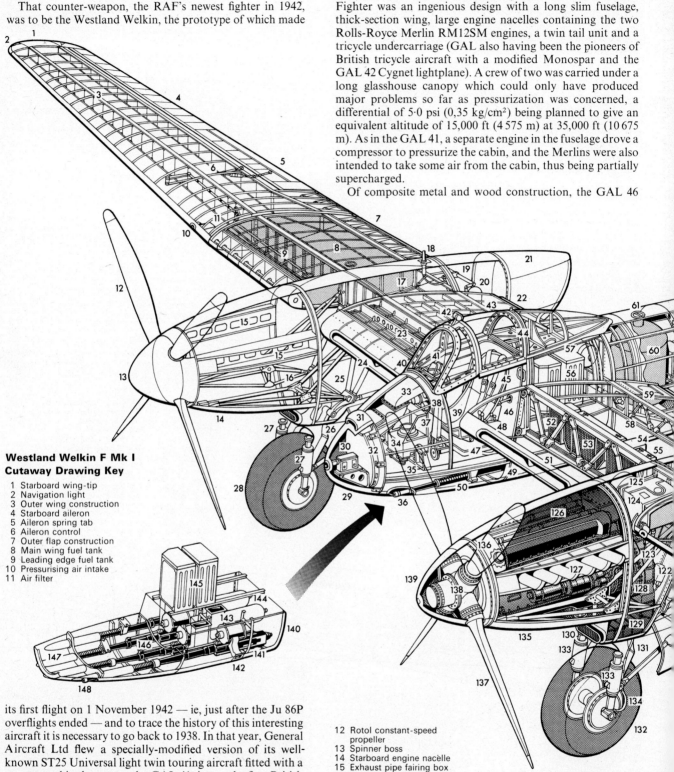

**Westland Welkin F Mk I
Cutaway Drawing Key**

1 Starboard wing-tip
2 Navigation light
3 Outer wing construction
4 Starboard aileron
5 Aileron spring tab
6 Aileron control
7 Outer flap construction
8 Main wing fuel tank
9 Leading edge fuel tank
10 Pressurising air intake
11 Air filter

its first flight on 1 November 1942 — ie, just after the Ju 86P overflights ended — and to trace the history of this interesting aircraft it is necessary to go back to 1938. In that year, General Aircraft Ltd flew a specially-modified version of its well-known ST25 Universal light twin touring aircraft fitted with a pressure cabin; known as the GAL 41, it was the first British pressurized aeroplane to fly. From the experience gained with this aircraft, General Aircraft designed a pressurized fuselage for a projected airliner for British Airways/BOAC (see Vol 3 No 3/September 1972) and the company also began project studies for a so-called Stratospheric Fighter and General Purpose Aircraft, the GAL 46.

On 18 October 1939, the company submitted details of the

12 Rotol constant-speed propeller
13 Spinner boss
14 Starboard engine nacèlle
15 Exhaust pipe fairing box
16 Engine mounting framework
17 Main undercarriage well
18 Undercarriage position indicator
19 Flap controls
20 Fire extinguisher
21 Nacelle tail fairing
22 Inboard flap section
23 Control cable runs
24 Radiator air intake
25 Nacelle framework

PILOT PRESS
COPYRIGHT
DRAWING

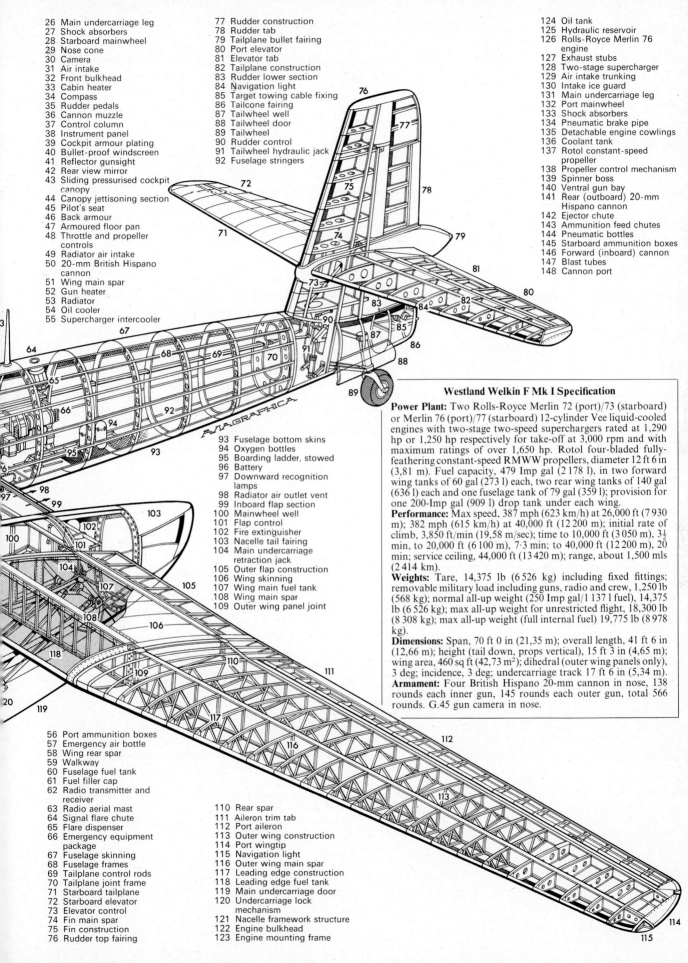

26 Main undercarriage leg
27 Shock absorbers
28 Starboard mainwheel
29 Nose cone
30 Camera
31 Air intake
32 Front bulkhead
33 Cabin heater
34 Compass
35 Rudder pedals
36 Cannon muzzle
37 Control column
38 Instrument panel
39 Cockpit armour plating
40 Bullet-proof windscreen
41 Reflector gunsight
42 Rear view mirror
43 Sliding pressurised cockpit canopy
44 Canopy jettisoning section
45 Pilot's seat
46 Back armour
47 Armoured floor pan
48 Throttle and propeller controls
49 Radiator air intake
50 20-mm British Hispano cannon
51 Wing main spar
52 Gun heater
53 Radiator
54 Oil cooler
55 Supercharger intercooler

77 Rudder construction
78 Rudder tab
79 Tailplane bullet fairing
80 Port elevator
81 Elevator tab
82 Tailplane construction
83 Rudder lower section
84 Navigation light
85 Target towing cable fixing
86 Tailcone fairing
87 Tailwheel well
88 Tailwheel door
89 Tailwheel
90 Rudder control
91 Tailwheel hydraulic jack
92 Fuselage stringers

93 Fuselage bottom skins
94 Oxygen bottles
95 Boarding ladder, stowed
96 Battery
97 Downward recognition lamps
98 Radiator air outlet vent
99 Inboard flap section
100 Mainwheel well
101 Flap control
102 Fire extinguisher
103 Nacelle tail fairing
104 Main undercarriage retraction jack
105 Outer flap construction
106 Wing skinning
107 Wing main fuel tank
108 Wing main spar
109 Outer wing panel joint

56 Port ammunition boxes
57 Emergency air bottle
58 Wing rear spar
59 Walkway
60 Fuselage fuel tank
61 Fuel filler cap
62 Radio transmitter and receiver
63 Radio aerial mast
64 Signal flare chute
65 Flare dispenser
66 Emergency equipment package
67 Fuselage skinning
68 Fuselage frames
69 Tailplane control rods
70 Tailplane joint frame
71 Starboard tailplane
72 Starboard elevator
73 Elevator control
74 Fin main spar
75 Fin construction
76 Rudder top fairing

110 Rear spar
111 Aileron trim tab
112 Port aileron
113 Outer wing construction
114 Port wingtip
115 Navigation light
116 Outer wing main spar
117 Leading edge construction
118 Leading edge fuel tank
119 Main undercarriage door
120 Undercarriage lock mechanism
121 Nacelle framework structure
122 Engine bulkhead
123 Engine mounting frame

124 Oil tank
125 Hydraulic reservoir
126 Rolls-Royce Merlin 76 engine
127 Exhaust stubs
128 Two-stage supercharger
129 Air intake trunking
130 Intake ice guard
131 Main undercarriage leg
132 Port mainwheel
133 Shock absorbers
134 Pneumatic brake pipe
135 Detachable engine cowlings
136 Coolant tank
137 Rotol constant-speed propeller
138 Propeller control mechanism
139 Spinner boss
140 Ventral gun bay
141 Rear (outboard) 20-mm Hispano cannon
142 Ejector chute
143 Ammunition feed chutes
144 Pneumatic bottles
145 Starboard ammunition boxes
146 Forward (inboard) cannon
147 Blast tubes
148 Cannon port

Westland Welkin F Mk I Specification

Power Plant: Two Rolls-Royce Merlin 72 (port)/73 (starboard) or Merlin 76 (port)/77 (starboard) 12-cylinder Vee liquid-cooled engines with two-stage two-speed superchargers rated at 1,290 hp or 1,250 hp respectively for take-off at 3,000 rpm and with maximum ratings of over 1,650 hp. Rotol four-bladed fully-feathering constant-speed RMWW propellers, diameter 12 ft 6 in (3,81 m). Fuel capacity, 479 Imp gal (2 178 l), in two forward wing tanks of 60 gal (273 l) each, two rear wing tanks of 140 gal (636 l) each and one fuselage tank of 79 gal (359 l); provision for one 200-Imp gal (909 l) drop tank under each wing.
Performance: Max speed, 387 mph (623 km/h) at 26,000 ft (7 930 m); 382 mph (615 km/h) at 40,000 ft (12 200 m); initial rate of climb, 3,850 ft/min (19,58 m/sec); time to 10,000 ft (3 050 m), 3¼ min; to 20,000 ft (6 100 m), 7·3 min; to 40,000 ft (12 200 m), 20 min; service ceiling, 44,000 ft (13 420 m); range, about 1,500 mls (2 414 km).
Weights: Tare, 14,375 lb (6 526 kg) including fixed fittings; removable military load including guns, radio and crew, 1,250 lb (568 kg); normal all-up weight (250 Imp gal/1 137 l fuel), 14,375 lb (6 526 kg); max all-up weight for unrestricted flight, 18,300 lb (8 308 kg); max all-up weight (full internal fuel) 19,775 lb (8 978 kg).
Dimensions: Span, 70 ft 0 in (21,35 m); overall length, 41 ft 6 in (12,66 m); height (tail down, props vertical), 15 ft 3 in (4,65 m); wing area, 460 sq ft (42,73 m²); dihedral (outer wing panels only), 3 deg; incidence, 3 deg; undercarriage track 17 ft 6 in (5,34 m).
Armament: Four British Hispano 20-mm cannon in nose, 138 rounds each inner gun, 145 rounds each outer gun, total 566 rounds. G.45 gun camera in nose.

AVIAGRAPHICA

	Westland P.17	Westland (Alternative)	General Aircraft	Hawker P.1004
DESIGN	Development of Whirlwind; 2e low-wing monoplane. Pressure cab built as separate unit.	2e in fuselage driving into common gearbox. Contra-rotating tractor propellers.	2e mid-wing monoplane. Pressure cabin built as separate unit.	Development of Typhoon; 1e low-wing monoplane. Pressure cab integral with central fuselage.
POWER PLANT	Two Merlin XX in wing nacelles	Two Merlin XX in fuselage	Two Merlin XX	One Sabre
UNDERCARRIAGE	Tailwheel	Tailwheel	Tricycle.	Tailwheel
ARMAMENT	Four 20-mm guns in fuselage, two in wing centre section; 120 rpg; Chatellerault feed.	Three 20-mm guns in each wing; 120 rpg; Chatellerault feed.	Three 20-mm guns each side of fuselage in centre section; 120 rpg; Chatellerault feed.	Three 20-mm guns in each wing; 120 rpg; Chatellerault feed.
CREW AND ARMOUR	Observer with back to pilot. Bullet-proof windscreen for both members. Bullet-proof pressure diaphragm in front and rear of pressure cab. Central section of cabin top jettisonable.	As P.17.	Observer behind pilot, forward facing but in pivoting seat for rear observation. Bullet-proof cabin hooding and windscreen panels. Fuselage nose built of heavy gauge plate. One side of cabin top hinges down for emergency exit.	Observer behind pilot, facing aft in pivoting seat for side observation. Bullet-proof windscreen for both members. Armour plate in front and behind pressure cabin. Sides and top of cabin jettisonable.
DIMENSIONS	Span, 60 ft (18,3 m); length, 41 ft 6 in (12,7 m); height, 14 ft 4 in (4,4 m).	Span, 58 ft (17,7 m); length, 46 ft 6 in (14,2 m); height, 15 ft 9 in (4,8 m).	Span, 59 ft (17,9 m); length, 48 ft 10 in (14,9 m); height, 15 ft 9 in (4,8 m).	Span, 52 ft (15,9 m); length, 39 ft 3 in (11,9 m); height, 12 ft 3 in (3,74 m).
GROSS WEIGHT	16,340 lb (7 418 kg)	16,420 lb (7 454 kg)	17,800 lb (8 081 kg)*	13,930 lb (6 324 kg)
WING LOADING	36·2 lb/sq ft (176,7 kg/m²)	36.5 lb/sq ft (178,2 kg/m²)	38·3 lb/sq ft (187.0 kg/m²)*	34·4 lb/sq ft (167,9 kg/m²)
FUEL CAPACITY	400 Imp gal (1 818 l)	400 Imp gal (1 818 l)	286 Imp gal (1 300 l)*	290 Imp gal (1 318 l)
MAX SPEED	368 mph (592 km/h) at 21,000 ft (6 405 m) 390 mph (628 km/h) at 35,000 ft (10 675 m)	398 mph (640 km/h) at 21,000 ft (6 405 m) 428 mph (689 km/h) at 35,000 ft (10 675 m)	373 mph (600 km/h) at 15,700 ft (4 788 m) 387 mph (623 km/h) at 25,000 ft (7 625 m)	380 mph (611 km/h) at 18,500 ft (5 643 m) † 430 mph (692 km/h) at 35,000 ft (10 675 m)
CRUISING RANGE	1,325 mls (2 130 km) at 225 mph (362 km/h)	1,425 mls (2 293 km) at 225 mph (362 km/h)	800 mls (1 287 km) at 348 mph (560 km/h)	1,500 mls (2 413 km/h) at 250 mph (402 km/h)
CLIMB	7·7 min to 15,000 ft (4 575 m) 18·1 min to 30,000 ft (9 150 m)	9·3 min to 20,000 ft (6 100 m) 16·2 min to 30,000 ft (9 150 m)	8·1 min to 20,000 ft (6 100 m) 14·5 min to 30,000 ft (9 150 m)	7·1 min to 15,000 ft (4 575 m) 18·9 min to 30,000 ft (9 150 m)
SERVICE CEILING	36,500 ft (11 132 m)	37,000 ft (11 285 m)	39,500 ft (12 048 m)	37,000 ft (11 285 m)
GENERAL COMMENTS	Good potential as short range project for high altitude in near term and to provide early experience of pressure cabin. Position of guns preferred. Pilot's view very good; observer satisfactory.	Pilot's view very poor; observer satisfactory. Questionable handling qualities for fighting. Possible difficulty in heating of guns.	Long nose spoils pilot's view. Observer's view satisfactory. Fighter handling qualities doubted. Tricycle undercarriage favoured but not at the cost of the long nose.	Of particular interest as short range project for early pressure cabin experience and against possible requirement for a high altitude fighter. Pilot's and observer's views satisfactory. Possible difficulty in heating guns.

*Alternative gross weight 21,600 lb (9 806 kg) with 755 Imp gal (3 430 l) fuel for 2,430-ml (3 910-km) range and with 180 rpg.
† Speed applies to version with high-altitude Sabre variant.

was to carry an armament of four 20-mm cannon in wing/fuselage fairings; these guns were described in the submission to DTD as being "reversible for rear defence", but this did not mean they could be pivoted in flight, only that they could be mounted to fire aft should the type of mission so require. Four drums of ammunition for each gun were carried in the wing leading edge, empty drums being stowed in the upper rear fuselage, and four 500-lb (227-kg) bombs could be carried in the lower fuselage, the rear crewman being able to serve as bomb aimer using a sighting panel under the forward cockpit. Fowler-type flaps were incorporated on the *upper* wing surface, extending aft to increase area for take-off, and drooping 35 deg for landing. The GAL 46 had a span of 52 ft (15,9 m) and an estimated speed of 395 mph (634 km/h) at 21,000 ft (6 405 m), the service ceiling being 37,000 ft (11 285 m).

Official reaction to this submission was that there was a good case for such a type, but only if the service ceiling was increased to 45,000 ft (13 725 m), as it was then considered that for most situations picked crews could operate on normal oxygen supplies in an unpressurized aircraft at 37,000 ft (11 285 m).* There was considerable disquiet over General Aircraft's ability, on the other hand; the work on the GAL 41 test-bed was described as "commendable but rather amateur-

rish" and the RAE Farnborough was quoted as being "not very happy" about GAL's work so far. Further unkind remarks were to be made later, but the immediate outcome of the GAL submission was that the Air Ministry agreed, in April 1940, to pursue the development of a high altitude fighter and to invite other companies to tender designs; the specification was issued as F.4/40 and it was stressed that this was "not in any way based on the GAL design". Tenders were invited from GAL, Fairey, Hawker, Vickers and Westland, to be submitted by 20 July 1940, but Fairey and Vickers did not respond.†

Birth of the Welkin

As was to be expected, the General Aircraft submission to the F.4/40 requirement was based closely upon the GAL 46 design, although the provision for bomb-carrying was deleted and the overall dimensions were increased. Hawker proposed a development of the Typhoon, somewhat larger but with similar aerodynamic and structural features, and Westland offered two designs — one being similar in layout to the Whirlwind and the other a highly experimental twin with two Merlins coupled in tandem in the nose to drive contra-props

*This view had changed by 1940, however, when an altitude of 35,000 ft (10 675 m) was said to be acceptable on oxygen alone if the crew was inactive, but insidious effects of such altitudes became more noticeable if the crew was active. Therefore, a pressure cabin came to be regarded as essential for such altitudes.

†Vickers, it should be noted, was already developing a twin-engined fighter — originally as the Type 414 to Specification F.22/39. This was a heavily-armed aircraft, carrying a 40-mm Vickers gun in a large dorsal turret, and two prototypes were ordered, later being modified as Type 420 to F.16/40 and eventually as Type 432 to F.7/41, in which form the fitting of a pressure cabin was intended and the turret was abandoned in favour of a ventral pack of 20-mm cannon. One prototype of the Type 432 flew but the pressure cabin was never made operational.

through a common gearbox. A summary of the Specification requirements and details of the four submissions appear separately in these pages. The various tenders were considered in detail at a design conference on 17 October 1940, when it was concluded that, from a structural point of view, the Hawker P.1004 was the most practical and easiest to produce; the conventional Westland twin had good points but "like the Whirlwind" was "rather fancy"; the second Westland design had very poor view for the pilot and engine development problems that made it "not promising" and the GAL proposal was "half-baked".

The conference concluded that the choice should be made at least in part on the basis of design capacity and ability to do the job. Hawker was judged best for rapid production but the design office was very busy; Westland had no new design work on hand and could be expected to produce a good effort while GAL was considered not to have had enough experience. By November 1940, only Westland was being seriously considered, and by this time the requirements had been changed to reduce the crew from two to only a pilot, and the armament from six to four 20-mm cannon, to permit the aircraft to be smaller and achieve a higher ceiling. The RAE and Vickers were to be invited to collaborate on pressure cabin design, on the basis of work being done on the Wellington V and VI. On 9 January 1941, Westland received a note direct from Lord Beaverbrook as Minister of Aircraft Production instructing the firm to go-ahead; two prototypes of the P.14 design (the "conventional" twin) were to be ordered at a total cost of about £160,000 (increased, a year later, to £215,000, to the considerable dismay of the Air Ministry!)

In close parallel to the evolution of the F.4/40, Gloster Aircraft launched development of the twin-engined fighter that was to become the Meteor — the first British jet to enter service. Specification F.9/40 was drawn up around Gloster's proposals during 1940 and prototypes were ordered in February 1941. Rightly, great hopes were held for the F.9/40, which was expected to have a high-altitude capability as well as better performance than its piston-engined counterparts, although a pressure cabin was not planned (a pressure suit was to be developed for the pilot instead). From 1941 onwards, therefore, the Westland P.14 came to be regarded as an insurance against failure of the "Gloster-Whittle fighter", as the Meteor was then referred to in official correspondence. This rôle was spelt out more fully in Specification F.7/41, to which the Welkin was eventually developed together with the Vickers 432 as already noted.

Designed by W E W "Teddy" Petter as Westland's technical director, in conjunction with chief designer Arthur Davenport, the P.14 — yet to be named Welkin when work started in earnest towards the end of 1940 — had the same overall configuration as the Whirlwind except that the wing was mounted in a mid position and the tailplane was not located so high on the fin.

At first designed with a span of 60 ft (18,3 m), the wing of the P.14 was extended to 65 ft (19,83 m) early in 1941, with increased aspect ratio, reducing the wing loading to 35 lb/sq ft (171 kg/m²) with a gross weight of 15,300 lb (6 946 kg). Subsequently the span was increased again, to 70 ft (21,35 m), and the weight increased to 18,300 lb (8 308 kg) by the time the prototype first flew, giving a wing loading of just under 40 lb/sq ft (195,3 kg/m²) and making it the largest single-seater ever attempted. The reduction of armament from six to four guns, with 150 rounds each, allowed an increase in fuel capacity. Among the early problems to be considered were the method of airframe de-icing, since ice accretion was likely otherwise to prove a serious handicap during the climb to height, and the possible requirement for a portable oxygen supply in the event of the pilot baling out. In February 1941, the top speed was estimated to be 385 mph (619 km/h) at 31,000 ft (9 455 m), the service ceiling was 43,400 ft (13 237 m) and the duration 3 hrs;

with the ultimate long-span wing, the stalling speed was 80 mph (129 km/h) and take-off distance was 585 yds (535 m). When the mock-up was inspected in March 1941, there was criticism of the view for search ahead and for landing in bad visibility and of the view astern because of canopy structure; the windscreen was considered to be too far away from the pilot's eyes.

The Welkin was of all-metal construction, the front fuselage incorporating the cabin being primarily of duralumin and the rear fuselage, of conventional frame and stringer construction, being largely of magnesium with the skin in longitudinal strips, the whole being flush riveted. The wing was of single spar construction, in three sections, the flat one-piece centre section extending to outboard of the nacelles and outer panels incorporating ailerons having dihedral. The relatively modest wing loading made it possible to meet the specified stalling speeds and landing requirements with the use of normal split flaps, located on the centre section of the wing only, both inboard and outboard of the nacelles and having a maximum deflection of 42 deg. The tail unit was of straightforward spar and rib construction, the high location of the tailplane being chosen to keep it clear of the disturbed flow in the wake of the flaps; a bullet fairing smoothed the airflow at the tailplane/fin junction. All control surfaces were manually operated by push-pull tubes.

The Merlin engines — Mk XXs when the type was first projected but two-stage two-speed Mk 61s in the prototype Welkins — were carried on bearers attached to the wing main spar and were enclosed in tight cowlings, the only excrescences on which were the ventral carburettor air intakes, with ice guards. The main engine radiators, oil coolers and supercharger intercoolers were located in the centre section each side of the fuselage, with intakes in the wing leading edge and a variable exit at the trailing edge controlled by the angular setting of the main landing flaps.

Specification F.4/40
Summary of Appendix 'B' requirements*

(a) Aircraft required as a high speed fighter for operations at great heights, with pressure cabin to provide cabin conditions equivalent to 10,000 ft (3 050 m) when aircraft is at 45,000 ft (13 725 m). To be as small as possible and flying weight not more than 16,000 lb (7 264 kg) if twin-engined.

(b) Target speed, 450 mph (724 km/h) at 25,000 ft (7 625 m); two-speed supercharger to be used to obtain high speed at lower altitudes also.

(c) Service ceiling, 34,000 ft (10 370 m) with engines immediately available and design for 45,000 ft (13 725 m) operation when suitably rated engines become available. Rolls-Royce RM6SM engines were preferred.

(d) Normal endurance, 2 hrs at max economic cruise at 25,000 ft (7 625 m) plus 30 min at max level flight power. Reinforcing range 1,200 mls (1 930 km) in overload conditions.

(e) Take-off distance to 50 ft (15,2 m) from grass in still air not to exceed 600 yds (550 m); landing distance from 50 ft (15,2 m) in still air with fuel for 500 mls (805 km) remaining, not to exceed 700 yds (640 m).

(f) Armament to be six forward firing cannon with 120 rounds each.

(g) Crew to comprise pilot and AI operator/lookout (short-range rôle) or W/T operator/navigator/lookout (long-range rôle).

(h) Use of a tricycle undercarriage optional; if used, to have a vertical velocity absorption rate of 12 ft/sec (3,7 m/sec).

(i) Crew to be protected against armour-piercing 0·303-in (7,7-mm) ammunition at a range of 200 yds (183 m) to cover a forward cone with an angle of 20 deg to the thrust line, and against similar ammunition fired from astern from a 10 deg angle above, below and on each side. Fuel tanks to be self-sealing.

*As initially circulated, dated 6 July 1940. Issue II of Appendix 'B', dated 3 June 1941, was generally similar but required a single-seat fighter and relaxed the pressure cabin requirement, to give a 25,000 ft (7 625 m) equivalent at 45,000 ft (13 725 m). A six-gun armament was still encouraged but "two of these guns will be treated as alternative load or an overload". Top speed was to be "not less than 400 mph or (644 km/h)"

Comparative views of the first prototype Welkin, DG558/G, as first flown (above) and after modification of the vertical tail surfaces and engine nacelles (below).

Fuel was carried in a cylindrical tank in the fuselage just aft of the cockpit, with a capacity of 79 Imp gal (359 l), and in a pair of tanks each side in the centre section outboard of the nacelles, having a combined capacity of 400 Imp gal (1 818 l); the fuselage tank was regarded as an auxiliary only required for long-range operation, when an additional 400 Imp gal (1 818 l) could be carried in two wing drop tanks. A 3,000 psi (211 kg/cm²) Dowty "live line" hydraulic system was fitted, and a Dunlop pneumatic system with a Heywood compressor. The armament, comprising four 20-mm British Hispano cannon, was grouped beneath the cockpit floor, keeping the nose of the aircraft extremely short and affording the pilot an excellent view forwards and downwards. A reflector gunsight was fitted, and a gun camera was located in the extreme nose.

A tail-wheel type undercarriage was adopted to avoid any untoward handling problems with the still relatively unknown tricycle type and to avoid nosewheel stowage complications in the short front fuselage. Main and tail undercarriage members had Lockheed oleo-pneumatic shock absorbers and Dunlop wheels, tyres and brakes.

Most interest in the design of the Welkin naturally centred upon the pressure cabin, for which a differential of 3·5 psi (0,25 kg/cm²) was adopted, to provide a cabin equivalent of 24,000 ft (7 320 m) at a height of 45,000 ft (13 725 m); this meant that the pilot would need to be provided with a continuous supply of oxygen. The cabin itself was constructed as an independent unit in heavy gauge bullet proof light alloy (up to $\frac{7}{16}$ in/11,11 mm in places), this being bolted to the main spar and completed at the rear by an armoured steel bulkhead. The transparencies comprised a thick double windscreen with airspace between and a half-cylindrical jettisonable and aft-sliding hood also of sandwich construction, the thick inner skin of which retained pressure and the outer shell of which served as a fairing. This canopy ended in a thick laminated glass pressure retaining bulkhead, behind which was an unpressurized rear cockpit fairing, and warm air was passed through the space between the two layers of the canopy and windscreen to keep it clear of ice and mist. An air heater and filter were located in the nose above the guns, with an intake for this cabin air on the nose fairing, and the warm air passed from the cabin into the rear fuselage to exit at the tail. Sealing of the canopy, when closed, was by means of a Dunlop rubber gasket which inflated automatically as cabin pressure increased.

Cabin pressurization was achieved by means of a Rotol blower on the starboard engine, air being taken from a small intake in the starboard wing leading edge through a Vokes filter to the blower, and then through an exhaust silencer to the cabin non-return valve mounted behind the rear bullet-proof bulkhead. To maintain pressure at the correct approximate value for any height, Westland developed an ingenious valve that controlled the exit of pressurization air to the atmosphere automatically, no action being required by the pilot once the system had been activated. Pressure glands had to be used in the cabin shell to carry control tubes, and electric runs were grouped at pressure-tight junction boxes.

Flight testing begins

As already noted, the first of the two prototypes of the Welkin assembled at Yeovil was flown there on 1 November 1942 by the company's chief test pilot Harald Penrose (who has contributed his personal account of Welkin test-flying, starting on page 98). The gross weight at this stage was 17,692 lb (8 032 kg) and the Merlin 61 engines were fitted with four-bladed de Havilland constant-speed non-feathering propellers of 13 ft (3,97-m) diameter. The latter were to prove a source of considerable trouble since the loss of oil pressure would mean that the propellers would return to full-fine pitch, with no capacity to coarsen. In practice, this meant that situations would arise in which an engine, having been closed down for some reason, would be "powered" by a windmilling propeller which, in fine pitch, would turn much faster than the revolutions normally permitted and thus cause problems on top of that causing the initial emergency!

Following the first flight, a second and third followed on 2 and 3 November, the longest being of 40 min duration. On the fourth flight, however — also on 3 November — the constant speed unit on the port propeller failed, allowing the propeller to overspeed and forcing a precipitate landing to be made at RAF Zeals. This was the first of what would be a total of five emergencies suffered by this prototype, DG558*, within the first 10 months, all attributable to engine or propeller problems. There were four other emergency landings made by production aircraft in the period up to the end of 1943 (ie, the first 13 months of test flying) and a subsequent analysis of causes showed that feathering propellers would probably have alleviated the problem in three and possibly six of those nine emergencies.

Some 11½ hrs of testing were completed in the first month and 7½ hrs in the next month. There were some stability problems and the elevator was unsatisfactory; all controls were too heavy at first, there was lack of trim definition at low speeds and the ailerons were overbalanced at moderate/high speeds but too heavy at low speeds. Among the steps taken to overcome some of these characteristics were a modification of the rear nacelle shape, which was lengthened and raised, a change of elevator aerofoil section, an increase in elevator balance area to 9 per cent and a reduction in rudder horn balance area, which "squared off" the top of the rudder.

The second prototype joined the programme in the early spring of 1943 and the first went to the A & AEE at Boscombe Down for the first time on 21 April. By then, it had demonstrated a service ceiling of 44,000 ft (13 420 m) and had been dived to 370 mph (595 km/h) IAS, although the level speed at FTH (full throttle height) was 30 mph (48 km/h) below estimate — probably because of propeller inefficiency and high drag of the thick wing roots. The onset of shock stall on the outer wings was detected during April, when heavy vibration occurred at 270 mph (434 km/h) indicated at 35,000 ft (10 675 m), disappearing when the speed was reduced to 220 mph (354 km/h). This led to a proposed limitation of

---

*The serial numbers actually carried by the two prototypes were DG558/G and DG562/G, the 'G' indicating that secret equipment was fitted (presumably the pressure cabin) that required an armed guard to be mounted on the aircraft when on the ground.

AIR International CLASSIFIED

ADVERTISEMENT RATES AND CONDITIONS OF ACCEPTANCE

Mach = 0·70, or 230 mph (370 km/h) IAS at 40,000 ft (12 200 m), since the phenomenon was not fully understood and modifications to overcome it could not be initiated.

By 28 May, DG558 was nearly through its preliminary trials at Boscombe Down but another propeller overspeed and consequent engine fire occurred (the prototype's fourth) while the aircraft was being flown by Flt Lt G Brunner. He had been conducting climbs and levels for performance measurements between 27,000 ft (8 235 m) and 40,000 ft (12 200 m) when the electric circuits serving the fuel gauges and trimmers failed at 27,000 ft (8 235 m). While descending to 25,000 ft (7 625 m) for level speed tests, he noted that the starboard prop rpm indicator suddenly increased to 5,500 (probably off the clock), and remained at 3,500 after he had throttled back and reduced speed to 120-140 mph (193-225 km/h). He then cut the switches and fuel to the engine, but with no rudder trim available (because of the earlier electrical failure), he could use only a little power from the "good" port engine.

Flt Lt Brunner's report said that he had "plenty of height" at this stage but the starboard engine was roasting with paint burning off the cowlings, there was much "grating and grinding" and smoke, and the oil temperature was off the clock. The control column suddenly went hard left and stayed there, the aircraft entering a steep spiral dive, in the course of which the pilot tried, without success, to bail out. Some control was regained after the nose was pulled up, but the starboard aileron was not moving, although the port aileron was normal. With insufficient control for single engined flight to be maintained, Brunner made a forced landing at RAF Upavon, where it was discovered that the starboard aileron control rod had failed in the heat, the original cause of the propeller runaway probably being oil starvation.

Notwithstanding this and other less "hairy" incidents, the preliminary Boscombe Down report said that the Welkin had no handling difficulties in normal conditions, but the ailerons still "must be improved" and the elevator lightened at high speeds. Duplication of the electric circuits to the trimmers (or a mechanical standby) was also called for — essential, said the A & AEE, for the rudder and preferable for the elevator also.

Production of the Welkin had been ordered soon after work on the prototype began, the initial order for 100 later being supplemented by a second for 200. The first of these (DX278) was at the A & AEE by mid-September 1943, following a month of armament trials on the second prototype that had

concluded on 9 September, this latter aircraft being damaged in a forced landing on its return flight to Yeovil on that date. DX278 completed 30 hrs of testing by 24 October, but then suffered loss of oil pressure and caught fire in the subsequent forced landing at Boscombe. Its task was taken over by DX279, which had reached the A & AEE on 23 October, supplemented by DX280 on 2 October, but the latter was written off in a forced landing on 11 December following an engine fire, and was in turn replaced by DX282 which had arrived at Boscombe Down on 7 November. Bad luck still dogged the Welkin, DX282 being damaged beyond repair in a ground collision with the Seafire III prototype at Boscombe on 21 January 1944. Consequently, DX279 was left to bear the brunt of the A & AEE testing, supplemented from time to time by the two prototypes. Other production aircraft were assigned to Boscombe during 1944 and 1945 for specific trial tasks.

The propeller situation gave cause for much concern during 1943, and it was eventually decided to standardise on four-bladed Rotol fully feathering units of 12 ft 6 in (3,81 m) diameter, although the first 50 aircraft would have three-bladed DH feathering propellers of the same diameter as used on the Mosquito. The larger diameter of the original propellers used on the prototypes gave them a tip speed of Mach 1·1 at 35,000 ft (10 675 m), leading to extreme vibration which was at the root of much of the trouble encountered. However, Westland's tests with the Mosquito units showed unacceptable vibration and it was preferred to soldier on with the non-feathering four-bladers until the feathering propellers became available. Engines in the production aircraft were Merlin 72 and 73 or Merlin 76 and 77 — the odd numbered mark in each case being the starboard engine with the cabin blower attached.

Boscombe Down comments on the production Welkin, made early in 1944, were not notable for their enthusiasm. For example, the ailerons were considered heavy and sluggish especially at altitude and had to be improved if manoeuvrability was to come up to that usually considered necessary for a fighter; rate of trim change was too slow, but accurate trimming became difficult if the action was speeded up; the elevator was too heavy for fighting at low levels; the instrument layout was poor, downward view was poor and forward view on the climb was poor because of the steep attitude.

The three-view drawing below depicts the Welkin F Mk I and the extra side view (bottom right) shows the Welkin NF Mk II prototype.

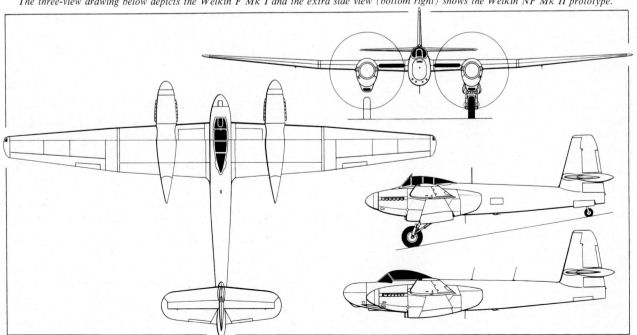

(Above) The original Welkin prototype carrying 200-Imp gal (909-l) underwing tanks and (below) the second prototype fitted with Merlin RM16SM engines and "beard" radiators.

(Below) The sole prototype of the Welkin NF Mk II in its original guise as PF370, converted from a Mk I production airframe. It later flew marked as P-17 and then as WE997.

The Welkin, said the Boscombe Down report, showed no inherent tendency to swing on take-off, but was very sensitive to power differences at similar throttle openings; also, the throttles were stiff to operate, so it was usual to taxi on the brakes with the engines set at 1,000-1,500 rpm. The aircraft was tail heavy when the undercarriage was retracting but then nose heavy with decrease of power or speed. Aileron effectiveness was poor at all speeds, a bank to 60 deg taking four seconds and a full roll, 12-15 sec; the aileron spring tab (fitted in the starboard aileron only, as a modification) needed further adjustment. Longitudinal stability was adequate with no tendency to tighten up in steep turns, and stalls, "clean" or "all-down", were fairly innocuous with no tendency to spin. Severe rudder oscillation was experienced in single-engined flight below 165 mph (265 km/h). Dives to 450 mph (724 km/h) at 10,000 ft (3 050 m) were steady but fore and aft vibration of the control column occurred above 440 mph (708 km/h) and at 315 mph (507 km/h) above 30,000 ft (9 150 m) the vibration and pitching motion increased to a point where the pilot was

---

Westland Welkin NF Mk II Specification
Power Plant: Two Rolls-Royce Merlin 76 (port)/77 (starboard); other details as Welkin I.
Performance: Max speed, 333 mph (536 km/h) at 40,000 ft (12 200 m), 346 mph (557 km/h) at 20,000 ft (6 100 m), 335 mph (539 km/h) at 10,000 ft (3 050 m); initial rate of climb, 2,650 ft/min (13,5 m/sec); time to 35,000 ft (10 675 m), 20 min; service ceiling, 41,000 ft (12 505 m); range, 1,050 mls (1 690 km) at 35,000 ft (10 675 m); take-off run, 2,250 ft (686 m); landing run, 3,345 ft (1 020 m).
Weights: Empty, 13,574 lb (6 162 kg); max take-off, 21,892 lb (9 939 kg).
Dimensions: As Welkin I except length, 44 ft 1 in (13,44 m).
Accommodation: Pilot and aft-facing observer in cockpit beneath aft-sliding one-piece canopy.
Armament: As Welkin I.

---

unable to hold the column or pull out of the dive until altitude was lost (and the same speed therefore represented a lower Mach number — this was an effect of the compressibility already mentioned).

Mock combats with a Mosquito IX and another Welkin at altitudes up to 35,000 ft (10 675 m) led to the comment that the Welkin had very poor aileron control for combat; it might be capable of dealing with a heavy bomber or reconnaissance aircraft but would be outmanoeuvred by single-engined aircraft, which would also be able to dive to avoid combat.

Changing requirements

Although Westland continued to devote considerable effort to the Welkin throughout 1944 and into 1945, RAF interest in the type was waning rapidly — partly, perhaps, because of its unpromising characteristics noted by Boscombe, but largely because the need for a high altitude interceptor had itself dwindled. Before the end of 1943, Fighter Command was already saying it saw "little or no use for the single-seat Welkin", but with the aircraft in production and so much effort already expended, possible alternative applications were naturally sought. One such possibility was long-range reconnaissance, needing a range of 1,850 mls (2 963 km) with provision for 15 min of combat at 35,000 ft (10 675 m). This required the use of two 200 Imp gal wing drop tanks (which were tested on the prototype DG558) and took the gross weight to 21,100 lb (9 580 kg), carrying 20-in or 36-in (50-cm or 93-cm) focal length F.8 or F.52 cameras.

The Air Ministry also requested Westland to study a fighter-bomber Welkin, carrying two 2,000-lb (908-kg) bombs; in October 1943 this was estimated to weigh 22,550 lb (10 238 kg) and to have a speed of 410 mph (660 km/h) at 30,000 ft (9 150 m), with a service ceiling of 46,600 ft (14 213 m). (The operational need for a fighter-bomber with this kind of altitude performance is no longer clear!) Various aerodynamic changes studied in this period included extending the wing chord forwards — but this led to difficulties over the engine exhaust manifolds — and the use of a Vee-tail unit.

Within the Westland design office, unofficial Mark numbers were applied to some of these projects. Welkin IIA was a two-seat high altitude fighter with Merlin 77s, while the IIB was a low altitude variant with Merlin RM14SMs. The Welkin III was a developed Mk IIA with a high speed wing planform and larger radiators to serve the Merlin RM15SMs and the Welkin IV, with further refinements, had a projected speed of 425 mph (684 km/h) and altitude of 50,300 ft (15 342 m) with a weight of 22,290 lb (10 120 kg). Jet versions of the Welkin were also studied by Petter during 1943, but he soon turned his attention to a jet powered bomber, the project designs for which he took with him in 1944 to English Electric, where they provided the basis of the Canberra.

None of these versions of the Welkin saw the light of day, but one version did go ahead in 1943, as a two-seat night fighter. This became the *official* Welkin NF Mk II, developed to Specification F.9/43 issued in April of that year to cover the work already put in hand at Yeovil — MAP had sanctioned a go-ahead on a two-seat Welkin on 4 February, to carry AI Mk VIII radar. The forward fuselage was lengthened, with provision for an observer facing aft behind the pilot, and radar scanner in the nose above the guns, and a mock-up was inspected on 13 May 1943 when the cockpit received much approbation.

Two prototypes of the Welkin NF Mk II were ordered, to be built by conversion of production Mk Is, and the possibility of converting all Mk I production to two-seaters was considered, the eventual decision being to change the final 60 of the second production contract to this configuration. The prototype flew on 23 October 1944, marked as PF370 (converted from DX386) but work on the second was abandoned, in common

continued on page 98

Countering Calamity

DISASTER is, of course, purely relative. There are some members of the modelling fraternity to whom a smear of cement on a clear canopy or a slip of a knife on a pristine wing surface is supreme calamity; to the more stoic, disaster is nothing less than the mishap announced by that heart-rending crunch signifying an inadvertent meeting between a lovingly-assembled model and an unyielding surface. Some modellers suffer profound distress and misery when accidents befall the objects of their creativity, while others shrug such off with a few imprecations and a vow to take greater care. But whatever one's reactions to such misfortunes—and we all experience the odd accident now and again—some positive action other than consigning the immediately salvageable parts to the spares box is called for, yet, from the correspondence that we receive, it is surprising how many modellers have little idea of how to go about the repair of accidental damage. *Nil desperandum*!

Let us take, for a start, the simplest and most common accident, the inadvertent cement smear. However great the temptation, *never* attempt to remove the unwanted cement while it is still wet. Allow it to dry overnight and then remove the cement by gentle scraping with a modelling knife and then rubbing it down with the finest of wet-and-dry emery paper. Now *Silvo*, or a similar liquid metal polish, may be applied with a soft cloth—first testing the effect of the polish on a piece of scrap plastic in case it should contain a solvent—and the surface carefully polished. This treatment will suffice for most surfaces, but for transparencies a final polish with tooth powder, or even toothpaste, will serve to provide the finishing touch. A word of caution about transparencies: these are usually moulded in rather brittle plastic and care should be taken in the amount of pressure applied and the vigour used in rubbing. It is possible to induce fatigue into the material with crazing or even disintegration resulting.

Extensive pitting of transparent surfaces is generally irremediable, but elsewhere may be dealt with by filling with body putty and then rubbing down to a smooth surface. Some surface detail may be lost in the process but this may be reinstated by ruling with a pointed metal scriber against a piece of flexible metal, such as a typewriter erasing shield or a piece of tinplate. If the detail on the original surface was engraved, then the problem is simple of solution. If, on the other hand, the panel lines are raised, then these cannot be simulated exactly, although the process of scribing does raise a small ridge which will blend well enough under a couple of coats of paint. Scratches or digs in plastic surfaces may be eradicated by use of the same treatment.

Damage resulting from dropping a model can vary tremendously in degree of severity, but the most common results of such accidents are sprung joints and the breaking off of such projections as propeller blades, pitot tubes, undercarriage members, etc. The sprung joint is best repaired by use of liquid cement applied with a fine brush as this is far less likely to damage the paintwork than is tube cement. Run the cement into the joint, clamp the parts together—or use adhesive tape—and allow plenty of time to dry. Small parts, such as undercarriage legs, can rarely be affixed as strongly as originally unless some reinforcement is applied. A broken part *can* be made even stronger than it was before by introducing a small hole in the end by means of a drill—Morse size 74 or thereabouts—chucked in a pin-vice and inserting a short length of wire as a dowel before cementing. Plastic pitot tubes and antennae are usually so weak that they are best replaced by components produced from wire in any case. Propeller blades can be dowelled and refitted in a similar fashion to the undercarriage legs.

If the paint job has been seriously damaged, there is little chance of retouching it successfully as paint, even if purporting to be of an identical shade, almost invariably differs slightly in tone and this can be very noticeable. Furthermore, there has probably been some fading of the paint since the model was originally finished, rendering precise matching out of the question. The best course, in such cases, is to rub down the entire model with "wet-and-dry", removing all the decals in the process, and make a fresh start with a new scheme and markings.

With many early kits no longer available and with suitable replacements yet to appear, a model should never be disposed of out of hand owing to its age, exposure to the ravages of time, or perhaps inadequacy of technique at the time of its construction. Part dismantling and reassembly with the incorporation of additional detail and a complete rub-down and new paint job can work wonders and transform a no-longer-acceptable model into an important item in the collection.

This month's colour subject

Ten years ago, on 27 June 1966, Westland announced receipt of the largest single contract ever to be obtained by the company—60 licence-built Sikorsky S-61D Sea King helicopters. Just short of three years later, on 7 May 1969, the first Westland production S-61D flew as the Sea King HAS Mk 1 and in the same month this (British) West Country cousin of the Stratford (Connecticut) classic logged its first export order—22 SAR models for the Federal German *Bundesmarine*—and has since gone from strength to strength as an export item, the British company being permitted, under the terms of its manufacturing licence, to sell the Sea King anywhere in the world outside of North America on a non-exclusive basis. Thus, the Yeovil-built Sea King has found itself in competition not only with basically similar helicopters built at Stratford but also those built by Sikorsky's Italian licensee, Agusta. Notwithstanding this competition, the British Sea King has accumulated a remarkable order book under its rotor blades, a fact to which the accompanying colour pages attest. So if choppers are your penchant, then what better than Westland's Sea King.

Only two kits have so far been produced for the Sea King, both representing the US Navy's SH-3D, but the external differences between this and the Westland-built models are minimal and, apart from having to find your own decals, no major modifications are called for, and thus we have a choice of Airfix's 1/72nd scale or Tamiya's 1/100th scale Sea Kings. Both are very good kits, accurately moulded in the basic US Navy white which presents no covering problems for any of the half-score schemes applicable to Westland-built Sea Kings illustrated on these pages, with the Westland-developed Commando Mk 2 tactical transport variant calling for only a modicum of adaptation. Because of its scale, the Airfix kit has more appeal than that from Tamiya, but both are well detailed and the latter, despite its smaller size, has a lot of charm. Both kits are generally available and can be confidently recommended.

A kit clearing house

Reverting to the subject of kits that are no longer readily available, Mark Grossman of Queens, New York, has written to us recently to bring to our attention a publication entitled *Kit Collectors Clearing House*. Comprising eight pages per issue and published monthly (from 3213 Hardy Drive, Edmond, Oklahoma 73034) with an overseas annual subscription rate of $7·50, the *Kit Collectors Clearing House* offers a free advertisement service for modellers seeking specific and no longer readily obtainable kits, includes news of both new kits and re-issues and is sent out by airmail. Published by a non-profit organisation, this little magazine could well provide a valuable service for those seeking the older and rarer kits and already has subscribers in a half-dozen countries.

Spectacular asiatic lightning

We have occasionally expressed doubts regarding the long-term prospects of 1/32nd as a scale owing to the storage problems that such large models entail, but we freely admit that, doubts or no, we cannot prevent ourselves drooling when a really *good* new kit to this scale appears on our workbench. It would seem that, even if little new in 1/32nd is being offered nowadays by western manufacturers, the Japanese are retaining their faith in such whoppers—this month we have two of them, the first of these, from Revell (Japan), representing the Kawanishi N1K1-J-Ko Shiden, or Violet Lightning. It would seem that Revell (Japan) is a law unto itself in producing kits of indigenous WW II aircraft which never seem to find their way into the UK catalogue, nor, as far as we can ascertain, that of the USA. It is to be hoped that this superb kit of Shiden—which, for those still experiencing difficulty in attaching Japanese names to

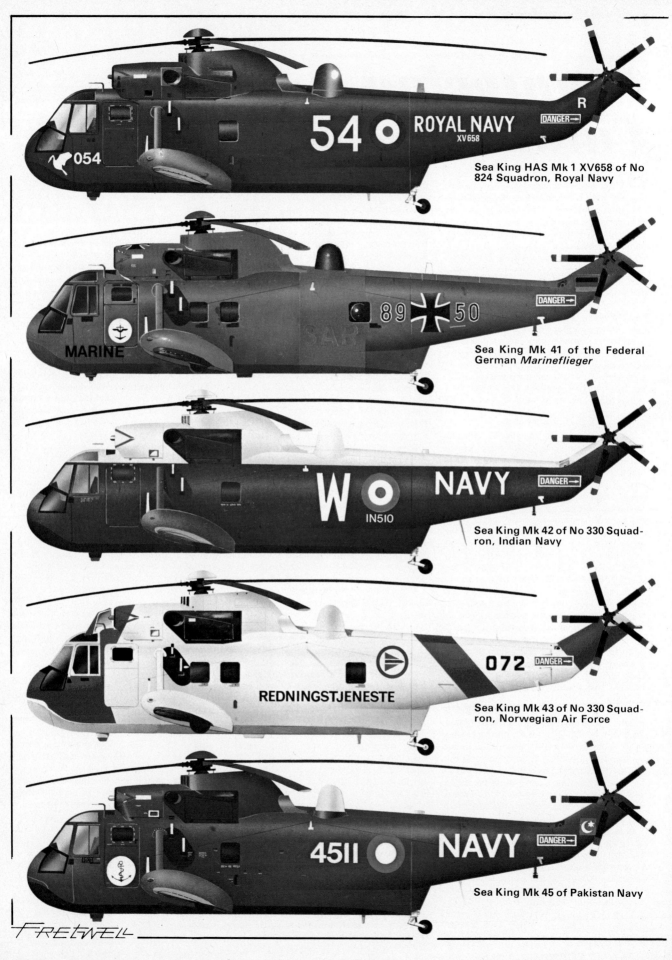

Sea King HAS Mk 1 XV658 of No 824 Squadron, Royal Navy

Sea King Mk 41 of the Federal German *Marineflieger*

Sea King Mk 42 of No 330 Squadron, Indian Navy

Sea King Mk 43 of No 330 Squadron, Norwegian Air Force

Sea King Mk 45 of Pakistan Navy

FRETWELL

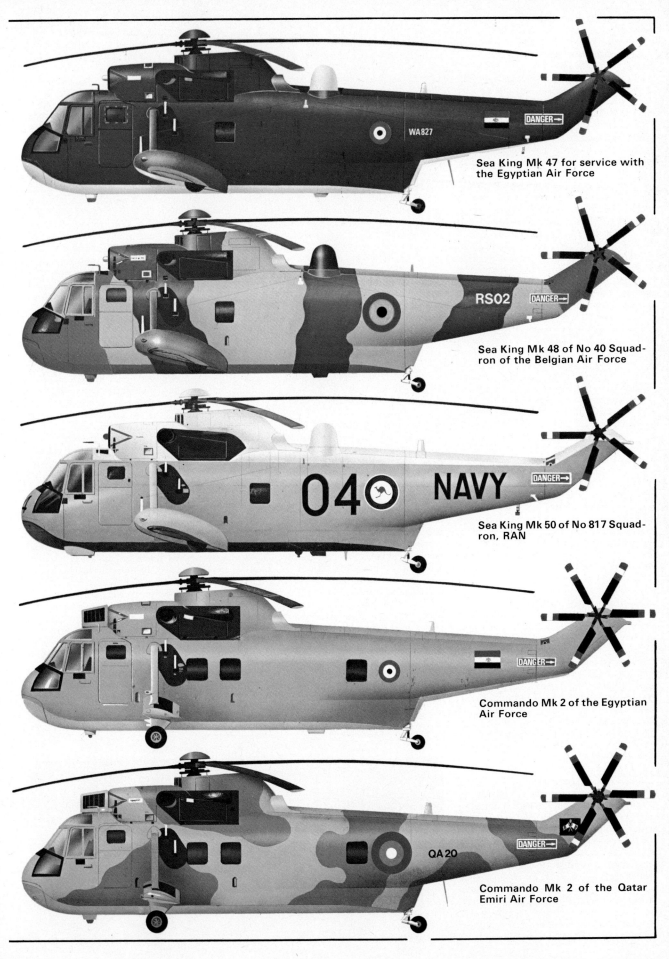

Sea King Mk 47 for service with the Egyptian Air Force

Sea King Mk 48 of No 40 Squadron of the Belgian Air Force

Sea King Mk 50 of No 817 Squadron, RAN

Commando Mk 2 of the Egyptian Air Force

Commando Mk 2 of the Qatar Emiri Air Force

specific aircraft types, was more prosaically dubbed *George* under the ATIU-SWP system of reporting names—will achieve somewhat wider dissemination than some other recent offerings from the same source.

Our records reveal no previous kits of the Shiden, although there are—or, at least, have been—many kits of the later N1K2-J Shiden-Kai, mostly of indifferent quality. This N1K1-J-Ko kit consists of 113 component parts, the major components being moulded in dark green and the smaller ones in light grey, plus a three-piece canopy and other transparencies for the navigation lights in the wingtips and rear fuselage. The fuselage contours of the Shiden have a subtlety that is not easy to capture, the section varying along its length, but Revell (Japan) has succeeded perfectly and we have nothing but praise for the overall accuracy and the superb surface detailing, the latter including rivetting reproduced exactly to scale and a subdued fabric effect on the control surfaces which looks just right. The interiors of the cockpit walls and the undercarriage wells all feature surface detailing and the overall effect could hardly have been bettered.

The interior of the spacious (by Japanese standards) cockpit comprises 12 parts, plus a pilot figure, the use of which is, in our opinion, detrimental to the finished model as it hides too much of the fine detail. The canopy may be assembled in the open position if desired. The instrument panel has engraved details but is also provided with a decal, and the gunsight has a transparent lens — even the cockpit floor incorporates rivet details! The engine is *really* something to see. The Homare 18-cylinder radial is fully modelled with pushrods separate from the cylinders and all of the complicated exhaust system. Assembled on the firewall as a power egg, it is a true model in its own right and comprises some 20 parts. The lower half of the cowling may be detached to display a substantial proportion of the engine. The undercarriage is to the same high standard and the propeller has four separate blades and a two-part spinner.

The wing flaps are operable without in any way distorting the outlines and there are alternative assembly positions for some component parts, but this is in no sense a "gimmicky" kit. The wing embodies a mainspar which adds stiffness and substance to the structure. There are external stores in the shape of two bombs and a centreline fuel tank—even the shackles for the latter are separate mouldings. A nice finishing touch is the provision of chocks to go under the wheels. The decal sheet offers markings for six different aircraft, but there is no choice of colour scheme, all Shidens being finished in the standard dark green (upper) and light grey (under) scheme.

Tomorrow's sky contender

In a few years' time, the General Dynamics F-16 will be a common enough sight in European and US skies, and currently bids fair to become familiar with Israeli, Iranian, South Korean and other skies, so we can expect quite a number of kits of this sprightly warplane in the years ahead, but we doubt that any will achieve greater economy in so far as the number of component parts is concerned than Monogram's new 1/48th scale offering. In fact, the main fuselage structure, complete with wings and horizontal tail surfaces, consists of only two parts! The kit possesses 51 parts in all,

these being moulded in flawless white plastic with superfine surface detailing, embossed for the main part, and nary a vestige of flash is anywhere to be seen. Assembly could not be more straightforward and the component parts fit with precision, despite the complicated shapes and sections. The accompanying instruction leaflet leaves nothing in doubt. The interiors of the cockpit, undercarriage wells, jet intake and efflux are all properly furnished and there is some commendable fine detailing in the undercarriage members and wheels — all landing gear doors embody internal detail.

External stores run to two Sidewinder AAMs, wingtip mounted, and two pylon-mounted underwing fuel tanks. The two-piece cockpit canopy is both thin and clear, and fits to a separately moulded section of fuselage decking. There is a clear plastic lens for the gunsight and the ejector seat, of semi-reclining type, is notable for its fine detail. There is some small embossed lettering under the trailing edge of the port wing flap and a little judicious filing is necessary to remove it. Full details are provided for the gaudy red, white and blue scheme that was briefly used by the prototypes for demonstration purposes and the achievement of a neat effect with this scheme will call for some careful masking but the finished effect is certainly impressive. Our sample kit was supplied by the UK distributor, A A Hales, and Monogram's F-16 is generally available from UK model shops at £1·85.

A quarter-inch bent-winged bird

The latest addition to the Japanese Otaki's much-respected 1/48th scale series of WW II kits represents the Chance Vought F4U-1A Corsair which fully maintains the already-established high Otaki standard and displays this company's usual economy in component parts. There are, in fact, only 54 parts, these being moulded in light grey plastic with the finest of etched surface details and a high degree of accuracy coupled with very precise mating. Everywhere that interior detailing is called for it is provided, and there is a nicely restrained surface and rib effect on the fabric-covered control surfaces.

The cockpit offers a floor and instrument panel with side consoles (engraved instruments), seat, controls, rear bulkhead and a very clear one-piece canopy. The complex tailwheel/arrester hook assembly is of the

raised type and the main undercarriage has all of the struts and door actuating gear faithfully reproduced. The engine is in half-relief and mounted on a bulkhead, but, being set well back inside the cowling it looks well. A drop tank is provided for mounting under the fuselage and there is a standing figure.

The decal sheet offers good colour reproduction, is matt finished and provides the markings of three different machines. The first of these is an F4U-1A of the US Marine Corps' VMF-11 *Devil Dogs*, this being "Olé 122" with 100 mission markers on the fuselage portside which was active in the Marshall Islands and featured the standard three-tone blue-grey finish of the period. The second aircraft is an unidentified Royal Navy Corsair II coded '8L' but lacking serial number, this sporting the standard temperate scheme, and the third aircraft belonged to the RNZAF and has the serial number NZ5218, but again the unit is unidentified. The last-mentioned aircraft has a similar overall finish to that of the USMC Corsair. A full-colour sheet is included with the kit, this offering side profiles to 1/48th scale of both the USMC and Royal Navy Corsairs.

The latest decals

The most recent decals received from Airline Publications and Sales are for a Thai Airways International DC-10 Series 30 registered HS-TGA. Intended for application to Revell's 1/144th scale kit, these decals are among the most colourful that we have so far seen, being in gold, purple and magenta, with a broad fuselage band which includes the windows, a large motif embracing part of the rear nacelle and part of the fin, the title of the airline for affixing in four positions and, of course, the registration of the particular aircraft, the overall effect being most striking. The decals are of top quality, being hand silk-screen printed in the style of those used for the models displayed by travel agents, and the adhesive qualities are very good. Unfortunately, the windows and doors on the decals do not coincide exactly with those on the model, so it is wise to fill those of the latter and rub them down smooth before painting. No diagrams or instructions are provided for positioning the decals, but the scheme is included in *Airliners No 2,* a booklet published by the same firm. The decal sheet is available in the UK at £1·00 plus postage. □   F J HENDERSON

Mr R A Woodling, of Redmond, Washington 98052, has sent us the photo below with the following comment: "Many thanks for your recent tips on scratch-building (April and June issues). For 26 years I have been a plastic kit 'basher', until this year, that is. I am enclosing a photo of a Boeing YC-14 model that I recently constructed from wood and plastic. The joy that I experienced in building this model far exceeded any that I had ever obtained from assembling plastic kits — and it did not prove a very difficult task. Before building my 1/144th scale YC-14, I discussed this venture with several professional model makers and incorporated some of their techniques". (Also in the photo is a 1/144th scale Airbus A-300 from the Airfix kit.)

DUXFORD'S LIVING MUSEUM

THINGS move fast at Duxford. This report on progress there, and at the Imperial War Museum in Lambeth, London, will almost certainly be out of date before it is published. What may be awkward for authors, however, is excellent for those who want to see historic aircraft not only preserved, but restored, displayed and, where possible, flown. At the very heart of the story is an unusual and singularly British experiment. This is the link-up between a national, government-financed museum — the IWM — and a band of dedicated volunteers — the Duxford Aviation Society or DAS. If this association continues to succeed, as it has done admirably so far, the UK could be providing an example for cash-starved aeronautical collections to follow in other parts of the world.

The Duxford story really started back in 1968 when the Ministry of Defence announced that Duxford Airfield, one of the RAF's oldest bases and one which had seen more than its share of military aviation history, would soon become surplus to Service requirements. This announcement sparked off a lengthy, and occasionally heated, debate in the area over what use would be made of the site. The local County Council, for example, had in mind a regional sports and recreation centre, while the Home Office hankered after another prison. These two uninspiring schemes might in fact have succeeded but for the almost forgotten action of a certain Flt Lt Richie of No 151 Squadron, RAF, who, on the night of 8 September 1942, shot down a *Luftwaffe* Dornier Do 217. This bomber's mission had started in occupied Holland but it ended in a Cambridgeshire field. When parts of the aircraft were turned up in ploughing during 1969, a newly formed local group of air enthusiasts, the East Anglian Aviation Society, decided to excavate the remaining wreckage.

While so engaged, the EAAS came into contact with Dr Rose of the IWM, who also wanted to establish the Dornier's identity. It soon transpired that while the EAAS was interested in restoring historical aircraft, the IWM ultimately aimed to establish a flying museum. Duxford seemed to provide a prospective venue for both groups and a close liaison rapidly developed between these two unlikely partners. In 1970, they approached the County Council with their idea, and the following February the whole issue came up before a Public Enquiry. In September 1971 the IWM and EAAS won at least temporary use of the airfield and, more importantly from the preservation point of view, its hangar facilities. Meanwhile, other plans for Duxford rapidly fell by the wayside.

Aircraft now started to arrive from the IWM's scattered storage facilities, but already certain strains were appearing inside the EAAS. The bulk of its membership, based around Basingbourne, proved to be more concerned with lectures and discussions than with the field work involved at Duxford and, following discreet recommendations from the directorship of the IWM, the Duxford group quietly separated itself from the Society. The new DAS group now hoped to concentrate its efforts on the restoration and preservation of aircraft and airfield facilities, and on the building up of what would one day be a full-scale aeronautical museum.

The Duxford Aviation Society, as it is now known, has grown to have a membership of many hundreds, mostly ex-RAF personnel and including a wide variety of occupations; doctors, designers, lawyers and housewives among them. Each of the senior "technical" members, the experts, are responsible for one or two aircraft. Not only do their duties cover the maintenance of the entire IWM collection at Duxford — which seems to grow week by week — but DAS members also work under various arrangements on other aircraft based at the field. Many of these are privately-owned and have been attracted by the free hangarage facilities and (at the time of writing) lack of landing fees. This set-up makes for an astonishing variety of aircraft at Duxford, while at the same time enabling DAS membership to widen its experience and expertize.

The heart of activity at Duxford continues to be, of course, the IWM collection. The Museum's aircraft at Duxford, in store elsewhere or still in the main museum building at Lambeth, must be among the finest in Europe. With few exceptions these will eventually all go to Duxford. As always, the elderly take precedence in receiving attention. In the IWM and at Duxford, this means aircraft of Great War or World War II vintage, though it certainly does not preclude restoration work being done on the products of a later age. One particular aircraft may be taken as representative of the IWM's future hopes, and of the Duxford Aviation Society's

Duxford's Junkers Ju 52/3m came to the UK from Portugal but is an original pre-war German specimen. One of the current restoration projects at Duxford, it lacks cowlings at present.

present tasks: the R.E.8 nick-named "A Paddy Bird from Ceylon" that has been a long-standing favourite with those who have been visiting the IWM for many years.

This Great War aircraft was not in fact delivered to the RAF until after the Armistice of 1918. Having been built by Daimler, R.E.8 serial number F3556 arrived at No 1 Coventry Air Park late in October 1918, powered by an RAF 4A engine. On the last day of that month, the aircraft was flown by Lt Halstead for 30 minutes and, after having had adjustments made to the rear cables of the outer wing extensions, F3556 was passed "OK" by the Chief Technical Officer, Sgt Marsh, to be crated and sent to the British Expeditionary Force in France. Within months, it was back in England, being stored at Tadcaster for a while before being sent by rail to Crystal Palace where the recently created Imperial War Museum had its first home.

This R.E.8 did not have a very inspiring service career, having logged only a few hours flying time, but as a result it arrived at the Museum in perfect condition. Some time before

World War II, all the rigging was lacquered and this has given it excellent protection, hardly a spot of rust being found anywhere. Although the R.E.8 hung from the Museum ceiling for some decades, the aircraft's weight was sensibly supported by the main engine bearers and the undercarriage struts — hence no damage was suffered. It was, however, apparently cannibalized at least once, but the IWM is confident of being able to replace the few missing parts from its own vast stores. Some four or five years ago, RAE Farnborough tested the R.E.8's woodwork and found it to be in good condition; not even brittle. Some slight warping had taken place and thin strips along the trailing edges had been strained, even in some cases cracked, by the contraction of the fabric; a few slightly cracked ribs will also have to be clamped and glued. The engine was complete and some of the remaining instruments were still full of their original alcohol. The tyres are, however, quite beyond recall.

All things considered, the condition of this aircraft was amazingly good. When the time came to move the R.E.8, the

The "Big Beautiful Doll" is one of Duxford's most prized exhibits, and was one of the first restoration projects of the group of enthusiasts that collaborates with the IWM. A P-51D, it is in the markings of Col J D Lander, who commanded the 78th FG at Duxford.

task was naturally undertaken with some trepidation, but the machine proved very easy to dismantle, the bolts being quite clean under a thin film of rust. The fabric was, of course, rotted and replacing it will be Duxford's first priority, though the original fabric will be retained as a historical record. The Falls Flax Spinning Co Ltd of Belfast, has been asked to provide new covering to the same specification as the old. This new fabric, with almost identical warp and weft as that woven in 1918, was recommended by Maurice Brett of the Shuttleworth Collection, who supervised the R.E.8's transfer from Lambeth to Duxford.

In fact the IWM's R.E.8 was given priority over the Museum's other Great War vintage aircraft because its condition was the worst — which serves to show how good the others are. The sole exception to this was a Short 184 seaplane, severely damaged in a German air-raid of 1941. This Short, serial number 8359, though still owned by the IWM, has now gone on long-term loan to the Fleet Air Arm Museum at Yeovilton, with which the IWM maintains a close working relationship.

Almost as old as the Short seaplane, and with a similarly active war career, is the B.E.2C serial 2699. This aircraft is known to have flown in defence of London, though no dates or times were recorded. Its wings were refurbished some years ago by the RAF, and at that time superficial appearance rather than accuracy of material was the order of the day — so the aircraft's undersides were painted a cream colour. Some of its sparse instrumentation has also disappeared over the years.

In the best condition, of the Great War types in the IWM collection, is the Bristol Fighter F2B, which has had the least done to it and is original in almost all aspects, including complete instrumentation. A Camel is in similarly excellent shape, although there is doubt in some quarters as to whether the single-seater's propeller is the original. The original fabric of this machine was stripped by the RAF long ago, but continuing research on the Camel shows that the undersides were originally painted a light blue. The colours of the upper

The Duxford team has completed assembly of one B-17G acquired by Euroworld in France and brought to the UK on a low-loader as illustrated. A second similar B-17G has been presented to the IWM and awaits complete restoration.

surfaces are as yet uncertain, while the original tri-colour rudder striping appears to have gone all the way around rudder and elevators. Twin Lewis guns were also understood to have been carried on the upper wing. This particular Camel is the aircraft flown by Gp Capt Cully when he destroyed Zeppelin L53 over the North Sea on 11 August 1918 after having taken off from a towed lighter.

It will not be necessary to renew the aircraft's present fabric, but the IWM does hope to restore this Camel, serial N6812, to its original appearance. All these aircraft, with the possible exception of the Bristol Fighter, are destined for display at Duxford, but at least one aircraft must remain at the IWM itself at Lambeth to illustrate the Great War in the air, while the Second War will be represented by Spitfire I R6915. Though destined to remain in London, these aircraft will probably come down from their present positions suspended from the ceilings, to be more visible on the ground.

The other Spitfire in the Duxford story is, in fact, owned by the Shuttleworth Trust, but has been loaned to the IWM for display at Duxford where it has been meticulously restored to flying condition by volunteers of the DAS. Without doubt this Spitfire VC AR501, has been Duxford's greatest triumph to date. Built in 1942 by Westland, it flew with No 310 (Czech) Squadron from Exeter and after seeing service with various other units, had its wings "clipped" by Air Service Training in

The P-51 (opposite page) does not fly, but the Dewoitine D 26 below, one of Duxford's more unusual exhibits, does. Privately-owned by Bob Willies, it was acquired in Switzerland some years ago and is in Swiss military colours.

1944. It was then also fitted with a Merlin 45M in place of the original Merlin 46. After various vicissitudes this Spitfire was acquired by the Shuttleworth Trust, featured in the film "Battle of Britain" (which was largely filmed at Duxford) and then arrived back at Duxford in a Hercules of the Canadian Armed Forces to be completely restored. It now appears in the markings of the original unit, the Czech 310 Squadron, whose motto was, most appropriately as it transpires, "We fight to rebuild". One other somewhat mysterious Spitfire, a Mark XVI owned by a private individual, can also be seen at Duxford and may one day be restored by the Society.

Already completed by the DAS, though only restored to a superficially original appearance, is one of two B-17 Flying Fortresses bought by Capt Donald Bullock of Euroworld from the French government, after being retired by the IGN. This completed aircraft will soon probably be sold, while the second B-17 has already been donated to the IWM. Completely civilianized for its photo-survey duties in France, this particular Flying Fortress will need a great deal done to it before it can be "un-civilianized" again. It may even fly, though this is by no means certain. A second American bomber of World War II vintage that spent some time at Duxford was the B-24J Liberator, *"Delectable Doris"*. This aircraft, having flown for RAF South-East Asia Command and subsequently the Indian Air Force, was lovingly restored to the condition and colours of the 389th Bomb Group, 2nd Air Division, USAAF 8th Air Force, by DAS volunteers before flying, last August, on to its ultimate home with the Yesterday's Air Force Museum at Chino, California. A third American bomber of similar vintage is an incomplete Martin B-26 Marauder rescued a short while ago from a scrap-heap, while a fourth will be an A-26 Invader. This civilianized machine, once also owned by Euroworld, was at the time of writing in the USA ready for shipment to Duxford.

Appropriately enough, one of the Society's first works of restoration, undertaken even before the splitting up of the East Anglian Aviation Society, was a completely refurbished P-51 Mustang. Though internal corrosion ensures that this aircraft cannot fly, it now stands resplendent in the colour scheme of Col J D Lander, commander of the 78th Fighter Group of the 8th Air Force at Duxford during World War II.

Other Allied aircraft of the IWM collection which will eventually be displayed at Duxford include a Fairey Swordfish III. The engine of this aircraft, being in excellent order, was swopped for that of the Royal Navy's Swordfish to enable the Senior Service's Historic Flight aircraft to keep flying. A Flettner towed autogyro designed for use from submarines was recently "rediscovered" by the IWM's staff in their Barking store. Together with military vehicles, tanks, artillery and two MTB from the now closed Barking store, this Flettner has been delivered to Duxford. The IWM's Hawker Typhoon and its Mosquito T Mk III, which is at present "stuck on a wall" at Lambeth with a large girder impaling one wing and the fuselage, will also be sent to Cambridgeshire one day. The Mosquito's other wing and engines are already at Duxford.

Finally, there is Duxford's C-47B. This aircraft, which is believed to have flown higher and farther than any other RAF Dakota, is actually the property of the DAS, but once it has been restored and repainted in the colours of SE Asia Command it will stand with the rest of the IWM's collection.

The most obvious enemy representative at Duxford is a corrugated Junkers Ju 52/3m. A special group from the DAS has dedicated itself to work on this magnificent old war-bird, even perhaps to get one engine operating so that the aircraft can taxi for the delight of visitors. This actual machine is basically a Ju 52/3m g3e, one of ten bought by Portugal in 1937 as bombers to equip the *Grupo de Esquadrilhas Bombardeamento Nocturno*. They remained in service as transports until the mid-1960s, although over the years many alterations were made to their basic structure. The present example

may now in fact be an amalgam of two aircraft, since many of the minor parts, including a licence-built BMW engine and various components identified as having been manufactured near Paris, clearly do not come from the pre-war original.

Even more ambitious are those members of the DAS now working on the IWM's Messerschmitt Bf 109F (*Werk Nr* 14120). This is a wreck, and it will need an incredible amount of work before it even resembles an aircraft again. Beyond hope of repair are the fragments of a Heinkel He 111 retrieved from a Norwegian lake some time ago by DAS enthusiasts and almost as bad is the IWM's Mitsubishi A6M2 Zero-Sen Model 52, of which only the engine, centre-section and cockpit survive. This aircraft is still at present at Lambeth.

Externally at least, the IWM's other enemy aircraft, plus a V2 and a V1 with its launcher, are in excellent condition. Most, however, lack many instruments and internal fittings, not all of which can be replaced from the IWM's stores. One yawning gap in the collection will remain very difficult to fill, this being representative enemy aircraft of the Great War period. At present, the IWM's main building at Lambeth contains only an engine from Von Richthofen's Fokker Triplane, the rudder from an Albatros D V, and twin-Maxim guns and mountings from another Albatros, probably a D III. World War II is better served, however, with an apparently complete Me 163 Komet, a Heinkel He 162 and a superb Focke-Wulf Fw 190A-3.

Somewhat out on its own in the IWM/DAS collection is the inter-war Dewoitine D 26. This splendid little parasol monoplane retrieved from Switzerland a few years ago, still flies. It is owned by Bob Willies and, being based at Duxford, is on loan to the IWM. Also from the inter-war era is one of Duxford's latest additions, a de Havilland Dragon Rapide — actually built in 1941 by Brush Motors but never used as a Dominie by the RAF.

Post-war aircraft, both piston-engined types and jets, are numerous at Duxford — too numerous to describe here in detail. New additions turn up almost monthly; most are in flying condition but many, like the English Electric Lightning, are clearly far too expensive for the Imperial War Museum to operate, let alone the part-time volunteers of the Duxford Aviation Society.

Despite its achievements and plans for the future, a cloud does hang over the future of Duxford, in the shape of a motorway — the proposed M.11 extension to Cambridge, which would chop off the north-eastern approach to the existing main runway. The presence of the IWM at Duxford carries a great deal of weight and will certainly strengthen those fighting to save the airfield, though the Museum is quite emphatic about not wishing to dominate Duxford. The IWM needs hangar space for its reserve collection, not only aircraft but also military equipment and naval craft; it has a certain amount of cash available, while the DAS has a great deal of enthusiasm and expertize, though needing aircraft on which to exercise its members' talents. Therein lies the basis of an effective working partnership.

The IWM has a small full-time professional staff at Duxford, certain existing buildings having already been earmarked for immediate restoration as offices, etc. A close liaison is also being developed between the IWM, the Shuttleworth Trust and the Science Museum at South Kensington. If, as is at present hoped, the derelict station cinema can be revived for the showing of documentary films, an educational service centre could be established. In fact Duxford might be opened to the public on a regular basis following the Duxford Aviation Society's "Duxford Vintage Day" of vehicles and aircraft in June. Britain will then have an historical aviation centre to rival those found anywhere else in the world; not only with aircraft but also with buildings of historical interest, a wide selection of original airfield equipment and vehicles, plus much of the IWM's unparalleled archive material. □   DAVID NICOLLE

IN PRINT

"Night Intruder"
by Jeremy Howard-Williams
David & Charles, Newton Abbot, Devon,
£4·95
184 pp, 5½ in by 8½ in, illustrated
AT ONE level, this book is a personal reminiscence of the night fighting between the RAF and the Luftwaffe in World War II, written in extended diary form and providing an interesting record of this particular aspect of the air war. The book is much more than "just another war story", however, for its author was closely involved in the development of night fighting techniques and the introduction of new equipment, becoming, after an operational tour, a flight commander of the NFDW (Night Fighting Development Wing) at Ford.

Out of his wide experience, Howard-Williams is able to interpret for the reader the significance of the various events he describes, and to trace the relative merits of British and German work as each pressed ahead with radar and other aids. The use of night-fighter pilots to fly Tempests for night interception of V-1s makes an interesting chapter. All told, this is a most readable and instructive book that adds human interest to previously published accounts of radar development and the night war.

"La Grande Aventure de Concorde"
by Henri Ziegler
Bernand Grasset, Paris
192 pp, 6 in by 9¼ in, illustrated
AMONG the growing literature of the Concorde, this volume is of particular note for its authorship. Henri Ziegler became president of Sud-Aviation (now Aérospatiale) on the last day of July 1968 and for the next seven years became Concorde's most energetic salesman and devoted advocate. At times, indeed, as faith in the Concorde wavered in Britain, it seemed as though Ziegler's personality and determination alone kept the project alive.

This history of the project from its inception to certification is therefore written from a singular viewpoint; no-one is in a better position to record the difficulties that have beset Concorde from within and without, and Ziegler does not flinch from discussing the problems and the set-backs, whilst also letting his pride in Concorde's achievement show through the whole time.

Serious students of the Concorde programme, which has had a profound effect upon the French and British aerospace industries for more than a decade, will wish to add this volume to their collection—even if they require the help of a French-English dictionary!

"British Homebuilt Aircraft Since 1920"
by Ken Ellis
Merseyside Aviation Society, £1·40
110 pp, 6 in by 8¼ in, illustrated
REPRESENTING the distilled results of an intensive five years' study of the subject, this compact little booklet is an example *par excellence* of the service that the various enthusiast organisations around the country now provide in the preservation of aviation history. In commercial publishing terms, this title would have had no prospects at all; yet it

is in fact quite invaluable for anyone with a genuine interest in the history of British civil aircraft or the homebuilt aircraft movement.

Of the several sections making up the whole volume, Part Two is the largest and most important, containing a type-by-type record of all British homebuilts since 1920: the term is interpreted as widely as possible, to include the products of small companies, as well as individuals, when there was no specific intention to put the type into series production, and the listing appears to be thorough and comprehensive. This alone would justify the book's inclusion in any reference library devoted to British aircraft: but there is more: a unique listing, for example, of all the Poux du Ciel (Flying Fleas) built or started in Britain between 1935 and 1939 (not all were given a civil registration and many have therefore escaped previous listings). Other sections list gliders, balloons and man-powered aircraft and there are useful appendices. Homebuilt gyroplanes are excluded, the author remarking that they need a work to themselves; this minor exception accepted, "British Homebuilt Aircraft Since 1920" cannot be too highly recommended in its particular field of interest.

Copies are available, at the price of £1·40 including postage, from the MAS Publications Department, 4 Willow Green, Liverpool, L25 4RR.

"EAA 'How To' Series"
EAA Air Museum Foundation Inc, USA
Motor Books & Accessories, London
THE WORK of the Experimental Aircraft Association in promoting the home-built aircraft movement in the USA is well-known, and its annual fly-in, originally at Rockford and now at Oshkosh, is world-famous for the variety and quantity of amateur-built aircraft it attracts. Other aspects of the EAA's work include the creation and maintenance of an excellent museum at Hales Corner, Wisconsin, publication of the monthly "Sport Aviation" and a range of other publications for the amateur constructor.

Readers in the UK and Europe may like to know that most EAA publications are now available from Motor Books & Accessories, at 33 St Martin's Court, St Martin's Lane, London, WC2. The range includes over two dozen titles in the "How To" series, details of

which can be obtained from Motor Books; in addition, *Sport Aviation,* which each month contains many articles and illustrations about the latest amateur designs, can be bought on an individual basis, or by subscription.

"A Very Special Lancaster"
by F E Dymond
Pitkin Pictorials Ltd, for RAF Museum 50p
32 pp, 7½ in by 8½ in, illustrated
AVRO Lancaster 1, R5868, is the Royal Air Force Museum's largest and, for many visitors, most popular aircraft exhibit. It is a worthy example of the most successful heavy bomber used by the Royal Air Force during the war of 1939-45 — worthy indeed, as very few bombers equalled R5868's remarkable record of 137 operational sorties.

The foregoing is the first paragraph in this booklet that sets out to record the history of R5868 — culled from its log book and given flesh and bone by the sympathetic and meticulous text of Mr Dymond. For good measure, the book contains colour reproduction of the crests of Nos 83 and 457 Squadrons, with which R5868 served; a colour photograph of the cockpit, a reproduction of J H Clark's original cutaway drawing of the Lancaster, two colour profiles of the Lancaster at different stages of its career, several half-tone photographs and a complete log of R5868's operational flying, quoting date, crew, bomb load and target.

It is to be hoped that this excellent and modestly priced volume will serve as the prototype for others dealing with more of the Museum's exhibits.

"Operation Nightfall"
by John Miles and Toni Morris
Souvenir Press, London, £3·25
210 pp, 8½ in by 5¼ in
A VERY readable novel, with plenty of action and an authentic background of airport operations and light aircraft flying. The plot's original, too, with four professional pilots and a couple of accomplices holding an airport to ransom as they fly three Cherokees overhead, each with enough explosive on board to give their threats teeth. They collect $3 million from airlines at the airport. Read the book to discover whether they get away with their masterplan!

The captured Messerschmitt Me 410A seen in company with a Mosquito NF Mk XVII — a photograph from the highly-recommended "Night Intruder" by Jeremy Howard-Williams, who was flying the Me 410 when this picture was taken.

PLANE FACTS

The French "Burnelli"

I am enclosing a photograph of an aircraft that I cannot identify. Can you please identify the aircraft depicted and publish details in your 'Plane Facts' column?

Philippe Aimar,
94 300 Vincennes, France

The aircraft depicted by your photograph (reproduced on this page), *Monsieur* Aimar, is the Dyle et Bacalan DB 10 Bn4 experimental twin-engined four-seat night bomber of 1925. The Société Anonyme des Travaux Dyle et Bacalan, an important naval dockyard in Bordeaux, entered the aircraft industry in 1925, its first product being the DB 10, which, built to the designs of Ing Létang, appeared in the same year and was exhibited at the *Salon de l'Aéronautique* in Paris in 1926. The DB 10 was particularly interesting in that it employed the "lifting fuselage" concept — the bulk of the fuselage possessing an aerofoil section and contributing substantially to total lift — which was being developed simultaneously (and apparently independently) in the USA by Vincent J Burnelli.

The DB 10 was of all-metal construction and powered by two 480 hp Gnôme-Rhône Jupiter nine-cylinder air-cooled radial engines attached to the extremities of the aerofoil-section fuselage. Pilot and co-pilot were accommodated by separate tandem cockpits, a gunner was accommodated in an open turret over the leading edge of the central wing section, twin Lewis guns being mounted on a Scarff ring, and the navigator's compartment was contained within the wing centre section. An internal bomb load of 2,866 lb (1 300 kg) was carried.

The performance of the DB 10 included a max speed of 118 mph (190 km/h), a max cruise of 107 mph (173 km/h) at 13,125 ft (4 000 m) and a service ceiling of 18,045 ft (5 500 m). Empty and loaded weights were 6,944 lb (3 150 kg) and 12,346 lb (5 600 kg) respectively, and overall dimensions were: span 82 ft 0¼ in (25,00 m), length, 44 ft 7⅞ in (13,60 m), height, 12 ft 5⅜ in (3,80 m), wing area, 1,001·04 sq ft (93,00 m²).

Switzerland's "Jet Stork"

While perusing some mid-'sixties issues of a British aviation weekly, I came across a reference to the Swiss FFA P-16 fighter, the development of which was abandoned by the Swiss government in 1958. Can you possibly

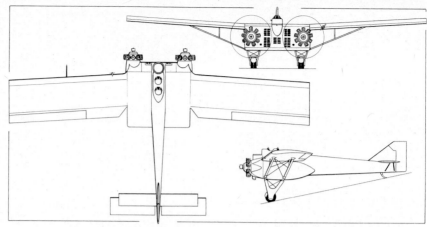

(Above and below) The Dyle et Bacalan DB 10 Bn4 experimental night bomber of 1925 which employed the 'lifting fuselage' concept. The photograph reproduced below is that accompanying Monsieur Aimar's letter.

provide details of the origins, development and reasons for cancellation of this aircraft?

Graham Rush
Acton, London W3

During the late 'forties, a project design team led by Dr-Ing Hans L Stüder at the Flug- und Fahrzeugwerke AG (FFA) of Altenrhein was engaged in a number of comparative studies with the aim of producing a transonic single-seat attack fighter capable of operating from short runways situated in high-altitude valleys, prerequisites being short take-off and landing distances, small turning radii and good low-speed handling. By 1949, three projects were being studied, the P-14.02, the P-15.01 and the P-16.01, the last-mentioned being selected for further development and becoming the subject of a contract placed on 24 July 1952 for two prototypes, these being designated P-16.04.

The P-16.04 featured a multi-spar low aspect

ratio (3·88) wing swept 20 deg on the leading edge, and carrying full-span leading-edge flaps rotating through 120 deg and large-area Fowler-type trailing-edge flaps, which, with a max travel of 45 deg, operated in conjunction with the ailerons. Fuel was accommodated in two non-jettisonable 208 Imp gal (945 l) wingtip tanks, which, acting as endplates, fed into a 133 Imp gal (605 l) collector tank in the fuselage, and power was provided by a 7,900 lb (3 583 kg) Armstrong Siddeley Sapphire ASSa 6 turbojet. The first prototype (J-3001) was flown by Lt Häfliger of the Federal Military Department on 28 April 1955, and quickly demonstrated remarkable shortfield characteristics which resulted in it being dubbed unofficially the *Dusenstorch* (Jet Stork). Unfortunately, after a public demonstration on 4 July 1955, a stone thrown up from the runway fractured the hydraulic brake supply line, the brakes failing and the undercarriage being written off when the aircraft ran across a railway track. The aircraft was repaired and resumed its test programme, but on its 22nd test flight on 31 August, Häfliger had to eject when a fatigue failure in the tank pressurization line resulted in a blow-out, the aircraft crashing in Lake Constance, having flown only 12 hr 38 min.

On the same day that the first prototype P-16.04 crashed, the FFA received a contract for a pre-series of four aircraft which were to embody various changes envisaged for the production model. The second prototype P-16.04 (J-3002) was flown on 16 June 1956, this differing from its predecessor primarily in having extended engine air intakes, large perforated air brakes attached to the sides of the aft fuselage, a parabrake housing over the

The first prototype P-16 attack fighter which flew for the first time on 28 April 1955 but crashed during its 22nd test flight on 31 August 1955 as a result of a fatigue failure in a tank pressurization line.

materialised and the flight test programme finally terminated on 26 June 1960, although some five years later, an attempt was to be made to resurrect the design with a Rolls-Royce Spey 250 (as the AR-7) or the General Electric J79-GE-11A (as the AJ-7).

The P-16 Mk III carried an armament of two 30-mm Hispano-Suiza 825 cannon with 120 rpg and a Matra 1000 launcher for 44 68-mm folding-fin rockets. This internal armament could be supplemented by external ordnance loads of up to 4,940 lb (2 240 kg). Performance included a max speed of M = 0·92 at 26,245 ft (8 000 m) — the maximum speed attained during testing was M = 1·1 in inclined flight — and an initial climb rate of 12,795 ft/min (65 m/sec). Range with 550 Imp gal (2 500 l) of fuel internally was 920 miles (1 480 km) at 36,090 ft (11 000 m), take-off and landing distances were both 547 yards (500 m), stalling speed was 115 mph (185 km/h) and minimum turn radius was 1,150 ft (350 m). Empty weight was 15,520 lb (7 040 kg), normal loaded weight was 20,503 lb (9 300 kg) and max overload weight was 25,838 lb (11 720 kg). Overall dimensions were as follows: span, 36 ft 7 in (11,14 m); length, 46 ft 11 in (14,30 m); height, 13 ft 11¾ in (4,25 m); wing area, 322·92 sq ft (30,00 m²).

The fourth example of the P-16 (X-HB-VAC), illustrated above and below, was the first in the series to be completed to definitive Mk III standards and flew for the first time on 8 July 1959. An order for 100 P-16 Mk III attack fighters was cancelled by the Swiss government shortly after being placed.

tailpipe and cannon armament. The very thorough test programme conducted with this aircraft — which was to accumulate 130 hr 37 min flying time in 310 flights by 7 March 1958 — was adjudged completely successful, and on 15 April 1957 it was joined by the third aircraft (J-3003), which, referred to as the P-16 Mk II, was powered by the 11,000 lb (4 990 kg) Sapphire ASSa 7 which was intended as the engine for the definitive P-16 Mk III.

In March 1958, the Swiss Parliament passed an order for 100 P-16 Mk III fighters — the placing of the order by no means receiving universal approbation and following much lobbying — but on the 25th of that month, the third aircraft crashed in Lake Constance after suffering a fatigue failure in the hydraulic system which resulted in a sudden transfer to manual control during a landing approach. The pilot failed to trim the aircraft correctly and ejected at 1,000 ft (305 m). The aircraft had flown a total of 50 hr 7 min during 102 flights prior to the accident. An investigation team appointed by the *Kriegstechniscke Abteilung* pronounced that the servo control system would have to be redesigned and the Swiss government promptly cancelled the entire development and production programme, citing as its reason the unacceptable delay in deliveries that would inevitably ensue if the servo system had to be redesigned.

Nevertheless, while endeavouring to persuade the Swiss government to reinstate P-16 production, the FFA continued development as a private venture, forming the AG für Flugzeugunternehmungen Altenrhein in the spring of 1959 specifically for this task and completing the fourth (X-HB-VAC) and fifth (X-HB-VAD) aircraft to P-16 Mk III standards, the first of these flying on 8 July

1959 and the second on 24 March 1960, subsequently flying 27 hr 25 min in 55 flights and 7 hr 14 min in 19 flights respectively. However, no customer for the P-16 Mk III

(Immediately above and above right) The fifth P-16 (X-HB-VAD) which flew for the first time only three months before the entire development programme was abandoned. (Below) The general arrangement drawing depicts the definitive P-16 Mk III.

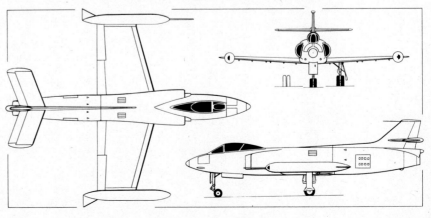

CURTISS HAWK III   USA

The export version of the BF2C-1, the Hawk III, differed from the US Navy fighter-bomber in reverting to the wooden wing structure of the F11C-2 (spruce beams with plywood webs and spruce ribs) and in having a Wright SR-1820F-53 Cyclone offering 785 hp for take-off and 745 hp at 9,600 ft (2 925 m). Gun armament comprised two synchronised 0·3-in (7,62-mm) weapons. The first export of the Hawk III was a single example to Turkey delivered in April 1935, deliveries of 24 to Thailand following from August 1935. In March 1936, the first of a total of 102 Hawk IIIs was delivered to China, 90 of these being assembled at the Central Government Aircraft Factory at Hangchow, and one other purchaser of the Hawk III was Argentina which took delivery of 10 from May 1936. The last-mentioned country also purchased the sole example of the Hawk IV in July 1936, this using a Hawk III airframe, a full sliding cockpit canopy, carburettor heating and an exhaust collector ring for the SR-1820F-56 Cyclone which delivered its maximum 745 hp at 12,500 ft (3 810 m). The Hawk IV attained 248 mph (399 km/h) at 12,500 ft (3 810 m) and 242 mph (390

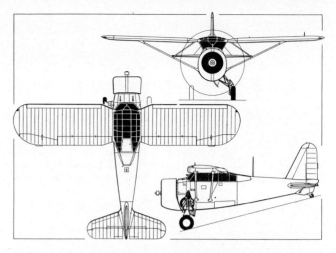

(Above and immediately below) The XF13C in its initial monoplane form (XF13C-1) in which it was tested by the US Navy for a year.

(Above) One of the total of 102 Hawk IIIs supplied to China, the majority of which were assembled by the Central Government Aircraft factory.

(Below) The XF13C in sesquiplane configuration (XF13C-2) in which it was flown briefly by the manufacturer before permanently adopting monoplane configuration.

(Above and below) The XF12C-1 with the single-row Cyclone engine and definitive engine cowling as tested by the US Navy in October 1933.

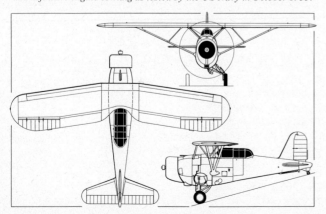

km/h) at 16,400 ft (5 000 m). The following data relate to the standard Hawk III. Max speed, 202 mph (325 km/h) at sea level, 240 mph (387 km/h) at 11,500 ft (3 505 m). Initial climb, 2,200 ft/min (11,18 m/sec). Normal range, 575 mls (925 km). Empty weight, 3,213 lb (1 457 kg). Loaded weight, 4,317 lb (1 958 kg). Span, 31 ft 6 in (9,60 m). Length, 23 ft 5 in (7,14 m). Height, 9 ft 9½ in (2,98 m). Wing area, 262 sq ft (24,34 m²).

CURTISS XF12C-1   USA

Based on a US Navy Bureau of Aeronautics design for a two-seat fighter, the XF12C-1 all-metal parasol monoplane ordered on 30 June 1932 featured aft-folding wings with leading-edge slats and trailing-edge flaps, and manually-operated retractable main undercarriage members. Completed in January 1933, the XF12C-1 was initially powered by a Wright R-1510-92 two-row radial rated at 625 hp at 6,000 ft (1 830 m). By the time it was tested by the US Navy in October 1933, the Twin Whirlwind engine had been replaced by a Wright SR-1820-80 Cyclone single-row radial and with the discarding of the two-seat fighter category it was redesignated XS4C-1 in December 1933 and XSBC-1 in January 1934 as a scout-bomber. It crashed during a preliminary demonstration on 14 June 1934, subsequently being replaced by the XSBC-2 biplane. The following data relate to the XF12C-1 with the R-1510-92 engine. Max speed, 217 mph (349 km/h) at 6,000 ft (1 830 m). Normal range, 738 mls (1 188 km). Empty weight, 3,884 lb (1 762 kg). Normal loaded weight, 5,461 lb (2 477 kg). Span, 41 ft 6 in (12,65 m). Length, 29 ft 1 in (8,86 m). Height, 12 ft 11 in (3,94 m). Wing area, 272 sq ft (25,27 m²).

CURTISS XF13C   USA
Perhaps the most unusual single-seat fighter developed by Curtiss was the model 70 which was designed from the outset to be flown either as a monoplane or as a biplane with the minimum of structural change. A metal semi-monocoque aircraft with fabric-covered wings, it was ordered on 23 November 1932 as the XF13C powered by a Wright SGR-1510-2 two-row radial rated at 600 hp at 10,000 ft (3 050 m), the designation XF13C-1 being assigned to it for test in monoplane form and XF13C-2 in biplane (or more strictly, sesquiplane) form. It was initially flown in December 1933 as a biplane, flying in monoplane form a month later and being delivered to the US Navy as the XF13C-1 on 10 February 1934. Featuring a manually-operated retractable undercarriage, an enclosed cockpit, retractable upper wing leading-edge slats and trailing-edge flaps, the XF13C did not revert to biplane standard but in February 1935 was returned to Curtiss for various modifications, including installation of an XR-1510-12 engine affording 700 hp at 7,000 ft (2 135 m), and with these changes was redesignated XF13C-3. In biplane configuration, the XF13C was 19 mph (30 km/h) slower than as a monoplane but possessed a shorter take-off run and better low-speed characteristics. Trials were terminated in October 1935, primarily owing to lack of engine spares. The following data relate to the fighter in XF13C-3 configuration. Max speed, 232 mph (373 km/h) at 7,000 ft (2 135 m). Time to 5,000 ft (1 525 m), 2·5 min. Endurance, 5·2 hrs. Loaded weight, 4,721 lb (2142 kg). Span, 35 ft 0 in (10,67 m). Length, 25 ft 9½ in (7,86 m). Height, 12 ft 9 in (3,88 m). Wing area, 205 sq ft (19,04 m²).

CURTISS MODEL 75   USA
Designed by Donovan R Berlin to participate in a USAAC fighter contest scheduled to take place on 27 May 1935, the Model 75 (the retroactive assignment of Model numbers to earlier designs being attempted at this time and the new fighter being the first design to receive a model designation from the outset) all-metal single-seat fighter was initiated in October 1934, flying mid-April 1935. Featuring a monocoque fuselage and a multi-spar wing, the Model 75 was powered by a 900 hp Wright XR-1670-5 14-cylinder two-row radial, proposed armament comprising one 0·5-in (12,7-mm) and one 0·3-in (7,62-mm) machine gun. The unsatisfactory behaviour of the Wright engine resulted in its replacement by a Pratt & Whitney R-1535 Twin Wasp Junior, but this, too, proved troublesome and was succeeded by a 950 hp Wright XR-1820-39 (G5) Cyclone nine-cylinder radial with which the prototype became the Model 75B. During USAAC trials, the Model 75B took second place to the Seversky SEV-1XP which was to enter

The Model 75B with Wright Cyclone engine as flown in the USAAC single-seat fighter contest.

(Above) One of the 30 P-36Cs built against the original contract and (below) the XP-36F with underwing 23-mm Danish Madsen cannon.

production as the P-35. The following data relate to the Model 75B. Max speed, 285 mph (459 km/h) at 10,000 ft (3 050 m). Time to 10,000 ft (3 050 m), 3·87 min. Range, 730 mls (1 175 km). Empty weight, 4,049 lb (1 837 kg). Loaded weight, 5,075 lb (2 302 kg). Span, 37 ft 3½ in (11,37 m). Length, 28 ft 1 in (8,56 m). Height, 9 ft 0 in (2,74 m). Wing area, 232 sq ft (21,55 m²).

CURTISS P-36   USA
Despite USAAC choice of the SEV-1XP in favour of the Model 75B, the Curtiss fighter was considered to possess sufficient merit to warrant an order being placed on 7 August 1936 for three evaluation examples powered by the Pratt & Whitney R-1830-13 Twin Wasp 14-cylinder radial rated at 900 hp at 12,000 ft (3 660 m), these being assigned the designation Y1P-36 (later changed to P-36) and the first being completed in February 1937. Successful trials resulted, on 7 July 1937, in a contract for 210 essentially similar P-36As, the first being delivered in April 1938. Armament comprised one 0·5-in (12,7-mm) and one 0·3-in (7,62-mm) gun, and the 15th and subsequent aircraft standardised on the R-1830-17 engine in place of the -13, the 20th being temporarily fitted with a 1,100 hp R-1830-25 as the P-36B (later reverting to P-36A standards). The fourth and tenth airframes were converted as the XP-42 and XP-40 respectively, the 85th made provision for an additional 0·3-in (7,62-mm) gun in each wing, the last 30 aircraft built against the original contract being completed to a similar standard as P-36Cs. The 174th airframe was fitted in 1939 with four belt-fed wing-mounted 0·3-in (7,62-mm) guns and two fuselage-mounted 0·5-in (12,7-mm) weapons as the XP-36D, the 147th airframe being modified to take eight wing-mounted 0·3-in (7,62-mm) guns and the 172nd airframe becoming the XP-36F when twin fuselage-mounted 0·5-in (12,7-mm) weapons were combined with two underwing 23-mm Danish Madsen cannon. During 1942-43, the USAAF was to purchase 30 survivors of 36 Hawk 75A-8s (Wright GR-1820-G205A Cyclone 9) originally ordered by the Norwegian government and subsequently used by the Norwegian flying training centre in Canada, these being assigned the designation P-36G and 28 being transferred to Peru under Lend-Lease. The following data relate to the P-36C but are typical for all models. Max speed, 311 mph (500 km/h) at 10,000 ft (3 050 m). Time to 15,000 ft (4 570 m), 4·9 min. Range, 820 mls (1 320 km) at 200 mph (322 km/h). Empty weight, 4,620 lb (2 095 kg). Normal loaded weight, 5,800 lb (2 631 kg). Span, 37 ft 3½ in (11,37 m). Length, 28 ft 6 in (8,69 m). Height, 12 ft 2 in (3,71 m). Wing area, 236 sq ft (21,92 m²).

eventually with production of the Mk I and the planned batch of Mk IIs.

This single Mk II became the only specimen of the Welkin to appear at a public event when it was displayed at the first post-war SBAC Display, held at Radlett in 1946; existence of the Welkin had, in fact, only been officially revealed in June 1945, the type having remained on the "Restricted" List for most of its flying life. For a time, the Welkin II was used by Westland on various tasks associated with pressure cabin development — which had become a major preoccupation for the Westland subsidiary Normalair — during which time it bore the marking P-17, before returning to Ministry of Supply ownership for a series of radar trials, when it acquired yet another identity as WE997.

In the course of 1945, Westland fitted Merlin 113/114 engines in one of the production Welkin 1s, and the prototype DG562 flew for a time with RM16SM engines and beard radiators replacing the wing root installation, gaining 11 mph (18 km/h) over the normal top speed in this guise. One other power plant trial concerned the use of liquid oxygen injection to the engines, also conducted on the second prototype. The highly unstable LOX was difficult to handle but, fed to the engines from a special tank replacing the rear fuselage fuel tank, it provided a valuable source of oxygen at high altitudes and boosted both the ceiling and the speed.

Two Welkin Is reached the RAF's Fighter Interception Unit at Wittering in May 1944, but remained for only two months, when the trials were terminated — indicating that official interest in the Welkin was virtually at an end. Among the pilots responsible for testing the Welkin at FIU was Flt Lt Jeremy Howard-Williams, whose diary for 8 May* reads as follows: "Altitude climb in the Welkin. I get to 40,000 ft (12 200m) in 19 min, which is a minute less than I took to get to 30,000 ft (9 150 m) in a Mossie Mk IX with Bill Maguire the other day — and we thought we were doing well then! They'd get a better performance from the Welkin if they didn't load it down with a

*Quoted from "Night Intruder" by J Howard-Williams, published by David & Charles, Newton Abbott, Devon.

lot of unnecessary weight. They were so proud of the ¼-in armour plate behind the pilot's seat when we saw over the factory. But who's going to shoot at you from behind when you're at angels forty? Certainly not a Ju 86P; we hope we'll be behind him. It is a clear day and, from 43,000 ft (13 115 m) over the middle of England, I can see the North Sea on one side and the Irish Sea on the other at the same time.

"The elevator trim is electrically operated so that the control can pass through the wall of the pressurised cockpit, and it fails to trim tail heavy. I don't discover this until I have wound on quite a bit of nose-heavy trim experimentally; my arm is aching by the time I have lost all that height hauling back on the stick all the way down."

The FIU was the nearest the Welkin got to RAF service. Apart from the two that went to Wittering and those used by Westland and at Boscombe Down, plus one or two used at the RAE Farnborough and by Rotol at Staverton for propeller development, the Welkin 1s coming off the Yeovil production line were mostly flown direct to No 5 MU at Kemble or No 18 MU at Dumfries (RAF Tinwald Downs). Occasionally test flown, they were stored in the open — some being moved from 18 MU to No 25 SLG (satellite landing ground) at Haddington before eventually being broken up in 1949-50. The last Welkin I to serve a useful purpose was DX330, one of the Rotol testbeds, which was scrapped at Staverton in August 1947.

During 1945, the production order for 60 Mk IIs was cancelled and the order for Mk Is, then standing at 238 (two airframes having been assigned to Mk II prototypes) was reduced to 75. However, the flow of components was such that Westland was allowed to go on completing airframes (less engines) beyond this point, the final production total being two prototypes, 75 production Mk Is (of which one became a Mk II) and 26 which were delivered minus engines. Never having fired its guns in anger or reached the point of equipping an operational unit, the Welkin lays small claim to fame as one of the significant aircraft of World War II — yet as the RAF's first production fighter to feature a pressure cabin, it has its place in history, and the experience of pressure cabin design that it provided was of value to Westland and the future of British aircraft development alike. □

Viewed from the Cockpit

by Harold J. Penrose, OBE

(formerly chief test pilot, Westland Aircraft Ltd)

LOG BOOKS, Pilot's Notes, Flight Reports and Technical Memos of war-time vintage vanished amid the clearance of 42 years' accumulation of paper work when I retired from Westland. I must rely on memory to give an impression of the Welkin — a name that conjures overwhelming recollection of vast vistas viewed from stratospheric heights which few men had previously attained yet now have become commonplace.

At the time I made the first flight of the prototype Welkin, the Battle of Britain had virtually been over for a year. Though there were still occasional intruders on hit-and-run daylight

raids, the weight of German attack concentrated on night bombing. Because of the complexity of aircraft identification and radar plotting, let along the intensity of terse W/T chatter, Welkin high flying was permitted only with due notification on the clearest days, and I flew in radio silence except for an occasional transmission to enable the flight plotters to fix my position. Often I would switch off the radio for 15 minutes or so, to be enfolded in what seemed sublime quietness, the dull note of the compressor and the growling of engines so familiar that they were forgotten. It was a bitter winter, but the cabin was warm and I flew with sunlight glowing through the window. Far away north, as I climbed, I might on occasion even see the twin estuaries of Dee and Mersey; or westward the entire peninsular of Cornwall might be framed in the bullet-proof front panel of my windscreen; and once, like a blue shadow beyond the glittering expanse of the English Channel, I saw the remote and hostile coast of Normandy, little dreaming that it would be the venue of a later epic of British landings. Mostly I flew west. The shadowed russet folds of Exmoor seemed as though a giant hand had crushed the skin of the land by pushing it from the south until it fell into alternate gentle slopes and steep drops which looked like a carelessly flung pile of ruffled velvet. Then, as I lifted higher, came Cornwall, projecting into the imperceptibly blended void of sky and sea like a wedge breaking the force of the waves before they battered the mainland of England. I would stare down at the onward roll of what seemed a vast impersonal force that was the very spirit of the waters — solemn, awe-inspiring, endless. But when I looked upward into the still vaster emptiness of the dark stratosphere I saw that, after all, the immensity of oceans was finite and circumscribed — for here, all around me and beyond imagination's furthest reach, was the infinity of a cosmography from which still vaster powers poured down upon man's little realm of land and ocean. Yet play of thought in this visual experience was no more than a subconscious background to the demands of testing. Except for a barograph there was no recording apparatus. All performance and engine data had to be written on a pad. Opening to full power, I would make a speed run, blind now to all else, aware only of the instruments, the increased roar of the engines and glare of the sun.

As a consequence of his ingenious design of the Lysander and the advanced structure of the Whirlwind, 32-year-old Teddy Petter had established himself as an oncoming and important designer whose concepts were far from commonplace. As a result he had been invited to formulate a design to the F.4/40 specification for a single-seat, fully armoured fighter, capable of climbing to heights giving a substantial margin of superiority over anything which the Germans might send over in the next few years; subsequently, to revised specification F.7/41, it was also an insurance against failure of the gamble on the novel turbine-jet propulsion to be utilized in the Gloster Meteor that was currently being designed.

A minimum altitude of 40,000 ft (12 200 m) was specified for the Westland machine, which was to be powered by two of the 1,290 hp Rolls-Royce Merlin 61 two-stage supercharged engines which were then being developed. A scaled-up version of the Whirlwind was indicated. A much higher aspect ratio would reduce the induced drag and therefore benefit climb analogously to the reduced rate of sink resulting from a sailplane's long wings. The major initial exercise was to determine the optimum aspect ratio for minimum structural weight, and the latter factor of course necessitated prior conception in extensive detail of the proposed structural system, so several layouts had to be drawn and analysed. Eventually a span of 70 ft (21,35 m) was selected with an aspect ratio (span² over area) of 10·6. It was calculated that this would result in a ceiling of 45,000 ft (13 725 m) at full load of 17,500 lb (6 935 kg), carrying four fixed 20-mm Hispano cannon. The crux would be the system of pressurization and design of a pressure cabin for the pilot.

Bill Widgery, the aerodynamicist who was in charge of all Westland's basic laboratory work at Yeovil, had a year or so earlier noted a description of the pressurization system used experimentally by Boeing for their Stratoliner in 1938 which had rubber gaskets sealing doors and windows and an aneroid capsule-operated spring-loaded discharge valve to hold constant pressure from an exhaust-turbo centrifugal blower. With Petter's interested approval, Widgery modified a standard altimeter to secure a similar result, and bench tests in a small air-exhausted Perspex chamber were sufficiently promising for Westland to secure an Air Ministry contract to modify a standard Spitfire fitted with a compressor. The modification was crudely made, sealing all cockpit air leaks with Bostik compound, and fitting the hood with a detachable section above the pilot's head, made air-tight with an inflatable gasket surround devised by Dunlop. Whether I flew this machine just before the war or in 1940 is beyond recollection, but this experiment must have increased the Air Ministry's confidence in Petter's proposed system for the Welkin.

After establishing the main parameters of the F.4/40, the usual wind-tunnel model was made to confirm the relative efficiencies of low wing and mid wing positions, and on settling for the latter there was similar experimentation to locate the tailplane clear of the wake from wings and flaps, resulting in a lower position than the Whirlwind's. Several sizes of tailplane were tested to measure the pitching moments and ensure

An early production Welkin I (the fifth aircraft, in fact) flying on test from Boscombe Down in November 1943. The day fighter colours (green and grey upper surfaces, light grey undersides) gave way to an overall blue finish on later Welkins — see page 76.

longitudinal stability, and similarly for the fin and rudder. More experiments were required to secure the effectiveness of the curiously shaped concave noses of the controls which ended in a rubber lip touching the arc-ed shroud of the fixed surface ahead. For the first flight the rudder had a horn balance based on that of the Whirlwind, though differing in having a central instead of off-set rudder hinge.

As always, by the time of the first flight every detail of the machine, except its span, had become familiar from sitting in the cockpit of the mock-up, and the evolution of the various auxiliary services had been followed up in the Drawing Office, which conveniently had transferred to near my home. There were also innumerable discussions with the RAF and RAE personnel, and the manufacturers of various components such as the undercarriage, propeller and engine, particularly in respect of cooling for the latter.

Preluded by several days of engine running and adjustments on Yeovil aerodrome, all was eventually ready for the first flight on 1 November 1942 in a gentle west wind — for an easterly might have caused delay because of the inadvisability of taking off across the town with an untried machine and powerplant. The usual crowd gathered rather anxiously, and I could see Teddy Petter peering from his window two floors up in the red brick office block midway along the factory frontage.

The machine ran in a well-sprung fashion and manoeuvred easily on the ground. Two full length runs were made for general familiarization and to judge effectiveness of elevators and rudder. From the cockpit, the wing span certainly seemed imposing. Then, with hood shut, the as yet unnamed Welkin was taxied to the east end of the aerodrome, turned, and a take-off made in remarkably short distance, followed by a climb to 5,000 ft (1 525 m) during which the controls were tentatively tried; then again in level flight when it was immediately found that the machine was directionally snaking if feet were taken off the rudder bar. Otherwise, controls seemed good, but the cabin was very hot and the heat increased when I turned the control handle on the starboard side of the seat to 'Pressure after closing Coupé', which not only began to pressurize the cabin but sent heated air into the cavity between the outer and inner windscreen glasses and between the double skins of the hood panels. However, the gaskets inflated as intended and the pressure maintained its differential as I climbed. By the time I returned for my landing circuit I was wet through from the intense heat, for it was as though one sat in a chair beside an open oven door. When I reported this to Petter after an easy landing and short run, he seemed remarkably unconcerned but I had to strip off my clothes and dry them on a radiator. It was the machine's performance which interested him and not that of the pilot — a matter long perceived by the A & AEE pilots responsible for assessing his earlier designs. Brilliant though he was, learning to fly had proved beyond him and his studious orientation debarred him from all athletic sports.

Succeeding flights in the F.4/40 prototype were chiefly

aimed at confirming that the machine attained its calculated performance, but it was a little down on speed. After each flight to high altitude I arrived back soaking with perspiration, for the cockpit temperature, due to heat of compressing the cockpit air, was higher than the Persian Gulf. Nothing was done about it. Came a day of bitter winter winds which struck me as I clambered from the machine to discuss matters of adjustment with the ground crew and pneumonia followed — luckily ameliorated by the recently discovered drug M & B. This complication certainly emphasized that the cockpit was dangerously hot and led to better cooling of the compressor and introduction of cold air to the cockpit. It also gave an opportunity to run further wind-tunnel tests, resulting in removal of the rudder horn balance and replacement with an inset sealed nose similar in design to the other controls. Drag tests with extended engine nacelles also showed a reduction, and the machine was therefore appropriately modified.

During the preceding tests near ceiling it had been found on some days that speed runs, after starting smoothly, suddenly suffered a novel type of vibration in which the wings and fuselage shook as though the machine was sliding along cobble-stones. On one of his routine visits to Westland, the Assistant Director of Technical Development, N E Rowe (known as 'Nero' to those who had worked with him at Martlesham when he was CTO), recognized that this was a new atmospheric phenomena, and asked for further investigation of what later became known as 'upper air turbulence'. The risk was that it might upset accurate aiming, but I found that it afforded an even more lethal snag when diving trials commenced after final establishment of controls, engine and propeller behaviour. The normal procedure is, of course, to increase diving speeds incrementally until the limiting condition is reached. A number of these were made quite smoothly, but on the fastest there was a sudden

Westland Welkin Cockpit Instrumentation Key

1 Three-way cock (fuselage tank)
2 Flaps lowering lever
3 Undercarriage emergency lowering lever
4 Undercarriage operating lever
5 Beam approach and landing lamp switches
6 Supercharger control switch
7 Positive coarse pitch stops
8 Friction adjusters
9 Propeller control levers
10 Slow-running cut-out control (port)
11 Junction boxes
12 Peg for harness leg-strap
13 Fuel tank instruction plate
14 Trim-tab motor switchbox
15 Throttle levers
16 Map case
17 Fuel cock switches
18 Booster push-buttons
19 Oil dilution push-buttons
20 Engine starting push-buttons
21 Compass card holder
22 Radio controller
23 Supercharger warning lamp
24 Magneto switches
25 Aileron and rudder tab position indicators
26 Elevator tab and flaps position indicators
27 Clock
28 Undercarriage position indicator
29 Engine speed-limitations plate
30 Undercarriage warning lamp (with test switch immediately above)
31 Lamp
32 Remote contactor
33 Gunsight switch
34 Gunsight socket
35 Cockpit lamp switch
36 Gunsight master switch
37 Gunsight mounting
38 Lamp
39 Oxygen regulator gauges
40 Compass lamp switch
41 Cockpit lamp switch
42 Compass lamp
43 ASI
44 Artificial horizon (partially obscured by grip)
45 Rate of climb/descent indicator
46 Altimeter
47 Direction indicator (partially obscured by grip)
48 Turning indicator
49 Gun and camera firing switches (on grip)
50 Brake lever
51 Rudder bar adjuster
52 Compass (partially obscured by column)
53 General data card plates (on glove box cover)
54 Rudder pedals
55 Control column
56 Pilot's seat

57 Engine fire-extinguisher push-buttons
58 Boost gauges
59 Engine speed indicators
60 Oil inlet temperature gauges
61 Oil pressure gauges
62 Fuselage fuel-tank pump warning lamp
63 Radiator temperature gauges
64 Canopy sliding hood operating handle
65 Generator warning lamp
66 Identification lamp switchbox
67 Remote contactor plug and socket
68 Lamp
69 Identification lamp selector switch

70 Wedge plate for camera indicator
71 Pneumatic high-pressure gauge
72 Brake triple-pressure gauge
73 Footage indicator plug stowage
74 Peg for harness leg-strap
75 Slow-running cut-out control (starboard)
76 Air temperature gauge
77 Voltmeter
78 Cabin pressure warning lamp
79 Suction pump gauge
80 Recognition lamps switch
81 Demolition push-buttons
82 Fuel contents gauges

83 Map case
84 ARI 525 switches
85 Pressure head, R/T supply, R/T contactor switches
86 Navigation lamps switch
87 Camera switch
88 Suction pump change-over cock
89 Junction boxes
90 Rounds counter
91 Cabin altimeter
92 Cabin pressure and ventilation control
93 Recognition signal firing lever and discharge damper
94 Crowbar stowage
95 Seat actuating lever
96 Harness release lever

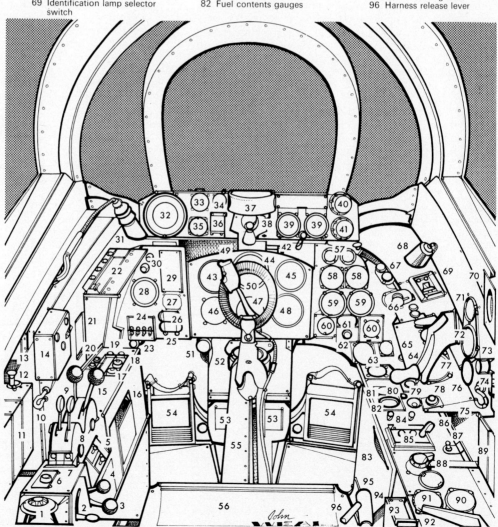

preliminary warning vibration and the wings began to flap with quick increase in amplitude to what appeared to be several feet at the tips, and it seemed that in a moment the wings would break off — though the vibration suddenly stopped during the process of easing from the dive as smoothly as possible.

Petter regarded the report somewhat suspiciously. "I'd like you to do another dive and see if it happens again," he said.

It did.

Since there was no easy solution to this problem, the decision was taken, as it had been with the Whirlwind and Lysander, to impose a limit on the diving speed of 20 mph (32,2 km/h) below that at which the fault occurred. That was still pretty fast for a machine of those days, and in retrospect it seems that this was an early instance of 'Mach' effect, for in order to secure necessary strength against bending, the spars, and therefore the wing section, had been made relatively deep, whereas a thin wing is the requisite for higher 'Mach' numbers.

There was the usual mixed bag of lesser troubles and modifications, such as air seals, inter-coolers, hydraulic functioning and occasional systems failures. On one, while making a speed run which had taken me 180 mls (290 km) from base, the steady pulse of the engines changed to noise rising in crescendo and a violent pressure on the rudder bar signalled the imminence of danger. Instinctively one tugs back the throttles. There was scarcely need to glance at the starboard propeller, shrieking in a blurred whirl while the other still rumbled round evenly and sedately. I checked the dashboard instruments. The runaway propeller was 2,000 rpm above maximum permissible. Oil pressure and temperature were normal. I pressed the feathering button. No result: the propeller still whistled on at dangerous speed, and ominously a film of oil began to spread across the engine cowling.

Similar things had happened before in the years of test-piloting. There was no immediate cause for concern; flight had merely become a little more difficult. I knew the source of trouble must be the complex hydraulic mechanism which was no longer adjusting the swivelling blade angle to match the aeroplane's speed. There was nothing I could do except switch off the starboard engine and fly home on the port. I reset the live throttle, dug my heel on the floor board against the unsymmetrical pull on the rudder, and adjusted the bias control to counteract the load. As I wrote at the time: "Winding the handle was arduous work and brought black and grey dots before my eyes. Inside the cabin there was unexpected quiet. I realized dimly that the cabin compressor must have failed when the engine raced away. Bereft of pressure, the atmosphere I breathed changed without warning from the equivalent of 7,000 ft (2 135 m) to a true height where life could only last a few more minutes. I groped for the oxygen regulator and turned it to maximum flow. Next moment I felt normal."

Oil was spreading across the cowling. A glance at the instruments showed that oil pressure was ominously low. With the engine windmilled uncontrollably by the propeller, bearings would quickly heat and seize if the oil escaped much faster. An immediate landing had become imperative. I called base and warned them. There was no answer. I called again. Nothing. Radio silence. More important things were happening. We were at war.

At this stage of hostilities, there were many new aerodromes. The difficulty was to find one. Half a mile of height was being lost in 60 seconds, and it would take five minutes to reach earth — too long, perhaps, for the ailing engine. I needed a little luck to guide me in one swoop to an aerodrome as yet hidden from my view. And then I saw it — just within reach. But would the engine seize? That could wrench it from the wing. It began to seem a race against time. The minutes flew. At 2,000 ft (610 m) I tried a warning call that I was on 'finals'. There was no reply. Then as the runway loomed clearer I saw

The Welkin NF Mk II prototype, everything down, photographed during the type's only public appearance, at the 1946 SBAC Display, Radlett.

that aircraft were taking off athwart my course, and that the wind was evidently at right angles to its direction at my home base. To try another circuit would entail raising flaps and undercarriage while opening up and trying to counteract the asymmetric pull, for her single engine safety threshold was at much higher speed. In any case there was that risk of the starboard engine seizing. The only hope was that airfield Control would see what was happening and stop other aircraft from taking off. Within seconds my wheels were rasping on the runway towards an eventual verbal rocket from a Duty Officer who clearly had no experience of the difficulties of a twin-engined aircraft approaching on one engine.

The hazards of such an approach were confirmed some months later in the course of further investigation of single engine performance, for the minimum safe speed and ease of control tends to vary between port and starboard engine and the associated direction in which the propeller is turning. To carry this to its logical conclusion I made my glide to Westland aerodrome for a landing with one engine stopped and its propeller fully feathered. The wind was north, and this entailed an approach over the hill-bluff preceding the aerodrome in order to land on the war-time southern extension which afforded a strip across the entrance road. At the last moment, with flaps and undercarriage down and speed below that at which the machine would fly under control on its single engine, the Works hooter must have blown and the men began to stream across the road. To go on would be to plough through them. I made an abrupt jiggling left and right turn whilst retracting the undercarriage; aimed at a field on top of the hill; was too fast; just cleared the intervening hedge, and flopped into the next field which terminated in a steep wooded gully, skidding to a stop just in time. When I walked to a gun-emplacement 50 yards (46 m) away, which was part of the defence of the Works, the soldiers had no idea that I had landed alongside.

One other crash landing proved the enormous safety of this machine in such circumstances. One of the great features of the design was not merely pressurization of the cabin but construction in thick bullet-resisting light alloy to prevent penetration of oblique gun-fire. The steel bulkhead behind the pilot and in the nose safeguarded direct attack, but the duralumin sides were built up of panels varying from $\frac{7}{16}$ in (11,1 mm) to 2 swg curved to the contour of the fuselage and supported from a large casting each side which carried the spar mounting lugs. Its great strength was demonstrated dramatically when Jimmy Ramsden, universally known for his horrific laugh, overshot on Yeovil aerodrome when landing with one engine out of action, tore across the all too short remainder of the aerodrome and went through the boundary fence where the railway line abruptly terminated progress. After rushing to the pile-up we found not only James unhurt but the pressure cabin portion still as good as new although it had butted the two rails into a gentle arc nearly a foot out of true.

Ten months after the prototype's initial flight the first production machine was flown, but throughout 1943 and 1944 the expected high flying German aircraft failed to materialize except for an occasional photographic-reconnaissance machine. Week by week the production Welkins were flown to a temporary airfield strip on the boundary of a Scottish laird's park, taxied to a hiding place under the trees and never flown again, although one went from Yeovil direct to Wittering for cannon gunnery trials, and experimental work continued on the development machines at Westland.

Thus the second prototype was eventually used for what was considered to be a somewhat dangerous project to use liquid oxygen injection for the specially modified Merlin engines. This necessitated considerable laboratory research in conjunction with the RAE and eventually a special oxygen tank was mounted in the fuselage bay behind the rear armoured bulkhead but because there had been several minor explosions when drops of liquid oxygen fell to the ground when being poured, one could not help feeling that this was a somewhat academic experiment because a single shot striking the tank would cause an immediate conflagration. Nor was the thought of leaking unions and broken pipes particularly cheering. However, this method of further energizing the engines considerably increased the ceiling, and to the best of recollection I attained 50,000 ft (15 250 m) and a speed of 400 mph (644 km/h).

There was also a two-seat night fighter version called up by specification F.9/43, with a lengthened nose to accommodate an AI Mk 8 radar, but more obviously the pilot's

cockpit was moved forward and a rearward facing seat fitted behind him for the observer. The slight rearrangement necessitated further experimentation with the rudder, which finally was made taller and reverted to a nose balance supplementing the previous arrangement. Otherwise, performance was much the same as the single-seater though the service ceiling was 3,000 ft (915 m) less because of the substantially increased weight. After the war I persuaded the directors to save this Mk 2 version of the Welkin together with a Whirlwind and a Lysander in view of their probable interest to later generations — but though the Welkin without its outer wings stood for several years at Merryfield, which had become our experimental flying base because of the open countryside, it was eventually sold for scrap, as was the Whirlwind after use by the Fire Brigade for practice in dealing with a burning aeroplane: the 'Lizzie' was stowed for ten years in the roof rafters of the Westland Dispersal Factory at Yeovilton yet it too finally was thrown away.

Meanwhile experimental work had continued, and in June 1945 I flew the still surviving second prototype fitted with more powerful RM16SM Merlins which had beard type radiators instead of the previous arrangement of mounting in the wing section and using long leading-edge ducts. This resulted in a speed of 398 mph (641 km/h) at 30,000 ft (9 150 m) compared with 387 mph (623 km/h) at 26,000 ft (7 930 m) of production aircraft. Photographic-reconnaissance was the intention, so that the redundant Mk I's could be modified for that purpose, but the PR version of the Mosquito could attain the same height and was 27 mph (43 km/h) faster, as well as being in quantity production, so the Welkin found no further use.

Yet though that costly wholesale scrapping of a type was but part of the huge wastefulness of war, the experiment of building the Welkin was not wholly lost, for its automatic pressure valve and pressurizing experience became the genesis of Westland's subsidiary, Normalair Ltd, initially managed by Bill Widgery, the original deviser. And for me there was that broader experience of exploring the unused stratosphere. Though 30 years later I flew in the comfort of pressurized airliners at great heights across the emptiness of the Atlantic, the memory of those explorations in the Welkin persists: the sublimity of those great heights; the isolation that had no memory of men fighting by land and sea far below; that first visual appreciation of the curvature of the earth's surface giving reality to knowledge that the world was but a small globe endlessly sailing the vastness of infinity. □

(Above left) A close-up of the RM16SM installation in DG562, the second Welkin prototype. This same aircraft was used for some trials in which liquid oxygen was carried in the fuselage tank and injected into the engines to boost performance at high altitude. The whole operation, including piping the LOX on board, illustrated below, was somewhat hazardous.

FRANCE

DASSAULT-BREGUET MERCURE 200

SINCE the publication of preliminary details of the Mercure 200 project earlier in the year (*AirData File*/February 1976), the design has undergone further development and refinement, primarily as a result of contacts between Dassault-Breguet and McDonnell Douglas. The latter company has shown considerable interest in a proposal to collaborate with Dassault-Breguet in the development and marketing of the Mercure 200 as an alternative to proposals to re-engine the DC-9 with the CFM-56 or similar engine. Details of the "definitive" Mercure 200, and of the proposed collaboration with McDonnell Douglas, were submitted to the French Ministry of Transport on 8 April, and the data quoted below are in respect of this current version.

Compared with the earlier Mercure 200 proposal, the type now has greater fuselage length; a modified aerofoil section for the wing in which the trailing edge is redesigned to obtain some characteristics of a supercritical section without changing the leading edge or central torsion box; short pylons to carry the engine pods, which were previously to be flush-fitting on the wing leading edge; small extension of the wing tip to increase the aspect ratio and improve take-off and high-altitude cruise performance; double-slotted flaps of Douglas design and, ultimately, uprated engines.

The engines remain GE/SNECMA CFM-56 "ten-tonne" turbofans, with an initial in-service thrust of 22,000 lb (10 000 kg), but the airframe will now be stressed to accept, without further modification, engines of 24,000 lb (10 900 kg) thrust which will be available two years later; with suitable modifications, it is expected that later CFM-56 variants rated at 25,000 lb st (11 350 kgp) and eventually 27,500 lb st (12 500 kgp) would be used in the Mercure 200 in due course.

Assuming a government decision in favour of the Mercure 200 by mid-1976, final definition of the project, in collaboration with McDonnell-Douglas and other possible partners in Europe, would be completed by October this year. With first orders being placed in 1977, an entry-into-service date sometime in 1980 is projected. Meanwhile, the 10 Mercure 100s continue in service with Air Inter and are building up a satisfactory record of operations, although no further examples are to be built. Commonality between the Mercure 100 and Mercure 200 is put at 77 per

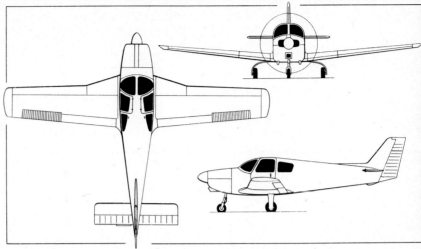

Three-view drawing of the Wassmer WA 80 Piranha.

cent for the structure and 95 per cent for the systems, excepting the powerplant and pods.

Power Plant: Two GE/SNECMA CFM-56 turbofans with initial rating of 22,000 lb st (10 000 kgp) and subsequent rating "steps" of 24,000 lb (10 900 kg), 25,000 lb (11 350 kg) and 27,500 lb (12 500 kg). Basic fuel capacity, 4,010 Imp gal (18 230 l); optional provision for 407 Imp gal (1 850 l) in fuselage tank.

Performance: VMO/MMO, 380 knots (704 km/h) EAS/Mach=0·85; economic cruise at 30,000 ft (9 150 m) Mach=0·77; take-off distance at 154,185-lb (70 000-kg) gross weight, 8,000 ft (2 450 m); range with 174 passengers, 1,750 mls (2 830 km) with standard fuel, 1,910 mls (3 085 km) with supplementary fuel. Range with 174 passengers and supplementary fuel with subsequent thrust increases (see "Power Plant" entry), 2,050 mls (3 297 km), 2,210 mls (3 554 km) and 2,570 mls (4 132 km) respectively.

Weights: Basic fuel, 32,500 lb (14 750 kg); supplementary fuel, 3,300 lb (1 500 kg); max ramp weight, 155,286 lb (70 500 kg); max take-off, 154,185 lb (70 000-kg); max landing, 138,767 lb (63 000 kg); max zero fuel, 129,956 lb (59 000 kg). Max take-off weights with subsequent thrust increases (see "Power Plant" entry), 156,390 lb (71 000 kg), 159,700 lb (72 500 kg) and 167,400 lb (76 000 kg) respectively.

Dimensions: Span, 104 ft 10 in (31,95 m); length, 134 ft 3½ in (40,93 m); wheelbase, 51 ft 6½ in (15,71 m); undercarriage track, 21 ft 8 in

(6,60 m); fuselage diameter, 12 ft 10 in (3,90 m); wing area, 1,277.7 sq ft (118,7 m²); aspect ratio, 8.6:1.

Accommodation: Typical mixed class layout for 16 first-class, four abreast at 38-in (96,5-cm) pitch and 144 economy-class six abreast at 34-in (86,4-cm) pitch; one-class seating for 174 at 34-in (86,4-cm) or 186 at 32-in (81,3-cm) pitch.

WASSMER WA 80 PIRANHA

WASSMER AVIATION has now added a two-seater to its range of plastics aircraft, and expects to begin deliveries of this new model, the WA 80 Piranha, before the end of this year, at an initial basic price of Fr 90,000 (about £11,000). To date, Wassmer has sold about 150 of its larger plastics-construction aircraft in three models—the WA 51 Pacific, WA 52 Europa and WA 54 Atlantic—with varying engine powers; two examples of the WA 80 have been built, of which the first flew last November and the second has been undergoing static testing at the CEAT.

Construction of the WA 80 follows Wassmer practice for its plastics aircraft, using resin-impregnated glassfibre (GRP) for all the main components, including the wing mainspar. One of the advantages of this form of construction is the very fine surface finish obtained, free from the usual joints, bolts and rivets. The airframe is stressed for +4.4 g and −2.2 g (or −1.0 g with flaps down). The undercarriage, which is of the fixed nosewheel type, differs from earlier Wassmer designs in that each main wheel is carried on a one-piece spring—polyester-resin leg attached to the wing root. Disc brakes of unusual design are fitted.

Access to the cabin is gained through upwards-hinged "gull-wing" doors each side, one of these being jettisonable for emergency exit. In addition to the initial 100 hp model of the Piranha, Wassmer plans to develop a version for glider towing, with a 160 hp Lycoming O-320.

Power Plant: One 100 hp Rolls-Royce Continental O-200-A flat-four air-cooled engine. Fuel capacity, 19.8 Imp gal (90-l) in tank behind cockpit.

Performance: Max speed, 115 mph (185 km/h) at sea level; initial rate of climb, 590 ft/min (3,0 m/sec); range, 528 mls (850 km); landing speed, 48 mph (78 km/h).

Weights: Empty, 1,073 lb (487 kg); useful load, 690 lb (313 kg); max take-off, 1,762 lb (800 kg).

Dimensions: Span, 30 ft 10 in (9,40 m); length, 24 ft 7 in (7,50 m); height, 8 ft 6½ in (2,60 m);

Three-view drawing of the Dassault-Breguet Mercure 200 as now projected.

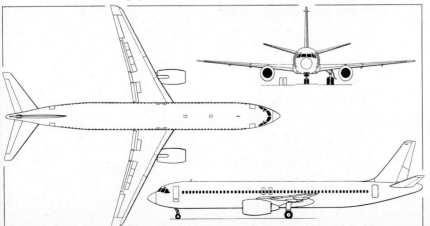

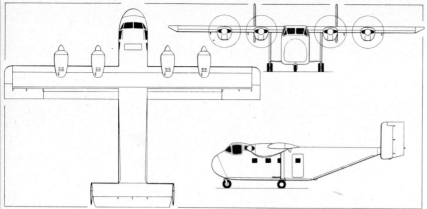

Three-view drawing of the piston-engined version of the Saab Transporter.

wing area, 133.5 sq ft (12,40 m²).

Accommodation: Pilot and passenger side by side; baggage space in rear of cabin.

SWEDEN

SAAB 108 TRANSPORTER

SAAB SCANIA has concluded that there is a potential market for some 2,000 light transport aircraft in the next 15 years, and has accordingly completed project designs for such an aircraft. At one time referred to as the Mulas, this design is now known as the Saab 108 Transporter, and both piston-engined and turboprop versions are being studied.

The basic configuration of the Transporter is similar to that of several other light utility transports already available or under development, with emphasis upon simple construction and ease of maintenance. Rear loading through a two-piece full-width upward-opening door is provided and the cabin offers a capacity of 515 cu ft (14,57 m³) in a length of 14.9 ft (4,54 m) and width of 5.65 ft (1,72 m).

Single-slotted flaps and pneumatically-operated lift dumpers are fitted on the wing, which has a basic NACA 63418 aerofoil section, modified at the leading edge for improved slow-flying. Designed to meet FAR 25 airworthiness standards, the Transporter will be able to operate with one pilot at weights up to 12,500 lb (5 670 kg) under FAR 135 as an air taxi, or at higher weights with two crew under FAR 121 for full commercial operation. The airframe is to be designed for a 25,000-hr life with 40,000 landings.

Total cost of the Transporter development programme is estimated to be SKr 100m (about £13m) and is within the resources of Saab-Scania, although participation by other companies and by the Swedish government is possible. Both the four-piston and twin-turboprop engined versions have particular merits in specific applications and further market studies are being made to assess the advisability of launching either one or both versions simultaneously. A decision is expected this year, with first flight of the prototype possible in 1978 and production deliveries in 1980. Data for the two alternative versions follow.

Power Plant: Four 320 hp Continental Tiara T6-320 piston engines. Fuel capacity, approx 330 Imp gal (1 500 l).

Performance: High speed cruise, 197 mph (316 km/h) at 10,000 ft (3 050 m); long-range cruise, 153 mph (246 km/h) at 10,000 ft (3 050 m); take-off distance to 50 ft (15,2 m), ISA sl, 1,380 ft (420 m); landing distance from 50 ft (15,2 m), ISA sl, 3-deg approach (FAR 121/135), 2,100

ft (640 m); range with 19 passengers, 115 mls (185 km); range with max fuel and 2,380 lb (1 080 kg) payload, 1,300 mls (2 090 km).

Weights: Operating weight empty, cargo config, one crew, 7,500 lb (3 400 kg); operating weight empty, 19 pass, two crew, 8,220 lb (3 730 kg); max fuel, 5,000 lb (2 270 kg); max payload, 5,000 lb (2 270 kg); normal take-off weight (FAR 135), 12,500 lb (5 670 kg); max take-off weight (FAR 121), 13,500 lb (6 120 kg); max landing weight, 12,500 lb (5 670 kg).

Power Plant: Two 850 shp Pratt & Whitney PT6A-45 or Garrett TPE 331 turboprops. Fuel capacity approx 330 Imp gal (1 500 l).

Performance: High speed cruise, 251 mph (403 km/h) at 10,000 ft (3 050 m); long range cruise, 212 mph (340 km/h) at 10,000 ft (3 050 m); take-off distance to 50 ft (15,2 m), ISA sl, 1,263 ft (385 m); landing distance from 50 ft (15,2 m), ISA sl, 3-deg approach (FAR 121/135), 2,100 ft (640 m); range with 19 passengers, 200 mls (324 km); range with max fuel and 2,380 lb (1 080 kg) payload, 645 mls (1 037 km).

Weights: Operating weight empty, cargo config, one crew, 6,724 lb (3 050 kg); operating

weight empty, 19 pass, two crew, 7,452 lb (3 380 kg); max payload, 5,622 lb (2 550 kg); other weights as piston-engined version above.

Dimensions: (both versions, approximate): Span 55 ft 9 in (17,0 m); length, 41 ft 10 in (12,75 m); height, 14 ft 5 in (4,4 m).

USA

GRUMMAN AG-CAT B

THE first major development of the Grumman Ag-Cat since this big agricultural biplane was introduced in 1958 has produced the Ag-Cat B, distinguished by an increase of nearly 4 ft (1,22 m) in the wing span. With the 450 hp engine retained, the Ag-Cat B can carry increased loads without extending the wing loading beyond reasonable limits, or can achieve improved take-off and climb performance for given weights.

The additional span is provided at both the wing roots and the tips. To retain acceptable handling characteristics, the Ag-Cat B also has an enlarged fin and rudder. A series of detailed refinements is also being introduced with the new model, and these items are being adopted for future production Ag-Cat As; they comprise an independently-sealed cockpit, one-piece wrap-around windshield, transparent canopy top, a baggage compartment and a large-volume ram-air cockpit ventilation system.

Extra wing span means that the Ag-Cat B lays a wider swath of insecticide, and can cover in eight passes the same area that earlier Ag-Cats would cover in 10 passes. The Ag-Cat A remains in production in both 450 hp and 600 hp versions, the latter having a Pratt & Whitney R-1340 engine. Production of all Ag-Cat models is handled by Schweizer Aircraft on behalf of Grumman American Aviation.

Power Plant: One 450 hp Pratt & Whitney R-985-AN (refurbished) nine-cylinder air-cooled radial engine. Hamilton Standard 2D30 two-blade propeller.

Performance (at 4,500 lb/2 041 kg gross weight at sea level: Typical working speed, 105 mph (169 km/h); take-off ground run, 465 ft (142 m); stalling speed, 60 mph (97 km/h); initial rate of climb, 1,060 ft/min (3,23 m/sec).

Weights: Empty (duster), 2,880 lb (1 306 kg); max certificated, normal operation, 4,500 lb (2 041 kg); max restricted category gross, 6,075 lb (2 756 kg).

Dimensions: Span, 42 ft 3 in (12,88 m); length, 25 ft 11 in (7,90 m); height, 11 ft (3,35 m); wing area, 392 sq ft (36,42 m²); undercarriage track, 8 ft 0 in (2,44 m).

Accommodation: Pilot only in enclosed cockpit. Hopper capacity, 300 US gal (1 136 l) liquid, 40 cu ft (1,13 m³) solid.

Photograph and three-view drawing of the Grumman Ag-Cat B.

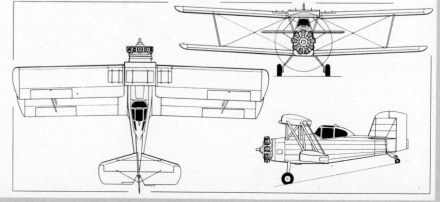

AIR International

Volume 11   Number 3   September 1976

Managing Editor .... William Green
Editor .... Gordon Swanborough
Modelling Editor .... Fred J Henderson
Contributing Artists .... Dennis Punnett
.... John Weal
Cover Art .... W R Hardy
Contributing Photographer
.... Stephen Peltz
Editorial Representative, Washington
.... Norman Polmar
Publisher .... Donald Hannah
Circulation Director .... Donald Syner
Financial Director .... John Gold
Subscription Manager .... Claire Sillette
Advertising/Public Relations
.... Elizabeth Baker

Editorial Offices:
The AIR INTERNATIONAL, PO Box 16, Bromley, BR2 7RB Kent.

Subscription, Advertising and Circulation Offices:
The AIR INTERNATIONAL, De Worde House, 283 Lonsdale Road, London SW13 9QW. Telephone 01-878 2454. US and Canadian readers may address subscriptions and general enquiries to AIR INTERNATIONAL PO Box 353, Whitestone, NY 11357 for onward transmission to the UK, from where all correspondence is answered and orders despatched.

MEMBER OF THE AUDIT
BUREAU OF CIRCULATIONS [ABC]

Subscription rates, inclusive of postage, direct from the publishers, per year:
United Kingdom .... £5·50
USA .... $17·50
Canada .... $17·50

Rates for other countries and for air mail subscriptions available on request from the Subscription Department at the above address.

The AIR INTERNATIONAL is published monthly by Fine Scroll Limited, distributed by Ducimus Books Ltd and printed by William Caple & Co Ltd, Chevron Press, Leicester, England. Editorial contents © 1976 by Pilot Press Limited. The views expressed by named contributors and correspondents are their own and do not necessarily reflect the views of the editors. Neither the editors nor the publishers accept responsibility for any loss or damage, however caused, to manuscripts or illustrations submitted to the AIR INTERNATIONAL.

Second Class postage approved at New York, NY. USA Mailing Agents: Air-Sea Freight Inc, 527 Madison Avenue, New York, NY 10022.

CONTENTS

WRENDEZVOUS
WITH WREN

"It comes as an executive kit, complete with adhesive and personal decals."

AIRSCENE

MILITARY AFFAIRS

ABU DHABI
Additional **helicopter procurement** is reportedly **planned** for the Abu Dhabi Air Force but will presumably not take place until the service's merger by the end of the year with the Dubai Defence Force — Police Air Wing and the Air Wing of the United Arab Emirates as the Union Air Force. The ADAF is currently operating seven SA 319 Alouette IIIs — from a total of 10 procured — in the utility rôle but with secondary close-support and anti-armour commitments with AS 11 and AS 12 missiles, and five SA 330 Pumas in the assault transport and logistic support rôles. Dubai has three Bell 206B JetRanger and four Bell 205A Iroquois helicopters which are used on liaison and communications tasks, and the Air Wing of the United Arab Emirates has three ex-ADAF AB 206 JetRangers for liaison and air observation post duties, four AB 205A-1s used in the troop transport rôle, together with a single AB 212, and is currently considering the procurement of four Bell HueyCobra gunships.

AUSTRALIA
It was anticipated that finance for a **supplementary** batch of two Lockheed P-3C **Orion** maritime patrol **aircraft** would be included in the 1976-77 budget which was to be announced last month (August), the two additional aircraft following on the eight previously ordered for the re-equipment of No 10 Squadron with deliveries scheduled to commence late next year and continuing at a rate of one per month through July 1978. There is now some doubt that the Australian Barra sonics system will be available in time for installation in the first of the RAAF's P-3C Orions which may initially operate the US Navy's DIFAR equipment on lease. A decision concerning the retrofit of No 11 Squadrons P-3B Orions with the Barra system has yet to be finalised.

AUSTRIA
The *Osterreichische Luftstreitkräfte* is apparently giving serious **consideration to** an Israel Aircraft Industries' offer of 18-20 **Kfir fighters** at a programme cost, including spares and technical support, of some £66m, or about 20 per cent less than other proposals for supersonic combat aircraft so far considered by Austria. An Austrian delegation was expected to visit Israel for further assessment of the Kfir at the time of closing for press.

BELGIUM
The *Aviation Légère de la Force Terrestre* (ALFT), the **Army** aviation component, **has** now **received half of its** 12 Britten-Norman BN-2A **Islanders,** these having been delivered to the 16e *Escadrille* based in Germany (and *not* the 15e *Escadrille* at Brasschaat as previously anticipated — see *Airscene*/April) and deliveries are continuing at a rate of one per month, some three months behind the original schedule.

BRAZIL
On 7 May, the *Fôrça Aérea Brasileira* took **delivery** from EMBRAER of the **first** two **EMB-110A** Bandeirante aircraft equipped for navaid checking and calibration, one of these being the 100th Bandeirante delivered. Current Bandeirante production for the FAB is centred on the EMB-110K freighter version incorporating a 31·5-in (80-cm) fuselage stretch, a strengthened freight floor and an enlarged cargo door. Twenty EMB-110Ks are on order, plus four photographic EMB-110Bs.

CANADA
The Canadian government finally signed the deferred **contract for** 18 **Lockheed Orions** on 21 July, the total value of the contract being put at $697m (about £398m). Following Canada's earlier selection of the CP-3C variant of the Orion to meet its long-outstanding requirement for a replacement for the maritime reconnaissance Canadair Argus fleet, difficulties were encountered in raising the necessary finance to cover the start-up costs (*Airscene*/July 1976) and the programme has now been revised to provide for deliveries a year later than previously planned, starting in May 1980 and continuing to March 1981. Coupled with other adjustments, this has reduced the sum needed for start-up to $50m (£28·5m), and it is understood that Lockheed has been able to obtain the backing of its creditor banks in this respect. The designation CP-140 Aurora has now been adopted for the Canadian Orions the total programme cost for which is $1,032m (£583m) including various ground facilities, simulators and support equipment.

EGYPT
Despite the urgency attached last year to the **procurement of western aircraft** for the re-equipment of the Egyptian Air Force and the apparent willingness of the UK, France and Italy to fulfil Egyptian requirements, little progress would so far seem to have been made in contractual negotiations, although reports from Paris suggest that agreement between the French and Egyptian government covering a firm order of 40 Alpha Jets and an option on a further 80, with finance furnished by Saudi Arabia, is only being held up by the "negative attitude" of the Federal German government. Egyptian interest has unofficially been reported in follow-on orders for the Westland Commando and Sea King helicopters — 30 Commandos (two VIP transport, five Mk 1 and 23 Mk 2 versions of the Commando) and six Sea King Mk 47s have so far been acquired by Egypt — and negotiations have taken place for the purchase of a substantial number of Agusta A 109 helicopters direct from the parent company followed by possible assembly and licence manufacture. The six Lockheed C-130 Hercules that the US government has agreed to supply to Egypt are now believed to include two EC-130E electronic countermeasures aircraft, although this has yet to be confirmed officially.

FEDERAL GERMANY
The *Marineflieger* has apparently **abandoned** its earlier **plans to acquire** 15 Lockheed S-3A **Vikings** to replace its current Atlantic maritime patrol aircraft and three options are now being considered: acquisition of the Atlantic Mk II, support for the proposed development of a maritime patrol version of the VFW 614 or the purchase of a version of the Fokker-VFW F.27 Maritime. A decision is expected to be taken during the first quarter of next year.

McDonnell Douglas is currently manufacturing 10 F-4E Phantoms for use by the *Luftwaffe* in training pilots at George AFB, California, and with their delivery the seven-year *Luftwaffe* **Phantom** production **programme** will be **completed.** The first of 88 RF-4E Phantoms was delivered to Germany in January 1971, these tactical reconnaissance aircraft being followed by 175 F-4F Phantoms for the intercept and fighter-bomber rôles, the last of which was delivered in April. The RF-4E equips two reconnaissance *Geschwader*, AG 51 at Bremgarten and AG 52 at Leck, while the F-4F is operated by two fighter-interceptor

Geschwader, JG 71 at Wittmundhafen and JG 74 at Neuburg, and by two fighter-bomber *Geschwader*, JaboG 35 and JaboG 36. JaboG 35 at Pferdsfeld was previously the G.91R-equipped LeKG 42, and with disbandment of LeKG 44 at Leipheim last year, the *Luftwaffe* now has only two light strike *Geschwader*, LeKG 41 at Husum and LeKG 43 at Oldenburg, both of which are scheduled to retain their **G.91Rs** until re-equipped from 1980 onwards with the Alpha Jet.

The *Flugbereitschaftsstaffel*, the special transport unit of the *Luftwaffe* responsible for VIP and other governmental transportation tasks, has recently taken **delivery of** the first of its three **VFW 614s** at Köln-Bonn and the remaining two aircraft are expected to have been taken into the inventory by February.

FINLAND
Although it was earlier believed that *Ilmavoimat* had as yet no definitive plans for the replacement of the aged MiG-21F fighters operated by HävLv 31 (the *Karjalan Lennosto*) at Rissala, under the new five-year plan (1977-1981) put forward by the Parliamentary Defence Committee, covering total military expenditure of the FMk 8,700m (£1,253·6m) of which about FMk 2,300m (£331·4m) covers procurement and about 45 per cent of this is to be allocated for the modernisation of the air defence system, it is **recommended** that an advanced, all-weather **Soviet interceptor** be procured for the re-equipment of HävLv 31. The favoured aircraft, up to 40 of which are required by 1980, is understood to be a version of the variable-geometry MiG-23 which has reportedly been on offer to Finland since 1974.

Deliveries to *Ilmavoimat* of nine **additional** Saab **Drakens** (see *Airscene*/July) began on 17 June with the arrival of the first two of three ex-*Flygvapen* S 35C Draken two-seaters which are to be followed by six low hour J 35F Draken single-seaters for operation by HävLv 21 (the *Satakunnan Lennosto*) next year. The two-seaters are being added to the inventory of HävLv 11 (the *Lapin Lennosto*) at Rovaniemi in Lapland, where the flight simulator included in the package is also to be installed.

FRANCE
In discussions concerning the NF502,440m (£58,782m) six-year (1977-1982) military programme recently approved by the National Assembly, it was revealed that the target **unit cost of** the initial batch of 127 Dassault-Breguet **Mirage 2000** air superiority fighters scheduled to be ordered for the *Armée de l'Air* in 1979 is NF80m (£9·36m), and that no delays will be acceptable if the in-service date of 1982 is to be achieved. To maintain *Armée de l'Air* strength at approximately 450 combat aircraft before the Mirage 2000 enters service, the total Mirage F1 order is to be increased to 225 aircraft, the retirement of earlier Mirages would otherwise result in a fall in the first-line inventory to about 370 aircraft.

The precise **number of Super Etendards** to be acquired by *Aéronavale* **remains uncertain.** When the programme was launched in January 1973, it was envisaged that about 100 aircraft would be involved, but changing circumstances, including the planned extension of the service lives of the Crusader interceptors and Etendard IVP reconnaissance aircraft until at least 1985, have reduced the requirement of Super Etendards to between 70 and 80 of which only 36 have been ordered up to Fiscal 1976.

The *Armée de l'Air* has now taken **delivery of** some 65 single-seat **Jaguar** As and all 40 of its two-seat Jaguar Es. The 100th Jaguar was accepted by the *Armée de l'Air* on 19 May at a ceremony at Toulouse-Colomiers and delivered to the 11e *Escadre* at Toul-Rosières.

GABON

It is now known that the *Force Aérienne Gabonaise* **order for Mirages** comprises five aircraft — three Mirage 5G strike-interceptors and two Mirage 5RG tactical reconnaissance aircraft — rather than the six that the Gabon government announced its intention of ordering last year (see *Airscene*/September 1975). No delivery dates have yet been announced. An additional SA 330 Puma helicopter has recently been delivered from France and the *Force Aérienne Gabonaise* expects to take delivery of its Lockheed L-100-20 Hercules (which will supplement a single L-100-30 already in the inventory) in December.

IRAN

The Iranian Imperial Air Force has reportedly placed an **order for** three **P-3C Orion** maritime patrol aircraft to supplement the six P-3F models currently in the inventory. The P-3C has a greater computing capacity than the P-3F which is used primarily for surface surveillance. Earlier, the IIAF was reportedly negotiating the purchase of two specially-configured P-3s for use in connection with the planned Ibex airborne and ground-based communications and radar monitoring system. The IIAF is understood to have a total requirement for 18 P-3 Orions for the maritime task. Iranian military expenditure for Fiscal 1976-1977 totals Rials 568,870m (£4,550m approx) and accounts for 27 per cent of the general budget and more than 12 per cent of Iran's gross national product.

IRAQ

The **US** Department of Defense **has** tentatively **approved** the **sale** to the Iraqi government for use by the Iraqi Air Force **of** two Lockheed **L-100-30 Hercules** and an option on the purchase of two additional transports of this type. According to reports from Paris, the French and Iraqi governments are continuing negotiations covering the purchase of 54 Mirage F1s and a similar quantity of SEPECAT Jaguars. The Iraqi Air Force has reportedly also evinced interest in the acquisition of up to 40 light strike aircraft in the Hawk/Alpha Jet category.

JAPAN

It is believed that the 50-day evaluation of current US fighters potentially able to meet the Air Self-Defence Force's **F-X requirement** and undertaken by an 11-man team headed by Gen Toshimitsu Komatsu has resulted in the McDonnell Douglas **F-15 Eagle** being placed at **frontrunner,** although the F-14 Tomcat and the F-16 still officially remain in the contest. High priority is now being allocated by the Defence Agency to the F-X decision and a definitive choice was believed imminent at the time of closing for press, the chosen aircraft being recipient of an order for 100-120 units.

Following retirement of its C-46 transport fleet, the Air Self-Defence Force is to modify one of its NAMC YS-11 transports for use as a **navigational trainer.** The converted aircraft will have six training stations — for C-1A and YS-11 navigators and for the rear-seat crew member of the RF-4EJ Phantom — and is scheduled to be completed by March. The ASDF is currently operating 12 YS-11s in the transport rôle and one as an ECM trainer.

The Defence Agency is to seek funding in the Fiscal 1977 budget for the further development of the small **XF-3 turbofan** designed by the Technical Research and Development In-

Two of the first illustrations to show the new V/STOL fighter developed for the Soviet Naval Air Force (Aviatsiya Voenno-morskovo Flota, *or AV-MF) and now serving aboard the* Kiev, *which as noted on this page, recently sailed into the Mediterranean on its first deployment outside Soviet home waters. Of similar overall configuration to the Harrier, the new AV-MF fighter makes use of a vectored thrust engine presumably derived from the power plant of the Yakovlev Yak-36 (Freehand) which served as a technology demonstrator. It has been widely assumed that the Yakovlev design bureau is responsible for the operational V/STOL type, but this has yet to be confirmed, and as these photographs show the airframe has nothing in common with that of the Yak-36. The photographs were taken by (above) a Nimrod of No 203 Squadron and (below) a Canberra of No 13 Squadron RAF, both based in Malta.*

stitute. The XF-3 has a thrust in the 2,645 lb (1 200 kg) category and a bypass ratio of 1·9. The primary target of the XF-3 programme is provision of a power plant for the proposed XT-3 replacement for the Fuji T-1 intermediate trainer. The ASDF's current planning calls for acquisition of the first two XT-3 trainers before 1981, and Fuji and Kawasaki are currently competing for a development contract. The production XF-3 is intended to be available within six years and will be manufactured by Ishikawajima-Harima. It is intended that the XT-3 will be powered by two XF-3 turbofans.

NEW ZEALAND

The New Zealand government has finally approved the **purchase of** 10 ex-RAF Hawker Siddeley **Andover** tactical transports at a total cost of approximately £8m, including spares, support and rôle equipment. Deliveries of the Andovers to New Zealand, after refurbishing, are expected to commence early next year and the RAF will assist in the training of RNZAF air and ground crews. Although being initially delivered to RAF standard, the Andovers may later be adapted to include maritime patrol among their tasks.

PAKISTAN

The entire PAF inventory of Chinese-built **MiG-19S** fighters is now being phased through a modification programme in which the somewhat primitive semi-automatic **ejection seat** is being **replaced** by the advanced-technology Martin-Baker Mk PKD 10 zero-zero auto-

matic ejection seat similar to that specified for the Panavia Tornado, Hawker Siddeley Hawk, etc. The PAF originally received 90 MiG-19S fighters in 1965-66 and a further 60 during March-April 1972, and substantially more than 100 are believed to remain in the inventory.

SOVIET UNION

The Soviet Navy's **first** genuine aircraft **carrier,** the 35,000-ton *Kiev,* passed **through** the **Bosporus** and entered the Mediterranean on 18 July, described euphemistically by the Russians as an "anti-submarine cruiser" in order to circumvent the 1936 Treaty of Montreux which effectively banned the strait to aircraft carriers and thus enable the Turkish government to state that the *Kiev's* passage conformed with the treaty, undoubtedly changes the balance of power in the Mediterranean. The *Kiev* has been working up in the Black Sea for the past year and may be expected to be joined late next year or early 1978 by her first sistership, the *Minsk* now nearing completion in the Nikolayev Nosenko yard where the *Kiev* was built, and by a second sistership (which, together with a fourth vessel, has been laid down in the Leningrad shipyards) in 1979-80. Aircraft carried by the *Kiev* include Ka-25 (Hormone) anti-submarine helicopters and the Soviet Union's first sea-going fixed-wing aircraft — V/STOL fighters apparently based on Yakovlev Yak-36 (Freehand) technology.

SYRIA

The placing of an **order for** two Lockheed L-

As noted in an accompanying news item, the prototype Lockheed US-3A COD aircraft recently made its first flight. Dimensionally the same as the S-3A Viking, the US-3A features a six-seat passenger cabin and underwing supply pods.

100-30 **Hercules** transports with an option on two more **has received** the tentative **approval** of the US Department of Defense.

TOGO

The **Togolaise** government is **expected** shortly **to** finalise a decision to **purchase** five Dassault-Breguet **Mirage 5** fighters for the *Force Aérienne Togolaise* which has recently taken delivery of five refurbished Magister jet trainers and is receiving assistance from the *Armée de l'Air* in the training of pilots and technicians. If the order for Mirages is finalised, deliveries are unlikely before late next year.

UGANDA

Libyan Minister of State Mohammed al-Zawi confirmed at a press conference held in Kuwait on 18 July that the **Libyan** government has sent **Mirage fighters** of the Libyan Arab Air Force **to Uganda** as part of its pledge to support President Amin in his confrontation with Kenya, although the type or quantity of Mirages were not specified. It would seem most probable that the aircraft deployed to Uganda are Mirage 5Ds and according to reports from Nairobi the number of aircraft involved is 30, although Col Muammar al-Kaddafi has allegedly promised to provide President Amin with 40 Mirages. It is probably as a result of the arrival of the Libyan Mirages that President Amin made his bellicose statement of 18 July in which he threatened to bomb the residence of President Kenyatta of Kenya. It may be assumed that the Mirages in Uganda are being flown by Libyan Arab Air Force pilots and serviced by Libyan groundcrews and that the aircraft are on indefinite deployment to Uganda rather than being a permanent addition to the Uganda Air Force's inventory.

UNITED KINGDOM

According to a recent Parliamentary answer, the **RAF** had a total **strength** of 1,908 aircraft on establishment as at 1 March compared with 2,021 a year earlier. The current total is somewhat lower, however, following the disbandment of 11 squadrons since the 1975 defence review and about one-third of the present total comprises combat aircraft.

The first of 13 Westland **Sea King Mk 2** helicopters for the Royal Navy began its **flight test** programme in July prior to delivery to the service later this year.

The RAF's two first-line **Hunter** FGA 9-equipped **squadrons**, Nos 45 and 58 at Wittering, were scheduled to be **disbanded** last month (August) and their aircraft transferred to RAF Brawdy to supplement the aircraft of the Tactical Weapons Unit.

The Royal Navy **retired** its last piston-engined

helicopter on 22 July, when **Whirlwind HAS Mk 7** XN299 was withdrawn from service at the Joint Warfare Establishment at Old Sarum and put into long-term storage at RNAY Wroughton. This Whirlwind may eventually join the RN Vintage Aircraft Flight.

USA

In recent tests over Eglin AFB, **F-15** Eagles have twice scored **"kills" on simulated MiG-25s,** Bomarc drones being used to simulate the Soviet aircraft. The first "kill" was gained when the F-15 launched an AIM-7F Sparrow AAM at a Bomarc travelling at M=2·7 at 71,000 ft (21 640 m) — which might be considered typical of the MiG-25 — and the missile, fitted with a dummy warhead, passed within lethal distance of the target. On the second occasion, the F-15 launched a live Sparrow at a Bomarc again travelling at M=2·7 but at an altitude of 68,000 ft (20 725 m), the target being destroyed.

AIRCRAFT AND INDUSTRY

CANADA

De Havilland Canada delivered the **500th Twin Otter** in a ceremony at the Downsview plant recently. Recipient was Metro Airlines of Houston, Texas, one of the many commuter airlines among the 171 Twin Otter operators.

FRANCE

Aérospatiale is studying the possibility of fitting **flight refuelling** probes to the new batch **of 25-30 Transall C-160s** that are to be built for *l'Armée de l'Air.* The 10 ft 4 in (3,16-m) probe will be located centrally above the windscreen and with a single refuelling the range of the Transall with a 22,000-lb (10 000 kg) payload will be increased from 2,800 mls (4 500 km) to 4,970 mls (8 000 km), or to 6,836 mls (11 000 km) with two refuellings. Use of the **Transall as a tanker** is also being studied, both for *l'Armée de l'Air* (which is also interested in a possible tanker version of the Airbus A300) and for export. As a tanker, the Transall would have two supplementary fuel tanks in the centre wing and provision for a fixed or pallet-mounted tank in the fuselage; part of the standard fuel capacity in the outer wings would also be transferable. The hose-and-reel unit — probably the Sargent Fletcher FR300B — would be located either in the rear fuselage or in the rear of the port wheel fairing and remotely controlled from a command post on the flight deck. As a tanker, the Transall could transfer 33,000 lb (15 000 kg) of fuel at a distance of 745 mls (1 200 km) from base, or 11,000 lb (5 000 kg) at a distance of 2,110 mls (3 400 km).

Both French and US **certification** has now been

obtained **for** the Aérospatiale **SA330J** version of the **Puma,** which is distinguished primarily by having main rotor blades of plastics construction. In addition to offering improved safety and reduced maintenance requirements, the new rotor permits an increase in maximum take-off weight from 15,420 lb (7 000 kg) for the SA 330G to 16,300 lb (7 400 kg). At the same time, the Puma's transmission has been recertificated for a maximum continuous rating of 2,240 hp in place of 2,130 hp.

INTERNATIONAL

According to Pentagon officials, the high cost proposals submitted by the companies from the four-nation General Dynamics **F-16** fighter consortium that were threatening to jeopardise the **programme** have now been trimmed to **competitive** levels in most areas and the cost of the F-16 to the USAF is projected as $4·41m (£2·48m) per aircraft. This figure is marginally *below* the original development concept threshold of $4·5m (£2·53m), this reduction being based on European participation. If only the 650 aircraft required by the USAF were built, the unit cost would be $4·63m (£2·6m). If the entire NATO consortium and USAF requirements for the F-16 were fulfilled in the USA, the cost of each fighter would be reduced to $4·24m (£2·38m). The projected unit cost of the 350 consortium aircraft is now $5·2m (£2·92m), representing 18 per cent more than the cost of the fighter if purchased direct from the USA.

Full series **production of the** Panavia **Tornado** was launched on 29 July with the signature of a Memorandum of Understanding by the governments of the UK, Federal Republic of Germany and Italy. On the same day, the NAMMA concluded contracts for an initial batch of 40 aircraft with Panavia, Turbo-Union and Mauser, covering the airframe, the RB.199 engines and the 27-mm cannon respectively. The total Tornado programme is now set at 809, excluding the nine prototypes and two of the six pre-series aircraft previously ordered (see "Tornado Takes Off", pages 118 *et seq*); of this total, 324 are for Germany, 100 for Italy and 385 for the UK, including 165 of the future Air Defence Variant.

US certification has been obtained **for** the B4 and B2K versions of the **Airbus A300,** with effect from 30 June. The B2 had previously been certificated, and the new approval clears the way for operation of the newer variants by US airlines.

The US State Department granted a licence on 22 July permitting Pratt & Whitney to proceed with its programme for **co-operative development of the JT10D** engine. Under terms of agreements already concluded, P & WA will direct and control the programme and will be responsible for 54 per cent of development effort and cost. Rolls-Royce will take a 34 per cent share, Motoren-und-Turbinen-Union of Germany, 10 per cent and Fiat in Italy, 2 per cent. Specific responsibilities will be: P & WA, HP compressor and HP turbine; Hamilton Standard, control system; R-R, burner, fan and associated components; MTU, LP turbine and Fiat, accessory gearbox. The JT10D is a "ten-tonne" engine competitive with the GE-SNECMA CFM-56 and P & WA says that market surveys indicate total potential business of $27,000m (£15,200m) for engines of this size over the life of the programme.

ISRAEL

To improve the **dog-fighting** capability of the IAI Kfir, fixed canard surfaces have been added to a version known as the **Kfir C2,** now in service with the *Heyl Ha'Avir.* First publicly demonstrated in Israel on 20 July, the Kfir C2 is reported to have first flown in 1973. The canards, attached to the air intake fairings just behind and below the cockpit, are considerably larger than the retractable surfaces originally developed by Dassault-Breguet for the Milan version of the Mirage 5, but serve the same purpose of improving the slow speed handling and therefore enhancing manoeuvrability; small strakes have also been added on each side of the nose of the Kfir C2, plus a dogtooth on each wing. The modifications add about 200 lb (91 kg) to the weight of the Kfir, which in its C2 version now has a max weight of 32,120 lb (14 600 kg). Typical weight for the dog-fight mission, with 50 per cent fuel, two Shafrir AAMs and a full load of 30-mm ammunition is 20,660 lb (9 380 kg).

ITALY
First flight of the **Piaggio P.166-DL3** was made on 3 July at Genoa, and this prototype was expected to be among the new aircraft exhibited at the Farnborough International show early this month (September). The P.166-DL3 is powered by 587 shp Lycoming LTP101-600 turboprops and is the first aircraft to fly with this engine in its turboprop, rather than turboshaft, form. The P.166-DL3 has an increased take-off weight of 9,470 lb (4 300 kg), a max payload of 2,860 lb (1 297 kg), a cruising speed of 259 mph (417 km/h) and a range of 1,116 mls (1 795 km) with standard tankage.

JAPAN
The maritime Self-Defence Force is studying the feasibility of **mating the ASW systems of** the Lockheed **S-3A** Viking **with the airframe of** the **Kawasaki GK-525** maritime patrol aircraft which has been under development for several years as a PX-L contender. The proposal has resulted from the undiminished resistance to the purchase of the P-3C Orion in the wake of the Lockheed bribery allegations. Nevertheless, the MSDF still favours acquisition of the P-3C and hopes that when current Japanese anti-Lockheed feeling fades, it will be possible to procure 41 P-3Cs with the first eight being included in the Fiscal 1977-78 budget. If anti-Lockheed feeling is maintained, the MSDF proposes to stretch P-2J procurement by ordering a further seven aircraft as an interim measure.

Linked with the latest BAC proposals for a short-haul STOL transport for use in Japan is a suggestion that the BAC **One-Eleven** might also be a **candidate for** the controversial **P-XL programme** to replace the JMSDF Kawasaki P-2Js. BAC efforts are now concentrated on the One-Eleven 475D, which, with a take-off weight of 80,000 lb (36 300 kg), would be able to carry 89 passengers out of 4,000-ft (1 200-m) runways. In military guise, the 475D would be fitted with two supplementary engines in underwing pods. The offer provides for up to 50 per cent participation by Japanese industry, but a smaller share would be acceptable to BAC.

McDonnell Douglas has **revised the specification of** its **DC-9QSF** proposal to meet Japan's short-haul STOL transport requirement (see *AirData File*/July 1976). The revised DC-9QSF-76 now has 10-ft (3,05-m) more wing span (added at the root) to eliminate the complicated leading-edge variable camber Krueger flaps. Containing an additional 2,100 US gal (8 085 l) of fuel, the enlarged wing allows the QSF-76 to offer a range of up to 2,000 mls (3 200 km).

POLAND
Aérospatiale has concluded an agreement with **Pezetel** in Poland providing for the latter **to produce and market** several models of the **Rallye** lightplane. The contract will become effective when ratified by the relevant government agencies in each country; meanwhile, one

Rallye has been delivered to Pezetel under the terms of the agreement.

UNITED KINGDOM
A marketing campaign has been initiated by Fairey Britten-Norman for a **military version of** the **Trislander.** The interior will be convertible for either troop transportation or freight carrying, 17 fully-equipped troops being carried over 253 miles (408 km) or 13 troops over 748 miles (1 205 km) and the seats being removable within five minutes to convert the aircraft as a freighter. The capacity of the military Trislander M is 328 cu ft (9,29 m³) with 27 ft (8,23 m) of unobstructed space. The maximum disposable load is 3,745 lb (1 699 kg) and the floor will be stressed to take loads at up to 120 lb/sq ft (585,84 kg/m²). The Trislander is also considered suitable for various maritime rôles and an endurance of up to 9 hours will be achieved with underwing fuel tanks.

In the course of the debate on the third reading of the Aircraft and Shipbuilding Industries Bill in the House of Commons on 29 July, it was announced that the government is making additional **funds** available to BAC and HSA **to support** work on the **One-Eleven and HS.146** respectively. Subject to contractual negotiations, an additional £3m will be made available to support the production of five One-Elevens beyond those already on firm order, and £3½m will be used to continue design work, research and development and structural testing relating to the HS.146 for a further period of six months. The Bill, allowing nationalisation of BAC, HSA and Scottish Aviation to go ahead, received its third reading with a government majority of three, and vesting day for the new British Aerospace Corporation to take over on behalf of the government is expected to be named in the near future.

First flight of the **Whittaker Excalibur** was made at Bodmin on 2 July and this interesting home-built prototype was subsequently displayed at the PFA Rally at Sywell the following week-end. Powered by a modified VW engine, the Excalibur makes use of a 34-in (86-cm) diameter Dowty-Rotol five-bladed ducted fan of glassfibre construction; the configuration is twin-boom, with a low wing, fixed tricycle undercarriage and the engine immediately behind the cockpit, driving the pusher fan. There are plans for building up to five more examples, with modifications that would include raising the tailplane to a high position, and alternative engines are being studied including a new 65 hp British two-stroke and a derated version of the Budworth Puffin turboprop.

Rolls-Royce Helicopter Engine Division at Leavesden is continuing to study the configuration of a **possible new turboprop** engine under the designation **RB.318.** The studies are being made in collaboration with Alfa Romeo in Italy and are concentrated upon an engine of about 600 hp, for fixed-wing applications.

USA
The **first** production model of the **improved E-2C** Hawkeye with General Electric APS-125 radar is scheduled to be delivered to the US Navy in December. The new radar can automatically detect and track low-flying targets over land as well as over water and reduces susceptibility to enemy noise-jamming through the antenna sidelobes as well as providing a modest increase in detection range. This improved radar is being fitted to the Hawkeyes being supplied to Israel's *Heyl Ha'Avir* (two on firm order and two on option), deliveries of which also commence in December. The APS-125 achieves greater clutter rejection than the APS-120 that it replaces as a result of the

introduction of a Doppler filtering technique for echoes slipping through the three-pulse AMTI (Airborne Moving Target Indicator). The pre-production APS-125 was first flown on 20 January 1973, and on the strength of the performance demonstrated, it was decided to fit this radar in the last aircraft in the Fiscal 1975 procurement — the 34th E-2C, to be delivered in December — and in all six Fiscal 1976 procurement aircraft.

A **go-ahead for the** prototype flight demonstration phase (FDP) of the **AV-8B Harrier** was approved by the Department of Defense on 27 July, and two existing AV-8As will be converted to YAV-8B configuration for first flight in November 1978 and a 120-hr test programme leading to a full-scale production decision by the end of May 1979. Two more prototypes would then precede production of 336 AV-8Bs for the US Marine Corps to replace three squadrons of AV-8As and five squadrons of A-4M Skyhawks, with initial operational capability achieved in 1984. The AV-8B will be built by McDonnell Douglas at St Louis with Hawker Siddeley/British Aerospace as a sub-contractor manufacturing major fuselage components; the Rolls-Royce Pegasus 11 engine (F402-RR-402) of 21,500 lb st (9 760 kgp) will probably be supplied from the UK.

First flight of the Lockheed **US-3A** COD version of the Viking was made early in July. Modified from one of the S-3A development aircraft, the US-3A was to enter Navy preliminary evaluation and carrier qualification tests on 27 August. The fuselage has been modified to carry six passengers, with a crew of two, or 7,500-lb (3 405-kg) of cargo, and large underwing pods accommodate an additional 1,000 lb (454 kg) each. Max gross weights range from 42,800 lb (19 430 kg) with internal fuel to 47,100 lb (21 380 kg) with auxiliary tanks, when the range is over 3,300 mls (5 370 km).

The USAF has informed the Defense Department that it anticipates incurring a **cost overrun of** approximately $1,000m (£561·8m) in the production and procurement of the **F-15 Eagle.** The impact of the cost increase will take place through 1982 aircraft deliveries. The USAF is procuring the Eagle at a rate of 108 aircraft per year with the objective of a total inventory of 729 fighters of this type. Congress has approved the Fiscal 1977 buy of F-15s while reducing the requested funding of $1,400m (£786·5m) by $30·1m (£16·9m) to reflect anticipated savings related to foreign military sales to Israel. The cost overrun calculation partially represents a more realistic estimate than that used previously of the escalation in labour and materials costs, but the service is planning no major programme change aimed at easing the impact of the higher forecast costs.

On 1 June, the **1,400th** Lockheed **Hercules,** a C-130H, was handed over to the USAF and accepted by a flight crew from the Military Airlift Command's 463rd Tactical Airlift Wing based at Dyess AFB, Abilene.

By early July, the two McDonnell Douglas **YC-15s** had **completed 360 hrs of testing** in over 165 flights, and results so far indicate flying qualities better than predicted and take-off and landing performance that "meet the design goals for an advanced STOL tactical transport". A total of 11½ hrs of night flying has been logged, including STOL landings on austerely-lighted 2,000-ft (610-m) runways. Simulated and "wet" refuelling has been accomplished with an Air Force KC-135 tanker and a YC-15 as a receiver, and the YC-15 has also acted as a tanker in simulated trials with a KC-135, a helicopter and several fighters including the F-4 Phantom and AV-8 Harrier. Comprehensive stall testing has been completed, totalling about 350 stalls in 60 different configurations. Other tests completed include flutter, noise, thrust reverser and cargo and troop door operation, vehicle loading, ground manoeuvring and definition of the stability and control augmentation system (SCAS).

The first McDonnell Douglas **YC-15** was scheduled to be flown from Edwards AFB back to Long Beach, Calif, last month (August) to have fitted the new, **longer-span wing** which has been designed primarily to provide information on proposed configurational changes for possible future civil transport derivatives. The new wing has a span of 132 ft 7 in (40,41 m) as compared with the original span of 110 ft 4 in (33,63 m), increasing gross wing area from 1,740 sq ft (161,65 m²) to 2,107 sq ft (197,75 m²) and aspect ratio to 9. Installation of the new wing is to begin this month and will take three-four months. While the new wing is being fitted in McDonnell Douglas's X-Shop facility, one of the Pratt & Whitney JT8D-17 engines will be replaced by a GE-SNECMA CFM-56 and flight testing will be resumed in the first quarter of next year. Later this year, a JT8D-209 will be installed in the other YC-15 in place of one of its JT8D-17s.

The US Defense Department has stated that the problems that led to runaway costs in the **E-4** advanced airborne command post programme have now been resolved. Projected cost increase from $550m (£308·99m) to $1,100m (£617·98m) for the seven-aircraft **programme** resulted in major **restructuring** last year and the programme is now expected to cost $872m (£489·9m). Whereas the programme was originally to have comprised three E-4A (modified Boeing 747-200s) with command and control communications equipment transferred from EC-135s, followed by four E-4Bs equipped to serve in either the NEACP (National Emergency Airborne Command Post) rôle, which is fulfilled by the E-4A, or the Strategic Air Command "Looking Glass" rôle, the three E-4As subsequently being converted to E-4B standard, the restructured programme eliminates one aircraft, is stretched by 40 months and makes greater use of equipment available from the EC-135. Furthermore, whereas the USAF had planned to use different aircraft to support the NEACP and SAC "Looking Glass" missions on a dedicated basis, the six aircraft remaining in the programme will be redesigned to perform either mission on an interchangeable basis. The three E-4As are currently being operated from Andrews AFB and the prototype E-4B is flying but is not scheduled to be delivered to the USAF until August 1979. The three E-4As will be reconfigured as E-4Bs after the three aircraft built as E-4Bs from the outset have been delivered, and the last of the reconfigured aircraft is now scheduled to be delivered in February 1983.

STC Engineering Co of Oklahoma, in conjunction with Reclyn Aircraft Inc, has developed a **modification of** the PA-36-285 **Pawnee Brave** in which a 350 hp Jacobs R755-S radial engine replaces the usual Continental of 285 hp, and full-span leading-edge flaps are fitted. Increased performance, improved low-speed control and a max permissible gross weight of 5,980 lb (2 715 kg) compared with 4,400 lb (2 000 kg), result from the modifications.

Cessna is reported to be planning the introduction of two new versions of the **Skyhawk** designed **to use 100-octane fuel** in place of the usual 80-octane on which the Lycoming O-320-E2D runs. One of the new models, the

Skyhawk 100, has a Lycoming O-320-H and the other will be powered by a 195 hp Continental IO-360-K. With the major oil companies phasing out 80 octane fuel, modifications require to be made to existing engines to allow them to operate on 100 octane fuel.

A **turboprop** version of the original **Great Lakes biplane** has been built by the Great Lakes Aircraft Company, which was formed in 1972 to put the piston-engined version back into production. Known as the Great Lakes X2T-1T, the turboprop version has a 400 shp Allison 250-B17B engine in place of the usual 180 hp Lycoming IO-360 in the Model 2T-1A.

CIVIL AFFAIRS

AUSTRALIA
Flying a home-built **Thorpe T18** (VH-CMC), Clive Canning arrived in the UK on 1 July at the end of a solo **flight from Australia** that took 98 airborne hours and had started on 16 June. The flight was the first from Australia to England by an aircraft of amateur construction and probably the longest point-to-point by such an aircraft. The route was by way of West Irian, Celebes, Southern Borneo, Sumatra, Singapore, Thailand, Burma, India, Pakistan, Iran, Bahrain, Saudi Arabia, Cyprus, Greece and France, to a UK landfall at Shoreham, and seven point-to-point records were established en route, subject to FAI ratification.

CANADA
Air Canada has decided to have three of its L-1011 **TriStars converted** by Lockheed **to L-1011-100** standard to permit their use on the North Atlantic. The -100 differs from the basic TriStar in carrying an additional 18,800 lb (8 535 kg) of fuel, to obtain an extra 900 mls (1 450 km) of range.

INTERNATIONAL
Latest IATA forecasts indicate an average **growth** rate **of 8 per cent in** world-wide **passenger traffic** up to 1981, although the number of passengers carried in 1975 was actually below the 1974 figure. The 8 per cent growth figure is lower than was achieved during the 'sixties, but higher rates are expected to apply in some sectors of the market — for example, 14·3 per cent between Europe and the Middle East and about 11 per cent on the mid-Atlantic and South Atlantic routes. Growth within Europe and on the North Atlantic is forecast to be below 6 per cent per year.

LEBANON
Middle East Airlines, having been forced to evacuate its main base at Beirut because of the civil war in Lebanon, after shelling of the airport destroyed one of its Boeing 720Bs, has **dispersed its fleet** to various European and Middle East airports and is concentrating upon making wet-lease arrangements with other airlines to keep its aircraft and crews busy pending a resumption of normal business. Three Boeing 707-320Cs and two 720Bs have been leased to Saudia and one 720B to Libyan Arab Airlines, and both Tunis Air and Air Algerie have been chartering time on the Boeing 747s. Efforts are being made to secure traffic rights from European cities to Middle Eastern destinations other than Beirut, and the company also hopes to acquire useful charter business during the Moslem Hadj pilgrimage later this year.

SCANDINAVIA
In addition to ordering two more DC-9 Srs 41s, as briefly noted in our previous issue, **SAS** has taken options on five other **DC-9s,** three for delivery in 1978 and two for 1979. One of these options may be converted later to cover a

palletized jet freighter variant of the DC-9. The two Srs 41s newly ordered in 1977 in a combined first and economy class seating arrangement for 108 passengers, and will bring the total of DC-9s purchased by SAS to 56; the airline is the largest DC-9 operator outside North America.

UNITED KINGDOM
All but one (very small) British airlines operating scheduled services have signed an agreement for a voluntary scheme to provide **compensation for passengers** who are prevented from taking a flight on which they have booked, **because of overbooking** by the airline. Twelve foreign airlines operating into the UK have also signed the agreement or have indicated their willingness to do so. Passengers will qualify for compensation of half the value of the ticket for the flight in question, within limits of £10 and £100, if they are unable to travel because of overbooking and the airline is unable to offer alternative transportation allowing the passenger to reach the intended destination within two hours (domestic) or four hours (international) of the original scheduled time of arrival.

CIVIL CONTRACTS AND SALES

Boeing 737: Southwest Airlines has ordered five 737-200s for mid-1977 delivery. □ Gulf Air's order for five Advanced 200s (this column, last month) was confirmed by Boeing on 16 July. Delivery will be in mid-1977 to replace BAC One-Elevens, and options have been taken on five more.

Boeing 720: One 720 previously operated by Air Viking is now flying for Eagle Air, a recently-formed charter company in Iceland.

Boeing 727: Braniff ordered four more Advanced 727s on 19 July, bringing its fleet of this type to 75 and taking the overall total of Boeing jetliner sales (all models) beyond the 3,000 mark.

Boeing 747: As yet unconfirmed by Boeing are reports of an order for two 747SPs for Jugoslovenski Aerotransport (JAT) and one for the personal use of King Khaled of Saudi Arabia. □ British Airways has ordered two more Rolls-Royce-engined 747-236Bs, making six in all; deliveries begin next year.

Fairchild Swearingen Metro: Southeast Airlines has one Metro in service on its route between Miami and Freeport, Bahamas.

Fokker F27: Ansett has ordered two more Mk 500s for use by its subsidiary Airlines of New South Wales. The Ansett Group has purchased a total of 29 Friendships since 1958. □ Air Niugini is reported to be acquiring four earlier F27s from Ansett Airlines, replacing four DC-3s.

Fokker F28: Fokker-VFW has confirmed the sale to Garuda International Airways of six more F28 Mk 1000s (one of which was previously listed as sold to an undisclosed customer). Deliveries are under way and will bring the total of Garuda Fellowships to 24.

McDonnell Douglas DC-9: British West Indian Airways has ordered two Srs 50s and a Srs 30F convertible freighter, for delivery mid-1977 and early 1978. Pending delivery, a Srs 50 is being leased by BWIA, for operations starting 1 August this year.

Vickers Vanguard: Europe Air Services of Perpignan has acquired three more V.952s, ex Invicta International, becoming the largest Vanguard operator in the process, with a fleet of 16 including two freighters.

Now another go-anywhere transport from de Havilland joins the U.S. Army... the UV-18A Twin Otter.

The U.S. forces had already chosen the Beaver, the Otter and the Caribou—more than 1,300 go-anywhere planes from de Havilland. They knew our performance first hand. And they had a very demanding order to fill, selecting transports for "command administrative, logistical and personnel flights from battalion headquarters to remote village sites throughout western and northern Alaska on a year-round basis."

It's no wonder they chose the Twin Otter. With their de Havilland experience. Plus these Twin Otter features:

It converts readily from wheels to wheel-skis, floats or high-flotation tires. (The U.S. is equipping each Twin Otter with all of these.)

It carries 19 troops in and out of rough, makeshift 300 m (1,000 ft) strips with room to spare.

In 15 minutes, two men can change it to a cargo plane that will carry a payload of more than two tons.

On a hundred-mile-radius reconnaissance or search and rescue mission, it can stay aloft for more than 6 hours because of its exceptional fuel economy.

It cruises at 182 knots at 10,000 feet. Or handles easily at 70 knots for pin-point paradropping of men or supplies.

The de Havilland Twin Otter. The go-anywhere plane that has proved its dependability, versatility and economy with 18 other defence, police and government organizations. And with 135 civil operators.

The de Havilland Aircraft of Canada Limited, Downsview, Ontario, M3K 1Y5. Telephone: (416) 633-7310. Telex: 0622128. Cable: Moth, Toronto.

Twin Otter: the standard of dependability and versatility in more than 50 countries.

de Havilland

In "appalling" weather...

A Jaguar of No 14 Squadron of the Royal Air Force which put up the best individual performance in the Salmond Trophy navigation and bombing competition arrived dead overhead of target, dead on time, and scored a direct hit. The weather was officially described as "appalling".

Jaguar – the best tactical strike aircraft in existence.

jaguar Designed and built by **S.E.P.E.C.A.T.**

BRAZIL STRESSES AIR CAPABILITY

by Roberto Pereira de Andrade

R EVOLUTIONS of the politically-motivated kind are scattered throughout the modern history of Latin America like so much confetti and the occasional forcible substitution of a government has been by no means unknown in Brazil as elsewhere on this vast continent where temperament has, rightly or wrongly, been credited with something of a reputation for volatility. But a revolution of a somewhat less traumatic nature is currently taking place in Brazil and has, indeed, been in progress for the past half-decade — it is a fundamental change in Brazil's air arm, the *Fôrça Aérea Brasileira,* or FAB, which is revolutionising its equipment inventory.

When the 'seventies dawned, the equipment of the FAB comprised hardware that, apart from a handful of light observation and liaison aircraft of indigenous design and a scattering of licence-built Fokker primary trainers, had been purchased abroad. Today, barely into the second half of the decade, the *Fôrça Aérea* can boast with complete justification that more than half of the service's inventory of upwards of 600 aircraft comprises aeroplanes of Brazilian manufacture and, for the most part, of Brazilian design! The "Brazilianization" of the FAB's equipment — which has paralleled the growth of Brazil's aerospace industry making its European début at the Farnborough Air Show this month when it exhibits its already widely-used Bandeirante utility twin — may appear undramatic to the more industrially advanced of countries, yet from virtual total dependence on imported aircraft to self-sufficiency in several important aircraft categories in a half-dozen or so years is no mean achievement by any standard and one in which Brazil justifiably takes pride.

As befits the largest South American nation, the FAB is today the most substantial of Latin American air arms, but size is, of course, purely relative. The fifth largest country in the world, covering 3,286,488 square miles (8 512 000 km²) of territory, with some 4,500 miles (7 240 km) of Atlantic

seaboard and stretching from north of the equator to south of the Tropic of Capricorn, Brazil presents fantastic climatic and topographical extremes with which the FAB must contend. Distances are vast, much of the terrain rugged and jungle-covered, and flying aids are sparse, and in such a country an air arm a half-dozen times the size of the *Fôrça Aérea* would have perforce to spread its resources thinly.

Brazil, in line with most western nations, has suffered and is still suffering the affliction of a high level of inflation, and stringent budgetary limitations, particularly in so far as the armed forces are concerned, have understandably exercised an inhibiting effect on the planned growth of the FAB. Nevertheless, if the FAB has expanded little in the numerical sense

(Head of page) An F-5E Tiger II of the I Grupo de Aviação de Caça based at Santa Cruz AFB, south-west of Rio de Janeiro, and (below) a Mirage IIIEBR interceptor of the 1ª Ala de Defesa Aérea which operates from the new Anápolis AFB, near Brasília.

during the present decade, its capability in virtually every sphere of activity in which it is engaged has increased to an unprecedented degree; there has been no period comparable with the past two or three years in its 36-year history as an autonomous force — with the possible exception of the early 'forties, when, after Brazil's declaration of war on Germany and Italy, and with US aid, the then-fledgeling FAB expanded from a mere token force to a substantial air arm — in which the *Fôrça Aérea* has expanded its faculties to such an extent.

In order to place the FAB in context, however, it should be understood that, whereas the primary task of most air forces is the defence of national airspace coupled with the ability to take retaliatory action in the event of an attack, the principal rôle of the FAB is seen in most Brazilian official circles — if not necessarily in the FAB itself — as an instrument of economic development; its missions are predominantly social and, in consequence, the average Brazilian thinks of the FAB not so much as a fighting force but as a state-owned enterprise for the transportation of passengers, mail and freight into and out of places to which commercial operators cannot or will not fly, for mitigating the effects of national disasters and for aeromedical tasks, including such hearts-and-minds duties as transporting doctors, vaccines and relief aid into the interior.

In consequence, much of the funding for re-equipment and modernisation available in recent years has been devoted to logistic support capability and to the acquisition of aircraft suitable for the ever-increasing communications commitment of Brazilian service aviation. Still largely undeveloped, Brazil lacks a really extensive network of railways and roads capable of accommodating heavy motor transport — the Trans-Amazonica road currently under construction could, if transported from Brazil and deposited in Europe, link Lisbon with Moscow! — and thus aviation is probably more vital a factor in its economic growth than in any other country. It is for this reason that the responsibilities of Brazil's Air Ministry

in Brasília embrace the entire spectrum of Brazilian aviation. Not only is this one Ministry responsible for the FAB, its tasks include the supervision and support of the national airlines and aero clubs, the construction and management of airports, the training of aeronautical engineers and technicians, in fact, virtually every facet of the aeronautical scene. Thus, while the Air Ministry came fourth of 16 ministries in so far as financial allocations from the 1976 federal budget were concerned, with some 3·3 per cent of total funding, equivalent to the not-insubstantial sum of around US$800m, this finance is spread over a wide-ranging array of departments, both civil and military, and the proportion allocated to the FAB must remain a matter for speculation.

While re-equipment emphasis has, of necessity, been placed in recent years on logistic support and communications aircraft, Latin American politics being such as they are — characterised by all the volatility popularly attributed to the Latin American temperament — the FAB has not, despite budgetary strictures, neglected either the defensive or counter-insurgency capabilities of the service, and of late has rationalised its combat components, largely phasing out and replacing the aged and obsolete aircraft that were pre-ponderant in their inventories until recently.

Command organisation

Possessing a nominal strength of 36,000 personnel, although currently some 8-10 per cent below this figure, and including 2,247 of commissioned rank, the FAB is headed by Lt Brig Deoclécio Lima de Siqueira as Chief-of-Staff with Headquarters in Brasília and responsible to the Air Minister, Lt Brig Joelmir Campos de Araripe Macedo. The FAB organisation includes a number of specialised Commands, those controlling combat units comprising the *Comando de Defesa Aérea*, which, based at Anápolis, near Brasília, controls the expand-ing air defence system; the *Comando Aerotático* controlling the tactical elements, including the counter-insurgency *Esquad-rãos*, and the *Comando Costeiro* which is responsible for the land-based maritime patrol units as well as the fixed-wing element aboard the Brazilian Navy's sole carrier, the *Minas Gerais*. Other Commands include the *Comando de Transportes Aéreos* which exercises overall control of all air transport elements, although these come under the direct control of the Regional Air Commands in which they are based; the *Comando Geral de Apoio*, responsible for repair, maintenance and storage depots; the *Comando Geral do Ar* which supervises all ground staff, FAB troops, etc, and the *Comando Geral de Pessoal* responsible for the FAB staff, general administrative tasks, etc.

(Above) An EMBRAER AT-26 Xavante serving in the light strike rôle with 7,62-mm gun pods and four 250-lb (113-kg) bombs, and (below) Bell UH-1H Iroquois helicopters of the 3° Esquadrão de Ligação e Observação based at Porto Alegre.

(Above) An RC-130E Hercules employed for SAR missions by the VI Grupo de Aviação based at Recife, Pernambuco, and (immediately below right) the DHC-5A Buffalo equips the 2° Esquadrão of the Grupo de Transporte de Tropas at Campo dos Afonços as well as the 5° and 6° Esquadrãos at Campo Grande and Manaus respectively.

Direct control of FAB elements is exercised by the Regional Air Command (COMAR) which is responsible for all aircraft, equipment, installations and personnel within its operational area and can operate, in effect, as an independent air arm should the need ever arise. Brazilian territory is divided between six COMARs as follows: 1° COMAR with Headquarters at Belém, Pará State, which covers the States of Amazonas, Pará and Acre, and the Federal Territories of Roraima, Rondônia and Amapá, which, combined, embrace an area almost half the size of Europe; 2° COMAR with Headquarters in Recife, Pernambuco State, covering the States of Piauí, Ceará, Rio Grande do Norte, Pernambuco, Alagoas, Sergipe, Bahia and the larger part of Maranhão, plus the territory of Fernando de Noronha, a group of mid-Atlantic islands; 3° COMAR with Headquarters in Rio de Janeiro and covering the States of Rio de Janeiro and the larger part of Minas Gerais; 4° COMAR with Headquarters at São Paulo and covering the States of São Paulo and all but the northern part of Mato Grosso State (which comes under the 1° COMAR); the 5° COMAR with Headquarters at Porto Alegre and covering the States of Rio Grande do Sul, Paraná and Santa Catarina, and the 6° COMAR with Headquarters in Brasília and embracing the Federal District of the capital, the State of Goiás, the western portion of the Minas Gerais State and a small area of Maranhão.

Several esquadrãos of the Comando de Transportes Aéreos are still either wholly or partly equipped with the reliable but venerable C-47 (above), and the Grupo de Transporte Especial includes eight HS.125s in its inventory, two of these being seen below.

First-stage air defence

While no serious threat of air attack is envisaged in the next decade or so from any neighbouring countries, a gesture towards an integrated air defence system which it is foreseen will embrace the whole of Brazil by the late 'eighties has been made and currently working up to full operational status is the SISDACTA computerised air traffic control and air defence radar system which has been installed under contract by the French Thomson-CSF concern. Known as DACTA I, the system so far established covers an area incorporating the cities of Brasília, São Paulo, Rio de Janeiro and Belo Horizonte, and within which some 60 per cent of all traffic movements take place. Next year, a start will be made on DACTA II which will extend the system to cover all of

AIRFIELDS AND BASES FROM WHICH THE FAB OPERATES ON A REGULAR BASIS (BUT NOT NECESSARILY ACCOMMODATING UNITS ON A PERMANENT BASIS)

southern Brazil, including the States of Rio Grande do Sul, Paraná and Santa Catarina.

In the long term it is envisaged that a substantial interceptor force and SAM batteries will be built up to complete an integrated defence system, but as yet the only intercept component is the so-called 1ª *Ala de Defesa Aérea* (ALADA), the FAB's first Air Defence Wing, which, based at the new Anapolis AFB, some 80 miles (130 km) from Brasilia, maintains a number of aircraft on permanent 24-hour standby but is only of *Esquadrão* strength with barely more than a dozen single- and two-seat Mirages. The 1ª ALADA was formed with 12 single-seat Mirage IIIEBRs and four two-seat IIIDBRs (known respectively as the F-103E and D to the FAB) ordered from France in 1970, but although follow-up orders were anticipated, these have not been forthcoming and as, at times, the readiness level of the 1ª ALADA has reportedly been disappointing owing to non-availability of certain spares, it would seem that any future expansion of the Mirage force is improbable and that the additional interceptor units envisaged will receive other equipment — the Israeli Kfir

is reputedly on offer and the FAB has allegedly been casting some envious glances in the direction of the General Dynamics F-16, but no funding for such a purchase would appear imminent.

Something of a fillip was given to the FAB fighter element earlier this year with the delivery to the Santa Cruz AFB, some miles south-west along the coast from Rio de Janeiro, of the last of the batch of Northrop F-5E Tiger IIs to the *I Grupo de Aviação de Caça* (GAvCa). In October 1974, a $72·3m contract was placed for 36 F-5E Tiger IIs and six two-seat F-5Bs, deliveries to the FAB commencing 18 months ago, on 12 March 1975, when the first three F-5Bs were ferried into Santa Cruz and the 1º *Esquadrão* of the GAvCa began the process of converting from the EMBRAER-built AT-26 Xavante. Original planning called for both *Esquadrãos* of the I GAvCa as well as the 2º *Esquadrão* of the XIV GAvCa to convert to the F-5E, but for economy reasons and to trim the requirements for ground technicians, all the aircraft have, in the event, been assigned to the I GAvCa, the Xavantes of its two component *Esquadrãos* being progressively transferred to the *Academia da*

Fôrça Aérea (AFA) at Pirassununga, São Paulo, where they are replacing the well-worn Cessna T-37Cs, which, with some eight-nine years of FAB service behind them, are presenting a growing spares problem. Two of the F-5s were lost during delivery flights to Santa Cruz and a third following a bird strike, and no replacements for these had been ordered at the time of writing, but the FAB is proposing the procurement of sufficient additional F-5Es to equip at least two further *Esquadrões* when budget considerations and trained technical manpower permit, and there is still a possibility that EMBRAER — which is contracted to manufacture for Northrop 100 sets of F-5 tail units and underwing weapon pylons — will eventually licence-manufacture the entire F-5E airframe.

The remaining fighter *Esquadrões* are now exclusively equipped with the AT-26 Xavante, as is the case with the 1° and 2° *Esquadrões* of the IV GAvCa at Fortaleza AFB, Ceará State, or in process of phasing out the aged Lockheed AT-33A in favour of the Xavante as is the FAB's other *Grupo de Aviação de Caça,* the XIV GAvCa, which currently comprises only a 1° *Esquadrão* at the Canoas AFB, near Porto Alegre in the Rio Grande do Sul State. Deliveries of the Xavante by EMBRAER against the original contract for 112 aircraft have been in process to the FAB since late 1971, peaking at two per month, and the confirmed follow-on contract for a further 40 aircraft will stretch Xavante deliveries through 1977. The FAB is well pleased with the performance and service record of the Xavante to date. Attrition has been low, the introduction of Aerotec-manufactured self-contained starter pods which can replace one of the Xavante's external fuel tanks is greatly increasing the number of airfields from which this type may be operated and the FAB has every reason to congratulate itself on its selection of the Xavante seven years ago.

Apart from the *Grupos de Aviação de Caça,* the Xavante is seeing increasing use with the counter-insurgency component of the *Comando Aerotático,* the *Esquadrões Mistos de Reconhecimento e Ataque* (Reconnaissance and Attack Squadrons), or EMRAs. There are currently five EMRAs of which more than half are now operating or phasing in the Xavante. The 3° EMRA at the Galeão AFB, Rio de Janeiro, and the 4° EMRA at the Cumbica AFB, São Paulo, are both now fully equipped with the Xavante, while the 5° EMRA at the Canoas AFB, Porto Alegre, is now phasing out the last of its aged T-6 Texans in favour of the Xavante.

The two remaining EMRAs, the 1° at Belém, Pará State, and the 2° at Recife, Pernambuco, still soldier on with the surviving T-6s, but current planning calls for their re-equipment during the course of next year with the armed version of the Neiva T-25 Universal, commencing with the 1° EMRA. While the Xavante provides an excellent backbone for the COIN force, the T-25 Universal offers the advantages of increased loiter time, albeit with a somewhat smaller offensive load, and the ability to operate from short, semi-prepared strips. The T-25 Universal was, of course, designed as a successor to the T-6 Texan for part of the basic training syllabus — Neiva having completed FAB contracts for 132 Universal Is by the end of 1974 — and this remains the primary function of the aircraft, but all Universals supplied to the FAB were delivered with provision for a weapons aiming sight and with a weapon selector box. The Universal II, with a 400 hp Avco Lycoming IO-720 engine and four wing strong points for gun pods, rocket clusters or bombs, has been under test for some time, and Neiva is hopeful of receiving a contract for this upgraded version as a successor to the T-6s of the 1° and 2° EMRAs.

Also possessing counter-insurgency capability are the *Esquadrão de Ligação e Observação* (Liaison and Observation Squadrons), or ELOs, which operate a mix of light aircraft and helicopters. The 1° ELO based at Campo dos Afonços, Rio de Janeiro, operates the Neiva L-42 Regente — the production of 40 of which for the FAB was completed in March 1971 — in concert with the Bell 206A JetRanger and a few Cessna O-1E Bird Dogs; the 2° ELO based at San Pedro de Aldea has Neiva T-25 Universal Is, and the 3° ELO at Porto Alegre possesses Bell UH-1H Iroquois helicopters, O-1E Bird Dogs and L-42 Regentes.

Maritime, SAR and transport

The FAB remains unique among air forces in that, although Brazil possesses a naval air component, the *Fôrça Aéronaval,* the service still fulfils a seagoing rôle by deploying aboard the carrier *Minas Gerais* six Grumman S-2 Trackers from its

The S-2A Trackers operated for the past 15 years by the Grupo de Aviação Embarcada were largely replaced recently by eight refurbished ex-US Navy S-2E Trackers, some of the older S-2As (such as that seen above right) now serving in the transportation rôle. The VII Grupo de Aviação operates the long-serving and recently-refurbished P-2E Neptune, one of which is seen below, and will continue to do so well into 1978.

The Mirage IIIEBR (above) has now seen some years of service in the intercept rôle with the 1ª ALADA, but spares support has allegedly fallen short of that desired and concern has been expressed over the high cost and extended time factor in the overhaul of the fighter's Atar engine. (Foot of page) The AT-26 Xavante has established a good performance and service record and production by EMBRAER will continue through 1977.

Grupo de Aviação Embarcada which, shore-based at Santa Cruz AFB, Rio de Janeiro, comprises only a 2° *Esquadrão* which has recently phased in eight refurbished ex-US Navy S-2E Trackers as replacements for the S-2A and CS2F-1 Trackers that it had been operating for the previous 15 years. The other principal component of the *Comando Costeiro* is the 1° *Esquadrão* of the *VII Grupo de Aviação* which operates seven long-serving Lockheed P-2E Neptunes in the maritime patrol rôle from Salvador, Bahia State.

It would now seem that the Neptunes are to soldier on into 1978, when deliveries may be expected to commence of the EMB-111 maritime patrol derivative of the Bandeirante light transport, 16 examples of which have recently been ordered for FAB use. Not that the FAB looks upon this EMBRAER-developed patroller, with its AN/APS-128 search radar, as a *replacement* for the Neptune, the service still being anxious to acquire an aircraft in the P-3 Orion category to equip one long-range maritime patrol *esquadrão*. Unfortunately, the funding of such a buy is currently presenting a near-insurmountable problem, even though the aircraft to be acquired will almost certainly be refurbished rather than new, and it could be well into the 'eighties before the *Comando Costeiro* will be able to deploy its envisaged force of one long-range patrol *esquadrão* and at least four EMB-111-equipped *esquadrãos*. Maritime

(Above) the 2° Esquadrão operates the six HS.748s with wide loading doors, deliveries of which began some two years ago and one of which is illustrated here. The DHC-5A Buffalo (below) provides the backbone of the Esquadrãos de Transporte de Tropas, while the Hercules fulfils the heavy logistic support rôle, a C-130E of the 1° Esquadrão of the I Grupo being illustrated bottom right.

patrol is an increasingly important commitment in so far as the FAB is concerned, and the EMB-111, which, in addition to its ASW rôle, will perform coastal fishery patrol, sonar search and shipping surveillance tasks, will provide a valuable addition to the service's inventory.

Search and rescue functions are fulfilled by the *VI Grupo de Aviação* based at Recife, Pernambuco, which performs long-range SAR missions as well as photographic tasks with three RC-130E Hercules and anticipates adding several EMB-111s to its inventory in due course. The *X Grupo de Aviação* operates its 2° *Escuadrão* from Florianopolis with a dozen SA-16A Albatross amphibians as the nucleus of the FAB's *Serviço de Busca e Salvamento* (Search and Rescue Service), its 3° *Escuadrão* having a mix of Bell SH-1D Iroquois and Bell 47G helicopters.

Transportation in all its forms provides the most important commitment of the FAB and the principal elements of the

——————————————— *continued on page 146*

TORNADO TAKES OFF

Europe's most significant military aircraft programme is the Panavia Tornado, under development for Germany, the United Kingdom and Italy. This account of Tornado progress and production plans coincides with the launching of full-scale production.

FOLLOWING a highly successful public début at the Hanover Air Show earlier this year, when daily flying demonstrations were made by one of the German prototypes and another provided a centre of interest in the static display, the Panavia Tornado is expected to be seen by an even wider public at Farnborough International '76, the biennial SBAC display which opens in Britain in the first week of September. Known until recently as the MRCA (Multi-rôle Combat Aircraft), the Tornado has emerged as Europe's most significant military aircraft of the current decade, with the necessary governmental approvals for full-scale production having been given in the course of the last few weeks to dispel any lingering beliefs that the MRCA might become just one more expensive project to pass into limbo before reaching maturity.

The three partner nations backing the Tornado — Britain, Germany and Italy — have an initial stated requirement, in total, for just over 800 examples of this new warplane, to be produced over the next 10 years or so. This alone establishes the programme as something out of the ordinary — no other military aircraft of European origin has entered production since the end of World War II with so large an *initial* commitment (although several have been produced, ultimately, in larger numbers) and no European aircraft production programme in the past or foreseeable future matches the Tornado in monetary value. Possibly more remarkable, however, than the sheer size of the programme, which embraces some 500 suppliers of material and equipment and will ultimately employ more than 50,000 workers in the three nations, is the fact that the Tornado meets the requirements of four military air arms (the Royal Air Force, the *Luftwaffe,* the *Marineflieger* and the *Aeronautica Militare Italiana*) for a warplane able to fulfil several different combat rôles. Never before have national air staffs been able to agree on an operational requirement that, notwithstanding some differences of emphasis upon specific rôles, allowed the design team to produce a satisfactory multi-national solution; and it

is this fact, of course, that has led to the 800-aircraft programme with its economies of scale.

If the integration of air staff requirements is remarkable, the degree of inter-government and industrial collaboration is no less so. Although collaboration is no novelty so far as the European aerospace companies are concerned (as such programmes as the Concorde, Jaguar, Airbus, Anglo-French helicopters, Adour, Mercure and Transall bear witness), it has been brought to a new high level of efficiency in the case of the Tornado, as AIR INTERNATIONAL was able to assess during a series of visits to the principal administration, manufacturing and test centres for the preparation of this account. Of key importance, in this respect, was the setting up of an international company, Panavia GmbH (headquartered in Munich and subject to German company law), jointly owned by the three principal airframe concerns — BAC (42½ per cent), MBB (42½ per cent) and Aeritalia (15 per cent).

Panavia has only 250 or so direct employees, and serves as a centralised management body, placing contracts on the three airframe companies — which in turn sub-contract as necessary — and upon the major equipment suppliers. It serves to exercise a close control over all aspects of the programme including, most importantly, cost, and maintains direct day-to-day contact with NAMMA (the NATO MRCA Management Agency) which is responsible for putting into effect the policy decisions of the three customer governments, and has its HQ in the same building as Panavia in Munich. NAMMA, staffed by government specialists, takes its directions in turn from NAMMO (NATO MRCA Management Organisation) which is made up of the senior government executives controlling the Tornado programme and is ultimately responsible for defining policy in accordance with government directives. On the engine side, Panavia is matched by Turbo-Union Ltd, set up by Fiat, MTU and Rolls-Royce. This company, with about 40 employees, has its HQ in Bristol and an office in Munich close to the Panavia office, and similarly places contracts on the three engine companies to implement the orders it receives direct from NAMMA. The Tornado's built-in armament is also regarded as a primary contract, NAMMA dealing direct with its designer, IWKA-Mauser.

The task of designing, developing, building and flight testing prototypes and launching full-scale production of the Tornado in three countries has gone ahead remarkably smoothly; more will be said later in this account of these aspects of the story. It is worth recording at this point, however, that the programme has also shown remarkable resilience in the political sphere, having already survived changes of government in all three sponsoring nations, one of which (Italy) has experienced a sharp swing towards communism without, at the time of writing, any indication that this will jeopardise its commitment to the Tornado. All three nations need the Tornado to meet clearly established defence requirements; the programme is providing substantial employment (a factor of special political importance in Italy and the UK); the aircraft is performing satisfactorily in flight test and there has been no serious cost overrun.

So far as costs are concerned, the most recent unit price quoted officially in Britain is £5·29m, at estimated 1976/77 prices. This compares with the £1·5m estimate at 1969 prices on which the MRCA was launched, but almost all of this increase is attributable to inflation; there has been a "real" increase of about £600,000 on the 1969 price. The figure involved here is a fly-away price for production aircraft, without allowing for R & D, and the equivalent price in Germany is reported to be DM26·4m*. When the German government gave its final approval to the Tornado production programme (on 2 June), a figure of DM15,500m was quoted as the total German investment for 322 aircraft — a systems cost of DM48·14m per aircraft. This figure is based on the unit price of DM32·2m (which is fly-away price plus pre-production costs and VAT) and various support items including documentation, ammunition, training, test and ground equipment and spares amounting to 50 per cent of the unit cost.

The story so far
Before describing the current status of production and flight test, a brief recap of the history of the Tornado will help to put the story in perspective. The origins of the MRCA can be traced back to before 1965, so far as the engineering evolution of variable sweep in the UK is concerned, but a better starting point for the story is 1967, in which year the French unilaterally left the Anglo-French VG programme in order to concentrate on the Mirage G as a wholly-national programme. While British defence policy underwent a major revision, with Far East commitments dropped, Germany was studying the development of a *Neuen Kampfflugzeug* (NKF — "new battleplane") and by 1968 had interested Italy, Belgium, the Netherlands and Canada in joining a consortium to study the requirement for and development of such an aircraft as a multi-national project. This became the MRA-75 (Multi-rôle Aircraft for 1975).

On 25 July 1968, the UK signed a Memorandum of Understanding with this consortium with a view to merging the British requirement with that of the European nations, and the project became known as the MRCA-75. Belgium, Canada and the Netherlands withdrew successively in 1968/69, for various reasons, but all three nations made distinctive contributions to the specification, the basic requirements of which had been agreed by the end of 1968. Further definition work was completed in the early months of 1969, basically to bring together the ideas of BAC and MBB, which in January 1969 were still somewhat in divergence over how to meet the requirement. Panavia was set up on 26 March, and on 16 May another Memorandum of Understanding was initialled by the UK, Germany and Italy, authorising the Definition Phase on MRCA to proceed; a formal competition was then conducted to select an engine — the choice being between Rolls-Royce and Pratt & Whitney — and the RB.199-34R, a brand new three-spool turbofan, was selected in September 1969.

The aeroplane that the RAF wanted was an interdictor/strike replacement for the Canberra, Vulcan and Buccaneer — the same requirement, in fact, for which the TSR-2 had been designed, although the subsequent change in the UK defence policy had rendered much of the TSR-2 specification out-of-date and the MRCA was designed to a different set of performance parameters. Germany wanted a similar aircraft for its *Marineflieger*, but the numerically larger

---

Direct conversions between German, British and Italian currencies at whatever rates prevail from day to day are almost meaningless in respect of the Tornado programme. A notional rate of £1=DM5·75 is used within Panavia for accounting purposes — some 20 per cent higher than the commercial rate of June 1976 — but the whole basis of the joint programme is that each nation funds its own work in its own currency and any necessary adjustments are made by more or less work being done, not by making monetary transfers.

Project drawings below show BAC (left) and MBB (right) proposals for a future combat aircraft as at the end of 1968. The fusing of these ideas produced the MRCA-75 in the form in which it was accepted by the three governments for further development in May 1969.

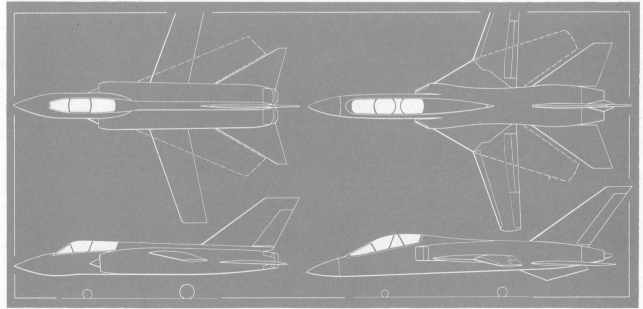

Varying aspects of the Tornado prototypes are seen here. The first British aircraft, P-02, is shown (left) with wings forward, (above) with wings fully swept and carrying 330-Imp gal (1 500-l) drop tanks and (below) with afterburners lit. The illustration below left shows P-03, the second British aircraft to fly and the first to appear in RAF camouflage.

German requirement was for a replacement for the *Luftwaffe's* F-104Gs in the battlefield interdiction and air superiority rôles. The Italian requirement, numerically the smallest, was for an air superiority fighter to replace the F-104G. All three nations needed a training variant of the aircraft that would eventually be developed to meet the requirement.

The wide spectrum of rôles for which the MRCA-75 was required made the choice of variable geometry virtually inevitable. Wings swept back gave supersonic capability, good acceleration and the low gust response rate essential for low-altitude contour-hugging flight in the interdiction/strike rôle; wings fully forward gave good take-off and landing performance (on which the *Luftwaffe* placed special emphasis), long range and long loiter capability over the target and good manoeuvrability, all characteristics required for the battlefield interdiction and air superiority rôles. In the early stages of the programme, the divergent requirements also led to the parallel development of single-seat (close air support and air superiority) and two-seat (interdictor strike) versions, with a high degree of commonality but different front fuselages. However, the extra R & D costs of a two-version programme proved excessive in relation to possible benefits, which became increasingly hard to justify in view of the demonstrated advantages (in such aircraft as the F-4 Phantom) of having a crew of two even for the CAS and air superiority rôles; and on 24 March 1970, the British and German defence ministers agreed to drop the single-seater, on the dual grounds that the two-seater was operationally more effective in all the required rôles and that there were substantial economies to be made by this course of action. Italy concurred in the decision and confirmed her intention of remaining in the programme a few months later.

The definition phase of the work having been satisfactorily completed by April 1970, the programme was subjected to a full critical review by the three governments and the development phase was launched, with a Memorandum of Understanding signed by the UK and German governments on 20 July 1970, and by the Italian government on 30 September. Included in this phase was the construction of the first nine aircraft (initially described as six prototypes and three pre-production, but now all called prototypes). A series of contractual check-points was established, with defined targets to be achieved before progressing to the next phase; at each point, a full government review takes place, and it is in the light of satisfactory reports at these check-points that the programme has moved steadily ahead, with a pre-production batch of six aircraft ordered in 1974 to follow on the prototypes, and the necessary contractual paperwork for the initial production batch (of about 40 aircraft) being prepared as this account went to press, following the full production go-ahead decision in June. Action to order long-leadtime material for these first aircraft has already been taken.

There had originally been some prospect of MRCA requirements totalling about 1,185, with Germany taking 600, the RAF 385 and Italy 200. By late 1970, however, these figures had been re-assessed on the basis of only the two-seat version being produced, and the final quantity, as still established today, comes out at 807, of which 210 are for the *Luftwaffe*, 112 for the *Marineflieger*, 385 for the RAF and 100 for the AMI. The RAF requirement has been further divided since the programme began, in the light of changing defence requirements, to embrace an air defence version (ADV) of the Tornado as well as the basic or IDS (interdictor strike) version. AST395 set out the need for a Lightning/Phantom replacement in the UK air defence rôle some three years ago, since which time a very careful evaluation has been made of the ADV version of the Tornado versus other available aircraft — notably the McDonnell Douglas F-15. The result of the evaluation was to confirm that the Tornado, suitably adapted, better meets the requirement than any other type — the requirement being primarily to defend the UK and the British Home Fleet from attack across the North Sea and Eastern Atlantic. This calls for the ability to fight at heights from very low level up to 80,000 ft (24 400 m) but with emphasis upon medium-to-low altitudes, with a speed of over Mach 2·0, outstanding manoeuvrability and an advanced radar/weapon system able to track and attack several targets simultaneously.

The Tornado ADV will have some 80 per cent commonality with the basic aircraft; its new features are the radar, the weapon system (which presumably will include advanced AAMs carried in recesses under the fuselage, *à la* F-15); a front fuselage lengthened by about 18 in (0,5 m) to facilitate the new weapon fit, plus the extra length of the new radome; increased fuel capacity derived from the lengthened front fuselage, and uprated engines. Since the requirement is wholly British, the ADV development will be funded from 1979 onwards, but manufacture will be shared in accordance with the overall work-division plan. It is currently expected that the RAF buy will include 165 of the ADV and 220 basic Tornadoes.

Details of the Tornado

As already indicated, the selection of VG for the MRCA was made almost inevitable by the spread of rôles it was expected to fulfil and especially by the emphasis placed upon the strike rôle. The need to combine Mach 2+ performance at high altitude with an exceptionally smooth ride for the crew in the critical low level attack mode at high subsonic speed also exerted considerable influence on the structural design and the selection of systems. The structure is designed for long fatigue life in low level transonic flight, with high g tolerance, and the wing attachment is a key area in this respect. The wing carry-through box is made of titanium, welded by means of an advanced electron beam technique that ensures strength whilst inducing a minimum of residual stresses. Loads are transferred from the carry-through box to the moving wing by self-aligning PTFE-coated spherical bearings and separate shear pick-up tracks.

The remainder of the airframe is manufactured mainly of conventional alloys using heavy frames and longerons to transfer loads throughout the structure. Wherever possible, these heavy pieces of structure are used to give additional protection from ground fire to vital systems, components and

(Above) Tornado P-03 is the first equipped as a dual control trainer and is currently engaged in stall and spin trials. (Below) The third British prototype, P-06, is assigned primarily to handling and weapons launching trials; it was the first to fly with the Mauser cannon fitted.

fuel. To simplify maintenance, more than 35 per cent of the Tornado's surface is made up of access panels to give quick and easy access to equipment. Almost all equipment is on a Line Replaceable Unit basis and requires no calibration when installed, and the diagnosis and location of faults is facilitated by use of Built-In Test Equipment (BITE) and Onboard (Check-out) and Monitoring System (OCAMS).

Much use is made of integrally-machined components throughout the Tornado airframe. Notably, the upper and lower skins of the outer wing panels are milled from single pieces of alloy, with integral lateral stiffeners. Among the Tornado's several structural features of special interest is the means adopted to seal the gap between the wing glove and the moving outer wing panels; this comprises a number of glass-reinforced plastics plates which open and close like a fan as the wing angle is varied. The fuselage slots into which the trailing edges move are closed by air-inflated flexible seals. Fuel is carried in integral tanks in the torsion box of each outer wing panel and in tanks grouped in the centre fuselage, fore and aft of the wing carry-through structure, which also carries fuel.

Flight control is by means of two large all-moving tailerons for pitch and roll, augmented by spoilers on the upper wing surfaces for extra roll control when the wings are at small sweep angles; there is a conventional fin and rudder, but no ailerons. To achieve near-STOL performance, the aircraft has trailing edge double-slotted flaps occupying the whole of the span in four sections each side, and leading-edge slots occupying the whole of the moving wing panels in three sections each side. The fixed leading edge wing roots have Krueger flaps. The spoilers, in two sections each side, operate also as lift dumpers after touch down and large air brakes are located on the upper surface of the rear fuselage, each side of the fin leading edge.

The primary flying control surfaces are actuated by electrically-controlled tandem hydraulic jacks, the basic control system being "fly-by-wire", and incorporating a Command and Stability Augmentation System (CSAS) which plays a major part in providing the crew with a comfortable ride in low-altitude, high-turbulent conditions. Potentiometers on the control columns feed triple electrical signals to the CSAS, which also receives feed-back signals from the control actuators, indicating their current positions, and pitch, roll and yaw rate signals sensed by gyros. These signals are processed within the CSAS, the triplexed signals being compared by voter-monitor units at various stages to detect and eliminate errors in any channel. Should two errors occur, the appropriate section of the CSAS is disengaged and the system reverts to straight electrical signalling. In the case of complete electrical signalling failure, the aircraft can be controlled on the tailplanes alone, using mechanical linkage between the control column and the tailplane's actuators.

The CSAS utilises artificial feel inputs and thus, with the appropriate feedback, ensures optimum control response throughout the flight envelope, with automatic compensation for configuration changes. As the system is all-electric, the interface with the autopilot is also much simplified. Marconi-Elliott Avionics is prime contractor for the CSAS, Elliotts being responsible for the autopilot and flight director system (APFD).

A comprehensive radar 'fit' is required to allow the Tornado to meet the demanding requirements of high-speed, all-weather, low-level penetration to a point target for a single-pass delivery of the selected weapon(s). The system includes forward-looking radar with terrain-following and ground-mapping facilities, plus air-to-air search, acquisition and lock-on, and air-to-air and air-to-ground ranging for missiles, bombs and cannon; in the basic Tornado, this radar is by Texas Instruments — the only major piece of equipment specified outside Europe — but the RAF's ADV version will have an all-new Marconi-Elliott Avionics air-intercept radar

The first two German prototypes of the Tornado, P-04 (above) and P-01 (below) are both finished in red-and-white test markings. P-04 is one of the primary avionics test aircraft.

The second avionics test aircraft, P-07, based with P-04 at the MBB flight test centre at Manching, near Munich (above), is finished in representative Luftwaffe colours and markings. The first Italian aircraft, P-05 (below), is expected to rejoin the programme later this year.

of increased performance. The heart of the nav/attack system is a doppler radar/inertial platform combination (Decca and Ferranti), both units feeding information to the main computer (by Litef).

Navigation information is communicated to the navigator on a combined radar/projected map (Ferranti) and television (Marconi-Elliott Avionics) displays. The pilot also receives the projected map display on a repeater unit, plus flight director and weapon aiming symbology on the Smiths head-up display.

Panavia Tornado Cutaway Drawing Key

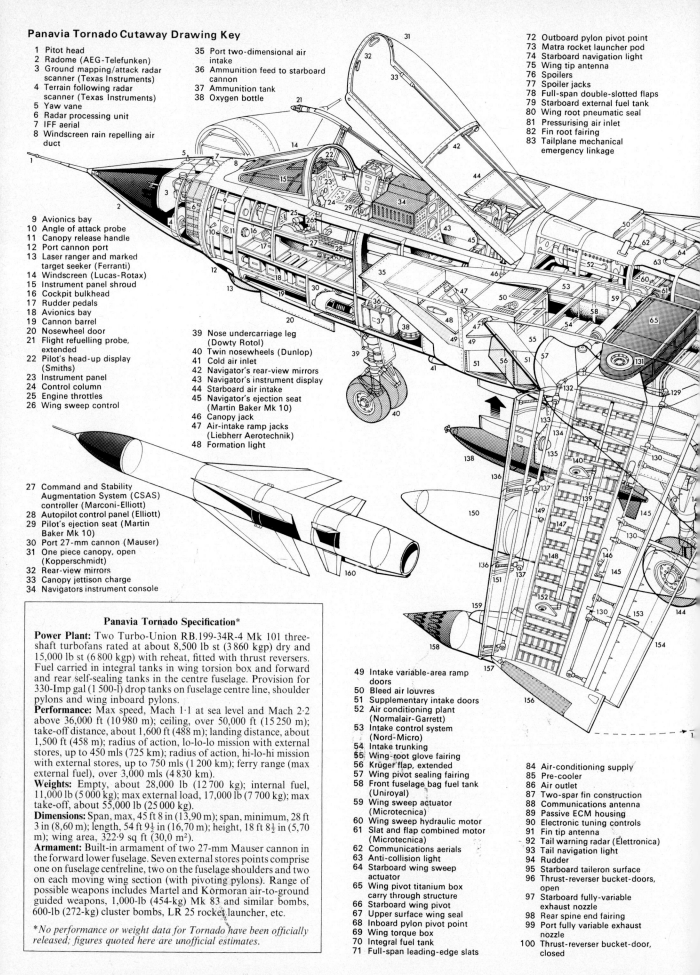

1 Pitot head
2 Radome (AEG-Telefunken)
3 Ground mapping/attack radar scanner (Texas Instruments)
4 Terrain following radar scanner (Texas Instruments)
5 Yaw vane
6 Radar processing unit
7 IFF aerial
8 Windscreen rain repelling air duct

9 Avionics bay
10 Angle of attack probe
11 Canopy release handle
12 Port cannon port
13 Laser ranger and marked target seeker (Ferranti)
14 Windscreen (Lucas-Rotax)
15 Instrument panel shroud
16 Cockpit bulkhead
17 Rudder pedals
18 Avionics bay
19 Cannon barrel
20 Nosewheel door
21 Flight refuelling probe, extended
22 Pilot's head-up display (Smiths)
23 Instrument panel
24 Control column
25 Engine throttles
26 Wing sweep control

27 Command and Stability Augmentation System (CSAS) controller (Marconi-Elliott)
28 Autopilot control panel (Elliott)
29 Pilot's ejection seat (Martin Baker Mk 10)
30 Port 27-mm cannon (Mauser)
31 One piece canopy, open (Kopperschmidt)
32 Rear-view mirrors
33 Canopy jettison charge
34 Navigators instrument console

35 Port two-dimensional air intake
36 Ammunition feed to starboard cannon
37 Ammunition tank
38 Oxygen bottle

39 Nose undercarriage leg (Dowty Rotol)
40 Twin nosewheels (Dunlop)
41 Cold air inlet
42 Navigator's rear-view mirrors
43 Navigator's instrument display
44 Starboard air intake
45 Navigator's ejection seat (Martin Baker Mk 10)
46 Canopy jack
47 Air-intake ramp jacks (Liebherr Aerotechnik)
48 Formation light

49 Intake variable-area ramp doors
50 Bleed air louvres
51 Supplementary intake doors
52 Air conditioning plant (Normalair-Garrett)
53 Intake control system (Nord-Micro)
54 Intake trunking
55 Wing-root glove fairing
56 Krüger flap, extended
57 Wing pivot sealing fairing
58 Front fuselage bag fuel tank (Uniroyal)
59 Wing sweep actuator (Microtecnica)
60 Wing sweep hydraulic motor
61 Slat and flap combined motor (Microtecnica)
62 Communications aerials
63 Anti-collision light
64 Starboard wing sweep actuator
65 Wing pivot titanium box carry through structure
66 Starboard wing pivot
67 Upper surface wing seal
68 Inboard pylon pivot point
69 Wing torque box
70 Integral fuel tank
71 Full-span leading-edge slats

72 Outboard pylon pivot point
73 Matra rocket launcher pod
74 Starboard navigation light
75 Wing tip antenna
76 Spoilers
77 Spoiler jacks
78 Full-span double-slotted flaps
79 Starboard external fuel tank
80 Wing root pneumatic seal
81 Pressurising air inlet
82 Fin root fairing
83 Tailplane mechanical emergency linkage

84 Air-conditioning supply
85 Pre-cooler
86 Air outlet
87 Two-spar fin construction
88 Communications antenna
89 Passive ECM housing
90 Electronic tuning controls
91 Fin tip antenna
92 Tail warning radar (Elettronica)
93 Tail navigation light
94 Rudder
95 Starboard taileron surface
96 Thrust-reverser bucket-doors, open
97 Starboard fully-variable exhaust nozzle
98 Rear spine end fairing
99 Port fully variable exhaust nozzle
100 Thrust-reverser bucket-door, closed

Panavia Tornado Specification*

Power Plant: Two Turbo-Union RB.199-34R-4 Mk 101 three-shaft turbofans rated at about 8,500 lb st (3 860 kgp) dry and 15,000 lb st (6 800 kgp) with reheat, fitted with thrust reversers. Fuel carried in integral tanks in wing torsion box and forward and rear self-sealing tanks in the centre fuselage. Provision for 330-Imp gal (1 500-l) drop tanks on fuselage centre line, shoulder pylons and wing inboard pylons.

Performance: Max speed, Mach 1·1 at sea level and Mach 2·2 above 36,000 ft (10 980 m); ceiling, over 50,000 ft (15 250 m); take-off distance, about 1,600 ft (488 m); landing distance, about 1,500 ft (458 m); radius of action, lo-lo-lo mission with external stores, up to 450 mls (725 km); radius of action, hi-lo-hi mission with external stores, up to 750 mls (1 200 km); ferry range (max external fuel), over 3,000 mls (4 830 km).

Weights: Empty, about 28,000 lb (12 700 kg); internal fuel, 11,000 lb (5 000 kg); max external load, 17,000 lb (7 700 kg); max take-off, about 55,000 lb (25 000 kg).

Dimensions: Span, max, 45 ft 8 in (13,90 m); span, minimum, 28 ft 3 in (8,60 m); length, 54 ft 9½ in (16,70 m); height, 18 ft 8½ in (5,70 m); wing area, 322·9 sq ft (30,0 m²).

Armament: Built-in armament of two 27-mm Mauser cannon in the forward lower fuselage. Seven external stores points comprise one on fuselage centreline, two on the fuselage shoulders and two on each moving wing section (with pivoting pylons). Range of possible weapons includes Martel and Kormoran air-to-ground guided weapons, 1,000-lb (454-kg) Mk 83 and similar bombs, 600-lb (272-kg) cluster bombs, LR 25 rocket launcher, etc.

No performance or weight data for Tornado have been officially released; figures quoted here are unofficial estimates.

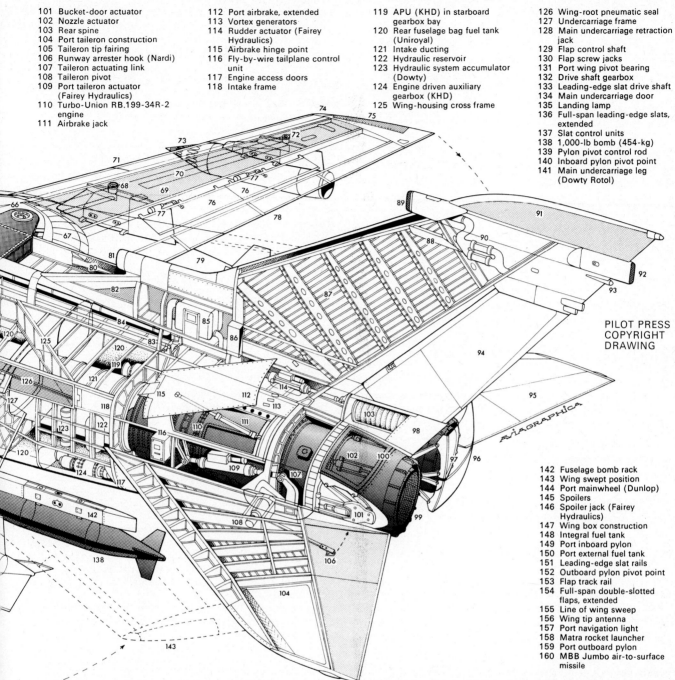

101 Bucket-door actuator
102 Nozzle actuator
103 Rear spine
104 Port taileron construction
105 Taileron tip fairing
106 Runway arrester hook (Nardi)
107 Taileron actuating link
108 Taileron pivot
109 Port taileron actuator (Fairey Hydraulics)
110 Turbo-Union RB.199-34R-2 engine
111 Airbrake jack

112 Port airbrake, extended
113 Vortex generators
114 Rudder actuator (Fairey Hydraulics)
115 Airbrake hinge point
116 Fly-by-wire tailplane control unit
117 Engine access doors
118 Intake frame

119 APU (KHD) in starboard gearbox bay
120 Rear fuselage bag fuel tank (Uniroyal)
121 Intake ducting
122 Hydraulic reservoir
123 Hydraulic system accumulator (Dowty)
124 Engine driven auxiliary gearbox (KHD)
125 Wing-housing cross frame

126 Wing-root pneumatic seal
127 Undercarriage frame
128 Main undercarriage retraction jack
129 Flap control shaft
130 Flap screw jacks
131 Port wing pivot bearing
132 Drive shaft gearbox
133 Leading-edge slat drive shaft
134 Main undercarriage door
135 Landing lamp
136 Full-span leading-edge slats, extended
137 Slat control units
138 1,000-lb bomb (454-kg)
139 Pylon pivot control rod
140 Inboard pylon pivot point
141 Main undercarriage leg (Dowty Rotol)

PILOT PRESS
COPYRIGHT
DRAWING

AVIAGRAPHICA

142 Fuselage bomb rack
143 Wing swept position
144 Port mainwheel (Dunlop)
145 Spoilers
146 Spoiler jack (Fairey Hydraulics)
147 Wing box construction
148 Integral fuel tank
149 Port inboard pylon
150 Port external fuel tank
151 Leading-edge slat rails
152 Outboard pylon pivot point
153 Flap track rail
154 Full-span double-slotted flaps, extended
155 Line of wing sweep
156 Wing tip antenna
157 Port navigation light
158 Matra rocket launcher
159 Port outboard pylon
160 MBB Jumbo air-to-surface missile

Panel-mounted instruments serve primarily as a back-up source for the HUD information.

The Tornado has a fully-duplicated hydraulic system pressurized by two pumps on the engine gearboxes, which have a cross drive so that both continue to run even if one engine stops. Items served by the hydraulic circuit, in addition to the flying controls, flaps and slats, are wing sweep, variable area air intakes, air brakes, undercarriage operation, brakes, nosewheel steering, canopy operation, flight-refuelling probe extension (when fitted), radar and laser range finding and target marker seeker. Brushless alternators on the engine gearboxes provide for both AC and DC power, each alternator being independently capable of supplying the entire power requirements of the aircraft.

Air is tapped from the high pressure compressor of the engine and after passing through heat exchangers is used for cockpit air conditioning, air ventilated suits, anti-g suits, wing and canopy seals, windscreen and canopy demisting, rain

dispersal and avionics bay cooling. The pilot and navigator/observer each have Martin Baker Mk 10 zero-zero ejection seats; canopy jettison is aided by rockets and the ejection sequence is always navigator first, either on his own command or on pilot command. A liquid oxygen system is fitted supplying a mixture of air and oxygen according to altitude, or pure oxygen in an emergency.

The Tornado carries a built-in armament of two 27-mm cannon, specially developed for the purpose by IWKA-Mauser in Germany and having a high velocity and high rate of fire to make them suitable for air-to-air and air-to-ground use. There are seven strong points for a wide variety of stores to be carried by the basic aircraft (the ADV will have its own special weapons fit), three on the fuselage and two on each wing, with pivoting pylons to keep the store normal to the flight axis regardless of wing sweep angle. The two outboard positions can carry only relatively light loads — up to about 1,000 lb (454 kg) each — and are not plumbed for fuel tanks; the two inner wing pylons and each of the three fuselage points can carry loads, judging by published photographs, of up to about 3,000 lb (1 362 kg), although not necessarily all at once, and all can carry fuel tanks when required. Tandem mounting of bombs on the fuselage pylons is possible and the total external load that can be carried is believed to be about 17,500 lb (7 945 kg), including bombs, rocket launchers and air-to-surface missiles. A reconnaissance pod is under development.

The power plant

The RB.199 engine, originally of Rolls-Royce concept but subsequently developed on a tri-national basis by Turbo-Union in the same way that the airframe is a product of Panavia and not of any single one of the contributing companies, was designed to match the Tornado's operating requirements. It therefore needed to have high reheat thrust to give the aircraft STOL performance, a good SEP, high supersonic speed at altitude and high manoeuvre capability; plus high dry thrust to obtain transonic performance at low altitude and low sfc to achieve the required radius of action. For at least one of the missions, 35 minutes continuous afterburner operation was required; also, extremely fast thrust response was needed — from flight idle to max dry thrust in less than 4 seconds, for example. These difficult and in some respects conflicting requirements have been met with a three-spool engine of modular design (to facilitate replacement of damaged, faulty or time-expired components for servicing), having a by-pass ratio of more than 1, a pressure ratio of over 20 and a thrust-to-weight ratio of better than 8. The dry thrust is of the order of 8,500 lb st (3 860 kgp), boosted in sea level static conditions to some 15,000 lb st (6 810 kgp) with the fully modulated reheat system. Notwithstanding the extremely tough design requirements, the RB.199 is remarkably compact, with an overall length of about 10 ft 6 in (3,2 m) and max diameter of about 34 in (0,87 m).

An integral target-type thrust reverser is used, the buckets of which are attached directly to the jetpipes and move aft before closing over the exhaust to deflect the hot efflux away from the fuselage and intakes. In the Tornado, the two engines are located side-by-side in the rear fuselage, receiving air from intakes that are set well ahead of the wing to minimize boundary layer effects and distortion of the inlet flow. The intakes are of two-dimensional horizontal double wedge type, the position of the variable inlet ramps being controlled by a fully automatic digital control system (by Nord-Micro) to best match the free stream Mach number and angle of attack at any given moment.

The RB.199 first ran on the test bed in September 1971, and flight testing began on 19 April 1973 with an engine mounted beneath a Vulcan test-bed. The installation in the Vulcan is especially interesting in that a complete replica of half an MRCA fuselage was fitted so that the performance of the RB.199 could be assessed behind a fully representative air intake. More recently, a Mauser cannon has been fitted in the correct position relative to the air intake, and has been fired in flight to investigate the effects of ingesting gases.

The two engines flown (individually) in the Vulcan came from the initial batch of 16 bench development engines, others of this batch having been used on eight sea level test beds (four in the UK, three in Germany and one in Italy) and four altitude beds (all in the UK). Initial flight testing used the engine of -01 standard, but these were later modified to -02 standard with increased core flow, flight clearance for this version being obtained towards the end of 1974. All the Tornado prototypes flown to date (P-01 to P-07) now have -02 engines, which, as noted in the description of flight-testing, do not produce the full specified thrust. The next important stage of engine development, therefore, is the introduction of the uprated -03 standard, expected to be flying in P-02 or P-06 by the time this account appears in print. These, like the -02 engines, come from a batch of 51 prototype and pre-production engines ordered for the 15 prototype and pre-series Tornadoes.

For the first production aircraft, Turbo-Union expects to deliver engines of -04 standard, known as RB.199 Mk 101s. These may have a thrust of 5-10 per cent more than the -03, which itself meets the original thrust specification, the increase being achieved without a major stretch of the engine. Improvements in the combustion chamber and an increase in compressor pressure ratio are among the new features of the -04, but at the time of writing decisions had still to be taken in respect of the possible use of shrouded turbine blades and the source of the master engine control unit (MECU). Relative merits and costs of shrouded or deshrouded blades were still being considered when AIR INTERNATIONAL visited Turbo-Union, with a shrouded blade apparently emerging as the preferred alternative.

The original MECU, using "fly-by-wire" principles, chosen for the RB.199 proved to pose a major development problem and was one of the factors causing delays in delivery of early flight engines. Rolls-Royce provided an alternative "bread-board" MECU at short notice and this has been functioning satisfactorily in all the prototypes flown so far, but it remains to be seen whether this design is productionized or an alternative is chosen.

It is a little early to talk of stretching the RB.199, but it is already clear that the RAF will want a more powerful variant for the ADV Tornado and there is talk in Turbo-Union of a Mk 102 and even a Mk 103. Use of deshrouded blades of wider chord is one possible way of increasing thrust in the longer term, and for the ADV, the higher thrust is also likely to be wanted at a higher altitude.

Flight testing

By the time this account is published, the MRCA prototypes are expected to be well over 500 hrs into the flight test programme (the 400th flight was logged towards the end of May) and after starting at a rate considerably lower than planned, the testing is now accelerating and has reached the point where in some areas it is ahead of schedule. Especially is this true of the avionics testing, for which MBB is primarily responsible at Manching (near Munich); although there have been some delays due to bad weather there — in the three mid-winter months, only five days allowed VFR operations, and at this relatively early stage in the programme, there are some restrictions on IFR flying with the Tornado prototypes — the avionics test flying has been less hampered by the lack of fully-rated engines than some of the performance and handling tests at Warton.

Details of the nine prototypes and their particular rôles are summarized separately; the overall programme is so divided that four prototypes are assembled and based in the UK, three in Germany and two in Italy. These aircraft will be joined, in 1977, by the six pre-production Tornadoes — three in the UK, two in Germany and one in Italy — which are referred to as P-11 to P-16 (P-10 now identifies the fatigue test airframe at Warton).

There is now an adequate supply of spare engines at each of the three test bases and this is no longer a pacing factor in the flying rate, as it was in the early days. Serviceability of the MECU and other items that gave trouble at first is now satisfactory also; it is not now uncommon for one or other of the prototypes to make three or four flights in one day. The Italian testing suffered a severe set-back when P-05 (the first of the two Italian prototypes) made a heavy landing at Caselle in January 1976, causing damage that will require a year to repair; the second Italian aircraft, P-09, has not yet entered flight test. The accident to P-05, which resulted from a problem with the CSAS that was quickly identified, was the most serious incident in the Tornado flight test programme, but there have been some lesser excitements and a number of problems, as would be expected of an advanced technology warplane powered by completely new engines.

One time-consuming problem has concerned directional stability at high transonic speed; at speeds between Mach 0·90 and Mach 0·95, the aircraft's stability was reduced — as evidenced by a lengthening of the Dutch roll period — to the point where it was considered to be unacceptable. Investigation with wool tufts revealed that there was flow break-away in the region of the rear spine and base of the fin, which was thereby rendered less effective. The solution to this problem proved less simple than its identification; twenty or more slightly different back end configurations have been flown to achieve an aerodynamically acceptable fairing of the original lines at the base of the fin, and additional work has been necessary to devise an acceptable engineering solution that allowed uninterrupted operation of the thrust reversers.

A loss of directional stability was experienced during some landings when maximum reverse thrust was used, this being caused by a break-down of the airflow over the fin. To overcome the problem, a system has been developed to pick yaw rate information off the CSAS circuit and use this to signal nosewheel steering. Early on, noise levels in the cockpit were excessive, the cause finally being traced to vibration of cockpit weather stripping at certain speeds and a cure being simply effected. The nosewheel doors also showed a tendency to protrude under air loads at high speeds, calling for some strengthening of the doors and operating linkage.

On one occasion at Warton, the wing sweep mechanism suffered a mechanical failure causing the wings to freeze at 41 deg of sweep. All previous landings had been made with the wings forward and although demonstration landings with wings fully swept to 65 deg will eventually be made, this incident necessitated a landing with partial sweep to be made earlier than planned! The landing was in fact uneventful. There have been two bird-strike incidents at Warton; one caused damage to an engine and a spoiler and the other (a herring gull) caused serious damage to the port engine during a run over the airfield at 250 knots (463 km/h) and 100 ft (30,5 m). The pilot, not unreasonably, selected full reheat and then combat power on the "good" engine, but was unaware that the reheat did not light (for reasons unconnected with the bird strike). With nozzle fully open, but no reheat combustion, the good engine gave considerably less than its maximum dry thrust and a potentially difficult situation was resolved only when the engine surged, the pilot instinctively responded by throttling back and the nozzle closed, whereupon thrust increased and the aircraft was able to climb away. Several modifications have been evolved in the light of this incident, and it has always been intended to provide a positive indication in the cockpit that reheat has lit and is burning.

One of the early problems with the RB.199 was the engine's tendency to shed high-pressure turbine blades, although in no case did this cause the engine to malfunction in flight and the pilot was usually unaware that the blades had failed. Modular design of the engine made it relatively easy to replace the HP turbine, once the initial shortage of engines and spares had been overcome, and modified blades have now been introduced to cure the problem. The engines can be "dropped out" of the airframe through access panels in the underside facilitating replacement of engines or modules.

The Tornado prototypes are instrumented to varying degrees according to their particular test missions, Panavia having opted to use a telemetry system in order to obtain the maximum value from each flying hour. Each of the three test centres is similarly equipped to monitor about 150 selected telemetered parameters at a time (the aircraft themselves having as many as 460 instrumented parameters for possible transmission). All the data transmitted is automatically recorded for subsequent analysis but the great value of the telemetry system is that it provides a voice link between the pilot, the test controller and one or more senior engineers who monitor the results of each test in real time on screens, pen recorders and dial indicators and can take immediate decisions

This view of P-02 clearly shows the revised fairing between the jet pipes at the base of the rudder, which has been evolved through flight testing to overcome a problem with directional stability at high transonic speeds.

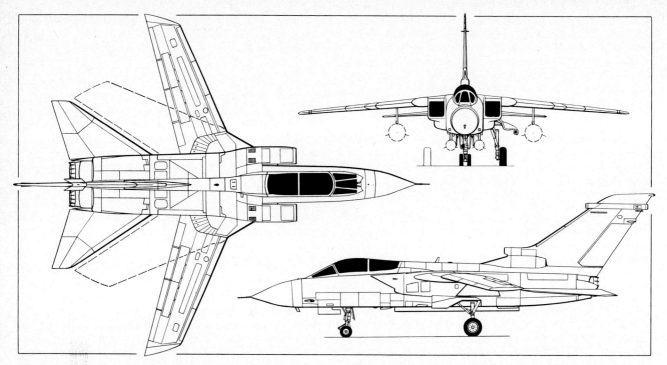

The three-view drawing above shows the Panavia Tornado as currently flying, with the new rear-end fairing. Bombs and drop tanks are indicated in the head-on view.

Two of the test aircraft involved in the Tornado programme — (above) the Vulcan with RB.199 in a Tornado "half fuselage" under the fuselage and (below) one of the two Buccaneers testing the MRCA avionics.

on the need to repeat manoeuvres and the safety of the next planned step in the programme, which can then be taken on the same flight.

Because fully rated engines have not been available, the whole of the Tornado flight envelope has not yet been opened up; speeds up to about Mach 1·3 and altitudes up to about 40,000 ft (12 200 m) represent the upper limits so far, but since a major part of the aircraft's mission profile is concerned with high subsonic flight at low altitude, plenty of useful work has been possible in this area of the envelope. Very satisfactory results have been obtained, with the aircraft proving to have excellent stability and behaving very well in turbulence. Exploration of the low-speed handling has already covered flying at angles of attack well beyond those required for approach and landing in both full CSAS and direct link, and the next phase of this work is to go through stall approaches and the full stall in 1g and accelerated flight, to spinning and roll coupling; for this phase, aircraft P.03 will have a spin recovery tail parachute (already fitted and tested in ground

deployment) and a mono-propellent emergency power unit to assist engine relighting in the event of a double flame-out. Such testing is, of course, essential to establish the aircraft's characteristics but in service Tornado will have a Panavia-designed spin prevention and incidence limiting (SPIL) system to prevent inadvertent stalling or spinning. This system serves to decrease the lateral authority of pilot control inputs progressively as incidence is increased, whilst leaving adequate control at all angles of attack that would normally be used; consequently, the pilot is able to use incidences well beyond the normal stall departure by provision of a powerful stability augmentation system without experiencing post-stall gyrations.

Preliminary flight refuelling trials were made in July 1975 with P.02, for which purpose the bolt-on probe pack was fitted on the starboard side of the fuselage adjacent to the cockpit; there is no built-in provision for flight refuelling as the probe would represent unnecessary weight on many missions, and the external fitting involves only a minor performance penalty on those missions when FR is required. Hook-ups were made without difficulty, with an RAF Victor tanker, and flight refuelling has subsequently been used on some occasions to benefit the test programme by allowing lengthy flights to be made and many test points to be covered without time-consuming intermediate landings. A good start has also been made on testing various external stores configurations, including subsonic 330-Imp gal (1 500 l) fuel tanks on the fuselage and inner wing points and various bombs on the fuselage and inner wing points with recording cameras on the outer pylons. These tests have been conducted on P-02, while preliminary dropping trials have started using P-06.

Chase aircraft are used as required, and usually comprise an F-104G or G.91R in Germany, a Lightning or Hunter 7 (replacing a Canberra previously used) in the UK, and F-104 and G.91 in Italy. A number of other aircraft test beds have been or are being used in connection with Tornado development, including the Vulcan engine test bed already described. Most important of the support aircraft are two Buccaneers modified (by Marshalls of Cambridge) to have MRCA avionics; based at Warton, one is primarily concerned with the

continued on page 145

PORTRAIT OF A DEFENCE BUDGET BEING WASTED.

The simple fact is Hawk will deliver more flying for your money.

Because Hawk is both trainer and ground-support fighter, a combination that makes operational and economic sense, and maintains pilot morale.

Fly it for basic instruction right through to squadron continuation training.

Fly it equipped for front-line combat duty.

Fly Hawk instead of doubling-up your aircraft strength. Especially as Hawker Siddeley designed it to need minimal maintenance, and for that to be simple.

If money matters to you, fly Hawk.

More flying for your money.

HS HAWK

HAWKER SIDDELEY AVIATION

Tornado...

Manufacture has begun of the tri-national requirement for a total of 809 Panavia Tornado multi-role combat aircraft — 385 for the Royal Air Force, 324 for the German Air Force and Navy, and 100 for the Italian Air Force. With eight prototypes already flying and the ninth scheduled for flight in the near future, a high flying rate has been maintained throughout 1976, and in all some 500 flights have now been completed. Already in advanced stages of final assembly are the six pre-series Tornado aircraft which will join the flight test programme in 1977 and which will be evaluated at the three Government flight test centres by Service pilots.

AVIONICS PROVING GOES AHEAD...
Virtually all avionics data necessary for production go-ahead was acquired by Tornado 04 in the course of 12 flights. Now, the second avionics aircraft, prototype 07, has joined 04 in extending the avionics test programme, which is one of the most important of all aspects of Tornado's development.

WEAPONS SYSTEM TESTING GOES AHEAD...
Proving of Tornado's ability to carry the complete range of NATO weapons is steadily progressing. Already, prototype 06 has successfully completed trials involving the dropping of external stores and is now moving on to gun-firing trials.

Tornado 06 successfully completed a series of external stores release flight tests in March, making a record 22 flights in the month.

Tornado 02 has carried out flutter tests with bombs and external tanks and tests on air brakes at various Mach numbers.

goes ahead

STATIC TESTING GOES AHEAD...

A Tornado airframe, including the fin, has completed static testing up to 95% of ultimate design load without failure, and loading is being increased to confirm the ultimate strength at production aircraft weight.

Tornado 04 is now sharing avionics development flying with the most recent aircraft to fly, prototype 07 (heading picture).

PANAVIA

Panavia Aircraft GmbH,
München, Arabellastrasse 16, Germany

AERITALIA

BRITISH AIRCRAFT CORPORATION

MESSERSCHMITT-BÖLKOW-BLOHM

PRODUCT OF EUROPE

The right concept for today and tomorrow!

The Viggen attack version was first introduced in the Swedish Air Force in 1971. This multi-role Viggen is now also in production in reconnaissance and fighter versions. The latter will enter into service in 1978 and continue in production at least until 1985. Today, yet another Viggen version is proposed by Sweden's defence planners for service starting in the mid-eighties. Tentatively designated the "A 20" it is a multi-role development of the new advanced technology JA37 fighter now in initial production.

SAAB
A product from Saab-Scania, Sweden

Scania medium-heavy and heavy diesel trucks, buses and diesel engines.

Saab-Scania AB, Scania Division, S-151 87 Södertälje, Sweden. Tel +46 0755-810 00.

Saab passenger cars in several models. The Saab 99 series, the Saab 95L and the Saab 96L.

Saab-Scania AB, Saab Car Division, S-611 01 Nyköping, Sweden. Tel +46 0155-807 00.

Saab aircraft, guided missiles, avionics and space equipment.

Saab-Scania AB, Aerospace Division, S-581 88 Linköping, Sweden. Tel +46 013-12 90 20.

Datasaab computers, terminal systems and other advanced electronics.

Saab-Scania AB, Datasaab Division, S-581 01 Linköping, Sweden. Tel +46 013-11 15 00.

Nordarmatur valves and instruments for the process industry, steam- and nuclear power plants and ships.

Saab-Scania AB, Nordarmatur Division, S-581 87 Linköping, Sweden. Tel +46 013-12 90 60.

Financial summary 1975
Consolidated sales
total   Skr 7,900 millions
Sales to markets
outside Sweden   42 %
Number of employees   37,500

Saab-Scania AB, Head Office, S-581 88 Linköping, Sweden. Tel +46 013-11 54 00.

HAL'S FIGHTERS...
...HOPE AND HAZARD

VIEWING the HF-24 project in perspective twenty years after it was initiated, it is manifest that its concept, in context of the skeletal aero industrial facilities then available in India, was extremely ambitious and that, if unlikely to go down in aviation history as one of the all time greats, it has certainly earned a place in aeronautical annals in terms of the development-persistence and longevity of effort of its creators. The HF-24 Marut is viewed by some as a flying monument to the tenacity of the designers and technicians at HAL who have never displayed faint heart or lost faith in the design potential of the aircraft despite years of official vacillation. The nation, too, waits gamely for the eventual *metamorphosis* of an unexceptional fighter-bomber of the 'sixties into a no more exceptional supersonic strike fighter of the 'eighties. There have been many aspiring Prince Charmings in the shape of compatible engines developing sufficient power, but none has yet breathed life into any of the successively-proposed supersonic HF-24 derivatives.

The first HF-24 prototype flew 15 years back, in June 1961, powered by a pair of Orpheus 703s which were the only immediately available and compatible engines. Although the decision to produce the transonic Mk I ensured that development efforts would not go by default, HAL cast around fairly widely for more powerful engines to exploit the latent potential of the HF-24 airframe. Various powerplants were considered, some fanciful such as the Egyptian E-300, and feasibility studies or even actual installation was endeavoured with types such as the Soviet VK-7 and RD-9F, while Bristol Siddeley proposed a hybrid Pegasus-Orpheus and US experts also investigated the problem. The RD.172/T.260 Adour turbofan was considered intermittently for some years from 1970, and a large proportion of the necessary revised airframe structural drawings were completed, as was also a rear fuselage mock-up. This proposal (the Mk II) was finally abandoned as resultant drag penalties made the Adour installation impractical and the augmented Adour was still some years away. The RB.153 turbofan was also studied, but HAL was unable to accept the terms of contract, nor consider the major re-design of the fuselage which would have been entailed. Meanwhile HAL and the Gas Turbine Research Establishment (GTRE)

Production of the HF-24 Marut in its single-seat ground-attack version (below) has been completed and this type now equips three squadrons of the Indian Air Force. Completion of a small batch of two-seat Marut Mk IT trainers means that all production of the type has now ended at Bangalore, but the company continues its search for a formula for a Marut development, as described in this account. One possibility, no longer current, was the HF-73, depicted in the heading illustration.

made efforts to adapt a reheat arrangement and the first Marut with Orpheus 703Rs (thrust increment of 27 per cent) was known as the Mk IA. Two more aircraft were completed as Mk IRs and about 250 test flights carried out, but achieved performance was not considered commensurate with the effort and expense.

Production programme

Production of HF-24 Mk I fighters meanwhile continued until this model was phased-out in late 1974, with the completion of a second-series order for 45 aircraft, and HAL is currently in the process of delivering the last of 20 tandem-seat HF-24 Mk IT trainers to the Indian Air Force. With this, HAL will have manufactured near 150 HF-24s, including the experimental aircraft, and although continuous modification, retrofit and overhaul activity will carry on, the production run of the Mk I may be assumed as over, with the IAF possessing three Marut ground attack squadrons (Nos 10, 31 and 220) in its order-of-battle.

Over the production period of a decade, a number of modifications were introduced, some incorporated retrospectively in service aircraft, these a result of user experience (the IAF's Maruts saw considerable action during the Indo-Pakistan conflict of December 1971), increasing indigenous substitution and component-improvement efforts. A major improvement was the extended-chord wing (by 10 per cent) to improve handling characteristics and provide a more

formalised in 1966, for an aircraft capable of carrying a weapons-load of 8,000 lb (3 629 kg) over a 450-mile (724-km) radius of action. The resulting design-proposal outlined a relatively large transonic fighter (38,000 lb/17 237 kg AUW) powered by two of the projected Rolls-Royce/SNECMA M.45Bs, but as supersonic capability was found desirable, the suggested engines were changed to M.45Gs and wind tunnel tests were carried out on models. Until 1970, the GAF proposals were studied and progressively amended, the ASR itself undergoing numerous modifications, but eventually the project was shelved.

In 1971, there was a luke-warm attempt to revive the GAF as the Advanced Strike Aircraft (ASA), to be powered by two RB.199s, and some preliminary design work was carried out. By mid-1972, however, Prof Kurt Tank, by now with MBB in Munich, who continued to maintain keen interest in the HF-24 and Indian aerospace efforts, made formal proposals on MBB's behalf to co-operate with HAL in an effort to meet the IAF's Deep Penetration Strike Aircraft (DPSA) requirement which had meanwhile superseded the ASA specification.

The initial proposal to re-engine the HF-24 with Rolls-Royce/MTU RB.199 turbofans came from Prof Kurt Tank in 1972, and Mr S C Das, HAL's Director of Design and Development, organised a project team to work on the concept. Preliminary studies were completed by late 1972, and a team of design specialists from MBB, headed by Herr

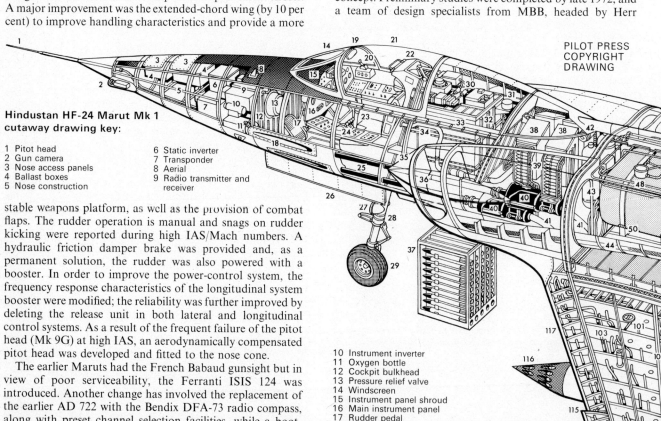

PILOT PRESS
COPYRIGHT
DRAWING

Hindustan HF-24 Marut Mk 1 cutaway drawing key:

1 Pitot head
2 Gun camera
3 Nose access panels
4 Ballast boxes
5 Nose construction
6 Static inverter
7 Transponder
8 Aerial
9 Radio transmitter and receiver

stable weapons platform, as well as the provision of combat flaps. The rudder operation is manual and snags on rudder kicking were reported during high IAS/Mach numbers. A hydraulic friction damper brake was provided and, as a permanent solution, the rudder was also powered with a booster. In order to improve the power-control system, the frequency response characteristics of the longitudinal system booster were modified; the reliability was further improved by deleting the release unit in both lateral and longitudinal control systems. As a result of the frequent failure of the pitot head (Mk 9G) at high IAS, an aerodynamically compensated pitot head was developed and fitted to the nose cone.

The earlier Maruts had the French Babaud gunsight but in view of poor serviceability, the Ferranti ISIS 124 was introduced. Another change has involved the replacement of the earlier AD 722 with the Bendix DFA-73 radio compass, along with preset channel selection facilities, while a bootstrap system was developed to improve cabin conditioning, this bringing down cabin temperature by about 10 deg C. In order to develop expertise and carry out field evaluation, a Marconi Elliot HUD and Weapon Release System was integrated in an HF-24 and limited trials conducted. A JATO device has also been adapted and fully-laden Maruts now employ this assistance as standard procedure.

The HF-73 proposal

While the production of HF-24 Mk Is was proceeding and HAL continued feasibility studies on new engines, another design cell was organised at HAL to develop a Ground Attack Fighter (GAF) against an Indian Air Force staff requirement,

10 Instrument inverter
11 Oxygen bottle
12 Cockpit bulkhead
13 Pressure relief valve
14 Windscreen
15 Instrument panel shroud
16 Main instrument panel
17 Rudder pedal
18 Cannon ports
19 Rearward vision mirror
20 Canopy control
21 Sliding canopy
22 Martin-Baker Mk S4C zero-altitude ejection seat
23 Control column
24 Engine throttles
25 Cannon barrels
26 Nosewheel door
27 Landing light
28 Nosewheel leg
29 Nosewheel
30 Electrical equipment
31 Canopy jettison reel
32 Pressurised box
33 Canopy rail
34 Cabin air conditioning supply

35 Port air intake
36 Intake centre-body
37 Retractable Matra Type 103 rocket pack (50 68-mm unguided rockets)
38 Ammunition boxes (130 rounds each)
39 Ammunition feed chutes
40 Port 30-mm Aden Mk 2 cannon

Herbst, spent some time at Bangalore working on details of the design proposals. By the end of February 1973, the feasibility studies were submitted to the Government of India.

While it has originally been the objective to retain much of the basic HF-24 design in order to cut time and expense, the new design that emerged required extensive changes to the forward fuselage, air intakes, tailplane and tailfin, the last mentioned incorporating a ram intake for conditioning air, as in the Panavia Tornado. In installing the two RB.199 engines, not only was the convergent nozzle of new design, but the overall length of the aircraft was increased and weight went up by some 12 per cent. Underwing and underfuselage weapon stations were cleared for the carriage of 4,000 lb (1 814 kg) of ordnance plus drop tanks, and the four 30-mm Aden cannon of the HF-24 were to be replaced by two 27-mm Mausers or alternative 30-mm weapons. The aircraft was to incorporate advanced state-of-the-art avionics, HUD, INAS, laser ranging equipment, etc.

Initially known as the HF-24 Mk III, the aircraft was formally designated the HSS-73 (for "Supersonic Strike"), the number 73 indicating the year in which the firm proposal was submitted. This designation was subsequently changed to the more familiar HF-73. The HF-73's performance parameters included a maximum speed of $M = 2 \cdot 0$ at altitude, a lo-lo-lo range of $300 +$ nautical miles $(556 + km)$ for the primary rôle

of deep penetration strike, while secondary tasks of air defence and tactical reconnaissance were specified. It was estimated that development time, to flight of first prototype, would be four to five years at a cost of Rs.60 Crores (then some $75m). Six prototypes and a ground test model of the HF-73 were planned and a total production run of over 200 aircraft was envisaged with squadron service by 1980-81. It was proposed by MBB to assign a design team to HAL to carry through the project well beyond the definition stage, with the Germans also reportedly keen to secure export rights of the definitive HF-73 for Europe and Latin America, while India would be clear to offer the type elsewhere. The effort was considered well justified as it would: (a) finally enable the HF-24 to achieve its optimum design/performance envelope; (b) cost the Indian Government no more than a quarter of what would be needed to finance an entirely new project, and (c) result in a great amount of contemporary design experience in matters of airframe, engines, avionics and weapon systems.

Even while the Government of India was examining the HF-73 proposal and deliberating on the costs involved, HAL continued to request detailed RB.199-34R data and, in order to proceed to the Project Definition Stage, two mock-up engines for installation in the full-scale HF-73 model. Being a multi-national programme, the acquiescence of three European Governments was involved, and although the Germans

41 Cartridge case ejection
   chutes
42 Canopy reel
43 Emergency pressure bottle
44 Air intake duct
45 Starboard air intake ducting
46 Control runs
47 Fuel system piping

90 Oil tank
91 Rear fuselage break point
92 Engine gearbox
93 Generator
94 Airbrake
95 Airbrake lever
96 Mainwheel door
97 Mainwheel well

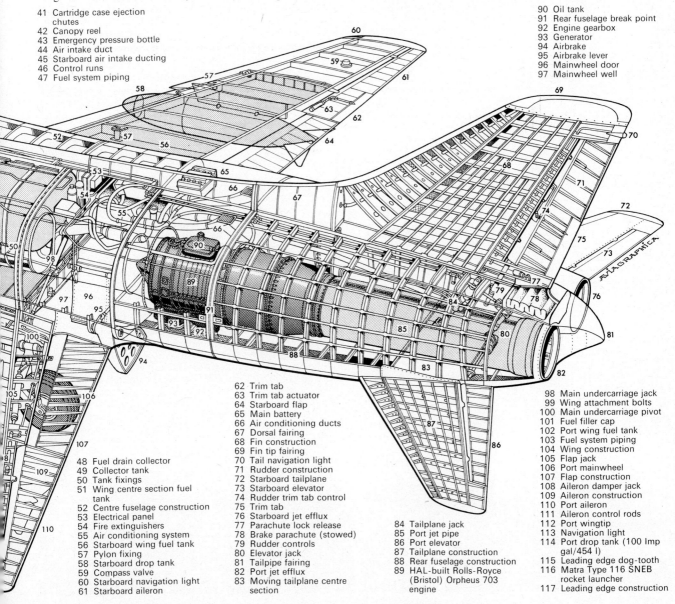

62 Trim tab
63 Trim tab actuator
64 Starboard flap
65 Main battery
66 Air conditioning ducts
67 Dorsal fairing
68 Fin construction
69 Fin tip fairing
70 Tail navigation light
71 Rudder construction
72 Starboard tailplane
73 Starboard elevator
74 Rudder trim tab control
75 Trim tab
76 Starboard jet efflux
77 Parachute lock release
78 Brake parachute (stowed)
79 Rudder controls
80 Elevator jack
81 Tailpipe fairing
82 Port jet efflux
83 Moving tailplane centre
   section

48 Fuel drain collector
49 Collector tank
50 Tank fixings
51 Wing centre section fuel
   tank
52 Centre fuselage construction
53 Electrical panel
54 Fire extinguishers
55 Air conditioning system
56 Starboard wing fuel tank
57 Pylon fixing
58 Starboard drop tank
59 Compass valve
60 Starboard navigation light
61 Starboard aileron

84 Tailplane jack
85 Port jet pipe
86 Port elevator
87 Tailplane construction
88 Rear fuselage construction
89 HAL-built Rolls-Royce
   (Bristol) Orpheus 703
   engine

98 Main undercarriage jack
99 Wing attachment bolts
100 Main undercarriage pivot
101 Fuel filler cap
102 Port wing fuel tank
103 Fuel system piping
104 Wing construction
105 Flap jack
106 Port mainwheel
107 Flap construction
108 Aileron damper jack
109 Aileron construction
110 Port aileron
111 Aileron control rods
112 Port wingtip
113 Navigation light
114 Port drop tank (100 Imp
    gal/454 l)
115 Leading edge dog-tooth
116 Matra Type 116 SNEB
    rocket launcher
117 Leading edge construction

had been said to have informally approved, British support was not immediately forthcoming and the RB.199's availability remained a matter of suspense through 1973 and 1974. Despite vigorous efforts made by both MBB and HAL, the Germans reportedly expressed regret on the RB.199's non-availability early in 1975, and the HF-73 project was reluctantly wound up soon thereafter.

A single powerplant

Greatly disappointing as this turn of events may have been — and the HF-73 project was once confidently viewed as a "winner" — HAL's design and development team did not lose heart, and continued studies with alternate powerplants. Although at one stage HAL had also considered the possibility of employing the SNECMA Atar 09K-53 turbojet, reconfiguration of the Marut to accept a single engine was then considered a major task and was not proceeded with. At a stage however, when engines of the right dimension and power were either not available for political, technical or economic reasons, HAL looked seriously at other possibilities, and with the SNECMA M.53 turbofan in mind, redesign work on the HF-24 for single-engine configuration was carried out in 1975. The French were willing to provide the M.53 on a commercial basis and even while the M.53's future hung in the balance in the wake of the "Arms Contract of the Century" struggle, HAL completed preliminary designs and went ahead with the fabrication of a full scale wooden mock-up. This retained considerably more commonality with the HF-24 than had the

HF-73 design — basically only the HF-24-M.53's rear fuselage was re-designed to incorporate a single engine installation. The resulting economies within the rear lateral fuselage also provided a bonus in terms of space for extra internal fuel tankage, thereby markedly improving the aircraft's endurance. The air intakes were modified for the higher air mass flow while the forward fuselage and nose section were also redesigned with consideration to the aircraft's intended primary ground attack function. A "Jaguar-type" nose section was suggested, with nose glazing for a laser installation, a clamshell type plexiglass cockpit canopy, twin barrelled cannon flush with the underside of the fuselage, HUD, air data computer, nav/attack electronics, etc, and multiple underwing weapons stations.

Once again, however, the element of uncertain developmental costs and lengthy gestation periods reared its nefarious head. The M.53 was being quoted, late in 1975, at a unit cost of near Rs16m and cost escalation was a very real factor to be considered. With the Mirage F1E future also hazy, the HF-24-M.53 proposal has, in all too familiar manner, and for reasons beyond HAL's control, had to be shelved. Nevertheless the intrepid men at Bangalore are reportedly continuing the study of a single-engined HF-24 married to a suitable engine of indigenous design or Soviet-origin. Whether the winds of fortune will blow favourably for this latest proposed development of the Marut is anybody's guess, but if success is in any way related to perseverance, then it certainly *should* succeed. □

TALKBACK

Phoenix phenomena

SINCE PUBLICATION of my story on Ansett's Fokker Phoenix (December 1975), it now transpires that the original open cockpit Fokker Universal, VH-UTO, of Ansett Airways Pty Ltd, was subsequently fitted with an enclosed cockpit in October 1936. Surprisingly, there is no record of this modification in the Department of Civil Aviation file for VH-UTO. The work was carried out by Ansett's chief engineer, J J Davies, at Hamilton Aerodrome, Victoria, under the supervision of the senior pilot, Captain Vernon Cerche, who complained that he almost froze to death in the open cockpit on the Hamilton-Melbourne flights. The new cockpit was very small, and it was jokingly claimed at the time that Vern Cerche purposely made it cramped to keep his job safe, as few others could fit into the new enclosed area. Thus, the US-built Universal, VH-UTO, operated with Ansett as an open cockpit monoplane from January to October 1936, and then with an enclosed cockpit until it was destroyed in the hangar fire at Essendon Aerodrome, Victoria, in February 1939.

Ansett Airlines of Australia kindly supplied two recently discovered photographs of VH-UTO with its enclosed cockpit (one of which is reproduced here). The other photograph is

full of historic interest, and shows Ansett's first hangar at Pedrina Park, the site of the original Hamilton Aerodrome, late in 1936. The hangar is still in use today as a workshop for the Roadways Division of Ansett Motors, having been moved from Pedrina Park to Gray Street, Hamilton. The aircraft outside the hangar are the enclosed cockpit Universal, VH-UTO, the Airspeed Envoy I, VH-UXM, (formerly Lord Nuffield's *Miss Wolseley*, G-ACVI), and the Porterfield 35/70, VH-UVH, with a 70 hp Le Blond radial engine, in which a young Reg Ansett won the Brisbane-Adelaide Air Race during 16-18 December 1936.

An enigma surrounds Ansett's Porterfield which—like the Universal's registration, VH-UTO—has a phoenix-type history. In 1936, Ansett Airways held the Australian agency for Porterfield aircraft, and two 35/70s were imported from America. VH-UVH (c/n 242) first appeared on the civil register in December 1936, followed by the second Porterfield, VH-ABP (c/n 355), in April 1938; this latter aircraft was partially destroyed in an accident prior to World War II, but Ansett was apparently remiss in not cancelling the registration until February 1942. Meanwhile, on 8 March 1939, DCA files recorded that Porterfield VH-UVH, Universal VH-UTO, D.H.60M Moth VH-

UNF, and Lockheed 10B VH-UZN, were all "completely destroyed by fire on 28 February 1939." On 9 March the certificates of registration and airworthiness for the four aircraft were returned by the Officer-in-Charge, Essendon Aerodrome, A E Shorland, to DCA for cancellation.

In the event, the fuselage and other salvaged sections of the fire-gutted VH-UVH were rebuilt, and amalgamated with portions of VH-ABP which had survived the accident, by the Ansett engineers under J J Davies. The resultant aircraft then reappeared on the civil register in April 1941 as VH-UVH. This machine is still in existence today, and is maintained in immaculate condition and perfect flying order. Although much modified since 1941, and powered by a flat-four 75 hp Continental A75, the Porterfield 35/70 Special—as it is now registered—still retains the original c/n 242. It is currently owned by Mr John Bange, a grazier and aviation enthusiast of Clifton, Queensland, who kindly supplied the accompanying photograph of VH-UVH, which he acquired in 1955.

In retrospect, perhaps I should have entitled my original article, Ansett's Burnt Birds!

Gp Capt Keith Isaacs, AFC, RAAF (Retd)
Lyneham, ACT, Australia

(left) The Fokker Universal VH-UTO with enclosed cockpit and (right) the Porterfield 35/70 Special VH-UVH, referred to in the letter above.

This year sees the 40th anniversary of the Supermarine Spitfire's first flight, which was made at Eastleigh Airport, near Southampton, on 5 March 1936. To mark the event, we present this personal view of Spitfire/Seafire development by Jeffrey Quill, who first flew the Spitfire prototype on 26 March 1936 as assistant to J "Mutt" Summers, then Vickers chief test pilot, and was to be closely associated with the testing of successive Spitfire variants for most of the war. Now Director of Marketing, Panavia, Mr Quill has recently presented several lectures on the Spitfire before members of the Royal Aeronautical Society and the account that follows is based upon a paper given at the Spitfire Symposium organised in Southampton last March by the Southampton Branch of the RAeS, with whose permission it is published here.

FORTY YEARS FAMOUS

THE STORY of the Spitfire is that of an aeroplane which was excellently designed in the first place, and was subsequently developed to an unprecedented extent. The same could be said of its engines — the Rolls-Royce Merlin and, later, Griffon: the Spitfire has a major debt to acknowledge to Rolls-Royce. It is appropriate to refer first to the man who headed up the team responsible for the initial design — Reginald Mitchell. Reg Mitchell died in 1937 when we had been flying the prototype Spitfire for just over one year. He was 42 years old and had been responsible for the design of some 25 aeroplanes.

The second man to whom I would like to pay tribute is the late Joseph Smith. He became chief designer shortly after Mitchell's death and it was he who inspired and supervised the

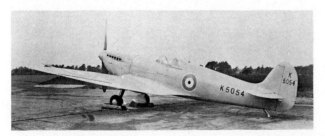

massive development effort on the Spitfire. He was a thoroughly practical engineer and a man of great drive, tenacity and courage. Without him, I think that much of the story I have to tell would not have taken place. He died in 1956. In referring to these two men I am, apart from paying them my own personal tribute, really drawing attention to the enormous influence that single individuals exerted over major aviation projects, and the companies involved, at that period. It was truly the era of the aviation giants — Mitchell, Camm, Pierson, Barnwell, J D North, Bishop and others.

To start the story of the Spitfire in more detail, let me spell out some of the simple, basic facts. The prototype was designed to Air Ministry Specification F.37/34 for a day and night fighter. It was not — as legend sometimes has it — a private venture; its design and construction were covered by Air Ministry Contract. There had, however, been private venture work involved in the early project design stages. Also, the 1,000 hp 12-cylinder Vee engine from Rolls-Royce, eventually to become the Merlin, started as a private venture, for there had been a time when Air Ministry policy in respect of its next generation of fighters was to develop the Kestrel, an engine of much lower capacity.

The prototype Spitfire, K5054, made its first flight on 5 March 1936 at Southampton in the hands of J "Mutt"

Contrasted in these photographs are (above left) the prototype Spitfire K5054 in its original overall pale blue finish, as it was first flown 40 years ago, and (below) a production model Spitfire F Mk 22. The heading photo shows Spitfire IXs patrolling over the Allied beachheads south-east of Rome in 1943.

The classical elliptical wing shape of the Spitfire, shown clearly above, was chosen by Mitchell for aerodynamic reasons at some expense in ease of production. It helped to make the Spitfire easily recognisable wherever it flew. In the author's opinion, the nicest Spitfire of all to fly was DP845, (below), the first prototype to be fitted with a Griffon engine.

Summers, then chief test pilot of Vickers Aviation Limited. Mutt Summers was a test pilot of extraordinary experience. He was very much a child of his own aviation generation in which prototype aircraft were produced at very frequent intervals, and when test flying was primarily a somewhat individual and qualitative business. Mutt had tested a very large number of prototype aircraft and had acquired a remarkable combination of experience and shrewd judgement of an aeroplane. I, as a very young pilot, learnt a great deal from him which stood me in good stead.

The first Air Ministry production contract, for 310 aircraft, was received in June 1936, and I flew the first production Spitfire — known as the Mk I — in May 1938. The first service aeroplane was delivered to the Royal Air Force at Duxford in August 1938. I flew it up there and handed it over to Sqn Ldr Cozens, the OC of No 19 (Fighter) Squadron. I doubt whether either of us realised at the time what an historic occasion this, in fact, was.

By the beginning of the "Battle of Britain" in August 1940, there were 19 squadrons of Spitfires operational in Fighter Command, compared with 38 squadrons of Hurricanes; in No 11 Group, which bore much of the brunt of the Battle, the ratio was more even, however, and the ratio of Spitfires to

Hurricanes also increased during the course of the Battle. However, it took both of these great aeroplanes to win this epic conflict, and it always grieves me when I hear people taking partisan views on this point. Let us always honour them both for the great fighters that they were.

A total of 22,759 Spitfires and Seafires was eventually built. They served in every theatre of war, ashore and afloat. The production engineering and management effort involved in building this quantity of aircraft was enormous and was greatly complicated in 1940 by the need to disperse it for protection against enemy action. No aircraft ever before or since has, I believe, been produced in such quantities in so short a period of time, with so many variants in production simultaneously. The men and women who performed this feat — and that is what it was — have gone largely unsung and unhonoured, and I am glad of this opportunity to pay tribute to them.

Thirty-six marks, or variants of marks, of Spitfire and Seafire were produced for operational service, and more were flown experimentally. The Spitfire had a front line operational life of some 14 years. The first time the Spitfire fired its guns against the enemy was in October 1939, over Scotland, when No 603 Squadron brought down a Heinkel He 111 in the sea off Port Seton, this victory being credited to Sqn Ldr E E Stevens.

The last time that the Spitfire fired its guns in anger was in 1951, when flown by No 60 Squadron, RAF, based in Malaya. The Squadron was led into action against terrorists in the jungle by my old and valued friend Sqn Ldr (later Group Captain) Duncan Smith, DSO, DFC, and to celebrate the Spitfire's last fight, Supermarine and Rolls-Royce gave No 60 Squadron a silver model of a Spitfire with the first verse of the "Nunc Dimittis" engraved in Latin on its plinth, which — when translated into English — says "Lord, now lettest thou thy servant depart in peace".

Well, maybe the Spitfire settled for peace when its fighting days were over — but it obstinately declined to depart. For although the vast bulk of those 22,000 Spitfires have now gone with the wind, some do in fact still survive in flying condition, in this country, in the United States and elsewhere. The Royal Air Force has four which are maintained with loving care by the "Battle of Britain" Historic Aircraft Flight at Coningsby. In the USA, there are two in the "Confederate Air Force", and at least one in the hands of a private collector, Bill Ross. There are several others in private ownership in England, and examples are flying in Israel and South Africa: in fact they seem to be on the increase — long may they fly!

The development story

I have said that this is a story of development. An accompanying illustration shows the prototype as we flew it in March 1936. I made my first flight in this aircraft on 26 March 1936, over 40 years ago and, no doubt, before many readers of this journal were born. I must also pay tribute here to George Pickering, who flew the prototype at about the same time as I did. With Mutt Summers and myself, he was the third member of the team, doing a great deal of Spitfire flying until 1941, when he suffered a catastrophic structural failure while diving a production Spitfire and was desperately injured. Sadly, he was killed a year later just after he was declared medically fit to fly again.

The prototype had a take-off weight of 5,400 lb (2 450 kg). Its Merlin engine produced 1,050 brake horsepower, which was converted into thrust by a two-bladed, fixed pitch wooden propeller driven through a 5:1 reduction gear. The wing area was 242 sq ft (22,48 m²) and the thickness chord ratio was 13 per cent at the root and 6 per cent at the tip. It had an unusually thin tailplane, of 9 per cent t/c ratio.

Now let us look at the last of the line in the development of this aeroplane — the Seafire 47. This had a maximum gross take-off weight of 12,500 lb (5 675 kg) carried on the same wing area, thus more than doubling its wing loading. Its Griffon engine gave 2,350 bhp, nearly 2·3 times the power of the prototype's Merlin III. Its maximum rate of climb had increased from the 2,500 ft/min (12,7 m/sec) of the prototype to nearly 5,000 ft/min (25,4 m/sec). Its range had increased threefold and its primary armament of four 20-mm cannon fired more than double the weight of projectiles per second than could be delivered by the Mk I's eight 0·303-in (7,7-mm) machine guns. In addition, it carried a large load of secondary armament in the form of bombs and rockets, and of course a selection of drop tanks. At its maximum gross take-off weight, the Seafire 47 was, in fact, equivalent to the Mk I Spitfire with the additional load of 32 "airline-standard" passengers each with 40 lb (18 kg) of baggage.

In between the first and the last of the line of Spitfires came a series of stage-by-stage developments providing, as I have said, no fewer than 36 distinct operational variants. The main line of development comprised, of course, the fighters but there was also a line of photographic reconnaissance types, and the Naval carrier-borne variants. I will refer in more detail to the main stages of development later, but it must first be stressed that the influence of engine development upon this whole process was profound. There were two fundamental stages of engine development, as it affected the Spitfire. These were, first, the change from single stage, single speed superchargers to two-stage, two-speed superchargers, with intercoolers and, second, the change from the 27-litre Merlin engine to the 37-litre Griffon. There were, of course, many specialised and detailed engine variants within this framework.

I have mentioned supercharger characteristics in particular because the power produced by a piston engine, as in a turbojet, is largely a function of mass flow. The more gas that can be pumped through in a given time, and burned efficiently, the greater the power that can be extracted. Since in any given engine the cylinder capacity is a fixed quantity, and since the rpm tends to be fixed by mechanical considerations (principally piston speed), the only way to increase the mass of the charge being burnt in the cylinders in a given time is to increase the capacity of the supercharger and raise the manifold pressure. Then, you have to cope with the ensuing cooling and

detonation problems by all sorts of design refinements and fuel developments, etc.

If all this sounds simple, then just ask anyone who was involved in engine development at Rolls-Royce at that time. Some accompanying diagrams illustrate the effects of supercharger developments and also the effect of the increased mass flows achieved by applying these blower developments to the larger capacity Griffon engines with which the later marks of Spitfire were fitted. In order to absorb these progressive increases in power provided by Rolls-Royce we had to provide larger propellers. We went through the whole gamut from two-blade fixed pitch through three-bladed variable pitch, three-, four- and five-blade constant speed to six-blade contra-props.

Racing seaplanes influence

Before discussing Spitfire development in greater detail, I would like to say something about the basic principles which influenced it, and the attitudes of mind which motivated the Supermarine design team throughout this period, as it seemed to me. At the time that the Spitfire was designed, Mitchell's design team, because of its previous involvement with the S.4, S.5, S.6 and S.6B Schneider Trophy racing seaplanes, had more practical knowledge of high speed aeronautics than any other design team in the world. They were mentally adjusted to, and dedicated to, the search for the ultimate in aerodynamic efficiency and the achievement of the highest possible speeds. They were not going to allow themselves to be constrained by convention or other extraneous considerations

(Above right) A Spitfire 24, the final production version, in the markings of No 80 Squadron, the last RAF unit to fly the type operationally. (Below) A far cry from the prototype K5054, this Seafire 47 with Griffon engine and contra-prop has long-range tanks and bombs under each wing, and another tank under the fuselage.

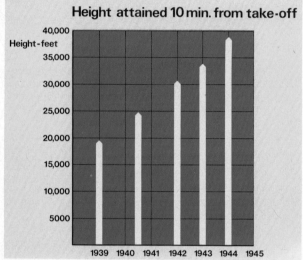

Height attained 10 min. from take-off

(chart showing height in feet, 1939–1945)

Height-feet

40,000
35,000
30,000
25,000
20,000
15,000
10,000
5000

1939 1940 1941 1942 1943 1944 1945

(Above) One of the several surviving Spitfires still airworthy in the United Kingdom, this is a Mk XVI now owned by Douglas Arnold (hence the D:A code letters on the fuselage) and used, before being retired from the RAF, by Air Chief Marshal Sir James Robb. (Left) An indication of the improvement in Spitfire climb performance in the course of the war and (bottom of page) a diagram showing wing and tailplane development.

from achieving these aims. They were young and, I believe, very single-minded.

From experience with the Schneider seaplanes, the Supermarine team learnt, amongst other things, that the most efficient aerodynamic shapes could be achieved in practice only by employing the most advanced engineering techniques in the design of the structures. This may sound today like a blinding glimpse of the obvious but in fact it was not unusual in those days for designers to try to achieve high aerodynamic efficiency whilst adopting pedestrian attitudes to structural design, and then to wonder why they failed. The different underlying design philosophies of the Spitfire and Hurricane make for an interesting comparison in this respect: the latter

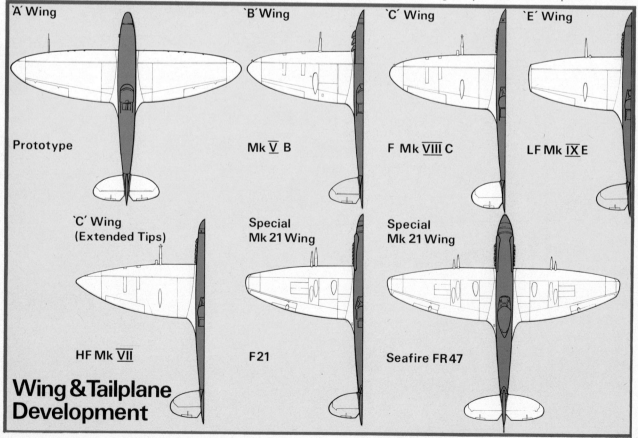

'A' Wing — Prototype

'B' Wing — Mk V B

'C' Wing — F Mk VIII C

'E' Wing — LF Mk IX E

'C' Wing (Extended Tips) — HF Mk VII

Special Mk 21 Wing — F21

Special Mk 21 Wing — Seafire FR 47

Wing & Tailplane Development

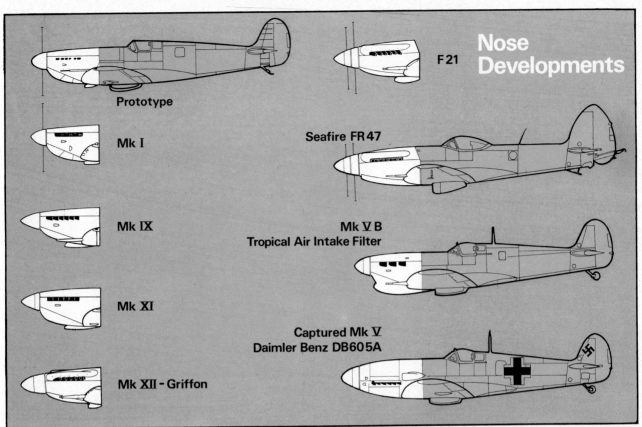

Nose Developments

Prototype

Mk I

Mk IX

Mk XI

Mk XII - Griffon

F 21

Seafire FR 47

Mk V B
Tropical Air Intake Filter

Captured Mk V
Daimler Benz DB605A

(Above) A diagram showing how the shape of the Spitfire's nose changed from the prototype to the Seafire 47, which was the last of the Spitfire family of variants to remain in production. The DB 605A installation was made in a Spitfire captured by Germany in 1944; in this guise, the Spitfire proved a little slower than the similarly-powered Bf 109. (Right) A plot of weight growth over 10 years, showing how the gross weight of the prototype was more than doubled by the Spitfire 24 and Seafire 47. (Below) Another of the airworthy Spitfires in the UK is this Mk IX owned by Airborne Taxi Services of Booker. At least a dozen others still fly in various parts of the World, and many examples are on static display in Museums and historic aircraft collections.

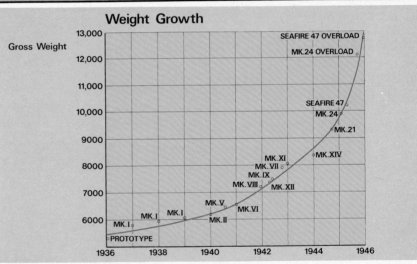

Weight Growth

Gross Weight

SEAFIRE 47 OVERLOAD
MK.24 OVERLOAD
SEAFIRE 47
MK.24
MK.21
MK.XIV
MK.XI
MK.VII
MK.IX
MK.VIII
MK.XII
MK.V
MK.VI
MK.I
MK.II
MK.I
MK.I
MK.I
PROTOTYPE

13,000
12,000
11,000
10,000
9000
8000
7000
6000

1936 1938 1940 1942 1944 1946

sacrificed some aerodynamic efficiency in order to achieve ease of production and as a result complemented the Spitfire.

The Supermarine S.4 is a good illustration of the Supermarine design philosophy. Built in 1925 — eleven years before the first flight of the Spitfire — it had a wooden stressed skin fuselage, a fully cantilever monoplane wing and a fully cantilever float structure. It had rigid tubular rods for the flying controls, ailerons operated through torque tubes, and trailing edge flaps on the wing to reduce its take-off and alighting speeds. I repeat that this was in 1925. Over-ambitious perhaps, as it turned out, because it crashed in Chesapeake

Bay — probably because of wing flutter — but not before it had set up a world speed record of 226·9 mph (365 km/h) on the 700 bhp of its Napier Lion engine. It was flown by that never-to-be-forgotten character Henri Biard, then chief test pilot of Supermarine.

The structural and engineering design of the S.6 series of seaplanes also merits careful study in the context of the general state of the art of the period. No radiators, as they were generally understood, were fitted but double skinned surface cooling was used for the main engine coolant in the wings with surface cooling for the oil along the fuselage sides, the oil tank being situated in the fin. The cockpit provided no direct forward view at all. Fuel was carried in the floats. A very light all-metal stressed skin structure was adopted, but with the

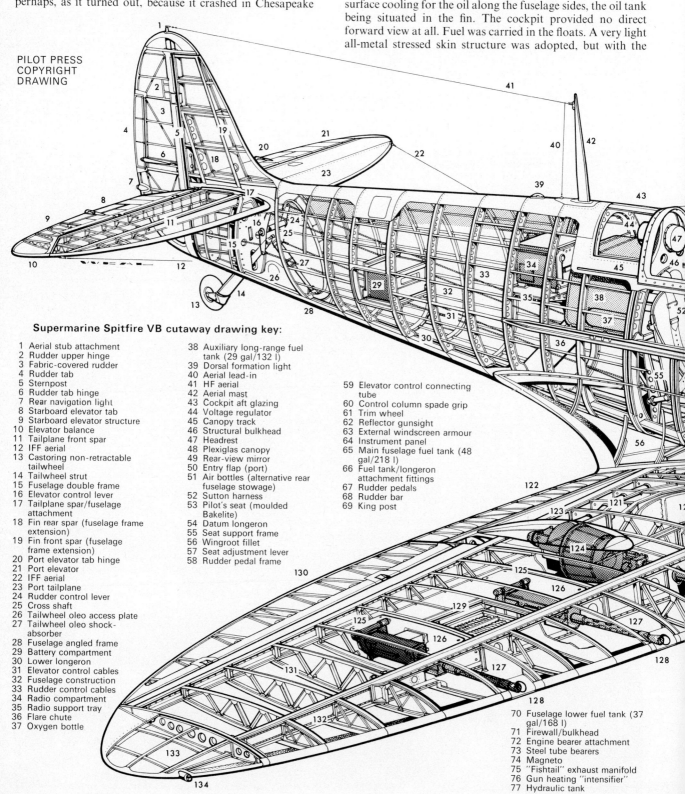

PILOT PRESS COPYRIGHT DRAWING

Supermarine Spitfire VB cutaway drawing key:

1 Aerial stub attachment
2 Rudder upper hinge
3 Fabric-covered rudder
4 Rudder tab
5 Sternpost
6 Rudder tab hinge
7 Rear navigation light
8 Starboard elevator tab
9 Starboard elevator structure
10 Elevator balance
11 Tailplane front spar
12 IFF aerial
13 Castoring non-retractable tailwheel
14 Tailwheel strut
15 Fuselage double frame
16 Elevator control lever
17 Tailplane spar/fuselage attachment
18 Fin rear spar (fuselage frame extension)
19 Fin front spar (fuselage frame extension)
20 Port elevator tab hinge
21 Port elevator
22 IFF aerial
23 Port tailplane
24 Rudder control lever
25 Cross shaft
26 Tailwheel oleo access plate
27 Tailwheel oleo shock-absorber
28 Fuselage angled frame
29 Battery compartment
30 Lower longeron
31 Elevator control cables
32 Fuselage construction
33 Rudder control cables
34 Radio compartment
35 Radio support tray
36 Flare chute
37 Oxygen bottle

38 Auxiliary long-range fuel tank (29 gal/132 l)
39 Dorsal formation light
40 Aerial lead-in
41 HF aerial
42 Aerial mast
43 Cockpit aft glazing
44 Voltage regulator
45 Canopy track
46 Structural bulkhead
47 Headrest
48 Plexiglas canopy
49 Rear-view mirror
50 Entry flap (port)
51 Air bottles (alternative rear fuselage stowage)
52 Sutton harness
53 Pilot's seat (moulded Bakelite)
54 Datum longeron
55 Seat support frame
56 Wingroot fillet
57 Seat adjustment lever
58 Rudder pedal frame

59 Elevator control connecting tube
60 Control column spade grip
61 Trim wheel
62 Reflector gunsight
63 External windscreen armour
64 Instrument panel
65 Main fuselage fuel tank (48 gal/218 l)
66 Fuel tank/longeron attachment fittings
67 Rudder pedals
68 Rudder bar
69 King post

70 Fuselage lower fuel tank (37 gal/168 l)
71 Firewall/bulkhead
72 Engine bearer attachment
73 Steel tube bearers
74 Magneto
75 "Fishtail" exhaust manifold
76 Gun heating "intensifier"
77 Hydraulic tank

wings and floats now wire-braced after the experience of the S.4. This aeroplane was of all-metal construction and had a percentage structure weight of 35 as against the 45 of the S.4. The S.6 won the Schneider Trophy in 1929, flown by the late Flt Lt Dick Waghorn and the S.6B took the world's speed record at 407 mph (654,8 km/h) in 1931, flown by the late Flt Lt George Stainforth, after winning the 1931 Schneider Trophy in the hands of the late Flt Lt John Boothman.

These racing seaplanes were the most advanced aeroplanes in the world at that time. They were designed by young men with an over-riding purpose to build the fastest aeroplanes in the world. As I have said, Reg Mitchell died at the age of 42, in 1937; in 1925 when the S.4 flew, he was 30. Members of his team still retained the basic attitudes acquired from the racing seaplane programmes throughout the life of the Spitfire. The Spitfire was a fighter — its job was to outperform and outfight all other aircraft in the world, and throughout its development, performance was given over-riding priority. I personally had no doubt whatever of the rightness of this attitude, which generally received the whole-hearted support of the production staff who cheerfully tackled all manner of production problems in order to support the basic philosophy which kept the Spitfire in the forefront of the battle for so long.

So, to continue with the story of the Spitfire, we started off in 1936 with a single prototype aeroplane of low drag configuration, having a very moderate wing loading in the circumstances, with good power to weight ratio (what today we might call SEP) and with a very advanced structure for those days, giving a low percentage structure weight allied with high strength factors. Aft of the main engine bulkhead, the Spitfire had a stressed skin structure built on frames and stringers, the material being copper-based light alloy. The wing had a single main spar at 25 per cent of the chord and the torsion box was formed by a 14-gauge flush-riveted leading edge skin structure. This gave a very efficient aerodynamic form to the wing leading edge. Only the control surfaces were fabric covered. The propeller was wooden and of fixed pitch.

From the very first day that we flew the prototype, we set out to get the maximum possible performance from it. This was done initially by propeller development (I recollect that we flight-tested some 15 to 20 different designs of wooden fixed pitch propeller on the prototype), but also by some other

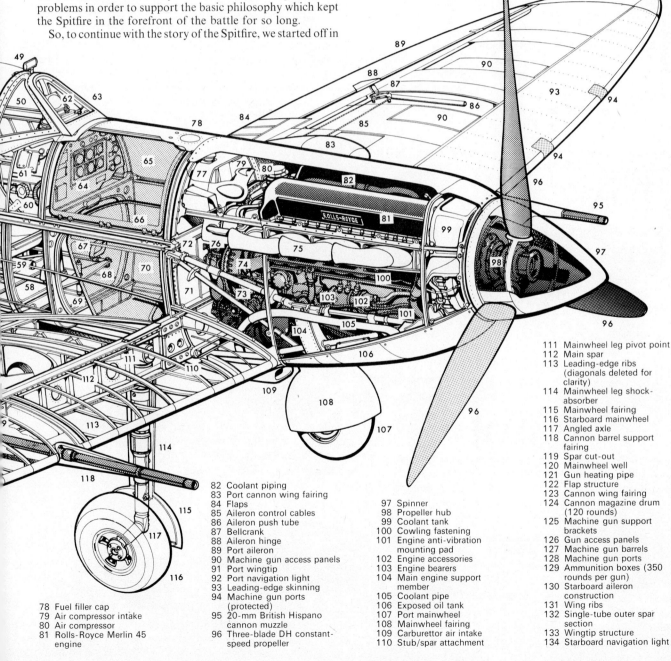

78 Fuel filler cap
79 Air compressor intake
80 Air compressor
81 Rolls-Royce Merlin 45 engine
82 Coolant piping
83 Port cannon wing fairing
84 Flaps
85 Aileron control cables
86 Aileron push tube
87 Bellcrank
88 Aileron hinge
89 Port aileron
90 Machine gun access panels
91 Port wingtip
92 Port navigation light
93 Leading-edge skinning
94 Machine gun ports (protected)
95 20-mm British Hispano cannon muzzle
96 Three-blade DH constant-speed propeller
97 Spinner
98 Propeller hub
99 Coolant tank
100 Cowling fastening
101 Engine anti-vibration mounting pad
102 Engine accessories
103 Engine bearers
104 Main engine support member
105 Coolant pipe
106 Exposed oil tank
107 Port mainwheel
108 Mainwheel fairing
109 Carburettor air intake
110 Stub/spar attachment
111 Mainwheel leg pivot point
112 Main spar
113 Leading-edge ribs (diagonals deleted for clarity)
114 Mainwheel leg shock-absorber
115 Mainwheel fairing
116 Starboard mainwheel
117 Angled axle
118 Cannon barrel support fairing
119 Spar cut-out
120 Mainwheel well
121 Gun heating pipe
122 Flap structure
123 Cannon wing fairing
124 Cannon magazine drum (120 rounds)
125 Machine gun support brackets
126 Gun access panels
127 Machine gun barrels
128 Machine gun ports
129 Ammunition boxes (350 rounds per gun)
130 Starboard aileron construction
131 Wing ribs
132 Single-tube outer spar section
133 Wingtip structure
134 Starboard navigation light

Engine Power Growth

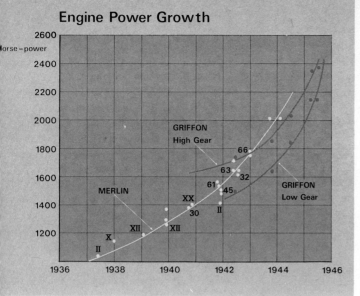

Drag at High Speed—RAE Tests

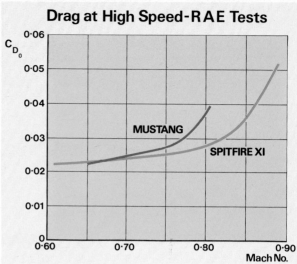

design refinements. We increased the maximum level speed of the prototype from 336 to 349 mph (541-562 km/h) at about 18,000 ft (5 490 m) before sending it for its official trials at Martlesham Heath — this, remember, was in the early summer of 1936.

One of the flight characteristics that became quickly apparent in the prototype was extremely docile behaviour at the stall, particularly under conditions of high *g*. Always claimed to be attributable to the elliptical shape of the wing,

this was one of the Spitfire's greatest features as a combat aircraft. You could pull it well beyond its buffet boundary and drag it round with full power and little airspeed; it would shudder and shake and rock from side to side, but if you handled it properly it would never get away from you. Whether they know it or not, there are many fighter pilots alive today who owe their survival to this remarkable quality of the Spitfire — and I think I am one of them.

Several diagrams accompanying this article illustrate the

(Below) These side views depict, top to bottom, Spitfire PR Mk IV N3117 of No 1 PRU, August 1941, Spitfire F Mk IX MH978 of No 132 Squadron, July 1944 and Spitfire IIB P8160 of AFDU, Wittering, April 1944.

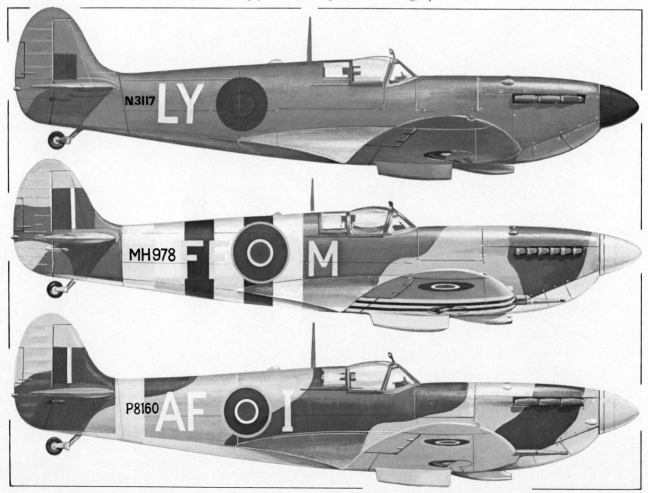

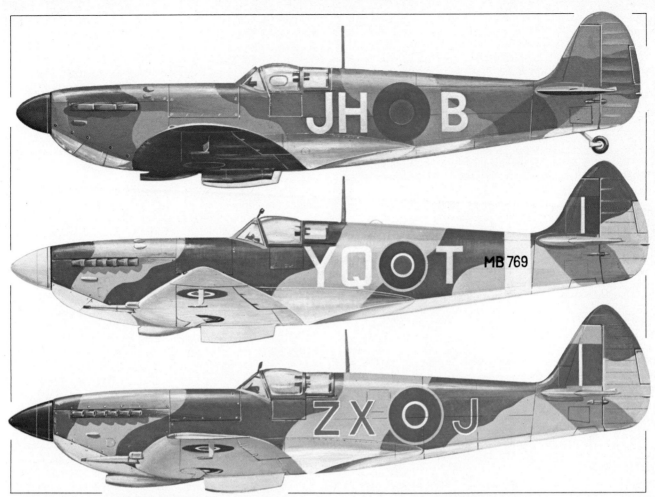

(Above) Illustrated, top to bottom, in these side views are: Spitfire I (K9927) of No 74 Squadron at Hornchurch in May 1939; Spitfire HF Mk VII MB769 of 616 Squadron, October 1943 and Spitfire LF Mk VIII (MT775) of No 145 Squadron serving in Italy 1944.

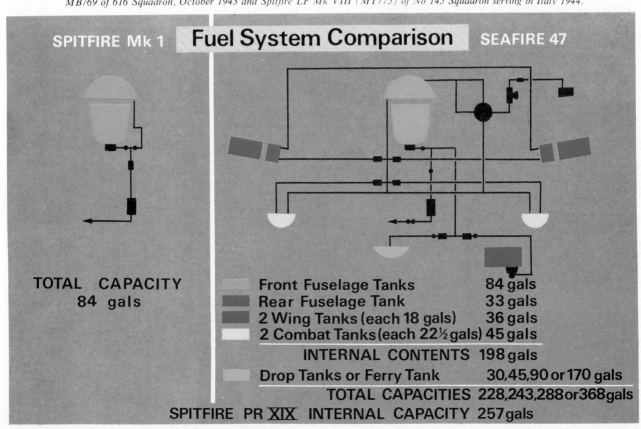

Fuel System Comparison

SPITFIRE Mk 1

SEAFIRE 47

TOTAL CAPACITY
84 gals

Front Fuselage Tanks	84 gals
Rear Fuselage Tank	33 gals
2 Wing Tanks (each 18 gals)	36 gals
2 Combat Tanks (each 22½ gals)	45 gals
INTERNAL CONTENTS	198 gals
Drop Tanks or Ferry Tank	30,45,90 or 170 gals
TOTAL CAPACITIES	228,243,288 or 368 gals

SPITFIRE PR XIX INTERNAL CAPACITY 257 gals

performance growth achieved with the Spitfire; the figures all come from A & AEE, Boscombe Down, reports and apply to production, in-service, aircraft and engines. The graphs for level speed performance show the Mk I aeroplane with fixed-pitch wooden propeller and Merlin III engine, followed by the Mk V with Merlin 45 and three-blade constant-speed propeller. Also shown is an LF Mk V with Merlin 50M engine, which had a cropped blower enabling it to develop high bhp at low altitudes (and at higher manifold pressures) at the expense of performance at altitude. This well illustrates the effect of supercharger characteristics on the speed/height parameter.

Then, the diagram shows, in curves for a Mk VIII and Mk IX, the impact of the Merlin 60 series engine with its two-speed two-stage supercharger, with intercoolers to lower the charge temperature. These curves illustrate the effect of varying the blower speed ratios in an otherwise identical engine. Finally, we move to the Mks XIV and 21 with their big Griffon engines having 10 litres more capacity — giving a basically increased mass flow — and also fitted with two-speed two-stage intercooled superchargers. This shows how the supercharger developments originated for the 27-litre Merlin engine could be effectively applied to the larger 37-litre Griffon engine — a good illustration perhaps, of the old adage that "A good big 'un will usually beat a good little 'un".

On the extreme right of the diagram is a spot indicating a performance of nearly 500 mph (805 km/h) which we achieved experimentally with a Spitfire-Spiteful hybrid having a laminar flow wing, a Griffon engine with a three-speed two-stage supercharger and a five-bladed propeller with metal blades of thin laminar flow section. It was not strictly a Spitfire, but it represented about the ultimate in speed development of piston engined aircraft. I must add that I believe a de Havilland Hornet later also achieved a speed of this order in an experimental configuration, with two Merlin engines.

Climb performance is shown in another diagram. This shows the growth of climb performance against a date baseline, stated in terms of height attained within 10 minutes of take-off. Engine power growth is also shown diagrammatically. It should be remembered that, as the power grew in the manner illustrated, there was an equally dramatic improvement in engine thrust-weight ratio. In the case of the Merlin, its dry weight ratio was just under 1·4 lb (0,64 kg)/bhp in 1937 and this was down to about 0·7 lb (0,32 kg)/bhp by the end of 1944. In other words, it's net dry weight per bhp was halved in seven years. This was a truly remarkable achievement on the part of Rolls-Royce.

A plot of the maximum performance achieved by Spitfire variants from the Mk 1 to the Mk 21, clearly showing the effect of different supercharging of the various Merlin and Griffon engines. The two spots on the left show the speed of the prototype, as first flown and after modification; that on the extreme right refers to a Spitfire/Spiteful hybrid.

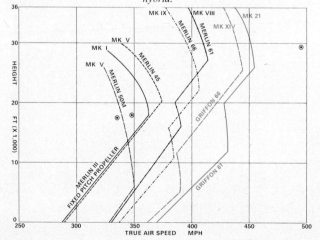

There was a series of basic stages in the development of the Spitfire airframe involving substantial structural design changes in order to accommodate the larger and more powerful engines as they came along and to accommodate increases in armament, fuel capacity and external stores. From each of these main stages — or stepping stones — branched out a whole series of sub-stages or variants or interim versions; fighters, reconnaissance and naval variants. Thirty-six different marks actually went into operational service, of which 23 were fitted with Merlin engines and 13 with Griffon. The principal stages of development are indicated on the diagram illustrating weight growth, and by other illustrations in these pages.

Flight handling

I would like to make the general point that almost every design change introduced in the course of the extremely rapid development of the Spitfire was in some way basically detrimental to the flight handling, usually in terms of longitudinal or directional stability. My main pre-occupation as chief test pilot was thus to ensure that the flight handling characteristics of the Spitfire remained within manageable limits, and it wasn't really possible in the prevailing circumstances to do more than this.

To keep the flight handling situation under control, many expedients were forced upon us by the immense pressures of the wartime production effort. The "elegant solutions" were usually not available to us, simply because of the pressures of time; solutions had to be found at once and therefore we improvised — generally with good success. But our expedients were not always entirely successful and the flight handling of the Spitfire sometimes left a certain amount to be desired. On the whole, however, we managed to keep things pretty well under control and in this process I must acknowledge the massive amount of help contributed by other test pilots who were my colleagues in the experimental flight development section at Supermarine, as well as the Service pilots at the RAE and A & AEE.

With the early production aeroplanes, high lateral stick forces at the higher airspeeds posed a serious problem, which became acute during the Battle of Britain. I blamed myself for not having made more of a song and dance about this characteristic before the war, although there were reasons for this. However, when I served in No 65 Squadron for a time in 1940 — to gain first hand experience of the Spitfire in combat — I made Joe Smith's life hell over this and with his usual energy and decisiveness he instituted a programme which produced a great improvement by 1941 — which all goes to show that there is no substitute for being shot at! However, in my view, the aileron problem was never completely solved until the Mk 21 wing came along, with a radically new aileron system.

Longitudinal stability, over the years, caused me more anxiety than anything else. We had to contend with some seriously destabilising influences, which included:

1 Longer and longer noses;
2 Progressive increases in propeller solidity (or blade area);
3 Increased moments of inertia due to increases in, and redistribution of, mass;
4 Extended flight envelopes in both speed and height;
5 The carriage of greatly increased loads of fuel and armament, both internal and external.

As I have said, all modifications made in the interests of handling had to be such as could be developed quickly and incorporated in the production line without slowing the ever-increasing tempo of production. More often than not, the obvious aerodynamic answer had to be abandoned because it meant too radical a change to be practical from the production/time viewpoint, and some sort of aerodynamic "fiddle" had to be adopted instead. On the whole, the inevitable conflict of interest between "design" and "production" was resolved by Supermarines as well and as successfully, I think, as was humanly possible. But it meant some give-and-take on all sides and some of the "give" inevitably had to be on the "handling" side.

It was none-the-less galling, on occasions, to encounter people whose sole pre-occupation in life was the study of flight characteristics and to be told something like "What you want to do with the Spitfire Mark so-and-so is to double the tailplane area". As if we didn't know . . .

High Mach number handling

The pilot's notes for the Spitfire Mk IX (1942) quoted a limiting Mach number of 0·85. Since Mach meters were not then available in service, the notes quoted the appropriate airspeeds against height associated with $M = 0.85$. As many readers will be aware, 0·85 is a higher critical Mach number than that of many of the subsequent jet aircraft produced after the war; I myself have flown at least three post-war jet aircraft which could not be controlled at Mach numbers lower than those at which I frequently flew Spitfires.

The Spitfire gave very good warning of impending Mach number trouble. At about $M = 0.85$ it started a longitudinal oscillation, sometimes associated with wing dropping. If Mach number was increased, the aircraft would eventually get into a severe nose down trim condition. The preliminary oscillation was only associated with certain elevator configurations.

In order to achieve these high Mach numbers it was necessary to climb to a great height and enter a steep dive. The rate of height loss in this dive was then so great that the Mach number relative to the IAS decayed rapidly and it was thus difficult to get into serious trouble. In fact, very few pilots even reached the initial oscillation stage. However, it is interesting that a critical Mach number of 0·85 should have been quoted in pilot's notes dated 1942. In those days, very few service pilots realised its significance nor indeed knew what a critical Mach number was, and I certainly did not deem it my business to go around telling them.

During 1942, some trials were conducted at the RAE, Farnborough, to measure drag and trim changes at high Mach numbers on a P-47 Thunderbolt, a P-51 Mustang and a Spitfire IX. The result of the drag measurements as between the Mustang and the Spitfire are interesting and are shown on an accompanying graph, taken from the RAE Report dated January 1944 (by Smelt and Charnley). The curves show drag coefficient measured against true Mach number, and the top extremities of the curves represent points actually achieved in flight. They show the Spitfire achieving a true Mach number of nearly 0·9 (34 years ago!) and the Mustang reaching only just beyond Mach 0·8. They also show the drag coefficient of the Spitfire (flown by the late Sqn Ldr Tobin) being lower than that of the Mustang from about 0·65 onwards. In a later series of dives — also at RAE — a Spitfire reached a Mach number of $M = 0.9$ in the hands of the late Sqn Ldr Martindale.

The Mustang had a thickness/chord ratio of 16 per cent as against the 13 per cent of the Spitfire, and it also had a more "draggy" cooling system, and a thicker tailplane. This probably accounted for the Spitfire's outstandingly better high Mach number behaviour. The RAE report noted: "It is, of course, not possible to decide the Mach number directly from ASI and altimeter readings by inspection, and a Mach meter was therefore fitted to both aircraft to indicate to the pilot when he had reached the maximum value. This was extremely useful on the Mustang but as it was calibrated only up to $M = 0.8$ it was off the scale during a good part of the Spitfire dives".

Armament and external stores

The Spitfire Mk I came out with eight 0·303-in (7,7-mm) Browning machine guns mounted in the wings and firing

(Above) A Spitfire PR Mk XIX, the final photographic reconnaissance version, with fuel carried in the wing to achieve a very long range. The oblique camera installation is clearly seen.

(Above) As part of the continuing quest for greater range, this Spitfire VC was tested with an outsize ventral tank, the capacity being 170 Imp gal (773 l); the oil tank was also enlarged, leading to the deepened cowl line beneath the spinner. (Below) Another experimental long-range Spitfire IX was this example fitted, in the USA, with P-51 wing drop tanks.

outside the propeller disc. The 300 rounds per gun gave a total firing time of about 20 seconds — which is in fact a great deal more than it sounds. This was considered at the time — and indeed it was — a very heavy armament. It meant a total rate of 7,200 rounds per minute, enough to blast any aeroplane out of the sky. I believe I am right in saying that the original decision to increase the requirement from four guns to eight guns for both the Spitfire and Hurricane was cooked up in 1934-35 between Wg Cdr Ralph Sorley — then responsible for RAF Operational Requirements — and Sydney Camm and Reg Mitchell. It was certainly a splendid decision. The Battle of Britain was fought and won by the Hurricanes and Spitfires with their eight Browning guns apiece.

However, early on in the war, the 20-mm Hispano cannon became available, due to the foresight of a number of men — a story which I have no space to tell in detail here. Suffice to say that we cobbled up an experimental installation of two 20-mm Hispano cannon each on 20 Mk I Spitfires. These guns had a drum feed and the whole thing was a bit of a dog's breakfast; the installation was subject to frequent stoppages, but operational trials proved the worth of the heavier armament. Eventually, the Spitfire VBs standardised on an armament installation consisting of two 20-mm cannon and four 0·303-in (7,7-mm) guns. The cannon installation was greatly improved by a belt feed system named after the French company Chattelerault, which developed it. The mixture of cannon and machine gun was one of those traditional, but extremely

A Spitfire IX carrying "Mod XXX Depth Charges" — a nick-name for barrels of Henty and Constable beer ferried across the channel to refresh the Allied troops soon after D-Day landings.

sound, British compromises. Some Spitfires were able to carry four 0·50-in (12,7-mm) calibre American machine guns instead of the four smaller calibre British guns, and from the Mark VC onwards, all Spitfires were able to carry four cannon. They did not always do so, but they had the capability, and towards the end of the war this became standard armament — the machine guns being finally eliminated from the Mark 21 series onwards.

Jettisonable fuel tanks came in 30, 45 and 90 Imp gallon (136, 205 and 409 l) sizes with a final jumbo version of 170 Imp gal (773 l). The 90- and 170-gallon varieties were for ferrying only. A whole range of bombs and RPs were finally accommodated. After "D"-Day in 1944, there was a problem about getting beer over to the Normandy airfields. Henty and Constable (the Sussex brewers) were happy to make the stuff available at the 83 Group Support Unit at Ford near Littlehampton. For some inexplicable reason, however, beer had a low priority rating on the available freight aircraft. So we adapted Spitfire bomb racks so that an 18-gallon (82-l) barrel could be carried under each wing of the Spitfires which were being ferried across from Ford to Normandy on a daily basis.

We were, in fact, a little concerned about the strength situation of the barrels, and on application to Henty and Constables for basic stressing data we were astonished to find that the eventuality of being flown on the bomb racks of a Spitfire was a case which had not been taken into consideration in the design of the barrels. However, flight tests proved them to be up to the job. This installation, incidentally, was known as Mod XXX Depth charge.

In conclusion

My early connection with the Spitfire was largely fortuitous but as it happened, from 1936 to 1945 — which was its period of glory — it completely dominated my life and my energies. It was my job primarily to criticise it, to find its defects and try to get something done about them. Believe me, I got to know this aeroplane intimately, not only as a test pilot but also as an operational pilot in both the Royal Air Force and the Fleet Air Arm. I never had any illusions about it, and I knew its many faults and shortcomings only too well.

Yet it is impossible to look back on the Spitfire without recognising it as something almost unique in aeronautical history. Through the tens of thousands of people who were in some way involved with it, the Spitfire cut through the fabric not only of this country, but of Europe and of a great overseas Empire. I refer to the people who in some way helped to design it, build it, maintain it, administer it, control it and fly it — and never ever forgetting those who died in it.

The Spitfire was flown in combat not only by Britons, but by Australians, Canadians, New Zealanders, South Africans, Rhodesians, Indians, Burmese; by free Frenchmen, Belgians, Dutchmen, Czechs, Poles, Danes, Norwegians and no doubt others I have not mentioned — not forgetting the Americans in the Eagle squadrons in 1940 and USAF squadrons in North Africa.

But it was in 1940 that the little Spitfires somehow captured the imagination of the British people at a time of near despair, becoming a symbol of defiance and of victory in what seemed a desperate and almost hopeless situation. To the people of Northern France, of Belgium and of Holland the sound of the Spitfires sweeping across their occupied countries in broad daylight in 1941, '42 and '43 brought the hope and prospect of freedom for the future.

Today, in all sorts of places in the world, I still meet men, ageing now, who come up and say "I flew Spitfires in the war". I have never heard it said without a strong note of pride. As I noted earlier, there are still Spitfires flying today, and no doubt many younger readers will have seen and heard one, or will do so in the future. What will never be heard again, however, is the unforgettable sound of a Wing of 36 Spitfires climbing out of an English airfield and heading south across the Channel. This was a sound that was never recorded, will never be heard again and can live only in the memories of those who heard it.

Looking back, from this distance of 40 years, it seems to me that of all the richly recorded achievements of this little aeroplane, perhaps the most significant, and certainly the least expected, was the very special place that it won, and still retains, in the hearts of men and women of all sorts of condition and nationality, all over the world. □

The author wishes to acknowledge his debt to the Technical Libraries of both the A & AEE and the RAE, whose records have survived better than those of Supermarine. Other information sources that have been used include the lecture "The Development of the Spitfire and Seafire" given by Joseph Smith before the RAeS on 19 December 1946, a lecture "The Development of the RR Merlin from 1939 to 1945" by Cyril Lovesay given at Hatfield in November 1945 and a paper on "Spitfire Stability and Control" by M P White. The research assistance of Mr Alec Lumsden is also acknowledged.

TORNADO —————————— *from page 128*

navigation system and the other is used mostly for TF development. A Mauser cannon was fitted in the ventral pack of a Lightning for subsonic and supersonic firing trials, also undertaken at Warton, and the Texas Instruments radar has been test flown, in the USA, in a Convair 240.

Production plans

The work sharing arrangements for the Tornado provide for BAC to build the front fuselage, rear fuselage and tail unit; MBB to build the centre fuselage and Aeritalia to build the wings — these same companies also having design authority for the respective components. There is no duplication of manufacture, but each nation maintains a final assembly line and will assemble and test fly the aircraft for national use; in the event of export orders being obtained, production will follow the same division, with final assembly arrangements to be agreed between the partners.

BAC is using the production facilities of its Military Aircraft Division, with the smaller parts being manufactured at Preston, the major components being built up at Samlesbury and final assembly taking place in a new hall now being erected at Warton, where flight testing also takes place. In Germany, MBB will undertake final assembly at Manching, for which purpose a large assembly hall currently used for F-104G overhaul is being modified; actual manufacture of the German components is further sub-divided with VFW-Fokker responsible for some 40 per cent of the MBB portion of the airframe. Similarly in Italy, Aeritalia has sub-contracted work on the wings to give a share to Piaggio, Aermacchi, Aeronavali, Saca and Siai-Marchetti. Final assembly and flight testing is at Turin.

Since the three nations have different total requirements and want their aircraft in somewhat different time scales, the rates of final assembly will differ, but the production rates of the components will, of course, be the same in all three countries. At present, it appears that planning is based on the production of between 100 and 150 aircraft per year at the peak — which will not be reached until the late 'seventies — and that production aircraft will be put in hand in batches of 40 at a time. The six pre-production Tornadoes, to fly next year, will probably be refurbished eventually and count as part of the production total, but the first true production aircraft will not appear until 1978. The first production batch will include aircraft for the RAF and the *Luftwaffe,* with the latter probably being the first service to receive a Tornado, late in 1978. Deliveries to Italy will not begin until 1979, and the ADV Tornado for the RAF will not appear until 1983.

In the *Luftwaffe,* the Tornado is scheduled to replace Lockheed F-104Gs in four wings (*Jabos* 31, 32, 33 and 34) and one training unit, and the *Marineflieger* will use the type to replace F-104Gs in MFG1 and MFG2. RAF Strike Command and RAF Germany currently have nine squadrons of Vulcans and Buccaneers (Nos 9, 12, 15, 16, 35, 44, 50, 101 and 617) earmarked for re-equipment with the Tornado and it is thought likely that No 617, the "Dam-Busters", will be the first to form on the type. The ADV variant will subsequently equip Strike Command squadrons flying Phantoms and Lightnings. In Italy, the AMI has scheduled four *Gruppi,* Nos 20, 102, 154 and 186, to re-equip on the Tornado from the F-104G and the G.91R. Plans are under way for the setting up of a tri-national OCU for the Tornado at RAF Cottesmore, and a weapons conversion unit at Decimomannu, Sardinia.

Although the supply of Tornadoes to the three sponsoring nations has top priority, production planning would certainly allow for the sale of export versions by the early 'eighties, and Panavia is now beginning to increase its marketing effort. The advent of the AD variant is seen as being of particular importance in this respect, since it allows the company to market the idea of a "mixed force" of Tornadoes in which the basic version would provide long range strike and reconnaissance functions and the ADV would provide strategic all-weather air defence. With growing awareness among air force staffs that the primary function of air power is its deployment in direct relation to a ground war (as shown in the Middle East and Vietnam) and not just to engage in traditional air-to-air combat with "hot rod" fighters, the sales prospects for an aircraft like the Tornado are improved, especially in view of its competitive cost. The Middle East is obviously one area with export prospects, but it should not be forgotten that Canada — one of the "founders" of the original MRCA specification — still has not ordered a new fighter and that, in the southern hemisphere, Australia is in process of evaluating new combat aircraft for the RAAF. If, as is fervently hoped, the rapid inflation of the last three years is now under control in Europe, the price of the MRCA will look considerably less formidable by the early 'eighties than it does today, and Europe's most important warplane of the present decade may take its place in the armouries of other nations. If versatility is a virtue, then the Tornado seems well placed to succeed, for there is no other single type of aircraft available today that can cover so broad a spectrum of operational rôles so effectively. □

Stores delivery trials made with Tornado P-06 shown in these photographs include dropping (above) external fuel tanks and (below) 1,000-lb (454-kg) bombs.

(Below) A close-up of the flight-refuelling probe on Tornado P-02 for the initial trials. The probe itself is retractable and the fairing into which it retracts, including the coupling to the aircraft's fuel system, is a "bolt-on" fitting, removed when flight refuelling missions are not being flown.

PAGE 145

transport component are the *I* and *II Grupos de Transporte,* the 1° *Grupo de Transporte de Tropas* and the *Grupo de Transporte Especial.* Both the *I* and *II Grupos* are based at the Galeão AFB, Rio de Janeiro, the former being the heavy logistic support element, its 1° *Esquadrão* operating seven C-130E, three C-130H and two KC-130H Hercules, the last-mentioned aircraft providing aerial refuelling support when necessary for the F-5E Tiger II *esquadrões,* and the latter *Grupo* having a mix of HS.748s, C-47s and C-95 Bandeirantes in its 1° *Esquadrão* and the six recently-delivered large-freight-door HS.748s as the equipment of its 2° *Esquadrão.* The *Grupo de Transporte de Tropas,* based at Campo dos Afonços, provides transport support for the Army's 1st Parachute Division and operates the few surviving Fairchild C-119Gs remaining in the FAB inventory in its 1° *Esquadrão* and DHC-5A Buffaloes in its 2° Esquadrão. The *Grupo de Transporte Especial* is responsible for governmental transport missions with two Boeing 737-200s, eight Hawker Siddeley HS.125s, a half-dozen Bell 206 JetRanger helicopters and several Bandeirantes, and is based at Brasília.

Other important components of the *Comando de Transportes Aéreos* are the independent *esquadrões* comprising the 1° *Esquadrãos de Transporte* at Belém, Pará State, now operating a mix of C-47s and Bandeirantes; the 2° *Esquadrão* with C-47s at Recife; the 3° *Esquadrão* at Galeão which will have phased out its few remaining C-47s by the end of the year when it will be completely Bandeirante equipped; the 4° *Esquadrão* at Cumbica AFB, São Paulo, which is now phasing out its C-47s and replacing them with Bandeirantes, and the 5° and 6° *Esquadrãos de Transporte de Tropas* based at Campo Grande and Manaus respectively with DHC-5A Buffaloes. The *II Grupo de Aviação* at Belém operates six venerable Consolidated PBY-5A Catalina amphibians for transport tasks in the Amazon. These aged aircraft, which have been recently refurbished in São Paulo, having undergone some structural strengthening, have been fitted with new avionics and are now flying with engines taken from the ex-Varig DC-6Bs after their withdrawal from FAB service. The Catalinas have given invaluable service over the years, fulfilling particularly arduous missions, but their replacement cannot be delayed for more than another year or two. The Canadair CL-215 and the Boeing Vertol CH-47 Chinook helicopter have been studied as potential successors but no decision has been taken.

In addition to the previously-listed transport units, each Command and major base has one or two Bandeirantes for utility transport tasks. The C-95 Bandeirante is rapidly becoming the FAB's maid-of-all-work and some 60 of the 80 general-purpose light transport model so far ordered for the service will have been taken into the inventory by the end of the year, the last 20 of these being of the stretched EMB-110K version with strengthened freight floor, enlarged freight door and revised avionics. In addition, the FAB is receiving four examples of the EMB-110B (RC-95) photographic version of the Bandeirante which has Doppler and inertial navigation equipment, and cabin floor apertures for various cameras.

The centre of helicopter activity is the *Centro de Instrução de Helicopteros* (Helicopter Training Centre) adjacent to the city of Santos, São Paulo, which is also the base of the so-called *Ala* 435 which is primarily a counter-insurgency unit with a half-dozen UH-1D Iroquois, four Bell 206 JetRanger and four Hughes OH-6 helicopters. It is agreed by general consensus that the helicopter element of the FAB must undergo substantial expansion over the coming years and the licence manufacture of helicopters for both the FAB and the *Fôrça Aéronaval* by EMBRAER has been under discussion for some considerable time past, various types having been considered with the UH-1H apparently being the current frontrunner, although discussions have been held with Aérospatiale.

Apart from the previously-mentioned Helicopter Training Centre at Santos, the principal training establishments are the *Academia da Fôrça Aérea* (AFA), the *Escola de Especialistas de Aeronáutica,* the *Centro de Formação de Pilotos Militares,* the *Centro de Aplicação Tática e Recomplementação de Equipagens* (CATRE), the *Escola de Sargentos Especialistas,* the *Escola Preparatório de Cadetes do Ar,* the *Escola de Comando e Estado Maior da Aeronáutica* (ECEMAR) and the *Centro Técnico de Aeronáutica* (CTA).

At the AFA at Pirassununga, between Rio de Janeiro and São Paulo, the pilot training syllabus for regular officers comprises some 350 hours up to a "wings" standard, including 150-200 hours on the Aerotec T-23 Uirapuru primary — this somewhat high number of hours being accounted for by the fact that the AFA course includes basic armament experience, etc. At the present time, the pupil pilots at the AFA progress from the T-23 Uirapuru to the Cessna T-37C for 150 hours, the latter now being progressively replaced by the Xavante. However, from next year, the AFA syllabus will be changed, the T-25 Universal I being interposed between the Uirapuru and the Xavante, and pilots will then fly 50 hours on the Uirapuru, 100-150 hours on the Universal and 100 hours on the Xavante. This syllabus is already employed by the *Centro de Formação de Pilotos Militares* at Natal, Rio Grande do Norte, where reserve pilots are achieving good results with the T-23 — T-25 — AT-25 sequence. Future transport pilots undertake twin conversion on the Bandeirante.

Both the Universal and the Xavante are utilised by the CATRE, also at Natal, for air-to-air and air-to-ground weapon training, this Centre possessing the largest of the FAB's firing ranges and utilises the latest techniques in computing the results of exercises. Every combat *esquadrão* flies to the CATRE each year; firing exercises and contests are held between the individual *esquadrões.* Technical sergeants, mechanics, flight controllers, etc, are trained at the *Escola de Especialistas* at Guaratinguetá, São Paulo; the *Centro Técnico* at São José dos Campos is responsible for the training of all aeronautical engineers and the ECEMAR in Rio de Janeiro provides command and administration training for higher-ranking officers.

The problems facing the *Fôrça Aérea Brasileira* are much the same as those faced by other national air arms to a greater or lesser degree and stemming from budgetary restrictions which enforce salary levels below those that are available from commercial organisations with recruiting problems as a result and the constant need in procurement of new equipment to balance one pressing demand against another equally pressing with the result that the fulfilment of all commitments demanded of the service is by no means easy. This latter is rendered the more complex by the immense part that the FAB is called upon to play in the economic development of Brazil — the service's non-military tasks are probably greater proportionately than such commitments fulfilled by any other of the world's major air arms — and by its social functions such as the operation of the *Correio Aéreo Nacional* (National Airmail Service), which is the direct responsibility of the *Comando de Transportes Aéreos,* the operation annually of the *Projeto Rondon* in which between one and two thousand university students are transported to the less accessible areas of Brazil for three weeks' social work among the local populace, the calibration of radio aids, photographic and survey operations over the interior, meteorological and oceanographic studies, and innumerable other tasks of a non-military nature.

However, although beset by wide-ranging problems, some of which appeared near-insurmountable but a few years ago, the FAB can claim without fear of contradiction to have made remarkable progress in its modernisation programme in recent years; a programme which is bringing about a dramatic improvement in operational capability. □

our trail in the sky

The G222 is today the
only medium range military transport
aircraft available on the market today.
Wide operational capabilities
and high reliability even in critical
flight conditions are guaranteed by the
advanced G.E. T64 P4D turbo-engines.
The most sophisticated avionics systems
and airborne instrumentation enable the aircraft
to operate in all weather conditions independently
of ground assistance. The G222 is certified
for operation with a crew of two and
can take-off and land on grass strips.
Its large volumetric capacity allows it to carry a wide range
of loads (up to 20,000 lbs.) or 44 fully equipped soldiers
and to parachute 32 paratroopers or to
air drop heavy loads up to 11,000 lbs.
The G222 can be rapidly converted to fulfil
rescue missions, aeromedical transport,
aerophotogrammetry, fire fighting and radio calibration.
And all the above at a very low operational cost.

AERITALIA

DIREZIONE GENERALE
80125 NAPOLI
PIAZZALE V. TECCHIO 51
TEL. 619.522 TELEX 71370

AIR International CLASSIFIED

ADVERTISEMENT RATES AND CONDITIONS OF ACCEPTANCE

Rates. Per word: UK 20p; Overseas 26p; USA/Canada 50 cents. Minimum: UK £2·40; Overseas £3·12; USA/Canada $6·50. Minimum charge applies for each paragraph. Name and address must be counted if included in the advertisement.

Semi-display advertisements, per single column centimetre (column width 55mm): UK £6·00; Overseas £6·25; USA/Canada $12·50. Minimum: UK £18·00; Overseas £18·75, USA/Canada $37·50.

Payment. All advertisements should be accompanied by payment and addressed to AIR International Classified Advertising, Barnack, Stamford, Lincs, PE9 3DN.

UK advertisers please remit by cheque or Postal Order. Overseas by International Postal/Money Order only. USA/Canada by cheque or International Postal/Money

Order. All cheques, Postal/Money Orders to be made payable to Finescroll Ltd.

Classified advertisements NOT accompanied by payment will be invoiced at an additional handling charge: UK 50p; Overseas 50p; USA/Canada $1·00.

Press Day. Classified advertisement copy must be received by the 20th of each month for publication last Friday of the month following, subject to space being available.

Box Numbers. For the convenience of advertisers, Box Number facilities are available at an additional charge: UK 80p; Overseas 80p; USA/Canada $2·00.

Replies should be addressed to the appropriate Box Number, c/o AIR International, Barnack, Stamford, Lincs PE9 3DN.

Series Discount. Advertisers who use this service regularly are allowed a discount of 5% for three, 10% for six, and 15% for twelve consecutive insertions.

Conditions of Acceptance. The Publishers retain the right to refuse or cancel advertisements at their discretion, and do not guarantee the insertion of any particular advertisement on a specified date. Although every care is taken to avoid mistakes, the Publishers do not accept liability for delay in publication, omissions, or for clerical or printers' errors however caused.

Advertisers are reminded of the requirements of the Trade Descriptions Act 1968, particularly regarding accurate descriptions of all goods offered for sale. Claims made in individual advertisements are the sole responsibility of the advertiser.

AIR International Classified Advertising, Barnack, Stamford, Lincs PE9 3DN
Telephone: Stamford (0780) 740373 or (London) 01-878 2454

AIR SHOWS

FARNBOROUGH INTERNATIONAL. 1976. Visit the Air International Stand. SF.32 in the South Hall, for your Finescroll, Ducimus and other aviation publications. Back issues, binders, bound volumes, etc. 5th to 12th September.
(1008HX)

SEE THE RED ARROWS. The internationally famous RAF aerobatic team will be appearing at the following venues in September: Biggin Hill and St Athan on 4th; Waterbeach and Rufforth 5th; Farnborough 9th-12th; Jersey and Guernsey 16th. Correct at time of going to press.
(1019JX)

HELICOPTERS

BELL JET RANGER AND HUGHES 300 spares, sales and service. CAA approved overhaul organisation. Bell and Allison spares always required. Heli Leeds, Refuge House, Bedford Street, Leeds 1.
(1014JX)

INFORMATION WANTED

AUTHOR wishes to interview aircrew members that flew as backseaters; (RIO's, WSO's) in the following aircraft: F-4, A-6, F-105F, during 1965-71 in Southeast Asia. AIRTITE PUBLISHING, Box 2366, San Francisco, CA 94126.
(1018JZ)

INSURANCE

INSURANCE. J. A. HARRISON (BROKERS) LTD. of Birmingham sell insurance. Our speciality aircraft insurance. A Century of Service. Phone, call or write: Security House, 160-161 Bromsgrove Street, Birmingham, B5 6NY. Tel. 021-692 1245 (10 lines).
(1002AY)

PUBLICATIONS

PLASTIC AIRCRAFT MODELS MAGAZINE. Specimen copy 40p. PAM NEWS, 22 Slayleigh Avenue, Sheffield, S10 3RB.
(1011LY)

AVIATION BOOKS. Out-of-print and current. State specific needs. JOHN ROBY, 3703R Nassau, San Diego, California 92115, U.S.A.
(1013KY)

PUBLICATIONS WANTED

WANTED — AVIATION BOOKS, MAGAZINES, RELICS. Details to Aeromart, 48 Marlborough Road, Ipswich.
(1012JY)

BOAC ANNUAL REPORTS for years ending up to 1952, 1954, 1957, 1960, 1961, 1966, 1967, 1968, 1972; BEA Reports for years ending up to 1952, 1954; any BSAA reports. Good prices paid. D. M. Hannah, Barnack, Stamford, Lincs, Tel. (0780) 740373.
(1017JX)

SOCIETIES

CLUB SECRETARIES. Club Ties, Blazer Badges, Drill Badges, Heraldic Shields, Brevets, Lapel Badges, Car Badges, Brochure from Club (Sales), 76 Greenford Avenue, Southall, Middlesex.
(1015LY)

LONDON SOCIETY OF AIR-BRITAIN. Wednesday, September 8th. "History of Airborne Early Warning Operations". An illustrated lecture presented by M. J. H. Lawrence. 7.00 p.m. Lecture Theatre, Holborn Central Library, Theobalds Road, London, WC1. Admission 35p. Visitors welcome.
(1020JX)

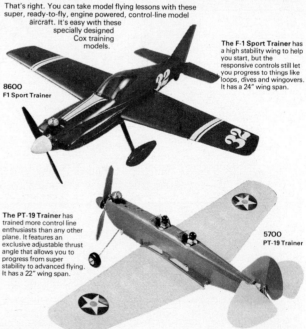

Eye of the beholder

WHILE we would hesitate to suggest that the recent revelation that Britain's postal services are celebrating a return to profitability is due to any great extent to the correspondence generated by this column, we *would* venture that at least a mite has been contributed by those many readers that have put pen or typewriter key to paper as a result of our recent references to scratch building! Indeed, no subject has resulted in so many letters being addressed to the *Model Enthusiast* column, serving to confirm our belief that the ranks of the do-it-yourself section of the modelling fraternity are growing apace.

These letters have been concerned with a variety of aspects of scratch-building, most of which we hope to discuss over the coming months, and quite a number have stressed what their writers consider to be a serious problem — a dearth of *suitable* drawings of the more esoteric aircraft types that whet their modelling appetites. For example, John M Bugary of Philadelphia writes as follows: "Many is the time that I have wished that I could model a B-15, say, or a B-23, but, alas, no kit. A return to a do-it-yourself approach to modelling is obviously the answer and we have an excellent magazine in AIR INTERNATIONAL in that it is packed every month with accurate three-view drawings, but these have one serious drawback — no cross-sections! If we really are to return to "doing-it-ourselves" with any chance of success, accurate drawings *with* cross-sections are an absolute necessity. Without such, who is to produce models of the more exotic aircraft of a quality and accuracy to stand alongside a collection of injection-moulded or vacuum-formed kit models?

"The size of the drawing is not important as any general arrangement drawing can easily be enlarged or reduced by the myriad of quick-print establishments here in the USA and, I suppose, elsewhere. Just as an example, consider the excellent *Fighter A to Z* series with its exquisite little three-views that can readily be enlarged, but they *do not include cross-sections!* May I suggest, therefore, that you insist from here on in that AIR INTERNATIONAL artists include cross sections in any and every general arrangement drawing that they prepare for your pages."

In reply to Mr Bugary and to quite a few other readers who have written to us in similar vein, we would suggest that scratch-building in fact commences with the preparation of the cross-sections of the chosen subject. Manufacturers drawings incorporating wing and fuselage cross-sections are, in truth, as rare as swimsuits in a nudist colony when it comes to anything other than the more mundane aircraft types and no plethora of such drawings for the latter survive. Thus, while a reasonably accurate general arrangement drawing of an aircraft type can be built up from photographs, assuming that basic dimensions are available

and the draughtsman possesses the necessary expertise, any cross-section drawings are *guesswork!* Apart from maximum depth and width — again assuming that *overall* dimensions are available — plan and sideview photographs will tell a draughtsman nothing of the fuselage cross-section, although a three-quarter view, and particularly one in which the frames or rivet lines can be discerned, will enable him to make an educated guess at the actual curvature, but it will be nothing more than an *educated guess!* The ellipses that he assumes to have been used could well differ appreciably from those arrived at by another and equally competent draughtsman. Wing cross-sections — without prior knowledge of the aerofoil section utilised — are a little easier to guesstimate and, of course, photos of the particular aircraft under construction are invaluable, but it must be stressed that in 99 cases out of every 100, cross-section drawings are no more than guesswork, and do not let anybody tell you that such drawings in a set of modelling plans — other than those very, very few exceptions that are based on genuine manufacturers drawings of the period — are anything *but* guesswork; *educated* guessing perhaps, but guessing nonetheless.

In short, it is a case of the eye of the beholder, which means the eye of the draughtsman preparing the drawing. His full elevations may be meticulous in their accuracy because he merely has to interpret as line what he can measure up with dividers from photographs, but when it comes to cross-sections . . . no way! We would therefore say again that scratch-building may well commence with the preparation of cross-sections of the subject aircraft, your guess probably being as good as that of any draughtsman provided that you have a 'feel' for the type that you have chosen to model — if it looks right, then it is probably as right as you are likely to get it.

Before leaving the subject of correspondence, we would again point out to readers that, with the best will in the world, we *cannot* offer a personal information service. We receive quite a number of letters from readers requesting that we furnish information calling for days and even weeks of research and to cope with such requests we would have to employ a large full-time research team. Other readers make requests that, to them, must appear relatively simple but, if they were to pause to think before committing pen to paper, they would perhaps realise that what they are asking verges on the impossible. Take, for example, Dr Spanoghe of Assebroek, Belgium, who wrote to us recently requesting that we provide him with the exact positioning of all the stencilled inscriptions appearing on the P-38 Lightning, the P-38 Airacobra, the P-40 Warhawk and the P-51 Mustang. Assuming that we *could* satisfy the good doctor's request,

we would have to provide him with little short of a hundred photographs! Sorry, Dr Spanoghe, no can do!

Finally we come to that hard core of what we refer to as our "veteran correspondents" — the VCs whose every repetitive turn of phrase, castigation and threat of ostracism from the "Lower Muddlecombe Modelling Society" or some such have become dear to our hearts. Our VCs make an invaluable contribution to the now-profitable postal services by writing to us month after month to assure us that *they* know better than we do; that they *personally* prefer this or that and as fellow modeller Fred next door agrees with them we cannot possibly know what we are talking about! To these we would say: Hard luck, chums! If *you* are so good why are we not reading *your* modelling column?

This month's colour subject

It is regretted that, owing to insurmountable technical problems, this month's colour subject — the Lockheed C-130 Hercules — has perforce become *next* month's colour subject! However, as a major part of this issue is devoted to the Vickers Supermarine Spitfire — the first among fighter immortals — which saw birth 40 years ago, some notes on Spitfire kits would not seem inappropriate this month.

The ballerina-like little Spitfire has understandably had a place in the catalogues from the earliest days of the plastic kit and has never lost its popularity, as is evidenced by the fact that rarely a year passes without at least one new Spitfire kit making its début. By our reckoning, Aurora was first in the field with a 1/48th scale kit, which, simple and quite inaccurate, was nevertheless considered to be acceptable by most of us who were around at the time. Soon afterwards, to the same scale or thereabouts, came a much better kit from Lindberg. As we recollect, it was somewhat *over*-scale, coming out at around 1/46th, but while in retrospect it may be seen to have still left much to be desired in providing a competent basis for a really sound model of the remarkable warplane that it purported to depict, it was hailed as quite something.

To 1/72nd scale, apart from the Frog Penguin kit of around 1939, which is really delving back into pre-history, the honour of being first fell to Airfix, the Spitfire being one of its very earliest aircraft kits, bearing a close resemblance to the larger-scale Aurora kit and being just as inaccurate! Of course, one was not too fussy about mark numbers and sub-types in those days, and all the aforementioned kits were probably meant to represent either the Spitfire Mk IA or Mk II. Over the years, Airfix has produced two more 1/72nd scale Spitfire kits; a somewhat poor and now rather elderly Mk IX and a recently-released and excellent Mk VB. Frog offered a Mk II early on which was quite good in its day, following this up with a nice — if not completely accurate — Mk XIV which comes with a V-1 flying bomb. More recently, Frog has come up with a very good Spitfire kit which may be completed either as a Mk VIII or a Mk IX.

Revell got into the 1/72nd scale Spitfire stakes quite some time ago with a passable Mk

II; Lesney has offered a very good "Matchbox" Mk IX and Heller offers a fine Mk VB, although this French company's earlier attempt at a Mk IA did not really come off as the model was too small, being to 1/75th scale. Somewhere along the line, still to 1/72nd scale, Hawk produced a Spitfire Mk 22, but this kit demands a great deal of work if it is to result in an acceptable model, as it possesses no undercarriage and the solid wings do not even have wheel wells, while the surface detailing is extremely coarse.

A very fine 1/72nd scale Spitfire Mk I is offered by Hasegawa and this includes, among its many attributes, alternative two-bladed wooden and three-bladed metal propellers. The Hasegawa Spitfire may certainly be considered definitive in so far as mark and scale are concerned. An odd-ball with regard to scale was the 1/70th Mk IX offered way back by Nichimo and which, if not well known, was quite a good kit for its period. Reverting to 1/48th scale, there is an elderly and not-too-accurate Mk IX by Monogram and a virtually identical offering from Marusan, but Otaki's recent Mk VIII heads the field in 1/48th scale.

Stepping up the scale, we find a good but by no means perfect Spitfire Mk IA from Revell to 1/32nd which has also been revised and re-issued as a Seafire Mk IB. This kit is easily eclipsed, however, by Airfix's magnificent 1/24th scale Mk IA which is truly a classic. Incidentally, a couple of years or so ago, John R Beaman Jr (2512 Overbrook Drive, Greensboro, NC 27408) published, after prodigious research, a book entitled "Calling all Spitfires". In this he offered conversion drawings and details for virtually every possible variation of Spitfire and Seafire based upon then-available kits. A number of new kits have since been released, but the book is still likely to prove invaluable to any modeller building up a collection of Spitfires.

A Concorde update
In the early days of Concorde development, a number of model kits were produced depicting 001 and 002, but with the progressive development of this Anglo-French aircraft over the years these kits have become obsolete. Included among these kits was an offering from Airfix which company has now completely revised its moulds to issue what is, to all intents and purposes, a new kit of the current production standard Concorde, the most noticeable feature being, of course, the much longer nose. While on the subject of this nose, we cannot but help wish that Airfix had gone to just a little more trouble and rendered this adjustable rather than mould it in with the rest of the fuselage so that it is rigidly fixed in the supersonic cruise attitude. Thus, when the model is assembled with the undercarriage extended, the nose angle and flight deck windows are incorrect. Rectifying this fault is a major operation indeed.

Even to 1/144th scale, this model has a length of 1 ft 5 in (43 cm) and the kit comprises 52 parts, moulded, apart from the clear windshield, in white plastic. No provision is made for glazing the cabin windows, but as these are so small, the omission is scarcely noticeable. In fact, it would perhaps have been better to have left the fuselage smooth and include the windows on the transfer sheet, thus avoiding the necessity of punching through the decal after it is affixed — by no means a foolproof method. Surface detailing is very

finely done, being sensibly contained to essentials, and the undercarriage is neatly modelled.

The intricate shape of the wing is well captured and the engine nacelles correctly depict those of the production standard aircraft. No problems should arise over assembly, for the component parts all fit well and the completed model has a most pleasing appearance, marred only by the previously-mentioned nose attitude if the model is standing rather than utilising the stand provided. The decal sheet offers markings for British Airways' G-BBDG plus, as an alternative, Air France's F-BVFA. In Airfix's Sky King Series 6, the kit retails in the UK at £1·40 and, as the only up-to-date Concorde kit, should find a ready market.

Aero alias Siebel
The largest and most ambitious kit yet to be released by Czechoslovakia's Kovozavody Prostejov represents the Aero C 3A twin-engined trainer and light utility transport which was, in fact, the German wartime Siebel Si 204D which was built in Czechoslovakia during the war years and continued in production into the postwar years, also being built in France as the Aerocentre NC 701.

Moulded primarily in light grey plastic and possessing 56 component parts, KP's kit is well detailed, accurate and easily assembled. The surfaces have embossed rivet detail but this is finely worked and by no means obtrusive. The flight deck is well endowed with bulkheads, instrument panels and consoles, seats, control columns and rudder pedals, and there is a large clear moulding for the nose, plus eight separate cabin windows. Another highly commendable feature is provided by the propellers, each of which forms three parts with the typical vaned spinner usually employed by the Argus provided as a separate moulding. The undercarriage may be assembled either extended or retracted, each pair of well doors being moulded as one and being separated by cutting along a grooved line if the modeller elects to have an extended undercarriage. Small details include the mass balances for the elevators — very delicate mouldings calling for care in handling.

A large decal sheet of good quality but thickly varnished provides markings for three aircraft — one military and two civil — all of postwar derivation. The Czechoslovak military example is coded UB-72 and has dark green upper surfaces and pale blue under-surfaces, and the civil models are registered OK-ZDJ and OK-ZDE, the former having the same colour scheme as the military example and having been used for pilot and parachutist training by SVAZARM in the 'fifties, and the latter being overall light grey-green and having been operated by CSA in the late 'forties. This is a fine kit and well up to the high standards that we have come to expect from this concern.

A mighty bantam
It is scarcely credible that nearly a quarter-century has elapsed since Ed Heinemann (then chief engineer of the Douglas Aircraft plant at El Segundo, California) first initiated work on his 'bantam bomber' which was to emerge on 22 June 1954 as the prototype Skyhawk. Parent company titles and US Navy designations have changed over the intervening years and this agile little aeroplane has seen combat over SE Asia and the Middle East, but,

progressively updated in so far as avionics, armament and power plant are concerned, and sporting a greater variety of national insignia with each passing year, it is still rolling off the assembly line for the USMC and for export, revealing little sign of its age.

Understandably, the Skyhawk has for long been a popular subject for the modeller, being offered in a variety of versions to 1/100th, 1/72nd, 1/50th and 1/48th scales—and now we have what simply must be the best of the lot, Hasegawa's kit to 1/32nd scale which may be completed either as an A-4E or an A-4F, the latter having been the first to feature the dorsal avionics pack. Oddly enough, two of the examples covered by the kit are a US Navy A-4E updated with the dorsal pack introduced by the A-4F and an A-4F flown by the *Blue Angels* aerobatic team not fitted with the pack and thus looking like an A-4E!

The kit comprises a total of 138 component parts, moulded in gull-grey plastic to the highest standards of precision, and assembly is straight-forward, despite the prodigious amount of detail. The surface detailing is finely engraved and includes rivets in perfect proportion, this being more readily achievable in 1/32nd than in smaller scales. Although a small aircraft by the standards of the day, the Skyhawk makes up into an impressive model with a length of 1 ft 3 in (38 cm) and a wing span of 10¼ in (26 cm). The cockpit and nosewheel housing form one sub-assembly and both have fully-detailed interiors. All controls are represented, the ejection seat is deserving of special mention—although the pilot figure intended to occupy this falls sadly short of the standard established by the remainder of the kit—and there is even a separate parachute back-pack.

The large fuselage half mouldings include the vertical tail surfaces and the lower wing panel is in one piece, and the mouldings are entirely free of all blemishes and flash. About a half-ounce (14 grammes) of weight is needed in the extreme nose to balance the tail, but as there is plenty of room to accommodate such a weight no problem is presented. The moulded piping and other detail in the wheel wells are notable and there are no voids anywhere in the model. Full marks are also due for the very sharp trailing edges of the wings and tail-planes. Transparencies are included for navigation, approach, landing and formation-keeping lights, and there are two rear-view mirrors inside the canopy. External appendages comprise two alternative in-flight re-fuelling probes, two Bullpup missiles, six 500-lb (226,8-kg) bombs with racks and two underwing fuel tanks.

The easily-followed instruction sheet is in English and incorporates detail views of the full-size aircraft and two pages of three-view drawings providing colour schemes and the positioning of the many decals. The large decal sheet covers a *Blue Angels* A-4F, an A-4E of VC-1 when based at Barker's Point, Oahu, Hawaii, and a camouflaged A-4E of Israel's *Heyl Ha'Avir*. A multitude of small markings is included, Federal Standard FS 595a reference numbers are quoted for the colours, and separate full-colour sheets covering the aircraft of VC-1 and the *Heyl Ha'Avir* are included, these incorporating very useful colour pictures of the cockpit interior and the ejection seat. This fine kit retails in the UK at £3·25 and it is, in our view, well worth the asking price. □   F J HENDERSON

PLANE FACTS

Hickory in the kindergarten

I am sending to you herewith two photographs of the remains of what I believe to be a WWII aircraft taken recently in the kindergarten at RAAF Fairbairn, Canberra. Can you possibly identify this aircraft and publish details and a general arrangement drawing.

N C Chequers
Sydney, Australia 2000

The aircraft fuselage seen in your photographs (reproduced here), Mr Chequers, belonged to a Tachikawa Ki.54-Hei, or Army Type 1 Transport Model Hei, known to the Allies under the ATIU-SWP reporting name system as Hickory. This particular fuselage in fact belonged to the aircraft that was used on 10 September 1945 to fly General Baba from the Sapong Estate, near Tenom, North Borneo, to Labuan Island off the north-west coast of Borneo, where the Japanese general surrendered to Maj Gen G F Wootten, General Officer Commanding, 9th Division Australian Imperial Force. This Ki.54-Hei was subsequently crated and despatched by No 81 Wing, RAAF, in an unserviceable condition, to No 1 Aircraft Depot, RAAF Laverton, in April 1946. Little is known of its history in Australia, but presumably it was originally sent to RAAF Fairbairn for possible transfer to the Australian War Memorial, Canberra, as an historic exhibit. Sadly, the derelict fuselage has languished in the kindergarten playground for several years, although there is still a possibility that it may be recovered and transferred to the RAAF Museum at Point Cook.

The Ki.54 was designed by Ryokichi Endo

The Ki.54-Hei fuselage in the kindergarten at RAAF Fairbairn as shown in one of the photographs accompanying Mr Chequers' letter and (below) this same aircraft sporting surrender crosses as used to transport General Baba to Labuan Island.

(Above) The Ki.54-Otsu crew trainer and (below) the standard Ki.54-Hei eight-seat liaison and communications model which was built in substantial numbers.

of Tachikawa to meet a *Koku Hombu* demand for a twin-engined multi-purpose trainer which could simulate the handling characteristics of the Imperial Army's twin-engined bombers, and the prototype was flown during the summer of 1940 with two Hitachi Ha-13-Ko (Army Type 98) nine-cylinder air-cooled radial engines which, rated at 510 hp for take-off and 470 hp at 5,575 ft (1 700 m), drove Sumitomo-Hamilton two-blade variable-pitch propellers. Of all-metal construction with fabric-skinned movable control surfaces, the Ki.54-Ko entered production as the Army Type 1 Advanced Trainer Model Ko and was intended primarily for pilot training. This was succeeded by the Ki.54-Otsu, or Army Type 1 Operations Trainer Model Otsu, which was a crew training variant suitable for the simultaneous training of the entire bomber's crew and having four gunnery stations each mounting a single 7,7-mm Type 89 machine gun, this being the principal production model. The Ki.54-Hei was an eight-seat liaison and communications model, while the Ki.54-Tei, or Army Type 1 Patrol Bomber Model Tei, was an anti-submarine patrol version with provision for eight 132-lb (60-kg) depth charges, the last-mentioned variant being built in small numbers during the closing stages of the war.

Production of the Ki.54 totalled 1,368 aircraft and performance included a maximum speed of 234 mph (376 km/h) at 6,560 ft (2 000 m), a cruising speed of 149 mph (240 km/h), a maximum range of 596 miles (960 km) and the ability to climb to 16,405 ft (5 000 m) in 20·3 min. Empty and loaded weights of the Ki.54-Hei were 6,512 lb (2 954 kg) and 8,591 lb (3 897 kg) respectively, and overall dimensions were: span, 58 ft 8⅔ in (17,90 m), length, 39 ft 2¹⁄₁₆ in (11,94 m), height, 11 ft 8⅞ in (3,58 m), wing area, 430·56 sq ft (40,00 m²).

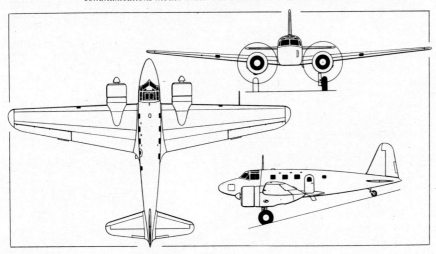

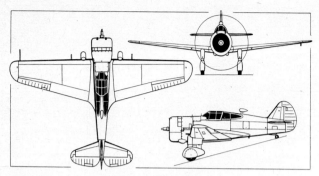

(Above and immediately below) The Hawk 75-O was the Argentine version of the basic fixed-gear Hawk monoplane. Twenty examples were manufactured under licence.

(Below) The so-called "China Demonstrator", the first example of the Hawk 75-H which was sold to China. The 30 Hawk 75-Ms that followed were similar.

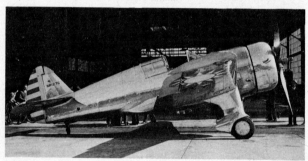

CURTISS HAWK 75   USA

Soon after receiving an order from the USAAC for an evaluation quantity of its Model 75 fighter, Curtiss began to consider the export potential of the basic design as a successor to the Hawk III biplane, evolving a simplified version with a fixed cantilever undercarriage for which the export appellation 'Hawk' was retained and to which the model number '75' was appended. Two demonstration examples of the Hawk 75 were built in parallel with the three Y1P-36s ordered by the USAAC, these being powered by the 875 hp Wright Cyclone GR-1820-G3 Cyclone nine-cylinder radial, one mounting an armament of one 0·5-in (12,7-mm) and one 0·3-in (7,62-mm) gun in the nose and the other supplementing this armament with a pair of wing-mounted 0·3-in (7,62-mm) weapons. The two demonstration aircraft were assigned the designation Hawk 75-H (Curtiss having adopted the practice of allocating suffix letters to each version of the basic design, the Y1P-36, for example, being the 75-E, the XP-37 being the 75-I, etc), the two-gun example being sold to Argentina and the four-gun example to China. The latter country was the first quantity

purchaser of the fixed-undercarriage Hawk 75, a total of 30 being delivered under the designation Hawk 75-M between May and August 1938. The delivery followed from November 1938 of 29 aircraft to Argentina under the designation Hawk 75-O, these having an armament of four 7,62-mm guns, and a further 20 examples were licence-built by the FMA. Delivered simultaneously to Thailand were 12 Hawk 75-Ns, these having two fuselage-mounted 7,62-mm guns and two underwing 23-mm Madsen cannon. The characteristics of all versions of the fixed-undercarriage Hawk 75 were essentially similar, the following data relating specifically to the Hawk 75-O. Max speed, 280 mph (451 km/h) at 10,700 ft (3 260 m). Initial climb, 2,340 ft/min (11,90 m/sec). Normal range, 547 mls (880 km). Empty weight, 3,975 lb (1 803 kg). Loaded weight, 5,172 lb (2 346 kg). Span, 37 ft 4 in (11,38 m). Length, 28 ft 7 in (8,71 m). Height, 9 ft 4 in (2.84 m). Wing area, 236 sq ft (21,92 m²).

CURTISS HAWK 75-R   USA

Completed late in 1938 as a company-owned demonstrator, the Hawk 75-R was essentially similar to the USAAC's P-36A, but its Pratt & Whitney R-1830-19 (SC2-G) Twin Wasp was fitted with a turbo-supercharger mounted beneath the nose, just aft of the engine cowling, with a ventrally-mounted inter-cooler. Extensively tested by the USAAC, the Hawk 75-R was eventually returned to Curtiss as the turbo-supercharger proved unreliable and the manual monitoring of the unit was considered impracticable in combat. The turbo-supercharger was subsequently removed and the aircraft re-engined with a Cyclone. Max speed, 330 mph (531 km/h) at 15,000 ft (4 570 m). Time to 15,000 ft (4 570 m), 4·75 min. Range, 600 mls (966 km). Empty weight, 5,074 lb (2 302 kg). Loaded weight, 6,163 lb (2 795 kg). Span, 37 ft 3½ in (11,37 m). Length, 28 ft 6 in (8,69 m). Height, 12 ft 2 in (3,71 m). Wing area, 236 sq ft (21,92 m²).

(Above) The Hawk 75-R was a company-owned demonstrator fitted with a turbo-supercharger. (Below) The P-36A was the initial production version of the USAAC's equivalent of the Hawk 75A and was described in Fighter A to Z *last month.*

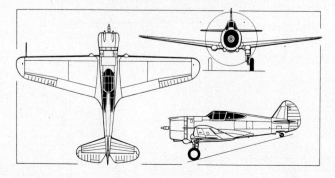

(Above) The Hawk 75A-3 was the last of the Twin Wasp-powered models ordered by France, and (below) the Hawk 75A-7 was the Cyclone-engined model supplied to the Netherlands East Indies.

CURTISS HAWK 75A   USA

In February 1938, the French government began negotiations for the purchase of what was essentially an export version of the USAAC's P-36 and, in May, signed a contract for an initial batch of 100 aircraft. At this point, a new system of designating variants was adopted by Curtiss, the suffix letter 'A' being assigned to all export models with the retractable under-carriage, numbers being appended in sequence to cover each successive contract. Thus, the aircraft covered by the initial French contract were designated Hawk 75A-1. This model was powered by a 950 hp Pratt & Whitney R-1830-SC-G Twin Wasp and carried two wing-mounted and two fuselage-mounted 7,5-mm FN-Browning guns, and the 100 Hawk 75A-1s were delivered between December 1938 and April 1939. A second contract called for 100 Hawk 75A-2s, the 41st and subsequent of this batch having two additional 7,5-mm wing guns and the 48th and subsequent having the 1,050 hp R-1830-SC3-G, these being delivered May-July 1939. In February 1940, deliveries began against a contract for 135 Hawk 75A-3s with the 1,200 hp R-1830-S1C3-G, but deliveries of 285 Hawk 75A-4s powered by the Wright GR-1820-G205A (R-1820-87) Cyclone had only just commenced to France at the time of the Armistice. A total of 227 Hawk 75As then found their way into the RAF inventory, mostly Hawk 75A-4s delivered directly from the USA and assigned the appellation Mohawk IV, small quantities of earlier models becoming Mohawk I (Hawk 75A-1), II (Hawk 75A-2) and III (Hawk 75A-3). Seventy-two of the Mohawk IVs were transferred to South Africa and 12 to Portugal. The Hawk 75A-5 (GR-1820-G205A) was assembled by CAMCO (30-40) in China after the supply of one pattern aircraft, a further five being assembled by HAL in India after a transfer of jigs, tools, assemblies and components; the Hawk 75A-6 was similar to the 75A-2 but with four 7,9-mm guns, 24 being ordered by Norway of which 12 were delivered (the remaining 12 being taken on charge by the RAF as Mohawk IIs); Hawk 75A-7 was the designation applied to 20 GR-1820-G205A-powered aircraft supplied to the Royal Netherlands Indies Army; the Hawk 75A-8 was a version for Norway (see P-36G) and the Hawk 75A-9 was a Cyclone-powered version for Iran, 10 being ordered and these being sequestered by the

Allies and issued to the RAF as Mohawk IVs. The following data relate to the Hawk 75A-4. Max speed, 323 mph (520 km/h) at 15,100 ft (4 877 m). Max range, 1,003 mls (1 614 km). Empty weight, 4,541 lb (2 060 kg). Normal loaded, 5,750 lb (2 608 kg). Span, 37 ft 4 in (11,38 m). Length, 28 ft 10 in (8,79 m). Height, 9 ft 6 in (2,89 m). Wing area, 236 sq ft (21,92 m²).

CURTISS P-37   USA

In the mid '30s, the USAAC held to its belief that liquid-cooled engines offered definite advantages over air-cooled engines for fighter aircraft. Having funded development of the 12-cylinder liquid-cooled Allison V-1710, the service placed an order with Curtiss on 16 February 1937 for an adaptation of the P-36 airframe with a V-1710-C7 engine as the XP-37 (Hawk 75-I). Although the basic airframe of the P-36 was retained, the cockpit was moved aft for CG reasons and the aircraft was powered by a V-1710-11 (C8) engine with a General Electric turbo-supercharger and affording 1,150 hp for take-off and 1,000 hp at 20,000 ft (6 095 m). Armament remained one 0·5-in (12,7-mm) and one 0·3-in (7,62-mm) gun. Delivered on 20 April 1937, the XP-37 succeeded in achieving 340 mph (547 km/h) at 20,000 ft (6 095 m) but suffered frequent turbo-supercharger malfunction. An order for 13 service test examples was placed on 11 December 1937. Powered by the V-1710-21 with an improved supercharger and rated at 1,000 hp for take-off and 880 hp at 25,000 ft (7 620 m), the service test model was designated YP-37 and featured a 1 ft 10 in (56 cm) longer fuselage and 457 lb (204,5 kg) and 539 lb (244 kg) increases in empty and normal gross weights. Delivered to the USAAC between 29 April 1939 and 5 December 1939, the YP-37s were dogged by mechanical problems and further development was discontinued. The following data relate to the YP-37. Max speed, 331 mph (533 km/h) at 20,000 ft (6 095 m). Initial climb, 2,920 ft/min (14,8 m/sec). Normal range, 570 mls (917 km). Empty weight, 5,723 lb (2 596 kg). Loaded weight, 6,889 lb (3 125 kg). Span, 37 ft 4 in (11,38 m). Length, 32 ft 10 in (10,01 m). Height, 9 ft 6 in (2,89 m). Wing area, 236 sq ft (21,92 m²).

(Above) The XP-37 which was delivered to the USAAC in April 1937, and (below) the service test YP-37 which embodied a lengthened rear fuselage and other changes.

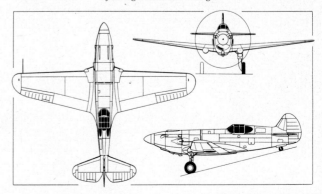

POLAND

PZL-106A KRUK

FOLLOWING extensive testing of three pro-totypes of the PZL-106 agricultural monoplane in Poland, a number of changes have been incorporated in the production version, shown in the three-view drawing on this page. The most obvious change in appearance concerns the tail unit; the tailplane is now located on the fuselage and has a modest degree of sweepback, whereas the prototypes had a straight tailplane mounted high on the fin. The shape of the rear fuselage has also been changed, the wing has been extended in span, an extra section of ailerons fitted each side, and the auxiliary aerofoil flaps on the trailing edge have been abandoned.

Design studies for an agricultural monoplane were begun at the WSK-Okecie works more than 10 years ago, the intention being to develop a replacement for the PZL-101 Gawron (Rook), 330 of which had been built between 1958 and 1973 at Okecie. The initial PZL-101M Kruk (Raven) proposal was an extensively revised Gawron with a 260 hp Ivchenko AI-14R radial engine, and further refinement led to the appearance of the PZL-106, the design of which began in detail in 1972 under the direction of Andrzej Frydrychewicz.

The first PZL-106 prototype flew on 17 April 1973 and was powered by a 400 hp Lycoming IO-720-A1B engine; the same engine was used in the second prototype, which had a number of small refinements and first flew in October 1973. The third prototype, flown in October 1974, was powered by an uncowled PZL-3S radial engine, this being a Polish-developed power plant derived from the Soviet AI-26W helicopter engine. Subsequently, a cowling was developed for this engine installation.

The PZL-106A carries an easily-removable glass-fibre reinforced plastics hopper or tank in the fuselage ahead of the cockpit and can carry up to 2,200 lb (1 000 kg) of dry or liquid chemicals, with a maximum capacity of 308 Imp gal (1 400 l). Liquids are distributed through spray bars and dry chemicals through a venturi distributor that can provide swath widths of 98-115 ft (30-35 m).

Data for the PZL-106A production version, some 600 examples of which are expected to be built for the member countries of the Council for Mutual Economic Aid, follow:

Power Plant: One 600 hp PZL-3S seven-cylinder radial supercharged air-cooled engine

An extensive redesign of the PZL-106 Kruk agricultural monoplane has been undertaken in Poland and production aircraft are now expected to have the configuration shown in this new three-view drawing.

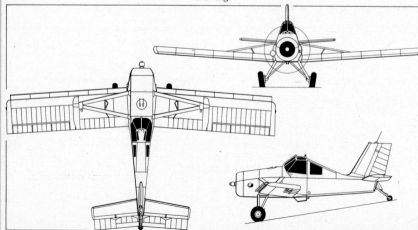

driving a four-bladed metal or glassfibre propeller of 8 ft 7½ in (2,62 m) diameter. Fuel capacity, 66 Imp gal (300 l).
Performance (at 6,170 lb/2 800 kg gross weight): Max speed, 124 mph (200 km/h) at 6,560 ft (2 000 m); max cruising speed, 119 mph (180 km/h), normal operating speed, 75-100 mph (120-160 km/h); initial rate of climb 825 ft/min (4,2 m/sec); take-off and landing run, 655 ft (200 m): range, 280 mls (450 km); ferry range (fuel in hopper), 1,120 mls (1 800 km).
Weights: Empty, 3,525 lb (1 600 kg); normal operating weight, 6,170 lb (2 800 kg); max take-off, normal category, 6,610 lb (3 000 kg).
Dimensions: Span, 48 ft 6 in (14,80 m); length, 29 ft 2 in (8,90 m); height, 11 ft 10 in (3,60 m); sweepback, 4 deg; wing area, 305·7 sq ft (28,4 m²); undercarriage track, 9 ft 2 in (2,8 m).

USA

BEECHCRAFT BARON 58TC

DELIVERIES of the turbo-supercharged Baron 58TC began during May and Beech Aircraft has now provided the first full specification for this addition to its range of business twins. Apart from having the supercharged Continental TSIO-520L engines, the Baron 58TC

The Beechcraft Baron 58TC has now joined other members of the Baron family, deliveries having started last May. Performance data for the turbo-supercharged Baron 58 appear on this page.

features some structural changes to permit greater loads to be carried in the baggage compartments and the cabin, the total useful load of 2,360 lb (1 071 kg) being the largest carried by any of the Baron variants. Another new feature is a two-stage propeller governor that provides an additional 100 rpm "burst of power" acceleration automatically during single-engined operation.

Provision is made in the Baron 58TC for an extra 24 US gal (92 l) of optional fuel capacity, and the internal arrangements have been changed to extend the rear baggage compartment, providing a 120-lb (55-kg) capacity. Smaller diameter propellers have been adopted to reduce tip speed and noise levels.
Power Plant: Two Continental TSIO-520L flat-six air-cooled engines rated at 301 hp each at 2,600 rpm and 310 hp at 2,700 rpm for single-engined operation. Three bladed propellers of 6 ft 4 in (1,93 m) diameter. Standard fuel capacity, 166 US gal (639 l); optional extra tankage, 24 US gal (92 l).
Performance: Max speed, 287 mph (462 km/h); cruising speeds at average weight at 20,000 ft (6 100 m), 267 mph (430 km/h) at max cruise power, 257 mph (414 km/h) at 74 per cent power, 242 mph (389 km/h) at 64 per cent power and 223 mph (359 km/h) at 55 per cent power; initial rate of climb, 1,461 ft/min (7,43 m/sec); single-engined climb rate, 204 ft/min (1,04 m/sec) at sea level; service ceiling, over 25,000 ft (7 625 m); single-engined ceiling, 14,400 ft (4 392 m); take-off distance to 50 ft (15,2 m), 2,495 ft (761 m); landing distance from 50 ft (15,2 m), 2,498 ft (762 m); cruising ranges (max fuel) with reserves, at 20,000 ft (6 100 m), 1,114-1,417 mls (1 792-2 280 km) according to speed.
Weights: Empty, including unusable fuel, oil and standard avionics, 3,780 lb (1 716 kg); useful load, 2,360 lb (1 071 kg); max take-off and landing, 6,100 lb (2 770 kg).
Dimensions: Span, 37 ft 10 in (11,55 m); length, 29 ft 10 in (9,11 m); height, 9 ft 6 in (2,89 m); wing area, 188·1 sq ft (17,47 m²); cabin length (including extended rear baggage compartment), 12 ft 7 in (3,84 m); cabin width, 3 ft 6 in (1,07 m); cabin height, 4 ft 2 in (1,27 m).
Accommodation: Pilot and up to five passengers in three pairs of seats side-by-side. Dual controls. Baggage compartments in nose, rear and extended rear compartments.

AIR International

Volume 11   Number 4   October 1976

Managing Editor   William Green
Editor   Gordon Swanborough
Modelling Editor   Fred J Henderson
Contributing Artists   Dennis Punnett
                         John Weal
Cover Art   W R Hardy
Contributing Photographer
                         Stephen Peltz
Editorial Representative, Washington
                         Norman Polmar
Publisher   Donald Hannah
Circulation Director   Donald Syner
Financial Director   John Gold
Subscription Manager   Claire Sillette
Advertising/Public Relations
                         Elizabeth Baker

Editorial Offices:
The AIR INTERNATIONAL, PO Box 16,
Bromley, BR2 7RB Kent.

**Subscription, Advertising and
Circulation Offices:**
The AIR INTERNATIONAL, De Worde
House, 283 Lonsdale Road, London
SW13 9QW. Telephone 01-878 2454.
US and Canadian readers may address
subscriptions and general enquiries to
AIR INTERNATIONAL PO Box 353, White-
stone, NY 11357 for onward transmis-
sion to the UK, from where all corres-
pondence is answered and orders
despatched.

MEMBER OF THE AUDIT
BUREAU OF CIRCULATIONS | ABC |

Subscription rates, inclusive of postage,
direct from the publishers, per year:
United Kingdom   £5·50
USA $17·50
Canada $17·50

Rates for other countries and for air mail
subscriptions available on request from
the Subscription Department at the
above address.

CONTENTS

**WRENDEZVOUS
WITH WREN**

*"One good thing about their
numerical superiority – there'll
be a lot more to shoot down!"*

AIRSCENE

MILITARY AFFAIRS

ARGENTINA

The Argentine **government has** recently **taken up** its **option on** a third Aeritalia **G.222** general-purpose military transport on behalf of the *Fuerza Aérea Argentina* (FAéA). Delivery of the first two G.222s to the FAéA is now anticipated for late 1977 with the third aircraft following in 1978. Another export customer for the G.222 is Dubai, which has placed a firm order for one aircraft and has taken an option on a second, and Tunisia is reportedly negotiating the purchase of three aircraft.

The Army's **air component,** the *Comando de Aviación Ejercito,* **has** recently **taken delivery of** two **Bell 212** Twin Two-Twelve **helicopters** to supplement its fleet of 20 UH-1H Iroquois helicopters which are operated primarily by Aviation Battalion 601, detachments of which are deployed as Aviation Sections with each Army Corps.

AUSTRALIA

The Department of Defence is currently engaged in a **study of** Australia's **new maritime patrol requirements** when a 200-nm (370-km) resources zone is declared around the continent. Aircraft under consideration include the Fokker F.27MPA Maritime, a proposed maritime patrol version of the VFW 614 and the DHC-7 Dash-7R, but a more likely interim arrangement is the purchase from US Navy surplus stocks of a number of Grumman S-2E Trackers. The Trackers, already included in the RAN inventory, would not demand any new infrastructure and this type is already being employed in the sovereignty surveillance rôle off NW Australia.

AUSTRIA

On 29 August, an Austrian all-party parliamentary **delegation** was flown to Israel by an IAI-supplied Westwind to **discuss** further details of the **proposed purchase** on behalf of the *Osterreichische Luftstreitkräfte* **of** some 20 IAI **Kfir-C2** fighters, which, favourably evaluated recently by an OLk team, including test pilot Maj Birnicker, are currently competing with a similar quantity of Northrop F-5E Tiger IIs for Austrian procurement. The Kfir-C2 is being offered at a basic unit price of approximately £2·53m ($4·5m), which, with the avionics being specified by the OLk, is expected to be increased to some £2·8m ($5m), and a substantial proportion of the programme cost is expected to be covered by some form of industrial offset. It was anticipated that details of the Kfir-C2 proposals would be placed before the Austrian parliament when it reconvened last month (September).

Delivery of the **last** of 12 Pilatus PC-6 **Turbo-Porters** to *III Geschwader* of *Fliegerregiment* 1 of the *Luftstreitkräfte* is expected shortly. Deliveries of the Turbo-Porters began in February.

BURMA

It has been reported that the Union of Burma Air Force has placed an **order** with SIAI-Marchetti **for** a half-dozen or so **SF-260W Warrior** armed trainers as the first stage in the replacement of its aged piston-engined Chipmunks and Provosts.

FRANCE

Although the two-seat Dassault-Breguet **Mirage F1B** was originally developed to meet export requirements, it would now seem almost certain that a batch of 10 aircraft of this type will be ordered for the *Armée de l'Air* **as a systems trainer** with a secondary combat rôle. The Mirage F1B retains the full operational capability of the single-seat F1C apart from a slight reduction in range, fuel capacity having been reduced from 946 to 846 Imp gal (4 300 to 3 850 l). The *Armée de l'Air* Mirage F1B will incorporate flight refuelling facilities and the avionics changes embodied by late production Mirage F1Cs now on the assembly line.

Plans announced earlier (see *Airscene*/July) for the **reorganisation of** the **Mirage IVA fleet** of the *Forces Aériennes Stratégiques* have resulted in the disbandment of the 93e *Escadre,* the FAS now comprising only the 91e and 94e *Escadres* with a total of six *Escadrons* operating 32 bombers dispersed among six bases. Formerly, each *Escadre* had its own *Escadron* of KC-135F tankers, but these *Escadrons de Ravitaillement en Vol* have now been grouped together at Istres. The bases at Cambrai, Creil and Istres formerly occupied by the 93e *Escadre* are being retained for Mirage IVA dispersal.

IRAN

The **Iranian** Imperial Air Force was expected to have taken about 18 Grumman **F-14 Tomcats** into its inventory by this month (October) of the 80 on order. A further 42 are scheduled to have been delivered by the end of next year with the remainder following during the first half of 1978. The F-14As are now expected to equip five squadrons but will operate from only two bases (Shiraz and Khatami) rather than the three originally planned. Support contracts and procurement of the Phoenix missile have brought the total Iranian F-14 weapons system cost to £1,291m ($2,300m). Other IIAF fighter procurement in recent years has included 32 F-4D Phantoms at a cost of £59·55m ($106m), 177 F-4E Phantoms at a cost of £481·5m ($857m) and 12 RF-4E Phantoms at a cost of £80·34m ($143m), plus 141 Northrop F-5E Tiger IIs at a cost of £211·8m ($377m) and 28 two-seat F-5Fs at a cost of £80·34m ($102m). The RF-4E Phantoms have still to be delivered to the IIAF, together with some two dozen of the F-4E Phantoms, but a substantial proportion of the F-5E Tiger IIs are now in the IIAF inventory, while deliveries of the F-5Fs began in August.

The Iranian **Navy** anticipates establishing an **independent logistics** and maintenance **capability for** its fleet of Sikorsky **RH-53D** Sea Stallion minesweeping helicopters in the early 'eighties. The Navy currently has plans to procure 12 RH-53Ds of which six have so far been ordered and deliveries of these are scheduled to commence shortly and continue into 1977. Procurement of 12 HH-53 search-and-rescue helicopters is also planned.

The Iranian Imperial **Army** anticipates **expanding** its **air component** from its current level of some 400 helicopters and fixed-wing aircraft with 8,000 personnel to more than 800 aircraft with 14,000 personnel by 1978. The Army has now taken delivery of more than half of the 202 Bell AH-1J gunships on order and about one-fifth of the 326 Bell 214 utility transport helicopters ordered.

JAPAN

Following the return to Japan of the 11-man fighter evaluation team and the submission of its report to the Chief of Air Staff early in August, it was anticipated that **definitive recommendations** concerning procurement of a fighter **to meet** the ASDF's **F-X requirement** would be submitted to the Defence Minister late last month (September) or early this month. Although the contents of the evaluation team's report have not been revealed at the time of closing for press, it is understood that the McDonnell Douglas F-15 Eagle remains frontrunner and that the Defence Agency hopes to obtain government approval for the procurement of this type before the end of the year. The ASDF hopes to request funding for 100-120 aircraft with the first batch being included in the Fiscal 1977 budget. The prime contractor for licence manufacture of the F-15 had not been announced as this issue

The Forger *V/STOL fighter, seen above while approaching the carrier* Kiev *for landing and illustrated by the general arrangement drawing below (and on page 193), remains of uncertain parentage although widely attributed to the Yakovlev design bureau.*

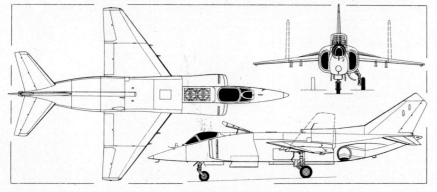

went to press but is virtually certain to be Mitsubishi.

The Ground Self-Defence Force, which is to procure Bell AH-1 gunship helicopters in the next five-year Defence Build-up Programme, now anticipates that the **AH-1 will be licence built** owing to the larger number of helicopters of this type now to be acquired. Initially, the GSDF is expected to form two independent squadrons each with 16 AH-1s and in the second phase of the programme will equip locally-based units with this type. The GSDF hopes to include the first four AH-1 helicopters in the Fiscal 1977 budget.

MALAYSIA
According to Prime Minister Datuk Hussein Onn, the Royal Malaysian Air Force *(Tentera Udara Diraja Malaysia)* is to procure a **further 20 helicopters** to supplement the service's fleet of Alouette IIIs, Sikorsky S-61As, Bell 206Bs and Agusta-Bell AB 212s. Neither the type nor category of helicopter has been announced.

With the delivery of its second Lockheed C-130H Hercules transport and arrival of a third imminent, the Royal Malaysian Air Force's newly-established **No 14 Squadron** at Kuala Lumpur is now **working up** to operational status and will attain full six-aircraft strength with delivery of the remaining three Hercules over the coming months. The RMAF is in process of phasing out its eight Herald freighters operated by No 4 Squadron and these are being offered for sale.

MOÇAMBIQUE
The fledgeling **Air Force** of the Moçambique Republic is **to increase** its **fleet of** Nord 2501 **Noratlas transports** from four to eight later this year with the delivery from Portugal of four aircraft currently being refurbished by OGMA as part of the Portuguese aid programme. Training assistance is being provided by the *Força Aérea Portuguesa* which has transferred to the new air arm, either as outright gifts or on indefinite lease, several Douglas C-47s and two Alouette III helicopters.

MOROCCO
Re-equipment and **expansion of** the Royal Maroc **Air Force** is steadily **accelerating** and Morocco will possess a substantial air arm by the end of the present decade. The helicopter force in particular has been greatly strengthened with, in service or in process of delivery, 40 SA 330 Pumas and a similar quantity of Agusta-Bell AB 205s, as well as quantities of AB 206 JetRangers and AB 212 Twin Two-Twelves. Deliveries are scheduled to commence next year of 12 Beech T-34C turboprop-powered trainers and it has been reported that orders for SIAI-Marchetti SF-260 trainers have been increased from two to 28. Orders for Lockheed C-130H Hercules transports were increased from three to nine aircraft earlier this year and it is now anticipated that deliveries of the 25 Dassault-Breguet Mirage F1s currently on firm order for the Royal Maroc Air Force will commence late next year. The purchase of 20 Rockwell T-2 Buckeye trainer/light strike aircraft is being negotiated at a cost of $88·9m (£49·9m).

NATO
Federal German Defence Minister Georg Leber recently disclosed that **NATO's defence planning committee has selected** the Boeing **E-3A** AWACS aircraft in preference to the modified Grumman E-2C Hawkeye or the proposed AEW version of the Nimrod to meet NATO's airborne warning and control requirement. Dr Leber reportedly told the parliamentary defence committee in Bonn that procurement of up to 32 E-3As at a cost of about £1,400m ($2,500m) will "help to balance out the quantitative superiority of the Warsaw

Pact forces". Formal endorsement of the decision is unlikely before the next meeting of the defence ministers of the participating NATO countries in December. It is claimed by Boeing that a single E-3A flying at 30,000 ft (9 145 m) over West Germany could detect every airborne target in an area between Paris and Warsaw.

NETHERLANDS
With the **completion of deliveries of** the 30 MBB **BO 105C** helicopters to the Light Aircraft Group *(Groep Lichte Vliegtuigen)*, which is operated and maintained by the KLu on behalf of the Army, plus the disbandment earlier this year of the remaining air reserve units, the KLu has finally retired its last remaining 44 Piper L-21Bs after more than two decades. The BO 105C helicopter now equips three flights each of Nos 298 and 299 squadrons at Soesterburg and Deelan, but it would seem that the third element of the Group, No 300 Squadron, is to continue to operate Alouette IIIs.

Three of the KLu's Fokker F.27 **Troopships** have been **assigned to** transport support of the **Navy** following the retirement by the *Marine Luchtvaartdienst* of five Beech TC-45Js.

PERU
It has now been confirmed that the Peruvian government has signed a **contract** with the Soviet union **for** the supply to the *Fuerza Aérea del Peru* of 36 variable-geometry **Sukhoi Su-22** strike fighters at a cost of $250m (£140·45m) payable over 10 years (with one year of grace) at an annual interest rate of two per cent. Assistance with conversion training and technical support for the FAP Sukhois is apparently being arranged with Cuba's air arm, the so-called *Fuerza Aérea Revolucionaria*, which, it is to be assumed, now includes similar aircraft in its inventory. The Su-22 is presumably a variant of the Su-20, which, in turn, is apparently the export version of the Su-17 serving with the V-VS. This marks the first Soviet penetration of the Latin American market with combat aircraft, although the FAP has been operating a substantial number of Mil Mi-8 helicopters for some considerable time.

An extraordinary order placed on behalf of the *Fuerza Aérea del Peru* covers **procurement of** six **Pitts Special** aerobatic biplanes for unspecified training duties, although it is believed that the aircraft will equip an FAP aerobatic demonstration team.

Peru's *Servicio Aéronavale* became the **first customer for** the Fokker **F.27MPA Maritime** coastal patrol and surveillance version of the Friendship, two having been ordered for delivery next year. The *Servicio Aéronavale* currently operates nine ex-US Navy Grumman S-2 Trackers and a small transport force of a half-dozen C-47s, and has a growing helicopter element with some 30 aircraft, including Alouette IIIs, UH-1D and UH-1H Iroquois and Bell 206B JetRangers.

SAUDI ARABIA
The Royal Saudi Air Force **requirement for** additional BAC 167 **Strikemasters** (see *Airscene/*July) has now crystallised into a firm order for a further eleven of these trainers. An early RSAF decision concerning a major new helicopter purchase was believed imminent at the time of closing for press. Strong contenders for orders to meet the RSAF's tactical transport and ASW requirements are reportedly Westland's Commando and Sea King, but smaller types, such as the Bell Model 214, the Lynx and the Gazelle are apparently being considered.

Following US Defense Department dis-

couragement of Saudi procurement of advanced fighters such as the F-14 Tomcat and F-15 Eagle — although the RSAF, which has evaluated both types, is understood to still plan procurement of 40-60 of one or other type during the next few years — the **Saudi government** has been unofficially **reported** as considering the **investment** of up to $300m (£168·5m) **in the F-18L,** the projected land-based derivative of the McDonnell Douglas/Northrop F-18 shipboard fighter, as a potential replacement for the Northrop F-5 in the RSAF inventory in the early 'eighties. The RSAF has so far received or is in process of receiving 20 two-seat F-5Bs at a cost of £16m ($28·5m), 70 F-5Es and 20 F-5Fs at a cost of £98·9m ($176·1m). All the F-5Bs and about half of the F-5Es and F-5Fs have so far been delivered.

SWITZERLAND
On 8 July, the 160th and **last Hunter** procured by the *Flugwaffe* was **handed over** to the service at Emmen. The *Flugwaffe* received its initial batch of 100 Hunter F Mk 58s from 1958 onwards, supplementing these by two further orders each for 30 refurbished examples in 1971 and 1973, the last batch including eight two-seat Hunter T Mk 68s. The Hunters currently equip nine *Fliegerstaffeln* (Nos 1, 4, 5, 7, 8, 11, 18, 19 and 21) and are expected to remain in service throughout the 'eighties.

SOVIET UNION
Tupolev *Backfire* variable-geometry **bombers**, using air-to-air refuelling, are **now performing maritime** reconnaissance **flights** from bases near Murmansk, some of them over US installations in the Azores. According to US intelligence sources, *Backfires* are operating with the AV-MF from bases on the Kola Peninsula and from Anadyr on the Bering Sea. The long-range operations on which *Backfire* has recently been engaged have buttressed the position held by US SALT negotiators who maintain that the aircraft is a strategic delivery system whereas the Soviet negotiators insist that *Backfire* is not a strategic weapon, should not be counted as part of the 2,400 strategic delivery systems permitted the Soviet Union under the Vladivostok arms limitation agreement and that its deployment should not be subject to restrictions.

THAILAND
Defence **spending** for 1977 at an estimated *Baht* 12,335m (£340m) represents a 26 per cent **increase** over the current year and reflects Thai military preoccupation with equipment and supplies following the US withdrawal. Included in the budget for Royal Thai Air Force procurement is the sum of about £28m for the purchase of 16 Northrop F-5E Tiger IIs and spares. Among items added to the RTAF inventory recently have been at least one Britten-Norman BN-2A Islander and five Transavia PL-12 Airtruck agricultural aircraft, and the last of a batch of 20 Fairchild AU-23A Peacemaker "minigunship" aircraft was formally handed over on 28 May, these bringing to 32 the number of Peacemakers in RTAF service.

TOGO
The *Force Aérienne Togolaise* has taken **delivery of** two of the six de Havilland Canada DHC-5D **Super Buffaloes** originally built for the *Force Aérienne Zaïroise* but cancelled before delivery to that air arm. The *Force Aérienne Togolaise* had previously requested the supply of a Transall C.160 from France but this was not forthcoming.

TAIWAN
Washington sources indicate that **approval** has now been given **for** the supply of a **further** 60 Northrop F-5E **Tiger II fighters** to the Chinese Nationalist Air Force. The Tiger IIs will follow

on completion in June 1978 of previous orders for 120 fighters of this type which are being part-manufactured and assembled by the Aero Industry Development Centre. Some 50 Tiger IIs were expected to have been delivered to the CNAF from the Taichung plant by the end of last month (September) and the supplementary order will carry the Tiger II programme through to 1980.

USA
Figures revealed recently by the **USAF** show a total **inventory of tactical aircraft** as at 31 December 1975 of 4,769 aircraft, of which 3,107 were in the active air force, 1,239 in the Air National Guard and 423 in the Air Force Reserve. Included in the totals for each type are active and non-active aircraft, those assigned to research and development and other special purpose aircraft. Type by type, the totals are: A-7D, 291 plus 101 in ANG; A-10A, 10; A-37B, six plus 46 ANG and 82 AFR; B-57E, four; EB-57E, 17; C-7A, 16 ANG and 32 AFR; KC-97L, 72 ANG; C/EC-121C/S, nine ANG; C-123J, eight ANG; C-123K, 64 AFR; C-130A, three plus 58 ANG and 60 AFR; AC-130A, one plus 12 AFR; DC-130A, five; RC-130A, one plus three ANG plus two AFR; C-130B, 23 ANG plus 60 AFR; C-130D, 11 ANG; C-130E, 251 plus 33 ANG plus 24 AFR; DC-130E, one; C-130H, 33; AC-130H, 10; EC-135, 16; F-4C, 275 plus 19 ANG; F-4D, 484; F-4E, 599; RF-4C, 273 plus 98 ANG; F-5A, two, F-5B, one; F-5E, 29; F-5F, two, F-15, 42; TF-15, 11; F-16A, two; F-100D, 329 ANG; F-100F, 91 ANG; F-101F, six ANG; RF-101, 56 ANG; F-104C, two ANG; F-104D, one ANG; F-105B, 21 ANG and 18 AFR; F-105D, 66 ANG and 51 AFR; F-105F, two plus 14 ANG and five AFR; F-105G, 47; F-111A, 103; F-111D, 93; F-111E, 87; F-111F, 95; EF-111A, two; UH-1N, seven; CH-3E, 11 plus eight AFR; CH-53C, 12; O-2A, 95 plus 149 ANG; O-2B, five ANG; OV-10A, 90; T-33A, 14 plus five AFR; T-38A, 80; T-39A/B/F, two ANG.

A number of changes in the **equipment** and responsibilities **of the US Naval Air Reserve** are planned for the next few years. In the course of Fiscal Year 1978 (ie, by September 1978), all Reserve fighter squadrons will be flying F-4B or F-4N Phantoms, and the sixth and last attack squadron will have converted from A-4L Skyhawks to A-7B Corsairs. Ten Reserve squadrons at present fly the P-3 Orion and the last squadron flying the SP-2H will convert to P-3s by FY80. During FY77, the E-1B Tracker will be replaced by the E-2 Hawkeye in Reserve units, and it is expected that EA-6s will begin to reach the Reserve in FY78-80. Reserve helicopter units ying SH-3A and SH-3G Sea Kings will re-equip successively with SH-3Ds and, starting in FY81, SH-3Hs; in addition, one squadron (HC-9) has recently formed on the HH-3A for combat search and rescue and riverine operations, and two others, HA(L)-4 and HA(L)-5, will equip on armed Bell HH-1Ks during FY77. Reserve units will cease to fly C-118 transports by the end of FY77, but a new reserve squadron, VR-55, was established on 1 April 1976 at NAS Alameda with three McDonnell Douglas C-9B Skytrain IIs and a second, similarly equipped, unit is to be formed later this year.

ZAÏRE
The *Force Aérienne Zaïroise* is receiving 15 Cessna 150 **Aerobats for** use in the **basic training** of officer cadets. A maintenance training programme on the Aerobats is to be operated at Kinshasa by Cessna.

The Zaïroise **government has reduced** its **order** from six to three de Havilland Canada DHC-5D **Super Buffalo** STOL transports which were to have been delivered to the *Force Aérienne Zaïroise*. Two of these aircraft have been taken over by Togo (see earlier news item).

AIRCRAFT AND INDUSTRY

CHINA
Strategic considerations are apparently leading **China to relocate** at least **part of** its **aircraft industry** to the vicinity of Sian, the capital of the Shensi Province, owing to the vulnerability of Shenyang, capital of the Liaoning Province, where virtually the entire aircraft industry is currently situated and which is only 405 miles (650 km) from the Soviet border. Some nine months ago, a Rolls-Royce team visited Sian to advise the Sino-Communist government on the establishment of a factory for the licence-manufacture of the Spey 202, which, it is generally assumed, is to be utilised by a range of new Chinese combat aircraft. Sian has the advantage of being in central China and less vulnerable to attack but lacks the industrial infrastructure of Shenyang. In recent years, China has become one of the major world purchasers of aluminium, a fact that is linked by some experts with the decision to develop and manufacture in quantity modern combat aircraft of entirely indigenous design, the only combat aircraft currently being manufactured in quantity in China being the F-6 (MiG-19S) and F-7 (MiG-19P) which are thoroughly obsolescent.

INTERNATIONAL
The French minister of transport, Marcel Cavaille, announced during August that the government had **approved** in principal the **launching of** the Dassault-Breguet **Mercure 200** (*AirData File*/August 1976), in co-operation with McDonnell Douglas. The decision appears to bring to an end the earlier discussions between Aérospatiale and Boeing centred upon development of the Boeing 7N7 and possibly an Airbus B10 derivative, but it has done little to solve the problems confronting the European industry as a whole in its attempt to launch one or more new airliners as collaborative ventures on the basis of anticipated European airline needs as assessed by the so-called Group of Seven manufacturers (which includes Dassault-Breguet). The Mercure 200 proposal provides for Dassault-Breguet to remain programme leader but to have only 5 per cent of the work; McDonnell Douglas would be responsible for 15 per cent and for marketing the aircraft in the USA. Aérospatiale would have 40 per cent of the work and the other 40 per cent would be made available to other European partners in the programme. It is understood that the French government will ask McDonnell Douglas, in return, to drop the DC-X-200 (*Air Data File*/August 1975) which is seen as a competitor for the Airbus, but the US company has made no commitment to do so. Final details of the Mercure 200 package are expected to be worked out over the next three months or so, during which time the plan will undoubtedly face severe criticism from within Europe including, it seems, the French aerospace trade unions.

Japan's Civil Transport Aircraft Development Association (CTADA) and Boeing reached an agreement during August to continue **joint work on the Y-X/7X7** new airliner concept. Basis of the agreement, which was to be signed at the end of the month, was creation of a new joint company by CTADA, Boeing and Aeritalia in the ratio of 20:60:20 with a view to finalising project design and launching production. The Japanese share, at 20 per cent of an estimated total $1,000m (£561,8m) launching cost, is much lower than previously planned, and the Japanese government is understood to be willing to contribute 75 per cent of this share, the balance to come from Japanese industry. The most optimistic time-scale now projects a start on prototype construction in October 1977 and first delivery in

1981; Boeing market forecasts are for the sale of 300-400 aircraft before 1985 and another 300 in the second half of the decade.

July was a **significant month for** the Panavia **Tornado.** In addition to the signing of the tri-national governmental Memorandum of Understanding on 29 July, as reported in our previous issue, the 500th test flight by a Tornado was achieved on the same day, this being made by prototype 01 in Germany. Prototype 08 made its first flight on 15 July; 03 made six flights in one day on 23 July and in the course of the month a total of 71 flights was made by all Tornadoes combined, exceeding by four the previous monthly total.

ISRAEL
Israel Aircraft Industries anticipate finalising **contracts** before the end of the year with at least two countries **for** the **Kfir-C2** multi-rôle fighter **and** are continuing negotiations with the Mexican government for the establishment of a **factory in Mexico** to assemble and part-manufacture the Kfir-C2 for the South and Central American market. Orders for a minimum quantity of 100 Kfirs from Latin American air forces are understood to be needed in order to render the project a practical proposition, the Mexican factory offering sales support and overhaul facilities. Tel Aviv sources have suggested that interest in the Kfir-C2 so far shown indicates that Latin America provides a potential market for substantially more than 100 fighters of this type; believing that sales efforts will be buttressed by the recent Peruvian purchase of Soviet variable-geometry strike fighters and claiming that the Kfir-C2 not only offers greater capability than any competitive aircraft that might be released on the Latin American market but is also substantially cheaper than potential competition. Furthermore, with Mexican-based assembly and overhaul facilities, Latin American purchasers of the Kfir are unlikely to experience the problems regarding spares support, etc, such as those of the Latin American users of the Mirage. If this project goes ahead, the Mexican facility is also likely to extend to the assembly of the Arava STOL utility transport, the bulk of the 45 of which so far sold having been supplied to Latin American customers. The Arava programme, together with that of the Westwind Eleven24, has recently come under fire in the *Knesset* (Parliament), the Israeli comptroller claiming that the R&D and production costs of the two programmes have so far cost some £34m whereas income derived from them has been merely £11m, 220 Aravas and 82 Westwinds needing to be sold to attain breakeven as compared with 45 and 13 sold respectively to date. IAI has responded by pointing out that their own profits and not government subsidies have gone into both the Arava and Westwind programmes and that, without them, Israel could never have developed the capability to produce the Kfir or the currently proposed new strike fighter (see following item). IAI is planning the further expension of its activities by moving into helicopter production and is discussing with various US companies possible licensing agreements. Current planning calls for IAI to initially produce dynamic components and eventually complete systems.

IAI is reportedly accelerating design **development** of a **strike fighter** as a hedge against difficulties that may be encountered in procuring the General Dynamics F-16 in the early 'eighties to replace the *Heyl Ha'Avir*'s current inventory of A-4 Skyhawks and F-4 Phantoms. The new aircraft is essentially a multi-rôle fighter with primary emphasis placed on attack capability, air superiority and reconnaissance being secondary functions. The aircraft is single-engined — the most likely power plant being the 25,000 lb (11 340 kg) class Pratt & Whitney F100 — and will have a small silhouette — the *Heyl Ha'Avir* has for long said that the F-4 Phantom offers too big a target in the Middle East environment. Features will include a reclining pilot seat, side-stick controller and fly-by-wire controls. If a decision is taken to proceed with full development, prototypes of the new strike fighter could by flying by 1980.

ITALY

Aermacchi announced that the **first flight of the MB 339** trainer derived from the MB 326, was made at Venegono, near Varese, on 12 August. It is the 25th distinct type to be powered by the Rolls-Royce Viper — in this case, the 4,000 lb st (1816 kgp) Viper 632 — and was expected to be displayed publicly for the first time at Farnborough International, as this issue went to press. Initial production contracts for the MB 339 have been placed by the AMI (Italian Air Force) which plans to use the new type as a replacement for its MB 326s in the advanced training rôle.

SOVIET UNION

Flying the new aerobatic **Yakovlev Yak-50** all-metal monoplanes, the Soviet Union made a clean sweep of the Eighth World Aerobatic Championships held in Kiev during August, winning the team prize and the men's and women's individual championships. Six Yak-50s were present at Kiev, and a few more **details** of the type are now to hand (see *Airscene*/August 1976). The engine is quoted as an M-14P, of Ivchenko origin and giving 360 hp. Span is 31 ft 2 in (9,50 m) and, length, 24 ft 5½ in (7,462 m) and wing area, 161·5 sq ft (15,0 m²). With a loaded weight of 1,320 lb (900 kg), the Yak-50 has a max speed of 186 mph (300 km/h), climbs at 3,150 ft/min (16 m/sec) and has take-off and landing runs, respectively, of 655 ft (200 m) and 820 ft (250 m).

UNITED KINGDOM

As forecast in our account of Westland **Lynx** development ("The Lynx Leaps Ahead", April 1976 p 203), a trial installation of the Pratt & Whitney PT6A-34 turboshaft has now been made, the first flight taking place at Yeovil on 19 July. The installation comprises a pair of 750 shp PT6A-34s in the first flying prototype of the Lynx, now registered G-BEAD as a company demonstrator.

Scottish Aviation's four-seat, retractable undercarriage version of the Bulldog trainer, the **Bullfinch**, made its **first flight** at Prestwick Airport on 20 August. First announced at the 1974 Farnborough International, the Bullfinch is to be marketed in both civil and military versions, the latter being known as the Bulldog 200 to stress its connection with the fixed-gear, two-seat Bulldog 100/120 family, more than 250 examples of which are now in service. Powered by a 200 hp Lycoming EAIO-360-A1B6 fuel-injection engine, the Bullfinch has Automotive Products nose and main gear shock absorbers, with Goodyear wheels and tyres, and an electro-mechanical retraction system. Compared with the Bulldog 120, the fuselage is 20 in (51 cm) longer, the extra length being equally distributed fore and aft of the main spar; the wing span is increased by 9·3 in (23,6 cm), overall height is decreased by 7·5 in (19,1 cm) and the tailplane is relocated 6 in (15,2 cm) higher on the rear fuselage. Full data for the Bullfinch, which was expected to make its public début at Farnborough International in September, will appear in our next issue.

Desmond Norman, co-founder of the Britten-Norman company that is now a subsidiary of the Fairey Group, is developing a new light aircraft, the **NOM-1 Firecracker**, at his home on the Isle of Wight. A tandem two-seater intended for use at military and civilian training schools and having wing strong-points to provide a counter-insurgency capability, the Firecracker is described as a "technology and industry/transfer aircraft" providing experience in software and management systems for countries wishing to start an aircraft industry. Two prototypes are under construction, the first of which is expected to fly by the beginning of 1977. The engine is a 260 hp Avco Lycoming IO-540 with aerobatic provision and the undercarriage is retractable.

A successful **first flight** was made **by** the **Cranfield A1** aerobatic monoplane on 23 August — too late to allow its use at the World Aerobatic Championships in Kiev during August. Powered by a 210 hp R-R/Continental IO-360 engine, the A1 has been designed and built at the College of Aeronautics in accordance with the ideas of Neil Williams, who achieved fourth place in the men's individual championships at Kiev flying a Pitts S-1S. An altitude of 4,000 ft (1 220 m) and 126 mph (203 km/h) were reached on first flight.

USA

British Airways ended several months of speculation, and intensive sales activity by both Lockheed and McDonnell Douglas, by placing an **order** on 18 August **for** long-range **L-1011-500 TriStars**. The type is intended as the replacement for British Airways Overseas Division's VC10s and early Boeing 707s and this is the "launching order" for the TriStar-500, which is to be powered by the 50,000 lb st (22 700 kgp) RB.211-524B, the version specified by British Airways for its new Boeing 747s. The initial BA order is for six TriStars previously ordered as L-1011-1s and now to be delivered as -500s, thus limiting the fleet of the earlier variant to nine examples (seven of which serve with European Division and two with Overseas Division); an option has been taken on six more TriStar-500s. The ultimate purchase of L-1011-500s by British Airways is expected to total at least 20 and Lockheed is confident that sales of aircraft of the TriStar-500 category will exceed 240 by 1985. McDonnell Douglas had offered to finance development of an RB.211-powered DC-10 Srs 30R if ordered by British Airways, believing that other sales of this variant could be expected to follow, but without that BA order it now seems unlikely that a Rolls-Royce engined DC-10 will materialize. Delivery of the new TriStars will begin in 1979, with the final two of the first batch in 1980. The TriStar-500 is 13 ft 6 in (4,11 m) shorter than the TriStar-1; it has a gross weight of 496,000 lb (224 982 kg) and aerodynamic and propulsion improvements that contribute to the reduced fuel consumption.

First flight of the **Boeing 747** fitted **with** 50,000 lb st (22 700 kgp) Rolls-Royce **RB.211-524Bs** was expected to be made at Paine Field on 3 September, as this issue went to press (see "Boeing's Behemoth" starting on page 167 of this issue); the engines are, however, cleared only for 48,000 lb (21 792 kg) thrust initially, and will be uprated later, probably in 1978. The first customer Lockheed L-1011-200 TriStar with the 48,000 lb st (21 792 kgp) RB.211-524s, one of a pair ordered by Saudia, is expected to fly early in October, although a Lockheed-owned TriStar has been flying with three of the new engines installed since 12 August. Earlier, this prototype had flown with a single RB.211-524 in one wing position, and then in the rear fuselage position, with the standard 42,000 lb st (19 068 kgp) RB.211-22Bs retained in the other positions.

New world records, including those for speed over a 15-25 km straight line and a 1,000-km (621·4-ml) closed circuit, have been **claimed by** a **Lockheed SR-71** flown by USAF crews. Three separate flights were made over California, with two records being set on each flight: these were for absolute closed circuit speed and a class record over 1,000 km at 2,086 mph (3 356 km/h); absolute speed and class record over 15-25 km straight course at 2,189 mph (3 522 km/h) and absolute altitude and class altitude record in horizontal flight at 86,000 ft (26 212 m). The previous closed circuit record was 1,853 mph (2 981 km/h), held by a MiG-25, and the previous straight line record was 2,070 mph (3 330 km/h), held by a Lockheed YF-12A.

First flight of the **Boeing YC-14** was made at Seattle on 9 August, a few days ahead of the revised schedule drawn up for this AMST contender after earlier funding cuts imposed a penalty of some seven months in the original programme, launched in November 1972 when contracts were placed with Boeing, and with McDonnell Douglas for the competing YC-15 design. Both prototypes of the YC-15 have already flown (the first a year ago) and have now completed the basic test programme required by the USAF. The second YC-14 is expected to fly before the end of this month (October) and will then join the first prototype at Edwards AFB for the completion of 365 hrs of testing by mid-1977. A full description of the YC-14, with a new cutaway drawing, will appear in our next issue.

The two McDonnell Douglas **YC-15** AMST prototypes returned to the company's facility at Long Beach on August 17 and 18, having **completed** a total of 473·2 hrs in 226 flights in the course of the **first phase of flight test** and evaluation by the joint McDonnell Douglas/USAF team. The first YC-15 is now to be fitted with a larger wing and a General Electric CFM-56 in place of one of the JT8D-17s at present installed; the second was to make a tour of Western Europe following its appearance at the Farnborough International Show early in September, and will then have a Pratt & Whitney JT8D-209 fitted in one engine position.

First flight of the Lockheed **JetStar II** was made at Marietta, Georgia, on 19 August, and Lockheed announced that it has a backlog of 18 orders for this new variant. Powered by four Garrett TFE731-3 turbofans, the JetStar II offers a non-stop range of 3,200 mls (5 150 km), and its production follows the completion by Lockheed of 163 of the earlier JetStar Is.

Under the title **Omnibus,** a number of **modifications** are being introduced **in** Marine Corps McDonnell Douglas **A-4M Skyhawks** to enhance their operational capability. Covered by Engineering Change Proposal 1120, and recently evaluated at NATC Patuxent River, the modifications include a laser spot tracker in the nose, new ECM equipment, indicated by a small fairing under the nose and a small "cap" on the fin, a redesigned cockpit layout to improve the head-up display presentation and provision for the installation of an angle-rate bombing system (ARBS) in due course. Total procurement of the A-4M is now set at 170 aircraft, including 17 purchased with funds resulting from the sale of 46 A-4E and A-4F Skyhawks to Israel during the Yom Kippur war. Of the total, 137 have been funded to date, with 21 more in the FY77 budget and a final 12 in FY 78-81. The USMC requirement is for five 16-aircraft squadrons of A-4Ms, plus 15 in a training squadron; with 13 pipeline aircraft and two for RDT & E, the total active inventory is 110, the balance of 60 being attributable to attrition over the service life of the aircraft.

Rockwell International has dropped its studies for a possible three-engined derivative of the Sabreliner and is now concentrating on development of a version of the **Sabreliner 60** **with** two **Garrett TFE 731** turbofans. The objective is to have a new version available by 1979, when new FAR 36 noise restrictions become applicable, and Rockwell is also discussing with the Raisbeck organisation a series of aerodynamic refinements that could be offered as a retrofit on existing Sabreliner 60s as well as being applicable to any new production version.

Flight **testing of the Bell 222** light twin helicopter began on 13 August with a 42-min flight by the first prototype; the second prototype was to enter a 200-hr ground running programme late in August and the third join the flight test programme in September. Two more examples are being produced for use as sales demonstrators and to build up service experience prior to customer deliveries starting in 1978. Powered by two 650 hp Avco Lycoming LTS101-650C turboshafts, the Bell 222 will be certificated to FAR Part 29 (for twin engined helicopters of more than 6,700 lb/3 042 kg gross weight) and eventually in Category A of this FAR, permitting flight to be continued to its destination by a twin-engined aircraft with redundant systems after failure of any single system.

CIVIL AFFAIRS

INTERNATIONAL
The Civil Aeronautics Board has recommended for Presidential approval applications by Delta Air Lines and Northwest Orient to operate **services across the North Atlantic,** and has also said that 11 more US cities should become gateways for transatlantic services in addition to the nine currently approved. The new gateways nominated are Atlanta, Tampa, New Orleans, Cleveland, Pittsburg, St Louis, Denver, Kansas City, Minneapolis-St Paul, Houston and Dallas-Fort Worth. The recommendation in respect of the new carriers is that Delta Air Lines should be awarded the Atlanta-London route, with single aircraft service between London and Dallas-Fort Worth/Houston, while Northwest would receive rights from six US gateways (including New York) to Scotland and five other countries in Europe. National, TWA and Pan American would all receive additional rights and/or routes under the proposal, which was backed by a three-to-one CAB decision with the chairman dissenting. Meanwhile, the UK has taken steps to renegotiate the bilateral air services agreement with the US by giving notice that it will renounce the existing (Bermuda) agreement. Talks on a new bilateral were scheduled to start in London on 9 September.

In renegotiating the Bermuda Agreement (see previous item) one of the principal British objectives will be to obtain an adequate **system of capacity regulation.** Recently, negotiations between Britain and the USA over capacity to be allowed for scheduled operations on the London-Miami and London-Chicago routes failed to reach agreement, and the Department of Trade consequently has imposed a limit for the coming winter season, of five "widebodied" return services each week by each airline on the London-Miami route, and four on the London-Chicago route. These limits are respectively two and one service below the level proposed by the US carriers (National and Pan American); although the British and US carriers agreed on estimates of traffic, the level of services proposed would have reduced average seat load factors, says the DoT, to 43 per cent on Miami and 39 per cent on Chicago.

UNITED KINGDOM
Laker Airways' long-standing attempt to introduce a low-cost, no-frills **Skytrain service** on the North Atlantic, having apparently suffered a fatal blow earlier this year in the Department of Trade's White Paper on Civil Aviation, was afforded a new **lease of life** at the end of July when a High Court judge ruled that the Secretary of State for Trade had exceeded his authority in seeking to revoke Laker's licence to operate the service. That licence had been granted by the Civil Aviation Authority on 1 January 1973, but inauguration of the service had to await US approval. This was on the point of being granted when the new UK civil aviation policy — based on "spheres of interest" rather than "dual designation" — was made the subject of a White Paper on 11 February 1976. Included in the White Paper was "guidance" from the DoT to the CAA, in effect calling upon the latter to take action in accordance with the new policy. It is on this point that the High Court has ruled that the DoT has exceeded its legal authority; although the Secretary of State is empowered under the Civil Aviation Act to reverse CAA decisions, he is not, in the view of the Court, entitled to direct the CAA to take decisions that effectively change the whole of UK civil aviation policy. Although the point at issue before the Court was the Laker Skytrain service, the ruling casts some doubt over the future of the route swopping between British Airways and B.CAL which was to follow the White Paper. At the time of going to press, both airlines were studying the effects of the High Court ruling, but were thought likely to proceed as both had agreed voluntarily to the new policy. The possibility of an appeal against the High Court order was also being considered by the DoT.

With the sale of two of its last four Carvairs, British Air Ferries is on the point of **phasing out** the last-remaining **cross-channel car ferry services,** for which there is now little demand. The two Carvairs that remain will be used primarily for cargo services, and BAF's passenger-carrying fleet has been augmented by three Heralds acquired from Transbrasil, making six in all. These new Heralds are to be operated in a mixed configuration, seating 26 passengers and 2¼ tons (2 550 kg) of cargo, and BAF is also reported to be negotiating for up to eight Herald 401s owned by the Royal Malaysian Air Force, for operation in the cargo rôle.

British Airways has finally succeeded in negotiating a **common Pilot Force** agreement to replace the previous separate agreements and schedules covering the old BOAC, BEA, Northeast and Cambrian pilots groups. The new agreement provides for creation of a single seniority system for all BA pilots, a basis for interchange of pilots and aircraft between Regional, European and Overseas divisions, arrangements for pilots and aircraft to "intermix" on Regional Division routes and rules for conversion and promotion of pilots from one aircraft type to another.

CIVIL CONTRACTS AND SALES

Boeing 707: Libyan Arab Airlines has taken delivery of one new -320C, to be operated on behalf of the government as a VIP transport. □ DanAir has added one second-hand -320C convertible to its fleet.

Boeing 727: Ansett Airlines ordered one additional Advanced 727. □ American Airlines ordered six more 727-223s, for delivery in July/August 1977 and to replace 707-123Bs on a one-for-one basis. □ Iran Air bought one Srs 100, ex-Lufthansa, through Omni Trading. □ Transbrasil bought two Srs 100s from Braniff.

Boeing 747: Qantas has confirmed an order for three more 747s to make a fleet total of 15. One of the new trio is a "combi" aircraft with side cargo door. Deliveries will be in September, November and December 1977.

EMBRAER EMB-110 Bandeirante: Top Taxis Aereo, the third level airline responsible with Varig for operations in southern Brazil (see *Airscene*/August 1976) has ordered six 18-seat EMB-110Ps.

Handley Page Herald: British Air Ferries acquired three more from Transbrasil and is reported to be negotiating to purchase eight Herald freighters from the Royal Malaysian Air Force.

Helicopters: Asahi Helicopters Co of Tokyo took recent delivery of a Bell 214 BigLifter, to be used in powerline construction activities in Japan. □ Offshore Helicopters has ordered a Bell 212 plus one on option, and is to order two Sikorsky S-61Ns to replace SA 330G Pumas that have been based in Norway to support offshore oil operations. □ Ansett Airlines ordered a second S-61N.

Lockheed L-1011 TriStar: British Airways has converted its outstanding order for six TriStar-1s to TriStar-500 versions and has taken an option on six more of the same type. Delivery of the first batch will be made in 1979 (four) and 1980 (two), these aircraft joining nine Tri-Star-1s already delivered (see separate news item also). □ Delta Air Lines took up an option on two L-1011-1s, for May and December 1978 delivery. □ Saudia's recently-announced order for additional TriStar-200s was reduced from three to two after re-assessment of future traffic growth.

McDonnell Douglas DC-8: Transmeridian Air Cargo is to acquire a DC-8F freighter, through the McDonnell Douglas conversion programme recently announced. □ Pelican Air Transport, based at Manchester, has acquired two Srs 55s from the manufacturer and will have them converted to cargo configuration at Tulsa before starting operations next spring.

McDonnell Douglas DC-10: Malaysian Airline Systems took delivery of the first of its two Srs 30s on 12 August and the aircraft set a new point-to-point record (subject to confirmation) between Honolulu and Kuala Lumpur, flying the 6,936·8 mls (11 163,3 km) in 12 hrs 26 min 35 sec.

MILITARY CONTRACTS

Aeritalia G.222: The *Fuerza Aérea Argentina* has taken up its option on a third aircraft for 1978 delivery.

Bell Model 212: Argentina's *Comando de Aviación Ejercito* has taken delivery of two for cargo and utility missions.

Cessna 150 Aerobat: The *Force Aérienne Zaïroise* has ordered 15 for basic flying training at Kinshasa.

De Havilland Canada DHC-5D: The *Force Aérienne Togolaise* has taken delivery of two (originally built against an order from Zaïre, now cancelled).

Fokker F.27MPA Maritime: Two ordered by the Peruvian *Servicio Aeronavale* for 1977 delivery. □ One ordered by Icelandic Coast Guard.

BAC 167 Strikemaster: Supplementary order placed on behalf of the Royal Saudi Air Force for 11 aircraft.

Pitts Special: Six ordered for the *Fuerza Aérea del Peru* for unspecified training rôle.

Sukhoi Su-22: Thirty-six Su-22 strike fighters orderd for the *Fuerza Aérea del Peru* at total programme cost of £140·45m ($250m).

THE FINE ART OF DISPLAY FLYING

The first part of this article, published in the August issue, gave an appreciation of solo display flying aimed at broadening the knowledge of the uninitiated, so that what impresses the professional is not lost on the layman. In this second and concluding part Wg Cdr Ian C H Dick, MBE, AFC, RAF, sets out to give readers a guide to the finer points of synchronised and formation display flying. The author was a member of the RAF's Red Arrows display team for six years and its leader for three.

As soon as more than one aircraft fly together in an aerobatic display, a whole new concept of display flying is opened up — the scope, flexibility and appeal of the display are increased considerably, although aircraft in formation are severely limited in what they can do. The automatic and instinctive attraction of a formation display cannot be denied; appeal exists for both the professional and for the layman. Most pilots know the difficulties in flying one aircraft in formation with another — to watch as many as nine aircraft manoeuvring in the sky as if painted on a card is awe-inspiring to the most blasé aviator. To the layman, the presence of a large number of aircraft in a small area of sky — looping and rolling in breath-taking unison — inevitably makes a spectacular sight. However, formation display flying requires different skills from those needed to perform solo aerobatics and draws its appeal in different ways.

As with solo display flying, what may be an impressive formation manoeuvre in the eyes of the professional may draw not so much as a sigh from the layman. How then does one judge and appreciate a formation aerobatic display; what is one looking for that is either impressive or spectacular or both? Before setting out to answer these questions by ex-

amining the components of the successful display, it is worth noting some of the formation and synchronised teams in existence at present, because it is these that most airshow spectators are likely to see and wish to appreciate.

As explained in the previous article, most types of aircraft are capable of putting on some form of solo flying display. However, formation display flying requires an aircraft to have well defined qualities of manoeuvrability and appearance. As with solo display flying, an ideal formation display aircraft will combine excellent manoeuvrability with an aesthetically pleasing appearance.

Manoeuvrability

The same factors affecting manoeuvrability of solo display aircraft affect formation aircraft although, for reasons explained below, many aircraft are unsuitable for formation aerobatic flying. A good power/weight ratio and responsive engine controls are essential for an aircraft used in formation, bearing in mind that the leader of the formation will have to manoeuvre using less than full power in order that his team members can keep up with him. A good ratio is also necessary because, the further an aircraft is away from the leader, the

Team	Country	Sponsor	Number and Type of Aircraft	Comments
Thunderbirds	USA	USAF	Six Northrop T-38A Talons	Full-time National Team
Blue Angels	USA	USN	Six McDonnell Douglas A-4E Skyhawks	Full-time National Team
Snowbirds	Canada	CAF	Nine Canadair Tutors	National Team
Carling	Canada	Carling Breweries	Four Pitts Specials	Civilian Team
Red Arrows	Great Britain	RAF	Nine Hawker Siddeley Gnats	Full-time National Team
Poachers	Great Britain	RAF	Four BAC Jet Provost 5As	Part-time RAF Team
Bulldogs	Great Britain	RAF	Two Scottish Aviation Bulldogs	Part-time Synchronised Pair
Vintage Pair	Great Britain	RAF	One Meteor T7 and one Vampire T11	Part-time Historical Pair
Rothmans	Great Britain	Rothmans Cigarettes	Four Pitts Specials	Civilian Team
Tiger Club	Great Britain	Tiger Club	Two Stampes	Part-time Synchronised Pair
Frecce Tricolori	Italy	IAF	Ten Fiat G91s	Full-time National Team
Patrouille de France	France	FAF	Eleven Fouga Magisters	Full-time National Team
Les Diables Rouges	Belgium	BAF	Six Fouga Magisters	Part-time National Team

(Below) The four Jet provosts of The Poachers, from RAF College Cranwell and (above) the nine Gnats of the Red Arrows. The better power/weight ratio of the Gnat makes it an easier aircraft to loop and roll tightly.

comparatively low power/weight ratio of the Jet Provost makes it difficult for the four-aircraft formation of the Poachers (the team from RAF College, Cranwell) to loop and roll tightly, whereas the Red Arrows' nine Gnats can do so with relative ease.

The power/weight ratio and engine response of an aircraft also affects its ability to execute formation changes — particularly during a manoeuvre. The Fiat G 91 is reasonably well endowed with power, enabling the AMI's *Frecce Tricolori* to execute quick and snappy formation changes without fear of anybody in the team sliding embarrassingly off the back of the formation! Surprisingly, though, high performance does not always mean good formation manoeuvrability. The USAF's Thunderbirds and USN's Blue Angels were severely limited when both teams flew the F-4 Phantom. Although the Phantom has plenty of power, it is so heavy that inertia forces are high and the engine response is not always positive enough to overcome them. Consequently, both teams were inhibited in the formation changes possible and, in fact mainly for this reason, very few formation changes were actually displayed in front of the crowd. On the other hand, the weight of the Phantom was advantageous in making the aircraft very stable in formation and allowing it to ride turbulent weather conditions relatively easily, whereas the lightness of the Gnat and sensitivity of its controls make it more difficult to keep steadily in formation when it is bumpy. This is one of the reasons why the American teams were able to fly so close together in their Phantoms, and they probably still fly closer in formation than any other team — less than 3 feet (0,92 m) apart on some occasions, although the Thunderbirds now fly Northrop T-38As and the Blue Angels are equipped with A-4 Skyhawks.

Although aircraft used for formation aerobatics do not require the high g limitations that are ideal for competition aerobatic aircraft, they still require to be well stressed so that tight manoeuvring can be a feature of the display. As a general guide, formation teams will pull up to 3-4 g in formation and 6 g or more in individual recoveries from bomb-bursts. By comparison, the pilots of the British Aerobatic Team and their international counterparts often pull 8 g and push -6 g in their solo displays. Any restrictions apart, aircraft often impose their own limits on what a pilot can do in formation. The Fiat G 91 and Gnat, for example, have powered controls with trimming at the flick of an electric switch on the control column; whereas the Jet Provost has manual controls and wheel trimming, which requires the pilot to take his hand off the throttle. Thus, formation aerobatics in the Jet Provost can require considerably more effort — in physical terms — and could be considered far more difficult, in some ways, than in the Gnat. On the other hand, the Gnat is not suitable for inverted formation flying because of the limited amount of control available with such a swept wing aircraft.

Obviously, size limits the type of aircraft used in formation aerobatics although there is perhaps nothing to match the impressiveness and presence of large, powerful aircraft in close proximity to each other; in practice the Phantom and Buccaneer are probably the largest aircraft capable of formation aerobatics. Any larger aircraft is unlikely to have the manoeuvrability required. The shape of an aircraft — as already discussed in the first part of this account — affects its manoeuvrability, but — again as with solo display flying — is perhaps more relevant to its appearance. The high performance, swept wing aircraft can be an impressive sight in a formation display but tight manoeuvring may not be a possibility and therefore the presentation of the display is spoilt by poor continuity. The Belgian Air Force "Slivers" — a synchro-pair of F-104G Starfighters — were capable of achieving very spectacular "crosses", but much of their display was taken up by enormous repositioning manoeuvres using extensive areas of sky — the fault not of the pilots but of the

greater the power and power changes required to stay in formation: the pilot flying at the back of a formation during a loop needs more power than anybody else in the formation to follow the leader. Therefore, if an aircraft does not have a good power/weight ratio and good engine response, formation manoeuvres will, at best, be restricted in the "tightness" with which they can be flown — thus affecting presentation — and, at worst, manoeuvres such as barrel rolls or loops may not be possible or aircraft numbers may be restricted. Thus, the

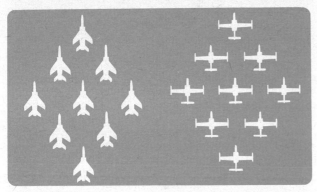

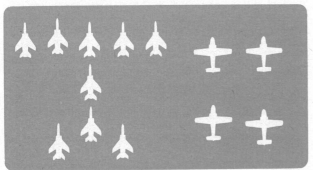

These diagrams, and those on succeeding pages, illustrate specific points made in the article. (Above) A comparison of "Diamond 9" formations with straight-wing and swept-wing aircraft. (Below) Imperfections in formations become more obvious with straight-wing aircraft.

aircraft. At the other end of the scale are the slower, straight wing aircraft such as the Fouga Magister and Jet Provost, which are capable of performing at slower speeds and therefore are able to keep their display nearer to the crowd — a loop done by the *Patrouille de France* takes up only 2,000-2,500 ft (610-765 m) whereas a loop by the *Frecce Tricolori* takes anything up to 7,000 ft (2 135 m). The straight wing shape tends to favour inverted flying, and this is where the Fouga Magister comes into its own as a formation aircraft; what it loses in speed and looks, it gains in inverted manoeuvrability, and the *Patrouille de France* and *Les Diables Rouges* teams both show how well this aircraft can be flown in inverted formations.

Appearance

Notwithstanding these factors, however, I still believe that the straight-wing aircraft is at a disadvantage when used for formation aerobatics. Most formation shapes flown are devised from a "diamond" pattern, and this is best and most naturally composed of aircraft that have swept wings. Imperfections in formation shapes also tend not to be so readily discernible when swept-wing aircraft are used. It is very easy to see if the Poachers are out of line, but not so easy to notice when the Red Arrows are out of position. Yet it is easier to fly a straight-wing aircraft in some formations — for example, line abreast — because the wing tip is readily seen and provides a good formation reference, whereas with a swept-wing aircraft the only reference for line abreast is the cockpit of one's neightbour.

The livery of a formation aerobatic team naturally contributes considerably to the team's appearance, and few teams do not have distinctive paint schemes to add colour to their display. In an attempt to overcome the gawkishness of the Jet Provost, the Poachers have adopted an angled motif to streamline and enhance the shape of their aircraft. Most National teams seem to favour a plain and simple livery which features a predominant colour — red for the Red Arrows and *Les Diables Rouges,* blue for the Blue Angels and *Frecce Tricolori.* I favour a simple colour scheme because once the air-

craft are in the air and away from the crowd one wants an overall picture of colour to create a striking impression. Fussy designs tend to become lost and meaningless when the aircraft are rolling and twisting through the three dimensions, and can break up the cohesive appearance of the formation as a whole.

Smoke unquestionably enhances the presentation of a formation aerobatic team, and few are without it. Not only is it useful for the team to establish a formation manoeuvre, thus leaving an imprint on the spectators' minds, but it is also essential for highlighting the "picture" manoeuvres used to give contrast in a display. Examples abound — the Red Arrows' "Twizzle", the *Frecce Tricolori's* "Bomba" and the *Patrouilles'* "Palm Tree" bomb-burst to mention but three — of manoeuvres that would pall without the signature of smoke.

Perhaps the greatest contribution to the impressive appearance of a formation aerobatic team is made by the number of aircraft it uses. I doubt if we shall ever return to the days of the late 'fifties and early 'sixties, when the Hunters of the RAF's Black Arrows and Blue Diamonds dominated European Air Displays with formations of up to 16 aircraft. Not only is the sight of so many aircraft in formation spectacular because of the sheer size and power of the formation, but it is also impressive because such large formations are difficult to fly. The famous Black Arrow loop of 22 Hunters at Farnborough in 1958 was not only a numerical record but was also a significant professional achievement. Besides large formations being more impressive and spectacular, they also

The two premier US aerobatic teams both sport distinctive colour schemes. (Above) the USAF Thunderbirds, flying Northrop T-38As, and (below) the US Navy's Blue Angels, flying McDonnell Douglas A-4E Skyhawks.

enable a greater variety of formation shapes to be flown and more flexibility can be achieved in the show by splitting-off a solo or pair of aircraft for synchronised aerobatics.

The sequence . . .

A display by a formation team must be considered in its entirety. Ideally, it is a balanced sequence of manoeuvres, choreographed to fill the aerial stage in a continuous performance. A typical sequence is likely to be composed of a mixture of three types of manoeuvre — formation, "picture" and synchronised — which we will now consider in greater detail.

Anybody can devise formation shapes for a particular number of aeroplanes; but which formation shapes are the more impressive to fly and what formation manoeuvres deserve the most applause? A square piece of paper is hardly an ideal flying shape, but fold it into a dart and you get a streamlined silhouette, which implies graceful speed and ease of flight. Thus, it is not surprising that, as a general principle of formation flying, sharp and pointed formations are more aesthetically pleasing than flat blunted ones, even though the latter tend to be more difficult to fly and so are inclined to be more impressive for the knowledgeable. The subtle difference between flying a "box" or "card" 4 formation may well be lost on the uninitiated. To many eyes, the "box" will be a more pleasing formation to watch and yet the "card" is more difficult to fly because it involves formating in line abreast — one of the more difficult kinds of formation to fly. Therefore, any formation shape which includes line abreast deserves extra marks for technical merit but may not always get praise for artistic appreciation. Inverted formation flying is equally — if not more — demanding of a pilot's skill, and the "mirror" slow roll of the *Patrouilles'* synchronised pair is one of the finest formation manoeuvres to be seen, as is the Rothmans' superb "box" formation slow roll. Typical shapes that can be

obtained from a nine-aircraft basic "diamond" pattern are shown in one of the accompanying diagrams.

The other factor which makes a particular formation shape more or less difficult to fly is the distance a particular pilot flies from the leader. The "whip-lash" effect of any movement in the formation is greatly increased the further a pilot is from the leader, and these pilots have to "finesse" their formation flying through the intervening aircraft on to the leader in order to have a steady datum on which to smooth out their own formation flying. An impressive example of such a formation is illustrated when the *Patrouille* run in to break and land at the completion of their display. The 11 aircraft are in line astern, which means that the last aircraft is nine steps removed from the leader; yet I have never seen any noticeable "whip-lash" effect, and the spacing between the aircraft is invariably immaculate. This is an impressive feat made all the more so by the leader being able to fly this unwieldy and deep formation in such a way that the bottom man is only about 100 ft (30 m) above the ground. But it is not only the formation shape that warrants close scrutiny; the manoeuvres which are performed in formation also have a bearing on the impressiveness or otherwise of the display. With the exception of something like the Rothmans' slow roll, manoeuvres in formation are mainly limited to fly-pasts, turns, wing-overs, loops and barrel rolls.

I have listed these manoeuvres more or less in ascending order of difficulty, and we shall examine their execution later. Meanwhile, it is worth noting that a formation display sequence should have a balanced and pleasing mixture of them all. Loop followed by roll followed by tight turning fly-past is the kind of rhythm that a display should aim to establish. The format of this part of the sequence should be designed so that one manoeuvre leads quickly and naturally into a contrasting one. As the manoeuvres are varied, so are the formation shapes by a contrast of changes — quick, slow and hidden. It is impossible to state the ideal format for a display; the successful one will consist of a logical blend of formation shapes, changes and manoeuvres.

"Picture" manoeuvres are those where the aircraft in the formation perform individually rather than as a formation. The result is that the close formation of the team is broken up to produce a "picture" in the sky. The most common example of this category is the bomb-burst, of which there are many varieties. These manoeuvres are an important feature of any formation display and should be used to contrast with the precision and closeness of the classical formation shapes. However, generally speaking, "picture" manoeuvres tend to

(Above left) "Box 4" (left) and "Card 4" (right) formations. (Below) Ten possible nine-aircraft formations, starting with the basic diamond (upper left) and showing its various derivatives.

be easier to perform than close formation ones; they concentrate more on giving a spectacular movement of aircraft — marked with a signature of smoke — rather than making an impression of professional skill. Nevertheless, some "picture" manoeuvres are considerably more difficult to do than others, and for this reason demand admiration from both the knowledgeable and the layman. The *Frecce Tricolori's* "Double Roll" is an example which readily springs to mind — an impressive and spectacular manoeuvre that has received the praise of other formation teams for many years and is still one of my favourite manoeuvres, which I always get a thrill from watching. Perhaps this is an area where the originality and ingenuity of a team are really highlighted, and because so many possibilities are available it is difficult to generalise or to introduce a scale of assessment. The character, style and skill of a team will be illustrated by the "picture" manoeuvres performed by it. Here is the free-style opportunity for a team to be truly spectacular and unique — performing manoeuvres that surprise everybody, defy imitation by other teams and reflect the creative imagination of those involved.

Finally, in examining the three types of manoeuvres available to a formation aerobatic team, we must not forget synchronised manoeuvres. I use "synchronised" in the broadest sense to cover not only those manoeuvres where one or more aircraft alternates with the main formation (ie, as a fill-in) but also opposition manoeuvres where aircraft or formations of aircraft synchronise together to fly in opposition to each other. The solo pilot of the *Frecce Tricolori* adorns the aerial stage with immaculate rolls whilst the rest of the team reassemble for their next manoeuvre. The Tiger Club Stampes, flown by Pete Jarvis and Karl Schofield, are an eloquent example of two aircraft flying together and in opposition in perfectly matched harmony. The synchronised pairs of the Red Arrows and *Patrouille de France* not only fill-in for the main formation but also execute their own synchronised ("mirror" slow roll) and opposition (opposition loop) manoeuvres.

Synchronised aerobatics exploit the flexibility provided by large formations. To my mind, they greatly enhance the sequence of a formation team by providing an exciting and unusual form of flying. On the one hand, two aircraft are not as limited when flying in formation and can therefore do things, for example "mirror" flying, which would be impossible for larger formations. On the other hand, and more importantly perhaps, two or more aircraft can fly in opposition to each other, thus achieving the illusion of an impending collision, which — it cannot be denied — has "gladiatorial" appeal to a great many spectators. Rightly or wrongly, there is little doubt that, when a team's performance includes synchronised aerobatics and the skilful and attractive presentation of formation shapes, the typical layman spectator's lasting impression will be of the adrenalin-inducing opposition "crosses" of the synchronised aircraft. This attraction cannot be denied, and therefore I firmly believe that, from a layman's viewpoint, a sequence which does not include opposition manoeuvres cannot match the spectacle of one that does.

. . . its execution . . .

Having looked at the types of manoeuvres that go to form an aerobatic team's sequence, we can now consider how these manoeuvres should be executed. There are three general points about formation flying for which spectators should always be on the lookout. First, and most importantly, there is the matter of position. It is an obvious feature of flying a formation shape that all the aircraft must be flown accurately in position to maintain the correct shape. A great deal of a team's practise time is spent in analysing and correcting individual formation positions so that errors are eliminated and team precision is achieved. High marks must be accorded in this respect to the American teams; their performance in this

The Red Arrows' seven-aircraft bomb-burst, appreciation of which is aided by the use of smoke, provides a contrast with precision formation manoeuvres.

respect epitomises precision, but it must be kept in mind that they use only six aircraft which are reasonably heavy and therefore have good stability in formation. Additionally, these teams tend to fly "set piece" manoeuvres involving flying well away from the crowd, and this helps to make actual formation keeping easier for the individuals.

Mention of stability brings us on to the second general point, which is steadiness in formation. In contrast to the seemingly effortless smoothness of the Blue Angels and Thunderbirds, "yugging" movements can sometimes be detected in the Red Arrows' formation as the individual pilots strive to overcome turbulence disturbing their light Gnats. The excellent response and sensitivity of the Gnat's controls do not contribute to the ease of the Red Arrows' task, and the "yug" (a good alliteration of the sudden up/down or rocking movement of the aircraft) is a common word in the team's vocabulary. Clearly, the less "yugging" in formation the better, but take account of the aircraft type and number, weather conditions and tightness of manoeuvre when judging the steadiness and smoothness of a formation aerobatic team.

Finally, formation shapes can be distorted by the way a team or its leader flies a manoeuvre. The most prevalent example of this error is the "dishing" of the formation during a barrel roll. The effect is that, as the formation rolls, the plane of the aircraft is different, thus giving the formation a saucer appearance — hence the term "dishing". It stands to reason that the wider the frontage of a formation, the more likely this error is to occur. However, "dishing" is not a particularly common error as professional teams should be so well practised that they know how to avoid it. Perhaps more common are distortions in formation shape owing to errors in depth. If, for example, during the pull-up to a loop, the g is too much or too quickly applied by the leader, aircraft will not be able to stay on plane and this will reveal itself as a distortion. Line abreast formations are particularly prone to this error, which is easily discernible in this case.

Rapid or unexpected power changes by the leader will tend to distort a formation by either squashing it up or stretching it out, but this kind of distortion in a professional team should be

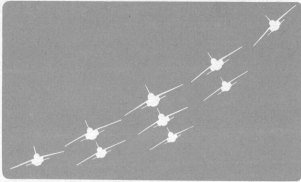

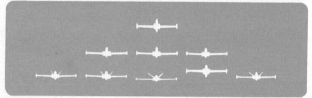

(Above) "Dishing" of a formation during a barrel roll is rarely seen in professional team presentations, but is an error the leader must always be on guard to prevent. (Below) Distortion in plane during the pull up from a loop, resulting from application of too much "g" by the leader.

(Below) An example of advanced mirror flying demonstrated by two outstanding US aerobatic pilots, Art Scholl and Skip Volk, in specially-modified Chipmunks.

rare as it is a very elementary error. Lastly, one must remember that the changing perspective of a particular formation shape as it loops, rolls and turns will give the illusion of distortion. Clearly, this is unavoidable in most cases but can be minimised in others by ensuring that the presentation of the formation is correct. The *Frecce Tricolori* are unique in that they fly their "Diamond Nine" formation so that it looks like a diamond from whichever angle it is viewed — a remarkable achievement from the professional point of view because it requires a great amount of co-ordination and control, but a facet of their display which probably and regretfully goes unnoticed by most. Remember also that, if as a spectator you are not standing exactly at the datum point, you are likely to get a distorted view of what the team is properly presenting to the centre of the crowd.

Horizontal Formation Manoeuvres

The fly-past and turn form the majority of horizontal manoeuvres which can be performed by a formation team. The fly-past should ideally be flown along the display line, in front of the crowd, so that the shape of the formation is clearly displayed. Unless adopting the *Frecce's* technique mentioned already, it is almost impossible to show off the shape of a formation in a straight and level fly-past; the crowd will mostly see the formation side on — hardly the most flattering angle. Thus, as with large singly-displayed aircraft like Concorde, fly-pasts should incorporate a turn so that the most pleasing view of the shape is presented to the crowd. Complete 360-deg turns are not widely used in a team's full display but are more relevant to poor weather displays when other manoeuvring is not possible. Nevertheless, a 360-deg turn is a quick and clear way of displaying formation shapes and changes. To be effective, the turn must be made at a high angle of bank so that the plan view of the formation is shown; it must be tightly flown so that the formation, when on the far side of the turn, is still easily visible. To help achieve all these features, the plane of the turn should be inclined slightly so that the lowest point is nearest the crowd and the highest is on the back straight of the turn. In this way, crowd proximity and a good plan view of the formation will be achieved. As I have already suggested on a number of occasions, inverted fly-pasts and turns in formation warrant additional applause. In these cases, one is more interested in the fact that the aircraft are flying upside down rather than in some specific shape. And are they all inverted? — if not, then it is not so impressive. Apart from watching how well the aircraft maintain their inverted formation, particularly watch for how easily all the aircraft get into and out of the inverted position. Do pairs of aircraft do it neatly and quickly — matched to each other and without moving a long way out of formation? Or does the whole thing have to be done well out of sight whilst something else distracts your attention? In my opinion, the *Patrouille* are the masters of this art.

Another example of "mirror flying", demonstrated by the Rothman's Team when flying its original Stampe biplanes.

I have already mentioned "mirror" flying, which is usually limited to turning or rolling in the horizontal plane; because of a number of limiting factors, one rarely sees a true "mirror" being flown these days. One can allude to the impression by flying slightly off-set either to the side or behind. The Gemini pair of Jet Provosts used to fly with slight lateral displacement, and the *Patrouille's* pair now have to fly with longitudinal displacement. Although, from the purists' viewpoint, these formations are not perfect "mirrors", it is still impressive to watch such manoeuvring; and one can still see really true "mirror" flying when watching the Tiger Club's Karl Schofield and Pete Jarvis, who provide an accurate example of this form of flying.

Clearly, a slow roll in formation should ideally have all the features discussed in the first part of this article, but its successful achievement is far more outstanding than a solo slow roll and deserves the highest credit.

Vertical Formation Manoeuvres

The manoeuvres I consider to be vertical — because they use the all-important vertical plane — are the wing-over, barrel roll and loop. The wing-over is a much maligned and often poorly executed manoeuvre mainly because it is used in a sequence as a positioning device rather than as a spectacle — but it is just because of this that the wing-over is so important. The main fault in its execution is that not enough use is made of the vertical. This has two unfortunate results: firstly, displacement from the crowd is greater, so that the formation is less visible and more side-on to the crowd. Secondly, a flat wing-over takes longer to complete than one making proper use of the vertical, and time is, of course, an important factor in the presentation of a display. Moreover, a tight wing-over starting with a good pitch-up into a steep climb, co-ordinated with a high angle of bank to give a good view of the formation and then a relatively steep recovery into the beginning of the next manoeuvre, is more impressive and attracts far more attention than a "wishy-washy" turnabout in the middle distance.

In my experience, the barrel roll is the most difficult manoeuvre to do with a formation of aircraft — something not readily appreciated from the ground. A careful co-ordination and combination of power, ailerons and elevators are necessary to achieve the desired manoeuvre which can be readily followed by the whole team. Ideally, the smoke pattern left by this manoeuvre should look as if it has been painted on the outside of a beer barrel. The manoeuvre, therefore, has length, breadth and height. Length to match the 2,000-yd (1 820-m) crowd line and breadth to height in equal measure. Usually and most effectively, this roll should be performed along the crowd line, which makes it difficult to judge the exact shape of the manoeuvre. However, one can get a good idea by looking at the smoke and seeing where the roll starts and where it ends. Very often it will be noticed from this that the axis of the roll is not parallel to the crowd line but angled slightly on or off crowd — probably on purpose to help the leader of the formation position the team for the next manoeuvre. What is more obvious to the eye is whether or not the roll starts and finishes at the same height; it should do. Related to this is the rate of roll. Does the rate stay constant from start to finish or does it start slowly, speed up over the top of the manoeuvre and then slow down again as the leader plays the formation down to the base height? The former is preferable and shows a more polished execution of the manoeuvre. It is also easier for wing men to follow and so should result in better formation keeping.

If the barrel roll is difficult for the team leader to execute, so too is it difficult for those flying on the edges of the formation. And in this context, the Red Arrows' "Wineglass Roll" — with five aircraft flying line abreast — is one of the most difficult manoeuvres they fly, as indicated by the fact that they are the

Les Diables Rouges, *the aerobatic team of the* Force Aérienne Belge, *performing a loop for the benefit of an accompanying photographer. Like the outstanding* Patrouille de France, Les Diables Rouges *fly* Potez Fouga Magisters.

only team to fly it — as much a reflection of the excellent handling characteristics of the Gnat as the pilots' skill.

Finally, there is the formation loop. Many of the points mentioned for solo display looping are applicable to a formation. The loop should be in the vertical plane — despite any wind — and the entry and exit should follow the same direction, ie, the loop has not been bent (unless done so on purpose to pick up a positioning line). The size of the loop should be kept as small as possible compatible with the performance of both aircraft and pilot. Large loops take time and height, which both detract from the presentation of the display. Loops are best done on the 45-deg or 90-deg line because the plan view of the formation is thus clearly seen by the crowd. A loop along the crowd line is generally going to obscure the shape of the formation from the audience and so lose a lot of its appeal. The actual outline of the loop matters little from a formation team's point of view; there is no

Possibly the foremost exponents of formation aerobatics outside of the armed forces, the Rothmans Team flies the highly manoeuvrable Pitts biplanes through a series of breathtaking evolutions at many air displays each season.

flexibility to make it a perfect circle. However, on a calm day, the best measure of a good loop is to see if the team exits through the smoke it left on its pull-up.

Formation Changes

In my view, there are three kinds of formation changes: those that give the impression of happening instantly, those that happen slowly and insidiously and the hidden or "now-you-see-it-now-you-don't" change. The most common example of the first kind is the "box change". A wide formation of say five aircraft is contracted to a longer, narrower formation by two aircraft rushing into the space behind the leader. This is how the change is best used — collapsing a wide formation into a narrow one or vice versa. It is easier and quicker to collapse than to expand a formation, although both can and are done effectively by a number of teams.

The slow change is far more subtle and, in my opinion, more difficult to do. Most teams do some sort of slow change — mainly to alter formation shape from the basic diamond to its derivatives. The Red Arrows' change from "Diamond" to "Super Concorde" is a prime example and, contrary to popular belief, is achieved by moving six aircraft backwards and not three forwards. Whether the formation changes are quick or slow, the same criteria apply. The most important thing is that the changes are matched on each side of the formation; movement must not be lopsided. After a rapid change, the formation should adopt its new shape without a lot of "wobbling" or adjustment. And, of course, the final ignominy of any change occurs if somebody falls out of the formation — not an uncommon occurrence in practice. In other words, formation changes should happen with polish — one formation shape being changed to another with the perfection and ease of a kaleidoscope. Finally, a word on the hidden change: it should be just that!

"Picture" Manoeuvres

Because there are so many types of "picture" manoeuvres, it is difficult to lay down criteria by which they should be judged. A suck of the breath is probably as good an indicator as any to judge the thrill of a particular manoeuvre. And yet I have already mentioned that some are easy and others difficult; how, then, to judge this difference? Very generally, a good guide is whether or not the formation stays together after the manoeuvre or whether it scatters to the corners of the display site. The latter — for example a downwards bomb-burst —

often requires little more skill than being able to divide the compass into the right number of degrees. On the other hand, the Thunderbirds' famous "Roll Back" requires considerably more skill because the aircraft rolling back have to rejoin the formation. It is also more difficult to perform a "picture" manoeuvre that does not have the ground readily available for reference. The *Patrouille's* vertical "Palm Tree" bomb-burst is a spectacular example of this type of manoeuvre. In judging how well a team performs a "picture" manoeuvre, there are two general points worth noting: the actual "picture" created and the symmetry in performing the manoeuvre. The names of the manoeuvres themselves often give the clue to the "picture" intended. "Palm Tree" hardly needs any explanation, and it goes without saying that, when performing this manoeuvre, the *Patrouille* should achieve the intended symbolism. The symmetry of these manoeuvres is achieved by matching the manoeuvre and spacing between the aircraft involved.

Synchronised Aerobatics

The most impressive and spectacular formation aerobatics I have ever watched were the remarkable synchronised displays of the Blue Diamonds and the Tigers at Farnborough in 1962. The sight of the sixteen blue Hunters of No 92 Squadron alternating with the nine Lightnings of No 74 Squadron provided a rare opportunity to see sensational synchronised aerobatics. Unfortunately, such days and displays remain only as a glorious memory. However, synchronised aerobatics are still to be seen — albeit on not such a lavish scale. What is one looking for in this type of manoeuvre? As far as the synchronised aspect is concerned, obviously the main factor is timing. As one formation leaves, so the next should arrive — the gap between them should ideally be no more than ten seconds. But it is the opposition aspect of synchronised aerobatics which warrants most attention in this article. The aim of opposition manoeuvring is simply to create the illusion of a near miss. One aircraft can achieve this by opposing the main formation, as shown in the *Frecce's* "Bomba". Alternatively, four aircraft can oppose five, and one manoeuvre I

continued on page 198

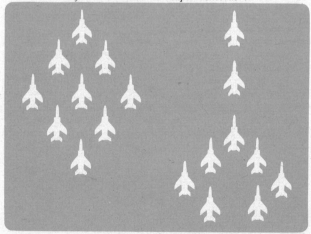

(Above) A diagram showing the relative aircraft positions in a change of formation from "Arrow" to "Box 5". (Below) The Red Arrows' change from "Diamond" to "Super Concorde".

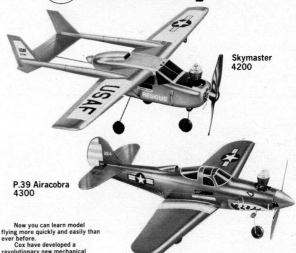

ROLLS-ROYCE
FROM THE WINGS
Military Aviation 1925–71

Heinkel 70 with Kestrel engine

176pp 244mm × 168mm £4·95
hardback 4 colour cover
SBN 0 902280 38 4

Publication date: 4 September

RONALD W. HARKER

Ronnie Harker served Rolls-Royce from 1925-71; forty-five years of unparalleled advance in technology and performance in aviation. The author and his contemporaries in engineering and aircraft design were involved with pre-war re-armament, war-time development, and post-war advance into the jet and V/STOL era, and supersonics.

The narrative describes the vital part that Rolls-Royce played in the development of military aircraft in World War II; how a most successful family of aero engines evolved from the Kestrel to become the 'R' engine which won the Schneider Trophy for Britain and the Merlin engine which powered all the British fighters in the Battle of Britain, and also the Lancaster, Halifax and Mosquito bombers. Probably the most significant personal contribution made by the author at this time was his realisation that the Merlin engine should be installed into the Mustang aeroplane. The Merlin Mustang became the most successful all-purpose fighter of the War and effectively turned the tide of the War in our favour.

When the War ended, a very serious slump in aircraft production was averted by the emergence of the jet engine, pioneered by Sir Frank Whittle and Rolls-Royce. The RAF had to be re-equipped and Rolls-Royce soon established a valuable export market in America and France (and inadvertently the USSR!). A civil market too was opened up and keen competition soon materialised with the US engine makers, who, by taking licences from Rolls-Royce, had quickly learned the necessary technology to produce them.

An insight is revealed into the tough battle for the military market of 1956 to the present day, when one gradually learned that the days of producing the best possible engine/plane combination for a direct operational requirement were over and that decisions were becoming complicated by economic, commercial and political pressures and by government policy. In spite of this however, successes were achieved; those described include the Spey Phantom, the Vertical Take Off Mirage and the LTV Corsair.

The final triumph, and tragically, the final downfall of the Company, was the production of the large fan engine, the RB-211 for the wide-bodied air liners. Towards the end of the author's career, the civil side had been absorbing increasing amounts of development and production time and money — often at the expense of military requirements — and the RB-211 engine finally sent the Company into bankruptcy at a time when the military side had won the order for the RB-199 engine for the European MRCA, and the Olympus engine was being produced for Concorde.

This book is essentially about Rolls-Royce; its principles and personalities, its contribution to military aviation, and its rise and fall as seen by the author. But because the author worked so closely with the RAF, the Royal Navy, the USAF and the plane makers in Britain, France and the USA, the book offers an essentially unique picture of military aviation during the 1925-71 period and should prove of real interest to anyone with a fascination for aviation history.

NAA Merlin Mustang

The BAC MRCA

The Author

Published by The Oxford Illustrated Press, "Rolls-Royce: From The Wings" is available direct from Ducimus Books Limited at £5·35 ($16·95) per copy inclusive of postage and packing. Place your order in writing or use the order form below.

BOEING'S BEHEMOTH

THE STORY OF THE 747

Visitors to the Renton, Washington, home of what was, in the mid 'sixties, the Airplane Division of the Boeing Company (the editor of AIR INTERNATIONAL among them) were prone to gaze with awe upon a large wooden hoop erected alongside one of the assembly shops. With a diameter of some 20 ft (6,1 m), this structure, representing the fuselage cross section of a projected future Boeing aeroplane, dwarfed the less-than-12 ft (3,66 m) diameter of the Boeing 707 section provided for comparison. The 707 was itself then still a relative newcomer to the airline scene, offering hitherto-unknown spaciousness as well as new standards of speed and comfort to the air traveller, and the prospect of an aeroplane of almost twice the size and weight of this first-generation jet transport was startling.

The project represented by the display at Renton was in fact Boeing's entry in the USAF's design competition for a strategic transport of outsize capability, identified as the CX-HLS (Experimental Cargo: Heavy Logistics System). Boeing had been conducting studies, since the middle of 1962, into the needs of USAF for an aircraft able to transport Army divisions including all their equipment, by air. Aircraft of gross weights ranging from 400,000 lb (181 600 kg) to over 1,000,000 lb (454 000 kg) were studied and by late 1962 a design with a weight of over 500,000 lb (227 000 kg) had been defined, capable of carrying 180,000 lb (81 720 kg) payloads over practicable ranges. This project provided the basis for Boeing's formal submission in the CX-HLS competition in May 1964, on the basis of which the company received a contract to undertake further design definition in a 90-day period.

A team of more than 500 engineers was deployed on this effort, out of which came a 4,272-page study submitted to the USAF on 14 September 1964. Further design studies and analysis followed, still under USAF contract. It was, therefore, a considerable blow to Boeing when, on 30 September 1965, the then Secretary of Defense Robert McNamara announced that Lockheed had won the contract to build 63 C-5A transports (including prototypes) with an option on a second batch of 57. But if Boeing was bloodied in this particular contest, it certainly emerged unbowed, and out of defeat emerged victory in the next round of the commercial jet transport battle, in the shape of the Boeing 747.

The commercial possibilities of a variant of the CX-HLS proposal had always been obvious at Renton, and the company's market research department had predicted the need for a passenger aircraft of, broadly, double the 707's capacity for service in the 'seventies. Even before the final USAF decision in favour of the Lockheed C-5A, Boeing had established, in August 1965, a formal preliminary design group to work on the commercial aeroplane and when the CX-HLS competition was lost, the efforts of this group were redoubled.

Whereas the military project had featured a high-wing configuration, to facilitate the required straight-in loading of large vehicles including tanks, the civil proposals under study at the end of 1965 favoured a mid-wing arrangement, in three possible sizes. Identified at this stage as the Model 747-3, -4 and -5, all three proposals were smaller than the CX-HLS design and with gross weights ranging from 532,000 lb (241 528 kg) to 599,400 lb (272 128 kg), they offered passenger capacities varying from 311 to 433 and ranges of about 5,700 mls (9 170 km) with full passenger payload. Engines of up to 40,000 lb st (18 160 kgp) were required (there was no final choice of power plant at this stage) and cruising speeds up to Mach = 0·9 were planned. One of the unusual features of these projects was the use of a "double bubble" fuselage with two

The family of Boeing 747 variants has grown steadily over the years, but only the 747SP (below) is immediately distinguishable externally, having an obviously shorter fuselage. A standard 747B is shown in the heading picture.

An artist's impression of the Boeing CX-HLS proposal, work on which helped the company to define the Model 747 configuration as finally adopted for the commercial market.

passenger decks, each 15 ft (4,58 m) wide to accommodate seven-abreast seating with two aisles.

Tests were made of this configuration from 5 to 10 October 1965 in Boeing's transonic wind tunnel at speeds from Mach 0·3 to Mach 1·05, these being the first such tests of an aircraft that is identifiable as a predecessor of the 747 as it is known today. However, initial airline reaction to the two-deck layouts was not enthusiastic and within four months Boeing had revised its 747 proposal to have a single-deck, low-wing configuration, with what was to become a characteristic "hump" fairing the raised flight deck into the fuselage, and allowing the main passenger deck to extend without interruption right to the nose of the aircraft.

In the early months of 1966, intensive marketing activity surrounded the development of a large capacity transport as represented by the Boeing 747 proposal. Lockheed was offering a commercial version of the C-5A as the L-500, but the principal competition for Boeing came from Douglas, which had also lost out in the CX-HLS competition and like Boeing was trying to make use of the design effort already expended, by developing a commercial airliner. Projects at Long Beach were known under the general title of DC-10 and were of the same mid-wing twin deck configuration that Boeing had at first considered. However, Douglas was in deep financial trouble at this time and poorly placed to launch a major new programme, and its market surveys in any case suggested that an aircraft of such large capacity was not really needed by the airlines until the mid 'seventies; consequently, the Douglas projects were dropped by the end of 1966 and the DC-10 designation was eventually re-adopted for the smaller tri-jet (see "The Tenth Dimension"/Vol 5 No 6 December 1973).

Unlike Douglas, Boeing believed the market would be ready for the outsize airliner by the beginning of the 'seventies and directed its energies to persuading the airlines accordingly. The proposal as of March 1966 was for an aeroplane with a fuselage having a near-circular cross section and a width at floor level of 19 ft 5 in (5,92 m) to permit comfortable nine-abreast seating with two aisles (and ten-abreast in high density arrangements), and providing 313 economy-class and 55 first-class seats in a typical layout. The low-mounted wing had a span of 183 ft 10 in (56,07 m) and a sweepback of about 40 deg; engines were in four individual pods under the wings, the choice of power plant lying at this stage between the General Electric CTF39 (commercial variant of the TF39 adopted to power the C-5A Galaxy), the Pratt & Whitney JT9D and the Rolls-Royce RB.178, the two last-mentioned both still being in the project stage. A basic gross weight of 625,000 lb (283 750 kg) was projected, with up to 675,000 lb (306 450 kg) for an all-freight 747F. To distribute this weight over existing runways, a 16-wheel main undercarriage was adopted, with four four-wheel bogies in line abreast under the fuselage and wing centre section.

An aeroplane as big as the Boeing 747 was clearly innovative, and Pan American was naturally looked upon as the airline most likely to place the first order, just as, ten years earlier, it had helped to launch both the Boeing 707 and

Douglas DC-8 with trend-setting contracts for fleets of both types. Boeing's management decided, before the end of March 1966, that the 747 programme should be allowed to proceed on a tentative basis, subject to review and firm approval at a later date. The first essential step towards that approval was taken less than a month later, on 13 April, when Pan American again assumed the mantle of world leader and ordered 25 Model 747s, but it was not until 25 July that the final commitment to production was made, after Lufthansa and JAL had each ordered three examples of the new Jumbo Jet, as the 747 quickly became known.

To meet the Pan American specification, the 747 as launched into production differed somewhat from the March 1966 definition described above. Span went up to 195 ft 9 in (59,66 m) and sweepback was reduced slightly to 37·5 deg; gross weight was set at 680,000 lb (308 720 kg), and the undercarriage units were "staggered" in side elevation, the wing units being behind those in the fuselage. Pan American opted for the JT9D at a rating of about 44,000 lb (19 976 kg), this decision putting a new Pratt & Whitney turbofan (initially developed as the JTF14) into production and effectively ending Rolls-Royce's hopes of launching the RB.168, that company's initial three-spool engine project.

To achieve a planned Mach 0·9 cruise, compared with Boeing 707's Mach 0·86, the 747 wing was of relatively thinner section but aerodynamically it was closely related to that of the 707, with double-slotted flaps, leading edge slats and Krueger flaps. First flight was projected to take place in the last quarter of 1968, with certification and initial deliveries to be made within 12 months of that date; the basic price tag for a basic all-passenger aircraft was of the order of $18·5m (equal to £6·6m in mid-1966). A pure freight variant was projected from the start, as well as a convertible passenger/freighter — respectively the 747F and 747C — with an upward hinged nose section (forward of the flight deck) to permit straight-in loading.

As the first Boeing 747 began to take shape and the production plans moved ahead, the sheer size of the programme became more and more impressive, although Boeing carefully avoided the use of unproven technical features that might have imposed delays in building and certificating the new aircraft. From the aerodynamic and structural points of view, the 747 was in many respects an enlarged 707, and it was designed to be operated within the same airline environment without making any special demands on the flight crew, which would comprise two pilots and an engineer (or three pilots) as in the smaller jet transports. The massive dimensions of the 747, however, meant that a completely new assembly plant was needed — Boeing's existing facilities were in any case already heavily committed to production of the 707, 727 and 737 — and this was established at Paine Field, Everett.

As early as June 1966, Boeing took an option on 780 acres at Everett, 30 mls (48 km) north of Seattle, and $200m has since been spent to establish what is now known as the 747 Division of the Commercial Airplane Group, including the world's largest volume building, of 200 million cu ft (5 663 400 m³) capacity and containing major portions of 747 manufacturing, sub-assembly, major and final assembly functions. Additional buildings house mock-ups, cleaning, sealing and painting plant, and static and fatigue test positions, plus offices, cafeteria, etc. Production activities began in this new facility on 1 May 1967, and the effort to get the first 747 — built on production tooling but assigned to Boeing as a test aircraft and demonstrator — began in earnest.

By September 1966, little more than a month after the formal decision to go ahead with the 747, Boeing had booked 56 orders from seven customers and it appeared that the world's airlines were about to embark upon another "jet buying spree" similar to that a decade earlier involving the Boeing 707 and Douglas DC-8. Two years later, the order book had reached 150 and market forecasts indicated sales of 488 could be achieved by 1977. This figure now appears to have been over optimistic, however, the mid-1976 sales total being 309, and there is no doubt that Boeing has suffered considerably as a result of the lower-than-predicted sales of the 747 and the consequently reduced production rate. This might be seen as some justification for the view of some industry and airline experts, at the time the 747 was launched, that an aircraft of this size was premature; but the decline in air traffic growth over the past few years, responding to world economic conditions, has also taken its toll of the market predictions.

The 747 and its JT9D engines also suffered a number of quite severe technical problems in the early years of the project, the first of these being Boeing's inability to hold the gross weight to the initially projected 680,000 lb (308 720 kg). Because of increases in the structure and systems weights, Boeing had to push the max take-off weight up, before the 747's first flight, first to 695,000 lb (312 200 kg) and then to 710,000 lb (322 050 kg) in order to meet the specified payload/range performance. Despite a strenuous weight reduction programme conducted by Boeing, this growth in turn required Pratt & Whitney to compress several planned future steps in JT9D power growth into a shorter time scale, and was perhaps in part responsible for the engine problems that would appear later.

The 747 had initially been based on using JT9D-1 engines rated at 41,000 lb (18 600 kgp) and it was intended that these engines would in due course be recertificated at 42,000 lb (19 050 kgp) while the JT9D-3 would become available eventually at 43,500 lb (19 730 kgp). By the time the first 747 flew, however, in February 1969, it had been decided that the JT9D-1 would be used in the flight test programme with a rating of 42,000 lb (19 050 kgp) and that the -3 would be ready by the time the 747 was certificated for airline service, at the initial 710,000 lb (322 050 kg) weight.*

From the start, the Boeing 747 handled well in the air and there were no major flight test problems. Jack Waddell made the first flight in the company-owned and appropriately-registered N7470† on 9 February 1969 and four more production aircraft joined the programme at short intervals for use in the flight test and certification programme, which was completed by the end of the year in some 1,400 hours of flying. Thus, although the original first flight target date had slipped by some three months, much of this lost time was recovered to obtain certification on 30 December 1969 and this allowed airline service to begin in January 1970, Pan American flying the 747's first revenue service on the New York-London route on 21 January.

Early days
The 747, with its ability to carry 500 passengers at a time (one-class, 10-abreast with two aisles) was a completely new concept in air transportation and it took some time for the airlines — and airports — to adjust to the problems of handling passengers in such large batches. In practice, most airlines began using their 747s with layouts for about 350 passengers, or even less, and for some time the average load factors even in these layouts were well below 50 per cent. This was possibly fortunate for the passengers, who could enjoy unprecedented spaciousness in the 747, and for airport managements, many of which had failed to make adequate provision for handling even one full 747 load, let alone two or three arriving simultaneously. For the airlines, however, these low load factors were bad news; the arrival of the 747 had co-incided with the first drop in the rate of airline traffic growth for many

*Maximum weights quoted throughout are those certificated for take-off. Max ramp weights are generally 3,000 lb (1 362 kg) greater, this being the allowance for fuel consumed during engine start, taxi and holding for take-off clearance.

†Later re-registered N1352B

years and the airlines were left introducing the most expensive and biggest new equipment in their history in a period of economic decline.

The overcapacity problem was aggravated, in the first year or so of 747 operations, by the engine problems. The JT9D, still early in its life and lacking the background of prior military operating experience enjoyed by almost every other new type of powerplant, was down on performance and had a high premature removal rate. Even before airline deliveries began there had been a major problem with the engine installation, attributable to lack of rigidity in the two-point-mounting of the engine to the pylon. This mounting was such that the turbine casing distorted in some flight conditions, causing loss of efficiency and high specific fuel consumption. At one point, in September 1969, when Boeing had rolled out 22 747s, 17 were still on the flight line at Everett awaiting the arrival of modified engines, and deliveries at this time were running some four weeks late.

Those 747s that did enter service in 1970 did so with engines still not fully up to standard, and it was not until the fully modified JT9D-3A was introduced that the problems began to be resolved. Subsequently, Pratt & Whitney made available a version of this engine, the JT9D-3AW, with water injection, allowing a take-off thrust of 45,000 lb (20 412 kg) to be developed, and Boeing took advantage of this to offer an optional increased weight for the 747 (without significant structural change) of 735,000 lb (333 390 kg).

When Pan American converted its initial fleet of Boeing 747s to have the -3AW engines, it adopted the designation 747A for these aircraft, but such designation was not an official Boeing one. Following earlier Boeing practice with the smaller members of its jet transport family, the early production 747s were identified as series 100s, each individual customer model having a separate "dash" number (eg, -121 for Pan American, -136 for British Airways etc) in which the first digit indicated the 100 series aircraft and the final two were specific to the customer.* All the 100 series 747s have the same fuel capacity of 47,210 US gal (178 690 l) regardless of take-off weight, but there are naturally differences in cabin layouts, ranging from Northwest Orient's spacious 57 first-class plus 261 tourist-class, to British Airways' 27 first-class plus 383

*After all possible two-digit numbers had been used for Boeing customers, a letter/number combination was adopted, running from A1 to A9, then B1 to B9 and so on, and is still used with the series indicator as a prefix. Thus, Wardair's Boeing 747 is a -1D1, a 100 series with D1 being specific to Wardair.

On its first flight, the company-owned Boeing 747 prototype was accompanied by Boeing's Canadair Sabre chase-plane. The undercarriage remained extended on the first flight.

economy class; associated with these differences are various numbers and locations of galleys and toilets. One of the innovations of the 747 cabin layout was the provision of an upper deck lounge behind the flight deck, reached by spiral staircase from the main deck; originally 16 and now 32 passengers may be seated in the upper lounge but many airlines opted to use this area as a cocktail bar, a feature proving especially popular with 747 passengers.

The family grows

Even before the first flight of a Boeing 747, the company had announced plans for a developed version with improved payload/range performance, obtained by increasing the gross weight yet again. This was called, in November 1968, the 747B (now the 747-200B) and was announced at a gross weight of 775,000 lb (351 530 kg) based on the use of JT9D-7 engines with a take-off rating of 45,500 lb st (20 657 kgp). Subsequently, Pratt & Whitney offered the JT9D-7W with water injection and a thrust of 47,900 lb (21 747 kg) flat rated to 86 deg F, compared to 80 deg F for the dry rating. Some changes were made in the structure and the undercarriage design to permit operation at the higher weight and provision was made for extra fuel in the wings to give a basic capacity of 51,430 US gal (194 660 l); overall dimensions and accommodation

remained the same as the 747-100. First flight of a 747-200 was made on 11 October 1970, and after certification on 23 December the same year, the second variant of Boeing's "Jumbo Jet" entered service (with KLM) early in 1971.

Further stages of engine development have subsequently allowed Boeing to improve the 747 in several steps. The JT9D-7A with a dry rating of 46,950 lb st (21 315 kgp) to 80 deg F became available and then the JT9D-7AW at 48,570 lb st (22 133 kgp) to 86 deg F, with water injection, allowed the gross weight to be increased to 785,000 lb (356 070 kg). El Al took delivery of the first 747 at this higher weight in April 1973, this being the 200th 747 delivered. Then, in 1975, came the JT9D-7F, at 48,000 lb st (21 790 kgp) dry to 80 deg F and 50,000 lb st (22 700 kgp) wet to 86 deg F, with another step up in certificated gross weight to 805,000 lb (365 470 kg). At their dry ratings, all these new engines could be applied to the 747-100, and some operators using both models of the 747 found it convenient to standardize on the power plant although the extra power was of little value in the 747-100. Other operators found it worthwhile to convert -3 engines to -7 configuration, when they became known as -7CNW (conversion, water-injection). With the higher gross weight, it also became possible to offer a further increase in fuel capacity, with 800 US gal (3 028 l) each in extended range tanks in the outer wings, plus some small changes in the standard tanks, increasing total capacity to 53,161 US gal (201 214 l). The first 747 delivered to Middle East Airlines, in May 1975, was also the first with JT9D-7FW engines and 805,000 lb (363 200 kg) gross weight, while Qantas was the first airline to receive an extended-range 747-200. The significance of these improvements was well shown when South African Airways decided to have the long-range tanks installed in its five 747-200s during 1975, with the engines uprated to -7FW standard at the same time; the result was that some 80 more passengers could be carried on the non-stop London-Johannesburg route by the modified aircraft.

Whilst Boeing was taking advantage of these engine developments — and with the prospect of still more power being offered not only by Pratt & Whitney but also by General Electric and Rolls-Royce, as noted later — other variations on the 747 theme were being studied in the context of specific customer requirements. The first such variant to emerge was the short-range 747SR, tailored to the needs of Japan Air Lines for an aeroplane of large-capacity operating over shorter ranges than those for which the 747-100 had been optimized. Although the 747SR retains the normal tankage of the -100,

To enhance the utility of the Boeing 747 in the freighting rôle, a hinged nose was developed, permitting straight-in loading to the main cabin. This feature is used on both the 747C convertible (above) and the 747F freighter (below), the latter having no cabin windows.

47,210 US gal (178 690 l), its gross weight is limited to a lower figure since full tanks are never required for the ranges flown; operating over shorter stage lengths, however, the SR experiences a greater frequency of take-offs and landings per flying hour than do other 747 variants and as a result some structural modifications were necessary. Japan Air Lines has acquired a total of seven 747SRs, the only examples built to date, and inaugurated service on the Tokyo-Okinawa route on 9 October 1973; powered by JT9D-7AW engines, two have a max permissible take-off weight of 610,000 lb (276 940 kg) and

the remainder are limited to 570,000 lb (258 780 kg), and three of these aircraft are arranged to carry 16 first-class and 482 tourist-class passengers — the largest capacity of any airliner in regular use.

Whereas the 747SR was optimized for short ranges, the next 747 variant, the 747SP, has been designed for operation on very long ranges, where the traffic density does not require the use of the fully-developed 747-200B. The SP designation indicates Special Performance, and this is the first Jumbo Jet to have different dimensions, the fuselage being shortened by 47

(Top of page) The first Boeing 747SP in Pan American colours, as used since March 1976 on routes from New York and Los Angeles to Tokyo. (Below) The first Boeing E-4A for the USAF, as originally flown with JT9D engines (see page 177 also).

ft (14,34 m) to allow a typical mixed-class accommodation of 288 and max high-density arrangement for 360. Using the JT9D-7A or -7F engine but with a gross weight of only 663,000 lb (301 000 kg), the 747SP has a greatly improved field performance, allowing it to fly out of relatively short, or hot/high, airfields with its full payload and still cover very long ranges. Fuel capacity is the same as for the basic 747-100.

As well as the shorter fuselage, the 747SP has a number of significant structural and other changes, among which are the use of single-slotted variable pivot type trailing edge flaps, reduced-gauge structural materials in the wing, small link fairings for the flap guides, revised wing/fuselage fairings and leading-edge fillets, tailplane span increased by 10 ft (3,05 m), fin height increased by 5 ft (1,52 m) and undercarriage structure weight reduced. The 747SP was announced by Boeing in September 1973 and on the 10th of that month Pan American ordered 10 of the new model (since reduced to five).

Boeing 747-200 cutaway drawing key

1 Radome
2 Radar dish
3 Pressure bulkhead
4 Radar scanner mounting
5 First class cabin, typically 32 seats
6 Windscreen
7 Instrument panel shroud
8 Rudder pedals
9 Control column
10 Flight-deck floor construction
11 First-class bar unit
12 Window panel
13 Nose undercarriage bay
14 Nosewheel door
15 Steering mechanism
16 Twin nosewheels
17 Radio and electronics racks
18 Captain's seat
19 Co-pilot's seat
20 Flight engineer's panel
21 Observer's seats
22 Upper deck door, port and starboard
23 Circular staircase between decks
24 Cockpit air conditioning duct
25 First-class galley
26 First-class toilets
27 Plug-type forward cabin door, No 1
28 First-class seats
29 Cabin dividing bulkhead
30 Anti-collision light
31 Cabin roof construction
32 Upper deck toilet
33 Upper deck seating, up to 32 passengers
34 Window panel
35 Air conditioning supply ducts
36 Forward fuselage construction
37 Baggage pallet containers
38 Forward under-floor freight compartment
39 Communications aerial
40 Upper deck galley
41 Meal trolley elevator
42 Lower deck forward galley
43 No 2 passenger door, port and starboard
44 Air conditioning system intake
45 Wing-root fairing

46 Air conditioning plant
47 Wing spar bulkhead
48 Fresh water tanks
49 Forward economy-class cabin, typically 141 seats
50 Wing centre section fuel tank, capacity 17,000 US gal (64 345 l)
51 Centre section stringer construction
52 Cabin floor construction
53 Fuselage frame and stringer construction
54 Main fuselage frame
55 Air distribution duct
56 Air conditioning cross-feed ducts
57 Risers to distribution ducts
58 Machined main frame
59 Sattelite navigation aerial
60 Starboard wing inboard fuel tank, capacity 12,300 US gal (46 555 l)

61 Fuel pumps
62 Engine bleed-air supply
63 Krueger flap operating jacks
64 Inboard Krueger flap
65 Starboard inner engine
66 Starboard inner engine pylon
67 Leading edge Krueger flap segments
68 Krueger flap drive mechanism
69 Krueger flap motors
70 Re-fuelling panel

71 Starboard wing outboard fuel tank, capacity 4,420 US gal (16 730 l)
72 Starboard outer engine
73 Starboard outer engine pylon
74 Outboard Krueger flap segments
75 Krueger flap drive mechanism
76 Extended range fuel tank, capacity 800 US gal (3 028 l) each wing
77 Surge tank
78 Starboard wing tip
79 Navigation light
80 VHF aerial boom
81 Fuel vent
82 Static dischargers
83 Outboard, low-speed, aileron
84 Outboard spoilers
85 Outboard slotted flaps
86 Flap drive mechanism
87 Inboard, high-speed, aileron
88 Trailing edge beam
89 Inboard spoilers
90 Inboard slotted flap
91 Flap drive mechanism
92 Centre fuselage construction
93 Starboard undercarriage bay housing
94 No 3 passenger door
95 Wing-mounted main undercarriage bay
96 Flap drive motors
97 Undercarriage beam
98 Fuselage-mounted main undercarriage bay
99 Main undercarriage jack
100 Floor panels
101 Seat rails
102 Cabin window trim panels
103 Centre cabin economy-class seating, typically 82 passengers
104 Nine-abreast seating
105 Air distribution ducts
106 No 4 passenger door, port and starboard

107 Centre cabin galley
108 Overhead baggage racks (with doors)
109 Main air supply duct
110 Rear cabin galley
111 Rear cabin seating, typically 114 passengers
112 Economy-class seating
113 Overhead baggage racks
114 Cabin roof panels
115 Control cable runs

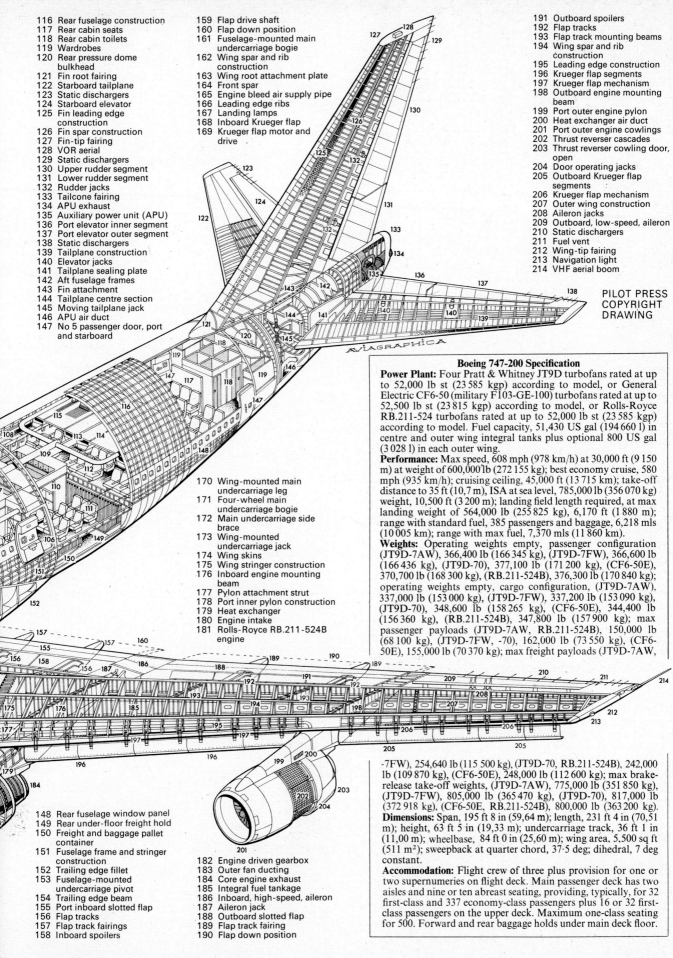

116 Rear fuselage construction
117 Rear cabin seats
118 Rear cabin toilets
119 Wardrobes
120 Rear pressure dome bulkhead
121 Fin root fairing
122 Starboard tailplane
123 Static dischargers
124 Starboard elevator
125 Fin leading edge construction
126 Fin spar construction
127 Fin-tip fairing
128 VOR aerial
129 Static dischargers
130 Upper rudder segment
131 Lower rudder segment
132 Rudder jacks
133 Tailcone fairing
134 APU exhaust
135 Auxiliary power unit (APU)
136 Port elevator inner segment
137 Port elevator outer segment
138 Static dischargers
139 Tailplane construction
140 Elevator jacks
141 Tailplane sealing plate
142 Aft fuselage frames
143 Fin attachment
144 Tailplane centre section
145 Moving tailplane jack
146 APU air duct
147 No 5 passenger door, port and starboard

159 Flap drive shaft
160 Flap down position
161 Fuselage-mounted main undercarriage bogie
162 Wing spar and rib construction
163 Wing root attachment plate
164 Front spar
165 Engine bleed air supply pipe
166 Leading edge ribs
167 Landing lamps
168 Inboard Krueger flap
169 Krueger flap motor and drive

191 Outboard spoilers
192 Flap tracks
193 Flap track mounting beams
194 Wing spar and rib construction
195 Leading edge construction
196 Krueger flap segments
197 Krueger flap mechanism
198 Outboard engine mounting beam
199 Port outer engine pylon
200 Heat exchanger air duct
201 Port outer engine cowlings
202 Thrust reverser cascades
203 Thrust reverser cowling door, open
204 Door operating jacks
205 Outboard Krueger flap segments
206 Krueger flap mechanism
207 Outer wing construction
208 Aileron jacks
209 Outboard, low-speed, aileron
210 Static dischargers
211 Fuel vent
212 Wing-tip fairing
213 Navigation light
214 VHF aerial boom

PILOT PRESS COPYRIGHT DRAWING

170 Wing-mounted main undercarriage leg
171 Four-wheel main undercarriage bogie
172 Main undercarriage side brace
173 Wing-mounted undercarriage jack
174 Wing skins
175 Wing stringer construction
176 Inboard engine mounting beam
177 Pylon attachment strut
178 Port inner pylon construction
179 Heat exchanger
180 Engine intake
181 Rolls-Royce RB.211-524B engine

148 Rear fuselage window panel
149 Rear under-floor freight hold
150 Freight and baggage pallet container
151 Fuselage frame and stringer construction
152 Trailing edge fillet
153 Fuselage-mounted undercarriage pivot
154 Trailing edge beam
155 Port inboard slotted flap
156 Flap tracks
157 Flap track fairings
158 Inboard spoilers

182 Engine driven gearbox
183 Outer fan ducting
184 Core engine exhaust
185 Integral fuel tankage
186 Inboard, high-speed, aileron
187 Aileron jack
188 Outboard slotted flap
189 Flap track fairing
190 Flap down position

Boeing 747-200 Specification

Power Plant: Four Pratt & Whitney JT9D turbofans rated at up to 52,000 lb st (23 585 kgp) according to model, or General Electric CF6-50 (military F103-GE-100) turbofans rated at up to 52,500 lb st (23 815 kgp) according to model, or Rolls-Royce RB.211-524 turbofans rated at up to 52,000 lb st (23 585 kgp) according to model. Fuel capacity, 51,430 US gal (194 660 l) in centre and outer wing integral tanks plus optional 800 US gal (3 028 l) in each outer wing.

Performance: Max speed, 608 mph (978 km/h) at 30,000 ft (9 150 m) at weight of 600,000 lb (272 155 kg); best economy cruise, 580 mph (935 km/h); cruising ceiling, 45,000 ft (13 715 km); take-off distance to 35 ft (10,7 m), ISA at sea level, 785,000 lb (356 070 kg) weight, 10,500 ft (3 200 m); landing field length required, at max landing weight of 564,000 lb (255 825 kg), 6,170 ft (1 880 m); range with standard fuel, 385 passengers and baggage, 6,218 mls (10 005 km); range with max fuel, 7,370 mls (11 860 km).

Weights: Operating weights empty, passenger configuration (JT9D-7AW), 366,400 lb (166 345 kg), (JT9D-7FW), 366,600 lb (166 436 kg), (JT9D-70), 377,100 lb (171 200 kg), (CF6-50E), 370,700 lb (168 300 kg), (RB.211-524B), 376,300 lb (170 840 kg); operating weights empty, cargo configuration, (JT9D-7AW), 337,000 lb (153 000 kg), (JT9D-7FW), 337,200 lb (153 090 kg), (JT9D-70), 348,600 lb (158 265 kg), (CF6-50E), 344,400 lb (156 360 kg), (RB.211-524B), 347,800 lb (157 900 kg); max passenger payloads (JT9D-7AW, RB.211-524B), 150,000 lb (68 100 kg), (JT9D-7FW, -70), 162,000 lb (73 550 kg), (CF6-50E), 155,000 lb (70 370 kg); max freight payloads (JT9D-7AW,

-7FW), 254,640 lb (115 500 kg), (JT9D-70, RB.211-524B), 242,000 lb (109 870 kg), (CF6-50E), 248,000 lb (112 600 kg); max brake-release take-off weights, (JT9D-7AW), 775,000 lb (351 850 kg), (JT9D-7FW), 805,000 lb (365 470 kg), (JT9D-70), 817,000 lb (372 918 kg), (CF6-50E, RB.211-524B), 800,000 lb (363 200 kg).

Dimensions: Span, 195 ft 8 in (59,64 m); length, 231 ft 4 in (70,51 m); height, 63 ft 5 in (19,33 m); undercarriage track, 36 ft 1 in (11,00 m); wheelbase, 84 ft 0 in (25,60 m); wing area, 5,500 sq ft (511 m²); sweepback at quarter chord, 37·5 deg; dihedral, 7 deg constant.

Accommodation: Flight crew of three plus provision for one or two supernumeries on flight deck. Main passenger deck has two aisles and nine or ten abreast seating, providing, typically, for 32 first-class and 337 economy-class passengers plus 16 or 32 first-class passengers on the upper deck. Maximum one-class seating for 500. Forward and rear baggage holds under main deck floor.

The Boeing 747 lends itself to the application of colourful airline markings, such as the new KLM scheme shown above. This is the first of KLM's Combi versions, with side cargo door and General Electric engines. Shown right is Japan Air Line's 747-246F all-freighter, with no cabin windows; this also has the side cargo door.

First flight was made on 4 July 1975 and this and two more SPs flew a total of 544 hrs 27 min by the end of the year to complete the FAA certification programme, while the fourth 747SP flew another 140 hrs on a round-the-world demonstration flight.

Full type certification was obtained for the "Junior Jumbo" on 4 February 1976 and Pan American took delivery of its first 747SP on 5 March — this being the 270th 747 delivered by Boeing to that date. Deliveries to Iranair and South African Airways followed in the same month and the SP began to show the special performance for which it had been designed — making, for example, a 40-hr round-the-world flight in Pan American service early in May with only two stops (at Delhi and Tokyo) between leaving and returning to New York, and a 10,290-ml (16557-km) delivery flight from Seattle to Cape Town in March, setting a world distance record for commercial aircraft.

Cargo and power plant developments

Boeing's original plans to produce front-loading cargo and convertible models of the 747 early in the production sequence — the 31st airframe had been intended to be the first convertible — were amended in the light of the early weight growth, which eroded the aircraft's utility in the cargo carrying rôle. Not until the 747-200 series aircraft became available did the Jumbo Freighter become a viable proposition, and the first 747 with the hinged nose flew on 30 November 1971, subsequently entering service with Lufthansa on 19 April 1972 after certification on 7 March. For the pure freighting rôle, the 747F has no fuselage windows and is provided with a fully

mechanized loading/off-loading system that makes it possible for a two-man team to handle and stow the maximum freight payload of 254,640 lb (115 500 kg) in 30 min.

In addition to 10 pure freighters sold by Boeing to five operators to date, three operators have bought six 747C convertibles, all of which also have the nose loading door. The two 747Cs sold to Iraqi Airways have, in addition to nose loading, a side-loading cargo door aft of the wing. This door, providing a clear opening 11 ft 2 in (3,40 m) wide and 10 ft 0 in (3,05 m) in height makes it possible to carry freight in the rear portion of the main cabin while passengers occupy the forward area (only the reverse arrangement being possible with the nose-loading convertibles) and its introduction by Boeing in 1973 represented a major addition to the flexibility of the 747 in airline service. To date, five airlines have ordered ten 747 Combis, with side loading but not nose loading doors, all these being basically series 200 aircraft. In addition, Sabena had its two -100s modified to Combi configuration, becoming the first to operate this variant in April 1974, and some two dozen other -100s have since been fitted with side doors to operate exclusively in the freighting rôle, being known as -100Fs.

The development by Pratt & Whitney of a still more powerful version of the JT9D has made it possible for the freighting potential of the 747 to be further enhanced. The JT9D-70, which is a major modification of the basic engine design featuring a larger diameter fan, an extra low-pressure supercharging stage, a new burner and other improvements, offers a dry thrust of 53,000 lb st (24 062 kgp) up to 86 deg F; available from mid-1976 onwards, it permits operation of the 747 at a gross weight of 817,000 lb (370 918 kg) and the first airline to take advantage of this improvement was Seaboard World, with an order for 747Fs which are specially equipped to carry up to 14 intermodel freight containers, each measuring 8 ft by 8 ft by 20 ft (2,4 m by 2,4 m by 6,1 m); the first of these "Containerships", as they are called by Seaboard, entered service in August 1974 with -7W engines and an

BOEING 747 CUSTOMER VARIANTS

CUSTOMER	MODEL	FIRST ORDER DATE	QUAN-TITY *	ENGINE	TAXI WEIGHT lb (kg) ×000	FIRST DELIVERY	NOTES
AEROLINEAS ARGENTINAS	287B	MAR 75	1	JT9D-7F	808 (366,8)	76	One -132 leased prior to this delivery, ex-Delta
AIR CANADA	133	FEB 68	5	JT9D-3A/7	713 (323,7)	FEB 71	
	233B	APR 74	1	JT9D-7	778 (353,2)	MAR 75	Side cargo door fitted
AIR FRANCE	128	SEP 66	16	JT9D-3/7W/7AW	738 (335,0)	MAR 70	Five with -3 engines converted to -7CNW; six with -7W; five with -7AW
	228F		1	JT9D-7AW	788 (357,8)	OCT 74	Side cargo door fitted
	228F	SEP 75	1	CF6-50E	803 (364,6)	76	
AIR INDIA	237B	MAR 67	5	JT9D-7W	778 (353,2)	MAR 71	
ALITALIA	143	DEC 66	2	JT9D-3	738 (335,0)	MAY 70	Engines converted to JT9D-7CNW
	243B		3	JT9D-3	778 (353,2)	MAR 71	Engines converted to JT9D-7CNW
AMERICAN	123	NOV 66	16	JT9D-3A	713 (323,7)	MAY 70	Two converted to -123F with side cargo door and 738 (335,0) weight; three sold to Flying Tiger, two to Trans-Mediterranean, one to NASA
BRITISH AIRWAYS	136	AUG 66	18	JT9D-3A/7	738 (335,0)	APR 70	First seven have -3A engine
	236B	JUN 75	6	RB.211-524B	803 (364,6)	77	
BRANIFF	127	JAN 68	1	JT9D-3A	713 (323,7)	JAN 71	
CHINA AIR	132	MAR 75	(2)	JT9D-7A	738 (335,0)	MAR 75	One bought, one leased from Boeing, ex-Delta
	SP-09	FEB 76	1	JT9D-7A	663 (301,0)	APR 77	
CONDOR	230B	APR 70	2	JT9D-3	778 (353,2)	APR 71	Engines converted to JT9D-7CNW
CONTINENTAL	124	OCT 66	4	JT9D-3A	713 (323,7)	MAY 70	Three sold to IIAF, one to Wardair (via Boeing)
CP AIR	217B	NOV 72	4	JT9D-7AW	778 (353,2)	NOV 73	
DELTA	132	JUL 67	5	JT9D-3A	713 (323,7)	SEP 70	One to Aerolineas, two to China Air (via Boeing)
EASTERN	131	JUN 67	(4)	JT9D-3AW	713 (323,7)	OCT 70	Sold to TWA before delivery, Eastern later leased 747-121s from Pan American
EL AL	258B	JAN 68	2	JT9D-7W	778 (353,2)	MAY 71	
	258B		1	JT9D-7AW	803 (364,6)	APR 73	
	258C	MAR 75	1	JT9D-7FW	808 (366,8)	DEC 75	Nose loading; no side cargo door
FLYING TIGER	123F	FEB 74	(3)	JT9D-3A	738 (335,0)	AUG 74	Purchased from American and converted with side freight door. Three more to be acquired
IBERIA	156	APR 68	2	JT9D-7W	738 (335,0)	OCT 70	
	256B		1	JT9D-7W	778 (353,2)		
IIAF	124F		(3)	JT9D-7AH	738 (335,0)		Purchased from Continental and converted with side freight door
	131F	FEB 75	(9)	JT9D-7AH	735 (335,0)	SEP 75	Purchased from TWA and converted with side freight door
IRISH	148	JAN 67	2	JT9D-3A	713 (323,7)	DEC 70	One leased by Air Siam
IRANAIR	SP-86	OCT 73	3	JT9D-7A	663 (301,0)	MAR 76	
	286B	APR 75	2	JT9D-7F	778 (353,2)	OCT 76	Side cargo door fitted
IRAQI AIRWAYS	270C	JAN 75	2	JT9D-7FW	808 (366,8)	76	Side cargo door fitted, plus nose loading
JAL	146	JUN 66	3	JT9D-3AW	713 (323,7)	APR 70	
	146		5	JT9D-7W/7AW	738 (335,0)		Fifth aircraft only with -7AW engines
	246B		12	JT9D-7W/7AW	778 (353,2)	FEB 71	Last three have -7AW engines
	246F		1	JT9D-7AW	778 (353,2)	SEP 74	Side cargo door fitted
	SR-46	OCT 72	2	JT9D-7AW	613 (278,3)	SEP 73	One seats 498, one seats 464
	SR-46		5	JT9D-7AW	573 (260,0)		Two seat 498, three seat 460
KLM	206B	MAR 67	7	JT9D-3AW/7W	778 (353,2)	JAN 71	
	206B	JUL 74	2	CF6-50E	803 (364,6)	OCT 75	Side cargo doors fitted
KOREAN	2B5B	JUN 70	2	JT9D-7W	778 (353,2)	MAY 73	Also one 747-100F with side cargo door leased from World
LUFTHANSA	130	MAY 66	3	JT9D-7W	738 (335,0)	MAR 70	
	230B		2	JT9D-7W	778 (353,2)	MAY 71	
	230F		1	JT9D-7W	778 (353,2)	APR 72	
	230B	MAY 75	2	CF6-50E	808 (366,8)		Side cargo doors fitted
MEA	2B4B	JUN 74	3	JT9D-7FW	808 (366,8)	MAY 75	Side cargo door fitted
NASA	123		(1)	JT9D-7AH	738 (335,0)	77	Purchased from American and modified to carry/launch space shuttle orbiter. Gross weight 778 (353,2) later
NATIONAL	135	FEB 67	2	JT9D-3AW	713 (323,7)	SEP 70	
NORTHWEST	151	NOV 66	10	JT9D-7	713 (323,7)	APR 70	
	251B		5	JT9D-7W	778 (353,2)	MAR 71	
	251F		4	JT9D-7F	778 (353,2)	JUL 75	
OLYMPIC	284B	MAR 73	2	JT9D-7AW	778 (353,2)	JUN 73	
PAN AMERICAN	121	APR 66	25	JT9D-3AW	713 (323,7)	DEC 69	One leased to Air Zaire. Three converted to have side cargo door
	121		8	JT9D-3A	738 (335,0)		Engines converted to JT9D-7CN
	SP-21	SEP 73	5	JT9D-7A	663 (301,0)	MAR 76	
QUANTAS	238B	NOV 67	15	JT9D-3A/7A/7F	778 (353,2)	JUL 71	First two only with -3A engines. Three have 53,030 US gal (200 720 l) fuel. One with side cargo door
SABENA	129	JAN 69	2	JT9D-3A	713 (323,7)	NOV 70	Converted to have side cargo doors and JT9D-7CNW engines in 1974
SAS	283B	DEC 67	2	JT9D-3AW/-7W	778 (353,2)	FEB 71	One each with -3AW and -7W engines
SEABOARD WORLD	245F	FEB 73	2	JT9D-7W/70	820 (372,3)	AUG 74	First delivered with -7W engines and 778 (353,2) weight. Side cargo door fitted
SINGAPORE	212B	JUL 72	5	JT9D-7A	778 (353,2)	JUL 73	
SAA	244B	MAR 68	5	JT9D-7W	778 (353,2)	OCT 71	Converted to have JT9D-7FW engines and 805 (365,5) weight with extra fuel
	SP-44	JUL 74	6	JT9D-7FW	666 (302,4)	MAR 76	
SWISSAIR	257B	DEC 67	2	JT9D-3AW	778 (353,2)	JAN 71	
SYRIAN ARAB	SP-94	DEC 74	2	JT9D-7A	663 (301,0)	MAY 76	
TAP	282B	SEP 70	4	JT9D-7/7A	778 (353,2)	FEB 72	Two with -7 engines. Two with -7A engines leased to Pakistan International 1976
TRANS-MEDITERRANEAN	123F		(2)	JT9D-3AW	738 (335,0)	MAY 75	Purchased from American, converted with side cargo door
TWA	131	SEP 66	19	JT9D-3AW	713 (323,7)	DEC 69	Engines converted to JT9D-7CN
UNITED	122	NOV 66	18	JT9D-3A	713 (323,7)	JUN 70	
USAF	E-4A	FEB 73	4	F103-GE-100	778 (353,2)	JUL 73	First two flown with JT9D-7W engines, later converted to have F103s. Fourth aircraft is E-4B, weight 803 (364,6)
WARDAIR	1D1	NOV 72	1	JT9D-3A	738 (335,0)	APR 73	Also one 747-124 purchased ex-Continental
WORLD	273C	MAR 72	3	JT9D-7AW	778 (353,2)	APR 73	One has been leased to Korean, one to Pan American

* Qualities in parentheses indicate re-sales, not counted in total of sales

(Above) The aerial refuelling capability of the 747 was shown in tests conducted in 1972, with a KC-135 type refuelling boom under the rear fuselage.
(Below right) Redesigned nacelles indicate that this Boeing E-4A has the definitive General Electric F103 turbofans adopted by the USAAF for its six aircraft of this type.

800,000 lb (363 200 kg) gross weight (for subsequent updating) and has since been joined by the first example with -70 engines.

As Boeing's need for more powerful engines developed, first General Electric and then Rolls-Royce re-entered the contest to provide power-plants of over 50,000 lb (22 700 kgp) for the 747, and with some success. Boeing and General Electric agreed in August 1972 to undertake the flight testing of a 747 version fitted with CF6-50 engines in order to "broaden the market potential for the airplane" and the company-owned 747 first flew with 51,000 lb st (23 154 kgp) CF6-50Ds installed on 26 June 1973. A 130-hr programme was flown, providing the basis for subsequent certification when a specific sale of CF6-50-powered 747s occurred, and Boeing began to offer versions of the Jumbo Jet with CF6-50D or E engines under the tentative designation of series 300 (since dropped) at a gross weight of 800,000 lb (363 200 kg). The first customer for this engine-airframe combination proved to be the USAF (as noted later) but Lufthansa, KLM and Air France have all now ordered 747 freighters or Combis with 52,500 lb (23 813 kg) thrust CF6-50Es, the first delivery having been made to KLM in October 1975.

Application of the Rolls-Royce RB.211 to the 747 came somewhat later and was made at the behest of British Airways, which wanted to standardize on the British engine (already used in its TriStars) whilst taking advantage of a further improvement in performance derived from the RB.211's excellent cruising sfc. For use in the 747-200B, however, the RB.211-524 needed to be uprated from its TriStar thrust of 48,000 lb (21 792 kg) to a minimum of 50,000 lb (22 700 kg) and this required British government backing for a development programme for the engine version known as the RB.211-524B. Between April 1974 and June 1975, the government withheld its approval pending a hoped-for second customer for the Rolls-engined 747 but a go-ahead on the RB.211-524B was eventually sanctioned on the basis of British Airways' order for four aircraft (now increased to six) and favourable market forecasts.

Flight testing of the RB.211 in the first 747 for British Airways was to begin in Seattle in September, with deliveries starting early in 1977. At the 50,000-lb (22 700-kg) rating, the RB.211-524B will allow operation of the 747 at weights up to 800,000 lb (363 200 kg); later, a 53,000-lb (24 062-kg) thrust RB.211-524D is expected to become available, permitting operation at 817,000 lb (372 918 kg). The entire range of Pratt & Whitney, GE and RR engines is offered by Boeing in all 747 versions, including freighters, Combis and SPs.

Military models — and others

Although well over 95 per cent of the 3,000 jetliners sold by Boeing since 1955 have been built for commercial use, the company has never neglected the military potential of its various types of aircraft. In the case of the 707, of course, Boeing sold 820 examples of the KC-135 that evolved from the same prototype (these being in addition to the commercial

total) and has also sold a useful number of 707s to the US and overseas governments for various military duties. The 727 has enjoyed little success in military rôles but the 737 was adopted as a navigation trainer by the USAF and it was natural therefore that military prospects for the 747 should be considered from an early stage in the programme.

The first success in this direction came early in 1973 when the USAF selected the 747-200 for its Advanced Airborne Command Post (AABNCP) programme, which provided for an eventual total of seven aircraft to replace EC-135s in use in the same rôle. The first two such aircraft, with the designation E-4A, were ordered on 27 February 1973 and were delivered in July and December the same year, with JT9D-7W engines and an interim avionics fit transferred from EC-135s. Two more AABNCPs were ordered in the course of 1973, however, of which the second was to be equipped to a more advanced standard as the E-4B, with the other three to be similarly modified in due course. USAF also decided to adopt the 52,500 lb st (23 835 kgp) General Electric CF6-50E engines (as the F103-GE-100) in all its E-4s, and the third E-4A flew with these engines on 6 June 1974, the two earlier aircraft being subsequently retrofitted to the same standard.

The E-4 programme has recently undergone some amendments in order to meet the available funding, and now embraces only six aircraft in all, each aircraft being equipped to serve either as an NEACP (National Emergency Airborne Command Post) or in the more specific Strategic Air Command "Looking Glass" rôle. The fourth aircraft (the first E-4B) is now flying but will not be delivered to the USAF until August 1979, and the three E-4As, now operating from Andrews AFB, will not be modified to E-4B configuration until after all three E-4Bs have been delivered, so that the full fleet of six E-4Bs will not be in service until February 1983.

A much larger potential military market exists for the 747 in the USAF's present Advanced Tanker Cargo Aircraft (ATCA) requirement, which is intended to enhance the strategic mobility of US forces. Increasing emphasis upon a national policy of quick response to overseas needs by US-based forces has brought a need for new tanker/transport

continued on page 200

GERMANY'S JAGUARS

The Anglo/French Jaguar strike/reconnaissance fighter is now in service with four squadrons in RAF Germany and two of these, Nos 14 and 17 at RAF Bruggen, have been declared operational to SACEUR. No 14 Squadron recently won, for the second year in succession, the RAF Germany navigation and bombing competition for the Salmond Trophy, with No 17 coming second. In the photograph above, one Jaguar GR Mk 1 from each squadron in Germany is seen being flown by the respective Squadron Commanders: leading, No 14 Squadron (Wg Cdr Anthony Mumford); left, No 31 Squadron, also at RAF Bruggen (Wg Cdr Terry J Nash); right, No 17 Squadron (Wg Cdr Roy Humphreyson) and far right, No 2 (AC) Squadron (Wg Cdr R A F Wilson). On the left is depicted a Jaguar of No 2 (AC) Squadron, showing the reconnaissance pod carried by the aircraft of this Laarbrüch-based unit, and below, a two-seat Jaguar T Mk 2 from No 14 Squadron.

TALKBACK

Spanish Bulldogs and Estonian Spitfires

WITH REGARD to the correspondence appearing in *Talkback* in the August and November 1973 and February 1974 issues, I recently came across British confirmation that, as previous correspondents had suggested, the Bristol Bulldogs participating in the aerial fighting over the Basque front in 1937 came from Estonia. This confirmation is in the form of a memorandum dated 9 August 1937 from Wg Cdr F M F West, air attaché in Helsingfors. At that time, air attachés everywhere were on the lookout for suspicious transfers of aircraft lest governments or private companies endeavoured to break the terms of the "Non-Intervention" agreements, hence the memo to the British Foreign Office.

West reported that, on 28 July, he had met Col Tomberg, Chief of the Estonian Air Force, and had requested permission to visit the fighter squadron at Tallinn and the army co-operation squadron at Rackvere. Col Tomberg had suggested that he visit Jågala instead. At the end of his visit to Jågala, West had observed that there was still time to visit the other airfields. Tomberg appeared somewhat uneasy, and then said: "Oh, I suppose you have heard about the sale of the Bulldog fighters and the Potez army co-operation aircraft." West indicated that he was aware of the sale and Tomberg explained that the Estonian government had been offered "such a wonderful price" for these obsolete aircraft — enough money, in fact, to purchase a dozen really modern fighters, such as Hurricanes — and eight Bulldogs and eight Potez 27s had been loaded aboard ship at Tallinn at the end of May.

In the event, the Estonians ordered 12 Spitfires and a training programme was, as stated by a previous correspondent, set up in the UK, but the contract was, not surprisingly, terminated on orders of the British government on 13 September 1939. This cancellation would seem extraordinarily late, considering that it must have long been obvious that these Spitfires, Britain's latest fighters, would, had they been delivered, have landed up in the hands of the Russians, or Germans, or both! Perhaps official cancellation of the order was overlooked in the general confusion that reigned at this time. However, on 14 December

In response to Mr Amendola's request below, our contributor Jack Bruce has supplied this photograph of Guynemer's Spad 13, taken at the Belgian field Les Moëres on 10 September 1917. On the next day, Guynemer was posted missing, probably but not definitely in this same aircraft. No complete photographs or full details of the colours and markings are known to exist.

1939, the British Air Ministry did approve the export of 25 wooden propellers to Estonia, with the comment: ". . . the political aspect of the supply is also recommended". Someone scribbled a note on the memorandum approving supply of the propellers: "I don't quite see why the AM should regard this as *politically* desirable." To this, another anonymous official had answered, "No, but the AM so seldom thinks *anything* politically desirable that I won't quarrel with them on that score!"

It would be interesting to know what happened to the money from Spain with which the Estonians were to have bought their Spitfires. The huge sum mentioned (and presumably paid for the ancient Bulldogs and Potez 27s) is indicative of the lengths to which the Spanish Republicans were willing to go to purchase virtually anything that flew. The murky traffic included the acquisition, at *enormously* inflated prices from nefarious dealers, of a variety of aircraft types that were of little or no use in the conflict taking place in Spain. Tarazona, the I-16 pilot who flew for a brief period on the northern front, subse-

quently recorded his constant anxiety for the crews of the old crocks that had been gathered together to form a squadron which had been given the affectionately derisive nickname of "The Circus Krone", the Bulldogs presumably being included in the inventory of this unit.

Incidentally, the eight former Estonian Bulldogs had been hidden aboard ship among sacks of potatoes and were apparently offloaded at a Spanish port at the end of June. Only two of these Bulldogs were surviving by the time the North fell to the Nationalists on 22 August.

Gerald Howson
London SE18 4LS

Guynemer's Spad

Allow me to compliment you on a splendid publication and your consistency of excellence. AIR INTERNATIONAL is always a constant source of accurate reference.

I especially enjoyed the current Spad articles and wondered if there is any information and photographs available of the Spad 13 that Georges Guynemer was lost in. I have been told that it was one of the first one or two Spad 13s built and that little or nothing is known of his aircraft. I would appreciate any information you can offer on Guynemer Spad 13, including colours.

John Amendola
Washington, USA

Surviving Waco

HAVING noted Pete Garland's request (*Plane Facts*/April 1976) for photos and information on the Waco Model D, I am enclosing photos of what is reported to be the last surviving airworthy example of the type. Photographed at Rochester, New Hampshire, on 15 June 1974, the aircraft is in immaculate condition with yellow wings and gloss black fuselage. Of note are the control linkage inspection windows just forward and slightly above the lower leading edge.

Thomas Hildreth
Mass, USA

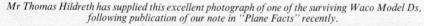

Mr Thomas Hildreth has supplied this excellent photograph of one of the surviving Waco Model Ds, following publication of our note in "Plane Facts" recently.

Why settle for one dish . . .

THERE IS, so we are told, an old Swedish axiom which, literally translated, asks: "Why settle for one dish when there's Smörgasbord?" The reader may well ask what this can possibly have to do with modelling, but it was brought to mind recently when first one and then, within a week, a half-score more readers' letters from every corner of the globe made essentially the same proposal; that we select an aircraft which, in our wisdom, we consider to be a suitable subject for the newcomer to the art of scratch-building and then describe in detail the progressive stages in recreating it in model form, simultaneously devoting our colour pages to general arrangement drawings to scale of one or more examples of the chosen aircraft type.

Since in this column (April issue) we first attempted to make a case for scratch-building, our postbag has furnished proof positive that, in so far as readers of AIR INTERNATIONAL are concerned, the pioneering spirit of at least a proportion of those following our chosen pastime has not been extinguished by the slap-'n-tickle brigade which considers itself worthy of the appellation of "modeller" solely on the strength of occasionally slapping together a plastic model kit and tickling it up with a spot of paint. This is heart-warming but those readers who feel that we should present a package which will enable them to take the first step in scratch-building without too much risk are, to our minds, missing the whole point. The essential ingredient of successful scratch-building is the desire to create something unique; a model that appears in no other collection. If we provide a blow-by-blow description of the construction of *one* individual aircraft type of our choice, the uniquity that only scratch-building can provide is lost and the modeller might as well remain just another "kit-basher".

Scratch-building is a very individual aspect of modelling; the novice can pick up helpful tips but trial and error play a major rôle and translate the tyro into the expert. The beginner should make a careful analysis of the aircraft types within his particular sphere of interest, select the one that he believes likely to prove within his capabilities, thoroughly research it until he has both ample reference and the "feel" of the chosen aircraft, and then commit himself. Why go for one aircraft type that is likely to be modelled by countless others; there are tens of thousands of types to choose from. In other words, why settle for one dish . . . ?

This month's colour subject

On 1 June, the 1,400th Lockheed Hercules to roll off the line, a C-130H, was handed over to the USAF Military Airlift Command's 463rd Tactical Airlift Wing based at Dyess AFB, Abilene, three months short of 22 years after the first flight of the first YC-130 prototype at Burbank on 23 August 1954 — 22 years in which this extraordinarily successful aircraft has repeatedly demonstrated how appropriate was the choice of the name of the legendary hero of Greek mythology as its appellation. It is doubtful if any transport aircraft, not excluding the immortal Douglas C-47, has ever demonstrated greater versatility than the C-130 Hercules and there would seem to be every likelihood that, given another dozen or so years, the Hercules will even emulate the smaller Douglas aircraft in the variety of national insignia that it will carry.

Some two score national air arms now include one or another version of the Hercules in their inventories or anticipate adding the C-130 to their logistic support components in the years immediately ahead, and thus this Lockheed-Georgia product — the story of which was told in very considerable detail in the November and December issues of AIR INTERNATIONAL — offers the modeller considerable variety of finish and insignia, only the surface of which is scratched by the colour profiles presented on the two following pages. The kit manufacturing industry has not given the modeller a wealth of choice on the other hand, as the only kit so far offered to an accepted standard scale is that to 1/72nd scale from Airfix.

Fortunately, few will wish to look further as Airfix's offering is a very good kit indeed and, although representing the C-130K, alias Hercules C Mk 1, of the RAF, it calls for virtually no modification to adapt it as a C-130E or C-130H. It makes up into a large model, with a span of more than 22 in (56 cm), but despite its size, it presents no constructional problems, although painting is best tackled with an airbrush as the large areas involved are by no means easily covered by hand brushing without leaving disfiguring brush marks. The decals accompanying the kit are, of course, for the RAF Hercules C Mk 1 and the camouflage suggested is the now-superseded desert-style scheme, but, as already said, a wide variety of markings and finishes are applicable.

The only other kit worth considering is that offered by Revell which originally appeared many years ago as a C-130A, was re-issued as the C-130B and then again as the "Blue Angels" support aircraft, a KC-130F, in which form it remains in the current catalogue. Despite the age of this kit, it makes up into an attractive and basically accurate model, but coming as it does from a period when scale was of little consideration, it does not fit *precisely* into any of the currently accepted scales, being to 1/140th. However, it is near enough to 1/144th to be acceptable to all but the most fastidious of scale addicts.

Belated termagant

Long, long ago, Frog produced a kit of the de Havilland D.H.110, the progenitor of the Hawker Siddeley Sea Vixen. Surprisingly two decades later — a score of years in which the Sea Vixen was developed, entered service, served and was duly retired — we are finally offered a kit of the production Sea Vixen FAW Mk 2. Belated, perhaps, but none-the-less welcome. A comparison of the original D.H.110 kit and that of the Sea Vixen is instructive in that it affords a clear indication of the transformation of the model kit state of the art that has taken place over the intervening years.

This 1/72nd scale kit in Frog's Orange Series comprises 65 component parts in this manufacturer's usual dark blue-grey plastic, these being well formed with very fine surface detailing of primarily the raised line variety. The kit assembles well and calls for very little filing or filling, but some care is needed to ensure the correct alignment of the tail surfaces with the wings as the tailbooms are separated just aft of the centre section. The cockpit interior could certainly make use of more detail, comprising, as it does, merely a floor, a seat and a pilot figure. However, interior detail is offered by the wells for the neat yet sturdy undercarriage. The nose needs to be weighted in order to balance the tail, but this problem is simplified by provision of a separate nose cone which, providing ample room for weights, can be affixed after the major assemblies are completed. We recall that Frog's early D.H.110 kit, while very basic and lacking the refinement of the latest product, *did* provide lead weights and a nose housing for them.

Four Red Top missiles are provided for the underwing pylons, with further external stores in the form of two Matra pods and two drop tanks. There is an in-flight refuelling probe to be located on the leading edge of the port wing and the outer wing panels may be assembled in the folded position if so desired, cover plates being included for the exposed roots — an admirable feature. The undercarriage may be assembled either extended or retracted. The decal sheet is good, with markings for two different aircraft, XJ580 while serving with No 899 Sqdn aboard HMS *Eagle* in January 1972 and sporting this unit's well-known "Gauntlet" emblem on the fins, and XN690 of No 829 Sqdn at RNAS Yeovilton in 1968.

A teutonic miscellany

The available range of German WW II aircraft is widened yet again by the Airmodel concern with the issue of four new vacuum-formed kits, two of which represent really offbeat subjects — the Blohm und Voss BV 40 glider fighter and the Junkers Ju 288 V3 — and the others, if somewhat more prosaic, representing two important but hitherto unavailable types, the Junkers Ju 90 and the Heinkel He 59. Simplest of the quartet, from the modelling viewpoint, is naturally the tiny BV 40 glider, the kit consisting of only seven component parts. These parts call for some rubbing down to remove unwanted pimples but are otherwise quite well moulded. Details of the take-off dolly and landing skid are provided by the instruction sheet, but these items must perforce be scratch-built by the modeller. The Ju 288 bore nothing more than a superficial

continued on page 184

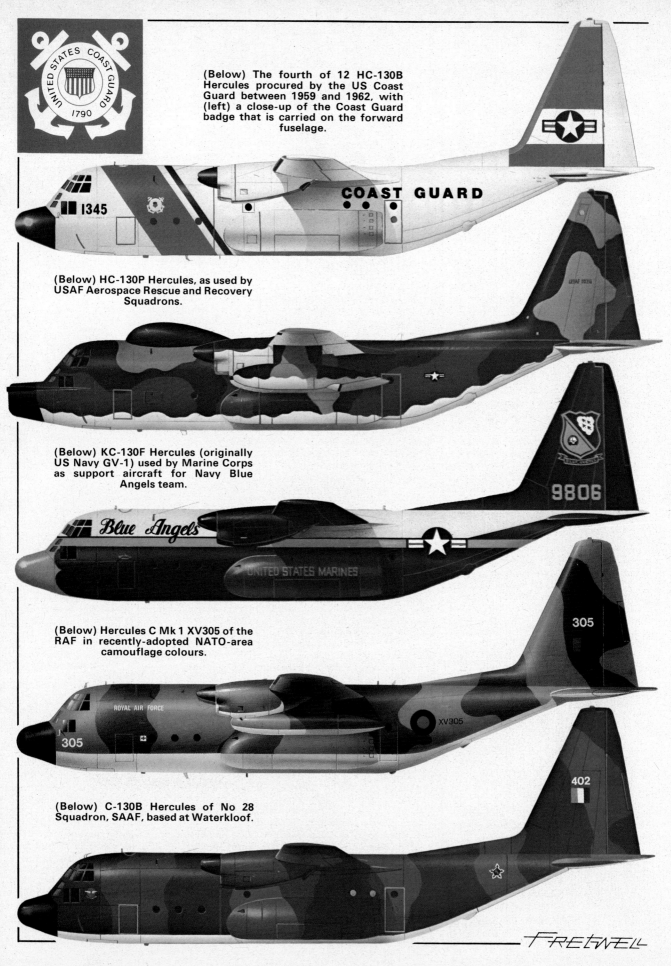

(Below) The fourth of 12 HC-130B Hercules procured by the US Coast Guard between 1959 and 1962, with (left) a close-up of the Coast Guard badge that is carried on the forward fuselage.

COAST GUARD

1345

(Below) HC-130P Hercules, as used by USAF Aerospace Rescue and Recovery Squadrons.

(Below) KC-130F Hercules (originally US Navy GV-1) used by Marine Corps as support aircraft for Navy Blue Angels team.

9806

Blue Angels

UNITED STATES MARINES

305

(Below) Hercules C Mk 1 XV305 of the RAF in recently-adopted NATO-area camouflage colours.

ROYAL AIR FORCE

305

XV305

402

(Below) C-130B Hercules of No 28 Squadron, SAAF, based at Waterkloof.

FRETWELL

(Below) C-130H Hercules of No 721 Squadron, Royal Danish Air Force, based at Værløse and (left) a close-up of the badge of No 721 Squadron.

(Below) One of the eight C-130H Hercules recently delivered to the Hellenic Air Force.

(Below) One of two C-130B Hercules delivered to the Jordanian Air Force from USAF stocks.

(Below) A Libyan Arab Air Force C-130H, one of eight delivered.

(Below) C-130E Hercules of No 16 Squadron, the Royal Saudi Air Force.

ENTHUSIAST——— *from page 181*

resemblance to its predecessor, the Ju 88, and this kit comprises 21 parts, but the modeller has to provide the engines (BMW 801Gs) and propellers, and produce from scratch the complex and somewhat ungainly four-wheel undercarriage. Full details of these parts and of the cockpit interior are provided. Incidentally, the big cockpit canopy is a very good one-piece moulding with nicely embossed framing.

The Ju 90 was, from several aspects, a pace-setter among pre-WW II commercial airliners, although the small numbers of this *grosse Dessauer* built were to see rather more extensive service with the *Luftwaffe* than with DLH for which they were intended. This kit is neatly moulded, the smaller parts being particularly clean and sharp, and with a total of 65 components, it is quite impressive. The typical Junkers "double-wing" trailing-edge flappery is included, as are also the wheels and engine cowlings, but the remainder of the undercarriage and the actual engines with their propellers must be provided by the modeller. Perhaps the most interesting of this quartet is the He 59 which was widely used by the *Luftwaffe* during WW II on second-line tasks, particularly air-sea rescue and navigational training — the kit offering alternative nose sections to enable the model to be completed as an example performing either of these duties. This is certainly no kit for the novice and will tax the skill of even an experienced modeller. All the major components of the He 59 are provided, the 24 component parts including fuselage, wings, tail surfaces, floats, engine nacelles and propellers, the modeller having to create lots of struts and other small components, but very clear instructions are provided, together with excellent assembly and general arrangement drawings. These kits will be available in the UK through the usual channels but we have no details of prices at the time of writing.

The 'Matchbox' Mitchell . . .

The North American B-25 Mitchell has now appeared in kit form more than a half-dozen times and it might be assumed, therefore, that the market has been satiated, an assumption which Lesney has evidently not made as this bomber provides the subject matter for the latest kit in the 'Matchbox' Red Range to be received. The B-25 is available in 1/72nd scale from both Airfix and Frog, and Monogram, apparently by accident rather than design, came close to this scale at 1/70th with its offering of this type. The Frog B-25D may now be somewhat difficult to obtain, but Airfix's B-25J and Monogram's B-25H should be generally available, so this new 'Matchbox' kit has some established competition.

How does this débutante compare with the other B-25 kits already on the market? In our opinion, it comes out very well and has the advantage of providing alternative component parts which permit either the "solid" nosed B-25H or the glazed nose B-25J to be produced. Comprising 81 parts sensibly moulded in basic olive drab, mid-green and black plastic, it is a comprehensive, accurate and well-detailed kit. There is not, as may be expected, a wealth of interior detail, but externally the model produced by this kit is more than adequate. The surface detailing is an odd mix of rather heavily engraved panelling lines on the wings with very fine raised lines elsewhere. Careful

attention has obviously been devoted to the problem of getting the cowling shape correct, each cowling having been moulded in three parts to enclose the one-piece engine. The fuselage-mounted forward-firing guns of the B-25H are moulded separately and there are very clear transparencies for both this and the B-25J, including landing lights in the wing leading edges.

The decal sheet is of good colour and register and provides three well-selected sets of markings covering a B-25H of the 1st Air Commando Group, USAAF 10th Air Force in the India-Burma theatre in 1944 (including some attractive individual nose art), a Mitchell III of No 180 Sqdn, RAF, when based at Brussels-Melsbroek late in 1944, and a similar model operated at around the same period by No 342 *Lorraine* Sqdn of the Free French Air Force. Adequate painting and marking detail is provided, and there is a very attractive box-top illustration of the USAAF B-25H in action against Japanese shipping off the Burmese coastline. The kit is, in our view, modestly priced at 95p.

The attention of the readers of this column is drawn to the fact that the Modelling Editor cannot reply to letters that are unaccompanied by return postage in the form of stamps (UK) or International Reply Coupon

---

. . . and a 'Matchbox' Messerschmitt

By coincidence, Lesney's companion offering in the 'Matchbox' Orange Range, the Messerschmitt Bf 110, faces up to competition from precisely the same three manufacturers as does the Mitchell and again the 'Matchbox' kit comes out well in the comparison. In this case, however, the competition is not quite so direct in that the Frog kit represents the Bf 110G and Monogram's the Bf 110E, leaving only the elderly Airfix Bf 110D kit to be effectively supplanted by the Lesney product which makes up as a Bf 110C or Bf 110D.

The kit has 70 component parts in light blue, yellow and brown plastic, and is moulded to a very high standard with finely raised panel lines, the rib effect on the control surfaces being particularly worthy of mention. The long, clear canopy reveals a moderate amount of interior detailing, but it will be necessary to augment this if the two crew figures are discarded. We were impressed with the fine moulding of the many small details, such as the aileron mass balances, the D/F loop, the supporting struts for the two 300-litre drop tanks and the exhaust manifolds. There are two bombs and a neatly-formed bomb rack to fit beneath the fuselage. Oddly enough, also provided is a single RZ 65 rocket tube which is intended to be fitted beneath the rear fuselage. Although no information is given regarding the actual deployment of this weapon, it would seem to have been fired at right angles to the line of flight! The undercarriage is quite sturdy without being too chunky — this can be a failing in a model of the Bf 110 if 1/72nd scale is strictly adhered to, so some tolerance is permissible. The decal sheet is again of good quality and provides markings for two aircraft, a Bf 110D-2 of 11./ZG 1 *Wespen* on the Eastern Front during the winter of 1941-42, this sporting the temporary white distemper finish and the characteristic 'wasp' emblem is a feature of the decals, and a Bf 110C-3 of 6./ZG 76 *Haifisch*

based at Le Mans in September 1940 and sporting the "Shark's Mouth" emblem. This is another highly recommended kit priced in the UK at 60p.

Building from scratch — II

Continuing our occasional notes on scratch-building in plastic sheet, we come to the construction of wings and tail surfaces. Unless one is prepared to indulge in some fairly advanced moulding processes, it is wise to keep to wings with constant chord or, at least, constant taper. Constant-chord wings are usually best constructed by the 'wrap-around' method — the upper and lower surfaces, joined at the leading edge, are drawn onto sheet plastic, due allowance being made for camber, and then the two surfaces are folded over and cemented along the trailing edge. This is something of a simplification but the principle is established. Some internal structure in the form of spars and ribs is necessary, and this should be mounted on the inside of the undersurface, the extent of the internal structure depending upon the size and thickness of the wing.

With thin wings, such as those found on most biplanes, a good method of providing strength is to build into the spar a length of OO/HO scale flat-bottomed nickel silver rail, epoxied to the bottom surface of the wing. This rail can be bent to conform to angles and thus serves a double purpose by fixing the dihedral. Where a ribbed effect is required, it should be ruled on the inside of the wing surfaces with a hard (HH) pencil or an empty ballpoint pen. If the material used for the wing is too thick for such treatment to be effective, the external surface may be scored with a fairly blunt modelling knife, thus raising fine ridges on each side of the score mark and then filling the groove with an equal mixture of tube and liquid cement applied with smooth brush strokes. Another method is to overlay thin strips of ·005-in plastic sheet, again using a brush but this time with neat liquid cement. If brushed on rapidly, the liquid cement will not damage the surface of the plastic.

Thicker wings can be built up on a substantial lower surface with a separate upper surface being added after inclusion of the internal structure. Some *very* thin wings can, of course, be single-surfaced but there is the ever-present danger of warping in such cases. Wing roots call for reinforcement where they are to be attached to the fuselage or centre section, and stiffening blocks should be built in wherever struts or other fixings have to be made.

The wingtips call for individual treatment, smaller pieces being cut to fit and moulded between finger and thumb to form curvature as needed. External surface detailing may be scribed on after assembly. Tapered wings are constructed in a similar manner but are rather more time-consuming to build owing to the preparation of tapered spars and variable-sized ribs. The opposite wing panels should always be built concurrently so that identical components are used and conformity thus ensured.

Surfaces in the smaller scales can sometimes be shaped from one or two thicknesses of sheet, and the scribing and filling method used for obtaining the rib effect, but larger scales and larger models will necessitate use of the previously-described 'wrap-around' system. □

F J HENDERSON

THE LAST SWALLOW OF SUMMER...

...THE EXTRAORDINARY STORY OF THE KI.100

SHORTLY AFTER MIDNIGHT, on 9-10 March 1945, the pathfinders of a force of 279 Marianas-based B-29 Superfortresses arrived at low altitude over Tokyo and began dropping M-47 incendiaries on a highly congested rectangular area of the Japanese capital. A high wind fanned the flames and, as the main force began to arrive over the city, dropping its M-69 clusters, the individual fires merged into one immense holocaust which was to gut almost 16 square miles (41,5 km²) of Tokyo's heart. It was with this inferno as a backdrop that one of the most extraordinary fighters in the annals of military aviation was to make its début.

Not that there was anything extraordinary in the *concept* of the fighter that flew its first operational mission that night against the B-29s bouncing about in the thermals generated by the heat of the conflagration produced in that first nocturnal assault on Tokyo. On the contrary, by the standards of the day, it *was* a thoroughly orthodox warplane. What *was* extraordinary about this débutante was the fact that its prototype had flown for the first time less than *six weeks* earlier, an event which, itself, had taken place barely *three months* from the initiation of design!

Admittedly, the 18th *Sentai*, flying from Kashiwa, Chiba, and to which went the distinction of blooding the new combat aircraft, was able to field only one example of the fighter on that fateful March night, in which more people were to lose their lives than were to be killed by either atomic blast at Hiroshima and Nagasaki three months later, but by the end of the month the bulk of the inventory of the *Sentai* was to be made up of this newly-created fighter and other *Sentais* had begun conversion, including the 244th, which, based at Chofu,

was commanded by the redoubtable Major Teruhiko Kobayashi. Indeed, in the three months that remained to Japan before final defeat, this fighter was to play a major rôle in the phrenetic battles that were to be fought in the skies over Honshu, Kyushu and Shikoku.

This newcomer to the combat scene was the end product of a prodigious engineering effort without parallel in aviation history; a creation that was purely the result of *force majeure* but a remarkable engineering achievement nonetheless. Through the 'twenties until the mid 'thirties, it had been common practice to offer potential customers for a fighter a choice of engine, air-cooled radial or liquid-cooled inline. As aerodynamic design advanced and airframes were designed more closely around a specific power plant, this practice became increasingly uncommon, and the number of types of single-seat fighter airframe that were to attain production with both air-cooled and liquid-cooled engines during WW II was singularly small, while no more than a couple gained such a status without major redesign of fundamental components.

In Germany, the Focke-Wulf Fw 190, created as a radial-engined fighter, was to be adapted to take an inline power plant, a metamorphosis facilitated by adoption of an annular radiator; in the Soviet Union a reversal of this process was to result from the adaptation by Semyon Lavochkin's design bureau of the inline-engined LaGG-3 to take a radial air-cooled power plant, thus creating the La-5, while in the UK, the Hawker Tempest was virtually conceived with alternative air-cooled and liquid-cooled engines in view. These were all marriages of choice rather than convenience, however, and it was the latter reason for marital union that was to bring about

WARBIRDS

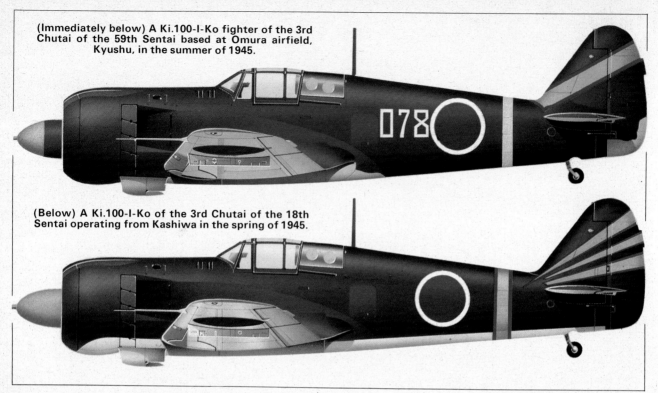

(Immediately below) A Ki.100-I-Ko fighter of the 3rd Chutai of the 59th Sentai based at Omura airfield, Kyushu, in the summer of 1945.

(Below) A Ki.100-I-Ko of the 3rd Chutai of the 18th Sentai operating from Kashiwa in the spring of 1945.

such a transformation in Japan — the creation of the radial-engined Ki.100, or Army Type 5 Fighter, from the inline-engined Ki.61 Hien (Swallow).

Takeo Doi and the Kawasaki design team had developed an excellent high-altitude interceptor fighter in the Ki.61-II-KAI Hien but one suffering an Achilles Heel in the form of a notoriously unreliable engine, the 12-cylinder inverted-vee liquid-cooled Ha-140. The problem presented by this poor reliability was compounded by the inability of Kawasaki's Akashi facility to fulfil delivery schedules, the assembly line being plagued by shortages of crankcases and cylinder blocks,

and more than half of the engines that *did* leave the assembly line failed to pass acceptance testing. By the late autumn of 1944, the number of engineless Ki.61-II-KAI airframes in open storage at the Kagamigahara factory was increasing with each passing day and the Akashi management could hold out little hope of any early improvement in the engine supply situation.

The *Koku Hombu* (Air Headquarters), in calling for drastic action to resolve this increasingly critical situation, suggested that the airframe of the Ki.61-II-KAI be adapted to take the most readily available and reliable engine of suitable power.

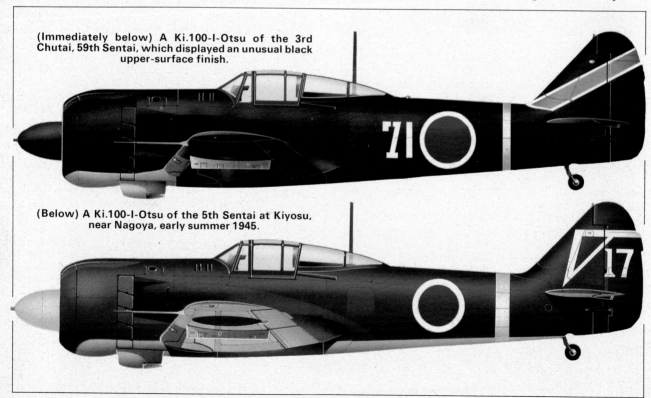

(Immediately below) A Ki.100-I-Otsu of the 3rd Chutai, 59th Sentai, which displayed an unusual black upper-surface finish.

(Below) A Ki.100-I-Otsu of the 5th Sentai at Kiyosu, near Nagoya, early summer 1945.

The Army Aerotechnical Research Institute suggested the Mitsubishi Ha-112-II 14-cylinder two-row radial and, after only tentative discussions with the Kawasaki team, the *Koku Hombu* authorised the use of this power plant on 24 October 1944.

The initial reaction of Takeo Doi to the proposal to use the Ha-112-II engine was unfavourable; he asserted that the mating of this 48-in (1,46-m) diameter power plant with the 33-in (0,84-m) fuselage width of the Ki.61-II-KAI airframe appeared on the surface impracticable without fundamental redesign of the basic fighter and such would be time-consuming in so far as his already overburdened design staff was concerned and, in his view, held out little possibility of success. Nevertheless, no acceptable alternative readily presented itself and, despite misgivings, the Kawasaki team placed tremendous impetus behind the project, which was assigned the *Kitai* (Experimental Airframe) designation Ki.100, work proceeding around the clock.

Transformation problems
The immediate problem posed by the translation of the Ki.61-II-KAI into the Ki.100, apart from the blending of the large-diameter engine with the narrow fuselage, was that of the differing thrust lines of the two power plants. The fact that the radial air-cooled engine was marginally lighter was no major problem, the weight difference being only 99 lb (45 kg), the Ha-140 weighing 1,587 lb (720 kg) and the Ha-112-II weighing 1,488 lb (675 kg), and the CG being restored when the radiator bath, rendered superfluous by the air-cooled engine, was removed.

Possessing little experience in the application of air-cooled radials to single-engined fighters, the Kawasaki team was assisted in the design of the mounting for the Ha-112-II by a study of the engine mount and cowl design of the Focke-Wulf Fw 190A which had been acquired earlier by the Imperial Army for comparison purposes and was now delivered to the Kagamigahara factory. The original fireproof bulkhead was extended forward to avoid inordinately long engine bearers and the exhaust pipes were aligned horizontally on each side of the fuselage *à la* Fw 190A, but stood proud of the airframe, the thrust augmentation thus provided being calculated as adding 6-9 mph (10-15 km/h) to maximum attainable speed.

Work began on the adaptation of three airframes to take the Ha-112-II engine and thus serve as Ki.100 prototypes during December 1944, by which time some 200 Ki.61-II-KAI engineless airframes were in open storage at Kagamigahara. Even more impetus was given to the programme when, on 19 January, Superfortresses attacked the Akashi plant and virtually stalled further production of the Ha-140 engine. On 1 February, only seven weeks after the actual conversion work had been initiated, the first Ki.100 prototype began its flight test programme, with the second joining it eight days later and the third, embodying minor changes introduced as a result of initial flight test results, flying before the end of the month.

By the time the third prototype had joined the test programme, the modification of all existing engineless Ki.61-II-KAI airframes to take the radial engine had been ordered, these being designated Ki.100-I-Ko, or Army Type 5 Model 1-Ko, such had been the success achieved during the first three weeks of flight trials. The Kawasaki team's most sanguine expectations had been bettered and by general consensus this improvisation was an *improvement* on its progenitor. Marginally slower than the Ki.61-II-KAI at all altitudes admittedly, the Ki.100 was more manoeuvrable and offered a better climb rate to operational altitude, thanks largely to a 628 lb (285 kg) reduction in normal loaded weight, while take-off and landing characteristics were adjudged greatly improved.

At Yokota, the Ki.100 was matched with a P-51C Mustang which had been captured by Japanese troops in Central China and taken to Japan for evaluation. It was ascertained that, if slower than the USAAF fighter, the Ki.100 enjoyed a distinct advantage in manoeuvrability and possessed superior diving characteristics. From the results of a series of mock combats between the two fighters it was concluded that, given pilots of comparable capability, the Kawasaki fighter should always emerge victorious from a dogfight, but it was admitted that the Mustang pilot could break off combat at will. In so far as the

(Below) The Ki.100-I-Otsu in service with the 5th Sentai which converted to the new fighter type from the Ki.45-KAI during May 1945, 39 Ki.100s being received and these being operated from the Kiyosu airfield for the defence of the Nagoya area. Criticism of aft view from the cockpit of the Ki.100-I-Ko was answered by the -I-Otsu with a cut-down rear fuselage and extended canopy shown clearly in this view (above right).

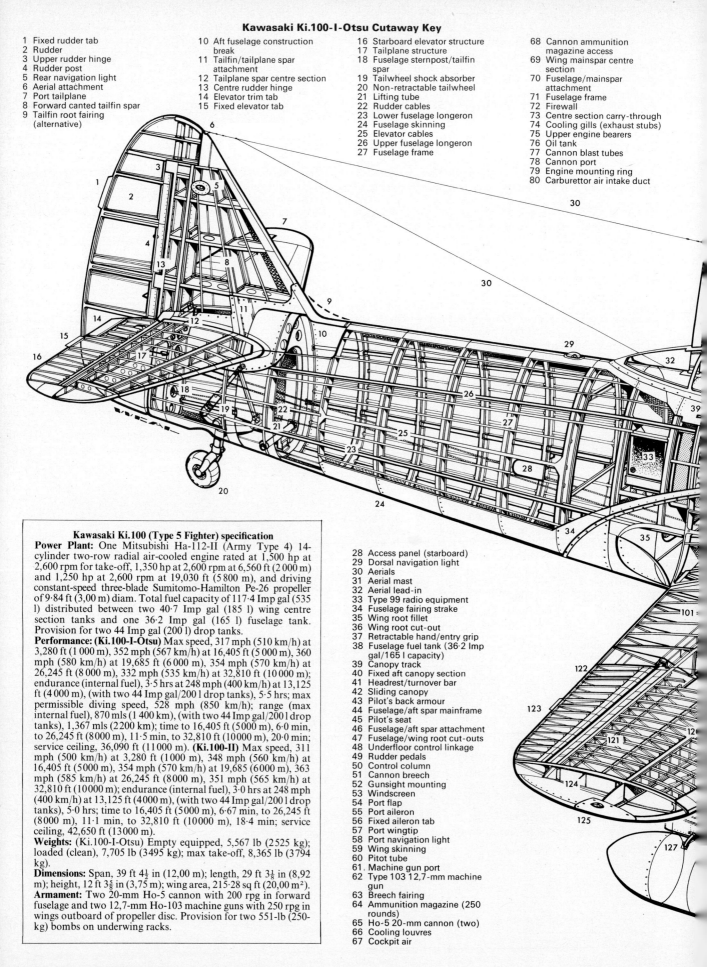

Kawasaki Ki.100-I-Otsu Cutaway Key

1 Fixed rudder tab
2 Rudder
3 Upper rudder hinge
4 Rudder post
5 Rear navigation light
6 Aerial attachment
7 Port tailplane
8 Forward canted tailfin spar
9 Tailfin root fairing (alternative)
10 Aft fuselage construction break
11 Tailfin/tailplane spar attachment
12 Tailplane spar centre section
13 Centre rudder hinge
14 Elevator trim tab
15 Fixed elevator tab
16 Starboard elevator structure
17 Tailplane structure
18 Fuselage sternpost/tailfin spar
19 Tailwheel shock absorber
20 Non-retractable tailwheel
21 Lifting tube
22 Rudder cables
23 Lower fuselage longeron
24 Fuselage skinning
25 Elevator cables
26 Upper fuselage longeron
27 Fuselage frame
28 Access panel (starboard)
29 Dorsal navigation light
30 Aerials
31 Aerial mast
32 Aerial lead-in
33 Type 99 radio equipment
34 Fuselage fairing strake
35 Wing root fillet
36 Wing root cut-out
37 Retractable hand/entry grip
38 Fuselage fuel tank (36·2 Imp gal/165 l capacity)
39 Canopy track
40 Fixed aft canopy section
41 Headrest/turnover bar
42 Sliding canopy
43 Pilot's back armour
44 Fuselage/aft spar mainframe
45 Pilot's seat
46 Fuselage/aft spar attachment
47 Fuselage/wing root cut-outs
48 Underfloor control linkage
49 Rudder pedals
50 Control column
51 Cannon breech
52 Gunsight mounting
53 Windscreen
54 Port flap
55 Port aileron
56 Fixed aileron tab
57 Port wingtip
58 Port navigation light
59 Wing skinning
60 Pitot tube
61 Machine gun port
62 Type 103 12,7-mm machine gun
63 Breech fairing
64 Ammunition magazine (250 rounds)
65 Ho-5 20-mm cannon (two)
66 Cooling louvres
67 Cockpit air
68 Cannon ammunition magazine access
69 Wing mainspar centre section
70 Fuselage/mainspar attachment
71 Fuselage frame
72 Firewall
73 Centre section carry-through
74 Cooling gills (exhaust stubs)
75 Upper engine bearers
76 Oil tank
77 Cannon blast tubes
78 Cannon port
79 Engine mounting ring
80 Carburettor air intake duct

Kawasaki Ki.100 (Type 5 Fighter) specification

Power Plant: One Mitsubishi Ha-112-II (Army Type 4) 14-cylinder two-row radial air-cooled engine rated at 1,500 hp at 2,600 rpm for take-off, 1,350 hp at 2,600 rpm at 6,560 ft (2 000 m) and 1,250 hp at 2,600 rpm at 19,030 ft (5 800 m), and driving constant-speed three-blade Sumitomo-Hamilton Pe-26 propeller of 9·84 ft (3,00 m) diam. Total fuel capacity of 117·4 Imp gal (535 l) distributed between two 40·7 Imp gal (185 l) wing centre section tanks and one 36·2 Imp gal (165 l) fuselage tank. Provision for two 44 Imp gal (200 l) drop tanks.

Performance: (Ki.100-I-Otsu) Max speed, 317 mph (510 km/h) at 3,280 ft (1 000 m), 352 mph (567 km/h) at 16,405 ft (5 000 m), 360 mph (580 km/h) at 19,685 ft (6 000 m), 354 mph (570 km/h) at 26,245 ft (8 000 m), 332 mph (535 km/h) at 32,810 ft (10 000 m); endurance (internal fuel), 3·5 hrs at 248 mph (400 km/h) at 13,125 ft (4 000 m), (with two 44 Imp gal/200 l drop tanks), 5·5 hrs; max permissible diving speed, 528 mph (850 km/h); range (max internal fuel), 870 mls (1 400 km), (with two 44 Imp gal/200 l drop tanks), 1,367 mls (2200 km); time to 16,405 ft (5 000 m), 6·0 min, to 26,245 ft (8000 m), 11·5 min, to 32,810 ft (10000 m), 20·0 min; service ceiling, 36,090 ft (11 000 m). **(Ki.100-II)** Max speed, 311 mph (500 km/h) at 3,280 ft (1 000 m), 348 mph (560 km/h) at 16,405 ft (5000 m), 354 mph (570 km/h) at 19,685 ft (6000 m), 363 mph (585 km/h) at 26,245 ft (8000 m), 351 mph (565 km/h) at 32,810 ft (10000 m); endurance (internal fuel), 3·0 hrs at 248 mph (400 km/h) at 13,125 ft (4000 m), (with two 44 Imp gal/200 l drop tanks), 5·0 hrs; time to 16,405 ft (5000 m), 6·67 min, to 26,245 ft (8000 m), 11·1 min, to 32,810 ft (10000 m), 18·4 min; service ceiling, 42,650 ft (13000 m).

Weights: (Ki.100-I-Otsu) Empty equipped, 5,567 lb (2525 kg); loaded (clean), 7,705 lb (3495 kg); max take-off, 8,365 lb (3794 kg).

Dimensions: Span, 39 ft 4½ in (12,00 m); length, 29 ft 3⅛ in (8,92 m); height, 12 ft 3⅝ in (3,75 m); wing area, 215·28 sq ft (20,00 m²).

Armament: Two 20-mm Ho-5 cannon with 200 rpg in forward fuselage and two 12,7-mm Ho-103 machine guns with 250 rpg in wings outboard of propeller disc. Provision for two 551-lb (250-kg) bombs on underwing racks.

F6F Hellcat was concerned, it was believed that the Ki.100 could best this US Navy shipboard fighter on all counts.

The fuel arrangement of the Ki.100-I-Ko was essentially unchanged from that of its predecessor, comprising two 40·7 Imp gal (185 l) tanks in the wing centre section and a single 36·2 Imp gal (165 l) tank immediately behind the pilot in the fuselage, the same Sumitomo-Hamilton propeller was employed and armament, too, was unchanged, consisting of two 20-mm Ho-5 cannon in the upper decking of the forward fuselage and two 12,7-mm Ho-103 machine guns in the wings, outboard of the propeller disc, fuselage and wing-mounted armament being provided with 200 and 250 rpg respectively.

Production of the Ki.61-II-KAI at Kagamigahara was terminated and the factory was authorised to switch immediately to manufacture of the Ki.100-I-Otsu (Type 5 Fighter Model 1-Otsu) and to establish a second assembly line at a new factory that had meanwhile been completed at Tsuiki. Every effort was now expended on re-engining the stock of some 270 Ki.61-II-KAI airframes in open storage, a task tackled with such energy that 36 Ki.100-I-Ko fighters were

delivered in March, followed by 86 in April and no fewer than 131 in May, the remaining 18 existing airframes being converted in June, in which month the Kagamigahara factory also delivered 74 new-build Ki.100-I-Otsu fighters.

On 22 June, Kagamigahara was seriously hit for the first time by B-29 Superfortresses which dropped 116 US tons (115·2 tonnes) of bombs, following this up four days later with an even more damaging raid in which the plant was almost completely destroyed. Some airframe assembly had already been dispersed throughout the surrounding woods and to a shrine a half-mile from the factory, and these dispersed units completed the assembly of components and carried these piece by piece to the ruins of the factory for final assembly. In this fashion, a further 23 fighters were to be completed in July and another 10 during August. The Tsuiki factory, which was, in fact, a former spinning mill, had succeeded in delivering its first five Ki.100s in May, a further four in June and three more in

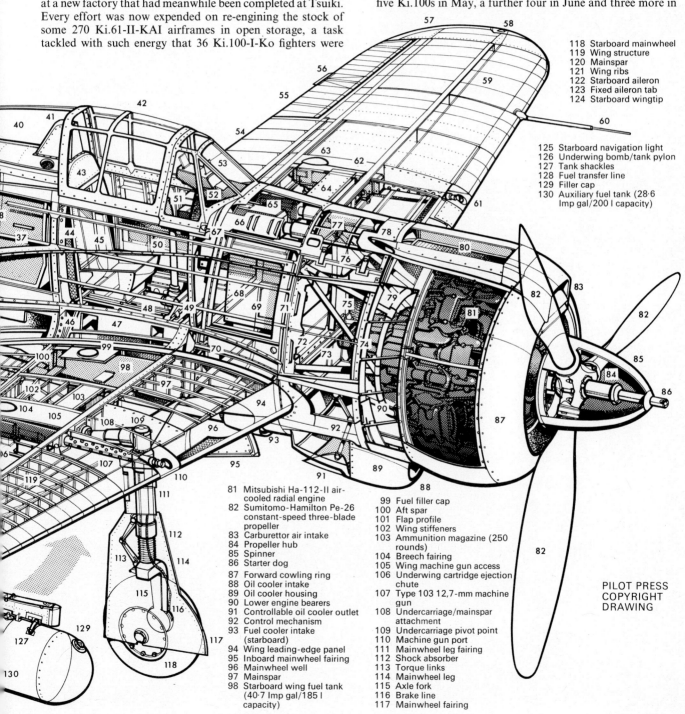

118 Starboard mainwheel
119 Wing structure
120 Mainspar
121 Wing ribs
122 Starboard aileron
123 Fixed aileron tab
124 Starboard wingtip

125 Starboard navigation light
126 Underwing bomb/tank pylon
127 Tank shackles
128 Fuel transfer line
129 Filler cap
130 Auxiliary fuel tank (28·6 Imp gal/200 l capacity)

81 Mitsubishi Ha-112-II air-cooled radial engine
82 Sumitomo-Hamilton Pe-26 constant-speed three-blade propeller
83 Carburettor air intake
84 Propeller hub
85 Spinner
86 Starter dog
87 Forward cowling ring
88 Oil cooler intake
89 Oil cooler housing
90 Lower engine bearers
91 Controllable oil cooler outlet
92 Control mechanism
93 Fuel cooler intake (starboard)
94 Wing leading-edge panel
95 Inboard mainwheel fairing
96 Mainwheel well
97 Mainspar
98 Starboard wing fuel tank (40·7 Imp gal/185 l capacity)

99 Fuel filler cap
100 Aft spar
101 Flap profile
102 Wing stiffeners
103 Ammunition magazine (250 rounds)
104 Breech fairing
105 Wing machine gun access
106 Underwing cartridge ejection chute
107 Type 103 12,7-mm machine gun
108 Undercarriage/mainspar attachment
109 Undercarriage pivot point
110 Machine gun port
111 Mainwheel leg fairing
112 Shock absorber
113 Torque links
114 Mainwheel leg
115 Axle fork
116 Brake line
117 Mainwheel fairing

PILOT PRESS
COPYRIGHT
DRAWING

This view (above) of the Ki.100-I-Otsu reveals the clean contours of the cowling of the Ha-112-II engine and the wide track of its undercarriage, creating the impression of refined sturdiness. (Below left) A Ki.100-I-Otsu serving with the 5th Sentai at Kiyosu airfield during the summer of 1945.

July when it, too, was knocked out. Thus, apart from the trio of prototypes, deliveries of the Ki.100-I fighter totalled 389 aircraft, this total consisting of 271 of the -Ko conversions and 118 of the new-build -Otsu model.

The Ki.100-I-Otsu differed from the -Ko conversion solely in its cockpit enclosure. Complaints concerning aft vision from the cockpit of the Ki.61 Hien had led to trials of one Ki.61-II-KAI with a cut-down rear fuselage and an extended canopy to provide all-round vision, this having originally been intended for the proposed Ki.61-III. These changes were embodied by the Ki.100-I-Otsu.

The Ki.100 joins combat

As fast as the Hien airframes could be fitted with the Ha-112-II engine they were issued to the fighter *Sentais,* the units receiving the new aircraft being allowed no working-up period before commencing operational flying. The first unit to fly the Ki.100 in action was, as previously recounted, the 18th *Sentai,* which, throughout the latter half of March 1945, operated this type from Kashiwa in concert with Ki.61s, but it was the 244th *Sentai* that became the first to completely convert to the new fighter, achieving this during April at Chofu and being redeployed to Chiran, Kyushu, on 20 May to provide cover for the special attack units operating from Kyushu against Okinawa.

The 244th, which had been formed late in the previous year

Ki.100-I-Ko fighters of the 59th Sentai at Omura airfield, Kyushu, in the summer of 1945. This former Ki.61 Hien unit was primarily devoted to B-29 intercept missions.

Those that made the grade...

and some that didn't.

INFORMATION WANTED

Location of photos of wartime BOAC aircraft: particularly Catalinas at Hythe, Rose Bay and Baltimore; Ansons at Montreal, Vaaldam and Northolt; Oxfords at Whitchurch, Hurn, Vaaldam and Cairo; Hudsons at Leuchars, Montreal, Asmara, Western Desert and Croydon; Halifaxes at Whitchurch; Albemarle at Lyneham; Beech AT-7 at Baltimore; Rapide, Ju 52/3m, Lockheed 10s and 14s in West Africa. Or any BOAC aircraft in RAF Transport Command markings with four letter codes. D. M. Hannah, Barnack, Stamford, Lincs. Tel. (0780) 740373.

(1021KX

Location of photos of Liberators used for repatriation of US servicemen interned in Sweden about 1944-45. Any information would be gratefully received by D. M. Hannah, Barnack, Stamford, Lincs. Tel. (0780) 740373.

(1022KX

INSURANCE

INSURANCE, J. A. HARRISON (BROKERS) LTD. of Birmingham sell insurance. Our speciality aircraft insurance. A Century of Service. Phone, call or write: Security House, 160-161 Bromsgrove Street, Birmingham, B5 6NY. Tel. 021-692 1245 (10 lines).

(1002AY

PUBLICATIONS

PLASTIC AIRCRAFT MODELS MAGAZINE. Specimen copy 40p. PAM NEWS, 22 Slayleigh Avenue, Sheffield, S10 3RB.

(1011LY

AVIATION BOOKS. Out-of-print and current. State specific needs. JOHN ROBY, 3703R Nassau, San Diego, California 92115, USA.

(1013KY

RAF SERIALS K1000–K9999. Full details, including fates, of this most interesting batch of service aircraft in a LIMITED PRINT RUN A4 size AIR-BRITAIN Monograph. 96 pages including 12 pages large photos. Price: Non-Members £3·00 or Members £2·00, post paid in Europe. Air-Britain Sales, Stone Cottage, Great Sampford, Saffron Walden, Essex CB10 2RS.

(1023KX

SOCIETIES

CLUB SECRETARIES. Club Ties, Blazer Badges, Drill Badges, Heraldic Shields, Brevets, Lapel Badges, Car Badges, Brochure from Club (Sales), 76 Greenford Avenue, Southall, Middlesex.

(1015LY

INCREASE YOUR AVAILABLE INFORMATION SOURCES. JOIN AIR-BRITAIN and get access to our specialist services, publications and library. Send 10p stamp for details (or 50p for sample House Journal) to H. B. Gwyther (A16), 208 Stock Road, Billericay, Essex CM12 0SH.

(1016KX

on the Ki.61, enjoyed considerable success in fighter-versus-fighter combat with its new mount. On 3 June, for example, the unit was to claim the destruction of seven F4U Corsairs in a pitched battle. Transferred to Yokaichi for the defence of the Osaka-Kobe area on 15 July, the 244th *Sentai* fought an epic conflict with a numerically superior formation of F6F Hellcats on 25 July, claiming 12 "kills". The 5th *Sentai* at Kiyosu, near Nagoya, began conversion to the Ki.100 from the Ki.45 Toryu during May, and for a period operated both types, two ex-Ki.61 *Sentais* to convert to the Ki.100 being the 17th and the 59th, the former being deployed to Taipei (Taiwan) from where it flew to Ishigaki Island in the Ryukyus to provide cover for attack aircraft engaged in the Okinawa battle and the latter flying B-29 intercept missions from Ashiya, Kyushu. One unit that flew the Ki.100 with somewhat less distinction was the 111th *Sentai,* which, not formed until 10 July 1945, possessed virtually no cadre of experienced pilots, being manned almost entirely by novices with 100 or fewer hours' flying training. Although the Ki.100, with its ease of handling and forgiving nature, gave even the least experienced pilot a fighting chance, those flying with the 111th from Komaki proved easy prey for marauding P-51D Mustangs, and the unit was quickly decimated.

In general, the Ki.100 enjoyed the popularity of pilots and ground crews alike, and was generally considered the most reliable combat aircraft in the entire Imperial Army inventory. At low- and medium-altitudes, the Ki.100 was superb and potentially the master of all fighter opponents other than the P-51D Mustang which began to appear over the home islands as a B-29 escort from 29 May 1945, flying from bases on Iwo Jima. The Ki.100 versus P-51D battles were ferocious and their outcome was usually determined by piloting skill and numerical advantage rather than any discrepancy between the relative capabilities of the fighter types involved.

Above 23,000 ft (7000 m), the performance of the Ki.100 fell off badly, the fighter thus being relatively ineffective against high-flying B-29s, but the need to improve the high-altitude capabilities of the aircraft had been appreciated from an early stage, and in March 1945, as soon as initial flight testing had indicated the potential of the re-engined Hien, Takeo Doi had attempted to make good the altitude shortcomings by mating the Ki.100 with a turbo-supercharger. The turbine was placed beneath the engine and the supercharger installation was similar to that previously employed by the Ki.102-Ko, this lending itself readily to Ki.100 application and calling only for the relocation of some fuel lines and accessories, and the transfer of the centrally-located ventral air scoop to starboard. Space restrictions prohibited the installation of an intercooler and associated ducting, and air was fed directly from the compressor to the carburettor. Provision was also made for the insertion aft of the cockpit of a 24·2 Imp gal (110 l) capacity tank for methanol-water, this being intended to boost power below the rated altitude of the engine, the mixture acting as an anti-detonant and enabling higher boost pressures to be used for short periods. This last installation was also intended to be applicable to the Ki.100-I.

The first of three prototypes to be fitted with the Ru-102 turbo-supercharger, designated Ki.100-II, was completed within six weeks of design work commencing, flying in May 1945, the second and third prototypes following at fortnightly intervals. Although the lack of intercooler restricted the high-altitude performance of the Ki.100-II, the turbo-supercharger-equipped fighter displayed a noteworthy improvement over the Ki.100-I, although the hand-made joints in the exhaust collector ring suffered excessive leakage with the result that the rated altitude of each prototype differed under test. Ordered to use A1 coated carbon steel for the exhaust system, Kawasaki considered this to have been a mistake and was considering the use of alternative materials when hostilities terminated together with the Ki.100-II test programme.

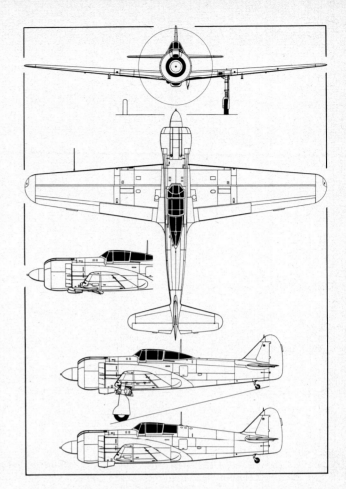

The general arrangement drawing above depicts the Ki.100-I-Otsu, the scrap view illustrating the Ki.100-II and the bottom sideview shows the Ki.100-I-Ko.

Being 386 lb (175 kg) heavier than the Ki.100-I, the Ki.100-II therefore suffered some performance penalty below 23,000 ft (7 000 m), but above that altitude a marked improvement in capability was to be seen, maximum speed being attained at 26,250 ft (8 000 m). Preparations were in hand for the series production of the Ki.100-II in place of the -I-Otsu during the summer of 1945, the production model featuring a wooden tail assembly which was being developed as part of a programme for the substitution of wood for more critical materials, but the war ended before any such plans could be implemented.

If the marriage between the Ki.61-II-KAI airframe and the Ha-112-II engine had been purely one of convenience, it was an outstandingly successful marital union; the 500 or so Ki.100 fighters in which it resulted gave an exceptionally good account of themselves in the closing months of the war despite operating almost continuously under conditions of enemy numerical supremacy and with a high proportion of relatively inexperienced pilots. Perhaps most remarkable was the fact that the life span of this fighter, from initial concept to final demise, had covered barely 10 months!

A former 18th *Sentai* pilot, Masashi Sumita, who was one of the first to fly the Ki.100 in combat, when asked recently to compare his former mount with the P-51D Mustang, commented: "In my view, the Ki.100 was capable of taking on two Mustangs at one time. Its turning capability was such that there was no problem in shaking a Mustang from one's tail. The engine of the Ki.100 was excellent and in my opinion the Kawasaki fighter suffered only two serious defects; the fuses of the electrical gun operating mechanism were prone to blowing and the radio equipment was virtually useless in many circumstances." □

ON RETAINING A NUMBER OF OPTIONS WHILE NOT RE-INVENTING THE WHEEL

M Y FRIENDS may characterise me as a slob for spending whole evenings glued to the tube, but I maintain that if we were not intended to watch TV, then we would not have been gifted with retention of vision. Nevertheless, it must be admitted that many programmes are evidently transmitted in the belief that if you are living in Leeds, then anything that happens in Los Angeles is worth seeing. For the record, I do not subscribe to this theory. I have been to Los Angeles many times, and you may judge its fascination from the fact that my knowledge is still limited to the stretch between the airport and the place where I get my head down, which must be all of three minutes' drive along Sepulveda Boulevard. When someone operates a 747SP non-stop between Heathrow and Honolulu, then for me LA will be obsolete, and they can bulldoze it straight into the ocean with my blessing. Perhaps they will then locate their TV scenarios in some more interesting place, such as Leeds, or Clapham.

I mention this possibility because I used to know a girl who lived in Clapham. In terms of looks, she was only a run-of-the-mill sex-bomb, but she happened to work in an office that sold missionary pots to Black Africa. These artifacts were listed on the official documentation (she assured me) not as "cooking pots, hand-finished, 500 litres", but simply as "Missionary Pots"! To come to the first point in this essay, in my personal view, when you have seen an Englishman selling missionary

pots in Black Africa, then you have truly witnessed the Brit at his best.

The second point emerged from a conversation I had many years ago with Fritz Hoffert, one of the brightest preliminary design men in Europe. I asked him why the Federal Government was then treating the industry like dirt, and he expounded a theory that the politicians of the day considered the true role of the German citizen to be putting Volkswagens together and leaving the crazy Americans to take all the risks of that highly unstable aviation business.

Extrapolating these two points into a coherent pattern, if we take it that all the people of the European nations have already found their true vocations in life, then WHAT IN HELL ARE WE DOING, ALL REDESIGNING THE F-16?

This innocent inquiry will doubtless bring an irate hail of semi-literate denials from the European industry's top brass, who probably couldn't recognise an F-16 anyway. However, having just completed a survey of every military project office between the Atlantic and the Urals, I can assure you that this is exactly what is happening! If I were David Lewis, I would be busting my gut laughing. Lewis works for General Dynamics, and is the only preliminary design man in living memory to have got anywhere, if you consider being the president of the corporation to be an advance on being a project engineer. We can debate that one some other time.

The F-16 affair raises all kinds of interesting questions. Will future historians conclude that the myopia of European air forces in drafting operational requirements has done more damage to industry than all the depradations of doctrinaire socialism? Is the fighter business about to go through a whole series of yawn-worthy non-innovations, such as the airliner business experienced after Sud Aviation unveiled the Caravelle? Should we instead go straight for some mind-boggling milestone designed around a new generation of technology? Would Europe be well advised to jettison its fighter development capability, and simply produce US aircraft under licence? Ought we to get out of the tin-bashing business altogether, and go back to marketing missionary pots, constructing cuckoo clocks and putting together people's cars? Can some compromise formula be found that serves the long-term defence interests of the Free World, and yet is acceptable economically to both Europe and the US? *Whatever happened to the girl from Clapham?*

Soviet Secrecy

The case for an independent European capability to develop military aerospace hardware rests on many factors, but one of the most important is the unprecedented secrecy in which the Soviet Union operates. As long as the Free World has to prepare its defences while largely in the dark about the potential enemy's future materiel, then a certain diversity of approach will remain essential for flexibility. The analogy may be dangerous, but for a gunfight in which you can't see your opponent, a sawn-off shotgun is probably more useful than a sniper's rifle. The objective must therefore be to retain a reasonable number of options in each class of equipment, yet to avoid unnecessary duplication of effort. In other words, don't re-invent the wheel!

Communist-block secrecy has been a problem for so long that its effects are often overlooked, and it is forgotten that in recent years the Soviet Union has become more furtive than ever. Up to 1961 an air show was held at Tushino (Moscow) almost every year, and in retrospect it appears that most aircraft were shown just as soon as they became available. Photography by the public and the foreign press was banned, but nonetheless took place using simple cameras. In that particular year, which happened to be the occasion for unveiling a new wave of military aircraft, a photographer (for whom the KGB are probably still looking) managed to get full coverage of the aircraft taking part, using professional equipment. According to stories that circulated after this event, British Technical Intelligence opposed publication on the grounds that it would scare the Russians off, but the photographs nevertheless appeared in a well-known US

weekly. Since the Tushino Show promptly disappeared without trace, it might be said that Tech Intelligence were right (for once), but publication did serve the useful purpose of drawing to the attention of a very large audience the impressive technical capabilities of the Soviet Union.

The next major show took place six years later at a different Moscow airfield (Domodedovo), when photography was permitted for the first time, and several jet lift and variable sweep aircraft were exhibited. However, following that event the security curtain clamped down once again, and this time it stayed down. The full range of Soviet military aircraft has consequently not been shown to the public for the last *nine years.*

It is important that the implications of this gap in our knowledge are recognised. Given minimal interference from the operator and his purchasing agency, any manufacturer should be able to fly a new fighter within three years of the start of design, and commence deliveries three years later. A nine-year gap in our flow of intelligence therefore means that the Soviet Union could easily be testing (and might conceivably have in limited service) several types of advanced aircraft of which the West has no knowledge whatever.

There are, of course, other sources of intelligence than air shows, but most come into play only when an aircraft is in widespread use. A great deal of Western information on Soviet developments comes from US satellite photographs (which presumably account for much of our knowledge of *Backfire*), but the usefulness of this system is limited by cloud cover, the large number of airfields available, photographic resolution, and the ease with which small fighters can be hidden. The situation may be further confused by the Soviet use of dummy aircraft. Once a new type has been issued to units in East Europe, there is no secret about its principal characteristics or status, but a small aircraft operated within Soviet territory might be kept totally secret for several years. The post-Domodedovo gap therefore means that there is now much more risk of the West being surprised by new Soviet fighter developments than was the case (for example) when the MiG-15 appeared in Korea in 1950, or the MiG-21 entered service in 1959, both of these aircraft having been seen previously Tushino.

The risk of the Soviets establishing a lead in some branch of development is particularly relevant to the case of V/STOL aircraft. Such information as is made generally available by the Russians indicates that jet lift projects (eg *Faithless, Flagon-B*) have been abandoned in favour of STOL aircraft with variable-sweep wings (Su-17/20, MiG-23 etc). On the other hand, the writer's occasional conversations with Soviet designers and officials have suggested that at least one VTOL

Seen hovering above the deck of the Soviet carrier Kiev, *the* Forger *is a subsonic V/STOL strike fighter of lift-plus-lift/cruise configuration, two vertically-disposed lift engines being mounted in tandem immediately aft of the cockpit and the vectored-thrust engine having twin nozzles just aft of the wing trailing edge. The swivelling nozzles are angled slightly forward in the hover and the lift engines are mounted at a slight aft sloping angle.*

close support aircraft and a jet lift STOL transport project have been initiated in recent years. The construction of the *Kiev*-class aircraft carriers without catapults (a fact confirmed with the appearance of the *Kiev* in the Mediterranean and the Atlantic) suggests that V/STOL fighters such as *Forger* recently revealed — albeit possibly so far in evaluation quantities — may well be used in the near future to provide Soviet naval air defence, surveillance, and support for amphibious landings.

The threat of the Russians secretly making major advances in V/STOL technology provides a good illustration of the benefits to Western defence of maintaining an independent military aircraft design capability in Europe. Experience over the last 20 years has proved that for the US, V/STOL has been worse than a blind spot. It has been an area of progress in which American willingness to attempt what appears to be impossible has rebounded with devastating effect, resulting in a series of projects which at best proved unsuitable for further development and at worst splattered aluminium over the landscape.

In contrast, European insistence on a simple powerplant concept has led (with some US financial assistance) to the only workable V/STOL fighter system known in the West, the Pegasus-engined Harrier. Although so far serving only with the RAF, USMC, and *Armada Española* (and slated for service with the Royal Navy), the Harrier has given the West invaluable experience of operating jet lift aircraft from a wide variety of ships and land bases in many parts of the world, and of using thrust vectoring in air combat. The project has thus provided, at comparatively little cost, not only a possible basis for later developments, but realistic operational data from which the future potential of this radical new concept may be assessed.

However, the Harrier programme also illustrates some of the problems that have plagued European progress in military aircraft. The most obvious potential customer for the Harrier has always been the German Air Force, since every *Luftwaffe* base would be vulnerable in the event of war and since Germany has the road network and forests that make dispersed operation feasible. The fact that Germany has never shown serious interest in purchasing Harriers might have been ascribed to nationalism in the early days of the project, but the most important and constant factor against this and any other European fighter has been US insistence on the purchase of arms from America to offset the balance of payments deficit

incurred by maintaining US forces in Germany. If Europe is to play its full part in military aircraft development, then not only must there be international collaboration in formulating operational requirements, but there must also be much more freedom of competition in the military market.

Bargaining Chips

It can be argued that the cost of maintaining an independent technological capability in Europe is far too high in relation to the value of the insurance that this provides against American omissions and failures. However, the danger of the Soviets exploiting loopholes in the US array of arms is only one of the arguments against relying on American equipment. Aside from the fact that US products are not necessarily well suited to foreign needs, Europeans can hardly be blamed for feeling that no-one ever got worthwhile arms from a super-power by negotiating from a position of weakness.

On the whole the US has acted perfectly rationally in supplying arms to friendly nations and (in particular) has shown far more restraint than Europeans in the present arms race in Latin America. If you want to be cynical, you can say that the F-5 is the only supersonic aircraft that the North Americans produce that the South Americans can afford, but I prefer to believe that the US has acted with the best of intentions in selling military aircraft in that area. However, anyone visiting Canada a few years ago heard a very different story about the supply of US fighters.

The way it was told to me in Ottawa, Canada had wanted to produce the F-4 under licence, but had been turned down flat by the US, and told that the only modern fighter available for foreign construction was the F-5, which (even Northrop will admit) is no F-4. Even before the CF-5 flew, the CAF was talking of using some for training, and putting the rest in storage! Soon afterwards, Japan was given licence rights on the F-4, the CF-5 ran into a teething problem (engine bay fires) and you might say it was fortunate that the CAF had nothing to go to war with! This was obviously an exceptional case, in which Canada had the worst of a sudden policy switch, but it is difficult to avoid the conclusion that, if Canada had been able to retain its own fighter design and development capability, then the CAF would have come out of the negotiations with something better than the CF-5.

Anyone who suggests today that Europeans should cancel the Panavia Tornado in favour of an American project might

The Hawker Siddeley Harrier, described by the author as "the only workable V/STOL fighter system known in the West", provides the best current example of European specialization proving superior to US technology. Illustrated is one of the two-seat TAV-8As recently delivered to the US Marine Corps.

The English Electric Canberra was the first post-war European aircraft purchased for service with the US forces and it also achieved good export sales elsewhere — justifying the effort expended in the UK to develop this jet bomber. Illustrated is an early licence-built Martin B-57A Canberra.

remember — aside from the fact that no American project has been designed to do the same job — that Canada cancelled its own Mach 2.3 CF-105, disbanded the Avro Canada team, was then sold by the US some Bomarc missiles with sand-filled warheads and ended up with the CF-5! In the late 1950s, Canada was as advanced as most European nations in aviation technology. Now it's a pretty good place for miniature totem-poles and soapstone walruses.

Of course, it can be argued that Canada has saved a great deal of money by exporting most of its aerospace engineers and by concentrating production on Indian and Eskimo souvenirs. On the other hand, France (for example) has benefited considerably in both economic and defence terms by putting effort into military aircraft developments. The French policy is simply to export arms with the minimum possible restraints, with a view not only to boosting employment and the balance of payments, but of increasing the scale of manufacture of equipment needed by its own forces. The result of arms exports in reducing unit prices is that France's defences can be increased in effectiveness and simultaneously reduced in overall cost.

Other European nations may feel that France has achieved these objectives largely by an irresponsible lack of restraint on arms exports, and that the country's cynical switches of allegiance between opposing nations will eventually backfire. However, in my view, within the next few years there must be some negotiated compromise between the unfettered export policy of France and the arguably over-restrictive policies of Britain, Germany and Sweden.

Given more realistic export policies, European military aircraft developments can not only enhance the security of the Free World, but also make a significant contribution to European economies. However, this is not to say that US products should be excluded from European inventories, when they offer significant advances over local counterparts. All of which brings us back to the F-16 affair.

The basic question is whether countries such as Britain, Germany and Sweden should be developing their own air superiority fighter, or whether US dogfight aircraft should be imported, pending a major technological advance (eg, using a much greater proportion of composite materials).

Unfortunately, the issue is complicated by differing national timescales and existing equipment, and by the fact that the various operational requirements are still being drafted. The broad timescale for this wave of replacements is officially around the late 1980s, which gives more than enough time for the development of a new fighter, yet *may* not be sufficiently behind the in-service dates of the F-16 (1978) and F-18L Cobra II (1983?) to permit a really major advance. A small interim buy of American fighters might well make sense, since (whatever the official timescales for new procurements) Britain, Germany and Sweden will undoubtedly be short of dogfight capability in the early 1980s, but can absorb few additional fighters under normal conditions. This "core force" would provide a basis for expansion, should a serious deterioration in the general defence climate warrant it.

However, this stop-gap response to the sudden swing in market demand must not prevent European powers from carrying out project studies of possible fighters for the late 1980s. American fighter powerplants have admittedly set standards that will be difficult to beat, but the airframes leave scope for improvements, and Europe can certainly produce a major advance in the field of armament. In my view, the potential gains are well worth the effort. Nevertheless, if it transpires that the best our present designers can produce is a crude rehash of the F-16 or Cobra II, then I say FORGET IT! *Missionary pot, anyone?* □

(Above) The XP-40 as originally flown with aft-positioned radiator bath and (below) an early production P-40 (there was no P-40A sub-type).

(Below) The P-40C sub-type was built in larger numbers for the AAF than any variant of the initial basic Allison-engined P-40 model.

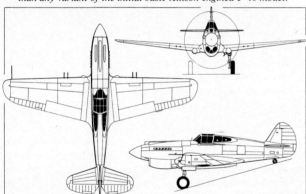

CURTISS P-40 — P-40C (HAWK 81A)　　　USA

Ordered in July 1937 as a rework of the 10th production P-36A with an Allison V-1710-19 (C-13) liquid-cooled engine, the XP-40 was flown on 14 October 1938, and an order placed for 524 production examples as the P-40 on 27 April 1939. The first P-40 flew a year later, on 4 April 1940, with a V-1710-33 (C-15) engine rated at 1,040 hp for take-off and two fuselage-mounted 0·5-in (12,7-mm) M-2 machine guns. A total of 199 P-40s was delivered, the remainder of the contract being made up with 131 P-40Bs with pilot armour, self-sealing tanks and armament augmented by two 0·3-in (7,62-mm) wing guns, 193 P-40Cs with an additional 0·3-in (7,62-mm) gun in each wing and provision for a ventral drop tank, and one P-40G. The last-mentioned sub-type was a P-40 fitted with Hawk 81A-2 wings, an additional 44 P-40s subsequently being converted to a similar standard. Hawk 81A was the export designation for the basic fighter, the Hawk 81A-1 being similar to the P-40 but having provision for four 7,5-mm wing guns and 230 being ordered by France. The first 140 completed against the French contract were transferred to the UK as Tomahawk Is, the remaining 90 (Hawk 81A-2s) having pilot armour and fuel tank protection, these being delivered as Tomahawk IIAs. British contracts called for 950 similar aircraft comprising 20 Tomahawk IIAs and the remainder as Tomahawk IIBs; of these 100 were released to the Chinese National Government,

195 were disposed of to the Soviet Union and others to Canada, Egypt and Turkey, the final 300 having increased ammunition capacity and a revised fuel system, and being referred to by the manufacturer as Hawk 81A-3s. The following data relate to the P-40C. Max speed, 345 mph (555 km/h) at 15,000 ft (4572 m). Initial climb, 2,690 ft/min (13,66 m/sec). Range (clean), 800 mls (1287 km). Empty weight, 5,812 lb (2636 kg). Loaded weight, 7,549 lb (3424 kg). Span, 37 ft 3½ in (11,37 m). Length, 31 ft 8½ in (9,66 m). Height, 10 ft 7 in (3,22 m). Wing area, 236 sq ft (21,92 m²).

CURTISS P-40D, E, K & M (HAWK 87A)　　　USA

The availability of the Allison V-1710-39 with an external spur reduction gear and a rating of 1,150 hp for take-off which was maintained at 11,700 ft (3565 m) prompted redesign of the basic Hawk 81A as the Hawk 87A, this being the recipient of a British contract for 560 aircraft in May 1940, the first example (Hawk 87A-1) flying on 22 May 1941 and being assigned the name Kittyhawk I by the RAF. After delivery of the first 20 Kittyhawk Is, armament was increased from four to six wing-mounted 0·5-in (12,7-mm) machine guns (Hawk 87A-2), a similar change being introduced on the parallel P-40D for the USAAF after completion of 22 aircraft, this change resulting in the assignment of the designation P-40E to the more heavily armed model. Orders were placed for 2,320 E-model fighters comprising 820 P-40Es (Hawk 87A-3) and 1,500 P-40E-1s (Hawk 87A-4), the latter being purchased from Lend-Lease funds for the RAF and other Commonwealth air arms as Kittyhawk IAs. The next Allison-engined production model was the P-40K with the V-1710-73 (F4R) engine rated at 1,325 hp for take-off and 1,150 hp at 11,800 ft (3595 m) but otherwise similar to the P-40E-1. Of 1,300 built, the bulk were supplied to the Soviet Union and to the USAAF in Asia and the Pacific. The P-40K-10 production batch introduced a 1 ft 7½ in (49,53 cm) increase in fuselage length. The P-40M differed from the P-40K in having a V-1710-81 engine offering 1,200 hp for take-off and 600 were built of which 595 were supplied to Commonwealth air forces as Kittyhawk IIIs. Performances of E, K and M models were generally similar and the following data relate to the P-40E-1. Max speed, 362 mph (582 km/h) at 15,000 ft (4572 m). Time to 5,000 ft (1525 m), 2·4 min. Max range (with drop tank), 850 mls (1368 km) at 207 mph (333 km/h). Empty weight, 6,900 lb (3130 kg). Loaded weight, 8,400 lb (3810 kg). Span, 37 ft 4 in (11,38 m). Length, 31 ft 9 in (9,68 m). Height, 12 ft 4 in (3,76 m). Wing area, 236 sq ft (21,92 m²).

The P-40E (above) was the first of the redesigned P-40s (raised engine thrust line, lowered cockpit sill and aft decking and revised radiator housing) to be supplied in quantity to the AAF, and the P-40F (below) was the first sub-type with a Merlin.

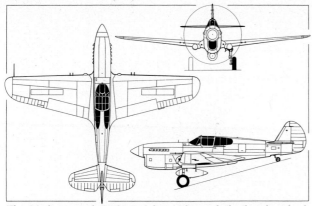

The Merlin-engined P-40L-5 (above) featured the lengthened aft fuselage first introduced by the P-40F-5 and P-40K-10.

(Above) A P-40K-1 which was similar to the P-40E-1 apart from an uprated Allison engine and (below) a P-40N-1 which introduced a new lightweight structure.

CURTISS P-40F & L WARHAWK   USA

The altitude capability of the P-40 was strictly limited by its Allison engine and in an attempt to overcome this the second P-40D airframe was fitted with a Rolls-Royce Merlin 28 and flown on 30 June 1941 as the XP-40F. Orders were subsequently placed for 1,311 P-40Fs powered by the Packard-built V-1650-1 Merlin rated at 1,300 hp for take-off, a similar armament to that of the Allison-engined models (six 0·50-in/12,7-mm wing guns) being fitted. The third production airframe was fitted with a deep, aft-positioned ventral radiator bath as the YP-40F, and the P-40F-5 and subsequent production batches featured a lengthened fuselage similar to that introduced by the P-40K-10. A total of 330 was allocated to the Commonwealth as Kittyhawk IIs but, in the event, only 117 served with the RAF, RAAF, and SAAF, and of the remainder, 100 were supplied to the Soviet Union. The final Merlin-engined model, the P-40L, was initially identical to the final production P-40F-20, but with the P-40L-5 production batch, two of the wing guns were removed, together with some fuel capacity as a weight-saving measure, but this produced only a 4 mph (6,43 km/h) increase in max speed at rated altitude. A total of 700 L-model Warhawks was built. Three hundred P-40Fs and P-40Ls were re-engined in 1944 with the Allison V-1710-81 as P-40R-1s and -2s owing to Merlin spares shortages. The following data relate to the P-40F-5 but are typical for Merlin-powered models. Max speed, 364 mph (585 km/h) at 20,000 ft (6095 m). Time to 5,000 ft (1525 m), 2·4 min. Max range (with drop tank), 1,500 mls (2414 km) at 208 mph (335 km/h). Empty weight, 7,000 lb (3175 kg). Loaded weight, 8,500 lb (3855 kg). Span, 37 ft 4 in (11,38 m). Length, 33 ft 4 in (10,16 m). Height, 12 ft 4 in (3,76 m). Wing area, 236 sq ft (21,92 m²).

CURTISS P-40N WARHAWK   USA

Built in substantially larger numbers than any other version of the Warhawk, the P-40N introduced a new lightweight structure and was successively fitted with the Allison V-1710-81, (P-40N-20) V-1710-99 and (P-40N-40) V-1710-115. The first 400 (P-40N-1) had four 0·5-in (12,7-mm) wing guns, subsequent aircraft having a six-gun armament, and the P-40N-5 introduced a frameless canopy and full-depth rear-vision panels. A total of 536 P-40Ns were allocated to the Commonwealth as Kittyhawk IVs and production comprised 5,216 aircraft, a further 784 being cancelled, the last production example — the 13,738th P-40 built — being completed in December 1944. The following data relate to the P-40N-20. Max speed, 350 mph (563 km/h) at 16,400 ft (5000 m). Max range (internal fuel), 600 mls (966 km). Time to 5,000 ft (1525 m), 2·4 min. Empty weight, 6,700 lb (3039 kg). Loaded weight, 8,400 lb (3810 kg). Span, 37 ft 4 in (11,38 m). Length, 33 ft 4 in (10,16 m). Height, 12 ft 4 in (3,76 m). Wing area, 236 sq ft (21,92 m²).

CURTISS P-40Q WARHAWK   USA

Prior to the final termination of P-40 development, effort was expended in combining aerodynamic refinement with increased power to produce a higher-performance model. A P-40K airframe was fitted with an Allison V-1710-121 engine rated at 1,425 hp for take-off and 1,100 hp at 25,000 ft (7620 m). Semi-flush low-drag radiators were incorporated in the wing centre section and a four-blade propeller was fitted, the designation XP-40Q being assigned. A second similarly re-engined P-40K for the P-40Q programme reintroduced the nose radiator scoop but featured an all-round vision bubble-type canopy (previously tested on a P-40N). The definitive XP-40Q (converted from a P-40N-25 airframe) had clipped wingtips, the cut-down aft fuselage with bubble canopy and coolant radiators faired into the wing leading edges. Four 0·5-in (12,7-mm) guns were carried but proposed production models were to have carried either six 0·5-in (12,7-mm) or four 20-mm weapons. No production was undertaken. The following data relate to the definitive prototype. Max speed, 422 mph (679 km/h) at 20,500 ft (6248 m). Time to 20,000 ft (6095 m), 4·8 min. Span, 35 ft 3 in (10,75 m). Length, 33 ft 4 in (10,77 m).

(Above and below) The second XP-40Q in its definitive form with clipped wingtips. Contrary to most references, the XP-40Q did not have a longer fuselage than the P-40N.

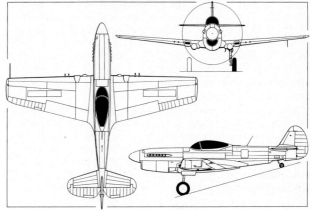

The famous Red Arrows cross-over, one of the most spectacular of all manoeuvres, is performed both in the horizontal plane (as illustrated above) and in the vertical plane (below).

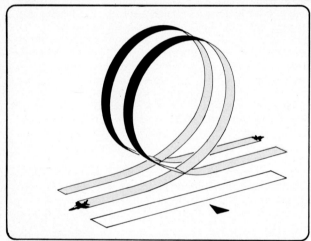

AEROBATICS ———————— *from page 166*

always wanted to try whilst flying with the Red Arrows was the upwards bomb-burst of four aircraft through the downwards break of five! Highly spectacular but probably impressively impracticable! Thus, the most common form of opposition aerobatics nowadays is a pair of aircraft individually opposing one another.

The most important thing for opposition aerobatics to achieve is the spectacular "cross". In its simplest form, a "cross" can be made by two aircraft flying past one another. It is immediately evident that, for the illusion to be successful, the aircraft must by flying parallel to each other and at the same height. They must also time their fly-pasts so that they pass each other in front of datum; an achievement made more difficult by any wind effect. Finally, the aircraft have to fly the "cross" reasonably close to each other so that parallax errors are not readily apparent to the crowd.

Having started with a simple fly-past, opposition manoeuvres can be developed and made more intricate and therefore more difficult. Progress leads to an inverted fly-past and then to a slow or hesitation roll, but perhaps the most spectacular manoeuvre to perform in the horizontal plane is the "Twinkle" roll (fast aileron roll) as the aircraft "cross", thus adding to the illusion of near collision with a flash of wings. Bearing in mind that they are the antonym of the graceful formation manoeuvres, opposition flying should consist of short, sharp punchy manoeuvres which have

spontaneous presence. Thus, opposition barrel rolls and turns should be small, tight manoeuvres taking up the minimum space and time. The two important things to look for are accuracy of "crosses" and symmetry of manoeuvre. To be accurate, the "crosses" should give the illusion of two aircraft passing close to each other in the same plane and should be exactly in front of datum. Obviously, to create the right spectacle, both aircraft must manoeuvre in exactly the same way — particularly when turning, rolling or looping — and so the manoeuvres of each aircraft should be matched precisely. Not an easy task — especially in the opposition loop where the difficult vertical plane is used and so many variables, for example wind, can affect each aircraft differently. In summary, when used as a fill-in for the main formation, synchronised aerobatics should provide a timely and snappy exhibition of exciting flying in complete contrast to that of the main formation. Opposition flying should aim to produce accurate "crosses" and precisely matched manoeuvres.

. . . and its presentation

As with solo display flying, by far the most important aspect of a formation aerobatic display is its presentation. The professional impressiveness and spectator appeal of a display will mainly depend on how well it is shown to an audience. All too often, this aspect of a display is given least thought and consideration — display design tends to rely more on "what *can* we do next" rather than "what *should* we do next". What, then, contributes to the showmanship of a display? The first feature is undoubtedly the concept and consequent design of the display. The sequence should be considered as a whole and not as a disjointed selection of separate spectacles; therefore, it should aim at providing an integration and balance of contrasting manoeuvres. A team should have a selection of sequences to provide the flexibility of performing in varying degrees of bad weather, and all but the thinnest cloud should be avoided. Not only does it make it more difficult to present and fly the display if cloud is penetrated, but also the team is out of sight and therefore of little attraction to the crowd.

Showmanship is an important part of the presentation although it may not directly contribute to the excellence or otherwise of the display. Disciplined drill in starting up procedures sets the tone for the rest of the display, neat taxying acts as an overture for the precision to come, attention to detail — for example the Red Arrows switching on their nose lights together just before take-off — may attract favourable comment. Smoke sequences should be designed so that the inevitable unevenness of individual smoke selections is hidden. Attention to detail may placate the most nit-picking critic; it will certainly enhance the professionalism of the display, and to this end, a well co-ordinated commentary will complement any flying display.

Before concluding, I must mention the less tangible and more difficult to appreciate aspects of display flying. Panache, flair and style are a few of the words often used to describe these characteristics of a display, whether it be solo or formation. One cannot measure such qualities; one can only feel them. Give the Italians a balmy, clear day on the Adriatic coast, and they will perform with Latin excitement. Give the French an intricate display site at Le Bourget, and they will display with typical chic and sophistication. Give the Americans a Texas plain, and they will fill it with thunder and speed. Give the Red Arrows a dank Farnborough day, and they will compromise the gaps in the clouds. The competition of display flying is not in seeing who can produce what out of the hat on the day, but who can best produce what has been carefully designed and practised over many months of winter training. The competition thus comes more in the concept and design of the sequence than in the execution of individual manoeuvres.

To finish, let me start at the beginning and take you, the reader, through my idea of an impressive and spectacular presentation of a display. A cracking arrival should be followed by a balance of rolling and looping formations — each shape being presented plan view to the crowd, each change being made clearly visible (or invisible). The aerial choreography should hold the rapt attention of the most disinterested observer. Manoeuvre should follow manoeuvre in a carefully regulated plan to entertain the spectator. Use of all the lines appropriate for various manoeuvres and tight flying by the leader will help maintain a rhythmic and flowing procession of manoeuvres, giving the team its opportunity to show off a large number of aesthetically pleasing and technically difficult formation manoeuvres. But interest wanes and combinations of formation shapes become exhausted. Interest can suddenly be regenerated at this moment by the scattering of the formation in a vivid bomb-burst; then, as the team gathers itself together, continuity is maintained with the rapid appearance of two aircraft rushing headlong towards each other on an apparent collision course.

Suddenly, interest and adrenalin reach a peak in both spectators and performers as the pair start an opposition manoeuvre, in sharp contrast to the elegance of the formation shapes so recently in view. The pair provide no more than a timely interlude of accurate "crosses", however, whilst the main formation reassembles (behind the crowd and not as a gaggle in front of it) for its next manoeuvre. Now with two fewer aircraft, it can do the more difficult and time-consuming "picture" manoeuvres to help add to the pace, vigour and spectacle of the display; the pair always remaining on hand to

Two display pairs currently provided by the RAF are (above) the Vintage Pair flying a Gloster Meteor T Mk 7 and a Vampire T Mk 11 and (below) The Bulldogs from No 3 FTS — the only RAF team flying piston-engined aircraft.

alternate with the main formation while they collect their thoughts and reposition.

But this cannot go on forever; repetition is the prime sin. Excitement is a short-lived commodity, so let the show finish whilst everybody is enjoying it most. A climatic finale — the *Frecce,* for example, perform a breathtaking thread-the-needle of all their aircraft — and suddenly all is over, leaving the crowd hungry for more, but resigned to licking leaking ice-creams! □

(Above right) The Italian Frecce Tricolori team, on Fiat G 91s, has made a speciality of the "Double Roll" manoeuvre, earning the appreciation of professionals and laymen alike. (Below) A cross-over demonstrated by Skyhawks of the Blue Angels.

aircraft with greater capabilities than offered by the ageing KC-135s. For example, during the 1973 Middle East crisis, USAF C-5s and C-141s relied heavily upon a refuelling stop in the Azores, without which the airlift would have been largely ineffective.

The ATCA will be an existing commercial wide-bodied freight aircraft with the addition of underfloor fuel tanks and air-refuelling equipment, providing the capability to project US forces on a near global basis without requiring third-country landing or overflight rights. The Boeing 747-200F is one of the primary candidates for ATCA (the other being the DC-10 Srs 30 CF) and is offered by Boeing at a gross weight of 820,000 lb (372 280 kg) with a choice of four engines — the CF6-50E or JT9D-70 previously described, the 54,000 lb st (24 500 kgp) CF6-50J or 56,000 lb st (25 400 kgp) JT9D-70D.

If chosen by the USAF, the 747 ATCA would most probably use General Electric engines. A total weight of 478,000 lb (217 012 kg) of fuel could be carried, of which 197,000 lb (88 438 kg) could be off-loaded at a radius of 2,875 mls (4 626 km). As a cargo transport, this aircraft could carry 36 standard USAF 463L pallets and could lift 195,000 lb (88 530 kg) a distance of 4,600 mls (7 400 km). Further increases in gross weight, to 880,000 lb (399 520 kg), are projected, and a 747 (the Boeing demonstrator) has already been tested, under USAF sponsorship, with a flight refuelling boom, a number of dry contacts with various receiver aircraft having been made. The USAF is currently conducting competitive source selection studies expected to lead to a decision by next spring and the production contract for 41 aircraft being placed by the beginning of 1978, with deliveries to begin in 1979.

One other military customer for the 747 has so far emerged, this being the Iranian Imperial Air Force. After considering the purchase of Lockheed C-5s, the IIAF finally decided, in 1974, to buy second-hand 747s on the commercial market and to have them converted for long-range freighting — primarily to ferry aircraft spares and other supplies from the US to Iran in support of its massive expansion programme. A total of 12 747-100s were acquired — nine from TWA and three from Continental — and these were fitted with the side cargo door

and other equipment for the freighting rôle before entering service with the IIAF earlier this year (one having subsequently been lost in an accident in Spain).

Another interesting rôle in which the Boeing 747 is destined to serve is that of ferry and launch aircraft for the Rockwell space shuttle orbiter. For this purpose, NASA purchased a 747-100 (from American Airlines) in 1974 and Boeing is now modifying it to carry the orbiter pick-a-back fashion, for ferry flights to Cape Canaveral in preparation for space launchings and also for air-launches to permit preliminary test-flights and landings to be conducted with the orbiter, which has no built-in take-off capability. A second 747 may later be modified to ferry the massive fuel tanks used by the booster for launching the orbiter into space orbit.

By the middle of 1976, Boeing had delivered 285 of the 309 Jumbo Jets on order and these aircraft had flown an estimated 3·7 million revenue hours, carrying 118 million passengers. These totals are currently growing at the rate of some 68,000 hrs and 2·3 million passengers per month, and 747s cover at least 34 million miles (55 million km) every four weeks; each aircraft is producing an average 21 million passenger/miles (34 million pass/km) per month — an output that is, thanks to the Jumbo Jet's size and high cruising speed, unmatched by any other commercial airliner. The decision to launch the Boeing 747 was undoubtedly a bold one, and the programme has not been devoid of problems, either for Boeing or for the user airlines; but the growing number of model options within the 747 family combined with the slow improvement in the airline traffic should ensure that the Jumbo will be in production for a good many years to come. It also seems likely that Boeing will eventually offer a "stretched" 747, as airline needs for greater capacity develop. Some indication of Boeing thinking in this respect is already available, with project studies for a 747/II with a fuselage stretch of 50 ft (15 m) to increase the passenger capacity to 526-704 according to layout, and the 747/III and 747/IV with a supercritical wing and even greater stretch. Developments such as these must await the commercial availability of 60,000 lb st (27 240 kgp) engines (a JT9D has already run at this thrust) but they indicate that Boeing has no intention of relinquishing its grip on the big capacity jet transport market, now firmly established with the Jumbo. □

A three-view drawing of the Boeing 747B with additional side-view of the 747SP, both with JT9D engine nacelles. The General Electric CF6-50 and Rolls-Royce RB.211-524 pods have longer forward ducts.

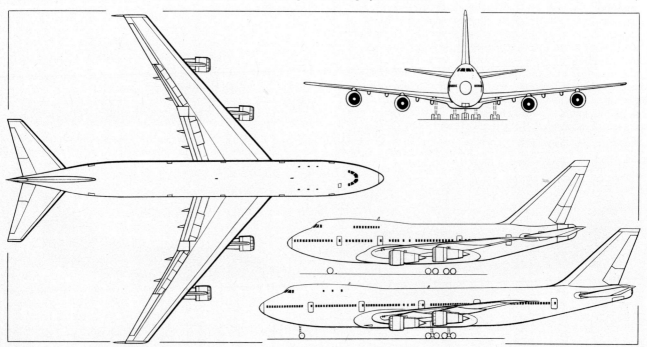

IN PRINT

"Twelfth Air Force Story"
by Kenn C Rust
Historical Aviation Album, California, $6·50
64 pp, 8½ in by 11 in, illustrated
THIS is the second of an intended 10-volume series which, when complete, will provide a concise history of the activities of each of the numbered US Air Forces in World War II. It summarises, in a readable manner, the story of the fighter and bomber units of the USAAF that served in the Mediterranean Area from November 1942 onwards, the Twelfth Air Force having been formed in August that year to take charge of the Army Air Force units that were to be committed to the Operation "Torch" landings in Northwest Africa.

The author has clearly gone to some lengths to obtain original photographs from personnel who served in the area and these are supplemented by a number of line drawings to illustrate markings. Several charts provide data on the units employed at various times from 1942 to late 1944, by which time many of the Twelfth Air Force groups and squadrons had been transferred to other commands, although a few flew on with the Twelfth in Italy until VE-Day.

Copies of this useful and authoritative guide can be ordered through Aviation Book Company at 555 W Glenoaks Blvd, Glendale, Calif 91202, USA. The overseas distributor is W E Hersant of 228 Archway Road, Highgate, London N6.

"Fighter Aces"
by Christopher Shores
Hamlyn Group, Feltham, Middlesex, £3·95
160 pp, 8½ in by 11¾ in, illustrated
AERIAL combat, particularly between individual fighting pilots, captured the public imagination in World War I, when it was often visualized (by those not exposed to the real thing) as an extension of the jousting between chivalrous knights of an earlier era. Both in the Great War and in subsequent conflicts in which air power has played a rôle, fighter pilots have tended to be thought of, as Christopher Shores says in this book, as "carefree young men rushing to their aircraft for another scramble" in their "gaudily-painted fighters".

However far removed from the truth this image may be, the subject of fighter aces continues to attract much attention, and it is a subject that both the author and the publisher have served well in this volume. The text, as to be expected, is readable and authoritative, and the many photographs of individual aces and their aircraft are supplemented by a series of 12 excellent, specially-commissioned paintings by Michael Turner, depicting memorable aerial combats.

Naturally, operations in World War II take up a large proportion of the book, but other conflicts are fully covered, including Korea, Vietnam, the Middle East and the Indo-Pakistan fighting, all of which have thrown up their quota of aces.

"Junkers 290"
by Thomas H Hitchcock
Monogram Aviation Publications,
Massachusetts, USA, $3·95
32 pp, 8¼ in by 10¼ in, illustrated
THIRD in Thomas Hitchcock's series of "Monogram Close-ups", devoted primarily to German aircraft of World War II, "Junkers 290" provides a summary of the aircraft's development story, comprehensive data, notes on operations and camouflage colours and a very fine collection of photographs. Side view line drawings depict each stage of development.

Published by Monogram, this volume can be ordered from Aviation Book Company, 555 W Glenoaks Blvd, Glendale, California 91202.

"Fighting Colours"
by Michael J F Bowyer
Patrick Stephens Ltd, Cambridge, £3·95
204 pp, 5¼ in by 8½ in, illustrated
A REVISED and updated edition of a volume first published in 1969 and recognised as a reliable guide to the camouflage and markings of RAF fighters since 1937. The new material deals, in particular, with the Lightning, Phantom and Harrier in the period from 1970 to 1975. Heavily illustrated throughout by photographs and line drawings, the volume is especially valuable for model-makers, much of the material having first appeared in *Airfix Magazine.*

"The Observer's Book of Aircraft"
by William Green
Frederick Warne & Co Ltd, London, 90p
254 pp, 3½ in by 5½ in
THE Sukhoi Su-19, the Boeing YC-14, the JuRom Orao and the Leko-70 are among the new aircraft that make their first appearance in the 1976 edition of this respected annual pocket-book. Other new entries are, for the most part, concerned with the latest variants of older aircraft types — in some cases, such as the T-34C Mentor, very much older.

The Observer's Book formula, the success of which has been amply demonstrated in 24 previous editions, is maintained without change, but all data have been checked and revised, all photographs replaced and silhouettes updated as necessary.

"Luftwaffe in Finland 1941-44"
by Ossi Anttonen and Hannu Valtonen
Kirja-Lento, Finland, FMK 39
144 pp, 6¾ in by 10 in, illustrated
ADDING to the flow of excellent historic aviation material emerging from Finland, this new title provides a heavily illustrated account of the operations of two *Luftflotten,* Nos 1 and 5, on the Finnish front, ranging from the Gulf of Finland to Petsamo in the Far North. The text, in both Finnish and English, summarises these operations on a month by month basis from July 1941 to December 1942, but it is the photographs (more than 250 of them, with captions also translated into English) that make the book a goldmine for the enthusiast with a special interest in the *Luftwaffe* in World War II. Typical colours and markings are shown in three pages of colour drawings and three pages of tone drawings.

Copies can be ordered from the publishers at PL40, 01531 Helsinki-Vantaa-Lento, Finland, price £5·00 or $10·00 inclusive of postage (add £0·50 or equivalent to cover bank charges if remitting by cheque).

"Elmer Sperry: Inventor and Engineer"
by Thomas Parkes Hughes
The Johns Hopkins University Press,
Baltimore, Md., and London, England,
$16.00
347 pages, 8 in by 10 in, illustrated
SPERRY: a name that is synonymous with gyrostabilisation, installed in ships (1912), and three years later in aeroplanes, to be dramatically demonstrated by his son Lawrence in Paris on 18 June 1914. Less known is that Elmer Sperry began his extraordinary career in electric lighting, power plants and trolley cars—among other things.

In these pages the career of this extraordinary man is treated in fascinating detail, the

The Junkers Ju 290A-6, which was the only true production example of the type, was intended to serve as Adolf Hitler's personal transport but was completed as a 50-seater and on 26 April 1945 flew secretly to Spain, where it was purchased in May 1950 by the Spanish government to serve at Salamanca-Matacan with the Escuela Superior de Vuelo (Advanced Flight School). Additional photographs of the Ju 290A-6 in Spanish markings appear in the Junkers 290 Monogram Close-Up noted on this page.

Two of the 44 Curtiss Hawk 75As that served with the Finnish Air Force, depicted here, were the ex-Norwegian 75A-6 CU-558 (left) and ex-French 75A-3 CU-562 (left). The whole story of Finland's Hawk 75As is told in great detail in the latest volume of Suomen Ilmavoimien Historia, *noted here.*

result being an absolutely marvellous book. Among other things, it describes Sperry's work in fire-control systems, bombsights, and an automatic-controlled "aerial torpedo" (father of the V-1; grandfather of the cruise missile), during World War I. And within this biography of Elmer is also that of his short-lived son Lawrence, an aviator, inventor and developer in his own right.

This is a remarkably good book. Well researched, well written, and (most unusual) well turned out editorially. Its excellent text is supplemented by a rich collection of more than 70 photos and 90 drawings. Anyone with an interest in the early development of aircraft instrumentation will be obliged to themselves to regard this volume as an absolute *must* for their library—RKS.

"Curtiss Hawk 75A"
by Kalevi Keskinen, Kari Stenman and Klaus Niska
Tietoteos, Helsinki, Finland,
99 pp, 7 in by 10 in, illustrated
FIFTH in the series of volumes devoted to the history of aircraft of the Finnish Air Force, this deals in fascinating detail with the 44 Hawk 75As purchased from Germany in 1941-43. The Curtiss fighters had been captured variously in Norway and France and had been refurbished in Germany for re-sale; those supplied to Finland included examples of the Hawk 75A-1, A-2, A-3, A-4 (all French versions) and A-6 (Norwegian).

The volume is largely pictorial, and includes a number of well-executed colour and line and tone drawings depicting markings and colour schemes. There is a summary of the text in English and a four-page appendix deals with the single P-40M operated by the Finnish Air Force — a Lend-Lease example supplied to the Soviet Union and captured intact after making a forced landing.

"Vintage Aircraft Directory, 1976"
by Gordon Riley
Distributed by Battle of Britain Prints, London, 85p
64 pp, 4¾ in by 7 in, illustrated
THE 1976 edition of this useful little pocket-book contains details of all types of aircraft in the UK that made their first flights in prototype form at least 25 years ago (prior to 31 December 1951). Aircraft still actively flying as well as those in museums or derelict but subject to possible restoration are included. Excluded are a number of aircraft still in current Service use, such as Chipmunks and Devons; details of ownership and location are given for the more than one thousand aircraft that are listed.

"Langley's Model Aero Engine of 1903"
by Robert B Meyer Jr
Aeroplanes & Engines Publishers Inc, Washington
114 pp, 8½ in by 9 in, illustrated
THE curator of the Smithsonian Air & Space Museum's Aeropropulsion Division provides an erudite note on the work of Samuel Langley, who came so close to pre-empting the Wright Brothers of their first powered, controlled flight. In 1901, following earlier successes with steam-driven model aircraft powered by a small petrol engine, this being the first petrol-powered aeroplane ever to fly.

The engine itself is among the Smithsonian Institution exhibits and is the subject of this book, originally published by the Smithsonian and now appearing in a revised edition. Details of price and how to order can be obtained from The Cumberland Press, 4926 Del Ray Avenue, Bethesda, Maryland 20014, USA.

"Famous Bombers of the Second World War"
by William Green
Macdonald and Jane's, London, £4·95
282 pp, 7¼ in by 9¾ in, illustrated
A SINGLE-VOLUME reprint of the two volumes originally published in 1959/60, providing development histories and operational details of the 25 most important bombers to see service between 1939 and 1945. There are no changes to the original text or illustrations but cutaway drawings of eight significant aircraft have been added.

"Wrecks & Relics"
Edited by Ken Ellis
Merseyside Aviation Society, Liverpool, £1·50
108 pp, 6¼ in by 9 in, illustrated
FIFTH EDITION of a guide to non-airworthy aircraft and bits of aircraft to be found scattered round the country. The catalogue is thorough, and the extent of the relics will probably come as a surprise to many. There are several useful appendices, listing, for example, aircraft on the BAPC register, the BAPC member groups, and a list of M (maintenance) serials applied to grounded RAF aircraft assigned to instructional use.

Copies can be purchased (adding 20p for post and packing) from MAS at 4 Willow Green, Liverpool, L25 4RR.

"Gloster Javelin Mks 1 to 6"
by Roger Lindsay, £1·60
32pp, 8¼ in by 11¼ in, illustrated
THE second monograph by this author (who is also the publisher), following the pattern of the successful booklet on the Venom/Sea Venom. This title deals with the "first generation" Javelins in great detail for the benefit of

enthusiasts. The descriptive text covers the evolution of the design, the individual prototypes and the production of the Mks 1 to 6. Details are given of each RAF squadron that used the type, with notes on its markings, and the history of every individual Javelin is related. The illustrations include 60 photographs and a series of 1/72nd scale drawings.

Copies can be obtained through specialist booksellers or from the author at 1 Chantry Close, Norton, Stockton-on-Tees, Cleveland, TS20 1EN, adding 15p for postage.

"Fiat G.50 Freccia"
by Pietro Tonizzo, Enzo Zaccavelli and G Paole Borelli
Stem Mucchi, Modena, Lire 500
240 pp, 9¼ in by 8¾ in, illustrated
AN ADDITION to the Stem Mucchi series of "profiles", with Italian text, many photographs and a three-view in colour.

"The Dragon's Wings"
by William M Leary, Jr
University of Georgia Press, Athens, Georgia, $12·00
279 pages, 6 in by 9 in, illustrated
SUBTITLED "The China National Aviation Corporation and Development of Commercial Aviation in China", this is certainly the "surprise" aviation book of the past quarter century. After the collapse of Nationalist China in 1949 who *ever* expected to see a history of CNAC? Much less one as substantial as this!

Most persons assume that CNAC was founded by Pan American Airways. In fact, it was an offshoot of the Curtiss-Wright empire that created the airline, in partnership with the Chinese government, in 1929, when operations started with five Loening amphibians. PanAm did not enter the picture until 1933, holding on until 1949 when it sold out to the Nationalist government on Formosa, which terminated the existence of CNAC. This book does an excellent job of detailing the airline's many trials and tribulations in the 20 years 1929-1949.

Through these pages fly Stinson Detroiters, Ford Trimotors, two ill-fated Sikorsky S.38s, Consolidated Commodore flying boats, Douglas Dolphin amphibians, Curtiss Condors and, of course, DC-2s and DC-3s. There are 14 pages with 22 photos, including one of the famous DC-2½ (a DC-3 with one DC-2 wing), and two route maps. The appendices provide a chronology and a wealth of statistical data.

This is certainly the finest piece of airline history to appear within the past ten years; no library of airline literature can claim to be complete without it.—RKS.

CANADA

CANADAIR LEARSTAR 600

SIGNIFICANT changes in the specification of the LearStar 600 have been announced by Canadair Ltd following acquisition of an option on design, production and marketing rights in this biz-jet (see *AirData File*/July 1976). Outright purchase of the rights depends on the results of market surveys and the Canadian company was hopeful that it could obtain 50 orders by 1 September (as this issue closed for press), allowing a positive decision to be made.

The gross weight of the LearStar 600 has gone up from 26,000 lb (11 804 kg) to 32,500 lb (14 755 kg) as a result of increasing the fuel capacity by 3,810 lb (1 730 kg), enlarging the fuselage diameter to 106 in (2,69 m) and making more accurate estimates of structural component and system weights. To match the weight growth, a developed version of the Avco Lycoming ALF 502 engine will be used, with a thrust of 7,500 lb (3 405 kg) compared with the 6,500 lb (2 950 kg) engines previously intended. The thrust-to-weight ratio remains outstanding, at 0·461:1, and the planned cruising speeds are, it is claimed, faster than those of any other biz-jet on the market.

The enlarged fuselage makes the LearStar 600 the first "widebody" biz-jet, with an inside cabin width 10 in (25,4 cm) greater than that of the Gulfstream II, and allows the wing to pass through the fuselage completely beneath the cabin floor. A headroom of 6 ft 1 in (1,85 m) is offered, greater than that in any other biz-jet.

The LearStar 600 will be marketed and supported direct from the Canadian factory and a full avionics package is included in the standard price, which has been set at $Can 4,275,000 (£2·44m). The avionics package is described as being "full Collins low profile or its equivalent" and will include completely dual flight director systems, weather radar, dual comms and navs, dual DME, dual compass systems, dual transponders, single ADF, single radio altimeter, dual audio systems, one ground proximity warning system and all antennas; space and power provisions will be made for an HF comm system, second ADF, third VHF, VLF navigation, inertial navigation, voice recorder and flight recorder.

The standard price, which Canadair will guarantee for the first 50 aircraft, together with performance specifications and delivery dates,

includes flight training of two captains and training of two mechanics, plus one year of factory-sponsored computerized maintenance.

Target date for prototype first flight is late 1977, followed by FAA certification by late 1978 with delivery of first production units in the second quarter of 1979.

Power Plant: Two Avco Lycoming ALF 502 turbofans rated at 7,500 lb (3 405 kg) each for take-off and 7,000 lb (3 223 kg) for max climb and cruise.

Performance: Max operating speed (M_{MO}) Mach 0·90 above 23,500 ft (7 168 m) and 375 knots (694 km/h) EAS above 10,000 ft (3 050 m); max operating speed (V_{MO}), 300 knots (556 km/h) up to 10,000 ft (3 050 m); high speed cruise, Mach 0·88 or 581 mph (935 km/h) above 36,000 ft (10 980 m); normal cruise, Mach 0·85 or 562 mph (904 km/h); long-range cruise, Mach 0·80 or 528 mph (850 km/h); time to climb to 40,000 ft (12 200 m), 15·5 min; FAR 25 take-off distance, 4,700 ft (1 434 m), ISA at sea level, max weight; landing distance, 4,400 ft (1 342 m), ISA at sea level, max weight; range, 4,020 naut mls (4627 km) with eight passengers at Mach 0·80, NBAA IFR reserve; range, 3,200 naut mls (5 926 km) with eight passengers at Mach 0·85, NBAA IFR reserves; range, 2,800 naut mls (5 185 km) with 14 passengers at Mach 0·85, NBAA IFR reserves.

Weights: Operating weight empty, 16,900 lb (7 673 kg); max fuel, 14,810 lb (6 724 kg); max payload, over 3,000 lb (1 362 kg); payload with max fuel, 940 lb (427 kg); max zero fuel weight, 24,400 lb (11 078 kg); max take-off, 32,500 lb (14 755 kg); max landing, 31,000 lb (14 074 kg).

Dimensions: Span, 59 ft 9 in (18,22 m); length, 63 ft 10 in (19,48 m); height, 19 ft 8½ in (6,01 m); fuselage diameter, 8 ft 10 in (2,71 m); wing area, 420 sq ft (39,02 m²); sweepback, 25 deg; undercarriage track, 9 ft 8 in (2,96 m); wheelbase, 26 ft 3 in (8,00 m); cabin internal length, 28 ft 3 in (8,62 m); cabin width, 8 ft 2 in (2,49 m); cabin headroom, 6 ft 1 in (1,85 m); cabin volume, 1,150 cu ft (32,56 m³).

Accommodation: Flight crew of two; typical executive layouts seat 10-11 passengers; max accommodation for 30 in commuter layout with four-abreast seating and central aisle. Baggage compartment at rear of cabin.

USA

BELL AH-1T SEACOBRA

FLIGHT testing of the latest version of the Bell H-1 series of helicopters, the US Marine Corps' AH-1T, began in June and together with a second prototype, this SeaCobra will

enter Navy preliminary evaluation in November, with full BIS trials starting next March. The AH-1T represents a major step-up in performance for the SeaCobra compared with the AH-1J version, of which the Marine Corps has already procured a total of 67 for its gunship squadrons.

The AH-1T was evolved from the AH-1J by introducing a number of new features, several of which had been developed by Bell for other members of the basic Iroquois family. Initially known as the Improved AH-1J and redesignated AH-1T in August 1975, the new variant uses the dynamic components of the Iranian Bell Model 214, an uprated engine initially developed for the Iranian AH-1J and some detailed improvements specific to the Marine Corps requirement. The Model 214 dynamics include a larger diameter main and tail rotor, the tail boom has been lengthened by 31 in (78,7 m) to obtain the necessary clearance and the fuselage has been lengthened by 12 in (30 cm) aft of the cockpit bulkhead, to allow for possible future growth without CG limitations.

The T400-WV-402 engine is rated at 1,970 shp compared with the 1,800 shp of the -400 in the AH-1J, and the drive system of the AH-1T is rated for 2,050 hp for take-off and 1,850 hp continuous, compared with 1,250 and 1,100 respectively for the AH-1J. The main rotor diameter increases from 44 ft (13,42 m) to 48 ft (14,64 m), with blade chord going up from 27 in (68,6 cm) to 33 in (83,8 cm), and the tail rotor diameter and blade chord increase to 9·7 ft (2,96 m) and 12 in (30 cm) from 8·5 ft (2,59 m) and 11·5 in (29,2 cm) respectively. As well as improving the overall performance at all temperatures and altitudes, the uprated engine makes possible a 40 per cent increase in the max weight of the AH-1T, and up to a three-fold increase in payload capability.

The Marine Corps plans to acquire 57 AH-1Ts in addition to the two prototypes (which were originally ordered as AH-1Js). Of the total, 24 have been funded, 23 are in the FY77 Defense Budget awaiting final Congressional approval and a final buy of eight will be made in FY78. One of the two prototypes is being configured to carry and fire TOW missiles (two on each side of the fuselage), and the final 23 production AH-1Ts will be built to this standard, incorporating a telescopic sight unit in a small nose fairing and provision for a helmet sight to be worn by the pilot. All earlier AH-1Ts will be capable of being converted to carry and launch TOWs if required.

Power Plant: One Pratt & Whitney (Canada) T400-WV-402 TwinPac coupled turboshaft rated at 1,970 shp for take-off.

Weights: Empty, 7,884 lb (3 580 kg); basic operating, 8,489 lb (3 854 kg); max useful load (fuel and disposable ordnance), 5,392 lb (2 448 kg); max take-off, 14,000 lb (6 356 kg).

Dimensions: Main rotor diameter, 48 ft (14,64 m); tail rotor diameter, 9 ft 8 in (2,96 m); overall length, 56 ft 11 in (17,36 m).

Accommodation: Pilot and observer/gunner in tandem.

Armament: General Electric XM-197 three-barrel 20-mm gun turret system in forward lower fuselage. Stub wings have four attachment points for various loads such as XM-157 or XM-159 rocket-pods or XM-18E1 7,62-mm Minigun pods. Provision for four TOW missiles in vertical pairs, one under each stub wing.

McDONNELL DOUGLAS/HSA AV-8B HARRIER

THE decision to proceed with a flight test programme for the improved version of the Hawker Siddeley Harrier required by the US Marine Corps, announced by the Deputy

A revised three-view drawing of the Canadair LearStar 600 as now projected.

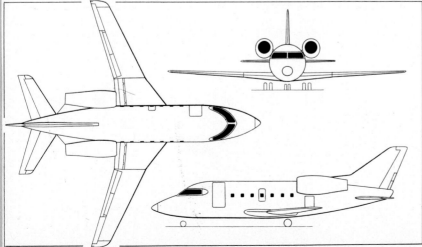

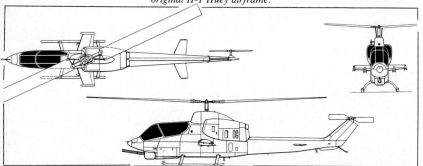

A photograph and three-view drawing of the Bell AH-1T SeaCobra, a major modification of the original H-1 Huey airframe.

Secretary of Defense William P Clements in Washington on 27 July, will lead to first flight of a YAV-8B prototype in November 1978. Two prototypes are currently scheduled to complete 120 hrs of testing by May 1979, allowing a full-scale development decision to be taken at the end of that month. These prototypes will be converted from AV-8As already delivered to the US Marine Corps.

Taking the place of the Advanced Harrier (AV-16) project of 1974, which was proposed for joint US/UK development, the AV-8B is a lower-cost alternative designed to meet specific US requirements after the UK indicated it was not willing to proceed with the AV-16. Although there is much current US Navy interest in the AV-8B, it has been evolved primarily to meet the Marine Corps AVX operational requirement for a new light attack aircraft having increased performance and supportability. Among the projected characteristics required were the ability to carry a 3,000 lb (1 362 kg) war load for 50 naut mls (92,6 km) from a VTO, and 8,000 lb (3 632 kg) for 275 naut mls (509 km) from an STO; the maintenance target was 10-15 man hours per flight hour.

A key cost-saving decision, by comparison with the AV-16, is the use of the existing Rolls-Royce Pegasus 11 engine, but with improvements that increase its thrust by 600 lb (272 kg) compared with the version as installed in the AV-8A. This improved Pegasus will be designated F402-RR-402 in US service and will deliver 21,500 lb st (9 760 kgp). A new supercritical wing made of graphite epoxy composite materials will be used in the AV-8B, this being lighter, less vulnerable, with more room for fuel and improved cruise performance. A new slotted flap design will induce positive circulation over the wing, this feature alone increasing the STOL capability by 6,700 lb (3 042 kg). Small strakes added to the gun pods under the fuselage also produce an improvement in lift, allowing the VTO weight to go up by about 1,200 lb (545 kg). A new engine inlet design gives increased recovery and better cruise efficiency.

An angle rate bombing system (ARBS) located in the nose will improve the weapon delivery accuracy. The AV-8B will have seven ordnance stations, with considerably increased load-carrying ability; the inner wing pylons will be stressed for 2,000 lb (908 kg) instead of 1,135 lb (515 kg); new intermediate pylons will carry up to 1,000 lb (454 kg) each and the outboard pylons remain unchanged with a 630-lb (286-kg) capacity. These seven stations can carry up to fourteen 500 lb (227 kg) bombs, compared with a maximum of five by the AV-8A.

Prime contractor for the AV-8B is McDonnell Douglas in St Louis, with Hawker Siddeley participating in development and in production as a major sub-contractor. The F402 engine will be built either by Rolls-Royce or under licence in the USA; in the latter case, a one-time royalty of about $20m (£11m) would be payable to Rolls-Royce. A royalty will also be payable on the airframes or portions of airframes built in the USA, comprising 5 per cent for the first 100 and 3 per cent thereafter, but with a cut-off in October 1984, no royalties being payable after that date. The projected AV-8B programme for the US Marine Corps in fact provides for only some 50 aircraft to be delivered by the cut-off date.

The Marine Corps requirement is for a total of 336 AV-8Bs, in addition to the two YAV-8Bs and two full-scale development prototypes, to be built only if a favourable production decision is made. Of this total, the basic front-line inventory is 160 for eight squadrons (three currently flying AV-8As and five flying A-4M Skyhawks); 25 would be assigned to training (these being single-seaters); 27 are described as "pipeline" aircraft and 124 are included in the total to cover attrition over the projected service lifetime (an attrition rate of 4½ per cent). If the programme proceeds as planned, production of a pilot batch of 24 AV-8Bs will begin early in 1980 followed by full-scale production in 1982, leading to IOC (initial operational capability) in the first half of 1984.

So far, $6·3m (£3·54m) has been allocated to the AV-8B development effort, and the 1977 defense budget includes $33m (£18·5m) for the flight demonstration phase to begin; sums of $59·8m (£33·6m) in 1978 and $122·1m (£68·6m) in 1979 will be needed to complete the flight testing. With procurement of an initial eight AV-8Bs in the 1980 budget, the projected cost in that year is $303·4m (£170·5m), followed by $280·9m (£157·8m) in 1981, when 16 aircraft will be ordered. With production reaching a maximum of three a month, the AV-8B unit flyaway cost is $4·5m (£2·53m), the unit production cost is $5·86m (£3·29m) and the unit acquisition cost is $6·81m (£3·83m), all in FY 1975 dollars.

Power Plant: One Rolls-Royce F402-RR-402 Pegasus vectored thrust turbofan rated at 21,500 lb st (9 760 kgp). Max internal fuel load, 7,500 lb (3 405 kg); max external fuel load, 8,078 lb (3 667 kg).

Performance: VTO radius, 200 naut mls (370 km) with 1,800 lb (817 kg) payload; STO radius, 400 naut mls (740 km) with 6,000 lb (2 724 kg) payload, 800 naut mls (1 480 km) with 2,000 lb (908 kg) payload; unrefuelled ferry range, 2,578 naut mls (4 774 km); mission radius from LHA ship with eight MK-82 bombs, 660 naut mls (1 222 km); mission radius from V/STOL strip with eight MK-82 bombs, 390 naut mls (722 km).

Weights: Operating weight empty, 12,550 lb (5 698 kg); flight design weight (7g), 22,750 lb (10 329 kg); max take-off weight, 29,550 lb (13 416 kg); VTO weight, 18,850 lb (8 558 kg); STO weight (1,000 ft/305 m), 27,950 lb (12 690 kg).

Dimensions: Span, 30 ft 4 in (9,25 m); length, 42 ft 10 in (13,08 m); height, 11 ft 3 in (3,43 m); wing area, 230 sq ft (21,37 m²).

Armament: Two 30-mm Aden cannon in detachable ventral pods. One pylon on fuselage centreline and six underwing pylons with combined total capacity of 8,000 lb (3 632 kg). Possible ordnance loads include 14 MK-81LD, MK-81SE, MK-82LD or MK-82SE bombs; six MK-83 bombs; two MK-83 LGB bombs; 11 Rockeye bombs; four AIM-9 Sidewinder AAMs; four Maverick ASMs or two "special stores".

The McDonnell Douglas/HSA AV-8B Harrier as at present projected.

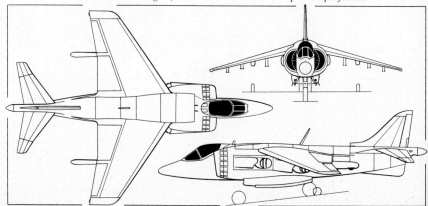

AIR International

Volume 11 · Number 5 · November 1976

Managing Editor · William Green
Editor · Gordon Swanborough
Modelling Editor · Fred J Henderson
Contributing Artists · Dennis Punnett
· John Weal
Cover Art · W R Hardy
Contributing Photographer
· Stephen Peltz
Editorial Representative, Washington
· Norman Polmar
Publisher · Donald Hannah
Circulation Director · Donald Syner
Financial Director · John Gold
Subscription Manager · Claire Sillette
Advertising/Public Relations
· Elizabeth Baker

Editorial Offices:
The AIR INTERNATIONAL, PO Box 16, Bromley, BR2 7RB Kent.

Subscription, Advertising and Circulation Offices:
The AIR INTERNATIONAL, De Worde House, 283 Lonsdale Road, London SW13 9QW. Telephone 01-878 2454. US and Canadian readers may address subscriptions and general enquiries to AIR INTERNATIONAL PO Box 353, Whitestone, NY 11357 for onward transmission to the UK, from where all correspondence is answered and orders despatched.

MEMBER OF THE AUDIT BUREAU OF CIRCULATIONS · ABC

Subscription rates, inclusive of postage, direct from the publishers, per year:
United Kingdom · £5·50
USA · $17·50
Canada · $17·50

Rates for other countries and for air mail subscriptions available on request from the Subscription Department at the above address.

The AIR INTERNATIONAL is published monthly by Fine Scroll Limited, distributed by Ducimus Books Ltd and printed by William Caple & Co Ltd, Chevron Press, Leicester, England. Editorial contents © 1976 by Pilot Press Limited. The views expressed by named contributors and correspondents are their own and do not necessarily reflect the views of the editors. Neither the editors nor the publishers accept responsibility for any loss or damage, however caused, to manuscripts or illustrations submitted to the AIR INTERNATIONAL.

Second Class postage approved at New York, NY. USA Mailing Agents: Air-Sea Freight Inc, 527 Madison Avenue, New York, NY 10022.

CONTENTS

WRENDEZVOUS WITH WREN

"Oh dear, George – we're having our first quarrel."

AIRSCENE

MILITARY AFFAIRS

ARGENTINA
Contrary to the report included in *Airscene* last month (October), the *Fuerza Aérea Argentina* is scheduled to take **delivery of** its first two Aeritalia **G.222** general-purpose **transports** *early* rather than late next year. The FAéA aircraft will be the eighth and ninth production examples of the G.222 and will be delivered in January and February respectively. The third FAéA G.222, the option on which was taken up recently, will be the 21st production aircraft and is expected to be delivered late next year. Aeritalia is understood to be endeavouring to interest the *Comando de Aviación Naval* in a multi-rôle version of the G.222 which will include maritime patrol in its repertoire as a potential successor to both the P-2H Neptunes and Douglas C-54s in the service's inventory. A prototype of this version is expected to be built during the next 18 months, primary interest currently being shown by the Philippine government, the Philippine Air Force having formulated a requirement for a number of aircraft (5–9) in this category.

AUSTRALIA
The 1976–77 defence budget of \$A2,178m (£1,555m), which represents a 17·6 per cent increase over the previous year, includes in the approximate \$A306m (£218·5m) allocated for equipment procurement provision for **follow-on procurement of** two Lockheed P-3C **Orion** maritime patrol aircraft at a cost of some \$A23·5m (£16·75m). Deliveries against the initial RAAF order for eight Orions are scheduled to commence late 1977, and the additional two will enable No 10 Squadron to attain its full 10-aircraft strength by early 1979.

Despite the increasing urgency attached to the **selection of** a **Mirage IIIO successor,** an early decision is considered unlikely, although Prime Minister Fraser is quoted as having said recently that he favours a US type in preference to a European alternative, and the RAAF apparently still hopes to obtain the McDonnell Douglas F-15 Eagle, despite its quoted unit cost of around \$20m (£14·3m).

The RAAF is still studying the possibility of **standardising on one aircraft** type as a replacement for its present fleet of DHC-4 Caribou, HS.748 and C-47 transports and to fulfil its emerging coastal patrol and surveillance requirement and is understood to be considering proposals made by Aeritalia for Australian part-manufacture and assembly of a multi-rôle version of the G.222. The RAAF has a requirement for 30–40 transport aircraft in the G.222 category, with deliveries commencing towards the end of the decade, and 15–20 coastal patrol and surveillance aircraft.

AUSTRIA
The *Luftstreitkräfte* has recently taken **delivery of** the 12 Bell **JetRanger** armed observation helicopters (equivalent to the US Army's OH-58B Kiowa) ordered last year. Armed with the 7,62-mm XM-27 minigun pod, these helicopters are to be used by the *Luftstreitkräfte* for armed escort and reconnaissance, target marking, liaison, SAR and observation duties.

BRAZIL
In a surprise move in September, the *Fôrça Aérea Brasileira* **permanently grounded** its remaining Lockheed P-2E **Neptune** maritime patrol aircraft which had been operated by the *VII Grupo de Aviação* from Salvador, Bahia State, the official explanation being lack of

sufficient funds for the procurement of the necessary spares to keep the seven remaining examples of this aged aircraft operational. It was previously expected that the Neptunes would soldier on into 1978 when the EMBRAER EMB-111 maritime patrol derivative of the Bandeirante light transport is expected to be placed in FAB service. The withdrawal of the Neptunes leaves the FAB without maritime patrol capability other than that provided by the ex-US Navy S-2E Trackers of the *Grupo de Aviação Embarcada.*

BURMA
Earlier reports that an order for the SIAI-Marchetti **SF-260 trainer** had been placed by the Union of Burma Air Force (see *Airscene*/October) have now been confirmed and the aircraft were, in fact, **delivered** to Burma by SIAI-Marchetti earlier this year, 10 aircraft being involved in the initial contract. The aircraft have been delivered in standard training configuration, but the UBAF is understood to be considering the conversion of all or part of the batch to armed SF-260W Warrior configuration at a unit conversion cost of approximately \$30,000 (£17,600). The current unit cost of the Warrior is \$140,000-\$150,000 (£82,300-£88,200), according to equipment standard specified, the SF-260 trainer being \$10,000-\$15,000 (£5,900-£8,800) less.

CHILE
The recent US Senate legislation placing a veto on the supply of arms to Chile from 1 October owing to the allegedly "repressive nature" of the Chilean government has not affected the **supply** to the *Fuerza Aérea de Chile* (FAC) **of the** 15 Northrop **F-5E Tiger IIs** and three two-seat F-5Fs ordered mid-1974, deliveries of which began in June and were expected to be completed before the embargo came into effect.

It is anticipated that the Chilean government will shortly place a **follow-on order** with EMBRAER **for** a further two-three EMB-110 **Bandeirante** light transport aircraft following recent delivery of an initial batch of three aircraft, these having been accepted by the *Aviacion Naval* at the EMBRAER factory on 2 July and flown to Chile after the completion of crew training in Brazil. The Chilean Navy Bandeirantes differ from aircraft delivered to the *Fôrça Aérea Brasileira* in having modified avionics to increase their suitability for flying in the Andes, the provision of IFF and full anti-icing equipment.

DUBAI
The Air Wing was scheduled to accept **delivery of** an Aeritalia **G.222** (the fourth production example) last month (October). A second example of this general-purpose transport is currently on option for the Air Wing.

EGYPT
The Egyptian **Air Force** is currently **evaluating** the FFA AS 202/18A **Bravo** as part of its programme to select a new primary-basic trainer, other contenders including the Scottish Aviation Bulldog 120 and the SIAI-Marchetti SF-260. The AS 202/18A Bravo, which has been developed jointly by the Flug-und Fahrzeugwerke in Switzerland and SIAI-Marchetti in Italy, has been flying in prototype form since 22 August 1974, although a production series of the lower-powered AS 202/15 is currently being built. Discussions with Egypt have concerned an initial supply of 20 Bravos by the FFA with subsequent aircraft being built in Egypt with a progressively increasing proportion of Egyptian-manufactured com-

ponents. Licence manufacture of up to 200 Bravos for the EAF is envisaged.

EIRE
It is now expected that **deliveries of** the 10 SIAI-Marchetti **SF-260W Warriors** ordered earlier this year for the Army Air Corps will begin next month (December), approximately three months behind the schedule announced at the time of the placing of the order, with the last aircraft being delivered in February. The Warriors will succeed the Chipmunk in the primary training rôle and will also fulfil the recently-formulated coastal patrol task.

FEDERAL GERMANY
The *Luftwaffe* has recently revealed its **plans for phasing into service** the **Alpha Jet** close air support aircraft, 84 examples of this version of the aircraft having so far been ordered against a planned total of 200. The first two Alpha Jets will be utilised for the technical training of ground personnel, while the third and fourth will be delivered to the flight test centre at Manching for extended service trials. The first actual unit to operate the Alpha Jet will be the *Waffenschule* 50 at Fürstenfeldbrück from February 1979 onwards for pilot conversion and tactical training, this unit subsequently being redesignated JaboG 49, with additional training and experimental responsibilities. The next Alpha Jets will enter service at the *Luftwaffe* Proving Ground at Decimomannu, Sardinia, in place of the current Fiat G.91Rs. The G.91R will also be replaced in the first of two combat *Geschwader* scheduled to receive the Alpha Jet, LeKG 43 at Oldenburg, from early 1981, with LeKG 41 following suit at Husum to complete the Alpha Jet re-equipment programme by November 1981, by which time the two *Geschwader* will have been redesignated JaboG 41 and 43. According to Brig-Gen Hans-Gunter Kannegieser, chief of the Armament Section of the *Luftwaffe,* the final total programme cost of the 200 Alpha Jets scheduled to enter the *Luftwaffe* inventory will be DM 3,301m (£754m), or a cost of DM 16·5m (£3·77m), but as Gen Kannegieser comments, these figures include non-recurring expenditure on personnel training and conversion, and the flyaway price cannot therefore be considered an exact equivalent as such would not normally include these costs, taxes, levies, etc.

The **updating of** the **RF-4E Phantoms** operated by the two reconnaissance *Geschwader,* AG 51 at Bremgarten and AG 52 at Leck, will result from the recent placing of a contract with Goodyear Aerospace for side-looking airborne radar. The contract, valued at nearly £50m, will include provision of a real-time data link and ground stations with correlator processors.

GHANA
The Ghana Air Force has placed a **contract** with Aermacchi **for** six **MB 326K** single-seat operational trainer/ground attack aircraft. This is the third Ghanaian contract for the MB 326, the first of which covered the acquisition of seven MB 326F two-seat trainers in 1966, and the second covering two additional aircraft to make up attrition. The MB 326Ks, which are expected to be based at Tamali, Northern Ghana, are to be used primarily in the light attack rôle and are the first combat aircraft to be taken into the Ghana Air Force inventory.

INDIA
The Indian Air Force anticipates phasing into service the **MiG-21bis** *(Fishbed-L)* by the turn

of the decade **to replace** the remaining **MiG-21FLs** and supplement the MiG-21Ms in the 13 IAF fighter squadrons currently operating the Soviet-designed Nasik-built aircraft. The MiG-21bis (this form of suffix — one of the many Latin words absorbed by the Soviet vocabulary — has not apparently been employed in the designations of Soviet military aircraft since its use by the MiG-15bis), which is in service with the V-VS, is scheduled to be phased into production by HAL at Nasik about 1979 with the completion of production of the MiG-21M, approximately half the contract for the earlier model fighter having so far been completed, and will continue through 1983-84. The IAF is understood to have a requirement for approximately 150 MiG-21bis fighters which will differ from the MiG-21M primarily in having the Tumansky R-25 engine of 16,535 lb (7 500 kg) thrust with reheat, updated avionics and more minor changes. Although still essentially an air combat fighter, the MiG-21bis will have improved ground attack capability.

Subject to successful service evaluation, the **HPT-32** has been **selected as** the **successor of** the **HT-2** for IAF and INA primary training, with deliveries commencing in 1979 and the aged HT-2 being phased out of service in 1980-81. The first of two prototypes of the HPT-32 — expected to be christened *Shipshak* (Pupil) — is now believed likely to commence its flight test programme next month (December), several months ahead of schedule, and production is likely to be launched mid-1978.

The first **deliveries of** production **Ajeet** light ground attack fighters to the Indian Air Force are scheduled to be made during the next two months against a total IAF requirement reportedly for 100 aircraft of this type. The tandem two-seat Ajeet trainer has now been finalised, the construction of two prototypes

will commence next year and the first of these is scheduled to fly in 1978.

The carrier INS *Vikrant* is to undergo modernisation but **no final decision concerning** its **flying equipment** has yet been taken. The Indian Navy has decided to phase out the remaining Breguet Alizé ASW aircraft next year and the veteran Sea Hawks are to be replaced by new multi-mission aircraft to be obtained from "willing friendly countries on liberal terms", which could mean the Soviet Union and the *Forger,* although the Indian Navy is still keen to obtain 12-15 Sea Harriers if the financial problems involved by the acquisition of these can be resolved.

Delivery to the Indian Navy of the **first** of four **Ilyushin Il-38** *(May)* long-range maritime patrol aircraft was reportedly imminent at the time of closing for press and a supplementary batch of two-three aircraft of this type has been promised for late-1977 or early-1978 delivery.

The **IAF** is understood to have finally **rejected** the Soviet offer of **MiG-23** *(Flogger)* multi-rôle fighters, largely on the basis of inadequate range to meet its requirements, and following the shelving of proposals for a SNECMA M53-powered derivative of the HF-24 Marut is now understood to be studying renewed HAL proposals but this time for a derivative of the HF-24 powered by the Tumansky R-25 engine.

INDONESIA
The Air Force of the Indonesian Armed Forces, *Tentara Nasional Indonesia-Angkatan Udara,* has begun taking **delivery of** 16 Rockwell **OV-10F Bronco** multi-mission counter-insurgency aircraft, the first having been handed over to the Indonesian Ambassador, Roesmin Nurjadin (a former Chief of Staff of the Air Force), at Columbus early in August.

Rockwell International reinstated Bronco production to meet the Indonesian order which was awarded early last year, and with completion of the Indonesian OV-10Fs will manufacture 24 OV-10G Broncos for the Republic of Korea Air Force under a $58·2m (£34·23m) contract.

The Indonesian Navy recently took **delivery of** the **last** two of six GAF N22 **Nomad Mission Masters** employed for off-shore maritime patrol and the surveillance of coastal waters. The Indonesian Nomad Mission Masters are equipped with search radar, flare racks, life rafts, drift sight, bulged aft windows and a navigator's station. External stores are carried on wing pylons, internal loads may be dropped via a floor hatch and long-range fuel tanks may be installed.

The Indonesian **air arm,** the TNI-AU, is understood to have completed its **analysis of** currently-available **multi-purpose trainer/light tactical aircraft** and to have selected a type for licence manufacture by the Indonesian aircraft industry. The selected type had not been revealed at the time of closing for press, at which time contracts were reportedly being finalised, but both two-seat trainer and single-seat light strike versions of the aircraft are to be built against TNI-AU requirements for 100-150 of the two models with initial deliveries (presumably from knocked-down airframes) commencing in 1978.

IRAN
Despite misgivings expressed by the Senate Foreign Relations Committee concerning the scale of the continuing arms purchases from the USA by Iran — which totalled $10,400m (£6,117·65m) between 1972 and 1976 — it has been confirmed that **agreement** has been reached **to supply** the Iranian Imperial Air Force with 160 **General Dynamics F-16** fighters

---

THE MIG-25 SAGA

In the most sensational defection of a combat aircraft pilot since Lt Noh Keun Suk flew his MiG-15bis into Kimpo 23 years ago, one Lt Viktor Ivanovich Belenko of the V-VS flew his MiG-25 *(Foxbat-A)* interceptor fighter to Japan on 6 September, landed at Hakodate airport and requested asylum in the USA. Lt Belenko had taken-off from a base at Sakharovka, some 125 miles (200 km) from Vladivostok, on a training exercise in concert with two other MiG-25 pilots. His aircraft carried its maximum internal fuel load of 30,865 lb (14 000 kg) and had no underwing stores (eg, *Apex* AAMs). Soon after taking-off, Belenko broke formation, dived to 150 ft (45 m) above the sea to avoid Soviet radar and flew eastward for some 250 miles (400 km). He then climbed to 24,400 ft (8 000 m) to locate the Japanese coastline, his intention being to land at Chitose, the ASDF's largest base on Hokkaido Island, some 87 miles (140 km) from Hakodate. He picked up the coastline but Chitose was covered by a thick layer of cloud and he therefore descended to low altitude and searched for a suitable place to land for nearly 30 minutes before discovering Hakodate airport through a break in the clouds.

In the meantime, four ASDF radars had picked up Belenko's MiG-25 some 185 miles (300 km) off the west coast of Hokkaido, at which time it was flying at 18,700 ft (5700 m) and 440 knots (815 km/h). The Air Defence Control Centre transmitted an international warning as the aircraft was heading for Japanese airspace and ordered the scramble of two F-4EJ Phantoms of the 2nd Air Wing at Chitose. The F-4EJs immediately took-off, but 15 minutes after the first appearance of the intruder on ASDF radar and six minutes after

the interceptors had been scrambled, the target disappeared. On the assumption that the unidentified aircraft had turned westward, the F-4EJs were ordered back to base.

Twenty-six minutes after its disappearance from the ASDF radar screens, the MiG-25 piloted by Lt Belenko appeared over Hakodate and then circled the airport. An ANA Boeing 727 was in process of taking-off and the Soviet fighter left the vicinity of the airport, returning three minutes later, made another circuit of the field and, after two low passes, touched-down about halfway along the 2,190-yard (2000 m) runway with full flap and drag chute deployed. The MiG-25 overran the threshold by 260 yards (240 m) and collided with an ILS monitor antenna, but suffered only minor damage to a nosewheel.

It was subsequently ascertained that Lt Belenko had joined the MiG-25 unit at Sakharovka in the autumn of 1975, having previously served as an instructor on the MiG-

17 and the Su-15 *(Flagon-E),* and had some 2,000 hours' flying experience, including 30 hours on the MiG-25. The aircraft was the standard interceptor version of the MiG-25 and, to the surprise of ASDF personnel performing a preliminary inspection of the fighter, the Machmeter was redlined at $M = 2·8$, suggesting that performance, while still exceptional, is not quite as high as had been believed in the west. Furthermore, it was discovered that the aircraft has no ejection seat and is manufactured from heavy steel rather than titanium. On 19 September, 64 Defence Agency personnel and 11 US experts began the task of dismantling the MiG-25 so that it could be loaded aboard a C-5 Galaxy for transportation to Hyakuri AFB, 50 miles (80 km) north-east of Tokyo, where detailed examination was expected to be completed by 5 October. Talks with Soviet Embassy officials began in Tokyo on 1 October with a view to handing back the MiG-25 late-October.

at a cost of a further $3,800m (£2,235·3m) calculated at anticipated 1980 values. State Secretary Dr Henry Kissinger, who confirmed the agreement, stressed that deliveries to the IIAF would not commence until 1979, when the first 10 two-seat F-16B trainers would be shipped to Iran for pilot conversion, and that the remaining 150 single-seat F-16s would follow on during the course of the next four years to 1983. It has been unofficially reported that the Iranian government is contemplating increasing its purchase of F-16s to an eventual total of 300 aircraft, but it is understood that no formal request for additional quantities of F-16s has yet been made to the US Defense Department. The IIAF plans to use the F-16 to supplement the F-5E Tiger II in the air superiority/air combat rôle with a secondary ground attack commitment, the service having now received all 141 of its F-5Es plus some 20 of its 28 two-seat F5Fs.

A letter of intent for the **purchase of** 250 Northrop/McDonnell Douglas **F-18L Cobra** (landbased derivative of the McDonnell Douglas/Northrop F-18 shipboard strike fighter) multirôle fighters to replace the F-4D and F-4E Phantoms in its inventory in the early 'eighties has been submitted to the US government. To be used by the IIAF primarily in the attack rôle, the F-18L Cobra, which will have 85-90 per cent commonality with the F-18NSF and is being quoted at a flyaway price of about $6m (£3·5m) in terms of 1975 prices, is expected to enter the Iranian inventory from 1982.

ISRAEL
The Israeli government is believed to be nearing **agreement concerning** the purchase of the General Dynamics **F-16A** as a successor to both the F-4 Phantom and the A-4 Skyhawk in the inventory of the *Heyl Ha'Avir*. Maj-Gen Benjamin Peled, C-in-C of the *Heyl Ha'Avir*, together with other high-ranking Israeli officers, was recently briefed in Washington on the training, logistics and support aspects of the F-16A which play a significant part in the proposals that have since been submitted to the Israeli government. The *Heyl Ha'Avir* would, it is understood, like to obtain a minimum of 200 F-16As with a possible eventual total of 400, deliveries to Israel commencing in 1980-81. While the *Heyl Ha'Avir* is currently planning on a second batch of 25 McDonnell Douglas F-15 Eagle fighters, with deliveries of the first batch of 25 expected to commence in January, the service apparently now adheres firmly to the "safety in numbers" principle, believing that larger numbers of the less sophisticated and less expensive F-16A are likely to be more efficaceous than smaller quantities of the F-15 Eagle.

JAPAN
The ASDF formed its **first** Mitsubishi **T-2A-equipped** advanced training **squadron**, the 21st *Hiko-tai* at the Matsushima air base on 1 October as part of the 4th Air Wing, some six months later than originally scheduled. The squadron, which has a statutory strength of 25 T-2As, replaces the F-86F Sabre-equipped 7th *Hiko-tai*, the ASDF now having only four Sabre-equipped squadrons, the 1st, 3rd, 6th and 8th, remaining in service. The second T-2A squadron, the 22nd *Hiko-tai*, is currently planned to be formed during the autumn of next year.

The ASDF anticipated that the Mitsubishi FS-T2kai single-seat close-support fighter would receive **official certification** last month (October) and be assigned the designation F-1. So far approval has been given to the procurement of only 26 of the close-support fighters, sufficient for only one squadron, but the ASDF hopes to form four F-1 squadrons with

a total of 80 aircraft and 37 are included in the Fiscal 1977 budget request. The long-range ASDF programme calls for a total of 14 fighter squadrons of which four will be equipped with the F-1, five with the F-4EJ Phantom and five with the still-to-be-selected F-X. The first F-1 squadron is expected to be formed late in 1977 or early in 1978.

The **Defence Agency** is **requesting** approximately £3,370·5m in **appropriations for** Fiscal **1977,** or some 13·7 per cent more than the current year. Of the total amount, £1,382·3m is for the Ground Self-Defence Force, £835·3m for the Air Self-Defence Force and £717·65m for the Maritime Self-Defence Force. Of these sums, a total of £330m is scheduled to be spent by the three services on aircraft procurement as follows: (Ground Self-Defence Force) 11 Kawasaki/Hughes OH-6J light helicopters, six Fuji/Bell UH-1H tactical helicopters, two Bell AH-1S assault helicopters, two Kawasaki V-107-II transport helicopters and two Mitsubishi LR-1 tactical reconnaissance/liaison aircraft; (Air Self-Defence Force) 37 Mitsubishi F-1 close-support fighters, four Kawasaki C-1A transports, 20 Fuji T-3 (KM-2B) primary trainers, two Kawasaki V-107-II rescue helicopters, two Mitsubishi MU-2K SAR aircraft and one MU-2J flight check aircraft; (Maritime Self-Defence Force) one Shinmeiwa PS-1 maritime patrol flying boat, one Shinmeiwa US-1 SAR amphibian, five Fuji KM-2 intermediate trainers, five Mitsubishi/Sikorsky SH-3 ASW helicopters, one Beech King Air C90 instrument trainer, one Mitsubishi/Sikorsky S-61A SAR helicopter and two Sikorsky RH-53D mine-sweeping helicopters. Additional funding will be required for the initial batch of 34 F-X interceptors, the ASDF having been unable to meet the deadline for budget request submission owing to the delay in type selection.

KOREA (SOUTH)
Latest procurement on behalf of the Republic of Korea Air Force comprises 24 Rockwell International **OV-10G Broncos** at a cost of $58·2m (£34·23m) with deliveries scheduled to commence early next year. Deliveries of the single-seat F-5E Tiger II and two-seat F-5F to the ROKAF are continuing against orders for 126 of the former and nine of the latter, approximately two-thirds of these having now been taken into the ROKAF inventory, these having followed 87 single-seat F-5As and 35 two-seat F-5Bs. The ROKAF also has 36 F-4D and 36 F-4E Phantoms in its first-line strength. Some 41,000 US servicemen are currently based in South Korea, which, in the coming fiscal year, is scheduled to receive £8·3m (£4·9m) in military grants from Washington plus $275m (£161·8m) in loans for the purchase of US military equipment.

KUWAIT
The Kuwait Air Force recently accepted **delivery of** the first three of 18 Dassault-Breguet **Mirage F1CK** air superiority/air combat fighters ordered from France in 1973 as successors to the Lightnings currently employed. The fighters, which it is anticipated will be armed with the Matra Super 530 and 550 Magic AAMs, are scheduled to be followed at a later date by two two-seat Mirage F1BK conversion trainers, and deliveries are scheduled to commence shortly against the order placed in 1974 for 36 McDonnell Douglas A-4M Skyhawk attack aircraft.

LIBYA
It has been unofficially reported that the Libyan Arab Air Force is about to accept **deliveries of** the Yugoslav SOKO **G2-A Galeb** two-seat basic jet trainer which was returned to production by SOKO a year ago in order to fulfil the LAAF order for an unspecified quantity of this type. Another new addition to

the LAAF inventory is the SIAI-Marchetti-built Boeing Vertol CH-47C Chinook medium transport helicopter which is now supplementing the fleet of SA 321 Super Frelon helicopters. The quantity of Italian-built Chinooks being supplied to the LAAF has not been revealed.

MAURITANIA
The Mauritanian Islamic Air Force has placed an **order** with Fairey Britten-Norman **for** two **additional Defenders** for border patrol, casualty evacuation, general transport and liaison duties. These will join two Defenders already operated by the MIAF from Nouakchott and from various desert strips.

PERU
There now seems to be **some doubt** that the Peruvian government *has* signed a **contract** with the Soviet Union for 36 **Sukhoi Su-22** strike fighters as previously reported (see *Airscene*/October) as several companies, including Dassault-Breguet (for the Mirage F1) and Israel Aircraft Industries (for the Kfir-C2), have been asked to tender new submissions. The report that the order for the Su-22 had been signed following months of negotiation and a recent nine-day visit to Lima by a high-level Soviet delegation emanated from Washington, but it is now admitted in the USA that it is not known with certainty if the contract has been signed. The Su-22 is reportedly an export variant of the Su-17 *(Fitter-C)* with somewhat less sophisticated equipment.

SOVIET UNION
Recent observations of the **operation of** *Forger* **V/STOL aircraft from** the **carrier** *Kiev* in the Atlantic suggest that they are being flown short of the limits of their performance envelope during their initial deployment and are in all probability a service test quantity as about a half-dozen of the aircraft display differing modifications, ranging from antennae to aerodynamic fences. The aircraft have been flown close to the carrier for short periods, presumably with reduced fuel loads, and with no external stores, and the take-off and landing operations have been referred to as conservative, the lack of any significant manoeuvring over the deck being interpreted variously as indicative of possible pitch/roll coupling problems associated with the gyroscopic forces of the lift/cruise engine or as indicating the existence of a highly refined flight control system. The transition from thrust-borne to wing-borne flight and vice-versa has been observed as about one-and-a-half minutes. Western assessments of the *Forger* suggest a clean loaded weight of the order of 21,500 lb (9752 kg) and it is believed that the lift/cruise engine affords a maximum thrust of some 18,000 lb (8 165 kg), total available thrust for take-off (including the two lift engines) being about 24,000 lb (10886 kg). Approximate overall dimensions for the single-seat *Forger* include a span of 23 ft (7,00 m), a wing area of 207 sq ft (19,23 m²) and an overall length of 50 ft (15,24 m), the tandem two-seat *Forger-B* conversion trainer having an overall length of some 58 ft (17,68 m). The *Forger*, the design bureau responsible for which is still uncertain, appears capable of transonic performance with a maximum level speed of the order of M = 1·05.

SWEDEN
The Saab **J 29**, nicknamed the *Tunnan* (Barrel), **flew** in *Flygvapen* service **for** the **last time** in late August during the 50th Anniversary celebrations. The J 29, which served in latter years with the target and towing elements of F 13, the weapons training wing at Malmslätt, first entered service with this same unit, then based at Norrköping and operating in the fighter rôle, just over 25 years ago, in May 1951, and a

Recently rolled out at Sao Paulo, the EMBRAER EMB-121 Xingu pressurised business twin (see AirData File/March 1976) should have entered flight test by the time this issue appears.

total of 656 aircraft of this type had been delivered when production terminated in April 1956.

SYRIA
The Syrian government is reported to be negotiating **contracts** with Agusta in Italy **for** a total of some 60 **helicopters** for the Syrian armed forces, one of the main items apparently being an anti-tank force of 24 Agusta A 109 Hirundos to be armed with either the Hughes TOW — if released by the US State Department — or the Euromissile HOT. Syria is also evincing interest in procurement of about a dozen Agusta-built Sikorsky SH-3D Sea King helicopters and a similar quantity of the smaller AB 212ASW helicopter to supplement its current ASW helicopter force of recently-procured Kamov Ka-25s *(Hormones)*, while for search-and-rescue six standard AB 212s and six Agusta-built Sikorsky AS-61A-4s are sought, the package being completed with technical assistance and aircrew and ground-crew training.

The Syrian Air Force is planning a follow-on **order for** 16 MBB 223K1 **Flamingo** basic **trainers.** The order will be placed via CASA in Spain which acquired the manufacturing rights of the Flamingo in 1972-73 and reportedly supplied 32 aircraft, including a number of single-seat aerobatic examples, to the Syrian Air Force from the batch of 50 Flamingos built in the facilities of the former Hispano Aviación SA (which was merged with CASA). The Iraqi Air Force is also reported to have a requirement for 16 Flamingo trainers.

The Syrian Air Force is understood to have received a **total of** 45 MiG-23 *(Flogger)* **aircraft** to-date and to have requested the supply of additional fighters of this type. One MiG-23 was recently flown to Iraq by a defecting Syrian Air Force pilot, Capt Mahmoud Yassin, after an unsuccessful attempt on the life of Syrian President Assad.

TUNISIA
An **order** has been placed on behalf of the Tunisian Republican Air Force *(Al Quwwat Aljawwiya Al-Djoumhouria Attunisia)* **for** four two-seat **Aeromacchi MB 326Gs and** six single-seat **MB 326Ks** for the re-equipment of the service's squadron of aged F-86F Sabres. This is the second Tunisian order for the MB 326, eight MB 326Bs having served in the basic training rôle with the Tunisian Republican Air Force for a number of years.

The Tunisian government is currently **negotiating** with Aeritalia **for** the purchase of three **G.222** general-purpose **transports** with a view to the delivery of the first aircraft at the end of 1977.

UNITED KINGDOM
The Westland/Aérospatiale **Lynx** HAS Mk 2 officially entered service **with the Royal Navy** with the formation on 17 September of No 700L Squadron at RNAS Yeovilton. A joint Royal Navy/Royal Netherlands Navy intensive flying trials unit, No 700L Squadron will, at full strength, have an inventory of six Royal Navy Lynx and two Royal Netherlands Navy Lynx.

AIRCRAFT AND INDUSTRY

AUSTRALIA
Government Aircraft Factories expected to begin flight testing of a **floatplane version of** the **Nomad** N22B at Inver Grove Heights, Minnesota, during October. The float conversion has been designed and installed to GAF requirements by Wipline Inc, which will become US dealer for Nomad floatplanes, a substantial market for which is believed to exist among bush operators in Canada and elsewhere. GAF also announced the appointment of Nordic Aviation AB of Stockholm as Nomad distributor for Scandinavia, Greenland, Iceland and the Faroe Islands; and of Eagle Aircraft Services as Nomad distributor for the UK, Ireland and the Benelux countries. A Nomad N22B demonstrator was exhibited at Farnborough International and British certification is now being obtained for both the N22B (the designation suffix indicating flat-rated Allison 250-B17 engines) and the stretched N24, the first example of which is expected in Britain in mid-1977.

CANADA
With design definition and choice of engine completed, Canadair was nearing a **decision point on** launching the **LearStar 600** as this issue went to press (see *AirData File/*October 1976). The original option to aquire worldwide exclusive rights from Bill Lear was to expire on 1 September but was to be extended by two months to off-set some delays at the start of the programme while final engine selection was made. The company says "substantial" firm orders, with deposits, have been placed for the LearStar 600, and it was hopeful of reaching the target of 50 by the 1 November deadline. First flight is scheduled for December 1977 with deliveries starting in mid-1979.

FEDERAL GERMANY
First flight of the new prototype of the RFB Fanliner was made on 4 September 1976 (see *AirData File/*August 1975). Identified as the **Fanliner 01,** to distinguish it from the earlier Fanliner 001, the new prototype is somewhat larger but of the same configuration, with a 150 hp Audi/NSU dual rotary piston engine (Wankel type) driving a ducted propeller, and wings and tail unit derived from the Grumman American lightplane range; a special feature is the styling of the forward fuselage by Luigi Colani. RFB, a subsidiary of VFW-Fokker, expects to reach a decision on series production of the Fanliner in 1977, with production starting in 1978. It is intended that RFB will build the fuselage and vertical tail, plus the engine installation, while Grumman will build wings, tailplane and some other components. Final assembly will be on two lines, one Grumman and one RFB, with Grumman American responsible for marketing.

FRANCE
With the designation **Robin R2000,** the Avions Pierre Robin company is testing a new two-seat lightplane derived from the all-metal HR200. First flown in July, the R2000 has a 160 hp Lycoming engine, refined wing, new tail surfaces and other modifications, including a reduction in the number of structural components to reduce assembly costs. A second prototype has been built for tests at the Centre du SFA at Challes-les-Eaux and an initial production batch has been put in hand, with deliveries to start by the end of this year.

Despite the high priority being allocated to development of the Dassault-Breguet **Mirage 2000,** the first of three prototypes of this interceptor is not now expected to commence its **flight test programme** until the end of 1978, with first production deliveries commencing in 1982 and initial operational status being achieved in 1984. The *Armée de l'Air* requirement for the Mirage 2000 is currently envisaged as 250-300 aircraft and peak production tempo is expected to be three-four per month. The 19,840 lb (9000 kg) plus version of the SNECMA M53 engine to power the Mirage 2000 will commence flight testing next year in the Mirage F1E test bed and a pulse doppler radar for the fighter is now being developed by Thomson-CSF.

INDIA
Hindustan Aeronautics has formed a **study group to define** the basic design of a new 18-20-seat twin-engined **utility transport.** To be powered by two Turboméca turboprops — probably Artouste derivatives — and of high-wing configuration, the new aircraft is being designed to meet an Indian Air Force requirement and it is anticipated that the Ministry of Defence will be asked to release funds during 1977 to enable a prototype test programme to commence in 1979-80. The IAF has a requirement for approximately 200 aircraft in this category.

The first of two **prototypes of** the HAL HJT-16 **Kiran Mk II** trainer, which was originally scheduled to fly last month (October), is not now expected to fly until early in the New Year, a second prototype following by mid-year. The Kiran Mk II differs from the Kiran currently serving with the IAF in having a de-rated Orpheus 701 turbojet in place of the Viper, built-in gun armament, updated avionics and four wing hardpoints. A Kiran Mk IA featuring the wing hardpoints commenced its flight test programme early in August.

HAL development of a **Light Armed Helicopter** (LAH) with Aérospatiale assistance has now reached a relatively advanced stage. Also known as the Advanced Light Helicopter (ALH), it is to be powered by an Astazou XX turboshaft and will feature a tail rotor of fenestron design. Designed to operate at altitudes as high as 19,685 ft (6 000 m), it will carry a variety of ordnance, including Indian-manufactured SS.11B anti-armour missiles, and is expected to be supplied in substantial quantities to both the IAF and Indian Navy by the mid 'eighties.

INTERNATIONAL
Responding to requests from Boeing for **engines in the 15-tonne category** required to match some of the permutations in the 7N7

family of projects (see *AirData File* page 256), both Rolls-Royce and General Electric have proposed so-called "cropped fan" versions of their big turbofans. Pratt & Whitney, whilst studying the possibility of similarly de-rating the JT9D, is concentrating on the prospect of increasing the thrust of the JT10D to the 15-tonne level, should this eventually prove to be required by Boeing. The Rolls-Royce proposal, identified as the RB.211-535, has a new fan of reduced diameter and a thrust of about 32,000 lb st (14 528 kgp). The core would be that of the RB.211-22B, and Rolls-Royce claim that noise levels would be even lower although there would be a small penalty in sfc due to the mismatching of fan and core. General Electric designates its proposal as the CF6-32, using the core of the CF6-6 (as used in the DC-10 Srs 10) with a new front fan and fan turbine components. This is initially rated at 30,000 lb (13608 kg), but the sizing of these projects remains flexible until precise airframe requirements are known.

Following its first flight on 9 July, **Concorde 209** was **delivered** to Air France on 3 August, bringing its fleet to three. Concorde 210 flew from Filton on 25 August and joined No 208 at Fairford, where the latter had been delayed for a number of weeks as a result of a labour dispute. Nos 208 and 210 have since been delivered to British Airways, and No 204 will return to Filton for refurbishing. The respective national fleets will be completed with deliveries of No 211 to Air France and 212 to British Airways.

ITALY
Aeritalia initiated operational trials with the second prototype **G.222** transport adapted for the **fire fighting rôle** during August and anticipated obtaining homologation during the course of September. The second and third production G.222 transports were scheduled to be delivered to the *Aeronautica Militare* in September, with the first production example following in December, this having been accepted by the AMI earlier in the year and returned to Aeritalia to complete its test programme. It is anticipated that the production tempo of the G.222 will attain two per month in March.

SIAI-Marchetti is currently evolving a **light trainer,** the S-211, **powered by** a single **turbofan** and anticipates taking a decision concerning the launching of prototype construction next year. The S-211 is considered as being complementary to the SF-260 rather than a replacement, sales of the piston-engined trainer still being buoyant with approximately 300 delivered to date.

Aermacchi is continuing design **definition studies** in collaboration with EMBRAER **for** the **MB 340** light close support aircraft which it is anticipated will be manufactured in Brazil from the early 'eighties. The MB 340 will be powered by a single high-bypass-ratio turbofan of about 7,000 lb (3175 kg), the Rolls-Royce M.45H being currently envisaged as the most likely engine. Armament will include a pair of 30-mm cannon and there will be six underwing hardpoints and probably wingtip missile stations. Studies have been narrowed down to two configurations and it is anticipated that a definitive choice between these will be made early in 1977 and the first metal cut on prototypes in 1978.

SOVIET UNION
According to Soviet sources, the **second prototype of** the Yakovlev **Yak-42** tri-jet airliner has 25 deg of wing sweepback, compared with 11 deg on the first prototype, which has been undergoing flight test since March 1975. Both prototypes had completed about 140 hrs of testing by July in parallel programmes in-

tended to establish which configuration had the best overall economics. Production deliveries are expected to begin by late 1978/early 1979 and the 114,640-lb (52 000-kg) Yak-42, powered by three 14,200 lb st (6 447 kgp) Lotarev D-36 turbofans, is emerging as one of the types upon which Soviet export efforts will be focussed in the next few years. The larger Ilyushin Il-86 airbus type scheduled to make its first flight by the end of this year, is also expected to be exported, as is the Antonov An-30, a specialised survey version of the An-24.

SWITZERLAND
The Pilatus Flugzeugwerke AG has now completed development of the **PC-7 Turbo-Trainer,** anticipates **certification** early next year **and** will launch a **pre-production batch** of 10 aircraft during the course of 1977 with first deliveries scheduled for 1978. An initial order (reportedly for seven aircraft) has been obtained from an unspecified Far Eastern country and current planning calls for follow-on batches of 50 aircraft subsequent to completion of the pre-production series. Although suitable for the light COIN rôle and incorporating six wing hardpoints, the Turbo-Trainer will not be delivered by the parent company with combat capability. The unit price is currently being quoted at approximately SwFr 1·0m (£256,000) and the principal competitor is the Beech T-34C Turbo Mentor. The Turbo-Trainer (see *AirData File/* August 1975) has been undergoing progressive structural and aerodynamic refinement for more than a decade, the first prototype (an adaptation of the first P-3 prototype) having flown with a PT6A-20 on 12 April 1966.

UNITED KINGDOM
Two new versions of the **Fairey Britten-Norman** Islander, represented at Farnborough International, are the **Agricultural Islander and** the **Firefighter.** The Agricultural Islander is offered as a quick-change aircraft, carrying solid or liquid fertiliser in flush fitting tanks beneath each wing, outboard of the engines. For liquids, a spray bar system is fitted, with rates of delivery adjustable between 50 and 250 US gal (190-946 l) per minute using Transland boom and nozzles, or Micronair rotary atomisers for low and ultra-low volume spraying. For solids, a Transland gate box (9·5 in by 25 in/24 cm by 63 cm) is used in place of the liquids pump, distribution from two underwing points serving to double the swath width normally achieved by a single spreader system. Retrospective installation is possible on all Islanders and the agricultural equipment can be removed when not in use to allow the aircraft to operate in its usual transport rôle. The Firefighter, a prototype of which has been recently tested, carries 176 Imp gal (800 l) of fire retardant in four separate but interconnected tanks in the fuselage, with individual inlets, outlets (in the underside of the fuselage) and vent systems. Dumping is activated by a lever between the two pilot seats and two or four tanks can be dumped simultaneously, in a maximum of 2·5 sec. Carrying the full load, the Firefighter has a patrol duration of 3 hrs at 7,000 ft (2 135 m) and flying at 75 mph (121 km/h) at 200 ft (61 m), it can drop the total load within an area of 328 ft (100 m) by 50 ft (15,2 m). An infra-red sensor can be carried, to detect hot spots that may be in imminent danger of bursting into flames.

Fairey Britten-Norman is to conduct tests with a **Trislander** fitted **with** a Canadian Bristol Aerojet 12NS-350CBA **solid rocket booster** to allow it to meet FAA requirements for aircraft of more than 10,000 lb (4 540 kg) gross weight. Offering a thrust of 1,320 lb (600 kg) in the event of failure of one of the aircraft's piston engines, the rocket motor fits in the rear of the centre engine fairing, with its nozzle projecting just aft of the rudder.

First details were released at Farnborough International of the work being undertaken by **Westland,** under Ministry of Defence contract, in the field of **remotely piloted helicopters.** This work began, on a private venture basis, in 1968 with a series of project studies, followed by wind-tunnel and other investigations in 1972 and a flight test programme in 1975 using a flying test bed aircraft known as the Mote, to prove the aerodynamic characteristics and help develop the control system. Under MoD contract, Westland has now built and started testing a small batch of larger drone helicopters, known as the Wisp, and has another contract covering the design definition of a still larger vehicle, the Wildeye. Wisp has an egg-shaped body of about 24-in (61-cm) diameter, a four-legged undercarriage and co-axial two-bladed rotors of 5-ft (1,53-m) diameter. Powered by two piston engines of US manufacture, it carries TV cameras or other sensors for battlefield reconnaissance under remote control from the ground. The contract to develop Wisp for British Army evaluation was won in competition with Shorts (which had previously developed the VTOL Skyspy RPV) and Canadair. Marconi-Elliott Avionic Systems Ltd, through its Electro-Optical Systems Division, has been appointed electronic systems contractor for the Westland RPVs.

Expected to have made its first flight by the time this issue appears, a de Havilland Chipmunk re-engined with a **Bonner Super Sapphire engine** was on show at Farnborough International. The engine is a six-cylinder Vee unit of completely new design, having a 3-litre capacity and rated at 200 hp at 5,500 rpm. Liquid-cooled by way of a ventral radiator, the Super Sapphire has fuel-injection and is turbo-supercharged; with a weight of 328 lb (149 kg), it drives the propeller through a 2-to-1 reduction gear and has an estimated consumption of 7·5 Imp gal (34 l) per 100 hp per hr. The Chipmunk test-bed, G-ARWB, is a one-time winner of the King's Cup Air Race and is known as the Chipmunk 200 with the Bonner engine.

The **name Venture** has been officially adopted **for** the **Slingsby T.61A** motor-gliders now on order for the ATC. The example that has been under evaluation for some years past is now the Venture T Mk 1 while 15 more to be delivered in 1977 will be Venture T Mk 2s. The T.61A is itself a license-built version of the Scheibe SF25B Motor-Falke.

USA
Rockwell International has clarified its plans for future **developments of the Sabreliner range** of biz-jets, with two new models to be introduced in 1978/79, and retrofit programmes available for existing models. Key to the new programmes is an advanced wing developed by the Raisbeck Group of Seattle, with chord increased by 5 in (12,7 cm), a blunt cambered leading edge in place of the leading edge slats on present models, and Fowler type flaps on the trailing edge. The new wing allows about 1,000 US lb (454 kg) more fuel to be carried forward of the front spar; a full modulated anti-skid brake system will also be fitted to the new and updated aircraft. Expected to be certificated early in 1978, the Sabreliner 80A will be the first version to use the new wing, and will have 4,500 lb st (2 043 kgp) General Electric CF700-2D-2 turbofans, like the existing Sabreliner 75A; conversion of the latter to Model 80A standard will be possible. A year later, in the first quarter of 1979, the Model 65A will be certificated, with 3,700 lb st (1 680 kgp) Garrett AiResearch TFE 731-3 engines. Existing Model 40A and Model 60 Sabreliners retrofitted with the new wing but retaining JT12A-8 engines will be redesignated Model 40B and Model 60A respectively, for certification in second quarter 1978 and fourth

quarter 1977 respectively, and Rockwell also plans to offer kits to re-engine these two models with the TFE331-3 turbofans, when they will become Model 45 and Model 65 respectively.

Cessna has adopted the names Citation 1 and Citation 2 for two **new models of the** current **Citation,** which they will succeed in production from the end of this year, **and Citation 3** for a brand-new swept-wing business twin aimed at the same market as the Falcon 50 and the LearStar 600. The Citation 1, deliveries of which are to begin in December, features a new wing of increased aspect ratio, span being 47 ft 1 in (14,36 m) compared with 43 ft 9 in (13,34 m). Engines will be 2,200 lb st (1 000 kgp) Pratt & Whitney Canada JT15D-1As and the Citation 1 will cruise at 404 mph (650 km/h) and will have a range of 1,535 mls (2 470 km) with six occupants. Citation 2 will be available from February 1978 with a stretched fuselage, 47 ft 3 in (14,41 m) compared with 43 ft 6 in (13,27 m) and the span further increased to 51 ft 8 in (15,76 m). With eight seats and 2,500 lb st (1 135 kgp) JT15D-4 engines, the Citation 2 will cruise at 420 mph (676 km/h) and have a range of 2,080 mls (3 347 km). Citation 3, scheduled to be available early in 1980, is designed to seat 12-15 and with two 3,700 lb st (1 680 kgp) Garrett AiResearch TFE731-3 turbofans, to have transcontinental and intercontinental versions with ranges, respectively of 2,760 mls (4 440 km) and 3,450 mls (5 550 km). Cruising speed will be 540 mph (869 km/h) and the wing, with 23 deg sweepback, will have an aspect ratio of 9.1:1, using supercritical aerofoil design by NASA and having a span of 50 ft 7 in (15,43 m). Advanced structural techniques and composite construction will be used. (The Citation III designation was previously used for the projected three-engined, straight-wing, T-tail Cessna 700, announced two years ago but now abandoned).

Cessna has given the **name Conquest to** its **Model 441,** the first turboprop twin in its range of aircraft (see *AirData File*/November 1975). Since flight testing began, the wing span has been increased by 3 ft (0,92 m) and the payload has been improved by the equivalent of two passengers for given ranges. Transcontinental range is now expected with pilot and six passengers. Deliveries are scheduled to begin in June 1977.

First flight of the **Boeing 747 with** Rolls-Royce **RB.211-524** engines was made at Everett (Snohomish County Airport), Washington, on 3 September. The aircraft is the first of six on order for British Airways, with first delivery scheduled for April 1977. Initial in-service rating of the RB.211-524 will be 48,000 lb st (21 792 kgp), rising to 50,000 lb (22 700 kg) in 1978, and the 747 will have a max ramp weight of 800,000 lb (363 200 kg). During 1980, Rolls-Royce expects to certificate the RB.211-524D at 53,000 lb st (24 062 kgp). By the time the Rolls-engined 747 flew, RB.211-524s installed in a Lockheed TriStar for engine development purposes, had totalled nearly 300 engine hours.

Northrop completed the **3,000th** T-38 Talon/ F-5 series **aircraft** on 4 November, this, an F-5E for Saudi Arabia bearing the tail number 1037, being scheduled to fly around the second week of the month, almost exactly 20 years from the date that Northrop began cutting metal on the T-38 prototype in December 1956.

Northrop is currently proposing a **dedicated reconnaissance version of the Tiger II,** the RF-5E. Previous reconnaissance versions of the F-5 series have resulted from the application of an interchangeable camera nose, but the RF-5E is designed to accommodate a variety of pallet-mounted sensors, the pallets being installed or exchanged either manually or by means of an adapted bomb loader during the course of normal refuelling and re-arming operations, permitting exceptional flexibility in mission-to-mission sensor selection. The pallets are nose mounted and their sensors are: (Pallet 1) a KA-95 medium/high altitude panoramic camera, a KA-56E low-altitude panoramic camera and an RS-702 infrared line-scanner, plus a KS-87B forward-oblique camera in the extreme nose compartment, or the KA-56E camera replaced in the pallet by a KS-87B; (Pallet 2) a KA-93 high-altitude panoramic stand-off camera and a KA-56E camera, plus a nose-mounted KS-87B, or (Pallet 3) a KA-108M long-range oblique (LOROP) frame camera. The RF-5E will include a chaff/flare dispenser system and will retain its ASG-29 lead-computing optical sight with 20-mm M-39 cannon and 280 rounds, provision for wingtip-mounted AIM-9 Sidewinder missiles and five stores stations.

The Northrop Corporation has initiated an international **sales campaign for** the **F-18L Cobra,** the land-based version of the F-18 shipboard fighter currently under development for the US Navy. The first flight of the shipboard F-18 is scheduled for mid-1978 and that of the F-18L Cobra will follow six-nine months later, five development aircraft being planned by the company, plus two static test airframes, and the flyaway unit price in terms of 1975 dollars being approximately $6m (£3·5m). A pilot production batch is planned, comprising six single-seaters and six two-seaters, and the first export deliveries are expected to begin in 1982. The F-18L about 6,000 lb (2 722 kg), or 20 per cent, lighter than the shipboard F-18, normal gross take-off weight being some 27,500 lb (12 474 kg) and maximum gross weight being 43,000 lb (19 504 kg). The thrust of the two General Electric F404 engines will be about 32,000 lb (14 514 kg) and the F-18L will thus possess the highest thrust-to-weight ratio of any western fighter at about 1.19 to 1.0. There will be between 85 and 90 per cent commonality between the F-18L and the shipboard F-18, the former having the arrester hook deleted, the main undercarriage simplified and a single nosewheel substituted for the twin nosewheels, deletion of the wingfold and its associated mechanism, the substitution of plain hinged flaperons for the more complex slotted flaps and the wing fuel tanks deleted. The external payload of the F-18L with full internal fuel will be 2,500 lb (1 134 kg) greater than that of the shipboard F-18 at 16,000 lb (7 257 kg), stores being carried on three underwing pylons per side as compared with two per side for the Navy F-18. The F-18L is aimed primarily as a successor to the F-4 Phantom, providing, it is claimed, twice the performance with five to six times the reliability, half the maintenance manhours and a third fewer maintenance personnel.

The **first** of eight **FSD** (Full-Scale Development) General Dynamics **F-16A/B fighters** was scheduled to be rolled-out of the assembly building last month (October) and will commence flight trials next month. The first FSD aircraft, a single-seat F-16A, is being closely followed by two further F-16As, the second of these being the first aircraft to have the complete avionics system with which it is scheduled to commence trials in June, by which time all FSD aircraft should have been completed, two of these being two-seat F-16Bs. Meanwhile, the second YF-16 has been equipped with the navigation, fire control and flight data display systems for a six-month avionics flight test programme prior to integration of these major avionics components in the third FSD F-16A, and General Dynamics is repairing the first YF-16 which was damaged in a landing accident at Edwards AFB while being flown as a control-configured vehicle (CCV) test-bed. The aircraft is being restored to CCV configuration and is expected to be ready to resume flight test in January.

Lockheed-Georgia Company has completed preliminary design of a new **Hercules freighter** variant with a total fuselage stretch of 35 ft (10,68 m), compared with the 15-ft (4,58-m) stretch of the L-100-30, the longest of the versions currently in use. As the **L-100-50,** the new project has an extra 20 ft (6,1 m) ahead of the wing and 15 ft (4,58 m) aft; other changes include a new wing spar and heavier skin panels and a revised landing gear with 12-in (30,1-cm) increased compression stroke. Retaining the standard Allison 501-D22A turboprops, the L-100-50 will have a gross weight of 170,000 lb (77 180 kg), up 15,000 lb (6810 kg) from the L-100-30, and field performance will suffer accordingly, take-off field length being 7,500 ft (2 288 m) and landing distance 6,000 ft (1 830 m). The L-100-50 is aimed primarily at airlines with scheduled cargo routes that are too short for economic operation by current turbojet freighters, being optimized for stage length of about 1,500 mls (2 414 km) carrying the max 60,000-lb (27 240-kg) payload.

Lockheed is understood to have a contract from the Defense Advanced Research Projects Agency to develop a so-called **Stealth Aircraft** which will have low visibility, low noise characteristics and a faint radar signature. A subsonic single-seater, it will have a gross weight of 12,115 lb (5 500 kg) and is expected to be flying before the end of 1978.

Swearingen Aviation Corp has developed a **"standby-power"** installation **for** use on the **Metro II** when operating at high altitude airfields. Comprising a continuous alcohol and water injection (CAWI) system, plus a standby 350-lb (159-kg) thrust solid rocket for use in the case of engine failure. The installation, for an additional 100 lb (45,4 kg) on the empty weight of the aircraft, allows the Metro II to operate at 12,500 lb (5 675 kg) at elevations up to 6,800 ft (2 074 m) amsl and temperatures up to ISA + 20 deg C; without it, the weight in these conditions is restricted to 11,400 lb (5 176 kg). Scenic Airlines has equipped all three of its recently acquired Metro IIs with the system.

First flight of a **Jetstream with** Garrett AiResearch **TPE331-3U-303 engines** replacing the Astazou XVIs was made at Van Nuys on 31 August (*Airscene*/May 1976). The conversion, now referred to as the Century Three Jetstream, was made by Volpar with technical assistance from Scottish Aviation and is supported by Apollo Airways which plans to have seven Jetstreams converted to this standard. Meanwhile, Commuter Airways has put into service two Jetstreams with PT6A-34 turboprops, as converted by Riley, on scheduled operations between Love Field and Oklahoma City.

CIVIL AFFAIRS

INTERNATIONAL

The FAA's third monthly report on **Concorde noise and exhaust emmissions** in operations at Dulles Airport, Washington, covering the 47 movements during July, showed noise levels in the range 120-131 PNdB at 3·5 naut mls (6,5 km) from the start of take-off roll, and 116-130 PNdB at 1 naut ml (1,9 km) from the threshold on the approach. These noise levels were slightly higher than the figures obtained in June, but there was a reduction in the number of complaints received by the FAA, 68 compared with 85. Carbon monoxide emissions from the Concorde during taxying were higher than those from other aircraft but all aircraft emissions reduced to such a low level before they reached the terminal that they were indistinguishable from all other sources.

LEBANON

Middle East Airlines, having been forced to evacuate from Beirut Airport (see *AirScene/* September 1976) has now set up its **maintenance** base **at Orly** Airport, Paris, with the help of Air France, a major shareholder in the Lebanese airline. More than 100 of MEA's top-grade technicians are now at Orly, including all senior engineering executives, and other maintenance personnel are based in Saudi Arabia, Cairo, Libya and other major European airports used by MEA aircraft. Most of the fleet of 20 Boeing jetliners are actively operating on a charter and lease basis and this traffic is in process of being increased. As a result of events in the Lebanon, MEA suffered a loss of £Leb 14m in 1975 and £Leb 57m in the first eight months of 1976; this compared with a profit of £Leb 36m in 1974. The losses to date are fully covered by the airline's accumulated profits and reserves.

UNITED KINGDOM

British Airways returned a **loss** of £16·3m in the year ended 30 March 1976, compared with £9·4m for the previous year. Almost all of the loss — £15·6m — could be attributed to the increased sterling cost of repaying foreign loans, resulting from the falling value of the pound, and before provision for tax and borrowings a profit of £10·1m was recorded, almost twice the previous year's figure. There was a three per cent increase in the number of passengers carried and 13 per cent gain in revenue passenger-miles. Overall load factor achieved was virtually unchanged at 55·5 per cent but freight ton-miles went down six per cent. The Concorde entered service during the year but by 31 March had completed only 174 commercial flying hours on the Bahrein route; a loss of £2·3m was recorded on these operations, of which £1·9m was attributable to non-recurring launch costs, a share of allocated overheads and amortisation.

First demonstrations of the Yakovlev **Yak-40 in the UK** took place during September, under the auspices of Aero Technical Supplies Ltd, distributor of the type in the UK and Europe. The aircraft left Moscow on 13 September and was demonstrated at Gatwick, Glasgow, Aberdeen, Sumburgh, Norwich, Southend, East Midlands, Stansted, Staverton, Southampton, Blackbushe and Jersey. Among the airlines showing interest in the Yak-40 was Intra Airways, which is seeking a replacement for six DC-3s; a special Jersey-Staverton-Jersey demonstration was flown for Intra, which has indicated that it would require the 32-seat version of the Yak-40, probably in a cargo/convertible configuration with side loading door and freight floor.

USA

Acquisition of **Overseas National Airways** by Alaska International Industries and its **merger with** the latter's wholly-owned subsidiary **Alaska International Air** has been "tentatively agreed in principle" by the two companies. Meanwhile, the merger between two other major US supplementals, Trans International and Saturn — was expected to become effective at the beginning of October.

CIVIL CONTRACTS AND SALES

Aérospatiale Corvette: DLT Luftverkehrs GmbH has acquired one Corvette on long-term lease for use as an executive taxi, based at Frankfurt.

BAC One-Eleven: Cyprus Airways has ordered two new S s 500s for early 1978 delivery and will meanwhile lease two One-Elevens from BAC.

Boeing 727: American Airlines increased its contract for Advanced 727s from six (this column last month) to 10 during September. All will be delivered between mid-1977 and early-1978. Since November 1955, American has now ordered 280 Boeing jetliners, to become the company's largest customer, with orders for 747s, 727s and 707/720s worth almost $2,000m. □ Eastern Air Lines ordered six Advanced 727s, for November/December delivery. International Flight Research purchased one Series 100C second-hand from Boeing for immediate resale to Faucett of Peru. □ The Government of Senegal purchased one 727-200 from Boeing, with executive interior, for use by President Leopold Senghor. □ Iranair purchased one Srs 100 ex-Lufthansa and leased a Srs 200 from TAA. United ordered 28 Advanced 727s for $350m (over £220m), to replace early DC-8s on a one-for-one basis.

Boeing 737: Pacific Western Airlines ordered one additional 737-200C convertible passenger/freighter, for December delivery. □ Nigeria Airways is leasing one -200 from NZNAC for nine months with an option to renew; this replaces the planned lease of the same aircraft by Britannia Airways (July issue).

Boeing 747: Air France ordered a 747-200B Combi with side-loading freight door, for passenger/cargo operations, with 52,500 lb st (23 835 kgp) General Electric CF6-50E engines. Delivery will be in April 1977, bringing the Air France fleet to 19. □ Singapore Airlines ordered its sixth 747-200B, for August 1977 delivery. □ SAS ordered a 747-200B Combi for October 1977 delivery, and took an option on a second 747 for late 1978. Powered by 53,000 lb st (24062 kgp) JT9D-70A engines, it will have a max ramp weight of 820,000 lb (372 280 kg) and will carry up to 400 passengers including 32 on the upper deck. The 747 sales total is now 312.

De Havilland Canada Twin Otter: DLT Luftverkehrs GmbH, a third-level operator flying scheduled services in Germany, ordered its fifth Twin Otter, for late 1976 delivery. □ Greenlandair ordered a ski-equipped Twin Otter, its second. Sales total for the type is now 518. □ Surinam Airways is leasing two from Alaska Airlines.

Fairchild Swearingen Metro II: Air Midwest ordered four Metro IIs for delivery late-1976, subject to a favourable CAB ruling. □ Air Wisconsin, biggest operator of the Metro, ordered its ninth example.

Fairey Britten-Norman Islander: Air-Inter Gabon ordered another Islander, its eighth, for scheduled and charter services within Gabon. □ Lutexfo, a forestry company in Gabon, ordered one, and another was ordered for use in the same area by Compagnie Equatorial des Boise.

Fairey Britten-Norman Trislander: Inter-Island Airways, independent Seychellois operator, ordered one Trislander for scheduled, charter and tourist flights from Victoria.

Fokker F28 Fellowship: Swedish domestic airline Linjeflyg ordered three more Mk 4000s, for summer 1977 delivery, adding to five of this mark already on order for 1976 delivery and three Mk 1000s delivered in 1973. Pending delivery of the new aircraft, the company is leasing a Mk 1000 from Martinair and the Mk 6000 prototype from Fokker-VFW. □ Burma Airways Corp has bought two used Mk 1000s from Fokker-VFW, both ex-Iberia. □ Aerolineas Argentinas has purchased from Fokker-VFW one Mk 1000, ex-Germanair, joining three F28s delivered in 1975.

GAF Nomad: Air Tasmania has acquired one N22B for scheduled internal services. □ Geosearch (WA) Pty Ltd has ordered an N22B, for use on geophysical exploration duties within Australia and elsewhere. □ Independent Air Transport of Wewak, New Guinea, has taken delivery of an N22B, to replace a Nomad that had been on lease from Nationwide Air Services, Australian distributors for the type. □ The Division of National Mapping of the Australian National Resources Department has taken delivery of an N22B specially equipped for large-scale mapping operations. □ GAF reports that it has a contract to supply components for 20 Nomads to be assembled under licence in an undisclosed country, understood unofficially to be Papua — New Guinea.

Lockheed Electra: American Jet Industries bought two from International Jet Air of Calgary, and the latter's third Electra has been leased to Northwest Territorial Airways of Yellowknife.

McDonnell Douglas DC-8: US supplemental Evergreen International purchased two Srs 52s from Air New Zealand.

McDonnell Douglas DC-9: Delta sold four Srs 30s to Ozark. □ Texas International acquired one Srs 32 from Swissair. □ BWIA's Srs 33RC now in service is ex-Balair, purchased through McDonnell Douglas.

McDonnell Douglas DC-10: Air Algerie is newest DC-10 customer, with an order for one. □ Aero Mexico is reported to be adding a third Srs 30 to its fleet. □ Lufthansa ordered one Srs 30 for December 1977 delivery— the eleventh of the type added to its fleet.

Yakovlev Yak-40: Three Yak-40s have been ordered from the USSR by Socan Aircraft Ltd, formed jointly by Allarco Developments Ltd of Calgary and Aviaexport. Delivery will be made next July and aircraft will be available for re-sale after Canadian certification.

MILITARY CONTRACTS

Aermacchi MB 326: The Ghana Air Force has placed a contract for six single-seat MB 326Ks. □ The Tunisian Republican Air Force has placed a contract for four two-seat MB 326Gs and six single-seat MB 326Ks.

Beech T-34C Turbo Mentor: On 1 September, the Beech Aircraft Corporation was awarded a $36·5m (£21·47m) definitive contract for US Navy procurement of 98 additional T-34C Turbo Mentor trainers. □ *The Fuerza Aérea Ecuatoriana* has ordered 14 T-34Cs at a cost of $5m (£3m) for late-1978 delivery.

Bell UH-1N: On 3 September the US Navy exercised an option to acquire six additional UH-1N Twin Huey utility helicopters on behalf of the US Marine Corps for delivery during the first quarter of 1978, contract value of the helicopters and kits being $4·28m (£2·52m).

Britten-Norman Defender: Repeat order for two Defenders placed on behalf of the Mauritanian Islamic Air Force.

Lockheed C-130H Hercules: *The Força Aérea Portuguesa* has ordered two C-130Hs, for delivery August/September 1977.

Rockwell OV-10G Bronco: Twenty-four OV-10G Bronco multi-mission counter-insurgency aircraft have been ordered for the Republic of Korea Air Force for 1977 delivery with a contractual value of $58·2m (£34·23m).

Which strike aircraft can make high-speed single-pass low-level attacks with pinpoint accuracy...

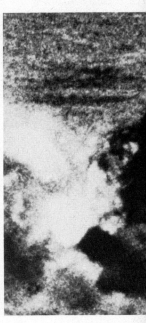

...and operate at full load from improvised strips?

Jaguar, with its integrated navigation and weapons aiming system, can operate at full weapons load from improvised airstrips close to the battle-line and strike with deadly precision, even in poor weather. Already the main tactical strike weapon of two of the world's most experienced air forces – the Royal Air Force and the Armée de l'Air – Jaguar is also in full production for the air forces of other nations. In terms of weapons load, operational range, survivability and maintainability, Jaguar is one of the most cost-effective tactical strike aircraft available today.

jaguar INTERNATIONAL

Designed and built by
S.E.P.E.C.A.T.
BRITISH AIRCRAFT CORPORATION
100 PALL MALL, LONDON, S.W.1.
AVIONS MARCEL DASSAULT
BREGUET AVIATION
B.P. 32 92 VAUCRESSON FRANCE

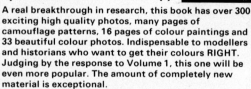

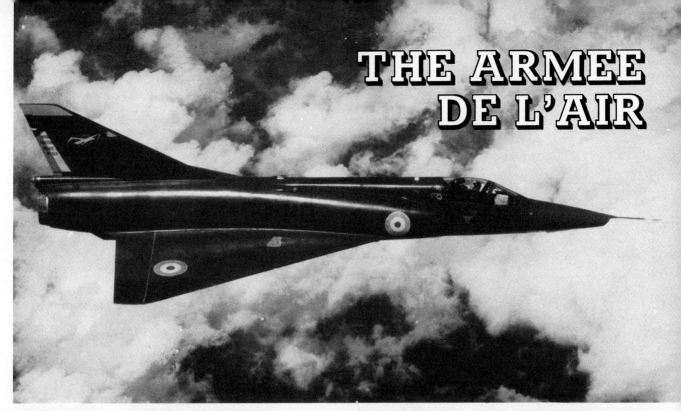

THE ARMEE DE L'AIR

MORE MIRAGES... FEWER ILLUSIONS

Paul A Jackson surveys France's very independent Armée de l'Air a decade after French withdrawal from the integrated military organisation of NATO and in the wake of fundamental changes in French defence policy.

THE REGION OF BRITTANY is probably the best known to the average tourist for the superlative scenery that it offers and accompanies with Breton cuisine; to most inhabitants of other regions of France, however, Brittany is equally well-known for the characteristic inflexibility with which the Breton is reputedly endowed. What Frenchman is unfamiliar with the dictum "As stubborn as a Breton"? In the wider sphere of West European defence, the French as a nation have, over the past decade, been increasingly likened in NATO circles to the Bretons owing to their intransigence in defence matters.

France's 10-year persistence in treading an independent path to that trodden by her neighbours and maintaining military liaison only at the highest levels has understandably incurred both the displeasure and the concern of the remaining participants in the integrated military organisation of NATO who believe a credible independent French defensive posture to be purely illusory. Primary cause for anxiety generated by French non-participation has, of course, been the reduction in effectiveness of NATO defensive capability that it has undeniably imparted, particularly at a time when major upgrading of Warsaw Treaty Organisation forces in qualitative if not quantitative terms has been continuous, paralleling the steady erosion of NATO forces as a result of swingeing budgetary restrictions on defence expenditure.

Gaullist-style nationalism — even jingoism — coupled with a deep-rooted distaste for what was viewed as NATO pragmatism and compounded by innate individualism have motivated France's attitude — though the less charitable have viewed the Ailleret *tous azimuts* concept of the late 'sixties as the product of a combination of naïveté and gallic obstinacy; a defence doctrine based on illusion. However, if individualists, the French are also realists and while there is as yet no evidence of a dramatic change of heart on the part of France, NATO is now taking comfort from a major shift in French defence policy encompassing the abandonment of the *tous azimuts* concept in favour of the more realistic acceptance that the

main threat in Europe can only be from the East and the discarding of the doctrine of inevitable nuclear retaliation in favour of a more flexible response.

Seen by some as inevitably the first step towards closer military links with NATO, the new policy, as recently expressed by Gen Guy Méry, French Chief of General Staff, allows for France to participate in a conventional conflict in NATO's forward area on the Czechoslovak and East German borders if France's own security is felt to be threatened, this being in direct contrast to the 'sanctuarization' concept of the past decade which held that French forces would be used only to defend the sanctuary of national territory. Although Gen Méry has emphasised that French forces will not be deployed in the forward defence zones of Federal Germany in peacetime, he recently commented: "It would be extremely dangerous for us to remain out of that first battle in which our own security would be at stake!"

This change of policy is accompanying increased emphasis

(Head of page) A Mirage IIIR of the 2ᵉ (Savoie) Escadron of the 33ᵉ Escadre de Reconnaissance based at Strasbourg, and (below) Mirage 5Fs of the 3ᵉ (Auvergne) Esadron of the 13ᵉ Escadre de Chasse based at Colmar.

(Above) Jaguar A strike fighters of the 1ᵉʳ (Provence) Escadron of the 7ᵉ Escadre de Chasse based at St Dizier, this having been the first Escadre to re-equip with the Jaguar.

(Above) A Mirage IIIE trailing a target and (below) a two-seat Mirage IIIBE of the 2ᵉ (Cote d'Or) Escadron of the 2ᵉ Escadre de Chasse at Dijon. This escadron serves as a Mirage OCU for both Armée de l'Air and foreign pilots.

on the build-up of conventional forces and is linked with a new six-year military programme (1977-82) in which defence expenditure will virtually double in terms of constant francs, from NF 58000m (£6,531m) in the 1977 Fiscal year to NF 114 575m (£12,902m) in 1982, the average annual rate of increase on defence spending over the six years being 14·8 per cent. This programme represents an increase as a proportion of the national budget from 17 to 20 per cent and as a percentage of the Gross National Product of roughly from 3·0 to 3·6 per cent.

In this programme, France's national air arm, the *Armée de l'Air,* will receive an average of something more than 22 per cent of the appropriations, as compared with 31 per cent for the Army, but, at this point in time, this is seen as sufficient to cover the replacement of the entire obsolescent element in the first-line hardware inventory while simultaneously maintaining numerical strength, significantly upgrading the conventional weapons capability of the service and, during the final year of the programme, commencing the phase-in of the next generation of combat aircraft. In fact, the completion of the programme will see the *Armée de l'Air* more completely equipped with aircraft of indigenous manufacture than at any time since the end of WW II — the only exceptions being a handful of long-range transports and tanker-transports — and reflecting the ever-increasing French self-sufficiency in military hardware.

Today roughly level-pegging with the RAF and the

Luftwaffe as numerically the world's fourth largest air arm, the *Armée de l'Air,* with Headquarters in Paris's Boulevard Victor, comprises some 80 squadrons and 102,000 personnel — including 39,000 one-year conscripts — divided between six principal commands, Strategic, Tactical, Air Defence, Transport, Training and Telecommunications, with *Général d'Armée Aérienne* Maurice Saint-Cricq as Chief of Staff in succession to Gen Claude Grigaut who recently retired on reaching the official age limit. Each command comprises administrative personnel and several *escadres* (wings), which, normally assigned one to each base, consist of two, three and occasionally four *escadrons* (squadrons) which are each further sub-divided into two *escadrilles* (flights), many of the *escadrons* being named after French provinces and their component *escadrilles* perpetuating WW I *escadrille* designations and insignia. An additional component of the fighter *escadres* is provided by the *Section de Liaison et de Vol Sans Visibilité* (SLVSV) operating a miscellany of aircraft ranging from the aged Broussard and Flamant to the equally-elderly Lockheed T-33A and Magister for communications and instrument-rating tasks.

The stategic component

Despite relinquishment of the *tous azimuts* ("all direction") concept that provided the cornerstone of the late Gen Charles de Gaulle's loftily independent strategy and increased emphasis on conventional weaponry, the French *Force Nucleaire Strategique* still commands as much as one-third of the total defence spending under the new six-year programme, although there is to be some tempo reduction in most strategic and tactical nuclear weapon production programmes, such as those for the Army's Pluton surface-to-surface missile and the AN-52. Production of the S-3 SSBS (*Sol-Sol Balistique Stratégique*) missile for the *Armée de l'Air* second-stage deterrent provided by the two nine-missile squadrons of the 1ᵉʳ *Groupement de Missiles Stratégiques* on the Plateau d'Albion, near Avignon, is unaffected, however, and these higher-yield extended-range missiles will replace the current 1,780-nm (3 300-km) 150 Kt S-2 missiles during 1978-82.

The first-stage deterrent is provided by the Mirage IVA fleet of the *Forces Aérienne Stratégiques,* which, with Headquarters at Taverny, near Paris, is commanded by *Général de Division Aérienne* Michel Delaval. Known at its inception as the *Force de Frappe* and subsequently under the less bellicose title of *Force de Dissuasion* when some rapprochement was reached between the French and Soviet governments — and perhaps also reflecting a more realistic assessment of the relative power of the armouries of the two countries — the Mirage IVA fleet has undergone some reorganisation during the course of this year with one of the three *escadres* (the 93ᵉ *Escadre de Bombardement* with Headquarters at Istres) being dissolved on 30 June, the number of *escadrons* being correspondingly reduced from nine to six and these operating a total of 32 bombers dispersed among six bases rather than nine as previously, although the three additional bases formerly used (by the 93ᵉ *Escadre*) at Cambrai, Creil and Istres are retaining the necessary support facilities and stocks of nuclear weapons so that they may still be utilised for Mirage IVA dispersal in an emergency.

This fixed-wing element of the *Force de Dissuasion* was completed in the mid 'sixties as a three-*escadre* force, each *escadre* comprising three four-aircraft *escadrons* plus an *Escadron de Ravitaillement en Vol* of four Boeing C-135F tankers, and the last of 62 Mirage IVAs being delivered in March 1968. The Mirage IVA fleet was originally intended to fly a high-level mission profile with M = 2·0 penetration with a 60 Kt free-falling nuclear bomb as the primary weapon, but the force is now orientated towards low-level penetration, each aircraft having been rotated through the necessary modification programme, and until last year, a single Mirage IVA from each *escadron* was maintained at 15-minute alert status, although this has now been scaled down. The force currently comprises the 91ᵉ *Escadre* with Headquarters at Mont-de-Marsan and *escadrons* also at Cazaux and Orange, and the 94ᵉ *Escadre* with Headquarters at Avord and *escadrons* also at St Dizier and Luxeuil. Each base has a *Dépôt-Atelier de Munitions Speciales* (DAMS) to store, maintain and assemble the nuclear weapons, but the C-135F *escadrons* are now grouped together at Istres. The FAS also includes a *Centre d'Instruction* (CIFAS 328) at Bordeaux with an inventory of eight Mirage IIIB conversion trainers, 10 Mirage IIIB-RV flight-refuelling trainers and four Mirage IVAs modified to take a 2,205-lb (1 000-kg) reconnaissance pod for strategic surveillance tasks. The *Centre* also possesses five N 2501SNB Noratlas *(Systeme Navigation-Bombardement)* systems trainers and Lockheed T-33A instrument rating aircraft which are detached to the *escadrons* as required. The 50 Mirage IVAs remaining in the FAS inventory are to continue in service until 1985 and no successor is intended.

A strong tactical element

Numerically the largest command of the *Armée de l'Air* in terms of aircraft and personnel (13,500) is the 1ᵉʳ *Commandement Aérien Tactique* (CATac) with Headquarters at Metz and, until 1966, deployed in Germany and NATO-committed as a component of 4ATAF. Possessing the tasks of ground attack, strike and reconnaissance, the 1ᵉʳ CATac forms a substantial force of 20 home-based operational and three training *escadrons,* plus one overseas-based operational *escadron* on permanent detachment in Djibouti, these being grouped in six *escadres de chasse* (EC), which include a tactical nuclear force of four *escadrons* equipped to carry the AN-52 nuclear weapon, and one *escadre de reconnaissance* (ER).

The backbone of the 1ᵉʳ CATac is, of course, provided by the Dassault-Breguet Mirage IIIE strike fighter, now some nine years old with phase-out scheduled to commence in 1978 although unlikely to be completed before 1985, and Mirage IIIR tactical reconnaissance aircraft, now nearly 15 years old and expected to be phased out by 1980-81. The smaller quantity of barely more youthful Mirage IIIRDs (eight years old and to remain in service until at least 1986) and rather newer Mirage 5Fs (which have an estimated 14 years of service life ahead of them) make a 1ᵉʳ CATac total of just short of 250 single-seat examples of the delta-winged Mirage, but the command is receiving a steady infusion of SEPECAT Jaguars —the 100th was taken over by the *Armée de l'Air* at Toulouse-Colomiers on 19 May — with a considerable upgrading of

strike capability in consequence. A total of 200 Jaguars is to be ordered for the *Armée de l'Air* comprising 40 two-seat Jaguar Es and 160 single-seat Jaguar As, the former all having been taken into the inventory with approximately half of the single-seaters so far delivered and 30 remaining to be ordered.

The first 1ᵉʳ CATac unit to convert to the Jaguar was the 7ᵉ *Escadre* at St Dizier (BA 113) which received its first aircraft on 24 May 1973, its component *escadrons*, 1/7 *Provence* and 3/7 *Languedoc*, relinquishing Mystère IVAs and taking on the rôle of nuclear strike. A third *escadron*, 2/7 *Argonne*, was subsequently formed to fulfil the functions of a Jaguar OCU and is equipped primarily with the two-seat Jaguar E, two or three examples of which are also assigned to the other component *escadrons*. The 11ᵉ *Escadre* started to follow suit during the course of 1975 at Toul-Rosières when it began to relinquish its F-100 Super Sabres, the first component

The Mirage IIIC (above) is seen in the markings of the 2ᵉ (Ile de France) Escadron of the 5ᵉ Escadre, this unit having converted to the Mirage F1C from late 1974, passing its Mirage IIICs to the 10ᵉ Escadre.

(Above right) Mirage F1C interceptors of the 3ᵉ (Lorraine) Escadron of the 30ᵉ Escadre de Chasse Tous Temps based at Reims, and (below) a Mirage IVA strategic bomber of the 91ᵉ Escadre de Bombardement which deploys its escadrons at Mont-de-Marsan, Cazaux and Orange.

escadron to convert being 3/11 *Corse* which subsequently operated as a conversion unit for 1/11 *Roussillon* and 2/11 *Vosages,* these operating Martel-armed Jaguars and which, it is anticipated, will eventually carry the proposed medium-range ASMP *(Air-sol moyenne-portée)* missile. The 11e *Escadre* is unusual in having a fourth *escadron*, this, 4/11 *Jura,* being on permanent detachment to Djibouti (BA 188) at *escadrille* strength with F-100D Super Sabres and not due to re-equip with (flight-refuelling capable) Jaguars until 1978.

The other tactical nuclear element of the 1er CATac is provided by two *escadrons* of Mirage IIIEs, this strike fighter equipping two of the three *escadrons* of the 2e *Escadre* at Dijon (BA 102), these being 1/2 *Cigognes* and 3/2 *Alsace,* each with 20 aircraft on charge; two of the three *escadrons* of the 3e *Escadre* (1/3 *Navarre* and 2/3 *Champagne et Brie*), each with 20 aircraft at Nancy (BA 133); the two *escadrons* of the 4e *Escadre* (1/4 *Dauphiné* and 2/4 *La Fayette*) at Luxeuil (BA 116) and two of the three *escadrons* (1/13 *Artois* and 2/13 *Alpes*) of the 13e *Escadre* at Colmar (BA 132). The third component *escadron* of the 2e *Escadre*, 2/2 *Cote d'Or*, acts as an OCU for Mirage pilots with an inventory of five single-seat Mirage IIICs and 25 two-seat Mirage IIIBs (nine) and IIIBEs (16) forming three *escadrilles*. Earlier this year, *Escadron* 2/2 *Cote d'Or* celebrated the graduation of its 1,000th student pilot to operational standards (more than 100 of these being pilots from foreign air forces). The third *escadron* of each of the 3e and 13e *Escadres* (3/3 *Ardennes* and 3/13 *Auvergne*) operate 20 Mirage 5Fs from the 50 taken into the *Armée de l'Air* after their export to Israel was embargoed by the French government in 1967, EC 3/13 having been formed with these on 1 May 1972 and EC 3/3 two years later, on 1 July 1974.

The remaining Mirages in the 1er CATac are operated in the tactical reconnaissance rôle by the 33e *Escadre de Reconnaissance* at Strasbourg (BA 124), 1/33 *Belfort* and 2/33 *Savoie* each having 20 Mirage IIIRs on strength and the third *escadron*, 3/33 *Moselle* operating 18 Doppler-equipped Mirage IIIRDs. With the exception of the Mirage 5Fs, the majority of the delta-winged Mirage fighters in the 1er CATac

(Above) A Nord 2501 Noratlas of the 62^e Escadre de Transport based at Reims and (below) Boeing C-135F tankers of one of the escadrons de Ravitaillement en Vol which have recently been grouped together at Istres.

inventory will reach the end of their useful lives during the next few years. Insufficient Jaguars are programmed to permit them to replace more than a small proportion of the Mirages and no further procurement of the Jaguar for the *Armée de l'Air* is contemplated subsequent to the delivery of the 200th aircraft in 1979. Thus a decision on a successor to the Mirage in the tactical strike and reconnaissance rôles must be taken in the not-so-distant future. The proposed Super Jaguar has been considered, apparently without a great deal of enthusiasm, and it could well be that, to adapt Donald Douglas's maxim, the only replacement for the Mirage is another Mirage! It would seem likely, therefore, that a proportion of the additional 109 swept-wing Mirage F1s that are to be funded under the new six-year programme as a follow-on to the 105 so far ordered in the F1C intercept variant will be optimised for the strike rôle and assigned to the 1er CATac, with a second-generation strike derivative of the Delta Mirage 2000 currently under consideration following-on in 1982-83.

An additional command within the *Forces Aériennes Tactiques* is the 2e CATac with Headquarters in Nancy, the sole permanent flying unit of which is the 92e *Escadre de Bombardement* with two component *escadrons*, 1/92 *Burgundy* and 2/92 *Aquitaine,* equipped with aged Vautour IIBs and

An N 262D Frégate operated by the 1er Escadron of the Groupe Aérien d'Entrainement et de Liaison, or the 65e Escadre de Transport, which operates from Villacoublay and is responsible for the training of communications pilots and for light transport and liaison tasks.

IINs, the remaining examples of which are to be retired next year. The 2e CATac is actually the aerial component of the tri-service *Force d'Intervention,* theoretically equivalent to NATO's ACE Mobile Force, and in times of emergency may be assigned *escadres* from other commands for rapid deployment in the so-called *Théâtre d'Operations Metropole-Méditerranée,* the 2e CATac exercising tactical control.

An upgraded air defence

The air defence of Metropolitan France is the responsibility of the *Commandement Air des Forces de Défense Aérienne* (CAFDA), which embraces 9,000 personnel, 10 battalions — of 20 programmed for air base defence — each with 80 Thomson-CSF/Matra R.440 Crotale surface-to-air missiles and eight squadrons of manned interceptors. For a number of years, the Mirage IIIC preponderated in the CAFDA *escadres de chasse,* but this initial production series model of the Dassault-Breguet delta-winged fighter, now considered to have only about three years of useful life remaining to it, has of late been surpassed numerically by the swept-wing Mirage F1C which is destined to provide the manned intercept capability backbone of CAFDA until the phase-in of the Delta Mirage 2000 from 1982.

Linked with NATO's NADGE network and commanded by *Général* Maurice Bret, the CAFDA interceptor force is controlled by the STRIDA II computerised warning and communications network, and will soon possess three Mirage F1C-equipped *escadres* and one *escadre* operating the Mirage IIIC and scheduled to convert to the later type towards the end of the decade. The first CAFDA *escadre* to re-equip with the Mirage F1C was the 30^e *Escadre de Chasse Tous Temps* at Reims (BA 112) where the first of its two *escadrons* (2/30 *Normandie* and 3/30 *Lorraine*) received its initial aircraft on 20

The Transall C.160, of which there are 48 included in the CoTAM fleet, equips the three escadrons of the 61ᵉ Escadre de Transport and is expected to remain in service until at least 1995, the Armée de l'Air having recently formulated a requirement for a further 30 aircraft of this type. (Below right) The DC-6B remains in service with the 82ᵉ Groupe Aerien Mixte at Papeete.

December 1973, both having completed conversion by mid-1974. The 5ᵉ *Escadre de Chasse* at Orange (BA 115) was the next to convert to the Mirage F1C, its component *escadrons* (1/5 *Vendee* and 2/5 *Ile de France*) each attaining full 15-aircraft statutory strength during 1975 and passing their surviving Mirage IIICs to the 10ᵉ *Escadre* at Creil (BA 110) where they augmented those already operated by 2/10 *Seine* and enabling 1/10 *Valois* to discard its Super Mystères. These, in turn, were assigned to the 12ᵉ *Escadre* at Cambrai (BA 103) until, in May this year, this *Escadre,* too, began conversion to the Mirage F1C, commencing with *Escadron 2/12 Cornouaille,* with 1/12 *Cambresis* due to follow suit in the coming summer.

Deliveries of the Mirage F1 to the *Armée de l'Air* during 1977-82 are scheduled to total 123 aircraft, leaving 23 of the additional 109 fighters of this type to be ordered under the new six-year programme to follow on thereafter, and it is likely that there will be included a small batch of two-seat Mirage F1Bs for use as systems trainers and retaining a secondary combat rôle. To supplement the Mirage F1C in the CAFDA in the first half of the 'eighties, orders are to be placed for an initial quantity of 127 Delta Mirage 2000 interceptors of which the first 10 will be delivered by 1982, with the first CAFDA *escadre* commencing working up on this type in the following year. The air defence system will also benefit from the introduction of new low-altitude radar equipment, improved electronic countermeasures and the balance of the Crotale low-level SAM system remaining as a shortfall from the 3ᵉ *loi-programme*.

A sizeable logistic support force

Logistic support for all French forces is provided by the *Commandement du Transport Aérien Militaire* (CoTAM), which, also responsible for communications and some rescue functions, has 7,400 personnel and some 20 squadrons and flights in five *Escadres de Transport*. The most numerous aircraft in the CoTAM transport fleet is the Nord 2501 Noratlas — of which more than 170 remain in the inventory of the *Armée de l'Air* — which had now seen something approaching a quarter-century of service and is currently being rotated through a modification and refurbishing programme aimed at extending its useful life until at least 1985. The Noratlas equips the two 18-aircraft *escadrons* (1/62 *Vercors* and 2/62 *Anjou*) of the 62ᵉ *Escadre de Transport* at Reims (BA 112) and two of the three *escadrons* (1/64 *Bearn* and 3/64 *Bigorre*) of the 64ᵉ *Escadre* at Evreux (BA 105), the other component *escadron* of the last-mentioned *Escadre* (2/64 *Mains*) flying equally elderly DC-6Bs which it anticipates replacing with three ex-Air France Caravelle 11Rs next year.

The Cessna 310N (above) serves in the communications rôle with the Centre d'Essais en Vol and its detachments. The MS 760 Paris (below) was repurchased by the Armée de l'Air from the Fôrça Aérea Brasileira and serves in the liaison rôle with the 2ᵉ Escadron of the 65ᵉ Escadre de Transport at Villacoublay.

The SA 330 Puma (below) is operated by the 67ᵉ Escadre d'Hélicoptères in which the principal CoTAM helicopter strength is concentrated.

The Alouette II (above) and Alouette III (immediately below) are concentrated primarily in the 67ᵉ Escadre d'Hélicoptères, but small numbers serve with the helicopter training centre at Chambery and other units.

The CAP 10 (above) is used for the initial selection of pupil pilots during a 17-hour course at Clermont-Ferrand, and two examples of the Falcon ST (immediately below) fitted with Mirage IIIE radar and navigational equipment serve in the systems training rôle.

Considered good for service until at least 1995 are CoTam's 48 Transall C.160s which equip the three *escadrons* (1/61 *Touraine,* 2/61 *Franche Comte* and 3/61 *Poitou*) of the 61ᵉ *Escadre* at Orleans (BA 123). Although the Transall has now been out of production for a number of years, the *Armée de l'Air* has formulated a requirement for a further 30 aircraft of this type* for the procurement of which provision is made in the 1977-82 programme. However, the delivery of the additional Transalls to CoTAM is apparently dependent on the receipt of export orders for at least a further 40 aircraft which are necessary in order to render the re-opening of the production line viable. If the *Armée de l'Air does* receive its additional Transalls, five of these are likely to be delivered as flight-fuelling tankers (for which Aérospatiale is already undertaking studies) and the remainder are probably to be supplied with in-flight refuelling capability.

Governmental transportation tasks are the domaine of the *Groupe des Liaisons Aériennes Ministérielles,* this consisting of the *Escadron de Transport* 1/60 at Villacoublay (BA 107) which operates the Presidential Caravelle, five Mystère 20s, and three Alouette III and two Puma helicopters, and *Escadron de Transport* 3/60, which, detached to Le Bourget (BA 104), operates four DC-8Fs for VIP transport and Pacific reinforcement rôles. The third component *escadron,* 2/60, attained autonomy in July 1972, was raised to *escadre* status as the 65ᵉ *Escadre de Transport* and now operates as the *Groupe Aerien d'Entrainement et de Liaison* with two *escadrons,* 1/65 with 18 Nord 262D Frégates and three Mystère 20s, and 2/65 with 24 MS 760 Paris light jet aircraft, a dozen Broussard utility aircraft and a single Rallye. The 65ᵉ *Escadre* is now responsible for the training of communications pilots and for light transport and liaison tasks from Villacoublay.

The 65ᵉ *Escadre* has a transport commitment to the 2ᵉ *Region Aérienne* (Paris), but other *Regions Aériennes,* including the 1ᵉʳ RA at Metz (BA 128), the 3ᵉ RA at Bordeaux and the 4ᵉ RA at Aix (BA 114) are respectively assigned the 41ᵉʳ, 43ᵉ and 44ᵉ *Escadrilles de Liaison Aériennes* under CoTAM control, each operating a mix of Paris, Broussard and Flamant aircraft, plus one Rallye 180GT, and 44ᵉ ELA also possesses a SAR rôle for which it operates two Puma helicopters, two Noratlas transports, a Broussard, a Sikorsky H-34 and an Alouette III from Solenzara (BA 126), Corsica.

The principal CoTAM helicopter strength, however, is concentrated within the 67ᵉ *Escadre d'Hélicoptères* with five *escadrons,* each of which has a normal inventory of five

---

This has aroused some cynical amusement in Federal Germany, the Luftwaffe having been prevented from cutting its original Transall order by 30 machines by vehement French opposition and, having no use for the aircraft, transferred 20 of them to Turkey.

The Magister trainer, seen in service below with the Ecole de l'Air at Salon-de-Provence, is currently being cycled through a refurbishing process with the aim of extending its useful life until at least 1985, but a successor, currently referred to as the Epsilon, is to be ordered during the 1977-82 programme.

The Mirage IVA, seen above approaching the refuelling drogue of a C-135F tanker, has formed the first-stage deterrent of the so-called Force de Dissuasion for a number of years and is currently scheduled to remain in the first-line inventory until 1985, no successor being intended.

Alouette IIs, four Alouette IIIs and two Pumas, 1/67 being based at Cazaux, 2/67 at Metz and St Dizier, 3/67 at Villacoublay, 4/67 which is deployed in support of the 1er *Groupement de Missiles Stratégiques* and 5/67 at Istres. Army responsibility for assault transport restricts *Armée de l'Air* helicopters to communications, SAR and airfield crash rescue, but the *Centre d'Instruction des Equipages d'Hélicoptères* at Chambery (BA 725) provides training for the pilots of the other services as well as for government departments with four Alouette IIs and six Alouette IIIs.

The training organisation
All flying, technical and administrative schools are subordinate to the *Commandement des Ecoles de l'Armée de l'Air* (CEAA). Initial selection of trainees is undertaken at the *Ecole de Formation Initiale du Personnel Navigant* at Clermont-Ferrand (BA 745) during a 17-hour course on 26 CAARP CAP 10 light trainers. Successful officer candidates then proceed to the *Ecole de l'Air* at Salon-de-Provence and other ranks to *Groupement Ecole* 315 at Cognac (BA 701) where they fly 150 hours basic training on the Magister. Advanced training of 100 hours on T-33As at *Groupement Ecole* 314 at Tours (BA 705) is followed by 150 hours of weapons training on Mystère IVAs with the 8e *Escadre de Transformation* at Cazaux. With the arrival of the first Alpha Jets at Tours in July 1978, the T-33A and Mystère IVA phases of the present syllabus will be combined into a single 130-hour course. Other of the Alpha Jets are earmarked for *Groupement Ecole* 313, the *Armée de l'Air* commitment being for 200 aircraft of this type, with final delivery scheduled for December 1983.

Operational conversion units within the 2e, 7e and 11e *continued on page 236*

continued on page 236

Shotgun marriage...
or love match?

ISRAEL'S PRIDE OF LIONS

W HEN, after the Israeli Cabinet had overruled the objections of the General Staff, Israel's indigenous derivative of France's Mirage fighter was publicly revealed at the Israel Aircraft Industries' plant at Lod (Ben Gurion) Airport on 14 April 1975, something of the remarkable screen of mystery and subterfuge that for years had enveloped Israeli activities in the sphere of fighter development appeared to have been dispelled. The existence of the J79-powered Mirage, now sporting the appellation of Kfir (Hebrew for Young Lion) had for long been postulated. Indeed, it had become one of the worst-kept secrets of a country in which military secrecy had perforce become a way of life. Thus, the removal of the security wraps was hardly calculated to create an international sensation.

Once the Kfir had been officially revealed, however, the artifice that had shrouded its development gave place to a smokescreen of rumour and innuendo designed to hide the true service status of the warplane. Most of the senior officers of the Israeli General Staff, including the C-in-C of the Israel Defence Force's air component, the *Heyl Ha'Avir,* Maj Gen Binyamin Peled, had staunchly opposed exposure of the Kfir. Not least among their objections was concern that the publicity that was the primary purpose of revealing the fighter might weaken Israel's argument that advanced new weapons,

Eighteen months ago, in April 1975, the air component of the Israel Defence Force, *Heyl Ha'Avir,* began to take into its first-line inventory what may well come to be looked upon in the annals of military aviation as the most extraordinary warplane of the 'seventies, the Israel Aircraft Industries-manufactured Kfir; extraordinary in that, as AIR INTERNATIONAL described it at the time, the Kfir is a mélange of French aerodynamic design and US engine technology fused by a good measure of Jewish *chochem* or astuteness. This is, of course, something of an over-simplification, for the Kfir is far more than a French Mirage airframe successfully mated with a US General Electric engine; it is the highest achievement to-date of an aircraft industry that had progressed from fledgling status to maturity within barely two decades — an aircraft industry that is already challenging those of the most technologically-advanced nations on the world's export markets.

such as the F-15 Eagle, were needed from the USA. It was also felt that the unveiling of the Kfir before it had even attained operational status with the *Heyl Ha'Avir* was tantamount to tipping one of the aces in Israel's pack. Premier Yitzhak Rabin and his cabinet had little recourse but to set aside these objections in the belief that the evidence of Israel's growing self-sufficiency in modern weaponry would provide a much-needed boost in public morale which was flagging under a combination of internal and external economic setbacks.

Thus, the Kfir was revealed against a background of unofficial — but undoubtedly *officially* inspired — reports that the Kfir had participated in the October 1973 conflict and that more than a hundred had already been taken on strength by the *Heyl Ha'Avir*; reports that were given due credence by the world's press. In fact, the occasion of the first public showing of the Kfir at Lod Airport coincided with the *first delivery* of the Kfir to the Israeli air arm!

Gestation of a polygenetic warplane
The delivery embargo imposed by the French government in 1967 on 50 Mirage 5J fighter-bombers for the *Heyl Ha'Avir* on which deposits had been paid and progress payments were continuing came as a traumatic shock to the Israeli government. France had for long been Israel's primary source of supply for weaponry and while the Israelis initially assumed the embargo to be a temporary measure, it rendered all too obvious their vulnerability to changes of the political wind when relying on a single source for supply. As the French attitude hardened in the following year, ostensibly as a result of the Israeli assault on Beirut Airport, and the embargo was *officially* extended to the supply of spares for French equipment already in the Israeli inventory, consideration was given as a matter of urgency to manufacturing the Mirage in Israel, despite the astronomically high cost of such a venture to so small a country.

The *Heyl Ha'Avir* had received a total of 72 Mirage IIICJ air superiority fighters (plus three two-seat Mirage IIIBJs) from France, the first two of these having been delivered on 7 April 1962, and over the years these had borne the brunt of much of the fighting to which the force had been committed, suffering inevitable attrition. Accordingly, a project was launched to extend the service lives of the remaining aircraft under the programme name *Salvo* — this designation being used in the connotation of an expedient for saving the aircraft — and at the same time, plans were formulated for the manufacture of the Mirage in Israel, presumably with the covert if not overt approval of Marcel Dassault.

The Mirage 5J had been evolved to Israeli specifications and its development and production had been closely monitored by the Israelis. Thus, a nucleus of Israeli engineers were thoroughly conversant with the structure and systems of the fighter. What structural and installation drawings were necessary were obtained clandestinely with the aid of Israeli sympathizers in France; the manufacture of jigs and tools began; contracts were placed abroad for such items as were still beyond the capability of Israeli industry, such as some forgings and pre-formed panels that were ordered from Metal Resourses of Gardena, California, and full manufacturing drawings for the SNECMA Atar 9C power plant were acquired from Switzerland* with a view to this being manufactured by Bet-Shemesh Engines, both to replace the time-expired engines in existing Mirages and to power the planned new-build Mirages which were to be based essentially on the Mirage 5J.

In the event, it was to prove possible, depite the embargo, to obtain adequate supplies of the Atar 9C for both the *Salvo* programme and at least the initial production run of new-build Mirages, and thus plans to manufacture the SNECMA engine were discarded, Israel Aircraft Industries setting its sights higher and acquiring a licence for the appreciably more advanced General Electric J79-GE-17 (which, incidentally, powered the F-4E Phantom which had meanwhile been ordered from the USA and was to start entering the Israeli inventory from September 1969) and initiating the redesign of the basic Mirage 5J airframe around this power plant.

US willingness to supplant France as the principal Israeli weaponry supplier, while removing some of the urgency from the Mirage programme, did not render it unnecessary, for the *Heyl Ha'Avir* had proved the French fighter to be a good, economical dogfight aircraft such as could not at that time be offered by US industry and thus, despite immense cost, Israel persisted with its plans to build the Mirage, simultaneously taking the opportunity provided by the J79-GE-17 engine to

make good some of the deficiencies in the French fighter in order to translate it into an air superiority and intercept aircraft capable of matching foreseeable Arab equipment through the second half of the 'seventies.

Thus, three individual programmes were pursued in parallel by Israel Aircraft Industries: the *Salvo* programme through which all remaining French-built Mirage IIICJ fighters were rotated and in which they were restored to zero-hours condition, various IAI-manufactured components being incorporated as necessary; a new-build programme covering an Atar 9C-engined multi-rôle fighter, which, dubbed Nesher (Eagle), was based closely on the Mirage 5J but embodied a dual fire control system for both air-to-air and air-to-ground tasks, and a development programme aimed at mating the Mirage airframe with the General Electric engine.

The prototype Nesher was flown at Lod in September 1969, this being based on a French-built airframe but incorporating IAI-manufactured components, some avionics produced at Ashdod by Elta Electronics, an IAI division, and a Martin-Baker JM 6 zero-zero ejection seat. The first delivery of the Nesher to the *Heyl Ha'Avir* took place in 1972, and some 40 were on strength when the force found itself committed to the *Yom Kippur* conflict in October 1973, serving primarily in the air superiority rôle armed with a pair of Israeli-manufactured 30-mm DEFA cannon and two Rafael Shafrir (Dragonfly) short-range air-to-air dogfight missiles. By this time, production of the Nesher had apparently attained a tempo of 2·5-

Alfred Fraunknecht, an engineer at the Sulzer Brothers plant where the Atar 9C-3 was being part-manufactured and assembled for the Mirage IIIS, delivered 20 cartons of drawings to Israel, via Germany, for which he received $200,000. He was subsequently sentenced by a Swiss federal court to four-and-a-half years imprisonment for industrial espionage.

(Head of opposite page and above right) The Kfir-C2 is the latest version of the IAI derivative of the Mirage 5 airframe and will shortly supplant in production the initial version of the Kfir seen below in service with a squadron of the Heyl Ha'Avir.

3·0 per month at IAI's Lod facility, and was to continue into the following year when the Atar 9C-powered Nesher was to give place on the assembly lines to the J79-powered model destined to emerge as the Kfir in 1975.

First and foremost a dogfighter

While much development effort was undoubtedly saved by adhering closely to Mirage aerodynamics, a prodigious effort was involved in manufacturing the jigs and tools, and in producing the detail drawings, and arranging the nuptials between the Mirage airframe and the General Electric turbojet was a task of considerable magnitude and a courageous effort by any standard, let alone an aircraft industry so youthful as that of Israel. By comparison with the Atar 9C, the J79-GE-17 was 25·31 in (64,28 cm) shorter in overall length at 208·69 in (5,30 m) and had a marginally smaller diameter at 39·06 in (99,20 cm), the diameter of the French engine being 40·2 in (1,02 m). Furthermore, at 3,835 lb (1 740 kg), the dry weight of the US engine was 715 lb (324,32 kg) higher. The 11 per cent greater mass flow of the General Electric engine dictated the provision of enlarged air intakes, but perhaps the greatest problem was that provided by the very much higher (954°C)

turbine inlet temperature of the J79 which manifested itself in an external wall temperature of roughly twice that of the Atar. Whereas the Atar incorporated a thermal shield, no such shield was fitted to the J79, and in order to avoid the creep that an all-aluminium alloy aircraft such as the Mirage would inevitably develop at such high temperatures, major local structural redesign was necessary and the necessary thermal insulation had to be provided in the form of a titanium shield.

A French-built airframe was modified to take a J79-GE-17 engine and was allegedly flown on 19 October 1970 — the R&D programme being referred to at this stage as *Black Curtain,* an allusion to the tight security wraps in which it was enshrouded — and reportedly problems with intake duct effectiveness, excessive drag generated by the new afterbody configuration necessitated by the introduction of a shorter engine and unacceptably high heat levels were swiftly encountered. Nevertheless, results of the initial flight test programme were apparently sufficiently promising to justify persisting with the development and a more definitive prototype utilising an early IAI-built airframe taken off the Nesher assembly line was flown in September 1971.

During the next two years, while IAI's Lod fighter assembly

Seen left and below in squadron service with the Heyl Ha'Avir, the initial production version of the Kfir entered service 18 months ago, in April 1975, and some 60–70 aircraft of this type are believed to have so far been delivered. The examples seen in these photographs all feature the nose configuration of the variant optimised for the air-to-ground rôle and are probably fitted with the APG-53A radar ranging and terrain clearance kit used by Heyl Ha'Avir Skyhawks. The large orange-and-black triangular markings on the vertical tail surfaces (and above and below the wings) are intended to assist Israeli pilots in differentiating between the Kfir and Arab-flown Mirages that may be encountered in combat.

line was cutting its teeth on the Nesher, considerable effort was being expended in refining its planned J79-engined successor which was to use essentially the same jigs and tools as those manufactured for the Nesher. Expertise gained in the production of the Nesher was fed into the programme, full advantage being taken of the considerable operating and combat experience with the Mirage accumulated by the *Heyl Ha'Avir,* and while the J79-engined fighter was looked upon first and foremost as a dogfighter, attention was given to enhancing secondary air-to-ground capability. By comparison with the Mirage, the layout of the cockpit was extensively revised as a result of research undertaken by a medico-technological team working at the Centre of Aviation Medicine and for which, on 28 April 1975, the team was to be awarded the annual *Ira Lahat* Memorial Prize; a head-up display and weapons sight of indigenous manufacture were introduced, much of the other instrumentation being of Israeli manufacture, and the Martin-Baker JM 6 zero-zero ejection seat was standardised. The immediately noticeable external changes compared with the Mirage were the introduction of a triangular dorsal air intake for afterburner cooling and a substantially cut-back aft fuselage to suit the shorter jetpipe of the J79. The vertical tail surfaces and wings of the Mirage were retained essentially unchanged, but a sturdier under-carriage with longer-stroke oleos was adopted to cater for higher operating weights.

When finally revealed in public on 14 April 1975 as the Kfir, this J79-powered derivative of the Mirage was seen in two versions which apparently differed in radar fit, one pre-sumably being optimised for the air-to-ground rôle and the other for the air superiority rôle, and both displaying a built-in

IAI Kfir-C2 Cutaway Drawing Key

1 Fin-tip UHF antenna
2 Rear navigation light
3 ECM antenna
4 Fin construction
5 Rudder construction
6 Rudder bellcrank
7 Rudder control rods
8 Fin spar

42 Leading edge fuel tank
43 Fuel supply piping
44 Fuselage fuel tanks
45 Turbojet intake
46 Engine starter
47 Port constant speed drive unit
48 Intake ducting
49 Fuselage frame construction
50 Pressure sensor
51 Inverted flight accumulator
52 Dorsal fairing
53 Oxygen bottles
54 Forward fuselage fuel tank

armament of two Israeli-manufactured 30-mm DEFA cannon. The nose of the former version appeared to accommodate a small radar — probably the APG-53A radar ranging and terrain clearance kit used by *Heyl Ha'Avir* A-4 Skyhawks — and was flattened on the underside to increase equipment space. A multi-mode nav-attack system was attributed to Elta Electronics and a substantial ventral outlet for avionics cooling air was to be seen immediately ahead of the Doppler housing.

As was to be expected, Israeli officials were not forthcoming with specifics regarding the Kfir's capabilities during the public unveiling at Ben Gurion International Airport 18 months ago and confined themselves to generalities apart from revealing that maximum take-off weight was 32,190 lb (14 600 kg), that a typical combat weight with 50 per cent internal fuel and two Shafrir AAMs was 20,515 lb (9 305 kg), that maximum attainable speed exceeded $M = 2·2$ and that stabilised combat loaded service ceiling was superior to 50,000 ft (15 240 m).

However, it was obvious that the increase in weight by comparison with, say, the Mirage IIIE as a result of the heavier engine and the marginally heavier structure were more than compensated for by the General Electric engine, the J79-GE-

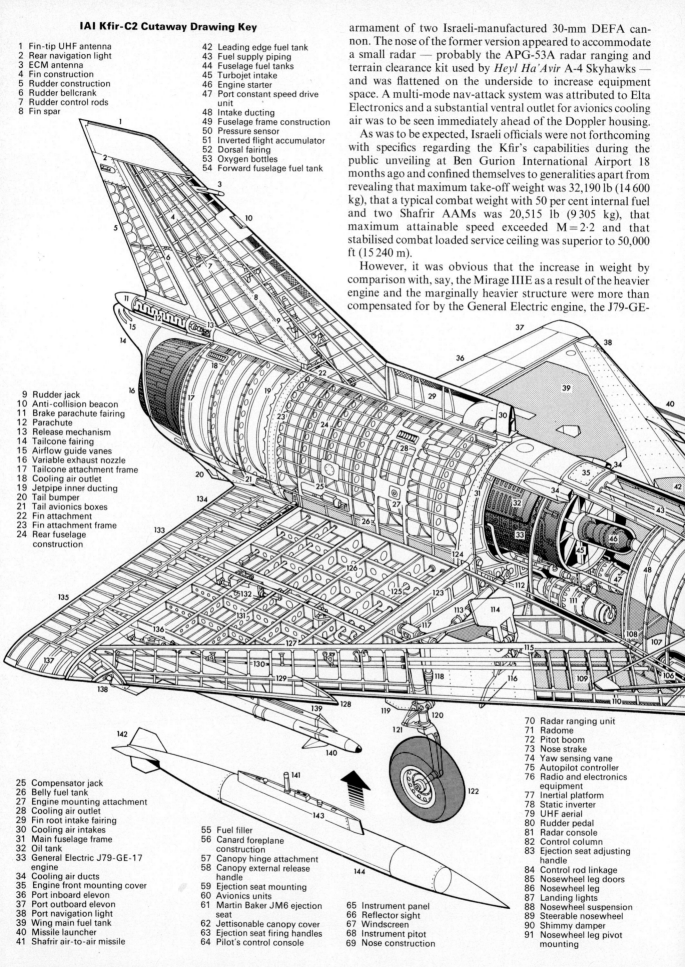

9 Rudder jack
10 Anti-collision beacon
11 Brake parachute fairing
12 Parachute
13 Release mechanism
14 Tailcone fairing
15 Airflow guide vanes
16 Variable exhaust nozzle
17 Tailcone attachment frame
18 Cooling air outlet
19 Jetpipe inner ducting
20 Tail bumper
21 Tail avionics boxes
22 Fin attachment
23 Fin attachment frame
24 Rear fuselage construction

25 Compensator jack
26 Belly fuel tank
27 Engine mounting attachment
28 Cooling air outlet
29 Fin root intake fairing
30 Cooling air intakes
31 Main fuselage frame
32 Oil tank
33 General Electric J79-GE-17 engine
34 Cooling air ducts
35 Engine front mounting cover
36 Port inboard elevon
37 Port outboard elevon
38 Port navigation light
39 Wing main fuel tank
40 Missile launcher
41 Shafrir air-to-air missile

55 Fuel filler
56 Canard foreplane construction
57 Canopy hinge attachment
58 Canopy external release handle
59 Ejection seat mounting
60 Avionics units
61 Martin Baker JM6 ejection seat
62 Jettisonable canopy cover
63 Ejection seat firing handles
64 Pilot's control console

65 Instrument panel
66 Reflector sight
67 Windscreen
68 Instrument pitot
69 Nose construction

70 Radar ranging unit
71 Radome
72 Pitot boom
73 Nose strake
74 Yaw sensing vane
75 Autopilot controller
76 Radio and electronics equipment
77 Inertial platform
78 Static inverter
79 UHF aerial
80 Rudder pedal
81 Radar console
82 Control column
83 Ejection seat adjusting handle
84 Control rod linkage
85 Nosewheel leg doors
86 Nosewheel leg
87 Landing lights
88 Nosewheel suspension
89 Steerable nosewheel
90 Shimmy damper
91 Nosewheel leg pivot mounting

17 delivering 17,900 lb (8 120 kg) with reheat as compared with 13,200 lb (6 000 kg) for the Atar 9C, the respective military ratings being 11,870 lb (5 385 kg) and 9,340 lb (4 280 kg). Lacking any evidence of some increase in internal tankage, it was to be assumed that this was much the same as the 770 Imp gal (3 500 l) of the Mirage, and while the specific fuel consumption of the J79 was notably better than that of the Atar 9C (0·84 lb/lb/hr as compared with 1·01 dry and 1·965 lb/lb/hr as compared with 2·03 with reheat) this was almost certainly offset by the fact that the higher-rated engine burned a greater overall amount, endurance thus possibly being slightly reduced. On the score of thrust-to-weight ratio, there was little comparison between the Kfir and its French progenitor, the Israeli derivative of the Mirage being immeasurably superior, this endowing the Kfir with commensurately improved intercept and dash performance — SEP (Specific Excess Power) in dogfight configuration with 50 per cent fuel was estimated as high as 800-850 ft/sec (245-260 m/sec) at low altitudes — and the débutante was acclaimed by general consensus as a highly potent dogfighter probably capable of besting anything that Israel's Arab neighbours were likely to field throughout the remainder of the 'seventies.

A still better dogfighter

On 15 July 1975, Israel's Air Force Day, Gen Binyamin Peled commented that the Kfir, of which deliveries to the *Heyl Ha'Avir* had begun three months earlier, was being integrated "with less than the usual growing pains", adding that, unless there was a dramatic improvement in Arab air capability, the Kfir was the answer to the Israeli air arm's needs for many years to come and could possibly cope with the variable-geometry MiG-23. The Kfir offered the advantage of substantial airframe spares commonality with the Nesher and also commonality with the F-4E Phantom's power-plant, and the *Heyl Ha'Avir* was already feeding back to IAI suggestions for improvements as a result of initial service experience. These were combined with changes suggested as a result of an evaluation programme conducted in IAI's new low-speed wind tunnel and the result was a further refinement of the basic design, the Kfir-C2, which was demonstrated publicly for the first time during this year's Air Force Day ceremonies at the Hatzerim training base in the Negev.

By comparison with the original Kfir, the C2 version that succeeds it in production embodies three aerodynamic modifications intended to improve still further the dogfighting capabilities of the fighter by aiding low-speed manoeuvrability. All three modifications take the form of fixed surfaces and thus demand no systems changes, facilitating their retrofit to existing aircraft. A combination of fixed canard surfaces above and aft of the engine air intakes and dogtooth extensions of the outboard wing leading edges generate additional lift at given angles of attack and enable higher angles of attack to be attained. the forward shift in the centre of lift and the accompanying reduction in the static-stability margin result in reduced trim drag, small strakes immediately aft of the nose radome countering any interference with the tail surfaces by the wake from the canards

—————————————————————— *continued on page 248*

IAI Kfir-C2 Specification

Power Plant: One Bet-Shemesh-built General Electric J79-GE-17 variable-stator single-shaft axial-flow turbojet rated at 11,870 lb (5 385 kg) thrust dry and 17,900 lb (8 120 kg) thrust with full reheat.

Performance: Max speed (with 50 % fuel and two Shafrir AAMs), M = 1·11 at 1,000 ft (305 m), M = 2·3 above 36,000 ft (10 970 m); max low-level climb rate (M = 0·8-0·95), 47,250 ft/min (240 m sec); time to 36,090 ft (11 000 m), 1·4 min; stabilised ceiling, 52,495 ft (16 000 m); max ceiling (zero rate of climb), 59,055 ft (18 000 m); radius of action with two 110 Imp gal/500 l drop tanks (air superiority mission), 323 mls (520 km), (M = 2·0 intercept mission), 217 mls (350 km), (ground attack hi-lo-hi), 745 mls (1 200 km).

Weights: Empty equipped, 16,072 lb (7 290 kg); combat (intercept with 50 % fuel and two Shafrir AAMs), 20,700 lb (9 390 kg); max take-off, 32,190 lb (14 600 kg).

Dimensions: Span, 26 ft 11¼ in (8,22 m); length, 51 ft 0¼ in (15,55 m); height, 13 ft 11½ in (4,25 m); wing area (excluding canard and dogtooth), 375·12 sq ft (34,85 m²).

Armament: Two 30-mm DEFA cannon with 125 rpg and (intercept) two or four Rafael Shafrir short-range dogfight air-to-air missiles, or (ground attack) up to 8,820 lb (4 000 kg) of external stores, including 2,000-lb (907-kg) Mk 84, 1,000-lb (453,5-kg) Mk 83, 500-lb (227-kg) Mk 82 or 250-lb (113,4-kg) Mk 81 bombs, 700-lb (317,5-kg) cluster bombs, LAU-51 (19 × 2·75-in) or LAU-10 (4 × 5-in) rocket pods, Hughes Maverick or Rockwell International Hobo ASMs or SUU-23 20-mm gun pods.

PILOT PRESS COPYRIGHT DRAWING

107 Ammunition feed chute
108 Front spar attachment
109 Leading edge fuel tank
110 Leading edge construction
111 Starboard constant speed drive unit
112 Mainwheel well
113 Main undercarriage jack
114 Upper surface airbrake
115 Airbrake jack

92 Locking cylinder
93 Air conditioning plant
94 Nosewheel door
95 Air intake centre-body half-cone
96 Starboard air intake
97 Intake half-cone operating jack
98 Boundary layer duct
99 Cannon muzzle blast shield
100 Air intake duct
101 Auxiliary intake
102 Canard foreplane root fairing
103 Electrical control unit
104 Electrical servicing panel
105 Cannon barrel
106 DEFA 30-mm cannon

116 Lower surface airbrake
117 Main undercarriage leg pivot
118 Damper strut
119 Main leg door
120 Shock absorber strut
121 Undercarriage scissors link

122 Mainwheel
123 Main spar
124 Main spar attachment
125 Fuel system piping
126 Main wing fuel tank
127 Leading edge spar
128 Leading edge dogtooth

129 Leading edge construction
130 Control rod linkage
131 Wing construction
132 Inboard elevon jack
133 Inboard elevon construction
134 Elevon compensator
135 Outboard elevon
136 Outboard elevon jack
137 Wing tip profile
138 Navigation light
139 Missile launcher
140 Shafrir air-to-air missile
141 Fuel tank pylon attachment
142 Fuel tank fins
143 Tank pylon
144 Fuel tank (110 Imp gal/500 l capacity)

THE CHAMPION

In appearance possibly the least attractive of all competing aircraft at the World Aerobatic Championships in Kiev earlier this year, the Yak-50 nevertheless justified its evolution by allowing Soviet pilots to take first place in the men's individual, women's individual and team events. A derivative of the familiar and distinctly elderly Yak-18 family, the Yak-50 is in many respects a totally new design. The engine is a 360 hp Ivchenko M-14P and other data include: span, 31 ft 2 in (9,50 m); length, 24 ft 5½ in (7,46 m); wing area, 161·5 sq ft (15,0 m²); gross weight, 1,982 lb (900 kg); max speed, 186 mph (300 km/h); rate of climb, 3,150 ft/min (16 m/sec); take-off run, 655 sq ft (200 m) and landing run, 320 ft (250 m). The photographs here were taken at Kiev by Roger Demeulle, and are published by courtesy of "Aviation Magazine International".

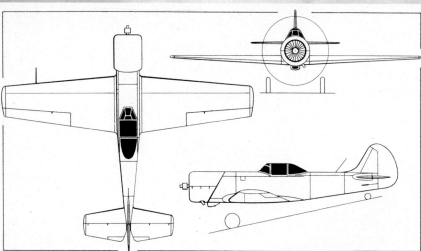

YC-14

ALL BLOW AND NO PUFF!

THE USAF's effort to obtain a successor for the ubiquitous C-130 Hercules came a step closer to fruition on 9 August with the first flight of the Boeing YC-14, the second of the AMST designs that are to be competitively evaluated in the course of the next few months. With the second YC-14 following some three months after the first, the flight test programme on the Boeing AMST is now likely to be pushed ahead rapidly, to allow Air Force evaluation of both the YC-14 and the competing McDonnell Douglas YC-15 (see *"A STOL Performer for the 'Eighties"*/Vol 9 No 6, Dec 1975) to be completed and source selection made by September 1977. The timetable provides for introduction of the selected type into service in 1983.

The AMST programme, which grew out of a Tactical Air Command requirement drawn up in 1970, has had a somewhat chequered history, with Congress reducing the funding that was required for construction of the prototypes to proceed as initially planned. Consequently, the original first flight target date for the YC-14 of November 1975 was put back by nine months (and of the YC-15 by five months, although in the event McDonnell Douglas improved on the revised schedule by a couple of months and flew the first YC-15 almost a full year before the first YC-14). The earlier hesitation on funding the AMST now seems to have been overcome, and the programme has produced two technically-advanced and (in the case of the YC-14 more especially) highly sophisticated tactical transport designs with short take-off and landing characteristics, offering a considerable advance in the state-of-the-art.

The case for replacing the Hercules — which is still selling steadily to a variety of customers around the world, with over 1,400 examples delivered to date — is based, so far as the USAF is concerned, upon the growing obsolescence and performance shortcomings of the Lockheed transport. In evidence given earlier this year before Congress in support of the FY 1977 Defense Appropriations, Lt Gen Alton D Slay, deputy chief of staff, USAF (Research and Development), indicated that the AMST was looked upon as the replacement

for a current fleet of 577 C-130s of assorted variants, as well as 64 Fairchild C-123 Providers and 48 de Havilland C-7 Caribou. By 1983, when it is hoped that the AMST will begin to enter service, all but a hundred or so of these aircraft will be more than 20 years old, the median age of each type then being as follows:

Aircraft	Quantity	Median age in 1983
C-7	48	21
C-123	64	27
C-130A/D	140	26
C-130B	84	22
C-130E (basic)	232	20
C-130E (attrition buys)	53	12
C-130H	68	8

So far as the C-130 is concerned, the performance limitations currently regarded as significant include its small cargo compartment cross-section; its low ('turboprop') speed; its need for relatively long runways; high maintenance costs; risk of damage in hard landings because of the relatively low designed sink rate and restricted off-runway capability. Special operating techniques could overcome some of these disadvantages, and Lockheed has also provided the USAF with data on a proposed improved C-130 with a strengthened wing, modified tail section, beefed up landing gear and rebuilt flight control system. This improved C-130 would have better payload characteristics and field performance but would still

The YC-14 made its initial flight at Seattle on 9 August and is seen below lifting off from Boeing Field/King County International Airport for the first time.

suffer several limitations, as indicated in the following table:

	C-130E/H	Improved C-130	AMST
Crew members	5	5	3
Cruise speed, kt (km/h)	290	290	400
	(537)	(537)	(741)
Cargo volume, cu ft (m³)	4,650	4,650	7,760
	(131,7)	(131,7)	(219,7)
Pallets plus troops	5+0	5+0	6+40
Allowable cabin load, 3·0g,lb (kg)	19,100	27,000	38,500
	(8 670)	(12 258)	(17 480)
Allowable cabin load, 2·5g,lb (kg)	39,100	47,000	60,00+
	(17 750)	(21 338)	(27 240+)
Thrust-to-weight ratio	0·3	0·3	0·6
Field length required, with 27,000 lb (12 258 kg) payload, SL at 103 deg F for 400 naut ml (740 km) radius, payload outbound only, ft (m)	3,700 (1 128)	2,800 (854)	1,800 (549)

The superiority of the AMST over the C-130 in performance terms is obvious enough, but it is the Hercules' limitations on load-carrying that is of particular concern to USAF. Since the

C-130 was first introduced, Army weapons and equipment have grown in size and weight to meet evolving combat mission requirements. Consequently, the Hercules can today carry only 55 per cent of all combat brigade vehicles in the "ready to fight" operational configuration whereas the AMST is dimensioned to carry 90 per cent. Excluded from the C-130 because of size are such important Army weapons as the eight-inch and 155-mm self propelled howitzers and the mechanised infantry combat vehicle (MICV). Although such items as these can be airlifted by the C-5, they can not be brought into small airfields in that aircraft; in terms of field performance, the AMST is considerably better than the C-130, being capable of operating into and out of many fields that would be unacceptable for the C-130. One specific study presented in Gen Slay's testimony showed that in West Germany alone there are more than twice as many airfields available to the AMST (offering a field length of at least 2,000 ft/610 m) than to the C-130 (offering 3,500 ft/1 068 m or more).

Funding of the AMST programme began in FY 1972 and up

Features of the YC-14 shown in the illustrations above and below include the four-piece rudder and double-hinged elevator, and the USB flaps on the inner wing section. When the latter are deflected for maximum lift, flow dividers extend into the exhaust flow over the wing, and the nozzles open up to spread the flow more widely over the surface.

The first of two YC-14s cruises over the Pacific Northwest on an early test flight. The second prototype was to join the test programme as this issue went to press.

to and including the FY 1977 request, a total of $224·4m (£126m) has been allocated to prototype design, construction and testing. An additional $12m (£6·7m) is also earmarked for 'transition' from prototype to full-scale development (FSD). Current plans are to seek funds for a start on FSD in the FY 1978 Budget, with this portion of the programme, costing more than $250m (£140m), extending over four years and being followed by production proper. The total investment cost to aquire a fleet of 277 AMSTs is currently put at $6,300m (£3,540m). The contracts for the AMST prototypes are of the so-called LOGO type (limit of government obligation); the original contract with Boeing was for $96·2m (£54m), with provision for a maximum overrun or $10m (£5·6m), and it is understood that the costs so far are within this ceiling.

The Boeing solution

The contract awards for both the YC-14 and YC-15 were made in November 1972, followed in January 1973 by definitive specifications established in an effort to keep the AMST within the overall fly-away cost goal of $5m for the 300th production example. An important change made at this time was to relax somewhat the overall cabin dimensions originally specified, but the size of the YC-14's cabin is still impressively large, with a fuselage diameter of 18 ft 10 in (5,4 cm), only a few inches less than the width of the Boeing 747, although in overall dimensions the YC-14 is more comparable to the Boeing 727.

To meet the stringent cost restraints inherent in the AMST programme, Boeing opted for a twin-engined design and after analysis of several alternative high-lift systems, selected upper surface blowing (USB) as a means of obtaining the required lift co-efficients and the necessary degree of control to obtain high angles in the initial climb and the approach to landing. USB involves mounting the engines in such a way as to obtain a flow of exhaust gases over the top surfaces of the wing; a simple,

externally-hinged two-segment flap on the trailing edge of the wing, when extended, deflects this flow downwards (by Coanda effect), recovering 92 per cent of the horizontal thrust with the flaps at 60 deg. To minimise the assymetric power situation in the case of an engine failure, the engines are located close together, as near the fuselage centreline as possible, and in this situation the two segments of the flap separate (being normally held closed by engine bleed air) to become a normal double-slotted flap and thus minimise lift loss.

Use of a single over-wing exhaust nozzle permitted the design of a simple target-type reverser, deflecting the exhaust stream upward and outward. For reverse thrust, the upper half of the exhaust nozzle is rotated by a single hydraulic actuator, yielding efficient performance down to zero velocity, uncompromised by hot gas infringement on structure or on adjacent engines, ground debris blowing, aerodynamic interference or loss of flap drag. This top-mounted reverser also increases braking effectiveness because of the resultant downward force, and the outward deflection allows good directional control during engine-out landings. An additional benefit of the reverser configuration is that, when operating on austere strips, thrust can be reversed without creating clouds of dust to obscure the vision of the crew.

A supercritical aerofoil was chosen for the YC-14, making it possible to achieve speeds of more than M = 0.7 with a wing having virtually no sweepback. Use of a high-mounted straight wing allows maximum advantage to be taken of aerodynamic lift potential and minimises the loss in lift due to ground effect. The wing is structurally simple, with a straight rear spar and a constant aerofoil and chord over the central one-third of the span, making it possible for the port and starboard engine installations to be identical. The detailed design of the centre section and the wing/fuselage junction called for special attention to minimise flow break-away, and since the design work started there have been several changes in this area, including moving the engines 6 in (15 cm) farther away from the fuselage and revising the trailing edge fillets and the undercarriage fairings.

Full span variable-camber Krueger flaps occupy the entire wing leading edge, and boundary layer control over the wing is aided by exhausting, through holes in the leading edge surfaces at the intersection of these flaps with the wing proper, air that has been bled from the engine. The BLC comes in when the flaps are deflected 30 deg, with 8th stage engine air being used; further deflection of the flaps for a STOL landing brings in 14th stage air as well, the two bleeds being mixed in a plenum chamber. There are small high speed ailerons on each wing, supplemented by four sections of spoiler on each wing

upper surface outboard of the centre section, used for direct lift control on the approach.

Another of the changes made during the detail design and wind tunnel testing phase was to delete the outboard flaperons that had been intended to supplement the ailerons and spoilers, primarily in the engine-out case. These flaperons were the outer portions of the trailing edge flaps, intended to operate both up and down, and differentially, but now having only the ordinary flap function. Comparison of the original three-view drawing of the YC-14 (see *AirData File*/August 1973) with that for the aircraft as now flown also shows a major change in the configuration of the rear fuselage and tail unit. The underline of the rear fuselage was raised to give better clearance for some items of Army equipment into the cabin through the rear cargo door and ramp, and the angle of sweepback on the fin was reduced from 35 deg to 25 deg, with a larger tailplane. Both the rudder and tailplane are double-hinged, multi-section components.

Boeing YC-14 Cutaway Drawing Key

1 Radome
2 Radar scanner
3 Nose bulkhead
4 Windscreen panels
5 Windscreen wipers
6 Instrument panel shroud
7 Nose section frames
8 Pilot's downward-view window
9 Nose undercarriage bay
10 Nose undercarriage leg (Boeing 707 unit)
11 Twin nosewheels
12 Nosewheel door
13 Crew entry door
14 Door operating cylinder
15 Flight-deck stairs
16 Handrail
17 Radio and electronic racks
18 Pilot's seat
19 Cabin roof window
20 Observers' seats
21 Ditching hatch
22 Air-conditioning supply pipe
23 Cabin bulkhead frame
24 Fuselage frame and stringer construction
25 Observation windows
26 Port engine intake
27 Main cargo floor
28 Cargo hold floor construction
29 Roller-track loading rails
30 Engine access panels
31 General Electric YF103-GE-100 turbofan
32 Engine mounting beam
33 Engine pylon frame
34 Bleed air pipes
35 Fan flow duct
36 Core engine
37 Firewall
38 Engine turbine section
39 Engine mounting struts
40 Reverser door jack
41 Wing centre-section construction
42 Engine pylon fairing

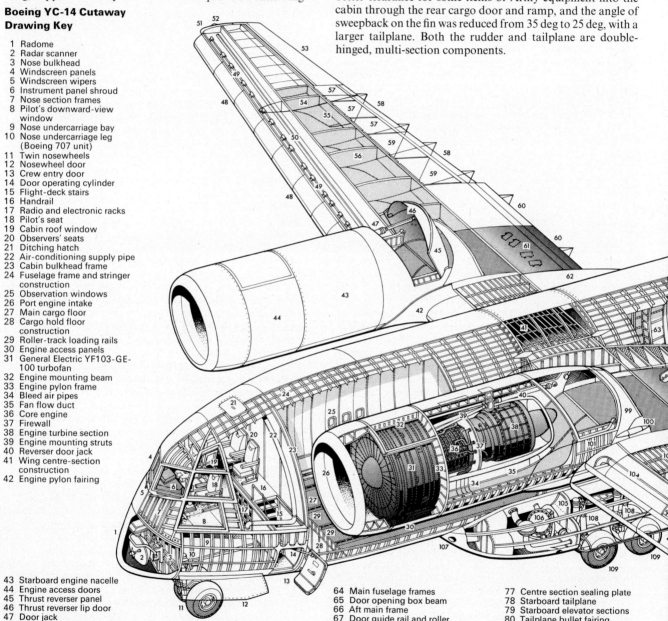

43 Starboard engine nacelle
44 Engine access doors
45 Thrust reverser panel
46 Thrust reverser lip door
47 Door jack
48 Leading edge Krueger flap sections (modified Boeing 747 units)
49 Krueger flap drive shafts
50 Boundary layer control air pipe
51 Starboard wingtip
52 Navigation light
53 Starboard aileron
54 Supercritical wing aerofoil profile
55 Flap actuating mechanism fairing

56 Starboard wing fuel tank
57 Outboard spoilers (Boeing 727 units)
58 Outboard flaps
59 Inboard spoilers (Boeing 747 units)
60 Inboard flaps
61 Vortex generators, closed
62 Trailing edge fairing
63 Fuselage semi-monocoque construction

64 Main fuselage frames
65 Door opening box beam
66 Aft main frame
67 Door guide rail and roller
68 Upward opening cargo hold door
69 Fin attachment frames
70 Constant section fin construction
71 Fin leading edge
72 Tailplane controls
73 Tail lighting
74 Fin/tailplane leading edge fairing
75 Tailplane jacks
76 Moving tailplane centre section

77 Centre section sealing plate
78 Starboard tailplane
79 Starboard elevator sections
80 Tailplane bullet fairing
81 Port elevator sections
82 Elevator controls
83 Honeycomb panels
84 Tailplane construction
85 Split rudder sections, three interchangeable units
86 Rudder jacks
87 Rudder honeycomb panels
88 Tailcone fairing
89 Cargo hold door hinge frame
90 Aft fuselage box beam
91 Cargo door construction
92 Door locking mechanism

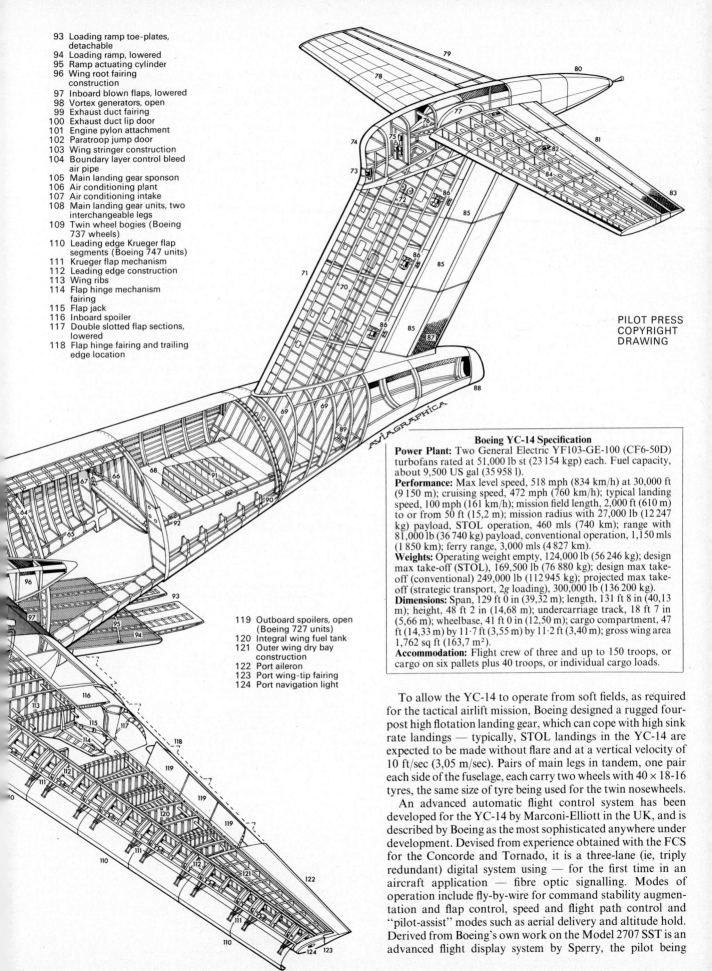

93 Loading ramp toe-plates, detachable
94 Loading ramp, lowered
95 Ramp actuating cylinder
96 Wing root fairing construction
97 Inboard blown flaps, lowered
98 Vortex generators, open
99 Exhaust duct fairing
100 Exhaust duct lip door
101 Engine pylon attachment
102 Paratroop jump door
103 Wing stringer construction
104 Boundary layer control bleed air pipe
105 Main landing gear sponson
106 Air conditioning plant
107 Air conditioning intake
108 Main landing gear units, two interchangeable legs
109 Twin wheel bogies (Boeing 737 wheels)
110 Leading edge Krueger flap segments (Boeing 747 units)
111 Krueger flap mechanism
112 Leading edge construction
113 Wing ribs
114 Flap hinge mechanism fairing
115 Flap jack
116 Inboard spoiler
117 Double slotted flap sections, lowered
118 Flap hinge fairing and trailing edge location

119 Outboard spoilers, open (Boeing 727 units)
120 Integral wing fuel tank
121 Outer wing dry bay construction
122 Port aileron
123 Port wing-tip fairing
124 Port navigation light

PILOT PRESS
COPYRIGHT
DRAWING

Boeing YC-14 Specification

Power Plant: Two General Electric YF103-GE-100 (CF6-50D) turbofans rated at 51,000 lb st (23 154 kgp) each. Fuel capacity, about 9,500 US gal (35 958 l).
Performance: Max level speed, 518 mph (834 km/h) at 30,000 ft (9 150 m); cruising speed, 472 mph (760 km/h); typical landing speed, 100 mph (161 km/h); mission field length, 2,000 ft (610 m) to or from 50 ft (15,2 m); mission radius with 27,000 lb (12 247 kg) payload, STOL operation, 460 mls (740 km); range with 81,000 lb (36 740 kg) payload, conventional operation, 1,150 mls (1 850 km); ferry range, 3,000 mls (4 827 km).
Weights: Operating weight empty, 124,000 lb (56 246 kg); design max take-off (STOL), 169,500 lb (76 880 kg); design max take-off (conventional) 249,000 lb (112 945 kg); projected max take-off (strategic transport, 2g loading), 300,000 lb (136 200 kg).
Dimensions: Span, 129 ft 0 in (39,32 m); length, 131 ft 8 in (40,13 m); height, 48 ft 2 in (14,68 m); undercarriage track, 18 ft 7 in (5,66 m); wheelbase, 41 ft 0 in (12,50 m); cargo compartment, 47 ft (14,33 m) by 11·7 ft (3,55 m) by 11·2 ft (3,40 m); gross wing area 1,762 sq ft (163,7 m²).
Accommodation: Flight crew of three and up to 150 troops, or cargo on six pallets plus 40 troops, or individual cargo loads.

To allow the YC-14 to operate from soft fields, as required for the tactical airlift mission, Boeing designed a rugged four-post high flotation landing gear, which can cope with high sink rate landings — typically, STOL landings in the YC-14 are expected to be made without flare and at a vertical velocity of 10 ft/sec (3,05 m/sec). Pairs of main legs in tandem, one pair each side of the fuselage, each carry two wheels with 40 × 18-16 tyres, the same size of tyre being used for the twin nosewheels.

An advanced automatic flight control system has been developed for the YC-14 by Marconi-Elliott in the UK, and is described by Boeing as the most sophisticated anywhere under development. Devised from experience obtained with the FCS for the Concorde and Tornado, it is a three-lane (ie, triply redundant) digital system using — for the first time in an aircraft application — fibre optic signalling. Modes of operation include fly-by-wire for command stability augmentation and flap control, speed and flight path control and "pilot-assist" modes such as aerial delivery and altitude hold. Derived from Boeing's own work on the Model 2707 SST is an advanced flight display system by Sperry, the pilot being provided with a TV picture of his landing field on which is superimposed cathode ray tube symbology to indicate altitude and position relative to the glideslope. This display has been adopted to help achieve the required touchdown accuracy of ±50 ft (15,2 m), more than usually difficult to achieve because of the high rates of descent associated with STOL techniques. Production aircraft (whichever AMST is chosen) may well have more sophisticated sensors and landing aids than those selected for the prototypes.

Boeing's choice of General Electric CF6-50 turbofans for the YC-14 prototypes could be changed, at USAF request, in any production version, since the Pratt & Whitney JT9D and Rolls-Royce RB.211 are capable of providing the required thrust. Most probably, however, since the airframe has been engineered with the GE engines, these would be retained — especially as USAF already has this engine in its inventory (in the Boeing E-4A and E-4B). CF6-50Ds are used in the Boeing prototypes, rated at 51,000 lb st (23 135 kgp) and with the military designation YF103-GE-100.

Mission requirement

The YC-14 is designed to meet the AMST requirements and, since it is in a competitive situation with the YC-15, may very well prove to exceed the specification in some respects. The mission requirement is to lift a 27,000 lb (12 258 kg) payload out of a 2,000 ft (610 m) field and to have a radius with this load of 460 mls (740 km). Carrying this payload, the YC-14 will approach a 2,000-ft (610-m) strip at 85 knots (157 km/h), or — if the risk of losing an engine is accepted, as it would be in a combat situation — at 72 knots (133 km/h), with the possibility of maintaining control down to 52 knots (96 km/h), "in extreme emergency". These figures assume operation at a 3g load factor; relaxing this to 2·5g would permit operation at higher gross weights and — using long range tanks carried externally on the wings — gives the possibility of flying a 50,000 lb (22 700 kg) payload a distance of 3,450 mls (5 550 km), using conventional take-off procedures.

Of the three types the AMST is designed to replace, only the C-130 can carry a payload as heavy as 27,000 lb (12 258 kg),

and it needs field-lengths almost twice as long as those required by the YC-14 to lift them into the air. The Boeing aircraft also has twice the rate of climb of the Hercules and from a standing start it is claimed that it can actually outclimb an F-4 Phantom to 10,000 ft (3 050 m). At a somewhat reduced rate of climb — about 1,500 ft/min (7,63 m/sec) — the YC-14 can spiral out of a forward landing strip that might be under enemy pressure, never flying outside a 4,000 ft (1 220 m) diameter circle.

For its first flight, the YC-14 was taken into the air by project pilot Ray McPherson accompanied by Major David Bittenbinder, USAF, at a weight of 171,000 lb (77 634 kg), and was flown for a little over an hour, in the course of which engine response, handling and systems were checked at speeds up to 170 kts (315 km/h), the undercarriage remaining down. During the second flight, the cargo door and ramp were opened in flight, and undercarriage and flaps were fully exercised. Following flutter testing and low-speed investigation early in the test programme, the behaviour of the Marconi-Elliot AFCS will receive special attention.

Initially at least, the USAF is expected to limit its buy of the winning AMST to 277 aircraft; since each AMST has double the productivity of the C-130, this quantity would more than replace the 577 Hercules in the inventory at present. It is clear, however, that whichever type goes into production it will have good prospects in the export field, selling as a Hercules successor in the 'eighties to at least some of the air forces now operating the Lockheed transport. In the longer term, the AMST might also replace the Lockheed C-141 StarLifter, since it has the same payload in conventional modes. Even if the civil potential of AMST derivatives is ignored — and that potential is probably limited to highly specialised types of commercial operation — the total prospective sales for an AMST type have been put as high as 1,500 by Boeing and even higher in some other market forecasts. The performance of the YC-14 — which is Boeing's first *new* military aircraft to fly since the prototype Stratofortress in 1952 — during the next few months will, in all the circumstances, be watched very carefully around Seattle — and with no less interest at Long Beach! □

A three-view general arrangement drawing depicting the YC-14 as first flown.

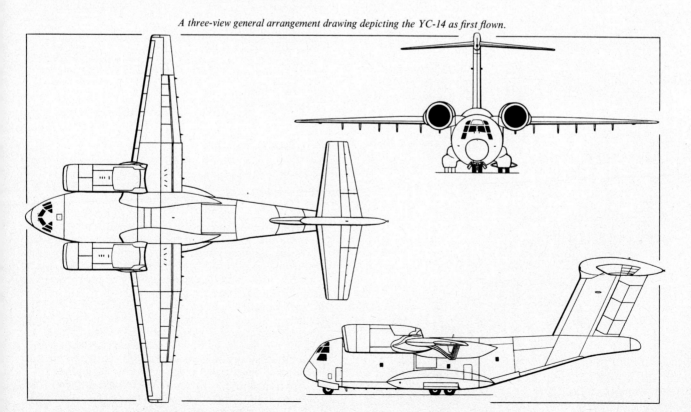

The proliferous kit

THE AVERAGE aircraft modeller is also an incurable optimist; were he not so, the plastic kit manufacturing industry would never have grown to its present size as the demand for its products would be substantially smaller than it in fact is. With each passing week the range of available kits proliferates — the sheer volume of new kits that reach our workbench leads us to speculate on the proportion of the millions, even billions (if one accepts the now widely-used definition of a thousand million), of kits that pour out of factories in most of the principal industrial countries that actually see completion as *finished models*. Forty per cent? A half?

Time and time again, we are asked the question: "How on earth do you find enough time to assemble all the kits that you review each month?" The simple answer is that *we don't!* It is physically impossible to assemble and finish *all* the new kits that reach us and some must, perforce, be put together only to a degree of completeness sufficient to permit a reasonably thorough assessment of the worth of the kit, but almost without exception, we nurture that pious hope that *one day* the time will be available for us to go back and finish these cursorily-assembled kits in the style to which they are entitled. We, like most modellers, are optimists, tucking away kits like squirrels with nuts, but the squirrel usually eats its nuts eventually, whereas the kits that we so optimistically put to one side for future attention must await that elusive period when adequate time is available.

How is it that so many model kits never make the transition to fully-fledged model? Many kits are, of course, acquired as a result of impulse buying, the box contents being appraised and perhaps even a dry run being attempted before the component parts are restored to their box to gather dust while they await that fondly-anticipated period when their purchaser finds the time to give them his attention. Others are roughly slapped together into some semblance of a model and, after knocking around the house for months and shedding parts at each flick of a duster, are finally consigned to the rubbish bin. Yet again, the assembly of many kits is begun in a flush of enthusiasm and then shelved, ostensibly temporarily, when a new and more intriguing kit captures the imagination.

Europe's recent long, hot summer was hardly conducive to furthering such indoor pastimes as modelling and now, with the onset of winter in the northern hemisphere at least, there will be more than the usual amount of dusting off kits accumulated during the summer months, yet the flood of new kits from the manufacturers seems never ending. Being incurable optimists, we will, despite the backlog of kits that have remained untouched during the summer and the amount of time-consuming work that their completion repre-sents, be reaching into our pockets to buy yet more kits as they make their débuts now that the modelling season is once again with us. And so the mountain of virgin polystyrene aircraft kit components grows and the cash registers of the kit stockists merrily tinkle. In so far as the kit manufacturers are concerned . . . *vive les optimistes!*

This month's colour subject

The "Bent-winged Bird", the "Sweetheart of Okinawa"; whatever the appellation unofficially bestowed on the Chance Vought F4U Corsair by the US forces in the Pacific Theatre, agreement was almost universal that it was an extraordinarily effective warplane. Operating from airstrips on Guadalcanal and the Solomon Islands, the US Marine Corps forged the Corsair into a superlative air superiority weapon which played a major rôle in turning the tide of air combat permanently in favour of the Allies. Understandably, this aircraft has always been a firm favourite among modellers and if its popularity can be adjudged by the number of kits that have been offered over the years — nearly a score to a variety of scales — then the Corsair can undoubtedly be numbered among the 'top ten'.

To 1/72nd scale, or thereabouts, there have been eight or nine versions of which several remain current if not necessarily readily available. Not all represent the same version of the fighter, so it is not really practicable to pick an overall "best", although we tend to favour Lesney's "Matchbox" offering of an F4U-4, which is also the latest to be released. Frog provides a very good F4U-1D which is rather better than the more elderly offerings of the same sub-type from Airfix and Revell, and also worth having — if it can be found — is Hawk's Marine Corps AU-1, originally issued as an F4U-1D but later modified as the only post-WW II variant to 1/72nd scale. Two Japanese kits that came close to 1/72nd were the Midori F4U-1D (1/69th) and the Fujimi F4U-4 (1/70th), the latter being a very good kit for its time. Hobbytime, in the USA, has listed an F4U-5N, but we have never seen an example of this kit and can offer no infor-mation concerning its quality or availability.

In so far as 1/48th scale is concerned, we know of three kits of which pride of place must inevitably go to the fairly recently issued F4U-1D from Otaki. This is a very fine, accurate and well detailed kit. Monogram's F4U-4, al-though of rather earlier vintage, is nevertheless a good kit and well worth having. The still earlier Lindberg kit is unlikely to be obtainable but, despite detail and finesse commensurate with its considerable age, it is at least novel in being a late production version, namely an F4U-5N. Incidentally, AMT in the USA has released a 1/48th scale kit of the Corsair, apparently an F4U-1, although we have not yet had an opportunity to appraise an example of this.

Stepping up to 1/32nd scale, there is a fine rendition of the F4U-5 alias Corsair II from Revell which offers much small detail, a good surface finish and a generally high standard of accuracy. There have been some other Corsair kits to smaller scales than those considered as standard for aircraft in this category, the smallest of these being 1/150th scale. Most of these have long since disappeared from the stockists' shelves and are unlikely to be missed, although a neat little kit to 1/96th scale of the F4U-5 is worthy of mention, this having been produced originally, if our memory serves us correctly, in Hong Kong and issued under the name of "Trim-Pak". It was later taken up by Lindberg which issued it in the USA.

A Franco-Teutonic trio

That eminent French manufacturer of kits, Heller, has recently added three WW II *Luftwaffe* types to its catalogue, these being the Bücker Bü 133C Jungmeister, the Mes-serschmitt Bf 108B Taifun and the Mes-serschmitt Bf 109K, all of which fill some gaps in the coverage of what is already the best represented era in the annals of military aviation in so far as the plastic kit is concerned.

All to 1/72nd scale, the gem of the trio is without doubt the diminutive Bü 133C, one of the smallest types yet offered as a plastic kit in this scale. Size is certainly not the main criterion, for this is a very accurate and beautifully detailed kit comprising 32 com-ponent parts neatly moulded in medium-grey plastic, plus a transparent windscreen. Every-thing goes well, the only tricky operation being the assembly of the top wing onto the centre-section 'N' struts and individual interplane struts — not really difficult but calling for care as the setting of the wings is vital to the appearance of the finished model.

The rib-and-stringer effect is first class and despite the miniscule dimensions of this model — its wing span is only 3·6 in (92 mm) — everything is to scale and even such small details as hand-holds in the wingtips and centre section are reproduced. The seven-cylinder Siemens Sh 14A-4 radial has a separate exhaust collector ring and a three-piece cowling, while the fixed undercarriage, with mudguards over the wheels, looks most realistic. The decal sheet offers markings for both a *Luftwaffe* trainer and for a Swiss-registered civil example.

A contemporary of the Jungmeister bearing some family resemblance to its illustrious stablemate, the Bf 109, the Bf 108B Taifun is another welcome kit and results in a fine model with accurate contours and just the right amount of surface detailing. The fuselage fits snugly on to the separate upper centre section of the wing and the one-piece lower wing panel, the appealing shape of the aircraft being convincingly captured. There are 36 com-ponent parts to the kit, including seats, controls, an instrument panel and a very clear four-piece canopy, and in its own way this kit is every bit as good as that for the Bü 133 previously reviewed. The decals provide for an example employed in the communications rôle by the *Luftwaffe* and, oddly enough, one serving with the Bulgarian air arm, the instruction sheet providing details of the colour schemes.

The third member of the trio represents one of the least-modelled variants of the immortal Messerschmitt fighter, the Bf 109K, with which the production career of this warplane finally came to a close. Unfortunately, Heller would seem to have been a little uncertain as to what actually constituted a Bf 109K as it has come up with something of a hybrid of this model and its production predecessor, the Bf 109G, complete with G-style tailwheel and nose gun bulges. There is adequate detailing inside the cockpit and which may be seen clearly through the two-piece canopy. A *Rüstsatz* 1 ventral ETC for a single 551-lb (250-kg) SC 250 bomb is provided, but the fins of this missile are a scale 5 in (12,7 cm) or so thick and call for removal and replacement by new fins cut from plastic sheet.

The kit posesses a total of 41 parts, some of which are very small and delicate, and call for careful handling. The surface detailing is of the best and the exterior finish of the component parts, as with those of the other Heller kits previously reviewed, has a most attractive matt effect. The decal sheet covers one aircraft only and the unit is not specified although the "Red heart on a white diamond" emblem suggests *Jagdgeschwader* 77.

A superior vac-form
On the occasions when we have reviewed new releases from Rareplanes, we have consistently been agreeably surprised by the advances that this manufacturer has made in the field of vacuum-formed kits to render them truly comparable in most respects with contemporary injection-moulded kits. Even Rareplanes early efforts were never as crude as those of some of its competitors and, by steadily improving on the state of the art, it has retained a substantial lead in what has now become an important market with a substantial following among more adventurous modellers. With its latest offering, the Douglas DC-4/C-54/R5D-3 Skymaster, Rareplanes has really excelled itself and we at last have a really worthy kit to 1/72nd scale of a type that has been completely ignored by the major manufacturers.

Possessing 82 parts moulded in white plastic sheet with a high gloss finish and of sufficient thickness to withstand moulding to a depth, as is the case with the fuselage halves, of 1·125 in (28,5 mm) while still retaining adequate strength, the kit offers sharply defined outlines and the standard of its surface detailing cannot be faulted, all panels being accurately and clearly delineated with finely engraved lines and the neatest of riveting. Inspection panels stand out just sufficiently to render them noticeable without being obtrusive and all the control surfaces are nicely formed.

The internal structure for the substantial fuselage comprises four bulkheads and a flight deck floor plus seats for the latter, and there is a transparency for the windshield through which the internal detail may be seen. There are also formed transparencies for the cabin windows, although it is debatable whether it is worthwhile cutting out the 24 oval openings in the fuselage so as to fit them from the inside; some modellers may feel that painting them on the outside will be effective enough. They are clearly indicated on the mouldings so the choice will be that of the individual.

The assembly instructions advise the insertion of a balsa spar in each wing half to maintain the correct thickness; this is undoubtedly necessary, and we would go further and advise fixing some additional stiffening around the wing roots and undercarriage attachment points. Furthermore, it would be wise to box in the nosewheel housing with plastic sheet and utilise the rest of the space in the extreme nose for the weights which will be needed to balance the tail. The undercarriage and well doors are all included, and the wheels are particularly noteworthy, incorporating very nice hub detailing. Each main undercarriage assembly comprises two halves between which must be cemented a reinforcement of wire or plastic rod which also forms the axles for the wheels, the overall result being the best undercarriage that we have yet seen on any vac-form.

The engine fronts provided are very effective when enclosed in the cowlings, but the propellers are a weak point as they cannot be moulded solid and they are not thick enough for two halves to be formed. They *can* be made to look acceptable but, if possible, it is better to use a set from a Revell B-17E to give a really neat appearance. An excellent feature of the kit is the inclusion of a set of Merlin engine cowlings which enable the kit to be assembled as a Canadair-built DC-4M (alias C-54GM). The instruction sheet is clear and comprehensive, including not only full assembly instructions but scale plans and information on colour schemes. The price of the kit in the UK is £4·50 from model shops or direct from Rareplanes. Decals are not included with the kit but are available separately for a Capital Airlines DC-4, a British Midland Airways DC-4M or a MATS C-54 Skymaster, the price of each sheet being £1·25 (US$3·00) plus postage.

Yet another Starfighter
Lockheed's famous, or infamous, depending upon your viewpoint, F-104 Starfighter has appeared in 1/72nd scale from Airfix, Hasegawa/Frog and Lesney over the years, and one might well consider that this subject has been recipient of adequate treatment. Heller evidently believes otherwise and its Starfighter kit is at least sufficiently superior to its predecessors to render its advent welcome. Consisting of 58 component parts, a number of which are alternatives to permit construction of either the single-seat F-104G or two-seat TF-104G, the kit offers finish and detailing of a very high standard. There are two forward fuselage sections with parts for one or two cockpits, and the joint line to the aft portion has been so arranged as to avoid any unsightly break. The cockpits are well equipped and the canopies are exceptionally clear with well-defined framing.

Clear landing lights are a feature and the undercarriage has its full complement of bracing with nicely-formed scale-thickness doors. The aft fuselage air brakes may be fixed in extended or retracted position and include actuating struts. The sharp edges and razor-thin sections of the wings and tailplane look very good, and four drop tanks are provided, two for mounting at the wingtips and the others on underwing pylons. Unfortunately, the decal sheet is not up to the same standard as the remainder of the kit, having a completely matt finish and suffering some lack of colour definition, but it is certainly extensive and covers no less than five different aircraft — Belgian and Danish two-seaters, and Dutch, Federal German and Canadian single-seaters — for which colour schemes are given in some detail on the reverse of the instruction sheet.

Decal reviews
When a new release from Modeldecal reaches us we are at something of a loss to say anything new in reviewing them as they are consistently of such a standard of excellence that we can hardly avoid repetition. Suffice it then to say that the latest sheets appear to be in every way of the same high standard that has characterised their predecessors. Modeldecal is certainly to be complimented also on its choice of subject matter, which, in the case of Sheet No 31, represents a completely new departure in that it represents a venture into the colourful world of the pre-WW II RAF.

The scale is, as usual, 1/72nd, and the very attractive quartet of aircraft represented are the Hawker Fury I (Matchbox), the Bristol Bulldog IIA (Airfix), the Gloster Gladiator I (Frog or Matchbox) and the Armstrong Whitworth Siskin IIIA (Matchbox). The markings offered for the Fury are the red outlines of No 1 Squadron; those for the Bulldog are No 23 Squadron's red-and-blue squares; the Gladiator's markings are the black bar with superimposed wavy green line of No 87 Squadron and the markings for the Siskin are the black-and-white chequers of No 43 Squadron. All sets of markings are complete with roundels and many small details, and the colours and their register are immaculate. Incidentally, the actual shade of blue used by the RAF during the period here represented has proved elusive to decal manufacturers the world over, but here we have the genuine article. Comprehensive instructions are provided for the location of the various decals, together with a sound photographic coverage.

Sheet No 32 covers a very different period and comprises a mixed bag which includes several different markings for the Royal Navy's Sea Vixen FAW Mk 2 (recently released by Frog), an F-100D Super Sabre of the Danish Nr 727 Sqdn in 1973, a Dassault Super Mystère B2 of *Escadron* 2/12 *Cornouaille* of the *Armée de l'Air* in 1971, a selection of *Armée de l'Air* Jaguar A and E variants in service in 1974-75. Application of the Jaguar markings calls for some modification of existing kits of this aircraft but these are described by the instructions and illustrated by the many photographs accompanying the decals. The price of each sheet in the UK is 60p plus 15p postage for one or two sheets. □

F J HENDERSON

We Get Letters ...
... and we are always pleased to hear from our readers, especially with comments or illustrations for use in our *Talkback* pages, or requests for information to be published in the *Plane Facts* section. Letters of a general nature, however, *must* be accompanied by return postage (or International Reply Coupon) if a reply is required and, sorry, but we cannot provide detailed information on specific aircraft on an individual basis by post.

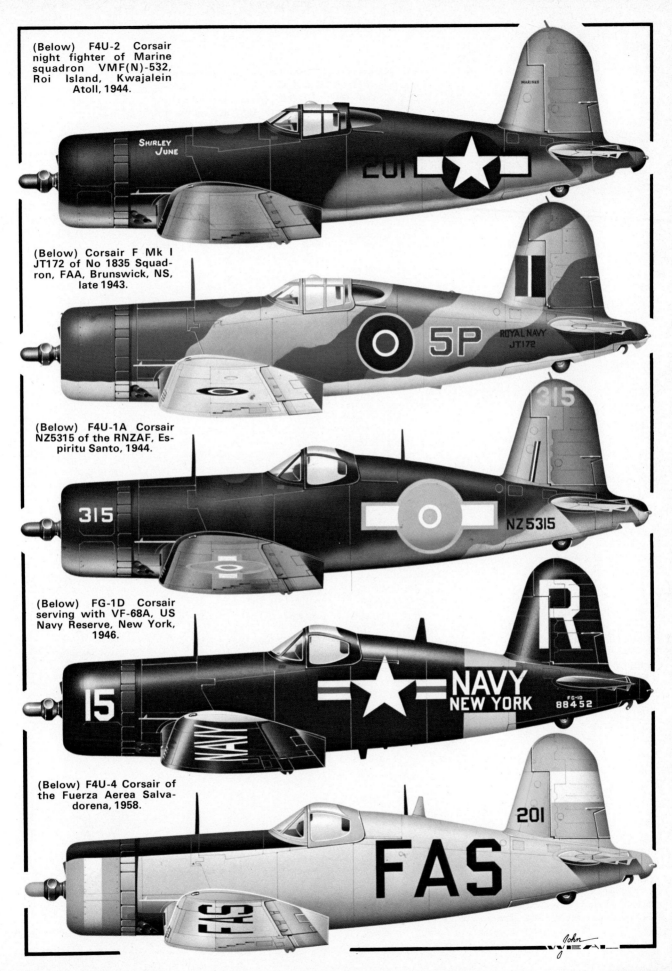

(Below) F4U-2 Corsair night fighter of Marine squadron VMF(N)-532, Roi Island, Kwajalein Atoll, 1944.

(Below) Corsair F Mk I JT172 of No 1835 Squadron, FAA, Brunswick, NS, late 1943.

(Below) F4U-1A Corsair NZ5315 of the RNZAF, Espiritu Santo, 1944.

(Below) FG-1D Corsair serving with VF-68A, US Navy Reserve, New York, 1946.

(Below) F4U-4 Corsair of the Fuerza Aerea Salvadorena, 1958.

(Above) The XP-42 in initially modified form with enlarged lower air intake and extended carburettor air intake, and (below) with conventional NACA C-type engine cowling, cooling fan and cuffs.

CURTISS XP-42 USA

Evolved in parallel with the XP-40 and delivered to the AAC on 5 March 1939, the XP-42 was effectively an exercise in drag reduction — an attempt to reduce the drag evoked by an air-cooled radial engine to approximately that of a liquid-cooled inline power plant. Utilising the fourth production P-36A airframe, the XP-42 had a 1,050 hp Pratt & Whitney R-1830-31 Twin Wasp with an 18-in (45,72-cm) extension shaft and enclosed by a close-fitting cowling which was, in effect, a streamlined prolongation of the propeller spinner. Inadequate cooling, carburettor ducting problems and extension shaft vibration proved troublesome, and much of the potential gain in performance from the improved streamlining was absorbed by the weight of the extension shaft and compensatory tail ballast. Both long and short high- and low-inlet-velocity cowlings coupled with propeller cuffs and a cooling fan were evaluated, the maximum level speed attained being 344 mph (554 km/h) at 14,500 ft (4 420 m), this being achieved with both long-nose high-inlet-velocity cowling with propeller cuffs and spinner, and with the short-nose low-inlet-velocity cowling with spinner only. Before trials were discontinued in 1942, the XP-42 was fitted with a slab-type all-moving tailplane. The following data relate to the definitive long-cowl XP-42. Max speed, 344 mph (554 km/h) at 14,500 ft (4 420 m). Empty weight, 4,818 lb (2 185 kg). Loaded weight, 6,100 lb (2 767 kg). Span, 37 ft 4 in (11,38 m). Length, 30 ft 3⅛ in (9,22 m). Height, 9 ft 9 in (2,67 m). Wing area, 236 sq ft (21,92 m²).

CURTISS XP-46 USA

In 1939, Donovan R Berlin attempted to combine what he considered to be some of the best features of the latest European fighters in a potential successor for the P-40, two prototypes being ordered on 29 September 1939 as the XP-46. Designed around the newly-developed Allison V-1710-39 (F3R) rated at 1,150 hp, the XP-46 was more compact than the earlier fighter and featured automatic wing leading-edge slats, an armament of twin fuselage-mounted 0·5-in (12,7-mm) guns and eight wing-mounted 0·3-in (7,62-mm) guns, and 65 lb (29,50 kg) of pilot armour. The second prototype, which was the first to fly (as the XP-46A) on 15 February 1941, was

delivered without armour, armament, radio and self-sealing fuel tanks, and in this stripped form met the specification speed of 410 mph (660 km/h), but when the fully-equipped first prototype was delivered on 22 September 1941, maximum speed was found to be 55 mph (88,5 km/h) down. Lacking supercharging, the XP-46 held no promise as a fighter at altitude and as a similarly-powered development of the P-40 had meanwhile been programmed (ie, P-40D), further development of the experimental fighter was abandoned. Max speed, 355 mph (571 km/h) at 12,200 ft (3 720 m). Time to 12,300 ft (3 750 m), 5·0 min. Empty weight, 5,625 lb (2 551 kg). Max loaded weight, 7,665 lb (3 477 kg). Span, 34 ft 4 in (10,46 m). Length, 30 ft 2 in (9,19 m). Height, 13 ft 0 in (3,96 m). Wing area, 208 sq ft (19,32 m²).

CURTISS XP-55 USA

One of three designs awarded development contracts as a result of an informal design contest for fighters of unconventional configuration — the others being the Consolidated-Vultee XP-54 (see *Fighter A to Z*/November 1975) and the Northrop XP-56 — the XP-55 was of radical canard configuration, albeit not a *true* canard in that it had no *fixed* forward control surfaces. Although originally intended for the experimental Pratt & Whitney X-1800-A3G (H-2600) liquid-cooled engine, the 1,275 hp Allison V-1710-95 (F23R) engine was eventually installed in the three prototypes contracted for on 10 July 1942. The first XP-55 was completed on 13 July 1943 but was lost during stall trials four months later, on 15 November. The second XP-55 flew on 9 January 1944, followed by the third on 25 April, the latter embodying extended wingtips with so-called 'trailerons' and increased elevator travel limits, the second prototype later being modified to the same standards. Armament comprised four 0·5-in (12,7-mm) nose-mounted guns. The XP-55 revealed a tendency to over-control at low speeds, stall behaviour was both unconventional and undesirable and engine cooling was critical, and it was concluded that the unorthodox configuration did not justify further development. Max speed, 390

(Above) The XP-46A, which, delivered without armour, armament, etc, flew in February 1941. The fully-equipped XP-46, illustrated by the general arrangement drawing below, joined the test programme during September.

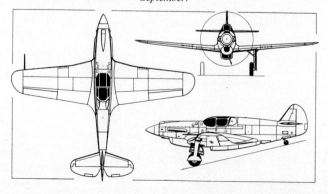

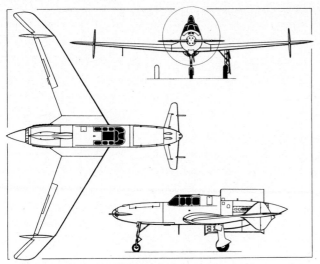

One of the most unconventional fighters of its era was the XP-55 illustrated by the general arrangement drawing above, the second prototype being depicted by the photograph below.

mph (628 km/h) at 19,300 ft (5 885 m). Time to 20,000 ft (6 095 m), 7·1 min. Normal range, 635 mls (1 022 km) at 296 mph (476 km/h). Empty weight, 6,354 lb (2 882 kg). Normal loaded weight, 7,330 lb (3 325 kg). Span, 44 ft 0½ in (13,42 m). Length, 29 ft 7 in (9,02 m). Height, 10 ft 0¾ in (3,22 m). Wing area, 235 sq ft (21,83 m²).

CURTISS XP-60(D)　　　　　　　　USA

Among proposals submitted to the AAC in the summer of 1940 for a successor to the P-40 was a development of the basic P-40 design with a Continental XIV-1430-3 engine, which was expected to afford 1,600 hp at 15,000 ft (4 570 m), and using a laminar-flow aerofoil. This was accepted by the AAC and two prototypes were ordered under the designation XP-53 on 1 October 1940. Subsequently, the decision was taken to complete the second XP-53 with a Merlin engine as the XP-60, the first XP-53 eventually becoming a static test airframe. A new inward-retracting undercarriage was introduced, together with enlarged vertical tail surfaces, and the XP-60 flew on 18 September 1941 with a British-built Merlin 28 engine, this aircraft later being fitted with six 0·5-in (12,7-mm) wing guns and self-sealing fuel tanks. Trials of the XP-60 proved that performance did not comply with the manufacturer's guarantees owing to a combination of insufficient wing smoothness and lower engine output than anticipated, and as the Merlin had meanwhile been selected for installation in other fighters and there was a likelihood of delays in deliveries of the Packard licence-built version, further development was concentrated on models powered by alternative engines. The XP-60 was returned to Curtiss-Wright for the installation of a Merlin 61 engine and in this form it was designated XP-60D. The following data relate to the XP-60. Max speed, 380 mph (611 km/h) at 20,000 ft (6 095 m). Time to 20,000 ft (6 095 m), 7·3 min. Range, 995 mls (1 601 km). Empty weight, 7,008 lb (3 180 kg). Loaded weight, 9,700 lb (4 400 kg). Span, 41 ft 5 in (12,62 m). Length, 33 ft 4 in (10,16 m). Height, 14 ft 4 in (4,37 m). Wing area, 275 sq ft (25,55 m²).

CURTISS XP-60A　　　　　　　　USA

On 31 October 1941, orders were placed for a total of 1,950 P-60A fighters in which the Merlin of the XP-60 was to be supplanted by an Allison V-1710-75 with General Electric B-14 turbo-supercharger and offering 1,425 hp at 25,000 ft (7 620 m). Shortly afterwards, on 17 November, it was realised that the Allison-engined P-60A would be underpowered, further work on this fighter subsequently being terminated and more powerful engines suitable for P-60 installation being sought. On 2 January 1942, it was decided that one XP-60A should be built (together with one XP-60B and one XP-60C) for development purposes with the turbo-supercharged Allison. Possessing little in common with the XP-60 other than the wing and undercarriage, the XP-60A finally flew on 1 November 1942, but without the turbo-supercharger which had been removed as a result of a fire in the previous month during ground trials. Armament of the XP-60A was to have comprised six 0·5-in (12,7-mm) wing-mounted guns, but without the turbo-supercharger installed, flight testing was confined to the investigation of control forces, and the wings, undercarriage and other items were subsequently applied to the XP-60E after it suffered damage in a forced landing. The following performance data are estimated for the XP-60A *with* turbo-supercharger. Max speed, 420 mph (676 km/h) at 29,000 ft (8 840 m). Time to 10,000 ft (3 050 m), 4·2 min. Empty weight, 7,806 lb (3 540 kg). Loaded weight, 9,616 lb (4 362 kg). Span, 41 ft 4 in (12,60 m). Length, 33 ft 8 in (10,26 m). Height, 12 ft 4 in (3,76 m). Wing area, 275 sq ft (25,55 m²).

(Above) The XP-60 photographed in November 1941 during the initial flight test phase. This prototype was later redesignated XP-60D after the application of a Merlin 61.

(Above and below) The XP-60A possessed little in common with the XP-60 other than the wing and undercarriage and was never flown with the turbo-supercharger for which it was intended.

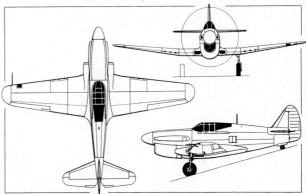

(Head of page) A Mirage IIIE of the 2ᵉ (Champagne) Escadron of the 3ᵉ Escadre de Chasse based at Nancy and (immediately above) a Mirage 5F of the 3ᵉ (Auvergne) Escadron of the 13ᵉ Escadre de Chasse based at Colmar.

MIRAGE ——————————————— from page 219

Escadres de Chasse complete the training of future tactical fighter pilots, while future transport pilots transfer to twin-engined Flamants at *Groupement Ecole* 319 at Avord (BA 702) and thereafter proceed to the *Centre d'Instruction des Equipages de Transport* at Toulouse which operates a dozen Noratlas transports together with four Transalls on loan from the 61ᵉ *Escadre*. Instructors and overseas students receive training with the three Magister-equipped *escadrons* of the *Groupement Ecole* 313, which, as previously-mentioned, is to receive Alpha Jets in the early 'eighties, and other specialist training functions are provided by the *Groupement Ecole* 316, a navigation school at Tolouse (BA 101) with 10 Noratlas transports and a handful of Flamants, and the *Centre d'Entrainement en Vol Sans Visibilitié* at Nancy (BA 121) with 20 T-33As.

Refurbishing of the 317 survivors of the 437 Magisters originally acquired by the *Armée de l'Air* is currently in process with the aim of extending their useful service until at least 1985, and a successor, so far referred to as the *Epsilon,* is to be

A Jaguar E two-seater of the 1^{er}(Provence) Escadron of the 7^e Escadre de Chasse operating from St Dizier and (foot of page) a Mirage F1C of the 2e (Normandie) Escadron of the 30e Escadre de Chasse Tous Temps based at Reims, this having been the first CAFDA escadre to re-equip with the new-generation swept-wing Mirage.

included in the 1977-82 programme with 60 to be ordered in that period for delivery after 1982. The *Armée de l'Air* has recently evinced some interest in the potential of the Bede BD-5J as a low-cost military trainer, this type being offered to non-US potential military customers by the French Microturbo company which produces the BD-5J's turbojet.

Apart from units based in Metropolitan France, the *Armée de l'Air* retains a small number of units in remaining overseas territories, aside from the *Escadron de Chasse* 4/11 *Jura* mentioned earlier as being on permanent detachment to Djibouti (BA 188), where is also stationed the 88e *Groupe d'Outre Mer* which provides logistic support and communications services for an Army counter-insurgency force of 2,000 men with six Noratlas transports, four Alouette II and two Puma helicopters and two Broussard utility aircraft. In addition, there is the 50^e *Groupe Aerien Mixte* at St Denis, Reunion, with Noratlas transports and Alouette II helicop-

ters; the 55^e *Escadron de Transport d'Outre Mer* at Dakar (BA 160) with Noratlas transports; the 58^e *Escadrille de Transport Antilles Guyane* which fulfils the transport and communications rôles in the West Indies from Pointe-a-Pitre with a mix of the Noratlas, Broussard and Alouette II, plus one Piper Aztec, and the 82e *Groupe Aerien Mixte* at Papeete which serves the French nuclear test centre in the Pacific, its inventory comprising six DC-6As and DC-6Bs, several Noratlas, 10 Alouette IIs and an Aztec.

With a total of some 1,600 aircraft of all types, including 450 first-line combat aircraft, the *Armée de l'Air* is today undeniably a very substantial force and the more realistic approach towards defence that would now seem to be emerging with the likelihood of closer collaboration with NATO forces than has been the case in recent years, its importance in counter balancing Warsaw Treaty Organisation air power cannot be too highly stressed. □

PLANE FACTS

The transitional Martin

Can you please publish in the 'Plane Facts' column photographs, general arrangement drawings and details of the Martin XB-48 six-jet bomber of the mid 'forties. G A Foot
Bretton, Peterborough

The Martin Model 223, or XB-48, was designed to meet the same requirement as the North American XB-45, the Consolidated XB-46 and the Boeing XB-47, design studies for all four bombers having been ordered early in 1945. A contract for two XB-48s (45-59585 and -59586) was approved on 13 December 1946, and the first of these was flown on 22 June 1947 powered by six 4,000 lb (1 814 kg) Allison J35 turbojets grouped in threes and underslung on the shoulder-mounted laminar-flow section wing. Apart from its undercarriage, which comprised dual mainwheel units retracting fore and aft of the weapons bay and small outrigger stabilising wheels, the XB-48 was of thoroughly conventional design and, being based on earlier piston-engined bomber projects, was very much a transitional type devoid of innovations. Three crew members were carried, comprising a navigator in the extreme nose, and pilot and co-pilot seated in tandem, the last-mentioned crew member being responsible for the aiming of twin 0·5-in (12,7-mm) which it was proposed to mount in a remotely-controlled tail barbette. The weapons bay was designed to accommodate a

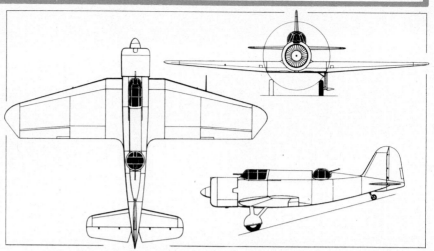

A general arrangement drawing of the Kharkov Aviation Institute's R-10 short-range tactical reconnaissance and light bombing aircraft which entered Soviet service in 1937.

maximum of 20,000 lb (9 072 kg) of bombs and total fuel capacity was 4,137 Imp gal (18 807 l).

The XB-48 had an empty equipped weight of 58,260 lb (26 426 kg) and a maximum take-off weight of 102,600 lb (46 538 kg), and performance included a maximum speed of 495 mph (796 km/h), a maximum range with an 8,000-lb (3 629 kg) bomb load of 2,400 miles (3 862 km)

and a service ceiling of 43,000 ft (13 106 m). An altitude of 35,000 ft (10 668 m) was attained in 13·3 min, take-off distance to clear a 50-ft (15,24-m) obstacle was 5,200 ft (1 585 m) and landing speed at 71,300 lb (32 341 kg) was 105 mph (169 km/h). Overall dimensions included a span of 108 ft 4 in (33,02 m), a length of 85 ft 8 in (26,11 m), a height of 26 ft 6 in (8,08 m) and a wing area of 1,330 sq ft (123,56 m²).

The performance achieved by the XB-48 was considered to provide an insufficient advance over existing piston-engined medium bombers to warrant further development and it was accordingly discontinued.

(Above) The first prototype Martin XB-48 which commenced its flight test programme on 22 June 1947, development being discarded when performance failed to measure up to expectations. A general arrangement drawing of the XB-48 (below) shows clearly the innovative (for its time) undercarriage of the XB-48.

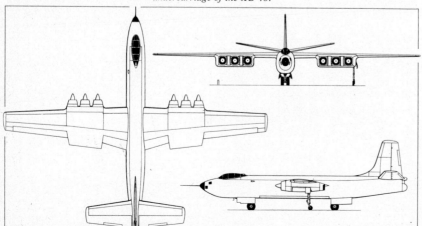

Ivanov from Kharkov

In a small booklet depicting the situation of several of the major combatant air forces in the summer of 1943, I have discovered a rather poor photograph of a somewhat odd-looking Soviet reconnaissance aircraft labelled R-10. This appears to be a single-seat low-wing monoplane with a retractable undercarriage and an air-cooled radial engine. Can you publish a general arrangement drawing, photographs and some information about this aircraft? J Soree
Venlo-Blerick, Netherlands

The *two*-seat R-10 short-range tactical reconnaissance and light bomber monoplane was designed by I G Nyeman of the Kharkov Aviation Institute (KhAI) and competed with designs by teams led by Polikarpov, Sukhoi and Grigorovich in the so-called *Ivanov* light reconnaissance-bomber contest announced at the beginning of 1936. Designated KhAI-5 by the Institute, the R-10 was essentially a military derivative of the KhAI-1 six-seat light transport of 1932, the performance of which had surpassed that of standard Soviet fighters of the day. The Khai-1 had subsequently been ordered into production for use on internal air routes and had understandably attracted the attention of the military authorities, approval being given to a proposed reconnaissance-bomber version, which, as the KhAI-5, entered development in 1935, before the *Ivanov* contest was promoted. Thus, three prototypes of Nyeman's design were available for testing by

— continued on page 249

Last of the Wartime Lavochkins

THE WARTIME development of the single-seat fighter in the Soviet Union was characterised by the continuous refinement of two fundamental designs bearing the appellations of Lavochkin and Yakovlev. In their initial production forms, they were established in service with the Soviet Union's Air Forces, the *Voenno-vozdushniye Sily* (V-VS), well before the *Wehrmacht* launched its onslaught. While other major combatants phased into service new fighter types as the conflict progressed, the Soviet Union alone was unable to afford such luxury; all effort had to be directed towards maximising fighter output and the disruption of assembly lines and ensuing loss of production inevitably associated with the introduction of an entirely new aircraft were not to be tolerated.

Thus, frontline demands for improvements in fighter capability to compensate for changing operational conditions and progressively more advanced enemy warplanes as they were committed to the air war over the Soviet Union had to be accommodated by a process of continuous refinement of existing aircraft; a process epitomized by the La-7, the last fighter created by Semyon A Lavochkin's design bureau to achieve operational status during WW II.

Lavochkin had risen to prominence when, after establishing his own OKB (*Opytno konstruktorskoye byuro* — Experimental Design Bureau), in which he had been joined by Vladimir P Gorbunov and Mikhail I Gudkov, he had created a new and promising 'frontal' fighter — a general-purpose tactical fighter with best combat altitude between 9,840 and 13,125 ft (3 000 and 4 000 m) — of wooden construction at a time when the Soviet aircraft industry was suffering critical shortages of steel tube and light alloy. This fighter, the LaGG-1, the first prototype of which had flown on 30 March 1940 with Aleksei I Nikashin at the controls, had displayed its full share of teething problems, but had, by general consensus, been considered an extraordinarily promising warplane, which, owing to the exigencies of the times and despite its immaturity, had been committed to large-scale production.

Entering service in modified form with the V-VS as the LaGG-3 in the spring of 1941, this fighter had soon revealed the painful fact that the defects seen in the prototypes had not only been fundamental but had been exacerbated by productionisation of the design. Within little more than a year, Lavochkin had found himself, if not in disgrace, certainly the subject of official disapproval owing to his apparent inability to exorcise the LaGG-3's defects; his OKB had been reduced to a bare nucleus and was no more than an unwelcome 'guest' in the Tbilisi factory to which it had been transferred from Gor'kiy.

V-VS pilots were attributing lethal propensities to the Lavochkin fighter, suggesting that the acronym "LaGG" stood for *"lakirovanny garantirovanny grob"* — varnished guaranteed coffin — rather than being indicative of the design team responsible for this ill-famed warplane! The LaGG-3 was undeniably overweight; it was also unforgiving. Its propensity for developing an unheralded and vicious spin from a steep banking turn, nosing-up during a landing approach and stalling at the least provocation — shortcomings compounded by the inexperience of the majority of its pilots — had resulted in a lack of élan and aggressiveness in its use.

Such was the pace of events in the early 'forties, however, that barely more than a further year had passed, when, on 21 June 1943, Semyon Lavochkin received the coveted title of Hero of Socialist Labour and his prestige as a fighter designer was at its zenith: an extraordinary metamorphosis but one no more dramatic than the transformation of the capabilities of his fighter that had brought about so radical a change in his standing. Indeed, the substitution of the Shvetsov-designed M-82 14-cylinder two-row radial air-cooled engine for the Klimov-designed M-105P 12-cylinder inline liquid-cooled power plant which had transformed the LaGG-3 into the La-5 had, fortuitously, resulted in what was to become one of the outstanding combat aircraft of WW II.

The progressive improvement of the M-82 engine as the M-82F and, finally, as the M-82FN on which the carburettor gave place to direct fuel injection, was paralleled by the development of the Lavochkin fighter, engine changes being accompanied by the redesign of the fuel system and structural refinements which were to culminate in the replacement by metal of the wooden spars. Whereas the LaGG-3 had garnered a reputation for unwieldiness, its radial-engined descendant,

while retaining the sturdiness of the earlier model, proved itself outstandingly manoeuvrable. A superlative low-to-medium altitude air superiority fighter, excelling in close-in high-*g* manoeuvring style of combat, the La-5 offered fine climb-and-dive characteristics. Its controls were sensitive; it could be looped and Immelmanned at low airspeeds; its only caprice was a tendency to emulate a kangaroo during landing. The combination of wing loading, power-to-weight ratio and aileron area — at 8·02 per cent of the total wing area this was proportionately larger than that of any contemporary — had resulted in the supreme dogfighter and a pilot's aeroplane *par excellence*.

The ultimate refinement

The Lavochkin design bureau had still to wring the last potential from the fundamental design, however, and this it did late in 1943 with the La-7; the ultimate refinement of the fighter that had begun its passage across the drawing boards of the small OKB established in *Zavod* 301 in the Moscow suburbs — a factory originally built for the manufacture of furniture for the Palace of the Soviets — in the winter of 1938-39.

Development of the La-7 was initiated in the autumn of 1943, when there was some reason to believe that the maxim

"Do not touch the production line" could shortly be relaxed. Despite the assignment of a new designation, the La-7 was anything but a new design. Launched under the design bureau designation La-120, or *Samolet* 120, the La-7 incorporated the results of a TsAGI wind tunnel programme aimed at defining areas in which the basic La-5FN could be aerodynamically improved. These were coupled with some refinements aimed at facilitating field maintenance, marginally less spartan equipment, an increase in firepower to overcome the only serious criticism of the La-5FN and the revised wing structure incorporating metal spars which was simultaneously being evolved for application to late production batches of the earlier fighter.

The La-7 was viewed by Lavochkin's bureau as essentially an interim measure, the aim being to provide the V-VS with an improved-performance fighter without any time-consuming redesign of principal components and pending availability of an entirely new all-metal fighter*, which, synthesising the operational experience gained with the earlier wooden- and mixed-construction Lavochkin fighter generation, was already on the drawing boards.

The La-7 retained the M-82FN engine of the definitive

This was to emerge in definitive form as the La-130 shortly after the end of WW II and enter production for the V-VS as the La-9.

The profiles at the head of the page and below illustrate three very different finishes applied to La-7s during the final year of fighting on Germany's Eastern Front. The aircraft illustrated above in the finish applied to many La-7s in the summer of 1944 was believed to have been flown by a squadron commander of the 163rd Guards IAP. The aircraft immediately below of an unidentified Guards IAP sported the two-tone grey upper surface finish widely used in the spring of 1945, and that at the foot of the page was that of Ivan Kozhedub while flying with the 176 Guards IAP during the winter of 1944-45.

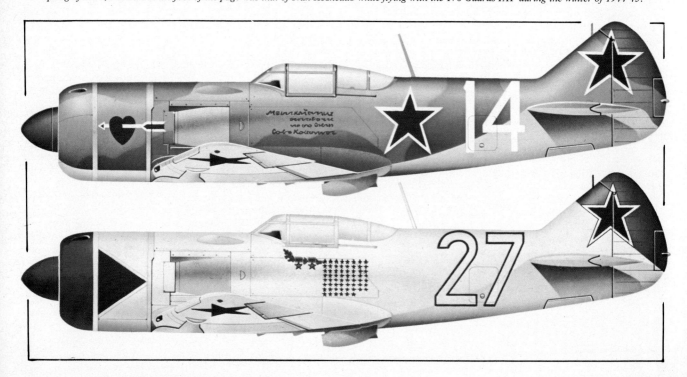

production version of the preceding fighter. This power plant, which owed much to the Wright Cyclone 14 but had a shorter stroke (155 mm), a smaller swept volume (41,2 l), a higher compression ratio (1:67) and smaller overall dimensions, had a dry weight of 2,046 lb (928 kg) and offered 1,850 hp for two minutes at 2,500 rpm, 1,630 hp being available at 5,085 ft (1 550 m) and 1,500 hp at 14,765 ft (4 500 m). Although cylinder head temperatures remained critical with this engine and there were still instances of cylinders *literally* losing their heads when the pilot failed to keep a wary eye on the cylinder head temperature gauge during the heat of combat, the M-82FN was considered a thoroughly reliable power plant, easily maintained under primitive conditions and capable of absorbing considerable punishment. This was mated with a VISh-105V-4 propeller of 10·17 ft (3,10 m) diameter.

Careful attention was paid to the refinement of the cowling enclosing the M-82FN. The long supercharger air intake fairing characteristic of the La-5FN was removed from the upper centreline of the cowling and replaced by a flush intake in the port wing root, and the oil cooler intake was transferred from the bottom of the cowling to a position under the aft fuselage, level with the wing trailing edge, to result in what was aerodynamically undoubtedly one of the cleanest radial engine cowlings ever applied to a fighter. The cowling itself — which, on the La-5FN, comprised four hinged and two fixed segments — consisted of only two sections aft of the front ring, both of these being hinged along the upper centreline to reveal the entire engine for maintenance and servicing. The anti-quated Hucks type starter dog incorporated in the propeller spinner of the La-5FN was discarded.

The fuselage structure of the La-7 was virtually identical to that of the La-5FN, this being a semi-monocoque of plywood-sheathed birch frames, triangular-section wooden stringers and bakelite ply skinning, and structurally the wing was similar to that of the late production La-5FN in which the two *delta-drevesina* (delta timber*) box spars had given place to spars employing chromansil still flanges and dural webs,

*Birch shpon, *or layers of birch strips glued cross-grained, impregnated with VIAM-B-3 phenol-formaldehyde resin, borax and boric acid.*

plywood ribs being retained except for those at the attachment points of the centre section and the outer panels which were of dural, skinning being of 6-mm bakelite ply†. The movable control surfaces were metal-framed and fabric-covered, and the flaps were of thick dural sheet on piano hinges. Continuous taper was applied to the wing centre section leading edge — the sharply-tapered root leading edges of the La-5FN being eliminated — and in addition to the supercharger intake, gun cooling apertures were introduced in the wing roots.

Further refinement resulted from the restoration of tail-wheel retraction (although the hydraulic system of the La-5FN had originally incorporated the tailwheel this had proved troublesome in operation and the tailwheel had almost invariably been disconnected from the system and locked in the extended position after delivery of the aircraft) and the provision of hinged flaps on the fuselage centre-line to enclose the previously-exposed portions of the mainwheels when retracted. The inadequate weight of fire offered by the twin 20-mm ShVAK cannon of the La-5FN was overcome in the La-7 by the substitution of a trio of lightweight 20-mm Berezina B-20 cannon mounted asymmetrically in the forward fuselage, two to port and one to starboard. These weapons, each weighing only 55 lb (25 kg) as compared with the 92·6 lb (42 kg) of the ShVAK, possessed the same muzzle velocity and

†*Layers of birch strip bonded at 150 deg C with bakelite film.*

The aerodynamically clean yet sturdy profile of the twin-cannon version of the La-7 is clearly illustrated by the photographs above right and below, the latter depicting one of the examples supplied during the final weeks of WW II in Europe to the 1st Czechoslovak Fighter Regiment as replacements for the unit's La-5FNs and photographed at Balice airfield, near Kraków, Poland, in April 1945. The La-7 was rather primitive by western standards of the day, but was ideally suited to the conditions under which it fought and was almost certainly the most manoeuvrable fighter used in Europe during world War II.

Lavochkin La-7 Cutaway Drawing Key

1 Propeller spinner
2 Three-blade controllable-pitch VISh-105V-4 metal propeller of 10·17 ft (3,10 m) diameter
3 Controllable frontal intake louvres
4 Semi-circular upward-hinging engine access panels (port and starboard)
5 ShVAK cannon port
6 Shvetsov M-82FN (ASh-82FN) 14-cylinder radial air-cooled engine
7 Exhaust pipe cluster (seven per side)
8 Cooling air exit louvre (port and starboard)
9 Tubular steel engine bearer
10 Port belt-fed gas-operated 20-mm ShVAK cannon (standard for 'Moskva La-7')
11 Port cannon ammunition tank (200 rounds)
12 Starboard cannon breech fairing
13 Oil tank
14 Laminated wooden block bulkhead reinforcement
15 Cockpit bulkhead
16 Armourglass (60-mm) windscreen
17 PBP-1a reflector sight
18 Pitot head
19 Starboard navigation light
20 Aft-sliding cockpit canopy
21 Instrument display panels
22 Control column
23 Engine throttle control
24 Engine air louvre controls
25 Oxygen regulator
26 Oil cooler control
27 Pilot's seat (parachute pan)
28 Armour (8-mm) plate
29 Armourglass (75-mm) screen
30 Radio packs (RSI-6 HF)
31 Oxygen bottle
32 Rear spar/fuselage attachment

40 Supercharger air intake (matching starboard auxiliary intake)
41 Dural rib structure mating outer panel and centre section
42 Forward wing spar (chromansil steel flanges and dural webs)
43 Wooden ribs
44 Automatic leading-edge slat (obliquely-operated)
45 Port navigation light
46 Dural-framed fabric-covered aileron
47 Aileron hinge datum line (showing underside leading-edge balancing)
48 Rear wing spar (chromansil steel flanges and dural webs)
49 Oleo-pneumatic mainwheel strut
50 Mainwheel cover plate
51 Mainwheel (650×200 mm)
52 Pilot's visual undercarriage position indicator
53 Port wing flap (plain dural sheet structure)
54 Flap shown lowered 30 deg
55 Flap actuating rod
56 Auxiliary spar (carrying control surfaces)
57 Fixed trailing edge
58 Wing root fairing

rate of fire as the heavier weapons that they replaced, thus providing a 50 per cent increase in weight of fire for a 40·5 per cent reduction in installed weight. In the event, shortfalls in deliveries of B-20 cannon were to result in the three-gun armament being applied to only those La-7s that were to be built in a factory at Yaroslavl — these being known unofficially as "Yaroslavl La-7s" — whereas those built in parallel at a Moscow factory had, perforce, to revert to the twin-ShVAK armament of the La-5FN*.

Apart from the relocation of some items of equipment and marginally less austere instrumentation, the revised fighter was in all other respects similar to the La-5FN, and the prototype flew as the La-120 with N V Adamovich at the controls in November 1943, immediately demonstrating a worthwhile improvement in performance. During the flight test programme conducted in the winter of 1943-44, the La-120 attained a maximum speed of 422 mph (680 km/h) at 9,840 ft (3 000 m) and proved capable of reaching 16,405 ft (5 000 m) within 4·45 minutes. Thus, in the spring of 1944, it was ordered into production as the La-7 *in parallel with* the La-5FN at factories in Yaroslavl and Moscow, a tandem two-seat version, the La-7UTI (or UTI-La-7) for conversion training and high-speed liaison tasks, being ordered simultaneously,

It was generally believed in the V-VS fighter regiments that, apart from superior armament, the 'Yaroslavl La-7s' were of a generally higher manufacturing standard than were the 'Moskva La-7s' — certainly one batch of Moscow-built La-7s had to undergo modification as a result of a series of spar attachment point failures in dives.

68 Accumulator
69 Rudder cables
70 Lift point
71 Wooden two-spar tailplane (plywood skin)
72 Metal-framed fabric-skinned elevator

73 Elevator trim tab
74 Tailplane/fuselage attachments
75 Wooden fin structure (integral with fuselage)

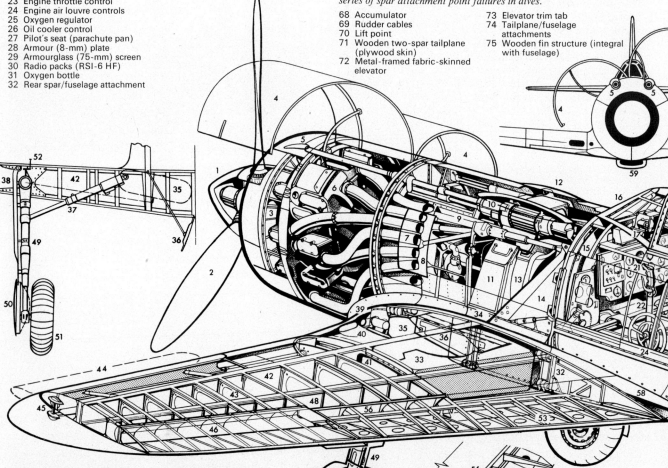

33 Port inter-spar fuel tank (matching centre and starboard tanks)
34 Mainspar/fuselage attachment
35 Mainwheel well
36 Mainwheel well doors
37 Hydraulic retraction jack
38 Undercarriage retraction pivot
39 Gun-cooling air intake (port and starboard)

59 Oil cooler air intake
60 Oil cooler
61 Variable air outlet
62 Compressed air filler cap
63 Compressed air bottles
64 Aerial mast
65 Bakelite-ply skinning
66 Semi-monocoque fuselage construction
67 Accumulator access panel

the suffix indicating *Uchebno-trenirovochny istrebitel* — literally "Instructional Training Fighter". The La-7UT1 was a straightforward adaptation of the single-seater in which a second cockpit was inserted aft of the radio bay, this being provided with duplicate control column and rudder pedals but only primary instrumentation. Both cockpits were enclosed by aft-sliding hoods, a fixed transparent section covering the radio bay and providing a continuous 'greenhouse' fairing into the normal aft fuselage decking. The tail surface control runs were rerouted, armament was restricted to a single 20-mm cannon in the portside of the upper nose decking and on some examples the oil cooler intake fairing was restored to the position that it had occupied on the La-5FN, necessitating slight modification of the hinged cowling sections.

The La-7 joins combat

Production La-7s began to reach the frontline V-VS regiments in the early summer of 1944, among the first to re-equip being the 176 (formerly 19) Guards (proskurovsky Order of the Red Banner and of Aleksandr Nevsky) IAP, an elite unit to which Ivan N Kozhedub — at that time the second ranking V-VS ace with 45 confirmed 'kills' — was transferred on 19 August when the IAP was based at Brest-Litovsk as part of Gen Rudenko's 16th Air Army. Kozhedub had become the V-VS's greatest exponent of the La-5FN and mounted on the La-7 — the flying characteristics of which were closely comparable with those of the earlier fighter but were to be described as "indefinably better" — he rapidly increased his score which stood at 57 'kills' by the end of the year. It was while flying the La-7 that, on 15 February 1945, Kozhedub encountered the first

Messerschmitt Me 262 to be reported over the Soviet Front, its pilot belatedly seeing the La-7 as Kozhedub fired a burst at maximum range which mortally damaged the German fighter. By this time, Kozhedub had surpassed Aleksandr I Pokryshkin's score to become the V-VS's leading ace and, incidentally the top-scoring ace of all Allied air forces.

Several other 'Guards' IAPs converted to the La-7 during the second half of 1944, and the fighter was to play a major rôle in the conflict over Germany during the final months of the war, being allegedly the master of any opponent at low and medium altitudes, assuming pilots of comparable capability. The La-7 was also issued to the 1st Czechoslovak Fighter Regiment during the closing weeks of the fighting in Europe as a replacement for the La-5FN but was not flown on operations by the Czechs.

Experimental versions of the La-7 evolved as part of a programme to counter a threat of a *Luftwaffe* high-altitude bombing offensive against the Soviet capital included rocket-boosted and turbo-supercharged variants. The first model to be equipped with a booster rocket was the La-7R (*Raketny* —

Lavochkin La-7 Specification

Power Plant: One Shvetsov M-82FN (ASh-82FN) 14-cylinder two-row radial air-cooled engine with two-stage supercharger and direct fuel injection rated at 1,850 hp at 2,500 rpm (for two minutes), 1,630 hp at 2,400 rpm at 5,085 ft (1 550 m) and 1,500 at 2,400 rpm at 14,765 ft (4 500 m), driving a VISh-105V-4 three-bladed controllable-pitch metal propeller of 10·17 ft (3,10 m) diameter. Total fuel capacity of 134 Imp gal (610 l) distributed between three flexible self-sealing tanks in wing centre section.
Performance: Max speed (at 7,010 lb/3 180 kg), 371 mph (597 km/h) at sea level, 379 mph (610 km/h) at 3,280 ft (1 000 m), 399 mph (643 km/h) at 6,560 ft (2 000 m), 416 mph (670 km/h) at 9,845 ft (3 000 m), 410 mph (660 km/h) at 13,125 ft (4 000 m), 423 mph (680 km/h) at 19,030 ft (5 800 m), 416 mph (670 km/h) at 21,325 ft (6 500 m); time to 16,405 ft (5 000 m), 4·52 min; service ceiling, 31,170 ft (9 500 m); range at econ cruise, 616 mls (990 km).
Weights: Empty equipped, 5,842 lb (2 650 kg); normal loaded, 7,496 lb (3 400 kg).
Dimensions: Span, 32 ft 11⅘ in (9,80 m); length, 28 ft 2⅖ in (8,60 m); height, 8 ft 6¼ in (2,60 m); wing area, 189·34 sq ft (17,59 m²).
Armament: Two 20-mm Shpital'ny-Vladimirov (ShVAK) cannon with 200 rpg or three 20-mm Berezina B-20 cannon with 170 rpg synchronised to fire through the propeller disc. Provision for two 220-lb (100-kg) bombs or six RS-82 rockets (82-mm) on underwing racks.

76 Aerial attachment stub
77 Rudder hinge post
78 Metal-framed fabric-skinned rudder
79 Rudder trim tab
80 Tail navigation light
81 Rudder hinge (lowest of three)
82 Aft-retracting tailwheel (300×125 mm)
83 Tailwheel doors
84 Oleo-pneumatic tailwheel leg pivot
85 Tailwheel retraction jack
86 Elevator control linkage rods

The photograph above depicts the two-gun version of the La-7 whereas that below illustrates an example of the three-gun version in Czechoslovak markings. It will be noted that the latter, photographed after withdrawal from postwar Czechoslovak service, features a D/F loop immediately aft of the radio mast.

The general arrangement drawing below illustrates the version of the La-7 fitted with three B-20 cannon, two offset to port and one to starboard.

'Rocket'), the development of which began in the early summer of 1944. Two prototypes of the La-7R were produced by the conversion of standard production airframes to take the RD-1KhZ auxiliary rocket motor developed by S P Korolev and V P Glushko. The RD-1KhZ operated on nitric acid and kerosene, and provided 660 lb (300 kg) thrust for up to three minutes. The RD-1KhZ was mounted in an extended rear fuselage, necessitating the cutting away of the base of the rudder and the heightening of the vertical surfaces to compensate. Rocket fuel was accommodated aft of the radio bay and, presumably for both CG reasons and simplicity, the supercharger air intake was restored to the engine cowling, and the ventral intake retained for cooling the rocket bay.

After protracted ground trials, an initial flight test was attempted in October 1944 by Georgi M Shiyanov. During the take-off run, however, a fuel pipe failed and the rocket motor exploded, the aircraft catching fire and Shiyanov 'baling out'. Shiyanov continued the flight test programme with the second prototype La-7R, but on one occasion, when the rocket motor was relit in flight, there was an explosion which left virtually no elevator surface and only 25 per cent of the rudder. Nevertheless, by skilful piloting, Shiyanov succeeded in landing the aircraft safely and, after repairs had been effected, managed to attain speeds as high as 435 mph (700 km/h) in level flight. Trials with the La-7R were to continue until February 1945 under low priority, the threat to Moscow of high-altitude bombing having meanwhile been removed, but were abandoned when the plywood skinning began to disintegrate as a result of the corrosive effect of the nitric acid vapour escaping from the inadequately-sealed tank.

A further rocket-boosted example — a conversion of one of the original prototype airframes and presumably for this reason designated as the La-120R — had, nevertheless, joined the test programme by this time, having been flown initially in January by A V Davidov. The La-120R had an improved version of the RD-1KhZ rocket (referred to as the ZhRD-1) and a revised installation, the local airframe structure having

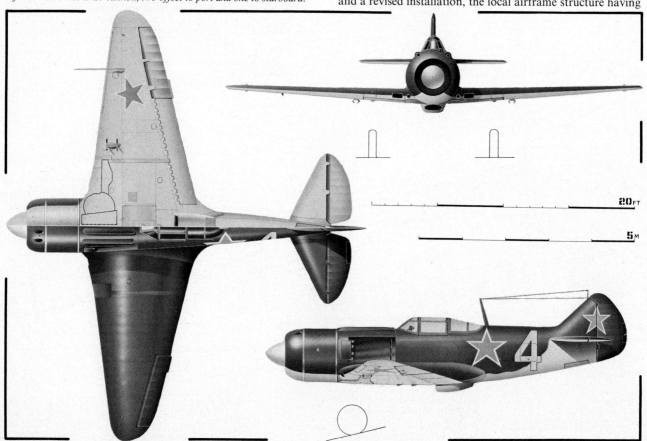

20 FT

5 M

The tandem two-seat La-7UTI (alias UTI-La-7) was produced in two versions, that illustrated left featuring an oil cooler intake fairing under the engine cowling and that illustrated right having this fairing mounted aft in a similar fashion to that of the standard single-seat model. The La-7UTI was employed more extensively for liaison and communications tasks than for conversion training.

been changed from wood to metal. Offering the same thrust and endurance, the ZhRD-1 boosted the maximum level speed of the La-120 R by 53 mph (85 km/h) to 461 mph (742 km/h) at 9,840 ft (3 000 m), and the test programme with this aircraft was to continue into the postwar years, the La-120R demonstrated publicly over Tushino in August 1946.

In parallel with the La-7R programme, the Lavochkin bureau endeavoured to improve the high-altitude intercept potential of the La-7 by fitting a turbo-supercharged version of the M-82FN engine. Designated La-7TK and test flown during July-August 1944, this experimental version was fitted with a pair of TsIAM-developed TK-3 turbo-superchargers and achieved a maximum speed of 420 mph (676 km/h) at 26,240 ft (8 000 m) during the test programme which terminated abruptly when one of the turbo-superchargers exploded and the aircraft was destroyed. Trials were also performed with one La-7 airframe fitted with a turbo-supercharged ASh-71TK engine of 2,000 hp but discontinued owing to the poor reliability of this Shvetsov engine and the erratic behaviour of the TsIAM turbo-supercharger. Yet a further experimental La-7 was fitted with a 2,000 hp ASh-83 engine and an armament of two 23-mm Nudelmann-Suranov cannon. Flown in February 1945, at a time the ASh-83 engine was being considered as a possible power plant for the La-7's successor, this La-7 achieved 450 mph (725 km/h) at 24,280 ft (7 400 m), but with the decision to discard the ASh-83, the test programme was discontinued.

By the end of 1944, the Lavochkin bureau had finally discontinued further development of the mixed-construction La-7 in favour of the entirely new all-metal design bearing only a configurational similarity to its immediate predecessor. Most of the features of this new fighter, the La-130, were tested individually by a series of experimental derivatives of the La-120, embodying varying degrees of metal construction, such as the La-126* which combined several of the individual features tested by earlier aircraft, such as an all-metal laminar-flow wing, revised engine cowling, etc, and was thus more a prototype for the La-130 (which was to enter production for the V-VS as the La-9) than a variant of the La-7, and did not commence its flight test programme until after the end of WW II.

Phased out of production early in 1946, by which time a total of 5,753 examples of this fighter had been delivered, the La-7, with its primarily wooden construction, relatively light armament and somewhat rudimentary equipment, was perhaps a rather primitive warplane by Western standards of the day. Primitive though it may have been, it was a most effective fighter ideally suited to the conditions under which it was operated. Its sturdy radial air-cooled engine endowed it with an advantage over those fighters equipped with liquid-cooled engines and which, under the harsh conditions of a Russian winter, were frequently immobilised by frozen glycol; its rugged, wide-track undercarriage was ideally suited for the

As the La-126PVRD, this aircraft was to be used as a test-bed for the Bondaryuk VRD-430 ramjet in the summer of 1946.

unprepared grass fields from which it operated more often than not and, perhaps surprisingly, in view of its largely wooden structure and ply skinning, it withstood climatic extremes on fields lacking the luxury of covered accommodation with extraordinary equanimity. Furthermore, it was less demanding in terms of field maintenance than virtually any contemporary. Finally withdrawn from first-line V-VS service late in 1947 — although it soldiered on somewhat longer with the *Československé letectvo* from which it was phased out in 1950 — the La-7 was almost certainly the most manoeuvrable fighter to see operational use in the European theatre during WW II. □

(Above and below) The La-7R which had a 660 lb (300 kg) Korolev-Glushko RD-1KhZ auxiliary rocket motor installed in the extreme rear fuselage. Taller vertical tail surfaces were applied and the supercharger air intake was fitted to the top of the engine cowling.

The photograph above and the general arrangement drawing on the opposite page show clearly the three features that distinguish the Kfir-C2 from the initial production model of the Kfir (illustrated below left), these being the fixed canards above and aft of the engine air intakes, the dogtooth extensions on the outboard wing leading edges and the small strakes immediately aft of the nose radome.

KFIR ——————————————————— *from page 225*

in yawed flight and ensuring even flow breakaway round the nose at high attack angles. These modifications also improve entry into manoeuvres, result in better sustained turning performance, reduce gust sensitivity at all operational altitudes and particularly during flight at minimum altitude, and also improve take-off and landing characteristics.

The new fixed surfaces weigh some 200 lb (91 kg), increasing combat weight with half-fuel and two Shafrir AAMs to 20,700 lb (9 390 kg), and it is anticipated that all Kfir fighters already in the *Heyl Ha'Avir* inventory will be retrospectively modified to C2 standard. In fact, Kfirs currently on the IAI assembly line are being completed with the dogtooth wing extension, a compound then being applied inboard to result in a straight leading edge. When the canards and fuselage strakes are applied, the compound will be removed. Canards or fore-planes were, of course, applied experimentally to the Mirage-Milan (see *Dassault Flies a Kite*/June 1971) in the late 'sixties to achieve a nose-up moment without using the elevons, but these, which, in their final form, incorporated slots and were retracted for high-speed flight, were somewhat smaller than those adopted for the Kfir-C2, the layout and position of which approximate more closely to those of the Saab 37 Viggen.

In addition to production of the Kfir-C2 for the *Heyl*

Ha'Avir, which is likely to start taking this model into its inventory during the first quarter of next year, IAI anticipates obtaining export sales for this fighter and is currently mounting a major marketing programme and offering deliveries in the second half of 1977. Israel is struggling to overcome financial problems which include soaring inflation and a weak Israeli pound, and thus, while the *Heyl Ha'Avir* enjoys priority in the procurement of hardware, budgetary purse strings are being pulled ever tighter. It is therefore likely to be several years before the service receives the full complement of 150 or so Kfir-C2s that it reportedly requires to replace the *Salvo*-Mirages and Neshers as the backbone of its air superiority component, for financial restraints are restricting IAI output to something of the order of half of its 4·5 aircraft-per-month capacity. Thus, relatively early export deliveries can be offered at the *highly* competitive unit price of $4·5m-$5·0m (£2·53m-£2·81m), according to equipment standard, but let it be said that the export unit price certainly does not reflect the non-recurring costs of the programme which must surely have been immense.

Political difficulties over the export of the Bet-Shemesh licence-built J79 engine — approximately 60 per cent of which is produced in Israel, including the blades and the IAI-designed titanium heat shield — are not anticipated and IAI is offering a "heavy package of support" to potential customers which is likely to prove particularly attractive to those air forces that have not hitherto operated modern, high-performance combat aircraft. While *primarily* an air super-iority fighter, the Kfir-C2 is being offered as a multi-rôle warplane with a broad mission spectrum, possessing rapid turnaround and rôle change capability — from interceptor to long-range combat patrol fighter or ground attack fighter without any change in onboard avionics. Promoting the Kfir-C2 as the "highest performance fighter aircraft" likely to be available on the international market for at least half-a-decade, an IAI spokesman has said that his company anticipates export sales running at 12-15 units annually for at least the next six years. Certainly if the interest being displayed

AIR International CLASSIFIED

ADVERTISEMENT RATES AND CONDITIONS OF ACCEPTANCE

BOOKS FOR SALE

AEROMART'S Autumn 1976 Aviation Booklist (now published) contains many rarities — new and old. Large s.a.e. please — 48 Marlborough Road, Ipswich.

(1024LY)

INFORMATION WANTED

AUTHOR wishes to interview aircrew members that flew as backseaters; (RIO's, WSO's) in the following aircraft: F-4, A-6, F-105F, during 1965-71 in Southeast Asia. AIRTITE PUBLISHING, Box 2366, San Francisco, CA 94126.

(1018JZ)

Location of photos of wartime BOAC aircraft: particularly Catalinas at Hythe, Rose Bay and Baltimore; Ansons at Montreal, Vaaldam and Northolt; Oxfords at Whitchurch, Hurn, Vaaldam and Cairo; Hudsons at Leuchars, Montreal, Asmara, Western Desert and Croydon; Halifaxes at Whitchurch; Albemarle at Lyneham; Beech AT-7 at Baltimore; Rapide, Ju 52/3m, Lockheed 10s and 14s in West Africa. Or any BOAC aircraft in RAF Transport Command markings with four letter codes. D. M. Hannah, Barnack, Stamford, Lincs. Tel. (0780) 740373.

(1021KX)

INSURANCE

INSURANCE, J. A. HARRISON (BROKERS) LTD. of Birmingham sell insurance. Our speciality aircraft insurance. A Century of Service. Phone, call or write: Security House, 160-161 Bromsgrove Street, Birmingham, B5 6NY. Tel. 021-692 1245 (10 lines).

(1002 AY)

CONSULT US FOR YOUR AIRCRAFT INSURANCE REQUIREMENTS. Quotations at competitive rates. Marlow Gardner & Cooke Insurance Brokers Ltd., 254 Lincoln Road, Peterborough, PE1 2ND. Telephone (0733) 64236.

(1029LX)

AIR International Cover Price

Despite ever increasing costs of materials and services, the publishers of AIR International have managed to keep the cover price constant for two years. However they much regret that they are now obliged to increase the UK price to 50p with effect from the January 1977 issue. Owing to the devaluation of the pound sterling against the US dollar, the cover price for North American readers in Canada and the USA will remain at $1·50. The postage included annual subscription rate has also to be increased for those starting or renewing with the January 1977 issue. The UK rate will be £6·50, the overseas rate £7·00, with the North American rate remaining at the present $17·50. All existing subscriptions will, of course, be honoured at the rates applicable when paid. Subscribers in the United States paying $17·50 get the benefit of container transport of AIR International to New York for onward transmission by post. This results in a considerable saving of time, compared with normal seamail posted in the UK.

REMEMBER . . .

AIR International offers you the largest circulation of any European-based aviation publication with an average net paid sale of 44,028 copies per month, ABC certified, and an average readership of 2·2 persons per copy. This means your advertising is seen by a total of 96,861 readers, world-wide. If you want to reach the widest possible audience, book space NOW. *Air International Classified* can meet all your sales requirements.

MAGAZINES FOR SALE

DISPOSING of fine quality issues of R.A.F. Flying Review, Flying Review International, and Air Enthusiast. Replies with s.a.e. Write Box 1025 Air International.

(1025LY)

MAGAZINES WANTED

WANTED. Air Enthusiast April 1972 issue. Peter Freeborn, Kopernicus Strasse 47, 28 Bremen, West Germany.

(1027LX)

AIR ENTHUSIAST for January 1972 wanted. Aldo M. Bellei, Via U. Balzani 8, 00162 Rome, Italy.

(1028LX)

PUBLICATIONS WANTED

ABC WORLD AIRLINE GUIDES, particularly up to mid 1960s, or Parts 1 of later issues with Advance Schedules Sections (orange pages). Also Bradshaw's Air Guides. Also airlines' own complete system timetables up to 1970, for major carriers such as BOAC, BEA, Air France, KLM, Sabena, Lufthansa, Alitalia, Iberia, SAS, Swissair, UTA. D. M. Hannah, Barnack, Stamford, Lincs, PE9 3DN. Telephone (0780) 740373.

(1031LX)

PUBLICATIONS

PLASTIC AIRCRAFT MODELS MAGAZINE. Specimen copy 40p. PAM NEWS, 22 Slayleigh Avenue, Sheffield, S10 3RB.

(1011LY)

SCALE MODELS

SCALE MODELS made to your own requirements by enthusiast specialising in WWI and WWII aircraft. For quote 'phone Maidenhead (Berks) 30506 or write Barfoot, 100 Aldebury Road, Maidenhead.

(1030LY)

SOCIETIES

CLUB SECRETARIES. Club Ties, Blazer Badges, Drill Badges, Heraldic Shields, Brevets, Lapel Badges, Car Badges, Brochure from Club (Sales), 76 Greenford Avenue, Southall, Middlesex.

(1015LY)

LONDON SOCIETY OF AIR-BRITAIN. Your own aviation society, Wednesday, 10th November, 22nd Annual Test Pilots Forum. Top entertainment value. 7.00 p.m. in the Lecture Theatre, Holborn Central Library, Theobalds Road, London, WC1. Visitors welcome. Admission 35p.

(1026LX)

INCREASE YOUR AVAILABLE INFORMATION SOURCES, JOIN AIR-BRITAIN and get access to our specialist services, publications and library. Send 10p stamp for details (or 50p for sample House Journal) to H. B. Gwyther (AI6), 208 Stock Road, Billericay, Essex CM12 0SH.

(1016KX)

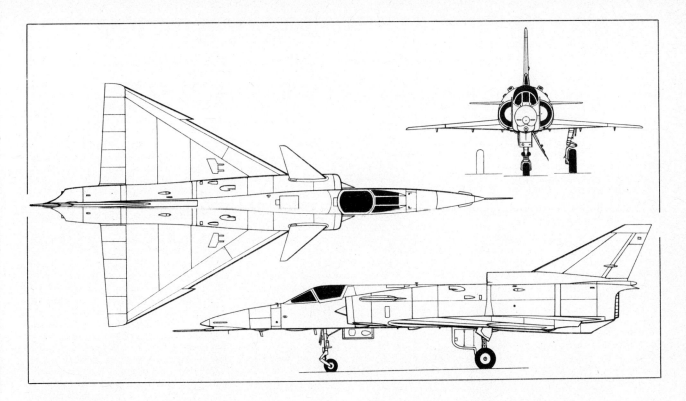

at the present time by several air forces crystallizes as firm orders, this anticipation will not have proved unduly optimistic.

There can be little doubt that, with the Kfir-C2, IAI has at least mitigated some of the well-known shortcomings of the tailless delta configuration, such as the rapid fall-off of SEP in turns owing to high induced drag, poor gust response, high approach speed and poor landing performance — if IAI literature is to be accepted *literally* these disadvantages would seem to have been completely overcome — and has come up with a dogfighter equal to and probably the superior of any warplane currently in service. There are those that would decry the fact that Israel has spent so much money on an aircraft

that, from the standpoint of configuration, has been *passé* a decade since, and there are some grounds for this view. Equally, there is no gainsaying that, when the Kfir programme was launched, Israel did not possess the necessary expertise to initiate the development of a dogfight aircraft of totally indigenous design, but the creation of an immensely improved Mirage not only provided the *Heyl Ha'Avir* with what is evidently an extremely competent warplane and a potentially valuable export; it enabled Israel's still youthful aircraft industry to cut its technological teeth and garner the experience with which the design of an entirely original multi-rôle fighter such as is now on the IAI drawing boards is well within its capability. □

PLANE FACTS ———————*from page* **240**
the time construction of prototypes of the other *Ivanov* contenders was launched, flight trials warranting the initiation of production as the R-10, although, in the event, the performances of the other reconnaissance-bombers designed specifically for participation in the *Ivanov* contest proved superior to that of the R-10.

Characterised by sharply tapered outer wing panels with straight trailing edges, the R-10 was powered by an M-25V nine-cylinder radial — a derivative of the Wright Cyclone SR-1820-F-3 adapted for Soviet production by

Arkadii D Shvetsov — rated at 775 hp at 2,200 rpm for take-off and 750 hp at 9,515 ft (2 900 m), and carried an armament of two or four 7,62-mm machine guns in the outer wing panels and a single 7,62-mm gun in a manually-operated dorsal turret, maximum bomb load being 661 lb (300 kg). The only armour protection comprised a small 8-mm plate to protect the head and shoulders of the pilot. The R-10 attained a maximum speed of 230 mph (370 km/h) at 9,840 ft (3 000 m) and maximum range was 904 miles (1 455 km), an altitude of 16,405 ft (5 000 m) being attained in 15.7 min and the service ceiling of 22,965 ft

(7 000 m) being reached in 38.5 min. Empty equipped and normal loaded weights were 4,707 lb (2135 kg) and 6,338 lb (2875 kg) respectively, max overload weight being 7,055 lb (3 200 kg), and overall dimensions were: span, 40 ft 0⅓ in (12,20 m); length, 30 ft 9⅞ in (9,40 m); wing area, 288.47 sq ft (26,8 m²).

Several hundred R-10 light reconnaissance-bombers were built during 1937-39, some being encountered during the Russo-Finnish conflict of 1939, but most had been assigned to second-line tasks or to less important command areas by the time the *Wehrmacht* onslaught on the Soviet Union began.

These photographs illustrate an example of the Nyeman-designed R-10 captured by Finnish forces during the so-called "Winter War". The performance of the R-10 rendered it obsolescent by the time that it was committed to combat.

TALKBACK

Omissions or no?

Far be it for me to criticise your superlative "Fighter A to Z" series — indeed, I am sure that no survey so complete of the world's fighters has ever before been attempted — but in the hope of being constructive, may I point out that you would seem to have omitted a number of the fighters designed in France by Louis Béchereau and flown during the 'twenties after this gentleman parted company with the Blériot concern.

John K Humphries
Guildford, Surrey

The designations of Louis Béchereau's fighter designs in the early 'twenties prior to his appointment as chief of the airframe design staff of the Salmson company (1923-26) are not entirely clear. Béchereau worked without manufacturing facilities during this period and his designs were built by various companies. Thus, there was a Letord-Béchereau single-seat fighter which was allegedly displayed at the 1922 Salon de l'Aéronautique in Paris but of which nothing further was heard. However, we would seem to have omitted from "Fighter A to Z" the Buscaylet-Béchereau C1, a single-seat fighter built by Buscaylet Père et Fils-Bobin. Béchereau's two-seat fighters were the SB 5 and SB 6 (Salmson-Béchereau), designed while with the Salmson company, and the SRAP 2 designed after Béchereau left the Salmson concern and the Société pour la Réalisation d'Appareils Prototypes was formed. We propose to include the Buscaylet-Béchereau C1 in an addendum to "Fighter A to Z" to be published shortly, and this will also include the Soviet Alekseev fighters of the late 'forties of which details and illustrations were not available earlier.

It has also been suggested to us that we have omitted the Borel CAn 2 two-seat night fighter of 1925 which is illustrated in L'Histoire des Essais en Vol by Louis Bonte (Docavia/Editions Lariviere). However, we doubt that the SCIM (Société Générale de Constructions Industrielles et Mécaniques) Borel two-seat sesquiplane was intended as a fighter as no French fighter prototype — even single-seat — appearing during the 1924-28 period had an engine of less than 400 hp, yet the SCIM Borel type, reportedly flown in 1924-25, had a 300 hp Hispano-Suiza 8Fb. As far as is known, the only other CAn 2 type of equivalent power and of comparable total weight was the LeO 8 parasol monoplane which flew in January-February 1923 with a 300 hp Renault 12F engine. If the SCIM Borel sesquiplane was actually a CAn 2, it would have been designed to a 1921 specification and it would seem odd that it should not have flown until 18 months or two years after its possible competitor, the LeO 8. — Ed.

Ju 52/3m origins

THE Ju 52 at Duxford (AIR INTERNATIONAL/August 1976) may well be an amalgam of two aircraft, or even an entirely French-built Ju 52. When the French armed forces relinquished their ageing Ju 52s still operating in North Africa and the Sahara some 16 years ago, a few machines went over to the Portuguese Air Force, but this transfer was never much publicised.

Therefore, the IWM Ju 52 — if definitely of original 1937 German vintage — may have incorporated some French licence-built components during the early 60s; or it may be an authentic French-built AAC-1 built by the Ateliers Aéronautiques de Colombes — (formerly the Amiot works, in the suburbs of Paris) either during the occupation of France or soon after the end of the World War II (see AIR International/August 1974 pp 82).

If this particular aircraft is an ex-French Aéronavale or Armée de l'Air machine, a clue might well be found in the wings or engine mounts which had been sub-contracted to SNCASO and might bring some further evidence of French manufacture.

By the way, it is a little-known fact that the Ateliers Aéronautiques de Colombes was also concerned with production of at least one other type of German aircraft, the Focke-Wulf Fw 190. Production of 60 was considered under the designation of AAC-6 but not followed up; however, a few Fw 190s were repaired by ACC and delivered as AAC-6s (more Fw 190s of the A-5 variant were also produced in France by the SNCAC as NC-900).

J P Dubois
Nice, France

Aussies in the desert—3

SUBSEQUENT to publication of my two previous letters under the above title (Talkback/December 1974 and May 1975), several more photographs of World War II enemy aircraft in the CV code markings of No 3 Squadron, RAAF, have been forwarded to me — mainly through the courtesy of Messrs David Vincent and Neville Parnell — and may be of interest to your readers.

No 3 Squadron came by a Messerschmitt Bf 109F soon after the opening of the Battle of El Alamein on 23 October 1942. It was test flown at Gambut by the Commanding officer, Squadron Leader R H Gibbes, who wrote in his diary (as recorded in James Sinclair's Sepik Pilot, 1971)—"a sweet little aircraft to fly, and a terrific performance. Reckon I should have joined the Luftwaffe!" Gibbes also tested a captured Bf 109G in RAAF markings (as pictured in Sepik Pilot) in November 1942, and mentioned "another 109F that we might be able to get serviceable. We'll have a Luftwaffe of our own before this battle is over!" The photograph (IWM CM4171) of the Messerschmitt, CV-V, about to take-off on a test flight could well be one of the 109Fs mentioned by Bobby Gibbes—although several other 109s came and went as the squadron advanced across the desert.

The Caproni Ca 309 Ghibli, (Desert Wind) was taken over (along with a Savoia-Marchetti SM 79-II torpedo bomber and a Caproni Ca 164 biplane trainer), by No 3 Squadron at Castel Benito, Tripolitania. On 2 February, Bobby Gibbes flew the Ghibli to Dufan to collect a new batch of pilots — "put six in the first time which, with myself and crew of one, made eight", recorded Gibbes in Sepik Pilot. "Trundled across the drome but couldn't get off. Taxied back and suggested that two pilots out to lighten the load. No trouble finding volunteers. Just got off the second time. When we got back I put the Ghibli in for a change of motors!" The Ca 309 remained in use as the squadron's communications aircraft, ferrying personnel and beer.

The photograph of the Macchi C 205V, MM9377, also coded CV-V (port fuselage), came from A Dawkins who, as a flying officer, flew the Italian fighter on 7 September 1943. His flying logbook recorded 50 minutes of aerobatics, with the comments, "lovely to handle—took off at 27″ (manifold pressure), cruised at ·9 (27″), 2250 revs, 250 mph." The C 205V was collected by No 3 Squadron on 24 August 1943, from Catania Main airfield and transported to Agnone, Sicily, where the

(Above) The Messerschmitt Bf 109F and (below) the Caproni Ca 309 in the 'CV' markings of No 3 Squadron RAAF, as described in the letter from Gp Capt Isaacs.

Two more No 3 Squadron's captured Italian aircraft: (above), the Macchi C 205V and (below) the Cant Z501.

squadron operated from 2 August to 14 September 1943.

The Cant Z.501 Gabbiano (Gull), shown with Pilot Officer J H Hooke and Flying Officer Dawkins aboard, was also acquired by No 3 Squadron while it was in Siciliy, August-September 1943. It is doubtful if the Z.501, with its CV squadron letters, was flown by the Australians but, apparently, it was taxied around the harbour on occasions.

The Caproni Ca 100, I-GUAS, was one of five such trainers previously used by the Catania Aero Club, Sicily, of which three went to No 112 Squadron, RAF, and one each to Nos 3 and 450 Squadrons, RAAF. It was flown at Agnone, August-September 1943 by Arthur Dawkins, and was used for taking maintenance personnel on joy rides.

The sixth photograph shows groundstaff members of No 3 Squadron inspecting de Pinedo's Savoia-Marchetti S.16ter flying boat at an airfield outside Rome in 1945. Even after 20 years, the RAAF Point Cook badge was still visible on the fuselage where it had been placed in 1925 (see *Plane Facts* October 1975).

Finally, astute readers might recall the photograph of the captured Fiat CR 42, with its unique serial number A421, which accompanied my first letter on No 3 Squadron ("Australian Gladiators", October 1973). Group Captain A C Rawlinson, RAAF (Retd), advised recently that it was planned to send this Italian biplane to Australia as a war trophy, with the locally coined number A(ustralia) (CR)42 (No)1. In the event, A421 was destroyed to prevent it falling back into enemy hands—or, perhaps I should say, friendly hands.

Gp Capt Keith Isaacs AFC, RAAF (Retd)
Lyneham, ACT, Australia

Silver Hadrians

HAVING just read your *Model Enthusiast* column in the April issue of AIR INTERNATIONAL, I noticed that you doubt the accuracy of the overall aluminium colour scheme suggested for the Italaerci kit of the CG-4A Hadrian.

Although I have not examined the said kit yet, I can assure you that the RAF *did* operate a couple of Hadrians in an overall silver doped finish, although the date was not 1950 as stated but somewhat earlier, probably around 1947. These Hadrians were actually ex-USAAF CG-4As, painted silver according to the late wartime instructions and originally intended for use in the Pacific, and they retained their original USAAF serial numbers.

John Andrade
Bewdley, Worcs.

A model Spitfire

I have now received an Otaki kit of the Spitfire Mk 8 and thought I should notify you and your readers of one major error in the colouring. The makers have apparently repeated the mistake first made by the Harleyford book "Spitfire", which I pointed out to its author, Bruce Robertson, at the time.

The code letters ZX:M on my aircraft MT928 should be dark *blue* edged in white, not red and white as shown. This error is a pity, as they have reproduced the rather odd shape of the 'M' very well and the squadron badge, which I did not expect to see, is included.

Minor criticism could be directed at the cockpit detail which bears very little resemblance to the real thing and the control column is a figment of someone's imagination! I might add that part number 10, pilot image, is somehow not quite me — I don't know what Sir William Dickson thinks! Anyway, after reading the hilarious assembly manual, I can forgive him most things.

For the record, all No 145 Squadron aircraft had the blue letters edged in white from some time in 1943 until the squadron was disbanded. One other squadron had similar markings, I believe it was No 111 but I now have no positive record.

Sqn Ldr G R S McKay (RAF, ret'd)
Tunbridge Wells, Kent.

(Above left) The Caproni Ca 100 I-GUAS mentioned in Gp Capt Isaacs' letter and (below) ground staff members of No 3 Squadron, RAAF, inspect the 1925 RAAF badge on de Pinedo's Savoia Marchetti S.16ter which they discovered near Rome in 1945.

IN PRINT

"The Grumman Story"
by Richard Thruelson
Praeger Publishers, New York, $14·95
401 pp, 7 in by 10 in, illustrated
ONE OF the most remarkable aircraft builders in the world is the Grumman Aircraft Engineering Co (which has, since this book was prepared, gone the 'aerospace' route). Just as the name of Douglas is synonymous with air transportation and Boeing with bombers and airliners, Grumman is synonymous with not just 'fighters', but Navy carrier-borne fighters and other carrier-type aircraft. It is a unique indentification.

A history of Grumman has been awaited for a long time. It still is. This is not a history of Grumman; as its title says, it's a 'story' — the kind of book a Grumman executive can hand to politicians, newsmen or prospective customers and say with that deplorable confidence which is born of ignorance, "it's all in *here!*" And the equally ignorant 'targets' will be properly impressed.

This book is essentially a Grumman public relations vehicle. But — just as Grumman has always built very good aeroplanes, it is a very good instrument of public information, even though a solid history of Grumman remains to be written.

For all practical purposes, the text is divided into five parts; the pre-1940 years; World War II; the postwar era and the 1950s; the decade of the 1960s; and thereafter. The treatment of the 1930s is by far the best. Dealing with World War II, the author becomes bogged down in regurgitating the combat records of Grumman aeroplanes — tales told better in dozens of other books. And as the text moves into the 1950s and 1960s (and as the 'story's' sources become more difficult to handle), its substance becomes thinner and thinner.

The book has at least one virtue which is undeniable: it provides an excellent overall view of Grumman and its many enterprises (canoes, truck bodies, stillborn lightplanes, crop-dusting aeroplanes, missiles, spacecraft, hydrofoils, *et al.*), which is not available elsewhere in one volume.

The text is well written (although not without many minor errors of fact and interpretation and some glaring omissions), and excellently illustrated by 10 drawings and more than 190 photos. An appendix of 18 pages

provides once-over-lightly summaries of each Grumman aircraft-type built, including general characteristics, numbers produced, and dates.

Anyone with the slightest interest in Grumman aircraft in particular and Navy carrier aircraft in general will not be disappointed in investing in the price of this book. It should be infinitely better; but in the country of the blind the one-eyed man is king, and there is nothing comparable in any 20 volumes to what is here compressed into a single binding. — RKS.

"British Independent Airlines Since 1946, Vol I"
by A C Merton Jones
Merseyside Aviation Society and LAAS, £2·35
120 pp, 8½ in by 11¾ in, illustrated
THE 'independents' have played an enormously important rôle in the development of British aviation in the 30 years since the end of World War II. The term is used — not wholly accurately — to embrace all those airline operators other than the State-owned BOAC, BEA, BSAAC and, now, British Airways. A very large number of companies has entered the arena during the three decades; some have flourished and, through mergers and acquisitions, have grown to maturity, but many have gone to the wall. And for almost the whole of the period, the precise rôle that should be played by the independents has been a subject for political argument, with as many changes of policy as there have been changes of government.

Recording the history of the independents on a day to day or season by season basis has been no easy matter; harder still is the task, now essayed by Tony Merton Jones, of putting down a comprehensive record of all the companies. The entire work is to occupy four volumes, of which the first has now appeared — and an excellent work it is, too. There is a short introduction to record the events of the first post-war decade, and then company-by-company histories, starting with ACE (Aviation Charter Enterprises) and continuing, in Vol I, to British Westpoint.

The accounts are succinct but comprehensive, with information (not always quite complete) on the personalities involved in the formation of the airline, its operational history and its fate — for few of the companies

listed in this volume are still operational. Here are the stories of many half-remembered names of the post-war years, and not a few that this reviewer scarcely remembers at all. In every case, fully detailed fleet lists are included and there is a good selection of photographs. A little surprisingly, in view of the title, airlines of the Republic of Ireland are included, which brings Aer Lingus in as something of an interloper among the genuine British independents.

Production of this volume brings added stature to the two enthusiasts organisations that have jointly published it — Merseyside Aviation Society, 4 Willow Green, Liverpool L25 4RR, and LAAS International, 21 Barchester Close, Uxbridge UB8 2JY. Copies can be ordered from either address.

"Curtiss P-40 in Action"
by Ernest R McDowell
Squadron/Signal Publications, Michigan, USA, $3·95
60pp, 11 in by 8¼ in, illustrated
FOR the 26th title in the "In Action" series, Squadron/Signal Publications has chosen one of the most famous fighters of World War II, adding eight pages to the usual allocation to allow the subject to be covered adequately. There is a summary of P-40 evolution, three-view line drawings or side-views of all the variants, 10 excellent colour profiles and a good selection of photographs, covering various developments of the type as well as the basic P-40s in all their many forms. In one or two places the text and captions suggest an incomplete knowledge of the subject, but this is more than compensated by the number of little-known illustrations included.

"Grumman Guidebook, Vol I"
by Mitch Mayborn and others
Flying Enterprise Publications, Dallas, Texas, $7·95 ($14·95 in hardback)
112 pp, 8½ in by 11 in, illustrated
WITH the authoritative Stearman, Cessna and Ryan Guidebooks behind it, Flying Enterprise Publications has launched into a Grumman coverage that is expected to require four volumes in all; Volume I covers the biplanes and the first few monoplanes, including the F4F Wildcat family.

There are four principal sections, two of which provide photographs of each type and variant, with fully detailed captions, and smaller illustrations to depict aircraft in action, odd markings and famous flights, pilots and so on. A third section is a 16-pp reprint of contemporary Grumman advertisements and magazine articles while Section IV comprises data tables listing the entire production of the aircraft types covered in this volume, with specifications and notes on individual owners and final dispositions.

There is much of interest in this volume, which comes up to the high standard achieved with previous titles in the series, although a few errors are noted in relation to the listing of Martlets (Wildcats) supplied to Britain. During 1940 and 1941, there were almost daily changes in the planned disposition of the G-36Bs built on British contract, ex-French G-36As re-assigned to Britain and a batch of US

A unique photograph of one of the 30 Grumman F4F-3As intended for Greece but diverted in 1941 to the Royal Navy, showing British markings applied immediately after its arrival in North Africa but with the USN serial 3876 still retained on the fuselage. The Grumman F4F Wildcat/Martlet family is fully described in "Grumman Guidebook" Vol I noted here and is also the subject of an extensive coverage in AE QUARTERLY/THREE.

Navy F4F-3As assigned to Greece under Lend-Lease but also diverted to Britain. The result was that paperwork often lagged behind events in the field and, indeed, there may well be no exact record in existence of the tie-up between RAF serial numbers and Martlet mark numbers and sources of origin. The list in Grumman Guidebook quotes c/ns for what is probably the correct number of Martlets assigned to Britain but it is in error in relating some specific serial numbers to certain batches of aircraft: there is, for example, both documentary and photographic evidence to show that the 'BJ' serialled aircraft were Cyclone-engined Mk Is in service in 1940, whereas this book says they were Twin-Wasp engined ex-Greek Mk IIIs; the latter, serving in the Middle East from 1941 onwards, were among the AX-serialled batches.

The second Northrop YF-17, originally built for the USAF LWF fly-off, now carries US Navy markings but retains its USAF serial number, 72-01570. Much new information on Navy serial numbers appears in the volume noted below.

"The Last of the Eagles"
by John R Beaman, Jr
Published by the author, Greensboro, NC, USA, $6·00
80 pp, 8½ in by 14 in, illustrated
INTENDED as a "scale modeller's guide to the Messerschmitt Bf 109G and K", this erudite volume will also interest all students of German aircraft of the World War II era. Profusely illustrated with highly-detailed line drawings — for the most part side views, but also some plan and head-on views, external details and cockpit layout drawings — the text contains a very concise analysis of the Gustav sub-variants. This provides the basis for the remainder of the book (more than one-half, in fact), which is devoted to a critical review of each Bf 109G/K kit on the market, showing, in the minutest detail, what is wrong with the kit and how it can be corrected. Also covered, in the same depth, is the subject of colours and markings for these aircraft.

Too esoteric for the average modeller, this volume is a good example of the lengths to which specialist enthusiasts will go to record the findings of their research in depth. The hours of loving labour that have gone into its preparation are obvious on every page, and in no way could commercial production of such a book be viable. By undertaking publication himself, Mr Beaman does a service to those fellow enthusiasts with a special interest in the Bf 109 (as he has previously on the subject of Spitfires and Mustangs). Copies may be ordered from John R Beaman, Jr, at 2512 Overbrook Drive, Greensboro, NC 27408, USA at $6·00 (for air mail delivery, the price is $8·25 to Europe, $9·25 to Asia and the Pacific; for 1st class delivery in the USA and Canada, the price is $7·25).

"The Boeing 727"
Edited by John Whittle, with William Lloyd, H J Nash and Harry Sievers
Air-Britain (Historians) Ltd, Saffron Walden, £1·60
104 pp, 7 in by 9¼ in, illustrated
THE Boeing 727 is, by a substantial margin, the World's best-selling jet transport, the current sales figure of 1,290 comparing with some 880 DC-9s sold to date. This new volume may not become Air-Britain's best-selling publication, but if it does not, this will be attributable to the level of reader interest in the subject, not to any shortcomings in the content. It is, indeed, hard to find any basis on which to criticise "The Boeing 727", which is very much more than just a production list — although full details

are, of course, included, of each aircraft built to date. Other sections are devoted to the airline operation of the 727, a general history of the design, a technical description, specifications, operating costs and a registration index: there are over 40 photographs. Top marks to John Whittle and his team for this one.

Copies can be ordered from the Air-Britain Sales Department, Stone Cottage, Great Sampford, Saffron Walden, Essex CB10 2RS; add £1·10p if airmail delivery is required outside of Europe.

"United States Navy Serials, 1941 to 1976"
Edited by Peter A Danby
Merseyside Aviation Society, Liverpool, £1·50
104 pp, 6½ in by 8 in, illustrated
THE THIRD edition of a little volume that must be rated 'indispensable' for anyone with an interest in US Navy aircraft and markings or more generally in the production of aircraft in the USA during World War II and since. More than just a serial number list, the book includes much general information on the disposition of individual aircraft, c/ns, etc plus sections on USCG aircraft, USN aircraft carriers and a good selection of photographs. Orders should be sent to Merseyside Aviation Society Publications Department, at 4 Willow Green, Liverpool L25 4RR.

"British Isles Airfield Guide"
Edited by P H Butler
Merseyside Aviation Society, Liverpool, 65p
28 pp, 6 in by 8¼ in, illustrated
THIS slender volume is the seventh edition of a useful listing of both active and disused airfields in the UK, giving precise locations and a note (in the case of the active ones) of the users. Also included are lists of gliding sites, Irish aerodromes, and a general location map. Orders should be sent to Merseyside Aviation Society Publications Department at 4 Willow Green, Liverpool L25 4RR.

"Beaufort Special"
by Bruce Robertson
Ian Allan Ltd, Shepperton, Middlesex, £2·50
80 pp, 8¼ in by 11¾ in, illustrated
CONTINUING the Ian Allan series of "Specials", this volume on the Beaufort gives a competent and well-illustrated account of one of World War II's less-well-known workhorses. Built in large numbers both in the UK and Australia, the Beaufort emerged as an off-shoot of the more famous Blenheim design and, as Bruce Robertson records in the first sentence of his text, it was intended as a torpedo-bomber but was used more often as an "ordinary" bomber,

it flew more hours on training sorties than on operations and it suffered more losses by accident than to enemy action. "Beaufort Special" contains little that has not been previously published but usefully puts the whole story together between one pair of covers.

"Curtiss P-40C v Mitsubishi A6M2"
Fighter Comparison Study No 1
by Murray Rubenstein
Gamescience Corporation, Miss, USA, $3·50
32 pp, 5½ in by 8¼ in, illustrated
USING techniques developed for a computer study conducted, some years ago, of the performance of Soviet and US jet fighters for USAF comparative purposes, Mr Rubenstein has made similar computer analyses of pairs of World War II fighters, of which this is the first. The results are shown in a number of graphs, and the text discusses the results in the context of widely-held and frequently-published beliefs and opinions about the two aircraft in question.

No 2 in the series is devoted to the Messerschmitt Bf 109E-3 and the Spitfire Mk I.

"Breda Ba.65"
by Pietro Tonizzo and Enzo Maio
STEM-Mucchi, Modena, Italy, Lire 500
24pp, 9¼ in by 8¾ in, illustrated
ONE of the less well-known types of aircraft serving with the *Regia Aeronautica* during World War II, the Breda Ba 65 is the subject of this latest STEM-Mucchi 'profile', with a good selection of photographs and a three-view in colour, plus (Italian) text describing the type's evolution and service.

"The Modern Air Racers in 3-Views"
by Charles A Mendenhall
Pylon Publications, Rochester, NY, $4·95
64 pp, 8½ in by 11 in, illustrated
THIS volume, says its author, is "written with the thought of providing all the modern racing aircraft under one cover" for the benefit of "pylon buffs, modellers, historians and enthusiasts". It should perhaps say 'drawn' rather than 'written', as the contents are primarily graphic, with three-view drawings fully annotated with notes on construction, performance, colour schemes, etc, and it should also be made clear that "all modern racing aircraft" means those flown in the USA and particularly at the National Air Races at Reno. Within these limits, the book amply achieves its author's goal.

Copies can be ordered from the Aviation Book Company, 555 W Glenoaks, Glendale, Calif 91202, USA.

ITALY

AERITALIA/PARTENAVIA P.68 TURBO

AERITALIA is sponsoring the development of a turboprop version of the Partenavia P.68B Victor with an eye on the potential military market for a multi-rôle light aircraft offering versatility at low cost. Basis of the proposal is the substitution of Allison 250-B17B turbo-props for the Victor's usual 200 hp Lycoming IO-360s, and the addition of six pylons of standard NATO configuration — four under the wing and one each side of the fuselage on a stub fairing.

Although the basic configuration of the P.68 Turbo is as illustrated here, various of the options available on the P.68B are also offered, including the Observer cockpit developed by Sportavia-Putzer in Germany (which would be especially appropriate to a sea surveillance version) and a retractable undercarriage. As a light commercial transport, the P.68 Turbo could carry six passengers, 360 lb (163 kg) of baggage and a crew of two a distance of 610 mls (980 km) at a cruising speed of 224 mph (360 km/h). Some 80 examples of the piston-engined Victor are now in service.

There is, at present, no commitment to the production of a prototype of the P.68 Turbo and the following data are the current design estimates.

Manufacturer: Partenavia Costruzioni Aero-nauticka SpA, Via Cava, CP 2179, 80026 Cossoria, Naples, Italy.

Power Plant: Two Allison 250-B17B turbo-props each rated at 320 shp for take-off. Hartzell three-bladed constant speed feathering propellers, diameter, 7 ft (2,13 m). Integral fuel tank in each outer wing, capacity 45 Imp gal (205 l) each, plus provision for two underwing fuel tanks of 45 Imp gal (205 l) each.

Performance (at max take-off weight): Max speed, 226 mph (362 km/h) at sea level; max cruise, 224 mph (360 km/h) at 10,000 ft (3 050 m); initial rate of climb, 1,580 ft/min (8,03 m/sec); service ceiling, 24,000 ft (7 315 m); single-engined ceiling, 8,000 ft (2 438 m); take-off distance to 50 ft (15,2 m), 2,000 ft (610 m); landing distance from 50 ft (15,2 m), 1,700 ft (518 m); range (VIP transport), 435 mls (700 km) with two passengers and one pilot, cruising at 228 mph (367 km/h) at 10,000 ft (3 050 m) with full reserves; radius (close support mission), 400 mls (644 km) carrying 1,400 lb (635 kg) of external stores at 150 mph (241 km/h) at 15,000 ft (4 575 m); ferry range, 910 mls (1 464 km) at 148 mph (238 km/h) at 15,000 ft (4 575 m); endurance (with external tanks, crew of two, 600-lb/272 kg equipment), 8 hrs.

Weights: Operating weight empty, 3,344 lb (1 520 kg); max fuel load, 980 lb (445 kg); max take-off, 5,720 lb (2 600 kg).

Dimensions: Span, 39 ft 4 in (12,0 m); length, 31 ft 4 in (9,55 m); height, 12 ft 4 in (3,76 m); wing area, 200·2 sq ft (18,6 m²); aspect ratio, 7·75:1; undercarriage track, 7 ft 10 in (2,30 m); wheelbase, 12 ft 0 in (3,66 m).

Accommodation: One or two pilots, up to six passengers.

Armament: Two hardpoints under each wing and one on each side of fuselage on stub sponsons. Wing pylons carry up to 400 lb (182 kg) each, fuselage pylons carry up to 250 lb (114 kg) each, typical stores including bombs, rocket pods, ASMs or mini-gun pods (wings only).

UNITED KINGDOM

CRANFIELD AEROBATIC AIRCRAFT

FOLLOWING its first flight at Cranfield on 23 August, the Cranfield A1 is now engaged in completing its flight test programme, to permit its use as a competition aerobatic aircraft next year. Known provisionally as the Cranfield A-1, this is the first aeroplane built in Britain solely for aerobatic flying at the World Championship level.

The concept of the A-1 is attributed to Neil Williams, ten times British aerobatic champion and winner of fourth place at this year's World Championships at Kiev, and was based, in his own words, on the best features of the Yak-18, the Zlin 226 and the Spinks Akromaster, which he short-listed as the three best aerobatic aeroplanes of the many he had sampled. During 1968, this specification was adopted by the College of Aeronautics at Cranfield as the basis for a project design study. Two students at the College, Bob Ward and Graham Potter, undertook preliminary design, under the supervision of Professor Dennis Howe, as part of their work for the award of a Master of Science degree.

Additional work was undertaken in the period up to 1974, on a very small budget, some as part of the College's regular activities and some in the students' spare time; Rolls-Royce provided an engine on favourable terms and apprentices at the Bristol Engine Division adapted the engine and fuel system for inverted flight. In this period Bob Ward became project designer, having joined the academic staff of the College meanwhile, and in mid-1975 the project received new impetus when financial assistance was offered by Alan Curtis. Jointly with the Institute, he formed Flight Invert Ltd as a non-profit making company to complete the prototype.

The original specification called for a high power-to-weight ratio to enable rapid changes in speed to be made and to give good penetration (the term used to describe the aircraft's performance in reaching vertical flight and holding as nearly as possible to it). A monoplane of moderate size was considered desirable to give the judges a good visual impression, and although speed was not considered to be of major importance the airframe needed to be robust and the controls light and positive.

For competition, the aircraft was required to have only one seat, but a second seat was deemed necessary for training and ferry flights. The pilot was to be placed low in the fuselage and close to the centre of gravity, to minimize the effects of angular motion, and at the same time to be located with his eyes immediately over the straight trailing edge of the wing so that he could use it as a reference along the horizon in vertical flight.

The form derived for the aircraft during the initial work by the two students was that of a conventional low-wing monoplane with tandem seating and a fixed landing gear. The gear was chosen for simplicity but has a secondary merit in that it can assist the judges to determine the attitude of the aircraft during complex manoeuvres; in the prototype, some Chipmunk undercarriage components have been utilized. The horizontal tail surface is placed across the top of the fuselage to ensure a strong attachment; a large rudder extending the full depth of the vertical tail and fuselage gives good spin recovery characteristics. The wing is designed and built in one piece to minimize the risk of structural failure and passes below the cockpit fuselage structure, and very large ailerons are used to obtain a good rate of roll. Provision has been made for the incidence of both wing and tailplane to be altered during flight testing of the prototype, and for aerodynamic balances to be added on the ailerons, should they prove necessary.

Large spats will be used to fair the wheels, not only to reduce air resistance but to provide side area in conjunction with the fuselage and vertical tail for the development of lift in horizontal flight, when the aircraft is on its side with the wing vertical. In the competition rôle, the aircraft is flown from the rear seat and the front cockpit is faired over.

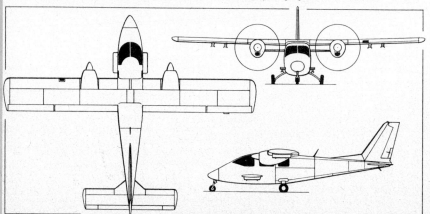

(Above) A piston-engined Partenavia P.68B with the Observer nose developed in Germany by Sportavia-Putzer and (below) three-view drawing of the projected P.68 Turbo.

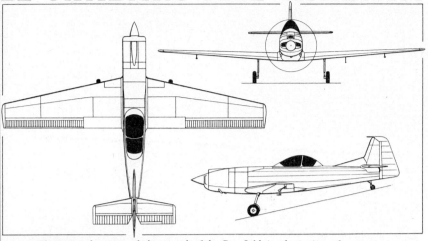

Three-view drawing and photograph of the Cranfield Aerobatic Aircraft prototype.

SCOTTISH AVIATION BULLDOG 200/BULLFINCH

SOME small changes have been made in the specification of the Scottish Aviation Bulldog 200 (military) and Bullfinch (civil) since the type was first announced at the Farnborough show in 1974. The prototype Bullfinch was first flown at Prestwick on 20 August and the public debut was made at Farnborough International '76, in the course of which the first sale was announced — to Alan Curtis, for delivery early in 1978.

The Bullfinch/Bulldog 200 is based on the current Bulldog 120 airframe, from which it differs primarily in having a retractable undercarriage and an enlarged cabin providing full four-seat accommodation. Fully aerobatic, the Bullfinch is offered as a sports and touring aircraft while the Bulldog 200 will be available as a primary trainer and multi-rôle light aircraft, with the option of underwing stores as already applied to the armed Bulldog 120.

Compared with the Bulldog 120, the Bullfinch/Bulldog 200 has the fuselage lengthened by 20 in (50,8 cm) — in equal parts fore and aft of mainspar; a redesigned cabin, engine cowling and centre section; span increased by 9·3 in (23,6 cm); tailplane located 6-in (15,2-cm) higher on the fuselage and overall height reduced by 7·5 in (19,05 cm). The cabin is lengthened by 13 in (33,02 cm) internally, and is 2 in (5,08 cm) wider and 3·5 in (8,9 cm) higher inside. An electro-mechanical retraction system is used for the undercarriage, the components of which are supplied by Automotive Products with Goodyear wheels and tyres. Dual controls are fitted as standard in both the Bullfinch and the Bulldog 200.

Manufacturer: Scottish Aviation Ltd, Prestwick International Airport, Ayrshire, Scotland.

Power Plant: One 200 hp Avco Lycoming AEIO-360-A1B6 fuel injection engine driving a Hartzell two-bladed metal constant-speed propeller, diameter 74 in (1,88 m). Fuel in two metal tanks in each wing, total capacity 32 Imp gal (145 l).

Performance (estimated): Max level speed, 173 mph (278 km/h) at sea level; cruising speed, 162 mph (261 km/h) at 4,000 ft (1 220 m) at 75 per cent power; initial rate of climb, 1,160 ft/min (5,9 m/sec); service ceiling, 18,500 ft (5 639 m); take-off distance to 50 ft (15,2 m), 1,280 ft (390 m); landing distance from 50 ft (15,2 m), 1,238 ft (377 m); range on max fuel at 55 per cent power, 622 mls (1 000 km); max endurance, 5 hrs.

Weights: Typical operating weight empty, 1,810 lb (820 kg); max take-off weight, 2,600 lb

As a competition aircraft spends more time inverted than upright, special attention had to be given to the design of the fuel and oil systems for inverted flight. The standard oil system for the IO-360D engine is of the wet sump type, which ceases to function after a few seconds of inverted flight when the pump inlet becomes exposed. This has been replaced by a dry sump system incorporating a separate oil tank with an engine outlet which automatically follows the movement of the fluid in it, thereby ensuring a continuous supply. The IO-360D has a direct injection fuel system able to operate at all attitudes, but the fuel supply from the aircraft tank has to contend with the same difficulties as does the oil system, and for this reason a single fuel tank is located just abaft the engine, the fuel outlet from which has a follower device not unlike that fitted in the oil tank.

Structurally, the A.1 is relatively simple and robust, high cost procedures having been avoided even where this has meant some increase in structure weight. The fuselage has a welded steel tubular framework around which are placed plywood formers and a plywood and fabric outer covering. The two-spar wing and tail surfaces are of light alloy stressed skin construction. To save weight, there are no flaps and no systems — even starting relies on an external power supply or hand-swinging of the propeller. Controls are of the push-rod type.

The A.1 wing is designed to an ultimate stress of 13·5g, which at a factor of 1·5 is equivalent to +9g and −6g when flown solo at aerobatic weight, and +7g/−5g as a two-seater. A total airframe life of not less than 2,000 hrs was the design target, half of which can be accumulated in fully aerobatic flight without exceeding the fatigue limits.

Power Plant: One Rolls-Royce Continental IO-360D flat-six piston engine rated at 210 hp for take-off, driving a two-blade variable pitch constant speed propeller.

Performance: Max speed, 152 mph (244,5 km/h); initial rate of climb, 1,440 ft/min (7,3 m/sec); stalling speed, 52 mph (84 km/h); take-off distance to 50 ft (15,2 m), 950 ft (280 m).

Weights: Max take-off, 2,020 lb (920 kg); max aerobatic weight, 1,690 lb (770 kg).

Dimensions: Span, 32 ft 9½ in (10 m); length, 26 ft 5 in (8,05 m); height, 8 ft 10½ in (2,7 m); wing area, 161 sq ft (15,0 m²); aspect ratio, 6·7:1.

Accommodation: Pilot in enclosed cockpit; provision for second occupant in optional front cockpit.

A three-view drawing of the Scottish Aviation Bullfinch/Bulldog 200, showing that it differs in many details from the fixed-undercarriage Bulldog 120 from which it has been developed.

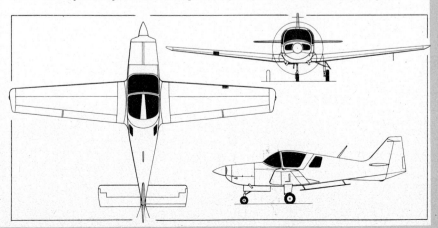

The prototype Scottish Aviation Bullfinch in flight.

(1 180 kg); max aerobatic weight, 2,304 lb (1 045 kg).

Dimensions: Span, 33 ft 9·3 in (10,29 m); length, 24 ft 11 in (7,59 m); height, 8 ft 4 in (2,54 m), undercarriage track, 7 ft 6 in (2,137 m); wheelbase, 5 ft 9 in (1,752 m); cabin internal width, 3 ft 11 in (1,19 cm).

Accommodation: Four individual seats in cabin, with dual controls for forward occupants.

USA

BOEING 7N7

THE continuing effort by Boeing's Commercial Airplane Company to have suitable new aircraft available for development at the time they are required by the airlines has led to the appearance of two distinct families of projects at the present time. One of these, known as the Boeing 7X7 (see *AirData File*/August 1975) is aimed primarily at the US domestic market and is, broadly, for the 180-195-passenger aeroplane with a gross weight of 300,000 lb (136 200 kg) and a design range of 3,100 mls (5 000 km).

There is still a wide range of engine options open for the 7X7 (in the development of which Aeritalia is participating with a one-fifth share, while negotiations between Boeing and Japanese manufacturers for a similar deal are making progress). The possibilities quoted by Boeing in the course of Farnborough International '76 included three General Electric CF6-32s or Pratt & Whitney JT10Ds, or two CF6-50s, JT9Ds or Rolls-Royce RB.211s. To date Boeing has spent more than $50m on the 7X7, and has completed, among much other test work, 1,950 hrs of wind tunnel testing and 1,000 hrs of propulsion/noise model and full scale engine tests.

The Boeing 7N7 family of projects has emerged more recently and is seen as complementary to the 7X7 — although this does not mean that Boeing expects to launch both types simultaneously or will *necessarily* build both types or either. Whereas the 7X7 is a wide-body type (up to eight-abreast with two aisles), the 7N7 makes use of the standard Boeing narrow body that has been retained through the 707/720/727/737 series. It is aimed at a band of somewhat shorter stage lengths, from 1,500 to 2,300 mls (2 413-3 700 km), with a capacity of 120 to 180 passengers (all-tourist) according to fuselage length.

Planned specifically as a derivative of the 727/737 family, the 7N7 introduces advanced wing technology, with improved aerofoils and higher aspect ratios; high by-pass engines and advanced cockpit systems. A twin-engined configuration has been adopted, but different sizes of aircraft are still under study — the Boeing presentations at Farnborough covering three possible fuselage lengths and two wing spans — and this in turn means that engine thrusts ranging from 22,000 lb (10 000 kg) to 30,000 lb (13 620 kg) or more are under review.

Carrying the Boeing type number 761, the variants of the 7N7 family under consideration, and their primary characteristics, are as follow; in the case of the largest variant, the 761-143, the engine options include the Pratt & Whitney JT10D-4 at 27,000 lb st (12 258 kgp) and the Rolls-Royce RB.211-535 at about 32,000 lb st (14 530 kgp).

Boeing 761-119

Power Plant: Two General Electric/SNECMA CFM-56/F1B1 or Pratt & Whitney JT10D-1 turbofans each rated at 22,000 lb st (10 000 kgp) with ATR (automatic thrust reserve).

Performance: Range, 1,500 mls (2 412 km) with full passenger payload; take-off field length, 6,800 ft (2 074 m); engine-out altitude on 575-ml (925 km) mission, 15,200 ft (4 636 m).

Weights: Max take-off, 138,000 lb (62 652 kg).

Dimensions: Span, 120 ft 0 in (36,6 m); length, 110 ft 6 in (33,70 m); height, 44 ft 2 in (13,46 m).

Accommodation: 125 passengers, all tourist-class, at 34-in (86,4-cm) seat pitch.

Boeing 761-120

Power Plant: Two General Electric/SNECMA CFM-56/F1B1 turbofans each rated at 22,000 lb st (10 000 kgp) with ATR.

Performance: Range, 1,850 mls (2 975 km) with full passenger payload, take-off field length, 8,900 ft (2 715 m); engine-out altitude on 595-ml (925-km) mission, 9,300 ft (2 837 m).

Weights: Max take-off, 163,000 lb (74 000 kg).

Dimensions: Span, 120 ft 0 in (36,6 m); length, 127 ft 5 in (38,87 m); height, 39 ft 9 in (12,12 m).

Accommodation: 160 passengers, all tourist-class at 34-in (86,4-cm) seat pitch.

Boeing 761-120B

Power Plant: Two Pratt & Whitney JT10D-2 turbofans each rated at 24,500 lb st (11 123 kgp) with ATR.

Performance: Range, 2,070 mls (3 330 km) with full passenger payload; take-off field length, 7,800 ft (2 379 m); engine-out altitude on 575-ml (925 km) mission, 13,400 ft (4 087 m).

Weights, Dimensions, Accommodation: As 761-120.

Boeing 761-143

Power Plant: Two General Electric CF6-32 turbofans each rated at 30,000 lb st (13 620 kgp) with ATR.

Performance: Range, 2,070 mls (3 330 km) with full passenger payload; take-off field length, 6,400 ft (1 952 m); engine-out altitude on 575-ml (925 km) mission, 16,700 ft (5 094 m).

Weights: Max take-off, 199,000 lb (90 346 kg).

Dimensions: Span, 127 ft 1 in (38,76 m); length, 145 ft 6 in (44,38 m); height, 42 ft 4 in (12,91 m).

Accommodation: 180 passengers, all tourist-class at 34-in (86,40 cm) seat pitch.

(Above left) The Boeing 7N7 compared with (above right) the 7X7 and (below) a three-view of the Boeing 7N7 Model 761-120.

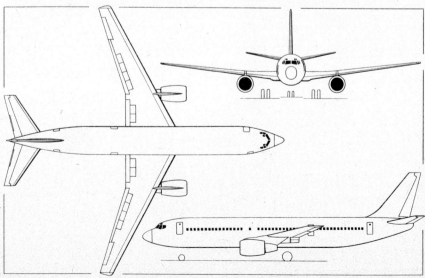

AIR International

Volume 11   Number 6   December 1976

Managing Editor — William Green
Editor — Gordon Swanborough
Modelling Editor — Fred J Henderson
Contributing Artists — Dennis Punnett
John Weal
Cover Art — W R Hardy
Contributing Photographer
Stephen Peltz
Editorial Representative, Washington
Norman Polmar
Publisher — Donald Hannah
Circulation Director — Donald Syner
Financial Director — John Gold
Subscription Manager — Claire Sillette
Advertising/Public Relations
Elizabeth Baker

Editorial Offices:
The AIR INTERNATIONAL, PO Box 16, Bromley, BR2 7RB Kent.

Subscription, Advertising and Circulation Offices:
The AIR INTERNATIONAL, De Worde House, 283 Lonsdale Road, London SW13 9QW. Telephone 01-878 2454. US and Canadian readers may address subscriptions and general enquiries to AIR INTERNATIONAL PO Box 353, Whitestone, NY 11357 for onward transmission to the UK, from where all correspondence is answered and orders despatched.

MEMBER OF THE AUDIT BUREAU OF CIRCULATIONS [ABC]

Subscription rates, inclusive of postage, direct from the publishers, per year:
United Kingdom — £5·50
USA — $17·50
Canada — $17·50

Rates for other countries and for air mail subscriptions available on request from the Subscription Department at the above address.

The AIR INTERNATIONAL is published monthly by Fine Scroll Limited, distributed by Ducimus Books Ltd and printed by William Caple & Co Ltd, Chevron Press, Leicester, England. Editorial contents © 1976 by Pilot Press Limited. The views expressed by named contributors and correspondents are their own and do not necessarily reflect the views of the editors. Neither the editors nor the publishers accept responsibility for any loss or damage, however caused, to manuscripts or illustrations submitted to the AIR INTERNATIONAL.

Second Class postage approved at New York, NY. USA Mailing Agents: Air-Sea Freight Inc, 527 Madison Avenue, New York, NY 10022.

CONTENTS

263 **THE SEA-SEARCHERS** Extension of territorial water limits to 200 mls (321 km), increasing utilisation of the sea's resources and the need to guard against smuggling and illegal immigration are among the reasons for the development of the new breed of medium-sized patrol aircraft described in this article.

269 **PETROL PUMPS IN THE SKY** The Victor, in its K Mk 2 version, is destined to serve the RAF until the late 'eighties. This article not only describes the latest tanker variant but also tells of the Victor's origins more than 20 years ago and records the several important variants that have preceded the tanker.

274 **MONOCOUPE!** Gene Smith, the owner of a Monocoupe 90AL, tells the story of a family of aircraft built more than 30 years ago, but still the centre of attention wherever they fly — a family that includes the Monocoupe 110 Specials, of which only seven were built but 10 now exist!

282 **THE SLOW AND THE 'FOOLPROOF'** In a postscript to his recent series on flying German aircraft of World War II, Capt Eric Brown recalls two novelties: the slow-flying Fieseler Storch and the even slower Zaunkoenig — an enterprising attempt to produce a really foolproof aeroplane.

258 **AIRSCENE** The monthly round-up of news and background to the news presented under section headings for Military Affairs, Aircraft and Industry, Civil Affairs and new Civil and Military Aircraft Contracts.

278 **TAKE AN EXPERT'S OPINION: THERE ARE NO EXPERTS!** Roy M Braybrook, in a further outpouring of his Personal View, goes in for a little debunking.

289 **MODEL ENTHUSIAST** Modelling comments, the latest kits reviewed and a page of colour profiles of the Lockheed P-3 Orion.

292 **FIGHTER A TO Z** Continuing the AIR INTERNATIONAL encyclopaedia of the world's fighter aircraft, from the Curtiss XP-60C to the Curtiss XF15C-1.

294 **IRAN'S MULTI-PURPOSE 707s** A photo-spread devoted to the unique Boeing 707 tanker transports of the Iranian Imperial Air Force.

306 **AIR DATA FILE** Technical data, photographs and general arrangement drawings for the BAC X-Eleven, Cessna Citation I, Citation II and Citation III, Rockwell Sabreliner 65A and 80A.

Veselé vánoce
a šťastný Nový rok
С Новым годом
Fröhliche Weihnachten
und Glückliches Neujahr
Merry Christmas
and Happy New Year
Joyeux Noël et Bonne Année

AIRSCENE

ARGENTINA
Although the *Fuerza Aérea Argentina* (FAA) had earlier anticipated having its first 12-aircraft *Escuadron de Ataque* equipped with the indigenous IA 58 **Pucara** twin-turboprop attack monoplane operational during the past summer as a component of the *Il Brigada,* **only two** additional production Pucaras have been **delivered since** the first was accepted by the FAA at Reconquista two years ago, on 15 **November 1974.** The fourth and fifth production aircraft are understood to have been completed at the Area de Material Córdoba (the former Fábrica Militar de Aviones), but development flying is continuing with the three prototypes at the *Centro de Ensayos en Vuelo,* suggesting that some teething troubles have still to be eliminated. Despite delivery delays, the FAA is continuing type conversion at Reconquista with those aircraft that have been accepted.

AUSTRALIA
Twenty-three Army Aviation Corps technicians and instructors recently graduated from the GAF Technical Training School in preparation for the full **service entry of** the **Nomad** Mission Master with the Corps during the coming year. A single Nomad has been undergoing operational tests with the Army Aviation Corps for the past year and 11 additional aircraft are on order.

BOLIVIA
One of the latest **purchasers of** the Lockheed **Hercules** is the *Fuerza Aérea Boliviano* which has ordered one C-130H for delivery in October next year. The aircraft is likely to be utilised by the *Transportes Aéreos Militares* (TAM) component of the FAéB which operates as a quasi-airline.

The FAéB has expressed **interest in** the Neiva **Universal II** and has a requirement for 40 aircraft of this type for the counter-insurgency rôle. Negotiations for these aircraft are expected to commence as soon as the Universal is returned to full production next year. Neiva has already started re-tooling for production of the Universal pending receipt of a contract.

BRAZIL
The *Fôrça Aérea Brasileira* (FAB) recently **retired** the last 21 **Douglas C-47** transports remaining in its inventory owing to spares shortages and engine maintenance problems. The oldest C-47 is being sent to the FAB's museum in Rio de Janeiro and the remaining 20 are being offered for sale at prices ranging from Cr 100,000 (£5,325) to Cr 350,000 (£18,640).

Neiva has received a **supplementary order** from the FAB **for** eight T-25 **Universal** basic trainers to make up attrition suffered over the past two years and pending release of a more substantial order for upwards of 150 additional Universals to be included in the 1977 budget. The eight additional aircraft are those remaining (semi-completed) from the original FAB contract for 150 which was subsequently reduced to 132, 10 of the surplus aircraft being sold to Chile.

CAMEROON
The Republic of Cameroon became the **39th country to order** the Lockheed **Hercules** when, on 2 September, this West African nation signed a contract for two C-130Hs for the *Armée de l'Air du Cameroun.* Personnel of the service will commence training on the Hercules at Lockheed-Georgia early in the New Year with delivery of the aircraft scheduled for mid- and late-1977.

CANADA
Pending a Canadian governmental decision concerning the possible procurement of the de Havilland Canada DHC-7R Ranger for the Canadian Armed Forces, 17 of the 30 CP-121 **Tracker** ASW aircraft currently included in the CAF inventory are **to be modified** at a cost of Can$11·5m (£7·2m) to improve their effectiveness in patrolling Canada's new 200-mile (322-km) fishing zone. At the present time, the CAF is operating 13 Trackers in VS 880 based at CFB *Shearwater,* near Dartmouth, NS, and three in VU 33 at Comox, BC. The remaining 14 are in storage at Saskatoon but four of these are to be withdrawn during the first quarter of 1977 to supplement those currently serving with VS 880 and *Shearwater* is also to be the base of a new Tracker reserve squadron, MR 420. All *Shearwater*-based Trackers are to have Omega VLF navigation, together with day and night photographic systems, VHF-FM marine-band radio, new radar and ILS.

CHILE
The Chilean **follow-on order** for the EMBRAER EMB-110 Bandeirante currently under negotiation (see *Airscene*/November) is now understood to be for a total of six aircraft and negotiations are also being conducted for approximately 20 Neiva Universals to supplement the 10 purchased for the *Fuerza Aérea de Chile* last year. Earlier negotiations for the supply to Chile of eight aircraft built against the original FAB contract (and now re-ordered) failed to see fruition, but now that the Universal is being returned to production negotiations have been resumed. The additional FAC aircraft are expected to be equipped for the dual training/counter-insurgency task and may be of the more powerful Universal II version.

GREECE
The Hellenic Air Force anticipates having received the last of the 60 LTV Aerospace A-7H **Corsair** attack aircraft currently on order by the second quarter of 1977, **and** with the continued deliveries of the 40 Dassault-Breguet **Mirage F1CG** interceptors, the service is phasing out its Convair F-102A Delta Daggers on a one-for-one basis. The HAF has also received some two-thirds of its 40 Rockwell International T-2E Buckeye trainers and recently took delivery of two McDonnell Douglas F-4E Phantoms to make up attrition suffered by the original 38 aircraft of this type delivered into the inventory.

HONDURAS
As a result of frontier clashes between Salvadorean and Honduran ground forces, the *Fuerza Aérea Hondurena* (FAH) was placed on full alert recently and the service's 10 airworthy **F4U-5 Corsairs** — the last examples of this WW II aircraft in service anywhere in the world — were bombed-up and placed **on operational standby** at Toncontin International Airport in case the border fighting should escalate. The FAH is apparently still operating one or two of the F-86K Sabres purchased from Venezuela in 1969, the only other combat equipment comprising three Lockheed RT-33As and four North American T-28Es.

ISRAEL
Israel's *Heyl Ha'Avir* has recently taken delivery of a KC-130H Hercules flight refuelling tanker and is awaiting delivery of a second KC-130H. The *Heyl Ha'Avir* has previously taken delivery of 12 C-130E Hercules and 12 C-130H Hercules as direct purchases, plus a batch of C-130Es transferred from the USAF during 1972.

JAPAN
The Air Self Defence Force finally selected the McDonnell Douglas **F-15 Eagle** on 14 October **to meet** its **F-X requirement** and official governmental approval is anticipated this month (December), although the total quantity of aircraft proposed by the ASDF will unquestionably be reduced. The ASDF proposal calls for total procurement of 170 Eagles with a unit cost of £12m-£14m for the first batch of 30-36 aircraft for which funding is to be requested in the Fiscal 1977 budget. This initial batch will include two complete Eagles supplied by the parent company as pattern aircraft and several in knock-down form, possibly including two two-seaters, for assembly by Mitsubishi which will licence-build the remaining aircraft required by the ASDF, Ishikawajima-Harima producing the F100 engine and Mitsubishi Electrics the fire control system. Current ASDF planning calls for the establishment of six 25-aircraft squadrons with 20 aircraft in reserve, but it is anticipated that total procurement will be cut to 100-120 aircraft, in which case it is likely that the number of squadrons will be reduced to five and their aircraft complement also reduced.

The Maritime Self-Defence Force was scheduled to send an evaluation group to the USA late October for the third and **final** technical and financial **evaluation of** the Lockheed **P-3 Orion** as its future P-XL. The MSDF reportedly still favours the Orion over the indigenous Kawasaki GK-525 project despite the inevitably adverse reaction that will result from the purchase of a Lockheed aircraft, but now accepts that the earlier plan, which called for the completion of the evaluation last month (November) in order to submit the report this month to the National Defence Conference and thus meet the deadline for the inclusion of an appropriation request in the Fiscal 1977 budget, is now impracticable. The P-XL programme has thus slipped yet another year and initial funding is now expected to be included in the Fiscal 1978 budget appropriations

NEW ZEALAND
The RNZAF anticipates having taken **delivery** before Christmas **of** all 10 Hawker Siddeley **Andover** C Mk 1 transports purchased from RAF surplus for the re-equipment of Nos 1 and 42 squadrons currently operating the 25-year old Bristol 170 Freighter from Whenuapai and the 31-year old Douglas C-47 from Ohakea respectively. Both Bristol 170s and C-47s are to be phased out soon after completion of Andover deliveries and passed to the Government Stores Board for disposal. The Bristol 170 entered RNZAF service in 1951-52 when eight aircraft were delivered, a repeat order for three being fulfilled in 1953 and one more being added in 1955 to replace an aircraft sold to Safe Air. The C-47 first saw service with the RNZAF eight years earlier than the Bristol 170, the first of 49 being delivered in March 1943. Twenty-six were eventually passed to NAC and others scrapped, and by 1953, the RNZAF was operating only two C-47s but four were returned to the service by NAC in the 'sixties as the airline re-equipped with Friendships.

PAKISTAN

Reports that the US State Department had agreed to the supply of 110 LTV Aerospace A-7 **Corsair** attack aircraft to the Pakistan Air Force if the Pakistan government abandoned **plans** to purchase a nuclear re-processing plant from France have been **vigorously denied** in Washington but would seem to have had some foundation in fact. Washington sources allege that the PAF has not yet decided between the A-7 Corsair, the A-10, the A-4 Skyhawk and the F-5E Tiger II, and Pakistani spokesmen have been at pains to point out that the PAF request for the A-7 Corsair was a matter of national security and in no way connected with the purchase of a nuclear reprocessing plant which was a part of an economic development programme.

PERU

Reports from Washington indicate that the new Peruvian **government** has finally decided **to accept** the **Soviet offer** of 36 variable-geometry Sukhoi Su-22 strike fighters (see *Airscene*/October and November) for the *Fuerza Aérea del Peru*. After the overthrow of the previous government, the new government renewed earlier requests to the US State Department for its approval of the sale of Northrop F-5E Tiger IIs to Peru — a succession of Peruvian governments have attempted to purchase the Northrop F-5 since 1965 but have been rebuffed by the US State Department on every occasion — but it is suggested that the State Department delayed too long in granting its approval, the Peruvian government, humiliated by the delay, finalising the contract with the Soviet Union. The Peruvian government reportedly requested a letter of offer in July for the purchase of 36 A-4 Skyhawks, but the State Department apparently did not ask the Naval Air Systems Command to quote a price until early October, three months later.

The *Fuerza Aérea del Peru* has decided to place an **order** with Dassault-Breguet **for** four **Mirage 5P** fighter-bombers to make up attrition suffered by the *Grupo de Caza Bombardeo* 13 since it introduced this type at Chiclayo in 1968. The FAP originally obtained 14 single-seat Mirage 5Ps and two two-seat Mirage 5DPs.

PORTUGAL

The two Lockheed **Hercules** ordered by the *Força Aérea Portuguesa* (see *Military Contracts*/November) are apparently of the "**Advanced H**" version, featuring an APU that may be utilised in the air, new meteorological radar and a new air conditioning system. The contract for the two aircraft was signed in Lisbon on 29 September, and when the aircraft are delivered in August and September next year, the FAP plans to retire 16 of the transport aircraft (DC-6s, Noratlases and Boeing 707s) currently in its inventory.

SOVIET UNION

V-VS changes in the German Democratic Republic include the **retirement,** last year, **of** the last **MiG-17s** flown by the Soviet service as a first-line unit **and the reintroduction of** a squadron of aged Ilyushin **Il-14** *(Crate)* piston-engined transports for ELINT and ECM missions along the border with the Federal German Republic.

The first Sukhoi **Su-19** *(Fencer)* equipped V-VS Regiment is **based at Chernyakhovsk,** near Kaliningrad (Königsberg) in the Baltic Military District, where a second Su-19 regiment is currently being formed, although deliveries are reported to be fairly slow.

The **range** of the *Backfire* variable-geometry bomber is resulting in major **differences of opinion** in the US intelligence community. The

The first photograph to be published of Backfire, *some 80 examples of which are now reportedly operational with the Soviet Air Forces. This aircraft is currently the subject of some controversy between US intelligence agencies, as recorded on this page, which are in disagreement concerning the range capability of* Backfire.

Soviet Union contends that *Backfire* is an intermediate-range bomber and cannot, therefore, be counted in the 2,400 strategic vehicle limit established during the Ford-Brezhnev Vladivostok accord providing guidelines for round two of the strategic arms limitations talks (SALT). US Defense Department intelligence officials are adamant in their belief that *Backfire* is potentially an intercontinental weapon with a range close to the original US intelligence estimate of 6,000 nautical miles (11 120 km), but the Central Intelligence Agency alleges that the range of *Backfire* is only about 3,000 nautical miles (5 560 km), supporting its claim with the results of a study conducted by McDonnell Douglas which estimates a 3,500 nautical mile (6 485 km) range. It has been suggested, however, that this McDonnell Douglas study was based on incomplete data, some information being withheld so that the results would support a behind-the-scenes concession made by Secretary of State Henry A Kissinger to Soviet negotiators that *Backfire* would not be considered as an intercontinental weapon in the renewed treaty negotiations. A similar study conducted by McDonnell Douglas from all the information available to the Defense Department apparently supports the Defense Department's contention concerning the range capability of *Backfire* as being in excess of 5,000 nautical miles (9 265 km) without use of in-flight refuelling. Edward Proctor, CIA Deputy Director for Intelligence, recently stated in congressional testimony that production of *Backfire* now stands at about 80 aircraft.

UGANDA

The Uganda **Air Force has sold back** to Israel 10 IAI-built **Magister trainers** for an undisclosed sum. The UAF orginally received 12 Magisters from Israel in the 'sixties when a *Heyl Ha'Avir* mission was responsible for training Ugandan pilots. It is believed that the trainers have not been used in recent years owing to lack of spares and the inability of UAF personnel to service the aircraft.

The IAI 1123 **Westwind** executive aircraft which has been operated by the Uganda Air Force as the personal transport of President Idi Amin since its delivery by Israel Aircraft Industries some five years ago and for which the Ugandan government failed to make full payment has now been **restored to IAI**. Two US pilots, who were purportedly to fly the Westwind to Europe for the repair of minor

damage sustained during the raid on Entebbe Airport, flew the aircraft from Entebbe to Israel via Khartoum, Cairo and Larnaca.

UNITED KINGDOM

The Ministry of Defence announced in October that 12 Scottish Aviation **Jetstreams** are to be converted **for operation by the Royal Navy** in the observer training rôle. Design and installation of the RN modifications is expected to take 18 months, the Jetstreams entering service during the course of 1978, and Scottish Aviation's total commitment including product support, training, design and other ancillary services. A further eight Jetstreams are to be returned to operations with the RAF in the multi-engine pilot training rôle from which it was withdrawn late in 1974 due to the reduction in the service's requirement for multi-engine pilots, and a further five Jetstreams are to be held in reserve.

Four Hawker Siddeley **Hawks** were **delivered to RAF Valley,** North Wales, in October, where they are now replacing the Gnat Trainer, and a further six Hawks are scheduled for delivery by the end of this year. At a later stage in the programme, the armed version of the Hawk will be introduced with the tactical weapons unit of Strike Command at RAF Brawdy, South Wales. In the RAF, advanced students will fly 150 hours on the Hawk after 100 hours basic training on the Jet Provost.

The RAF is understood to have a **requirement for** a **further** 18 Hawker Siddeley **Harriers** to make good attrition suffered since the introduction of the Harrier and maintain frontline strength, and has put proposals to the Treasury for purchase of the aircraft involved.

USA

The USAF has prepared **proposals** calling **for** the expenditure of $3,000m (£1,850m) over the next six years on approximately 170 **fighters to replace** the ageing F-106 **Delta Darts** currently serving with the interceptor squadrons of the Aerospace Defense Command. The proposals are based on the USAF contention that the USA can no longer safely assume that Soviet manned bombers are insufficient a threat to justify modernisation of the manned interceptor element of the ADC. The USAF proposal calls for initial funding of approximately $31m (£19m) for what is referred to as the "follow-on interceptor", expenditure increasing to $800m (£494m) in Fiscal 1981 and $850m (£525m) in Fiscal 1982.

Pentagon sources indicate that the McDonnell Douglas F-15 Eagle is currently the front runner as the "follow-on interceptor", one reason being that the USAF has already received funding to increase the fuel capacity of the F-15 and this will endow the aircraft with sufficient range to suit it for the ADC rôle. Last January, Defense Secretary Donald H Rumsfield told Congress that the F-106 was wearing out and would have to be replaced, starting at the end of the present decade. He commented: The Soviet strategic bomber program has not changed appreciably since last year, nor has the tanker force . . . the *Backfire* continues to be the only new *heavy* Soviet bomber in production but this can strike the United States."

AIRCRAFT AND INDUSTRY

FRANCE
The second prototype of the Dassault-Breguet **Mercure 100** flew **to the USA** in late October, to be present at Long Beach during a symposium held by McDonnell Douglas for 240 airline executives to undertake "a critical appraisal of preliminary designs for an advanced short-to-medium range commercial jet transport". Invitations to the symposium were extended jointly by McDonnell Douglas and Dassault-Breguet and the principal subject of the meeting on 21-23 October was the Mercure 200 proposal as currently defined by MDD and D-B. Although the French government has approved a proposed agreement between the two companies that would give the US manufacturer a 15 per cent share in the programme, no final decisions have yet been taken. The aircraft is now referred to as the ASMR (advanced short-to-medium range) transport, being substantially similar to the Mercure 200 as described in *AirData File* in our August issue.

INDIA
The first **production HAL Ajeet** (Unconquerable) lightweight fighter derived from the Gnat was **flown** on 30 September and HAL remains confident of meeting the delivery schedule to the Indian Air Force despite some delays in delivery of the special Martin-Baker GF4 ejection seat and the Lucas-manufactured Hobson PFC 1003 longitudinal control unit. The Ajeet differs from the Gnat primarily in having integral wing tanks of 110 Imp gal (500 l) capacity, Ferranti ISIS weapons aiming, updated avionics, a new feed system for the Aden cannon, a reinforced wing structure, the new lightweight ejector seat (zero level 90 knots) and an increase of 150 lb (68 kg) thrust from its Orpheus engine. By comparison with the HAL-built Gnat, the Ajeet embodies some 50 changes and all up weight is increased by 300 lb (136 kg). The first Ajeet prototype (which incorporated all the major modifications but lacked the new ejection seat) was flown on 6 March 1975, a second prototype following in November 1975.

ITALY
The **Fiat** company has decided **to withdraw from** the state-controlled **Aeritalia** and will sell its stake in that company to Finmeccanica, a state-owned holding company. All the original Fiat facilities previously contributed to Aeritalia will remain with the latter, and a new Fiat subsidiary, Fiat Aviazione SpA, is to be formed to replace the company's aero-engine division, which is outside of Aeritalia.

JAPAN
Japan's National Aerospace Laboratory (NAL) is seeking funds in the Fiscal 1977 budget to begin a new **experimental STOL aircraft** programme which would lead to first flight in 1982 and completion of flight testing by 1985. Basis of the project is to use a

Kawasaki C-1A transport fuselage and wing, with four FJR-710/20 experimental turbofans in an installation similar to that of the engines in the Boeing YC-14, with upper-surface blowing. The ailerons would be replaced by larger flaperons, a double-hinged rudder would be fitted, a stability augmentor system and a variable stability system would be fitted, all control surfaces would be modified to have hydraulic operation, and structures and landing gear would be strengthened.

NETHERLANDS
Fokker-VFW is reported to be showing some interest in the Japanese **FJR-710** engine as a **possible power plant for** its projected **F-29** successor to the **F-28**. With an initial rating of about 10,500 lb st (4763 kgp) and potential for development to 13,200 lb st (5987 kgp) and beyond, the FJR-710 seems to be well matched to the needs of the F29, which is seen as a stretched-fuselage F28 with supercritical wing. However, a factor in the Dutch company's current interest in the Japanese engine, two prototypes of which have been bench-tested to date, may be the effort to promote the F28 as a YS-11 replacement for use by Japan's domestic airlines, in competition with the BAC One-Eleven 670 and McDonnell Douglas DC-9-QSF.

NEW ZEALAND
The New Zealand government has directed that **production of the Aerospace CT/4 Airtrainer should cease** by the end of the year, following a study of the continued viability of the company in the absence of new orders for the Airtrainer. Delivery of 13 CT/4Bs ordered by the RNZAF to replace Harvards in the Flying Training Wing at Wigram began in July and was to be completed by the time this issue appeared in print, but the eventual fate of 14 Airtrainers built against an order placed by an intermediary on behalf of the Rhodesian Air Force remains uncertain. Export of the aircraft — which were completed and crated at Hamilton Airport earlier this year — was blocked by the NZ government, and it is believed that they may pass eventually to the RNZAF and/or the RAAF.

SOVIET UNION
It would now seem virtually certain that the *Forger* shipboard strike and reconnaissance **fighter** deployed aboard the carrier *Kiev* (see *Airscene*/November) is **restricted to VTOL** operation and is incapable of STOL operation. The configuration of the vectoring nozzles behind the wing, balanced by two downward-blowing direct lift engines behind the cockpit, would pose formidable balance and safety problems in STOL modes. The US Secretary of the Navy, J William Middendorf II, recently stated that *Forger* ". . . is superior to the British-built AV-8A Harrier now being flown by the Marines", and suggested that US intelligence had underestimated the capabilities of the Soviet aircraft, adding that *Forger* ". . . is a much more effective aircraft than we were led to believe. It has a 300-mile [480-km] radius as compared to 200 miles [320 km] for the Harrier and can carry more weapons".

It is understood that *Flogger-D* is officially designated **MiG-27** and *not* Mig-23B as has been previously believed. The version of the basic multi-rôle fighter design optimised for the battlefield interdiction and counterair missions from dispersed sites, the MiG-27 differs from the MiG-23, as represented by the single-seat air superiority and air intercept *Flogger-B*, in having simplified fixed air intakes (in place of the variable-area intakes of the MiG-23) and a shorter, simpler exhaust nozzle, presumably indicating a different engine variant and lower boost reheat; repositioned (further outboard) fuselage weapon pylons and a 23-mm six-barrel rotary cannon

in place of the similar-calibre twin-barrel GSh-23; a sturdier undercarriage and bulged undercarriage doors to accommodate low-pressure tyres, and a redesigned nose (not unlike that of the Jaguar) apparently housing a laser ranger.

The **MiG-25** *(Foxbat)* interceptor, whose pilot defected to Japan on 6 September (see *Airscene*/December), was **crated** after examination by Japanese and US teams in October, and transported to the port of Hitachi from where it was to be collected by a Soviet vessel **for return to the USSR.** The aircraft had undergone detailed examination at the Hyakuri Air Force Base, during which the Tumansky R-31 turbojets were run. These revealed a ground static thrust of 24,250 lb (11000 kg) during a 1 hr 20 min run on 3 October and apparently have a five-stage compressor of 3·28 ft (1,0 m) length, the overall length of the engine being 19·68 ft (6,0 m), and utilise a water-methanol injection system and electrically-controlled variable ramp-type intakes, intake width being 35·4 in (90 cm). With the somewhat higher-than-anticipated max take-off weight of 77,160 lb (35000 kg), the Tumansky engines apparently afford a thrust-to-weight ratio of only 0·63:1·0. This unexpectedly high weight is due to the primarily nickel steel construction of the aircraft, titanium being restricted to such components as the wing leading edges and the engine air intakes and exhaust nozzles. Empty weight is slightly more than 44,090 lb (20000 kg) and take-off weight, which includes 30,865 lb (14000 kg) of fuel, results in a wing loading of 128 lb/sq ft (625 kg/m²), gross wing area being 602·8 sq ft (56,0 m²). The fuel is distributed between integral wing tanks and three fuselage tanks aft of the cockpit, and there is no provision for external tankage, the four underwing pylons being intended only for missiles. Earlier reports that no ejection seat was provided proved erroneous, the MiG-25 have an essentially similar seat to that of the MiG-21, but cockpit instrumentation was found to be spartan by Western standards and restricted to the essential — surprise was evinced that there were only three engine instruments compared with 10 in the F-4 Phantom. Avionics were described as primitive, relying on vacuum tubes and making no use of solid-state circuitry, and being scattered in a complex manner rather than packaged in plug-in boxes. The *Fox Fire* search and tracking radar was found to be of phased-array configuration with a 33·46-in (85-cm) nose antenna, a range of 56 miles (90 km) and minimal look-down capability.

A technical and flight-test team from the Civil Aviation Authority was scheduled to visit the USSR early this month (December) to take **British certification of the Yak-40** a stage further. Following the recent demonstrations of a Yak-40 in the UK (*Airscene*/November), modifications have been introduced in another example of the aircraft at the Saratov production plant, and this Yak-40 is to be inspected and test-flown by the CAA team. Modifications are extensive but mostly of a minor nature, relating to the electric and fuel systems and the flying controls. It is expected that any Yak-40s for the UK market will have the King Gold Crown KFC-300 flight director system, in place of the Collins 108 series planned for installation when British certification was first projected in October 1972; Collins ProLine equipment is a possible alternative. Airlines to which the Yak-40 was demonstrated in the UK were British Airways Regional Division, Dan-Air, British Island Airways, Intra Airways, Loganair, Peters Aviation, Air Anglia, Alidair, British Caledonian (on behalf of Air Liberia) and the CAA's civil aviation flying unit based at Stansted.

USA

McDonnell Douglas is currently promoting a **reconnaissance version of** the **F-15 Eagle** for use by the USAF, describing this proposed RF-15 as a "high-commonality, low-cost derivative of the F/TF-15A Eagle fighter weapon system". Without degrading the air-to-air modes of the current Hughes APG-63 radar, it is proposed to add terrain-following/terrain-avoidance (TF/TA) modes for low-altitude, high-speed penetration into high-threat areas, and Doppler beam-sharpening (DBS) and synthetic aperture radar (SAR) modes to provide high resolution ground mapping for navigation and target location. An integrated FLIR/EO sensor would be fitted in the centre fuselage, for identification of tactical size targets. A two-seater like the TF-15A, the RF-15 would have an integrated sensor/data management system in the rear cockpit, using multiple CRTs, side-mounted hand controllers, a digital computer, recorders and a data link. Use of FAST (Fuel and Sensor Tactical) packs would give the RF-15 a long cruise radius and additional volume for conventional sensors and specialised mission equipment.

Beech Aircraft Corp has decided to put its PD285 single-engined T-tail two-seat lightplane (see *AirData File*/December 1975) into **production** as **Model 77,** for initial deliveries in 1978. The prototype PD285 first flew on 6 February 1975, powered by a 100 hp Continental O-200 flat-four engine and having a low-mounted tailplane; a T-tail was fitted subsequently and the company has decided to adopt the 115 hp Lycoming O-235 engine for production. Final assembly of the Model 77 will be at Liberal, Kansas, to relieve pressure upon the main Beech production centre at Wichita. The company has also confirmed that deliveries will begin late in 1977 of the **Model 76,** a light-twin that also features the T-tail (*AirData File*/December 1975). Two airframes for static and fatigue testing are now under construction and the fourth airframe will be flying by mid-1977, to join the prototype that has been under test since late-1974. In the course of the recent Beech annual international sales meeting, dealers and distributors placed orders for more than 200 Model 76s, including 25 for export.

Rockwell International has announced a series of **improvements** in five **1977 model Commander** business and touring **aircraft,** comprising the 7-10 seat turboprop Commander 690B, the piston-engined Strike Commander and three single-engined four-seaters, the Commander 112B, 112TC-A and 114. All models benefit from an 18-month engineering test and development programme that has reduced sound levels in the aircraft and improved their payloads and performance. The Commander 690B has noise levels in the cabin comparable to the acceptable level established by ALPA for the cockpit area alone; a wholly new interior configuration with toilet at the rear; reduced empty weight and gross weight increased to 10,375 lb (4 710 kg) to give a net improvement of 126 lb (57 kg) in useful load; cruising speed increased by 8 mph (13 km/h) to 329 mph (529 km/h). The Commander 112B has increased gross weight of 2,800 lb (1 271 kg), an increase of 34 in (86 cm) in wing span, larger wheels and tyres with new brakes and higher max and cruising speeds. The turbo-supercharged Commander 112TC-A already has the longer wing span but gross weight is increased to 2,950 lb (1 319 kg), max and cruising speeds go up to 196 mph (315 km/h) and 188 mph (302 km/h) respectively. The Commander 114, which is "top of the line" with a 260-hp engine, has similar drag-reducing refinements with benefit to the overall performance. The Commander 700 (Fuji FA300) is to be added to the range in 1977.

On the specific instructions of President Ford, the Rockwell **space shuttle** orbiter, rolled out on 17 September, has been **named Enterprise,** after the space ship that has gained international fame in the TV series *Star Trek.* The president overruled NASA's plan to name the orbiter Constitution. First flights of the Enterprise are expected next March or April, mounted on the back of a specially-modified NASA-owned Boeing 747. Captive tests will be followed by the first drop tests, with a two-man flight crew, in July, with a total of eight such flights scheduled, each concluding with a conventional landing at Edwards AFB. Operational weight of the orbiter is about 150,000 lb (68 100 kg), and it has a span of 78 ft (23,79 m) and length of 122 ft (37,21 m). The prototype Enterprise will be used for ground vibration tests, mounted vertically, after completing the approach and landing tests; the first orbiter to go into space will be the second example completed and is due for launching on the first manned orbital flight in March 1979, with a crew of four. Launching will be vertical with the aid of two 2·65 million lb (1 203 000 kg) thrust solid booster rockets to supplement the orbiter's three 470,000 lb (213 380 kg) thrust liquid oxygen/liquid hydrogen rocket engines mounted in the rear fuselage.

First flight of a fully-configured **OV-10D** NOS (night observation surveillance) version of the Rockwell Bronco was made at Columbus on 8 October. The aircraft — one of two original YOV-10Ds that were converted as night observation gunship systems (NOGS) — is the first to fly with 1,040 shp Garrett AiResearch T76-G-420/421 turboprops; other NOS features comprise the installation of FLIR, a laser ranger designator and a ventral 20-mm gun turret. The wing pylons have been modified to carry external fuel tanks and modifications made to the electrical system.

FAA certification for the **Mohawk 298** was obtained on 19 October. First flown on 7 January 1975, this re-engined Nord 262 is now expected to enter service on the Allegheny Airlines third-level route network in the first quarter of 1977 and further conversions will be undertaken in the USA.

First flight of a Lockheed **L-1011-200 TriStar** was made at Palmdale on 8 October. Powered by three 50,000 lb st (22 680 kgp) RB.211-524s, the TriStar 200 operates at a gross weight of 466,000 lb (211 374 kg) and has a range of 4,450 mls (7 160 km). The first aircraft is for Saudia, which has also confirmed that it will eventually convert all its TriStars to 200-series.

First flight of the Sikorsky **S-72** Rotor Systems Research Aircraft was made on 12 October (*Airscene*/August 1976). Powered by two General Electric T58 turboshaft engines, the S-72 flew without the wings that will be fitted for subsequent research, together with two TF34-GE-400A turbofans on the fuselage sides.

The submissions of four manufacturers to meet the requirements of the **US Coast Guard** for its new medium-range **surveillance aircraft** were scheduled to be opened in Washington on 28 October, with the possibility that the winner would be announced shortly after the US Presidential election on 2 November (and after this issue went to press). The submissions comprise modified versions of the VFW 614 (Rolls-Royce M45H engines) and Dassault-Breguet Falcon 20G (Garrett AiResearch ATF3-6), a derivative of the Lockheed JetStar II powered by the General Electric CF34 (see subsequent news item), and the Rockwell Sea Sabre 75C, a much modified Sabreliner with ATF-3 engines. Rockwell has also studied a Sea Sabre variant with the much more powerful Lycoming ALF-520R engines, in case the ATF3 does not go ahead.

Ted Smith Aerostar Corp of Santa Maria, California is **flight testing** a new version of its Model 601 business twin known as the **Aerostar 800.** It differs in having a 32-in (81-cm) fuselage stretch and two 400 hp Lycoming engines with four-bladed propellers, and is reported to have recorded a speed of 330 mph (531 km/h). Current Aerostar 601s also differ from the initial standard in having 3 ft (0,92-m) greater wing span and a number of other improvements.

General Electric has confirmed that it intends to offer for **commercial** use versions of the TF34 turbofan and T700 turboshaft engines, to be known respectively as the **CF-34 and CT7.** The CF34 is a high by-pass turbofan in the 7,000-8,000 lb st (3 175-3 629 kgp) class, essentially the same as the TF34-GE-100 used in the Fairchild A-10A with changes necessary for FAA certification. It has been specified, at a rating of 7,990 lb st (3 624 kgp) to 73 deg F at sea level, by Lockheed for its submission in the US Coast Guard MRS programme and timing of CF34 development is related to that requirement, with FAA certification in late 1978 and first aircraft delivery in March/April 1979. The CF34 has also been offered by General Electric to Grumman for a three-engined version of the Gulfstream and data have been provided to Fokker VFW, Boeing, McDonnell Douglas and Dassault-Breguet for studies that could involve use using the CF34. The CT7 is quoted with a max (2½-min) rating of 1,536 shp, take-off (5-min) rating of 1,420 shp, engine-out (30-min) rating of 1,420 shp and max cruise of 1,175 shp. Certification is scheduled for the second quarter of 1977 with first production delivery in mid-1978. Initial applications are expected to be in commercial versions of the Boeing Vertol and Sikorsky UTTAS helicopters, which are each powered by two T700s.

CIVIL AFFAIRS

BANGLADESH
Tempair International has won a contract — initially for a period of three months — **to operate services** for Bangladesh Biman. Starting on 19 October, the arrangement covers the provision of a Boeing 707 with flight deck crews, operations and engineering back up for services from Dacca to London, Bombay, Bangkok, Karachi and Dubai, as well as the Haj operations.

GILBERT ISLANDS
As a major step towards the **establishment of** a national **internal airline,** the Government of the Gilbert Islands has taken delivery of a Fairey Britten-Norman Trislander and expects to obtain a second by year-end. The first aircraft was handed over late-September by Air Pacific. The new company, still in process of formation, is expected to operate as a subsidiary of the island's Development Authority.

INTERNATIONAL
While **negotiations** between the UK and the USA **to revise** the bilateral air transport agreement (known as the **Bermuda agreement**) continue, a compromise has been negotiated in respect of capacity on the Atlantic routes between London and Miami and London and Chicago (*Airscene*/October 1976). The capacity agreed is less than the one quarter a day planned by US airlines on the Miami route and five a week on the Chicago route, but more than the five and four services a week, respectively, sought by the Department of Trade. The first round of negotiations to revise the Bermuda agreement, which expires on 21 June next, was held in London during September, followed by a second round in Washington in the second half of October. Further meetings will take place monthly, alternating

between the UK and the USA, with the prospect of tough bargaining to achieve an agreed sharing of capacity on the North Atlantic and the possibility that an interim agreement may be necessary to meet the June deadline.

Concorde 203, one of the Air France fleet, was leased by the manufacturers to make a sales **tour of the Far East** during November, leaving Paris on the 2nd to fly to Manila via Bahrein and Singapore. Demonstrations were being made in Hong Kong, Jakarta and Seoul before the return via Singapore, Bahrein and London. The visit to Singapore was timed to coincide with the AGM of IATA on 8-10 November. Air France took final delivery of Concorde 205 on 26 September; since being used for the initial Concorde passenger services early in 1976 this aircraft has undergone a complete overhaul and modifications at Toulouse.

JAPAN
BAC's **One-Eleven 475** demonstrator (G-ASYD) made a series of **demonstration flights in Japan** during October as part of the effort to sell the type to the nation's three domestic airlines. Flights were made over a number of routes from Iruma to domestic airfields with runways down to 4,000 ft (1 200 m) in length, and on similar routes from Naha in Okinawa. The 91-seat variant on offer to Japan is now identified as the One-Eleven 670, being basically a Series 475 with minor modifications to allow it to meet the Japanese requirement, including a small extension to the wing span, a revised wing leading edge profile and wide-chord Fowler flaps. Japanese manufacturers are being invited to participate in development and construction.

PARAGUAY
A feasibility study is being conducted in Paraguay with a view to establishing **airports at eight** of the nation's most important **population centres**. The study, undertaken with financial assistance from the International Bank for Reconstruction and Development, includes consideration of the economic justification and optimum timing for the development of the eight airports, the needs for aeronautical communications and navigational aid requirements and the effects of introducing replacement aircraft for the DC-3s at present used by *Transportes Aéreos Militars* (TAM), which provides domestic services in Paraguay. Sites of the eight projected new airports are Puerto Presidente Stroessner (close to the Itaipu hydro-electric scheme on the Parana River), Encarnacion (serving another hydro scheme on the same river), Bahia Negra, Filadelfia, Mariscal Estigarribia, Concepcion, Pedro Juan Caballero and Salto del Guaira. Retained to undertake the study are Brian Colquhoun & Partners, consulting engineers; Cable Wireless Ltd, international telecommunications operator; Coopers and Lybrand Ltd, management and economic consultants and Ingaer SRL, a Paraguayan company of consulting engineers.

UNITED KINGDOM
The route **exchange between British Airways and B.Cal** under the terms of the Civil Aviation Review earlier this year, took effect at the end of October. British Airways has relinquished its services from the UK to Peru (Lima), Colombia (Bogota) and Venezuela (Caracas) in favour of B.Cal, most of the BA staff in those countries transferring to the latter airline. B.Cal operated its first Boeing 707 service to Caracas and Lima on 26 October, and the first to Bogota on the 28th. B.Cal has in turn relinquished some of its African services, and to provide an all-cargo service to Nairobi in place of the Africargo operation, British Airways was modifying, during November, a fourth 707-336C to all-freight configuration.

CIVIL CONTRACTS AND SALES

Aérospatiale Nord 262: Swift Aire, a Los Angeles-based commuter airline, has purchased three Nord 262s to replace Herons. Previously operated by Filipinas Orient, they were acquired and refurbished by American Jet Industries at Van Nuys. ☐ Ransome Airlines acquired one more to make eight in all.

Airbus A300: Lufthansa has decided in principal to take up two of its eight options on A300B-4s. Subject to approval by the Lufthansa supervisory board, the order provides for delivery in April 1978 and brings the total of Airbus orders and options to 57.

BAC VC10: As part of its deal to purchase additional Boeing 747s, British Airways traded in five Standard VC10s to Boeing. They are thought to have no more than scrap value and will probably be broken up at Heathrow, two already having been so treated.

BAC Viscount: Two Air Rhodesia Viscounts are reported to have been acquired by Swazi Air. ☐ Skyline of Sweden increased its Viscount fleet to three with the purchase of one from Ghana Airways.

Boeing 707: Nigeria Airways ordered one additional -320C, for delivery next November, joining two already in service on routes to Europe. ☐ Nusantara Airlines of Indonesia acquired one -120B from Braniff. ☐ Aero Condor purchased a second -120B from American Airlines.

Boeing 720: Belize Airways, newly founded, has acquired four 720s from United (the last of its fleet).

Boeing 727: Nigeria Airways became the 83rd customer for the 727 with an order for two Advanced -200s, for delivery in August and September. They will operate as 139-seaters on the airline's African route network. ☐ TransBrasil bought four -200s from Pan Am. ☐ Braniff ordered two more Advanced 727s for September 1977 delivery, bringing the total fleet of this type to 77. ☐Northwest Orient ordered five Advanced -200s to bring its 727 fleet to 73; deliveries will be made September-December 1977.

Boeing 747: Avianca ordered one Srs 100, with delivery made in late November and first service on 5 December. The aircraft is reported to be ex-Continental and one of three previously earmarked for the IIAF.

Convair 880: Bahamas World Airlines has leased five 880-Ms, ex-Cathay Pacific Airlines, for use on the Nassau-Brussels route and, later, on new routes to South America. Among other CV-880s currently available are two owned by American Jet Industries and TWA's fleet of 25, retired some years ago but for which no buyers have been found.

EMBRAER EMB-110 Bandeirante: Four 18-seat EMB-110P have been ordered by VOTEC, the third level/air taxi company based in Rio de Janeiro. ☐ The State Governments of Pernambuco and Minas Gerais have each ordered one EMB-110E executive.

Fairchild Swearingen Metro II: Scheduled Skyways Inc, a commuter airline operating in Arkansas and Oklahoma, has ordered two Metro IIs with an option on a third, deliveries to begin in February.

Fairchild FH-227: The last four FH-227s operating in Brazil have been sold to Indonesia: all originally used by Paraense they

later operated on the São Paulo-Rio de Janeiro air bridge and two have more recently operated in the colours of TABA pending delivery of Bandeirantes.

Fokker F28 Fellowship: Burma Airways ordered one Mk 4000 for mid-1977 delivery, to join two Mk 1000s recently acquired second-hand.

Handley Page HPR-7 Herald: British Air Ferries bought the last two Dart Heralds flying in Brazil, previously operated by Sadia.

Hawker Siddeley D.H.106 Comet: Dan-Air acquired three from Egyptair, becoming the only remaining major Comet operator in the process.

Hawker Siddeley HS.748: Mount Cook Airlines added a fourth HS.748 to its fleet in October, having acquired a Srs 2A (owned but unused since October 1973 by the late Howard Hughes) from Hawker Siddeley. ☐ Dan-Air acquired one Srs 2 from Air Pacific.

Lockheed Electra: TACA Airways bought two from American Jet Industries, converted for freighting. ☐ Varig purchased another Electra from Aero Condor of Colombia for use on the São Paulo-Rio de Janeiro Air Bridge.

Lockheed L-1011 TriStar: LTU in Germany has ordered two new L-1011-1s and an L-1011-100. The aircraft in question are those originally built for but not delivered to Pacific Southwest Airlines. Delivery will be made in March 1977, at which time LTU's two existing TriStars will be traded back to Lockheed. The two L-1011-1s will have 315 seats and will operate at the same 430,000 lb (195 045 kg) gross weight as the current aircraft; the third will be a 466,000-lb (211 374-kg) L-1011-100 and will have transatlantic capability.

Lockheed Hercules: Transmeridian Air Cargo is leasing time on three L-100-30s of Saturn Airways to supplement its outsize freight capacity. ☐ IAS Cargo Airlines has taken a part-lease on a Hercules for the current winter season.

McDonnell Douglas DC-8: Air New Zealand sold two Srs 50s to Evergreen International (previously Johnson Flying Service), after conversion in Auckland to have one-class 186-seat interiors. ☐ Cyprus Airways, which has been leasing one Srs 50 (ex Air New Zealand) from McDonnell Douglas, is ending the lease.

McDonnell Douglas DC-9: Toa Domestic Airlines (TDA) ordered four 118-seat single-class Srs 40s, for delivery December 1977-April 1978. Current TDA fleet of 14 DC-9s will be supplemented by one leased new Srs 50 (with 135 seats) pending delivery of the new Srs 40s. ☐ LAV took delivery of the first of three Srs 50s on 15 October, to become the ninth airline to operate the longest of the DC-9 variants. All three, plus three additional Srs 30s, were scheduled for delivery by year-end, joining two Srs 30 and four Srs 10s in service. ☐ Avensa purchased a Srs 10 from LAV and acquired the LAV share in a Srs 30 operated jointly. ☐ Texas International bought a Srs 32 from Swissair (the third oldest DC-9 in its fleet) and a Srs 14 from an unspecified US airline. ☐ Ozark Air Lines bought one Srs 30 from McDonnell Douglas to join four bought from Delta; deliveries of all five will be made March through December.

McDonnell Douglas DC-10: Nigeria Airways took delivery of a Srs 30 — its first — on 14 October and planned to use it initially on Haj operations to Jeddah in a 300-seat one-class configuration. Later it will be reconfigured to have 272 seats in two classes.

PAV 23

The go-anywhere tactical transport now has more muscle.

Higher gross weight. Increased payload. Improved "hot and high" performance.

The Buffalo now in production is a better, even more versatile Buffalo. With a new gross weight of 22,300 kg (49,200 lbs).

It features a significantly improved version of the General Electric T64 turboprop. The 820-4.

With these efficient, fuel-saving engines, the Buffalo will lift 41 passengers or 5,400 kg (6 tons) of cargo from a makeshift strip as short as 300 m (1,000 ft). Or an 8,200 kg (9 ton) payload from a 600 m (2,000 ft) gravel airstrip. And it combines these payload capabilities with improved "hot and high" performance. *At sea level, for example, it now maintains full takeoff power up to 33° C (92° F).*

Additional improvements include airframe and system changes that mean even greater mission reliability. Plus other modifications for reduced maintenance requirements.

More than ever, the Buffalo is the ideal multi-purpose transport.

Its huge rear door and adjustable ramps give you the fastest possible handling of troops, vehicles or cargo.

Its STOL capability means that it can get into areas that no other large plane can reach.

It cruises at 245 knots, and can stay up for 12 hours on a reconnaisance or search and rescue mission.

At 90 knots it's a remarkably stable platform for photography. Or for pinpoint parachute drops of men or supplies.

In short, the "go-anywhere" Buffalo is practically a "do-anything" plane. It started out great—and just got better.
The de Havilland Aircraft of Canada Limited, Downsview, Ontario M3K 1Y5.
Telephone: (416) 633-7310. Telex: 0622128.
Cable: Moth, Toronto.

de Havilland
The STOL company.

THE SEA-SEARCHERS

A status report on the new breed of maritime patrol aircraft

Four-fifths of the Earth's surface is covered by ocean; as the world's burgeoning population struggles to survive on the land masses that account for the remaining one fifth, more and more ways are being found of exploiting the sea and its animal, vegetable and mineral resources. This, in turn, brings new requirements for policing, patrolling, guarding and surveilling large tracts of ocean — requirements that are most easily met by the deployment of suitably-equipped aircraft.

The rôle of maritime reconnaissance is not in itself new, but has hitherto been largely identified with military operations — the protection of friendly shipping has called for the use of aircraft equipped to detect, identify and destroy enemy vessels, including submarines. At the upper end of the MR spectrum, this requirement has produced today's highly sophisticated and very expensive aircraft such as the Lockheed P-3 Orion and Hawker Siddeley Nimrod, able to fly long overwater missions in any weather, carrying a variety of sensors and weapons to combat — primarily — the underwater threat.

There is now developing, however, a whole range of maritime rôles in which the use of an Orion or a Nimrod would be like taking a sledgehammer to crack a nut — rôles such as fishery protection (anti-poaching operations and protection of home fleets), pollution control (pollution detection and tracking and identification of the responsible vessels), contraband control (co-operation with surface vessels in detection and arrest of suspect ships) and off-shore oilfield patrol (monitoring the safety and security of rigs and oil exploration operations on a routine patrol basis). Additionally, there are search and rescue responsibilities imposed by the regular airline operations across the ocean as well as more local operations necessary for shipping protection around the coastlines. Whilst the military MR aircraft are well equipped to undertake most of these duties, few nations could contemplate their purchase unless there were overriding military requirements to be fulfilled also. Consequently, there has been a flurry of activity among the world's aircraft manufacturers in the last year or two to produce suitably-

equipped variants of existing commercial aircraft that can be offered to governments and non-military agencies with responsibility for this type of off-shore operations.

With the increasing awareness of the need to protect the sea's resources, the extension of national fishing limits to distances up to 200 mls (321 km) from the coastline, the large number of off-shore oilfields currently being developed and the need to control smuggling and illegal immigration, almost every country with a coastline can be said to need a maritime reconnaissance aeroplane of some type. With a market so potentially large, there is naturally a wide variety of ideas on how the requirements can best be filled — with first cost and operating cost playing as important a part as the technical specification of the aircraft. Some of the rôles set out in the preceding paragraph could, indeed, be fulfilled — after a fashion — by the cheapest of single-engined aircraft with no more sophisticated sensors than the pilot's eyeballs; equally, as already noted, they could be fulfilled very adequately indeed — if over-expensively — by the military MR types. It is to provide something between these two extremes that most of the current activity is concentrated, and the remainder of this account will be devoted to a status report on four of the types most likely to enter service in the sea-search rôle in the next few years.

This quartet is made up of medium-sized turboprop-powered aircraft — variants of the Fokker F27, the Hawker Siddeley HS.748, the EMBRAER Bandeirante and the de

The Indonesian Navy is operating six GAF Nomad Mission Masters for off-shore maritime patrol and surveillance of Indonesian waters. They differ from standard Nomads in having nose-mounted search radar, bubble observation windows, flares and flare launcher, life rafts and other special equipment.

Havilland Canada Dash 7 — but there are other candidates in the field, including piston and jet types also. The US Coast Guard, for example, is currently seeking a sea surveillance aircraft in this same general category and has specified a twin-turbofan configuration; this has drawn proposals for modified and suitably-equipped versions of the Rockwell Sabre 75, Lockheed JetStar II, Grumman Gulfstream II, VFW 614 and Dassault Breguet Falcon 20. Whichever of these types eventually wins the USCG contract, expected to be for about 40 aircraft, will have a toe-hold in the market and with some changes of equipment should prove attractive to other potential customers. Israel Aircraft Industries has projected a similar MR version of its Westwind 1124 and, going up the scale somewhat, Aeritalia is proposing a variant of the G.222 including the maritime rôle in its repertoire.

At the piston-engined end of the spectrum, Fairey Britten-Norman Islanders are already being used by some governments for coastal patrol and this has led the company to offer, more specifically for this rôle, a suitably equipped version of the Trislander M. Other aircraft of similar size and performance could be adapted in the same way. Among the smaller turboprop twins, the GAF Nomad has already been supplied to the Indonesian Navy, equipped with search radar, bubble windows, signal flares, life rafts and survival equipment to serve in the off-shore maritime patrol rôle over Indonesian waters; and Piaggio is offering similarly equipped versions of its new Piaggio P.166DL-3.

Fokker F27 Maritime

Of the "middle range" of civil maritime patrol aircraft now under development, the F27 Maritime is the first to fly, a demonstration prototype having flown for the first time on 25 March 1976 and recently completed Phase 1 of its flight test and development programme in some 50 hrs. The prototype — which made its first public appearance at Farnborough International — is an elderly Mk 100 F27, returned to Fokker-VFW after serving with THY Turkish Airlines, and is therefore not wholly representative of the production Maritime, which will be based on the Mk 200 airframe with more powerful Dart RDa7s and the latest standard of systems. It has been fitted, however, with fully representative avionics and radar and in the next phase of testing a number of specific customer-required items of equipment will be added.

The search radar selected by Fokker is the Litton Systems (Canada) APS-503F, the antenna for which is located in a radome under the forward fuselage, where it achieves an uninterrupted 360-deg scan. In the course of Phase 1 testing, the behaviour of the aircraft with the radome added has been investigated, and a new radome shape has been evolved. The radar — which can be used for navigational guidance and weather avoidance as well as sea search — has a narrow pencil beam to direct maximum power at shipping under observation, whilst minimising sea clutter. Variation of pulse width obtains optimum trade-off between resolution and range.

Two displays are provided: a pilot's bright display used primarily for weather information (with a range of up to 200 naut mls/370 km) and a high-resolution display for use by the radar operator in search and mapping. Radar operator and navigator are located side-by-side in the cabin aft of the wing and sideways-facing, with the navigator usually acting as mission commander responsible for tactical control, data correlation and mission navigation. In addition to two pilots, the crew normally includes two observers in the rear of the cabin, seated alongside bubble windows (one each side) for visual search; their duties also include the dropping of stores, upon command of the controller or pilots. A universal chute is fitted in the rear cabin to drop marine markers of various types and a flare launching system, comprising a 16-flare rack in each engine nacelle, can be provided on customer option.

To meet the long-range navigation and search requirements of the F27 Maritime, a Litton Aero Products Division LTN-72 inertial navigation system is fitted, and the flight control system is slaved to the INS to allow the crew complete tactical freedom. Navigation to a pre-selected position is conducted automatically and independently of outside aids, and the pilot can turn, change speeds, climb or perform other flight manoeuvres without introducing errors. The INS computer is programmed to allow the aircraft to fly selected search patterns including a sector square, expanding square or ladder.

Typically, the avionics fit of the F27 Maritime will include a standby altitude reference system, TAS computer, dual gyro compass, dual VOR/ILS, marker beacon receiver, dual ADF, radar altimeter and ATC transponder. Among the miscellaneous new items is a windscreen de-salting system to prevent salt accumulation during prolonged operation at low levels over the sea.

The Maritime has a maximum fuel capacity of 2,460 US gal (9 310 l), using both an optional centre-wing tank and two underwing pylon tanks of the type previously used for F27 delivery flights. Operating within the F27's normal certificated max take-off weight of 45,000 lb (20 410 kg), the Maritime will have a range of 2,220 naut mls (4 100 km) cruising at 20,000 ft (6 100 m) with 5 per cent flight fuel reserve and 30 min loiter, equivalent to an endurance of 11 hrs. The typical search speed (1.1 V_{MD}) is 145 kt (270 km/h) TAS at 2,000 ft (610 m), although lower speeds — down to 100 kt (185 km/h) — are usable if necessary, according to the manufacturers.

Fokker-VFW believes there is a market for at least 50 F27 Maritimes, a useful addition to the 600-plus F27s of all types sold to date. At the time of writing, the company has concluded a contract to sell two Maritimes to an "unspecified South American country" (understood to be Peru for its *Servicio Aeronavale*) with first delivery to be made in the summer of 1977. Negotiations are proceeding with another 10 or so potential customers; it is worth noting, however, that the specially-equipped F27 ordered in September 1976 by the Icelandic government for patrol duty over fishing waters and for search and rescue duties, is *not* a Maritime. For delivery at the end of this year, it will join another F27, modified in Iceland, which has been serving with that nation's coastguard since 1972.

The HS.748 Coastguarder

In a programme closely comparable to that undertaken by Fokker, Hawker Siddeley's Manchester division has designed a maritime patrol version of the HS.748, for which the name Coastguarder has been adopted. A prototype conversion for a company-owned 748 demonstrator is now under way (at the HSA Chester factory) with first flight to take place next Spring, followed by an initial public showing at the Paris Air Show. Basic aircraft for the Coastguarder is the HS.748 Srs 2A which,

like the F27 Mk 200, is powered by the RDa7 variant of the Rolls-Royce Dart; it has a fully fail-safe structure which is protected both metallurgically and chemically from salt-water corrosion.

The Coastguarder's radar is MEL Marec (ARI-5955), derived from a helicopter radar already in world-wide use, with the 36-in (91,5-cm) scanner located in a radome under the forward fuselage, with full 360-deg scan. Weather information is expected to be derived from the aircraft's standard nose-mounted radar, the output from Marec being presented only on a 17-in (43-cm) diameter main display unit located in the rear portion of the cabin. There are three display modes as follow, each of which is north-stabilised by inputs from the Sperry C14 compass:

1. A plan position indicator display in which the aircraft remains at the centre of the screen and the radar returns move across the screen as the aircraft moves over the surface below;

2. A ground stabilised display, using inputs from the aircraft's Decca 72 doppler, in which the aircraft position moves across the screen;

3. A ground stabilised mode in which the aircraft position can be manually offset to gain extra radar range in any particular direction.

Sector scan is available, centred on any required bearing, to improve radar performance for better contact resolution under marginal conditions and five display ranges are available, ranging from 125 naut mls (231 km) at 15 naut mls/in (28 km/cm) to 8·5 naut mls (16 km) at 0·5 naut mls/in (0,93 km/cm).

The Coastguarder is designed to be operated by a basic crew of five — two pilots, a tactical navigator and two observer/

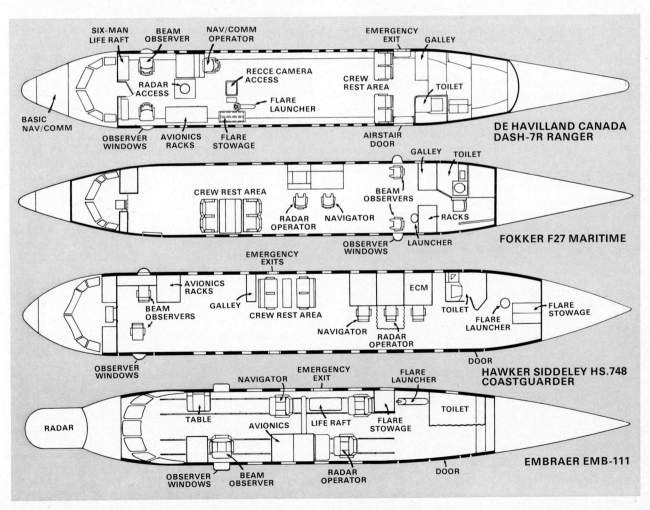

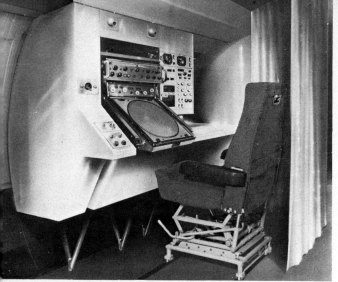

A mock-up of the Coastguarder tactical navigation console, incorporating a 17-in (43,18-m) diameter MEL Marec radar plotting display.

despatchers. A routine navigator can be carried if required, accommodation being provided alongside the radar console. The two observers occupy the forward cabin area, having large bubble windows (one each side) for visual scanning. The stores launch area is at the rear of the cabin with a launching chute for flares and sea markers; this is large enough for four-man dinghies to be despatched when the aircraft is used in the search and rescue rôle.

The tactical navigation system comprises the Decca Doppler and Sperry C14 compass already mentioned plus Decca Tactical Air Navigation System (TANS), this being fully integrated with the Marec radar. The latter also has an interface with the pilot-controlled Omega VLF long-range navigation system. The basic radio fit comprises dual VHF communications, dual VOR/ILS, dual ADF, single marker, single HF, VHF communications and interphone/cabin address.

There are a number of options available for Coastguarder customers, including an extra 750 Imp gal (3 410 l) of fuel to bring total capacity to 2,190 Imp gal (9 956 l). Four underwing strong points can be provided for the carriage of external stores, rescue equipment and air-to-surface weapons, should they be required, and the inner starboard pylon can carry a pod-mounted searchlight, controlled by the second pilot. Provision has been made for a passive ECM system to be fitted, with an operator's console in the cabin alongside the navigator's station, and IFF transponder and/or interrogator can be carried. If large rescue dinghies are required to be

The radar and navigation console in the prototype Fokker F27 Maritime, showing the operator using the high-resolution display of the Litton APS-503F radar.

carried, it is necessary for the Coastguarder to be fitted with the HS.748's optional side-loading cargo door; in this case, enough 30-man dinghies can be carried and dropped to rescue the entire complement of a ditched "jumbo jet".

Designed to operate at the HS.748's normal take-off weight of 46,500 lb (31 092 kg), the Coastguarder will have an endurance in excess of 12 hrs and at a typical mission radius of 200 naut mls (370 km) will be able to remain on station for 8·5 hrs, using the optional extra fuel capacity. With the Marec radar providing information out to a range of 200 naut mls (370 km), Coastguarder can search an area of ocean well in excess of 500,000 sq naut mls (1·7 million km²) in a single sortie. Active marketing has begun and deliveries could begin early in 1978; like Fokker, Hawker Siddeley is optimistic that useful additional business can be obtained for the HS.748 with the addition of the MR variant to the range on offer.

EMBRAER EMB-111 Bandeirante

Expected to begin flight testing by the end of this year, the EMB-111 is in a slightly different category from the other "sea searchers" described in this article, being both smaller and intended, in the first instance, for specifically military operations. The rôle, however, in the hands of the *Força Aérea Brasileira,* is similar to that envisaged for the MR versions of the F27 and HS.748, and with the type established in production, it may well be ordered by government agencies and others for non-military use.

The EMB-111 was evolved by EMBRAER from the EMB-110 light transport specifically to meet the requirements of the FAB's *Commando Costeiro* (Coastal Command) and represents a low-cost approach to the problem of replacing that Command's Lockheed P-2 Neptunes, recently-retired. Powered by 750 shp Pratt & Whitney of Canada PT6A-34 turboprops (compared with the basic Bandeirante's 680 shp PT6A-27s), the EMB-111 carries AIL AN/APS-128 patrol search radar in the nose, there being insufficient ground clearance for the ideal ventral location. Range is extended by the use of fixed wing-tip tanks of 67 Imp gal (305 l) capacity each.

A 10-million candlepower searchlight is carried in a small ventral pod and underwing provision is made for eight air-to-surface unguided rocket projectiles. A flare chute in the rear cabin allows up to six Mk 6 smoke grenades to be launched. The EMB-111's avionics include a Collins INS-61B inertial navigation system, Collins VIR-30A VOR/ILS receiver, Collins DF-301E VHF/DF, RCA AVQ-75 DME, dual Bendix DFA-73-A-1 ADF, Collins ALT-50 radio altimeter and Collins PN-101 gyro-magnetic compass.

Orders and options have been placed by the FAB for 16 EMB-111s, including two prototypes, with deliveries to begin in 1978. Performance details have not been revealed, but it may be assumed, from the known performance of the commercial EMB-110, that the maritime version, with more fuel but operating at a higher gross weight, has a range of not less than 1,750 mls (2 816 km) and a probable endurance of about 8 hrs.

De Havilland Canada Dash 7R Ranger

With 1,000 hrs of flight-testing completed on the two prototypes and the first production Dash 7 airliner scheduled to fly early in 1977, de Havilland Canada announced details of a proposed maritime patrol and reconnaissance version of the design at Farnborough International. Named the Ranger, this Dash 7R version is the subject of current engineering design work and marketing activities, and the first example could be flying by the autumn of 1978 if a launch decision is taken soon.

Using the same airframe as the Dash 7 airliner, the Ranger has increased fuel capacity, search radar and other necessary equipment for the rôle; crew stations, however, are installed on a modular basis to permit their rapid removal and the aircraft

Illustrations above and below depict the prototype F27 Maritime on an early test flight. Phase 1 testing has now been completed and the installation and testing of customer-specified items of equipment is now proceeding.

can be easily reconfigured for all passenger or passenger/cargo operations if desired. Without removing any of the special equipment, 26 passengers can be carried in the rear of the cabin, although the seats would not normally be fitted for specifically reconnaissance rôles.

The Ranger's radar is Litton LASR-2, with the aerial in a radome under the forward fuselage, providing 360-deg scan. Bubble windows are provided for the two observers in the forward end of the cabin, and the nav/comm operator is seated (forward-facing) at a console on the starboard side, just aft of the observer on that side. A fuselage-mounted vertical camera is installed aft of the radome, to provide photographic evidence of suspected intruders in restricted waters, with a photo annotation system which records on the film the

appropriate position using data from the aircraft's navigation system. Close to the camera is a flare launcher and stowage for flares.

The LASR-2 radar is similar to the Litton equipment adopted for the F27 Maritime and already described, with such features as pencil beam for optimum search, weather mapping and station keeping; variable pulse width, sector scan of variable width; ground stabilisation and off-set sweep. A Litton LTN-72 inertial navigation system is optional equipment in the Ranger, as an alternative to the recommended primary Omega VLF (Canadian Marconi) with dual VHR and ADF; when fitted, the LTN-72 can be pre-programmed to conduct search patterns through the auto-pilot. Other options include Doppler navigation system, ONTRAC III VLF

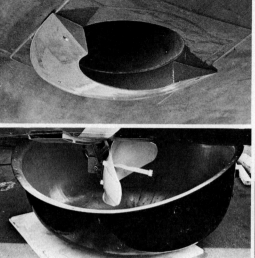

Features of the F27 Maritime shown in close-up here are (left) the observation window; (top centre) the flare chute exit in the fuselage underside; (bottom centre) the radar aerial, with radome removed and (right) retractable searchlight in the fuselage side.

navigation system, electronic emission measuring equipment, multi-spectral sensor and independent nose-mounted weather radar.

Operating at a gross weight of 45,000 lb (20 408 kg), the Ranger carries 17,050 lb (7 982 kg) of fuel and has a maximum payload of 9,550 lb (4 331 kg). At a radius of 200 naut mls (370 km) the Ranger has a time on station of just over 8 hrs, reducing to about 4½ hrs at 600 naut mls (1 110 km), total endurance being in excess of 10 hrs. These figures assume the transit is made at 10,000 ft (3 050 m) or more, followed by radar search on station at 5,000 ft (1 525 m) and 30 min inspection at 1,000 ft (305 m); if the entire operation is conducted at 2,000 ft (610 m), the time on station reduces to 6½ hrs at 200 naut mls (370 km) and 2½ hrs at 600 naut mls (1 110 km). Carrying 26 passengers, the Ranger will fly 1,500 naut mls (2 780 km), cruising at 5,000 ft (1 525 m) at 80 per cent of the MCR with 45 min reserves.

Ranger has a max cruising speed of 233 kt (432 km/h) in ISA and will operate comfortably from a 3,000 ft (915-m) gravel strip in temperatures up to ISA plus 15 deg C with its max payload. A bonus point claimed for the aircraft by de Havilland, insofar as long endurance missions are concerned, relates to the very low noise level in the cabin, resulting in low crew fatigue and therefore higher efficiency. The low external noise levels, deriving from the use of four 1,120 shp Pratt & Whitney Canada PT6A-50 engines turning Hamilton Standard propellers with glassfibre blades, gives an added advantage in helping undetected approach during missions seeking intruders; the four engine configuration — unique to the Ranger in maritime patrol aircraft of its class — is claimed to provide an added safety factor on long overwater missions and in the unlikely event of an engine failure, the mission can be continued without the need to abort.

There is adequate space and payload margin in the Ranger for various specialised sensors to be fitted at customer demand. A freight door can be fitted in the forward port side of the fuselage to allow freight pallets to be loaded (with the patrol crew stations and equipment removed) and another option is an air operable rear door, required for search and rescue duties. □

Depicted to scale in these side view drawings are a number of the medium-sized aircraft currently available or under development for maritime duties.

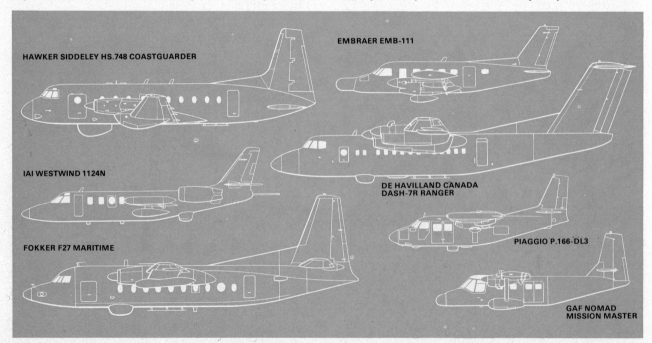

Petrol Pumps in the Sky

The RAF's Victor K Mk 2 tanker and its predecessors described

A T ALMOST any time of the day or night, somewhere over one of six training areas (identified as "towlines") around the coast of the United Kingdom, a Victor of RAF Strike Command's Tanker Force will be airborne, exercising its crews and those of a number of receiver aircraft programmed to make contact with it in the course of a single sortie. Comprising three squadrons sharing a total fleet of only 24 Victors, the tanker force is one of the most élite within the RAF, as well as being one of the most hard-working, for in addition to their regular training commitment, the tankers are required to participate in virtually every exercise conducted by the operational aircraft of Strike Command, all of which are equipped for air-to-air refuelling.

A typical tanker sortie begins some three hours before the scheduled take-off time at RAF Marham, Norfolk, the home base of the three tanker squadrons (Nos 55, 57 and 214), when the crew goes to the self-briefing room in the Operations Block to collect the necessary general data, weather information and specific details of any air traffic control or other problems that might interfere with the flight plan. The crew comprises the captain (P1), who is primarily concerned with flying the Victor as well as being in overall command of the operation; the co-pilot (P2), who is responsible for fuel management and distribution of fuel between the tanks to ensure that sufficient remains at all times for the tanker's own needs; an air electronics officer (AEO), who handles communications and looks after the aircraft electrical system, and two navigators — a nav-plotter who performs the basic navigation and a nav-radar who handles the rendezvous equipment and controls the transfer of fuel to the receiving aircraft through any or all of the three hose and drogue units (one in the fuselage and one under each wing). A jump-seat allows a crew chief or other supernumerary to be carried.

Self-briefing completed, the tanker crew will have all the information necessary, including such items as time on and off the rendezvous point (RV), radio frequency to be used, controlling ground radar station and its frequency, number of

aircraft to receive fuel, their home base(s) and the fuel transfer details. Time is then available for a pre-flight meal before the crew board the Victor an hour or so before take-off — long enough to allow for any minor snags to be overcome, should they arise, without jeopardising the planned take-off time, which is critical if the RV is to be kept.

Arrived on station at the appropriate towline, the Victor, flying at a steady Mach = 0·76, trails the hose and drogue (each of the three units is separately controlled) a few minutes before the arrival of the receiver aircraft, and communication between tanker and receiver begins. Three types of RV are possible — radar controlled (through the ground station), tanker controlled or receiver controlled, the two last-mentioned requiring no reference to an outside controller. In peace-time, the ground radar station is normally involved, as a safety measure if for no other operational reason.

The receiver — typically on a training exercise these would be a pair of Phantoms or Lightnings — close on the tanker 2,000 ft (610 m) below, until visual contact is made and confirmed over the radio, using a separate frequency so that ATC and other frequencies are not cluttered up with the exchanges between tanker and receivers. Having identified the tanker, the leader of the pair of receivers will confirm: "Foxtrot 27 (or whatever call-sign applies) – visual contact with tanker", receiving the response "27 clear to join port".

The pair of Phantoms join formation, slightly ahead on the port side at a distance of about 400 yds (366 m), where they can be seen by the tanker's captain, who then gives the command: "Foxtrot 27 cleared astern the starboard" and "Foxtrot 28 cleared astern the port". The receivers drop back to their appropriate positions behind the aircraft, watched by the nav-radar through a periscope, and confirm that they are ready to move in to make contact by calling "astern port" and "astern starboard". Finally, the captain checks that the refuelling systems are "go" with the drogues out and refuelling circuits open, whereupon he clears the receiver to make contact: "Foxtrot 27 ready for contact starboard wet to full" (if only a

The Victor K Mk 2, depicted in the three illustrations on these pages, is the ultimate service version of a design that had its origins more than 30 years ago, in the months immediately following the end of World War II. As a tanker, it is destined to continue in RAF service until the end of the 'eighties.

practice contact is being made, he will specify "dry" instead of "wet", and if only a partial refilling of the receiver's tanks is planned, this will also be indicated).

To help the receivers make contact with the drogues from the underwing pods, sighting aids are painted on the underside of the Victor in the form of two right-angled marks. The receiver takes up a position some 20 ft (6,1 m) behind and below the drogue, where the two marks appear to the pilot as a '+', and he then edges his aircraft upwards and forwards, watching the reference marks rather than the drogue itself the whole time until contact is made, and confirmed with the call "contact starboard" or "contact port". Fuel flows automatically when the receiver has nudged some 7 ft (2,12 m) of the hose back into the drum unit and is indicated by a green light adjacent to the hose exit from the aircraft. The light is at amber during the approach prior to fuel flowing, and if it turns to red, contact must be broken off immediately – simply achieved, in either emergency or routine separations, by retarding the throttle slightly while staying in the correct position relative to the tanker.

The flow of fuel from the tanker to receiver(s) is controlled by the nav-plotter, with checks being called after each 2,000 lb

(908 kg) of fuel has been transferred — or each 5,000 lb (2 270 kg) in the case of large aircraft such as the Vulcan or VC10, which would use the fuselage-mounted drogue. Maximum rates of flow are, 1,200 lb/min (545 kg/min) through the wing-mounted units and 4,000 lb/min (1 816 kg/min) through the fuselage unit, but the rates are slowed down to a trickle for the last couple of hundred pounds.

It is customary for fighter and strike aircraft to refuel from the Victor in pairs, although contact with the wing tip drogues is normally made in succession so that each hook-up can be monitored by the nav-radar. Separation is usually simultaneous, however, upon the command of the captain after completion of refuelling has been confirmed: "Foxtrot 27, 28, clear to break" and the two Phantoms then rejoin formation on the port side before departing. Depending on fuel states and mission requirements, the Victor stays on station — flying a "racecourse" pattern with two long sides available for refuelling contacts — to await the arrival of the next receivers or returns to base.

Tanker origins

The RAF's first tankers were converted Vickers Valiant bombers, the operational mission of which in the first instance was to enhance the range of the V-force strategic bombers. The emergence of the Victor as a tanker occurred at very short notice at the end of 1964 when fatigue cracks were discovered

in the wing spars of several Valiants — the result of sustained operations at lower altitudes than those for which the aircraft had been designed — and the entire fleet was grounded three years earlier than planned.

It had already been planned to develop a Victor tanker as a replacement for the Valiants in the 1966/67 timescale, using Victor Mk 1 airframes that had been rendered surplus to the V-Force with the delivery of B Mk 2s, and a trial installation had been made (on the second production aircraft, XA918) of Flight Refuelling F.R. Mk 20B hose-and-drogue pods mounted under the wings, plus an F.R. Mk 17 in the fuselage bay originally designed to carry flash bombs. To meet the serious lack of tankers which ensued when the Valiants were withdrawn, however, Handley Page undertook a "crash" programme to fit the wing pods only to six Victor B Mk 1As, and the first of these flew at Radlett on 28 April 1965. As the bomb-bay refuelling unit was not installed, these aircraft were designated Victor B(K) Mk 1As (retaining a bombing capability, if bomb-bay fuel tanks were removed) but they were assigned exclusively to the tanker rôle, entering service with No 55 Squadron at Marham in May 1965.

As soon as this initial batch of six aircraft had been delivered, Handley Page proceeded to work on the three-point tanker variant, which not only featured the fuselage-mounted F.R.17 hose-and-drogue unit but also had increased fuel

continued on page 300

Handley Page Victor K2 Cutaway drawing key

1 Nose probe
2 Control feel system pressure intake
3 Nose compartment windows
4 Nose construction
5 In-flight refuelling probe
6 Windscreen
7 Refuelling searchlights
8 Jettisonable roof hatch
9 Co-pilot's Martin-Baker ejection seat
10 Pilot's roof hatch windows
11 Pilot's Martin-Baker ejection seat
12 Control column
13 Instrument panel
14 Rudder pedals
15 Air intake to air-conditioning system
16 Radome
17 Throttles
18 Pilot's side console
19 Cockpit floor
20 External door handle
21 H₂S radar scanner
22 Radar mounting and equipment
23 Rearward facing crew members seats — AEO port, nav-plotter centre, nav-radar starboard
24 Cockpit door
25 Entry steps
26 Front fuselage construction
27 Rear view periscope
28 Rearward facing crew members work table
29 Cabin side window
30 Air conditioning system

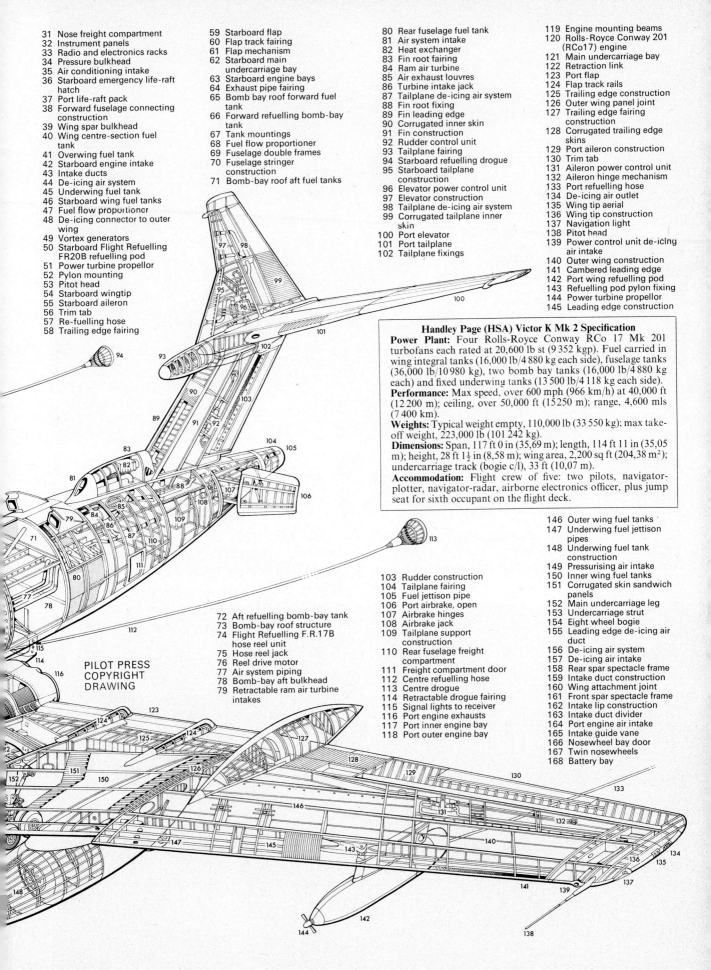

31 Nose freight compartment
32 Instrument panels
33 Radio and electronics racks
34 Pressure bulkhead
35 Air conditioning intake
36 Starboard emergency life-raft hatch
37 Port life-raft pack
38 Forward fuselage connecting construction
39 Wing spar bulkhead
40 Wing centre-section fuel tank
41 Overwing fuel tank
42 Starboard engine intake
43 Intake ducts
44 De-icing air system
45 Underwing fuel tank
46 Starboard wing fuel tanks
47 Fuel flow proportioner
48 De-icing connector to outer wing
49 Vortex generators
50 Starboard Flight Refuelling FR20B refuelling pod
51 Power turbine propellor
52 Pylon mounting
53 Pitot head
54 Starboard wingtip
55 Starboard aileron
56 Trim tab
57 Re-fuelling hose
58 Trailing edge fairing

59 Starboard flap
60 Flap track fairing
61 Flap mechanism
62 Starboard main undercarriage bay
63 Starboard engine bays
64 Exhaust pipe fairing
65 Bomb bay roof forward fuel tank
66 Forward refuelling bomb-bay tank
67 Tank mountings
68 Fuel flow proportioner
69 Fuselage double frames
70 Fuselage stringer construction
71 Bomb-bay roof aft fuel tanks

80 Rear fuselage fuel tank
81 Air system intake
82 Heat exchanger
83 Fin root fairing
84 Ram air turbine
85 Air exhaust louvres
86 Turbine intake jack
87 Tailplane de-icing air system
88 Fin root fixing
89 Fin leading edge
90 Corrugated inner skin
91 Fin construction
92 Rudder control unit
93 Tailplane fairing
94 Starboard refuelling drogue
95 Starboard tailplane construction
96 Elevator power control unit
97 Elevator construction
98 Tailplane de-icing air system
99 Corrugated tailplane inner skin
100 Port elevator
101 Port tailplane
102 Tailplane fixings

119 Engine mounting beams
120 Rolls-Royce Conway 201 (RCo17) engine
121 Main undercarriage bay
122 Retraction link
123 Port flap
124 Flap track rails
125 Trailing edge construction
126 Outer wing panel joint
127 Trailing edge fairing construction
128 Corrugated trailing edge skins
129 Port aileron construction
130 Trim tab
131 Aileron power control unit
132 Aileron hinge mechanism
133 Port refuelling hose
134 De-icing air outlet
135 Wing tip aerial
136 Wing tip construction
137 Navigation light
138 Pitot head
139 Power control unit de-icing air intake
140 Outer wing construction
141 Cambered leading edge
142 Port wing refuelling pod
143 Refuelling pod pylon fixing
144 Power turbine propellor
145 Leading edge construction

Handley Page (HSA) Victor K Mk 2 Specification

Power Plant: Four Rolls-Royce Conway RCo 17 Mk 201 turbofans each rated at 20,600 lb st (9 352 kgp). Fuel carried in wing integral tanks (16,000 lb/4 880 kg each side), fuselage tanks (36,000 lb/10 980 kg), two bomb bay tanks (16,000 lb/4 880 kg each) and fixed underwing tanks (13 500 lb/4 118 kg each side).

Performance: Max speed, over 600 mph (966 km/h) at 40,000 ft (12 200 m); ceiling, over 50,000 ft (15 250 m); range, 4,600 mls (7 400 km).

Weights: Typical weight empty, 110,000 lb (33 550 kg); max take-off weight, 223,000 lb (101 242 kg).

Dimensions: Span, 117 ft 0 in (35,69 m); length, 114 ft 11 in (35,05 m); height, 28 ft 1½ in (8,58 m); wing area, 2,200 sq ft (204,38 m²); undercarriage track (bogie c/l), 33 ft (10,07 m).

Accommodation: Flight crew of five: two pilots, navigator-plotter, navigator-radar, airborne electronics officer, plus jump seat for sixth occupant on the flight deck.

PILOT PRESS
COPYRIGHT
DRAWING

72 Aft refuelling bomb-bay tank
73 Bomb-bay roof structure
74 Flight Refuelling F.R.17B hose reel unit
75 Hose reel jack
76 Reel drive motor
77 Air system piping
78 Bomb-bay aft bulkhead
79 Retractable ram air turbine intakes

103 Rudder construction
104 Tailplane fairing
105 Fuel jettison pipe
106 Port airbrake, open
107 Airbrake hinges
108 Airbrake jack
109 Tailplane support construction
110 Rear fuselage freight compartment
111 Freight compartment door
112 Centre refuelling hose
113 Centre drogue
114 Retractable drogue fairing
115 Signal lights to receiver
116 Port engine exhausts
117 Port inner engine bay
118 Port outer engine bay

146 Outer wing fuel tanks
147 Underwing fuel jettison pipes
148 Underwing fuel tank construction
149 Pressurising air intake
150 Inner wing fuel tanks
151 Corrugated skin sandwich panels
152 Main undercarriage leg
153 Undercarriage strut
154 Eight wheel bogie
155 Leading edge de-icing air duct
156 De-icing air system
157 De-icing air intake
158 Rear spar spectacle frame
159 Intake duct construction
160 Wing attachment joint
161 Front spar spectacle frame
162 Intake lip construction
163 Intake duct divider
164 Port engine air intake
165 Intake guide vane
166 Nosewheel bay door
167 Twin nosewheels
168 Battery bay

MONOCOUPE!

Gene Smith, who owns a Monocoupe 90AL, tells the story of a family of aircraft built more than 30 years ago but still the centre of attention wherever they fly, a family that includes the Monocoupe 110 Specials – of which only seven were built but 10 now exist!

THE American Airlines DC-3 was a little more than halfway along its 140-mile (225-km) leg from Chicago to Fort Wayne, Ind, when the straining little red-and-yellow pursuer overtook it. The big man in the cockpit of the tiny two-seater grinned and leaned forward, nodding at the airliner well ahead and slightly below him. "Watch this," he said to the slim 15-year-old youth beside him.

Ron Kendall let the cowling of the 145-hp Warner radial dip a few degrees below the horizon. The Monocoupe, already nudging the 200-mph (322 km/h) mark, took the bit between its teeth. It came howling down the sky in a long slant and levelled out just astern and to one side of the cruising airliner. The Monocoupe's speed was now on the high side of 250 mph (402 km/h) as Kendall rolled it smoothly inverted and flashed past the DC-3, waving to the passengers and crew.

The Monocoupe was well in the lead, wheel pants still skyward, before Kendall rolled back to normal flight. With the 145 Warner still wrapped up tight, the little aeroplane simply flew off and left the Douglas, arriving at Fort Wayne far enough ahead to allow Kendall to park NC2347 and hide behind a hangar door with his passenger, well before the DC-3 landed. "The crew piled out as soon as they got the door open," recalls Al Allin, the boy who had shared in Kendall's fun that day. "They were all over that airplane, wanting to know what it was and what it would do."

Allin has never forgotten that ride with Kendall, and the many other things he saw the 110 Special do in the big man's hands. Today he owns a sports car racing shop in Grand Haven, Mich — and NC501W, the very first Clipwing built, winner of a dozen Cleveland air races in 1931 and 1932, and holder of a world speed record for its class in 1933.

The factory advertised a 200 mph (322 km/h) top speed for its 145-hp Monocoupe 110 Special, and it did not exaggerate — although "normal" performance specifications indicate a cruise of 162 mph (261 km/h) and a top speed of 186 mph (299 km/h). Specials, thus powered and swinging a fixed-pitch Curtiss-Reed propeller, have turned its timed speeds of better than 240 mph (386 km/h) on the flat in pylon races.

The late John H Livingston, most famous of the Mono-coupe race pilots and the father of the Clipwing, once explained how it was done, remarking casually that some other pilots were turning their 145 hp Warners (in different aeroplanes) up to 3,500 rpm. "Personally, I never found it necessary to turn more than 3,000," he added. The engine is red-lined at 2,050!

All Monocoupes — there were 772 of them built — were remarkable aeroplanes, but the 110 Specials in particular have fascinated pilots and laymen alike for more than 40 years. There are three apparent reasons: they are fast (and the records are in the books to prove it), they are strong and they are agile — a 110 Special won the world aerobatic championship in 1948. Furthermore, they possess a sporty air of competence seldom seen before or since. They have tiny tails, pinched-in fuselages and 23 feet (7,02 m) of wing, and that big radial engine blotting out the world. They look, in fact, rather like a winged bulldog drawn by Walt Disney.

Only seven 110 Specials were built in a 20-year production span that ended in 1950. One was never flown much. The other six have killed four pilots, have been "totally destroyed" half a dozen times and merely badly damaged as many times again. Yet there are 10 now in existence, for three men, unable to buy a "real" 110 Special, built their own from parts of other Monocoupes — a perfectly legal and logical (if complicated) process, since even the factory Specials were the end result of a series of modifications to an earlier model.

Monocoupe origins

The Clipwings are only the most glamorous examples of a rare and fetching breed. The whole Monocoupe clan served as the progenitor of ten thousand similarly-configured aeroplanes — high-wing, strut-braced, enclosed-cabin monoplanes with side-by-side seating — now to be found throughout the world. They were the first such designs to find commercial success, the first really economical primary trainers, winners of a bookful of racing honours, aerobatic mounts *par excellence,* glamour queens of the 'thirties sports 'plane set. Even today, they are unbeaten for sheer performance in their class.

There were a couple of Monocoupe forays into larger

(Below) The Monocoupe 110 Special "Little Butch" was built in 1941 and won the World Aerobatic Championship at Miami in 1948; it is now owned by Capt John McCulloch. (Opposite page, top.) The author's Lycoming-engined Monocoupe 90AL N87618, photographed in 1972 and (opposite page, bottom) R Sheldon Stewart's D-145 N86570 in 1973.

Owner/pilot Harold Neumann, of Leawood, Kansas, climbs vertically while putting on a demonstration in his "Little Mulligan", a Monocoupe 90AF converted to have a 145 hp Warner engine.

aeroplanes, exemplified by the 21 good but unlucky four-place Monocoaches of 1928-29, the even more hapless twins of 1936 and 1956 (the latter launched by a successor company) and the low-wing Dart digression spawned by designer Al Mooney (also responsible for the Monocoach twin). But the marque's name and fame rests squarely upon the high-wing two-seaters.

These, from first to last, provide what is probably general aviation's best illustration of endless development and adaptation of a single good idea — a process which resulted in such dissimilar products as the mothlike "personal planes" of the late 'twenties, the fierce and fearsome racers of the mid-'thirties and the somewhat demanding "sport planes" of the late 'thirties and 'forties. Among them, they provide a case history of personality change in a linear aeroplane family.

Despite the series' 23 years of production and a hatful of accomplishments, there are professional flyers active today who have never heard of Monocoupe, for the company went quietly bankrupt a quarter of a century ago after teetering on the thin edge of financial disaster for almost two decades. Even so, to the knowledgeable, Monocoupe is still a name to conjure with. Curiously, then, the Monocoupe's enduring reputation is not the kind its creators sought.

They were "primarily interested in building an aircraft that was easy to fly, inexpensive and efficient," as the late Phoebe Fairgrave Omlie remarked in a private letter to the author. "IT WAS NOT FOR RACING." However, the resulting aircraft "was so far superior to all competitors in its class that many used it for races that popped up all over the country after 1929, and [it] became known as a racing machine. As far as cost of operation, adaptability and efficiency are concerned, nothing has equalled it to this day." Mrs Omlie knew, for she was an early contributor to that reputation — flying one of two early Velie Monocoupes which went twice across the Rockies in the gruelling 6,300-mile (10 137-km) 1928 Ford National Air Tour from Detroit to California, up the coast to Oregon and return.

The first Monocoupe lifted off the spring grass of a Davenport, Iowa, field some 50 years ago, unlikely offspring of a chance mating between the ideas of a flying advertising man,

Luscombe, and a self-taught farm boy, Folkerts. It was an instant success; a sprightly canary in a colony of crows, but soon to prove itself a hot canary.

Hooked on aviation while serving in France in 1917 as an ambulance driver, Donald A Luscombe had purchased a war-surplus Curtiss JN-4D "Jenny" in 1924, but soon grew tired of manhandling it in and out of the hangar, and dissatisfied with both its slowness and lack of creature comforts. One ought, he felt, to be able to fly in a hat instead of a helmet, and without the weather smiting one in the face.

Luscombe made a mock-up side-by-side cabin for two, using wood lath and cardboard, with old oil cans for seats. The seating arrangement was dictated by his desire to concentrate the weight on the centre of gravity. He wanted a steel-tube fuselage for strength with low weight, like the renowned Fokker fighters. Aside from that he was flexible in his ideas, though he had been impressed with some features of the 1924 Belgian Demonty-Poncelot, a sort of powered ukelele with wings and tail.

Clayton Folkerts, a genius at eyeball engineering, had built four aircraft of his own design over the preceding eight years. The last two actually flew and the final one was an advanced shoulder-wing monoplane of geodetic construction. Unable to find backers for a two-seat growth version of this geodetic midget, Folkerts agreed to Luscombe's offer of a one-year contract to serve as designer for the new Central States Aero Co* at $35 per week, and supervised the building of the first "Monocoupe" around Luscombe's cabin design in four-and-a-half months.

Powered by a 75 hp five-cylinder Detroit Air Cat radial engine, it had a 30-ft (9,15-m) one-piece wing with a Clark "Y" aerofoil and 143 sq ft (13,28 m²) of area, weighed 650 lb (295 kg) empty and 1,134 lb (515 kg) fully loaded, and took-off in less than 100 ft (30,5 m). Performance was remarkable for the time, with a cruise of 85 mph (137 km/h), a top speed of 102 mph (164 km/h), a stall of 45 mph (72 km/h) and a 700 ft/min (3,56 m/sec) initial climb rate — but its most outstanding attribute was a lightness and responsiveness of control shared by no other design of the period. Test Pilot E K "Rusty" Campbell made only one short flight before predicting a great future for the new product. Luscombe believed the aircraft's speed was due to the quick reduction in fuselage cross section aft of the cabin, likening it to the teal, fastest of the duck family. A flight of three stylized teal thus became the Monocoupe trademark, retained through the production life of the series.

Monocoupes underwent many changes between 1927's first production model and that sad day in 1950 when Carl Poston had to buy a truck to haul away his still-unfinished last aeroplane from a dying factory. But two things never changed — the side-by-side, high-wing layout and the distinctive recurved lines of the rectangular-section aft fuselage. For the initiate, there is no mistaking that recedent fuselage, copied by two famous later designs, the Howard and the Beech Staggerwing. Ben Howard's mighty *Mister Mulligan*, the DGA-6 racer, was a frank and unabashed scaled-up copy of the clipwing Monocoupe, while the planform of the Beech 17's wings has always looked suspiciously familiar to owners of later 'coupes, as well.

The Air Cat engine proved to possess bad habits; overheating, detonating and consuming pushrods and sparkplugs like popcorn. Worse, the Detroit company was foundering and

---

The company building the Monocoupe underwent several changes of name — becoming Mono Aircraft Corporation in 1927, Monocoupe Corporation in 1929, and Lambert Aircraft Corporation, at Lambert Field, St Louis, in 1934. By 1939, it was once again the Monocoupe Corporation, taken over in 1940 by Monocoupe Aeroplane Engine Corporation, which in turn became a part of Universal Moulded Products Corporation in 1941, and was re-established under its former name in Melbourne, Florida, in 1948 to resume production of the Model 90 and Model 110 Special.

engine deliveries rapidly fell behind, leaving CSA with plenty of demand for its new Monocoupe but many troubles in meeting orders.

When the Detroit company finally collapsed late in 1927, Luscombe persuaded auto-maker Willard L Velie to produce a substitute engine. Velie had been almost driven out of the motor car market by General Motors, and was ready to listen. He had the first Velie M-5 in flight test by March 1928, and as it was almost a duplicate of the Air Cat, it at first shared the same problems, but these were soon reduced by the use of aluminium heads, sodium valves and a new Stromberg carburettor. Rated at 20 hp less (METO) than the Air Cat, its service life was greater and CSA was soon producing 10 Monocoupes a week. Tony Fokker stunted in a borrowed Monocoupe. Col Charles A Lindbergh bought one (though he insisted on brakes being fitted — a modified motorcycle rig that was among the first ever fitted to an aircraft). Monocoupes competed well in the 1928 National Air Races; pulling 60 hp from the Velie (take-off rating), they averaged between 95 and 101 mph (153 and 163 km/h) over the closed course.

Racing experience produced the first of a seemingly never-ending series of refinements, which led from the original Model 70 to the Model 113, the Monosport and eventually, in January 1930, to the first Model 90, powered by the new 90 hp Lambert R-266. The Lambert concern was the Velie company reorganised after the death of Willard Velie and the sale of his aircraft interests to a St Louis combine; it subsequently acquired the Monocoupe design rights also. About 370 of the assorted early aeroplanes were built, including 60 open-sided Monoprep trainers designed at the behest of Jack Frye, later president of TWA, who was then running a California aviation enterprise. The Model 90 series was next most numerous, at 350 and continued through the Lycoming-powered 90AL-115, produced (on and off) until 1948. Of 37 Monocoupes still flying today, the "90" series accounts for 29, having thus proved the most durable of the line.

Adaptation, of course, also began immediately at the factory. The Model 110, a 90 modified to take a 110 hp Warner engine, was certificated in June 1930, and the first example left immediately for England, where owner Lord Carberry placed sixth among 60 aircraft in the two-week *Challenge de Tourisme International* the following month. Had he been able to dismantle the one-piece wing and strap it alongside the fuselage for the required roadability test, the Monocoupe would most probably have won; Carberry and his mechanic removed the wing in the allotted time, but were unable to mount it for towing. That same summer, at the US National Air Races, assorted Monocoupes took first place in 11 out of 15 events they entered, second in 10 and third in nine. They also took first positions in three cross-country events and claimed 63 per cent of the total prize money in events in which they competed.

Enter the Special

John Livingston, flying a stock 110, returned a speed of 146·1 mph (235 km/h) around the pylons in 1930. The next year, his mount having meanwhile progressed from having a Townend ring to a pressure cowling and with strut fairings to cut drag, he upped that performance to 149 mph (240 km/h) — but the competition, too, was getting faster. He sent the aircraft back to the factory with instructions to "cut the wing to 20 ft (6,1 m)" from its stock 32-ft (9,76-m) span. The manufacturer complied, but not exactly as Livingstone had intended; he meant simply to chop the existing wing to 20 ft (6,1 m), tip to tip. What he got was 20 ft (6,1 m) of *new* wing, with bigger ailerons and the same number of ribs as the original! The span, tip to tip, actually came out at 23 ft 2½ in (7,08 m). The new wing was to become a feature of all subsequent 110 Specials.

Livingston sold his NC501W to John Henry "Jack" Wright, a Utica, NY, insurance man, in 1933. Wright promptly sent it back to the factory for further refinement and an approved type certificate (2-452) was obtained for the new model. It was Wright who clipped the empennage surfaces, subsequent 110 Specials also following this pattern. Thus, factory statistics in the late '30s show the 90A with 132·2 sq ft (12,28 m²) of wing, 13·5 sq ft (1,25 m²) of aileron, 4·1 sq ft (0,38 m²) of fin, 5·8 sq ft (0,54 m²) of rudder, 10·6 sq ft (0,98 m²) of stabilizer and 9.2 sq ft (0,85 m²) of elevator. The 110 Special, by comparison, made do with 94 sq ft (8,73 m²) of wing, 16 sq ft (1,49 m²) of which was aileron; the fin measured 3·5 sq ft (0,33 m²), the rudder 5·0 sq ft (0,46 m²), the stabilizer 10 sq ft (0,93 m²) and the elevator 7·0 sq ft (0,65 m²).

Wright quickly won three speed events at the American Air Races in Chicago, earning more than $2,600 and setting an unofficial world speed record of 180·47 mph (290,38 km/h) for

continued on page 296

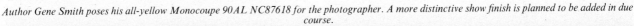

Author Gene Smith poses his all-yellow Monocoupe 90AL NC87618 for the photographer. A more distinctive show finish is planned to be added in due course.

TAKE AN EXPERT'S OPINION: THERE ARE NO EXPERTS!

ROY 'INFALLIBILITY' BRAYBROOK SELF-CONFESSED EXPERT!! Ask him a question – any question!

JUST outside Lima there is a military flying training base called Las Palmas. At present it is also used by FAP (*Fuerza Aérea del Perú*) as a home for some fine old aeroplanes pending completion of the aviation museum alongside the *Ministerio de Aeronáutica*. For practical purposes it never rains there, so with regular polishing any piece of aluminium that FAP decides to preserve *al aire libre* is soon looking better than when it was nailed together at the factory.

I went there to see if it was worth making an offer for the squadron of B-26Cs, which — contrary to various "authoritative" guides to the world's air forces — has been awaiting disposal since 1969. After the serious work was over (no, I didn't buy them!), I was taken to see FAP's two main exhibits in front of the officers' college: the Blériot monoplane in which Jorge Chávez (after whom Lima International is named) made the first aerial crossing of the Alps, and a beautiful old fighter that my guide described as an NA-50A.

Having previously researched what was worth seeing in the area, I assured him that, whatever FAP (or its predecessor: *Cuerpo de Aeronáutica del Perú*) may have called it, that particular example of the tin-basher's art was known in Europe as the Hawk 75A. With the confidence that frequently accompanies total ignorance, I drivelled on about what nice aeroplanes Curtiss used to put together, the contribution the '75A made to the Battle of France, etc, while this poor *Mayor-General* looked more and more confused!

If my old friend William Green had been present, he would at this stage have been rolling around the ground, clutching his gut, near-paralysed with mirth, since (as you may know) there

"There is (as you know) . . . not the slightest connection between the North American NA-50A and the Curtiss Hawk 75A." Examples of the Hawk 75A (above) and NA-50A (below) discovered in Peru confused our contributing expert!

is not the slightest connection between the North American NA-50A and the Curtiss Hawk 75A! He would, incidentally, have been finished off completely a few minutes later, when (for the title shot for "Historic Aircraft of Perú") ace photographer Braybrook carefully arranged two *llamas* in front of Armando Revoredo's DB-8A-3P, and then snapped away for half an hour with his brand-new piece of Japanese technology that did everything *except* wind the film!

Now the reason for this blow-by-blow account of a fairly average day in my life is not merely to hint to Aero Perú that I would welcome a chance to get back there with a better camera. My message is that there are too many innocents hooked on the idea that certain characters (perhaps including this writer) "know all about aviation". I am painfully aware that there is a vastly greater number of the opinion that the writer knows *nothing whatever* about aviation, but this article happens to be addressed to the credulous minority. **The truth about aviation is that it is an incredibly complex subject and very few people have the faintest knowledge about even the smallest corner of it.** That sentence is the best thing that you will ever read in an aviation magazine. No need to applaud: just throw money!

My friends will doubtless point out that the examples quoted are not evidence of an absence of experts, and that the writer's failings are already recorded for posterity in countless publications. *Who* (they will ask) *guessed the Fouga 90 would be powered by Aubisques? Who was the colour-blind imbecile that said the Mirage F1CZ is camouflaged sand and brown? Who wrote that the designers of the CASA C.101 would be out of their skulls to choose anything but the Viper 600?*

Well, such criticisms are justified, but my vast experience in aviation tells me that everyone else's track record is just as patchy and that of some people is even worse! On arriving back from Perú, I thought I would run a check on the 150-hp engined Oriole with which Faucett SA are reported to have kicked off their service in 1928. Naturally, I got on the horn to Green and Swanborough and flew it over them. Believe it or not, the best these two dum-dums could suggest was that it had been some aeroplane on which someone happened to have painted the word *Oriole*! He might have written *Spirit of St Louis, Enola Gay, Southern Cross,* or *Winnie May,* but that day he felt like writing *Oriole*! I can only say it would serve Green and Swanborough right if all those valiant pilots who poled their trusty Curtiss Orioles around the skies were to write in and bury them with irate mail. Even the expert's experts aren't expert!

Aha! – you may respond – *but writers, editors and journalists are known for their fallibility. One distinguished Fleet Street air correspondent is famous for his undiluted hogwash and the rest are a pretty disreputable bunch. Fortunately, the captains of industry are of a different ilk!*

Now that is a beautiful idea, but it simply isn't true. The first thing an aviation enthusiast learns on joining the industry is that anyone who takes the trouble regularly to read one good aviation journal cover-to-cover will soon know far more about the subject *in general* than any faceless wonder from the front office.

Will things be any worse under nationalisation? A good question. For the benefit of overseas readers, I should explain that the idea of nationalising the British aircraft industry arose as a peculiarly personal crusade by the then Industry Secretary, the Right Honorable Anthony Wedgwood Benn, MP. Having read at length the Aircraft and Shipbuilding Industries Bill (which runs a close second to the telephone directory for interest and excitement), I feel it should have been established right at the outset, precisely how much those concerned really knew about the industry and its products. You might visualise the enquiry being held in public as a TV quiz: **"Okay, Tony baby, an easy question: Why did the Javelin have a worse take-off performance with afterburner than without?"**

Are things just as bad in the States? Yes, America leads the world in aviation non-expertise, as in everything else. The well-known cargo door could easily become for future engineering students what the Tacoma Narrows Bridge was for my generation. I am speaking of the first design, of course, not the present one, in either case. As for the USAF, my life-long ambition is to run a research project to establish whether their flying training can really be what people say!

Americans have also trail-blazed the lemming-like rush to specialisation, which has resulted in the industry being almost entirely staffed by people who know increasingly less about their own products, and nothing whatever about the competition and the opposition. Today's typical aviation employee could well be a world authority on (say) cryogenic stress corrosion in die-cast molybdenum bolts, but whose concept of an F-4 is a pencil or someone who failed his medical. (Ed: That's one more reader down the pan!)

Assuming all this is true, how is it that aircraft have become the world's safest form of transport? This puzzled me too, for many years. Aside from the microscopic level of intelligence applied to all alternatives, I believe that modern aviation wins largely by virtue of the comprehensive checks used at each stage of aircraft development and by the numerous stand-by systems employed in the final product. When the Madison Avenue types portray aviation as a magnificent edifice firmly based on the twin supports of Brilliance and Bravery, you might remember that what stops the shiny facade falling flat on its face is a third little prop labelled Scepticism and Fear. If ever you meet an aeronautical engineer who unquestioningly accepts whatever the computer spews out, or a pilot who doesn't care about living forever, then run for your life!

What is all this frankness and honesty leading up to? I thought you'd never ask. The message is that if the reader accepts aviation for what it really is – **a multi-dimensional maze that demands the closest questioning at every turn** – then he will

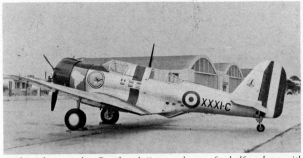

Author/photographer Braybrook "snapped away for half-an-hour with his brand-new piece of Japanese technology" but failed to preserve an FAP Douglas DB-8A on film; AIR INTERNATIONAL's files filled the gap.

firstly expect nothing more from this column than an informal (and inevitably fallible) Personal View. Secondly, he will not expect me to produce sure-fire solutions to his questions! For example, a surprising number of people want to know how to become aviation writers. Others expect me to tell them how to make fortunes from their inventions. Someone the other day asked me how I manage to drink so much, but I believe that was more in the nature of an oblique complaint about the floor area I was covering, rather than a request for technical expertise.

The Literary Bent

Just for the hell of it, let's look at the problems of entering the writing game. Firstly, does the questioner want to become a genuine aviation journalist? If so, the best bet is to contact his national *weekly* mag, because it employs four times as many people as any monthly and can absorb one extra with proportionally less of a squeeze. If it currently has no vacancies, the editor might still advise on what sort of recruits he looks for and how often. Editors *are* human beings, even if writers get a warm glow from knowing that Stevenson's archetypal pirate (Long John Silver) was based on a real-life magazine editor.

If the question is how to become a free-lance writer, the inevitable reply is WHY? Only Richard Bach ever got rich by writing about flying, and you can forget the stories of beautiful air hostesses giving you the keys to their apartments. I have travelled around the world many times, borrowing such distinguished names as John Fricker, Bill Gunston, John Taylor and Derek Wood, and it never once got me to first base. I would try calling myself Richard Bach, but they might ask me to fly the aeroplane!

The most important fact to take on board is that free-lancing works largely on the basis of personal contacts, so it is best to have some special writing gimmick to warrant an introduction. This who-knows-who business is not as anti-social as it sounds, since mutual trust is essential to the operation. When AIR INTERNATIONAL gets on the horn to this writer, it is not because — out of the entire world population

" . . . why did the Javelin have a worse take-off performance with afterburner than without?"

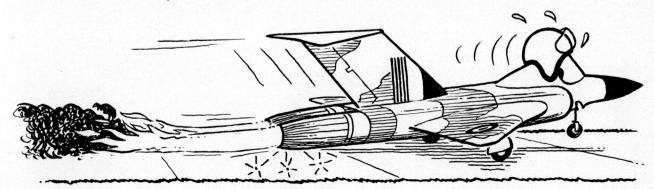

"... the 150-hp engined Oriole with which Faucett SA ... kicked off their service in 1928". The editors of AIR INTERNATIONAL apologise to author Braybrook for their temporary lapse of memory; they have now recalled that this three-passenger sportplane had a gross weight of 2,028 lb (921 kg), a span of 36 ft (10,98 m) and a max speed of 85 mph (137 km/h).

— he is best qualified to write on the required subject. (That thought may have already occurred to you). No, it is because the editors trust me to deliver the necessary words *on time*. They also know they can rely on me to "frag" their offices if they're one day late with the cheque! How could some turgid legal contract substitute for a fine personal relationship like that?

If all you want is to see your name on a by-line, there are plenty of magazines that will use any aviation article, but pay a rock-bottom fee. They are run by perfectly nice people, whose beautiful wives will scratch my eyes out if their publications close down tomorrow, but I believe that many such products needlessly dilute the revenues of more serious (ie, better-paying) journals. The other side of the story is that these low-budget mags provide healthy competition for the major ones and useful opportunities for new writers, and that one or two journals cannot adequately cover both the present and past of aviation. On balance, I am willing to dig in my pocket to support an essentially *different* concept, but too many aircraft magazines are just a repetitive waste of good timber and I would not encourage you to write for them.

How do you develop a special writing gimmick? In my own case, the gimmick was experience of analysing competitors' high performance aircraft. It happened that in the early 1960s a great deal of raw information on Soviet military aircraft became available, but none of the established writers had the expertise (or perhaps the time) to analyse it. Combining the editor's collection of photographs and information, my own guessing stick, and some excellent drawing by Dennis Punnett, we put together a series of design analyses which kept me in white convertibles for several years.

That the articles were entirely responsible for the subsequent demise of that magazine, I still doubt. I prefer to believe that they usefully focussed attention on Soviet progress, and needled RAF Technical Intelligence out of their post-war dream world. They certainly needled someone, as the editorial director of the day received a visit at home from two poker-faced gentlemen apparently suspecting a direct line to Moscow! Digressing, I consider it the duty of RAF officers to disguise themselves as perimeter fences on Soviet airfields and research such matters as Su-19 availability rate, and whether Tu-26 crews wear flak vests, but that **the analysis of information on Soviet aircraft designs should be left entirely to designers.**

In the bad old days, the RAF would typically yank someone out of the cockpit of a Swift, and pretend for the next two years that he was an expert on Soviet aircraft! They also had a bizarre preference for snaps apparently taken by their own attaché with a Minox stuffed up his sleeve, while rejecting photographs taken by a civilian professional armed with a Nikon and a 1000 mm lens! Finally, the people at the sharp end in RAF Germany complained that they were learning more

from Punnett's drawings than from the Intelligence reports, and things began to change.

In the last year there has appeared another generation of young writers specialising in design analysis (all with sinister foreign-sounding names, which was a gimmick I missed), so any newcomer would have to find something different. It is no secret that I have a protégé who is a financial specialist, the only person I know who knows both aviation and money. A few years of post-graduate training in the art of the studied insult and the unanswerable question, and this kid is going to be the terror of every management in the business!

No Profits for Prophets

Any PRO will tell you that writers and journalists are the lowest form of humanity. If you see yourself as an inventor, there are two simple steps that you can take to avoid being similarly categorised. Firstly, find out what constitutes an invention, and secondly, file at least a provisional patent specification before offering the idea to a manufacturer.

The majority of amateur inventors fail to grasp the fact that a patent grants the owner certain monopolistic rights for a limited period of time (about 16 years, but you can apply for extensions) in exchange for revealing *how* to achieve some difficult yet desirable objective. Many claim to have invented something when they have only defined the end product. Likewise an invention will not stand up in court if it is obvious or a simple combination of known ideas. There are countless people who have written to aircraft constructors on the lines of, "I have this brilliant idea for a rocket-powered canard. You may buy sole rights for a mere zillion dollars". Since no-one has ever built such an aircraft, they imagine they have an invention and resent the company declining their offer. They get even more bitter and twisted when the company builds a rocket-powered canard!

It is because the inventor has not only to solve a problem, but firstly to appreciate that the problem is going to arise, that makes it difficult for an aviation inventor to exist outside this fast-moving business. There have been plenty of examples of an outsider completely misunderstanding the technicalities. One chap got the garbled message that the next major problem after the "sound barrier" would be the "thermal thicket", caused by the air scrubbing against the external surfaces. He proposed to overcome this by building the aircraft in the form of a series of overlapping planks, with the sawn-off ends

"... the duty of RAF officers to disguise themselves as perimeter fences on Soviet airfields ..."

projecting forwards to stop the local airflow and thus prevent the heat problem!

The vast majority of ideas offered to a manufacturer are easily rejected. The real problem is the occasional proposal that might conceivably have something in it, yet would take a great deal of money to evaluate. Without wishing to sound too discouraging, I have never heard of a major invention applicable to advanced aircraft that has originated outside the business. If you nonetheless feel that you have a worthwhile idea, read some books on patents; if possible visit your national patents library and get a feel for these documents, and file at least a provisional patent specification. This serves the interests of all parties. The only inventor who is really given a hard time is one who claims *unreasonably* that a manufacturer has stolen his idea.

It is impracticable to go into detail on how to obtain a patent, since procedures vary from country to country. You can patent almost anything in the UK as the examination process is relatively easy-going. Try a half-baked invention on the *Patentamt* in Munich and the examiners will throw you straight in the river! Consequently a German patent is a very durable document, but you may have no idea how good a British one is until it comes up in court!

How much money is made from patent royalties is one of the darker secrets of aviation. Handley Page clearly made a nice income pre-war from leading edge slats, and more recently someone (United Aircraft?) is popularly supposed to have received one dollar for each vortex generator installed. Fairey is said to have collected for the drooping noses of early Concordes, an idea patented at the time of the FD.2. The Caravelle powerplant arrangement owned (then) by Sud Aviation was initially not taken very seriously abroad, as there had been various rear-engined German wartime projects, and as someone was supposed to have tested a J85 on the rear fuselage of a P-51 Mustang long before the Caravelle ever surfaced. However, Boeing (who were looking for a V/STOL deal with the French) coughed up a royalty on the 727, so everyone caved in and paid, with some mumbling curses at Seattle.

Has the writer invented anything? Yes, I am the proud originator of a flak gun (*Flab,* if you happen to be Swiss) that fires wake-stabilised ammunition, producing in aircraft structures a devastating linear perforation similar to the effect

"Fairey is said to have collected for the drooping noses . . . patented at the time of the FD.2."

of a continuous rod warhead. If anyone hasn't grasped the idea, it fires so fast that each round follows precisely in the wake of its predecessor. As you may have noticed there are nowadays no low-flying Soviet military aircraft over Western Europe, which can hardly be regarded as coincidental. You can acquire sole rights for a mere zillion dollars.

Is it advisable to take an invention to an expert for advice? This question brings us full circle and I will reply by means of a real-life case history, from which you may draw your own conclusions.

I used to work for the late Sir Sydney Camm, who was (in my personal view) the greatest fighter designer of all time, taking in combination the quality and quantity of his products. In his last years he would come round most days, shoot a bit of a line about how he had once again massacred young Sir George Edwards at golf, and fly his latest ideas over me. At the very start of the Airbus programme (when a Caravelle layout was the official front-runner) Sir Sydney produced the (then) completely new idea of having two engines under the wings and a third at the rear. Always quick to spot a no-go project, I told him that this combined all the worst features of every airliner in existence. It had the rear cabin noise and the FOD problems of underwing engines, it had powerplant systems spread out all over the aircraft, and it had the thousand screaming agonies of the centre-line intake! **There was no way** (I assured him) **that anyone would ever get into a bag of nails like that.**

As you know, the Airbus finally came together as a scaled-up 737. (Strange how the brochures miss the simple and direct descriptions, isn't it?) You will also know that years after that conversation, Lockheed produced the L-1011 TriStar. Just answer me this: would that great corporation have got into its recent financial mess if they had had the sense to come to an expert? □

TALKBACK

Those Estonian Spitfires

REFERENCE the correspondence that has developed in your *Talkback* column concerning the Estonian Spitfire order, it is interesting that the British Air Attaché in Finland should have seen the Chief of the Estonian Air Force on 28 July 1937 to arrange a visit to see the Estonian fighter squadron, for Air Ministry files show that Vickers-Supermarine first received an enquiry from Estonia about a possible supply of Spitfires on the 8th of that month. This suggests that it was the enquiry itself which set wheels in motion and alerted the Air Attaché to the need to look into reports that Estonia had sold its Bulldogs to Republican Spain.

Estonia's request was for 12 Spitfires, six to be delivered in August/September 1938 and six in the Spring of 1939. These dates were not then so unrealistic as they were later to appear for at the time production deliveries of Spitfires to the RAF were expected to start in December 1937 and the first 150, which the Air Ministry insisted should be delivered before exports could be considered, were expected by October 1938. Even so, these forecasts were, quite

rightly as it turned out, regarded as rather optimistic and Vickers was informed that no releases to meet foreign orders could be considered before 1939. There matters rested for the time being, but towards the end of 1938 the company, which was keen to accept the order, again approached the Air Ministry.

The Air Staff was by then opposed to *any* release of Spitfires, but after first obtaining the advice of the Foreign Office the Government ruled in December 1938 that two Spitfires could be released from Air Ministry contracts for export to Estonia in July 1939, two more in February 1940 and eight in June 1940.

Negotiations between Vickers and the Estonian Government then proceeded apace and a contract was received on 2 March 1939. This called for the first two aircraft to be delivered by 31 August 1939, followed by two more by 29 February 1940 and the remaining eight by 30 June 1940. The contract price was £151,255 10s 0d.

The Air Ministry agreed to release the 260th and 261st RAF aircraft (L1046 and L1047) to meet the first delivery, but by the time these

aircraft were ready early in July. Estonia had already concluded a non-aggression pact with Germany on 31 May and the two aircraft were included in a block allocation to the RAF made on 22 June and they were delivered into store at No 19 MU, St Athan, on 10 and 11 July 1939.

The eventual decision on 13 September 1939 not to supply Spitfires to Estonia was made by the Air Ministry as part of a general review on that date of all outstanding orders from abroad for military aircraft and I do not think that any seeming delay can be attributed to confusion said to be reigning at the outbreak of War, as suggested by Mr Howson. Until War actually began there was always the chance that diplomacy might restore the position in the Baltic and the supply of modern fighters to Estonia might still serve a useful purpose.

The two aircraft held at St Athan were issued to No 603 Squadron, RAF on 18 and 20 September 1939.

Peter H Pimblett
Sale, Cheshire

THE SLOW AND THE 'FOOLPROOF'

WHATEVER conclusions history may draw from Germany's ill-fated Third Reich, it cannot but conclude that this period in German history witnessed a most extraordinary upsurge in creativity and inventiveness on the part of that nation's industry in general and aircraft industry in particular. The innovatory developments that saw birth on the drawing boards of German aircraft designers between the mid 'thirties and mid 'forties were legion; many of these provided patterns for international development.

I was to have the good fortune to fly virtually all the aircraft types that saw service with the *Luftwaffe* during WW II as a result of this German prolificity of idea and have, over the years, recorded in the pages of AIR INTERNATIONAL my impressions of such relatively prosaic types as the Fw 200 Condor, the Do 217 and the He 111, to extravagantly audacious creations ranging from the bizarre Do 335 Pfeil and exotic Me 163 Komet to the epoch-marking Me 262 and Ar 234 Blitz, and that oversize example of the modeller's art, the He 162 *Volksjäger* – aircraft which, to the conventionalist, vied one with another in whimsicality.

German aircraft designers of the period were not, however, pre-occupied with the attainment of dramatic advances in high-speed performance and combat capability to the exclusion of all else, and two of the German wartime aircraft from which I derived the most pleasure represented the antithesis of all those types that I have described hitherto and

yet were, in their own fashion, just as innovative. These were the Fieseler Fi 156 Storch (Stork), the progenitor of the really practical STOL light aeroplane, and the Zaunkönig (Wren), which probably came as close to being a *foolproof* single-seat trainer as any aircraft before or since.

The genesis of the Storch dated back to the early 'thirties, and the ideas of Gerhard Fieseler and his chief designer, Reinhold Mewes, for achieving exceptionally short take-off and landing distances, and extremely low stalling speeds by combining long-span Handley Page automatic slots with the so-called *Fieseler-Rollflügel* — extendable flaps moving aft and downward to produce a respectable increase in gross wing area. This combination was applied by the Fieseler Flugzeug-bau, as it was then known, to the Fi 97, an attractive little low-wing four-seat cabin monoplane which gave a dramatic demonstration of its capabilities in the 1934 *Europarundflug* and set the stage for Fieseler to take his ideas for slotted-and-flapped slow-flying aircraft a further step.

This step took shape on the Kassel-Bettenhausen drawing boards as the Fi 156, or Storch as it was soon to become popularly known, in the summer of 1935, almost exactly a decade before I was to find the opportunity to settle myself behind the controls of this angularly ugly monoplane and peer through its extraordinarily panoramic windscreen for the first time; a decade in which the Storch, despite an unpretentious appearance, was to receive almost universal acclaim. The

Storch certainly possessed some outstanding attributes: it could be flown under full control in still air at 31 mph (50 km/h) and with a fair headwind could virtually hover; the take-off run into an 8 mph (13 km/h) wind barely exceeded 55 yards (50 m) and the landing run into the same wind demanded a mere 17 yards (15 m). During trials with a medium-strength wind blowing, the Storch demonstrated its ability to land in a ploughed field within a distance of *five yards*!

It would have been singularly strange had not the military potential of the Storch been immediately obvious to the Technical Department of the *Reichsluftfahrtministerium,* but oddly enough, a requirement for an army co-operation and observation aircraft with performance parameters provided by the Storch was promptly framed. There was no shortage of contenders: the Siebel Flugzeugwerke submitted the Si 201 monoplane with an aft-mounted engine driving a pusher propeller above a slim tailboom; Focke-Wulf proposed the Fw 186 jump-start gyroplane and the Bayerische Flugzeugwerke tendered the Bf 163 of closely similar concept to the Storch apart from the added innovation of a variable-incidence wing. Whether or not these competitors could emulate the Storch's performance was, in the event, to become a matter of purely academic interest, for the RLM had opted for the "bird-in-hand" before the potential competition flew in prototype form!

The Storch made its public début in the summer of 1937, when one of the ten pre-production Fi 156A-0 aircraft was demonstrated at the 4th International Flying Meeting held at Zürich-Dübendorf and from that point on its success was unqualified. Production had attained a rate of three per week by the end of 1938, the bulk of these going to the *Luftwaffe* which accepted a total of 227 in the following year. A Storch was presented to both Yosef Stalin and Benito Mussolini, the latter at that time blissfully unaware of the rôle that this gawky monoplane was to play in his subsequent fate. Stalin, for his part, so impressed by the capabilities of the Storch, issued instructions for the design to be adapted for Soviet production, a task assigned to Oleg K Antonov who was later to achieve an international reputation for his own designs. However, deliveries had still to commence from an assembly line set up at Kaunas, Lithuania, when the *Wehrmacht* invaded the Soviet Union, the factory being turned over to MiG-3 repairs and shortly thereafter overrun by the German forces.

Licence manufacture was later to be undertaken by the ICAR factory in Romania and there was certainly no lack of potential export customers, Yugoslavia, for example, ordering 34, but one of the principal effects of the Storch's début was to send designers scurrying to drawing boards all over the world

Viewed from the Cockpit

by Captain Eric Brown, CBE, DSC, AFC, RN

to produce "chinese copies" — in France such types as the SFAN 11 and Levasseur PL-400 appeared, the IMAM Ro 63 was evolved in Italy, while in Japan, Kobe produced the Type Te-Go and Nippon Kokusai developed the Ki.76. Indeed, if emulation can be regarded as the sincerest form of flattery, then the Storch was perhaps the most flattered aircraft of its era.

During the war years, the Storch became omnipresent; wherever the *Wehrmacht* was to be found so was to be found the Storch. It was already in Spanish service, examples used by the *Legion Condor* as staff transports and utility aircraft having been left behind with the end of the civil war, and it now appeared in service with the forces of Bulgaria, Croatia, Finland, Hungary, Romania, Slovakia and even Switzerland. From April 1942, production of the Storch by the parent company was supplemented by output from the former Morane-Saulnier plant at Puteaux and in the autumn of 1943, all jigs and tools were transferred by Fieseler to the Mraz factory at Chocen in Czechoslovakia. During the period 1937-

Among several examples of the Storch flown to the UK were Air Ministry 99 (VD + TD), an Fi 156C-3 subsequently shipped to South Africa (above right), and VP546, formerly Air Ministry 101 (below) which was flown by the author and is the subject of the accompanying handling notes. (Head of opposite page) An early production Fi 156C-1 (upper) and the LF 1 Zaunkönig V2 being flown as G-ALUA.

Few aircraft have seen use in a wider variety of countries than the Storch, the examples illustrated above being seen in Swedish service (as the S 14) in the 'fifties.

45, the *Luftwaffe* was to accept just short of 2,900 examples of the Storch — production was, of course, to continue well into the postwar years in both France and Czechoslovakia — and during the course of its war-time career the Storch was to perform some remarkable feats, not least of which was the rescue of Mussolini from imprisonment in the hotel at the peak of the Gran Sasso Massif in the Abrussi Molise, or Hanna Reitsch's landing in the rubble-strewn streets of Berlin in front of the *Führerbunker* in an attempt to snatch Hitler from the clutches of the advancing Soviet troops only to find that her *Führer* had already adopted the ultimate solution — suicide.

One of the most successful . . .

This, then, was the extraordinary background of the Fi 156 Storch by the time I first made my acquaintance with this slightly bizarre braced monoplane with its bulged transparent

"conservatory" and spindly long-stroke undercarriage legs in the summer of 1945. Much of this history I was to learn later, but I knew enough to appreciate that the Storch could justifiably be numbered among the world's classics; a member of that élite group of the most successful aircraft ever created.

I had never found an opportunity to fly the Storch in Germany and was, in consequence, delighted to get my hands on the sole example that we had at Farnborough. Assigned to the RAE's Aerodynamics Flight for communications work and special duties in connection with slow speed flight investigation, our Fi 156C had, so I was led to believe, been brought to the UK by a senior RAF officer who had used it as a personal hack until the postwar inventory system of captured enemy hardware had caught up with him and reallocated the aircraft to more productive tasks as Air Ministry 101. Thus, the history of this particular Fi 156C-1 (*Werk-Nr* 475061) was somewhat indeterminate, although from mid-May 1946 it was to take on a more positive identity when it was assigned the serial VP546 which it retained thereafter. However, it was still AM101 when, in September 1945, I demonstrated its near-unique slow flying capability for the first time in public at Hendon.

Few would suggest that the appellation Storch was not appropriate to this aircraft — when landing with flaps fully extended it bore for me a startling resemblance to a stork landing, such as I have seen so many times, on its chimney-top nest in Schleswig-Holstein. Structurally there was nothing unconventional about the Storch, with its rectangular-section welded steel-tube fabric-skinned fuselage, two-spar fabric-covered wooden wings and plywood-covered wooden tail surfaces, but its main undercarriage members, designed to absorb the impact of high vertical descent rates, appeared inordinately long at first sight, particularly when under no

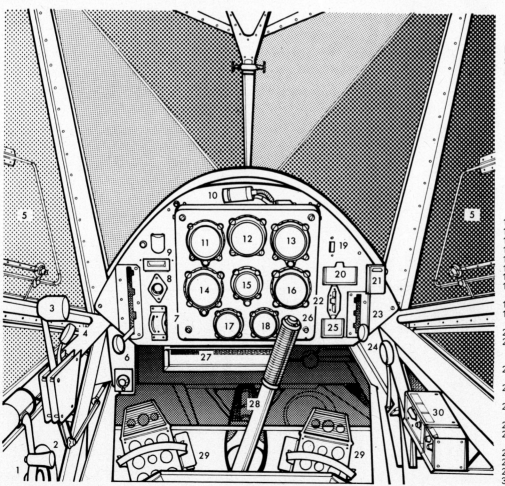

Fieseler Fi 156C Storch cockpit instrumentation key

1 Tailplane adjustment handwheel
2 Landing flap actuating handcrank
3 Throttle lever
4 Mixture control lever
5 Ventilation/clear vision side panels
6 Gate for petrol cock selection (four positions)
7 Ignition switch
8 Remote isolator switch push-button
9 Pitot tube heating indicator
10 Instrument panel light
11 Airspeed indicator
12 Turn-and-bank indicator
13 Variometer
14 Altimeter
15 Clock
16 Rev counter
17 Multi-manometer (pressure indicator)
18 Oil temperature gauge
19 Compass and instrument panel lighting switch
20 Speed data table
21 Automatic bomb-release control (fitted to Fi 156P version only)
22 Compass deviation/systems data table
23 Valve accumulator adjustment lever
24 Gate for main battery selection (three positions)
25 Trim data tables
26 B-Knopf XI bomb-release button (on control grip)
27 Map/document shelf
28 Control column
29 Rudder pedals
30 Mains switch box

compression. There were two compression legs incorporating long-stroke steel-spring oil-damping shock absorbers, the upper ends of which were attached to the apices of two pyramid structures built out from the sides of the fuselage, with the lower ends hinged to the underside of the fuselage centreline by steel-tube vees.

The cabin was a roomy, comfortable affair, entered by an automobile-style door, the entire sides and roof being glazed and the side panels sloping outward at an acute angle as an aid to downward vision. It offered a marvellous all-round view and reminded me of a small bay window. The instrument panel was, as one would imagine, the essence of simplicity, and behind the pilot's seat were two passenger seats in tandem. The Argus As 10C eight-cylinder inverted-vee air-cooled engine was rated at 240 hp for take-off. Starting it was a very basic procedure. The petrol cock was set to P1 + P2, thus opening the two wing root fuel tanks, which had a combined total capacity of 32·5 Imp gal (148 l); the generator and main battery switch was set ON and the main battery master lever pulled fully aft; the starter switch was turned to ON and the ignition switch set to SPÄT (retard); the internal primer was operated and finally the direct cranking starter was activated. The little Argus rarely failed to start first time and its sewing machine-like purr was delightful. I can believe that it was one of the few power plants used extensively by the *Luftwaffe* that could be urged into life fairly easily during winter operations on the Eastern Front.

After warming up to an oil temperature of 35°C, taxying could commence. Oddly enough, there were pitfalls in taxying to guard against. For a start, the wheels were extremely small and it was therefore advisable to avoid ruts and stones. Sharp turns were inadvisable as the tailwheel was always under heavy load owing to the extreme forward position of the mainwheels, and taxying with flaps down was to be avoided as a strong sidewind could roll the Storch over. Preparation for take-off involved lowering the flaps 20 degrees as seen on the gauge mounted just above the pilot's head and setting the elevator trim one division tail heavy and the ignition to FRÜH (advance). The Storch could be held on the hydraulic foot brakes until virtually the full 2,000 rpm was reached, and using this technique and without passengers, I did a measured take-off on a tarmac runway of 96 yards (88 m) in zero wind and +15°C temperature. With 40 degrees of flap I cut the take-off distance to 82 yards (75 m).

On reaching 53 mph (85 km/h) on the initial climb, it was possible to begin retracting the flaps slowly by winding a handle on the portside of the cockpit and a climbing speed of 56 mph (90 km/h) at 1,900 rpm was then established. However, if obstacles had to be cleared on take-off, the steepest angle of climb was attained with 15 degrees of flap at 47 mph (75 km/h). I found that, in general, cruising speeds were somewhat lower than claimed, being 74·5 mph (120 km/h) at 1,800 rpm, while the maximum range of 240 miles (385 km) could only be achieved by throttling back to around 62 mph (100 km/h).

Of course, speed was not intended to be the forte of the Storch, its *pièce de résistance* being its *slow* flying ability and this was the nearest thing to helicoptering in my experience then and since. With full flap and the Argus throttled back to about 1,300 rpm, it could be flown under full control at 43·5 mph (70 km/h), the nose high and forward view very poor in consequence. But by making gentle turns a superlative view of the ground was offered through the cockpit side windows. The Storch felt comfortable at this speed in calm conditions except that the rudder was sloppy and called for large movement for effect. In turbulence the flaps had to be retracted to the 15 deg position and the speed stepped up to 53 mph (85 km/h).

Stalling the Storch *was* possible, but the elevator was still so effective that recovery was immediate from a straight dropping of the nose. Just occasionally, however, it would drop a wing and then some caution was called for as rudder effectiveness

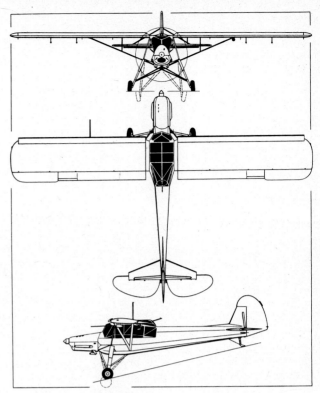

This general arrangement drawing depicts the Fi 156C-1 Storch.

was poor at this point. I derived infinite pleasure from attempting to reduce the distance taken for successive landings. The flaps were lowered 20 degrees at 74·5 mph (120 km/h) for the turn on to finals when full flap was selected and the tail trimmer set full back, an engine-assisted approach being made at 40 mph (65 km/h). On touch-down the brakes could be applied fully to produce ridiculously short landing distances, such as when, on 28 May 1946, I *literally* landed the Storch on the aft lift of the carrier HMS *Triumph!* The aircraft stayed exactly where I touched down and the flight deck crew simply folded the wings and then struck the Storch down into the hangar without having to move it an inch.

At the RAE we exploited the versatility of the Storch by using it as a consort aircraft in a series of fascinating experiments observing the airflow patterns produced by the early Sikorsky R-4B helicopter with results still regarded as classic of their kind.

How does one assess so remarkable an aeroplane? It was even by standards of today a near-unique slow flying aircraft and it certainly served the *Wehrmacht* well. It was probably easier to shoot down from the ground than from the air and

The LF 1 Zaunkönig V2 as flown by the author at Farnborough. After passing through many hands, this Zaunkönig is now registered in Eire.

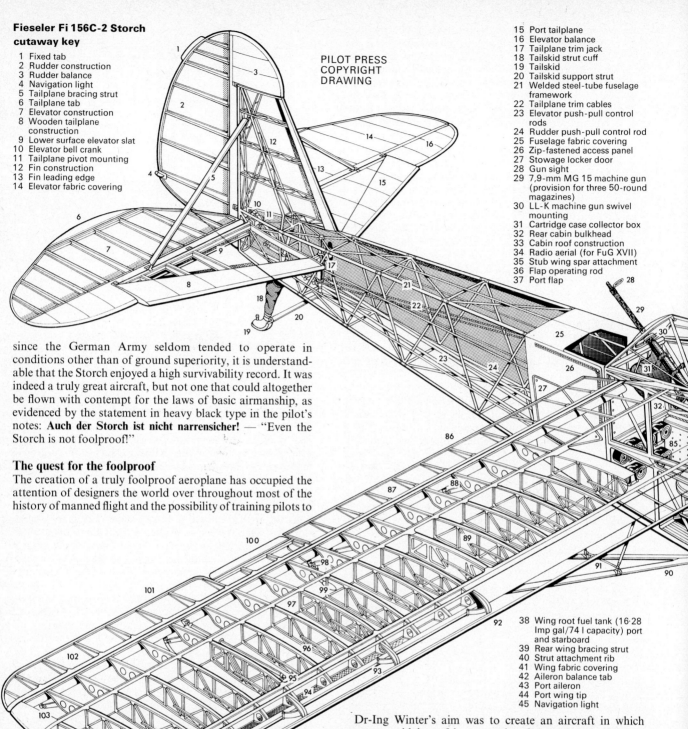

Fieseler Fi 156C-2 Storch
cutaway key

1 Fixed tab
2 Rudder construction
3 Rudder balance
4 Navigation light
5 Tailplane bracing strut
6 Tailplane tab
7 Elevator construction
8 Wooden tailplane
   construction
9 Lower surface elevator slat
10 Elevator bell crank
11 Tailplane pivot mounting
12 Fin construction
13 Fin leading edge
14 Elevator fabric covering

PILOT PRESS
COPYRIGHT
DRAWING

15 Port tailplane
16 Elevator balance
17 Tailplane trim jack
18 Tailskid strut cuff
19 Tailskid
20 Tailskid support strut
21 Welded steel-tube fuselage
   framework
22 Tailplane trim cables
23 Elevator push-pull control
   rods
24 Rudder push-pull control rod
25 Fuselage fabric covering
26 Zip-fastened access panel
27 Stowage locker door
28 Gun sight
29 7,9-mm MG 15 machine gun
   (provision for three 50-round
   magazines)
30 LL-K machine gun swivel
   mounting
31 Cartridge case collector box
32 Rear cabin bulkhead
33 Cabin roof construction
34 Radio aerial (for FuG XVII)
35 Stub wing spar attachment
36 Flap operating rod
37 Port flap

38 Wing root fuel tank (16·28
   Imp gal/74 l capacity) port
   and starboard
39 Rear wing bracing strut
40 Strut attachment rib
41 Wing fabric covering
42 Aileron balance tab
43 Port aileron
44 Port wing tip
45 Navigation light

since the German Army seldom tended to operate in conditions other than of ground superiority, it is understandable that the Storch enjoyed a high survivability record. It was indeed a truly great aircraft, but not one that could altogether be flown with contempt for the laws of basic airmanship, as evidenced by the statement in heavy black type in the pilot's notes: **Auch der Storch ist nicht narrensicher!** — "Even the Storch is not foolproof!"

The quest for the foolproof
The creation of a truly foolproof aeroplane has occupied the attention of designers the world over throughout most of the history of manned flight and the possibility of training pilots to

fly powered aircraft without dual instruction has been debated for almost as long. Henri Mignet believed mistakenly that he had created the foolproof *ab initio* single-seat trainer with the *Pou-du-ciel* and Robert Kronfeld was equally positive that his BAC Drone provided a basis for such an estimable aeroplane. In my view, the only designer to have come *really* close to achieving this objective was one Dr-Ing Hermann Winter, who, hardly by coincidence, worked on the original development of the Storch at the Fieseler Flugzeugbau.

Dr-Ing Winter's aim was to create an aircraft in which anyone could be safely sent solo after a mere half-hour's ground instruction, or five minutes in the case of anyone that had flown a glider. Pre-requisites were docility and simplicity, and the result was the LF 1 Zaunkönig built to Winter's designs by his students at the Brunswick Technical High School. A little parasol monoplane with an elliptical cross-section wooden monocoque fuselage and an angular wooden wing of 7·52 aspect ratio, the Zaunkönig was powered by a 51 hp Zündapp Z9-92 four-cylinder air-cooled engine and had full-span fixed slots, semi-span slotted flaps and drooping slotted ailerons, the latter drooping 15 degrees as the former lowered to the full 40 degrees. A tank accommodating some six Imp gal (27 l) of fuel was located immediately aft of the fireproof bulkhead.

The first prototype Zaunkönig was apparently tested in the full-scale Chalais-Meudon wind tunnel in Paris during 1943, but subsequent flight testing at the Brunswick-Waggum

75

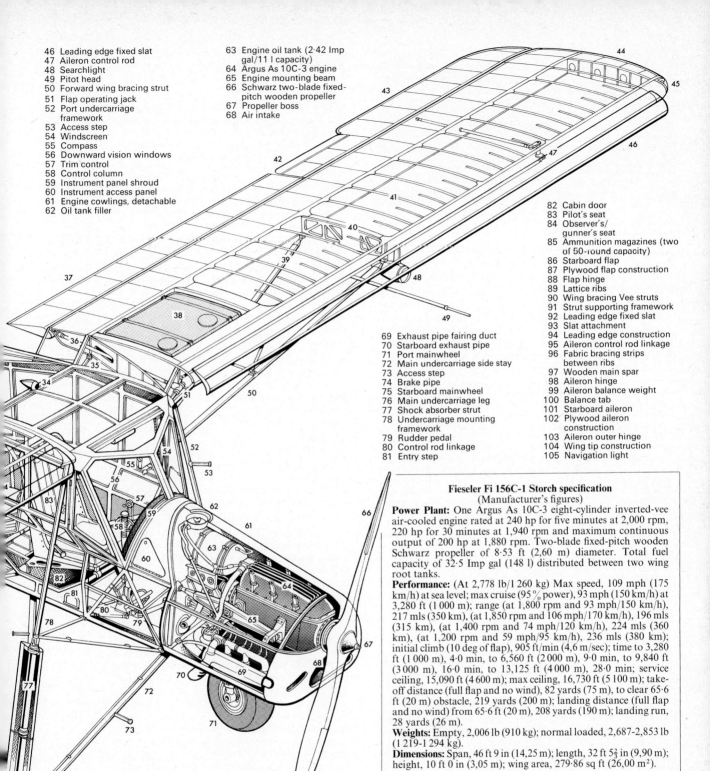

46 Leading edge fixed slat
47 Aileron control rod
48 Searchlight
49 Pitot head
50 Forward wing bracing strut
51 Flap operating jack
52 Port undercarriage framework
53 Access step
54 Windscreen
55 Compass
56 Downward vision windows
57 Trim control
58 Control column
59 Instrument panel shroud
60 Instrument access panel
61 Engine cowlings, detachable
62 Oil tank filler

63 Engine oil tank (2·42 Imp gal/11 l capacity)
64 Argus As 10C-3 engine
65 Engine mounting beam
66 Schwarz two-blade fixed-pitch wooden propeller
67 Propeller boss
68 Air intake

69 Exhaust pipe fairing duct
70 Starboard exhaust pipe
71 Port mainwheel
72 Main undercarriage side stay
73 Access step
74 Brake pipe
75 Starboard mainwheel
76 Main undercarriage leg
77 Shock absorber strut
78 Undercarriage mounting framework
79 Rudder pedal
80 Control rod linkage
81 Entry step

82 Cabin door
83 Pilot's seat
84 Observer's/gunner's seat
85 Ammunition magazines (two of 50-round capacity)
86 Starboard flap
87 Plywood flap construction
88 Flap hinge
89 Lattice ribs
90 Wing bracing Vee struts
91 Strut supporting framework
92 Leading edge fixed slat
93 Slat attachment
94 Leading edge construction
95 Aileron control rod linkage
96 Fabric bracing strips between ribs
97 Wooden main spar
98 Aileron hinge
99 Aileron balance weight
100 Balance tab
101 Starboard aileron
102 Plywood aileron construction
103 Aileron outer hinge
104 Wing tip construction
105 Navigation light

Fieseler Fi 156C-1 Storch specification
(Manufacturer's figures)

Power Plant: One Argus As 10C-3 eight-cylinder inverted-vee air-cooled engine rated at 240 hp for five minutes at 2,000 rpm, 220 hp for 30 minutes at 1,940 rpm and maximum continuous output of 200 hp at 1,880 rpm. Two-blade fixed-pitch wooden Schwarz propeller of 8·53 ft (2,60 m) diameter. Total fuel capacity of 32·5 Imp gal (148 l) distributed between two wing root tanks.

Performance: (At 2,778 lb/1 260 kg) Max speed, 109 mph (175 km/h) at sea level; max cruise (95% power), 93 mph (150 km/h) at 3,280 ft (1 000 m); range (at 1,800 rpm and 93 mph/150 km/h), 217 mls (350 km), (at 1,850 rpm and 106 mph/170 km/h), 196 mls (315 km), (at 1,400 rpm and 74 mph/120 km/h), 224 mls (360 km), (at 1,200 rpm and 59 mph/95 km/h), 236 mls (380 km); initial climb (10 deg of flap), 905 ft/min (4,6 m/sec); time to 3,280 ft (1 000 m), 4·0 min, to 6,560 ft (2 000 m), 9·0 min, to 9,840 ft (3 000 m), 16·0 min, to 13,125 ft (4 000 m), 28·0 min; service ceiling, 15,090 ft (4 600 m); max ceiling, 16,730 ft (5 100 m); take-off distance (full flap and no wind), 82 yards (75 m), to clear 65·6 ft (20 m) obstacle, 219 yards (200 m); landing distance (full flap and no wind) from 65·6 ft (20 m), 208 yards (190 m); landing run, 28 yards (26 m).

Weights: Empty, 2,006 lb (910 kg); normal loaded, 2,687-2,853 lb (1 219-1 294 kg).

Dimensions: Span, 46 ft 9 in (14,25 m); length, 32 ft 5¾ in (9,90 m); height, 10 ft 0 in (3,05 m); wing area, 279·86 sq ft (26,00 m²).

airfield was terminated abruptly when the aircraft reportedly spun in. A second prototype, the LF 1 Zaunkönig V2, was then built and completed early in 1945, the war situation dictating its evacuation to Bad Harzburg, where, with the registration D-YBAR, it is reported to have made a few flights with Dr-Ing Winter at the controls. It was eventually disassembled, crated and sent to Farnborough where I watched its re-assembly with more than passing interest as I was to make the first test flight of this little oddity, this taking place at the RAE on 18 September 1947, by which time the Zaunkönig had acquired the serial VX190.

Simplicity was the essence of the Zaunkönig, although

climbing into the cockpit called for a certain amount of dexterity owing to its close proximity to the wing, an exercise in which my modest stature was of some value. To start the little Zündapp engine, a yellow knob on the righthand side of the cockpit was pulled down and back to turn on the fuel, the throttle was then pumped three or four times until the fuel started running out, indicating that the engine was primed, and a key was inserted in the single magneto. A ground crewman then cranked the starter by hand until the engine purred into life. The fuel and oil pressure gauges were combined in a single instrument and it was only necessary to check that the needles were within the marked limitations.

The Zaunkönig was extremely simple to taxi, the view from the cockpit being good and the rudder effective. Foot brakes

(Above) The first of two postwar Zaunkönigs built in Federal Germany, this example (D-EBAR) having first flown on 28 April 1957. The Zaunkönig is illustrated by the general arrangement drawing at the foot of this column.

were fitted but tended to be too powerful for so light an aeroplane. There was no noticeable tendency to swing on take-off, the drag of the tailskid probably acting as a tailwheel lock to negate any slight slipstream effect. With the stick held just aft of neutral, the aircraft flew itself off at 45 mph (72 km/h) with flaps up and at 31 mph (50 km/h) with flaps down, the take-off distances being approximately 110 yards (100 m) and 55 yards (50 m) respectively in a 4 mph (6·5 km/h) wind. If the

---

LF 1 Zaunkönig specification

Power Plant: One Zündapp Z9-92 four-cylinder inline air-cooled engine rated at 51 hp at 2,350 rpm for take-off and driving a Schwarz two-bladed wooden propeller.
Performance: Maximum speed, 87·5 mph (141 km/h); econ cruise, 53 mph (85 km/h); initial climb, 562 ft/min (2,85 m/sec); approx service ceiling, 12,550 ft (3 820 m); range, 218 mls (350 km); take-off speed (flaps up) 45 mph (72 km/h), (flaps down), 31 mph (50 km/h); landing speed (engine off), (flaps up) 44 mph (71 km/h), (flaps down), 37 mph (60 km/h).
Weights: Empty, 553 lb (251 kg); max loaded, 776 lb (355 kg).
Dimensions: Span, 26 ft 4¾ in (8,02 m); length, 19 ft 10½ in (6,08 m); height, 7 ft 10¼ in (2,38 m); wing area, 91·38 sq ft (8,49 m²).

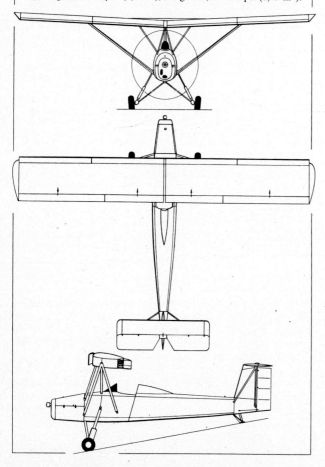

aircraft was *pulled* off it unstuck at 42 mph (67 km/h) and 30 mph (48 km/h). When take-off was effected with the flaps fully depressed, the mainwheels seemed to unstick first and then, when the aircraft became completely airborne, it did so at a steep angle of attack and a fair amount of forward pressure had to be applied to the stick in order to assume a comfortable climbing attitude.

There were no trimmers on the Zaunkönig, but a climb speed of 47 mph (75 km/h) at 1,850 rpm gave a comfortable attitude with only a slight pull force, this having to be maintained at its cruising speed of 53 mph (85 km/h) at 1,700 rpm. Harmony of control was good in manoeuvring, and stick free stability was laterally neutral and directionally positive, with controls centering rapidly after release. A dive to the maximum permissible speed of 99 mph (160 km/h) revealed a need for a slight pull force in order to hold the speed, while a dive to the limiting speed of 74·5 mph (120 km/h) with flaps down called for a fair push force. No vibration or buffeting was apparent at these speeds.

The Zaunkönig could not be stalled normally. With flaps up, a steady rate of descent was maintained at a minimum speed of 38 mph (61 km/h) and with flaps wound down at 31 mph (50 km/h). In each case, the rate of descent seemed very small and probably reasonable enough to permit a heavy landing to be made straight from it. The elevator was the heaviest of the three controls, but only heavied up slightly with speed as did also the ailerons which were extremely light up to 62 mph (100 km/h) and remained effective at all speeds. The rudder, too, was extremely light, but was rather ineffective at low speeds.

Landing was extremely simple and straightforward. Approach speeds with engine off of 47 mph (75 km/h) with flaps up and 40 mph (65 km/h) with flaps down allowed sufficiently for the rate of sink to be checked easily and touch-down occurred at 3 mph (5 km/h) below approach speed. There was no tendency to bounce as the long-stroke undercarriage absorbed the rebound energy fully, and the Zaunkönig had no tendency to swing after touching down. During landing there was a marked increase in lift as the flaps were depressed and this was not just an impression imparted by the nose-up change of trim, and the spring-loaded throttle lever tended to open itself unless the friction nut was screwed up fairly tightly.

Did Dr-Ing Winter achieve his objective with the Zaunkönig? In essence I would say that he did, although I would have always had qualms about sending off a complete beginner after only half-an-hour's ground instruction. I actually did send off a very famous aerodynamicist on his first solo in the Zaunkönig, but he had had already had two or three hours dual in a Miles Magister and I therefore had not the slightest worry about his safety. It is just as well that the Zaunkönig *was* a safe little aeroplane as the aerodynamicist concerned now leads the UK's Concorde team!

At a point in time other than the vacuum left by a world war, the Zaunkönig *could* have revolutionised private flying in Europe and have succeeded where the *Pou-du-ciel* failed. Sadly, Dr-Ing Winter's delightful little creation appeared at the wrong time and only two more examples were to be built, these being D-EBAR flown on 28 April 1957 and D-ECER flown in the following October. In so far as VX190 (alias D-YBAR) was concerned, after we had finished with it at Farnborough it was sold to R W Clegg and used by the Ultra Light Association as G-ALUA. It subsequently passed through a number of hands, going to P J Sullivan at Denham in 1966, and to Vintage Aircraft Flying Limited in 1969, seeing much flying. Later in 1969, it was completely rebuilt by M Loyal and resumed its career at Fairoaks in 1971, passing in the following year to Fairoaks Aviation Services with whom it remained until May 1974, when it resumed its travels, going to Commander Jet Sales of Kilkenny in Eire where it remains to this day as EI-AYU. □

Trends? What trends?

A DAY OR SO before these words were penned, the editor voiced his assumption that, with another year tottering to its close, we would this month be surveying the eleven that have preceded it in so far as the modelling scene has been concerned and metaphorically dabble in a little crystal gazing by indicating the trends. After ruminating for a while on the likelihood of the next plane to be hijacked and the chances of getting the editor aboard, we browsed through the last half-score-and-one editions of *Model Enthusiast* to refresh our memories and to see if any trends were readily discernible. A nauseating occupation do we hear someone comment? OK, so our prose may not scintillate . . . but then, who reads this column for its literary style?

An hour's browsing and four cups of unsweetened coffee later — kicking this sugar thing really should have been one of *next* year's resolutions — we had a reasonable picture of what had gone on in the year past, but as for trends . . . nary a one! Apart from the fact that kit prices have been slowly escalating — and that will hardly come as news to any modeller, unless he happens to have passed the year ensconced in a monastery or detained at Her Majesty's pleasure — no indication of what may be expected in the year ahead immediately presented itself. A quick round of our half-dozen tame kit stockists produced as many contradictory opinions regarding sales trends and as for the manufacturers, well, from past experience we knew that everything would come up smelling of roses.

So where did that leave us? Could we conclude that the modelling world, or at least that portion of it concerned with the plastic aircraft kit, had merely maintained some sort of *status quo* during this year of grace nineteen hundred and seventy-six? A total of 66 new kits had passed across our workbench during the course of the year as compared with 71 in the previous twelve months — a drop of seven per cent but hardly a trend towards fewer new issues if we take into account the fact that not *all* kits are submitted to us for review. Admittedly, the proportion of vac-forms among these kits *seemed* to have risen from approximately 20 to no less than 35 per cent, but this *could* have been accounted for by better distribution, and lack of distribution might account for the substantially fewer kits — eleven as compared with 21 — received from Japan. France, Italy and Czechoslovakia have all made significant contributions, as they did in the preceding year, and the output of kits from the USA has remained depressingly low, while the major British producers have been level-pegging with their previous year's output as regards individual aircraft types portrayed in kit form — the size of the production runs

on these kits is as closely guarded a secret as next year's Paris fashions. The ratio of kits of one scale to those of another, too, has remained virtually unchanged with 1/72nd scale retaining its dominant position and accounting for some 80 per cent of all new kits issued, with 1/48th and 1/32nd trailing far behind with five each, and, at the opposite ends of the scale range, 1/24th and 1/144th having one and two to their credit respectively.

So what's new? At first sight, nothing; but then a little cogitation over the actual aircraft types represented by the kits issued over the past year *revealed* a trend — the proportion of types never previously available in kit form to those considered as *standards* has risen dramatically! No less than 70 per cent come into this much-desired category, a fact which must surely warm the cockles of any serious modeller's heart. Some of these new issues have been, by kit manufacturer's standards if not those of the modeller, decidedly off-beat, and we can only hope that the sales response has been sufficient to encourage these more adventurous companies and ensure that this highly desirable trend is maintained through 1977. It is nice to have updated *standards,* but such are unlikely to start the true modeller's adrenalin flowing as rapidly as entirely original ventures.

Super Stuka

It has been our privilege to review many fine kits over the past years, but with Airfix's 1/24th scale kit of the Junkers Ju 87B-2 we are willing to metaphorically stick our neck out and say this is *the* finest! Of course this kit is impressive, if only on the score of size and complexity, but it is in finish and accuracy that Airfix has excelled and the prodigious research, tooling and production effort that has spanned some two years has, in our view, borne fruit in the finest plastic model aircraft kit yet produced anywhere! If Father Christmas, Papa Noël, St Nicholas, or whatever you happen to call that red-coated white-bearded character in your neck of the woods, does not drop liberal quantities of *this* kit down modellers' chimneys during that certain night, well, I for one will never hang up my stocking again. No modeller worthy of his salt will be able to resist this one, regardless of normal scale preferences.

Airfix has captured every nuance of the relatively complex contours of this evil-looking warplane that Dipl-Ing Hermann Pohlmann created at Dessau four-score-and-two years ago; contours that have perhaps never been captured in their entirety by a plastic model until now. No warplane has ever enjoyed greater notoriety or aroused greater controversy and it was to be expected that it would provide an obvious choice of subject

matter for kit manufacturers throughout the world. Many have been the kits and various the scales, and when Revell offered the angularly ugly Junkers in 1/32nd scale it seemed that the ultimate had been reached, but even that sterling effort pales into something approaching insignificance beside this Airfix kit.

Spanning 1 ft 10⅝ in (57,47 cm) and possessing an overall length of 1 ft 6¼ in (46,35 cm), this kit comprises no less than 344 component parts, plus a stand, so if at first you balk at the UK retail price of £6·29, just think what is being offered for this admittedly substantial hunk of change. Other than the transparencies and tyres, the parts are all moulded in pale blue plastic — an excellent match for the *hellblau* of the *Luftwaffe* — and all the external surfaces have a most realistic matt finish. We really cannot see how the surface detailing could possibly be improved upon; every panel line is neatly engraved or embossed, as appropriate, and perfectly in scale. In fact, the only surface faults that we could find were two very small sinkings, close together just ahead of and below the pilot's windscreen on the port side, which call for a little filling.

The fuselage halves include the fin and the engine bearers, and these, despite their size, are a perfect fit. The interior of the cockpit embodies virtually everything that could be embodied and all items are correctly modelled to type. For example, the tubular framing and swivel base of the gunner's seat, the instrument panel with a clear plastic insert to represent the instruments and the gun sight with its clear lens. It is pointless to list everything, but one thing is certain, the super-detail *buffs* will have their homework cut out finding anything to add to this one!

The Junkers Jumo 211Da 12-cylinder liquid-cooled engine is a model within a model. It can be fitted with a small electric motor (not, incidentally, included in the kit) to drive the propeller, and should the model be so motorised, a simplified model of the Jumo engine can be made. The propeller has separate blades, a two-piece hub and a two-piece spinner. The rudder incorporates three tiny, separate hinges and is moveable, as are also the elevators.

By the time the fuselage halves are ready to be cemented together, one has assembled around 130 parts and the inclusion of everything will have called for a modicum of care, but so good is the design of this kit and so precise the mouldings that everything fits like a dream. The gulled sections of the wings are separate from the outer panels, and the flaps and ailerons of the typical Junkers "double wing" are all separately moulded, with finely detailed brackets and actuating rods. Removeable panels in the wing upper surfaces give access to the gun bays, and there is a landing light inside a transparent cover in the leading edge of the port wing.

A choice of bomb cradles for either 551-lb (250-kg) or 1,102-lb (500-kg) bombs is provided for the ventral position and these swing out and down to clear the propeller disc. The bombs are excellent, each having separate fins and fin bracings, and there are also four 110-lb (50-kg) bombs for mounting on wing racks which have separate shackles. The mainwheel tyres are black soft-vinyl mouldings, properly treaded and very realistic. The wheels revolve and the tailwheel castors. An interesting feature of the undercarriage is the slipstream-driven dive-bombing siren — which had such a shattering psychological effect on the recipients of the attention of the full-scale original — which is an optional fitment and has a revolving propeller. The five-piece canopy is beautifully clear and has internal bracing in the centre portion; the pilot's canopy slides and there are alternative machine gun mountings to cater for the model employed during the "Battle of Britain" and the tropicalised version. There are also variations in the air intakes and filters.

The instruction booklet is fully comprehensive with regard to every aspect of construction and finish, and includes four-view colour drawings of two schemes: a Ju 87B-2 of 3./StG 2 based at St Malo/Lannion in August 1940, and a Ju 87B-2/trop of 3./StG 1 based at Derna, Libya, in the following year. All of the necessary markings are included on the large, matt-finished decal sheet.

In our book, this is the kit of the year and while our little crystal ball does not show any sign that this "Super Stuka" will launch a trend towards larger and more complex kits of this nature (nor, for that matter, does it indicate that the Managing Editor will be more liberal with the largesse this Christmas), it has made modelling history and given 1976 some significance in modelling annals.

This month's colour subject

For some inexplicable reason, the long-range maritime patrol aircraft lacks *glamour*, or so the principal model kit manufacturers — who link this indefinable quality with commercial viability — would have us believe. Thus, this ever-more-vital item in the inventories of the major air forces fares poorly at their hands — we would give our back teeth to see a 1/72nd scale kit of the Nimrod! Even Lockheed's P-3 Orion, the world's most *widely-used* maritime patrol aircraft, has failed to establish itself in the favours of those grey eminences that determine kit subject matter, yet, on the score of ubiquity if nothing else, one might assume that this warplane would be an important item in the lists of several kit producers.

In so far as the Orion is concerned, there is at least *one* kit of this type on the market, however, but sadly its odd scale will put it right out of court for the modeller priding himself on his adherence to constant scale. Indeed, this kit is to a *very* odd scale, namely 1/110th, and do not be misled by the accompanying instruction leaflet claiming 1/144th scale, for the model's wing span comes out at $10\frac{13}{16}$ in (276 mm) against the full-scale machine's 99 ft 8 in (30,37 m) and unless our pocket calculator has gone on the blink . . .! This kit originates, of course, from the Revell company and stems indirectly from the bad old days before it realised that the constant-scale principle, wisely adopted from the outset by such firms as Airfix and Frog, was the real basis for success in producing model kits. Revell had produced a kit of the Lockheed Electra and emulated Lockheed, which used the Electra as a basis for the Orion, in that it re-worked the Electra kit to produce an Orion, but was naturally unable to change the scale in the process.

For those modellers willing to accept such an off-beat scale, the kit provides at least a reasonable representation of the P-3A Orion, both in outline and external detail, and conversion to the P-3B or P-3C versions is a relatively simple matter. The surface detailing on the model is quite acceptable, although there are lots of rivets which could well have been omitted from a large aeroplane such as this — they are not *too* obtrusive but will benefit from being lightly rubbed-down. A major cause for complaint, however, is Revell's failure to provide a transparency for the flight deck, leaving just empty apertures where the windows should be. Any modeller worth his salt can rectify this omission, but lack of a transparency as a component of the kit is inexcusable in this day and age.

The fit of the component parts is really very good and assembly presents no problems. A full undercarriage is included but plenty of weight should be added in the nose in order to balance the tail — a supporting stand is provided but this does not look very elegant. There are seven underwing stores pylons, but nothing to hang from these, and a searchlight pod is provided for mounting beneath the starboard wing. Currently available in the UK at around 90p, this kit has its shortcomings but nevertheless gives a reasonable impression of the Orion and, unless the kit manufacturers undergo a change of heart towards the maritime patrol aircraft, it would seem that we are unlikely to be presented with a better kit of this particular aircraft type in the near future.

A feline chopper

There have previously been two 1/72nd scale kits of the Westland-Aérospatiale Lynx helicopter and these had two major features in common; they both represented prototypes and they both offered alternative parts for the versions for the British Army and Royal Navy — these kits were, in fact, discussed in the April issue when both the Army and Navy production versions were illustrated in colour. Unlike Frog and Lesney, the manufacturers of the two previously-mentioned kits, Airfix has bided its time and has now offered a kit of the genuine production article while confining itself to the Army version only. On balance, we feel that Airfix has been wise, but it is generally accepted that the market for helicopter kits falls somewhat short of that for fixed-wing aircraft and only time will tell if Frog and Lesney, with their earlier offerings, have creamed off the bulk of the sales potential. At least, the Airfix kit renders the competition obsolescent.

Included in Series 3, the kit comprises 97 component parts moulded in olive drab plastic, and is both accurate and meticulously detailed, many of the parts being extremely delicate. Surface detailing is as fine as could be desired and the cabin interior would seem to be virtually as complete as scale considerations allow, including floor, controls, console, instrument panel, missile sight, pilots' and troop seats, and a rear bulkhead. There are also two well-sculptured figures. There is much fine detailing in the rotorhead, there are 12 parts for the main rotor and the blades have the correct contours. There are 11 very clear transparencies, each window being separate and calling for careful assembly and neat cementing to ensure that clarity is not marred by excess cement.

The armament comprises six launching tubes for anti-armour missiles grouped three per side on realistic racks. We like the realistic fashion in which both doors slide and the way in which the landing skids are mounted on four separate panels fitted into the underside of the fuselage. For those modellers intent on having the naval version, which, incidentally, officially entered Royal Navy service on 17 September with the formation of No 700L Squadron at RNAS Yeovilton, it will no doubt be possible to utilise parts from either the Frog or the Lesney kit, but this will undoubtedly be a fairly complex operation and we have not considered the possibilities in any detail.

The decal sheet accompanying the kit offers markings for two machines but these differ only in their serial numbers, and the camouflage scheme is given as drab olive green and black — a scheme finally chosen by the Army after some vacillation and since the preparation of the drawings that appeared in this column in April — which will be sported by the first Lynx AH Mk 1s when they roll off the Yeovil assembly line early in the New Year. This is, without doubt, a very good kit and, in so far as the UK is concerned, reasonably priced at 62p.

A larger Natter

The Bachem BP-20 Natter (Adder), or Ba 349, would seem to hold some fascination for the designers of vac-forms, for, having previously been presented with two different vac-forms of this type to 1/72nd scale, Horizon Conversions of Malton, Ontario, now offers this venomous little brute — a semi-expendable piloted *missile* — to 1/48th scale. Priced at Can$3·50, this is a neatly-formed and accurate kit consisting of 18 parts, including a transparent nose cap but, surprisingly, no cockpit canopy, the cockpit having to be glazed with parts cut from a piece of transparent material included — the windscreen and other panels are flat so the method is certainly practicable, but we do consider that a moulded canopy *should* have been included.

Assembly is quite simple provided that spars are made for the wings and tailplane to impart the necessary strength, and it would be wise, also, to insert a couple of bulkheads in the fuselage. Alternative ventral fins are included in the mistaken belief that this permits either the early *Versuchs* Natters or the production Ba 349A to be built — there were, in fact, various other changes to the upper tail surfaces and the elevons — but this makes an attractive modelling subject and this larger scale for so tiny an aircraft is certainly preferable. The instructions include a good four-view drawing of the Natter and also, for those desirous of mounting the aircraft in a realistic setting, full drawings of the vertical launching tower.

Decals for the DC-4

Following upon the recent release of Rareplane's kit for the Douglas DC-4 (reviewed in this column last month) we have now received samples of the three sets of decals produced by Airline Publications and Sales specifically for the kit. Priced at £1·25 each, plus postage, these decals are silk screen printed and include the windows and doors. Of first class quality and colour, and in superlative register, these sheets provide the markings of a Capital Airlines DC-4 in red, white and pale blue, a DC-4M in the light and dark blue livery of British Midland Airways and a C-54 of the USAF's Military Air Transport Service, Pacific Division, with dark blue cheat lines, blue-and-yellow logos and various other decorations. □   F J HENDERSON

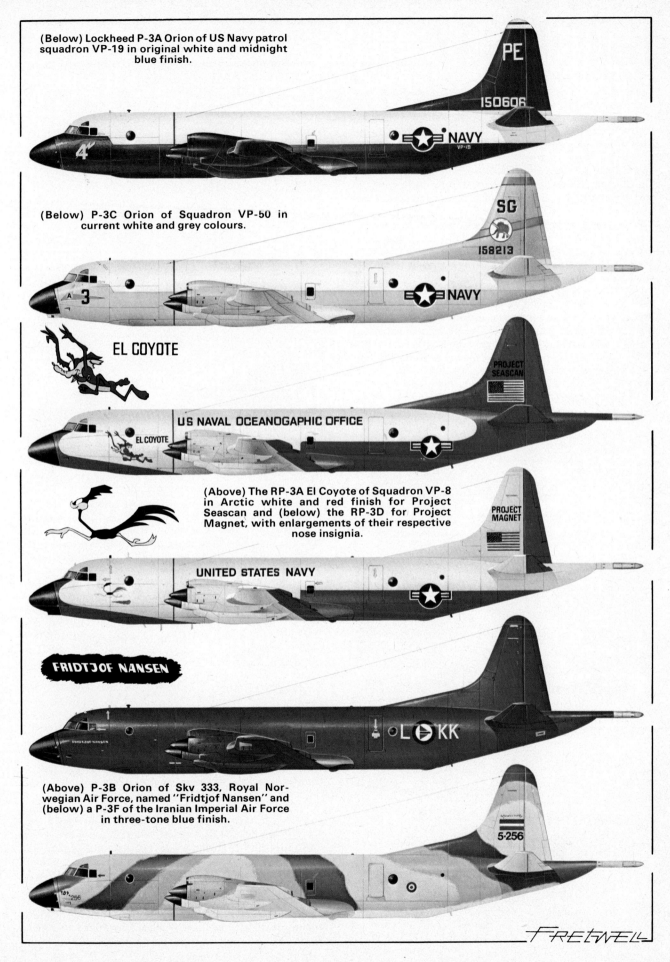

(Below) Lockheed P-3A Orion of US Navy patrol squadron VP-19 in original white and midnight blue finish.

(Below) P-3C Orion of Squadron VP-50 in current white and grey colours.

EL COYOTE

US NAVAL OCEANOGAPHIC OFFICE

PROJECT SEASCAN

(Above) The RP-3A El Coyote of Squadron VP-8 in Arctic white and red finish for Project Seascan and (below) the RP-3D for Project Magnet, with enlargements of their respective nose insignia.

PROJECT MAGNET

UNITED STATES NAVY

FRIDTJOF NANSEN

(Above) P-3B Orion of Skv 333, Royal Norwegian Air Force, named "Fridtjof Nansen" and (below) a P-3F of the Iranian Imperial Air Force in three-tone blue finish.

FRETWELL

FIGHTER A TO Z

CURTISS XP-60C(E)　　　　　　　　　USA

Ordered simultaneously with the XP-60A, the XP-60C was intended to have a Chrysler XIV-2220 16-cylinder engine of 2,300 hp but studies revealed that several hundred pounds of lead would have to be installed in the tail as ballast in order to avoid total fuselage re-design and as the status of the XIV-2220 engine was questionable, in August 1942 it was proposed that a Pratt & Whitney R-2800 18-cylinder air-cooled radial should be substituted. The potential performance of this model was such that, in November 1942, a letter contract was prepared covering 500 R-2800-powered P-60A-1 fighters. The XP-60C was flown on 27 January 1943 with a 2,000 hp R-2800-53 engine driving contra-rotating propellers, and as it appeared that the contraprops and necessary gearing would be unavailable for production aircraft, the XP-60B (originally intended for an Allison V-1710-75 engine with a Wright SU-504-2 turbo-supercharger) was modified before completion to take an R-2800-10 engine of similar power driving a four-bladed propeller, thus providing a direct comparison with the XP-60C installation, the former XP-60B being redesignated XP-60E. Owing to the lighter propeller installation of the XP-60E, it was found necessary to move the engine 10 in (25,40 cm) forward by comparison with that of the XP-60C. The XP-60E flew on 26 May 1943, but three months later, on 14 August,

(Above) The XP-60C with contra-rotating propellers and R-2800-53 engine was otherwise essentially similar to the XP-60A (see Fighter A to Z/November).

The YP-60E (above and below) brought the Curtiss P-60 series to a close, only two flight tests being conducted before development was abandoned.

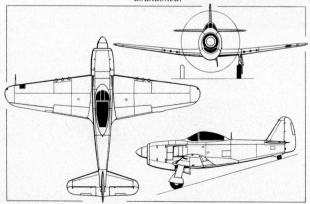

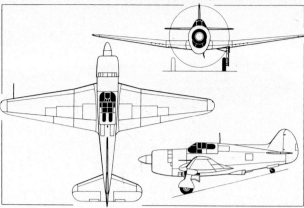

The XP-62 (above and below) bore no relationship to the P-60 series other than a common design origin and was an appreciably larger and heavier fighter.

just prior to scheduled release to the AAF for official trials, the prototype was damaged in a forced landing. Curtiss was then asked to remove the -53 engine and contraprops from the XP-60C and install a -10 engine with four-bladed propeller, the XP-60C thus becoming an XP-60E, while repair of the original XP-60E with the wings, undercarriage and other items from the XP-60A and the installation of a -53 engine and contraprops turned this into an XP-60C. The following data relate to the XP-60C. Max speed, 414 mph (666 km/h) at 20,350 ft (6 205 m). Initial climb, 3,890 ft/min (19,75 m/sec). Empty weight, 8,600 lb (3 901 kg). Loaded weight, 10,525 lb (4 777 kg). Span, 41 ft 4 in (12,60 m). Length, 33 ft 11 in (10,34 m). Height, 12 ft 6 in (3,81 m). Wing area, 275 sq ft (25,55 m²).

CURTISS YP-60E　　　　　　　　　　USA

In May 1944, Curtiss indicated to the AAF that it wished to abandon further work on the P-60 series fighters owing to the disappointing results achieved with the XP-60C and XP-60E. Earlier, the P-60 had been eliminated from the production schedules, the aircraft previously contracted for having been reduced to two. However, the AAF insisted on completion of one of the two aircraft still on contract, these, originally ordered as YP-60As, having been redesignated as YP-60Es owing to the fact that the design modifications incorporated were most directly descended from the XP-60E. The YP-60E differed from the XP-60E principally in having a 2,100 hp R-2800-18 engine, a deeper cowling incorporating the ventral cooler intake, a cut-down rear fuselage and a bubble-type cockpit canopy. The sole YP-60E completed was flown on 13 July 1944, but only one further test was flown before the aircraft was transferred to Wright Field where it was eventually disposed of without further testing. Armament comprised six wing-mounted 0·5-in (12,7-mm) machine guns. Max speed, 405 mph (652 km/h) at 24,500 ft (7 465 m). Initial climb, 4,200 ft/min (21,33 m/sec). Empty weight, 8,285 lb (3 758 kg). Loaded weight, 10,270 lb (4 658 kg). Span, 41 ft 4 in (12,60 m). Length, 33 ft 11 in (10,34 m). Height, 12 ft 6 in (3,81 m). Wing area, 275 sq ft (22,55 m²).

CURTISS XP-62   USA

At the beginning of 1941, design work was initiated on a heavily-armed high-performance fighter featuring a pressure cabin and powered by the 18-cylinder two-row Wright R-3350 radial engine with an exhaust-driven turbo-supercharger and driving a six-bladed contraprop. Continuous revision of the specification seriously delayed the programme and a letter contract for 100 P-62s approved on 25 May 1942 was terminated two months later, the first flight test of the XP-62 not taking place until 21 July 1943, owing to non-availability of the pressure cabin, one of the first such installations in an interceptor fighter. Initial trials were conducted, in the event, without the pressure cabin, and although a decision to install this was taken in February 1944, the XP-62 was assigned low priority and the sole prototype was scrapped in the autumn of 1944, before pressure cabin installation was completed. The proposed armament comprised four or eight 20-mm cannon, but no guns were installed and flight testing was insufficient to secure full performance characteristics, the following data being based on manufacturer's estimates. Max speed, 448 mph (721 km/h) at 27,000 ft (8 230 m), 358 mph (576 km/h) at 5,000 ft (1 525 m). Normal range, 900 mls (1 448 km). Time to 15,000 ft (4 570 m), 6·9 min. Empty weight, 11,773 lb (5 340 kg). Normal loaded weight, 14,660 lb (6 622 kg). Span, 53 ft 7¾ in (16,35 m). Length, 39 ft 6 in (12,04 m). Height, 16 ft 3 in (4,95 m). Wing area, 420 sq ft (39,02 m²).

CURTISS XF14C-2   USA

On 30 June 1941, Curtiss received a prototype development contract for the XF14C-1 single-seat shipboard fighter designed around the 2,200 hp Lycoming XH-2470-4 liquid-cooled engine, but at a relatively early stage in the programme the unsatisfactory state of development of the Lycoming engine led to the redesign of the fighter to accept an 18-cylinder two-row Wright R-3350 as the XF14C-2, this engine driving a

The XF14C-2 (above and below) was abandoned owing to its failure to meet specified performance and the difficulties experienced in eradicating excessive vibration.

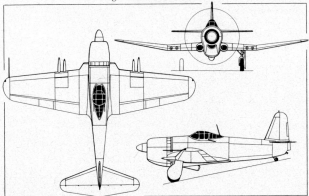

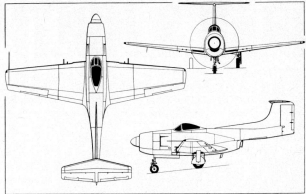

The general arrangement drawing above depicts the XF15C-1 in its definitive form and the photograph below illustrates the first prototype with the H-1B installed.

six-blade contraprop. Powered by an XR-3350-16 engine rated at 2,300 hp and carrying an armament of four 20-mm cannon, the XF14C-2 was flown for the first time in July 1944. Performance proved to be substantially below that specified and the prototype suffered excessive vibration. In consequence, further development of the XF14C-2 was abandoned. Max speed, 380 mph (611 km/h) at 20,000 ft (6 095 m), 392 mph (630 km/h) at 32,000 ft (9 755 m). Range, 1,355 mls (2 180 km) at 162 mph (261 km/h). Time to 20,000 ft (6 095 m), 7·9 min. Empty weight, 10,582 lb (4 800 kg). Normal loaded weight, 13,405 lb (6 084 kg). Span, 46 ft 0 in (14,02 m). Length, 37 ft 9 in (11,51 m). Height, 12 ft 4 in (3,76 m). Wing area, 375 sq ft (34,84 m²).

CURTISS XF15C-1   USA

US Navy interest in the mixed-power concept for shipboard fighters — aircraft employing a piston engine for cruise and an auxiliary turbojet to provide supplementary power for take-off, climb and maximum speed — which had resulted in orders for three prototypes of the Ryan XFR-1 and 100 production FR-1s, was taken a stage further on 7 April 1944 with the placing with Curtiss of a contract for three prototypes of the appreciably more powerful XF15C-1 which was to be powered by a 2,100 hp Pratt & Whitney R-2800-34W 18-cylinder two-row radial and a 2,700 lb (1 226 kg) Allis-Chalmers J36 (Halford H-1B) turbojet. Armament was to comprise four wing-mounted 20-mm cannon. The first XF15C-1 was flown on 27 February 1945 without the turbojet installed, this being fitted by April but the aircraft being lost on 8 May when it crashed during a landing approach. The second XF15C-1 flew on 9 July 1945 and was joined soon after by the third, both subsequently having their low-set horizontal tail surfaces replaced by a T-tail arrangement. The flight test programme continued until October 1946, by which time the US Navy had lost interest in the mixed power arrangement and cancelled further development. Max speed, 432 mph (695 km/h) at sea level, 469 mph (755 km/h) at 25,000 ft (7 715 m). Initial climb, 5,020 ft/min (25,5 m/sec). Range, 1,385 mls (2 228 km). Empty weight, 12,648 lb (5 742 kg). Normal loaded weight, 16,630 lb (7 550 kg). Span, 48 ft 0 in (14,64 m). Length, 44 ft 0 in (13,42 m). Height, 15 ft 3 in (4,65 m). Wing area, 400 sq ft (37,16 m²).

IRAN'S MULTI-MISSION 707S

T HE Iranian Imperial Air Force, still in the midst of a major expansion programme that will make it among the World's largest and most potently-equipped by the end of the present decade, has recently added a unique type of tanker/transport to its inventory. Although Boeing 707 tankers were first delivered to the IIAF as long ago as 1974, they were initially fitted only with "flying boom" refuelling equipment, as used by the USAF and compatible with the Iranian McDonnell Douglas F-4E Phantom, 177 of which have been delivered. The installation of the "flying boom" on what was basically a commercial Boeing 707 airframe was itself unique, since the only other users of the equipment operated only the slightly smaller KC-135 tankers (the USAF and the *Armée de l'Air*) or the KC-97 (USAF and Spain's *Ejército del Aire*). However, the more recent decision of the IIAF to acquire Grumman F-14 Tomcats posed a problem in that these aircraft were intended for the probe-and-drogue refuelling system favoured by the US Navy.

To meet this additional requirement, the IIAF has ordered the installation of Beech Model 1080 hose-and-drogue refuelling pods under each wing tip of its Boeing 707s, this applying both to those aircraft already delivered and others still in production. An initial order for six Model 707-3J9Cs was placed by the IIAF in September 1973 after protracted negotiations, and a second batch of six was ordered early in 1975; it is believed that another three have been ordered subsequently. Boeing conducted flight tests of a 707 with the wing-tip Beech stores from the USN Patuxent River facility in May of this year, to check compatibility with the F-14, and an example of the dual mode tanker made its first public appearance at Farnborough International in September. (Two Boeing 707s operated by the Canadian Armed Forces were modified in 1971 to carry similar Beech pods, to refuel Canadair CF-5s, but do not have the "flying boom").

In addition to their unique ability to refuel other aircraft by either of the two accepted methods, the Boeing 707-3J9Cs have numerous other special features. Fuel capacity in the fuselage has been increased by 5,000 US gal (18 925 l) to a total of more than 28,000 US gal (109 008 l) and advanced military mission electronics for communications, navigation and refuelling rendezvous is installed. The aircraft are fitted with the standard cargo door of the commercial 707-320C, measuring 11 ft by 7·6 ft (3,4 m by 2,3 m), and have a cargo tie-down and net system to allow up to 13 freight pallets to be carried.

The wing-tip pods can be removed when refuelling missions are not being flown and Boeing is supplying kits to provide the IIAF 707s with full passenger capability or executive interiors. The flying boom and operator's station do not intrude onto the main deck and are retained at all times.

In addition to its fleet of Boeing 707s, the IIAF is in course of taking delivery of 12 Boeing 747s, purchased second-hand in the commercial market. An unspecified number of these aircraft is also being fitted with flying boom equipment and extra fuel tanks in the lower cargo holds, while some others are being fitted with in-flight refuelling receptacles above and behind the cockpit. □

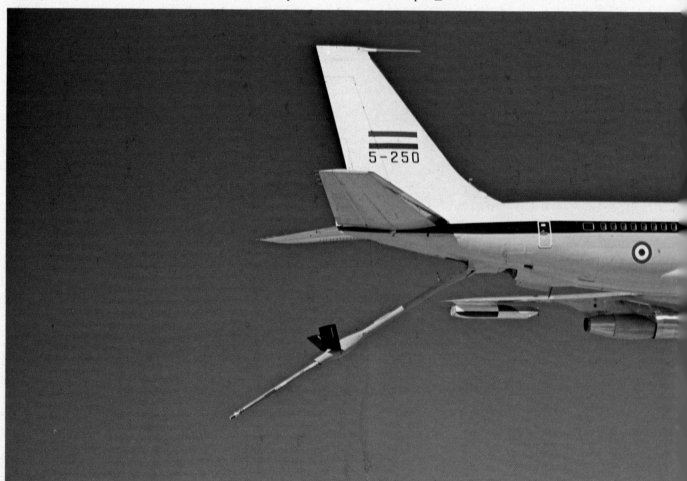

aircraft under 1,000 lb (454 kg) empty weight. In 1934, at Miami, Wright set an official world speed record of 169·9 mph (273,37 km/h) with a passenger, and that autumn he and co-pilot John Polande, from Lynn, Mass, took the 'coupe (now sporting an attractive new red-white-blue paint job and the name *Baby Ruth*) to London for the epic Mac-Robertson London-to-Melbourne Race. They failed to finish after being jailed by Persian police as a result of a misunderstanding.

Back home, Wright loaned the Monocoupe to Helen MacCloskey, of Pittsburgh, Pa. In January 1935, Miss MacCloskey averaged 166·67 mph (268,17 km/h) over the 100-km Miami closed course to set a women's lightplane speed record. Shortly afterward, Wright sold NC501W to Ruth Barron who was fated to be the first to die in a Clipwing.

A hard-charging, 25-year-old aviatrix "of good family" from upstate New York, Miss Barron painted out the *Baby* and added *Barron*, presumably in anticipation of new conquests. She never found them; a chain smoker, she is believed to have ignited the nitrate dope in the aircraft's finish with a cigarette. In any event, she had not owned it long when it caught fire in the airport traffic pattern at Omaha, Nebraska, only the fire-blackened metal parts surviving to be dug out of the soft earth by a local mechanic, who stored them in a corner of his shop, where they gathered dust for 25 years. Then James P Heim of Saugus, California, himself confined to a wheelchair as a result of an earlier landing accident in a Monocoupe, began the laborious task of tracking down NC501W's paperwork and parts.

He succeeded, bought title from the last surviving Barron heir, rebuilt the aeroplane, installed hand controls and successfully flew the Clipwing from a 30-foot (9,15 m) wide paved runway. He even did some aerobatics with it. But, knowing it was "only a matter of time," as he puts it, he finally sold NC501W. "I've been sick about it ever since," he adds. He sold it, of course, to Al Allin, the skinny lad who had been so impressed by Ron Kendall and NC2347!

Second to die in a Clipwing was Leonard Peterson, famed in the 'thirties as an airshow and racing pilot and an ordained Presbyterian minister — killed in October 1941, while doing his air show routine at Richmond, Virginia. Peterson had a stunt which involved touching his wheels on the runway, then pulling straight up for a vertical roll. This time, something happened, and he went almost straight into the runway. Peterson was flung through the skylight as the aircraft tumbled down the runway, tearing itself to bits. That aeroplane, laboriously rebuilt, flies today as N606G, owned by John Glatz of St Charles, Illinois.

(Above) An early Monocoupe with Le Blond engine and (below) a standard Warner-engined Model 90AW.

Originally a conversion from a stock Model 110, made especially for society sportsman Reginald "Pete" Brooks of Long Island, this Special had been completed in the spring of 1936 as NC2064 and dubbed *Spirit of Dynamite* by its owner. Brooks, an occasional Monocoupe salesman among the Country Club set, was enthused about the Clipwing, but did not keep it long. Caught in a flood and under water for several days, NC2064 was traded back to the factory by Brooks for the one-off 90AW, powered by a 90 hp Warner engine (significantly, the 90AW cruised at only 115 mph/185 km/h, but landed at a much more comfortable 45 mph/72 km/h, down from the Special's 75 mph/121 km/h). At the factory, workman hacksawed open every fuselage tube at mid-bay to drain the water out of the Special, then welded them back together. NC2064 remained in factory hands for nearly two years as a demonstrator, until Peterson flew it to victory in a famous head-to-head dual with a similarly-powered Dart G fielded by wealthy aviation backer Knight K Culver, who inherited both Al Mooney and the Dart when then-Monocoupe President Clare W Bunch elected to drop production of the low-wing model that it had launched as the Monosport, only five of which were built. The photo-finish not only won Peterson the race but permanent possession of the Clipwing, and he flew it constantly until his death.

Dallas Warren, a 38-year-old retired Marine sergeant who operated a small motel and trailer court at Pataskala, Ohio, bought NC2347, third of the Specials, from Ron Kendall in 1960 for $5,000. Kendall, an alcoholic, was a polished flyer who sometimes flew the Clipwing when he couldn't walk. He passed out on the upside of a hammerhead one rainy day and spread aeroplane pieces, himself and a cockpit full of dirty laundry all over a field, waking up three days later in a hospital unharmed but sober. Kendall re-built the Clipwing himself, using a 90A fuselage (which differs in the door area) but, in failing health and needing money, he finally sold it to Warren, a self-proclaimed daredevil with a bushy Guardsman moustache and a strong yen for flying.

Warren added the last few pieces needed for the rebuild and flew it for four years from his own 1,600-foot (488-m) airstrip. On the evening of 16 July 1964, the aircraft failed to recover from a low-level vertical manoeuvre and plunged into the woods just off Warren's runway. Margaret Warren salvaged the throttle knob and her husband's body, and asked a friend to bulldoze the balance of the wreckage into the hole it had dug and cover it over. He complied. Nevertheless, Richard P "Dick" Austin of High Point, North Carolina, says he is now reconstructing both that aeroplane and N101H, the Special in which L A "Rusty" Heard was killed.

The latter was originally NC511, *Nervous Energy III,* fourth Clipwing and the first actually built as such, constructed in 1938 as Clare Bunch's personal aircraft. Edna Gardner Whyte, a highly successful 'thirties aviatrix, twice used it to win the Culver Trophy in Miami. She recalls Clare Bunch telephoning her and offering the use of his Clipwing in 1939, proclaiming it a "chance to get some of that Culver money." Even today, Mrs Whyte, who now operates her own airfield in Texas, praises the performance and handling qualities of the Clipwing, but recalls Bunch had installed narrow landing gear for more speed and its landing behaviour was consequently "vicious." Mrs Whyte was one of several women to fly the Clipwing successfully. Others were pretty, blonde Florence Klingen-smith, later killed in the crash of a different type aircraft; Helen MacCloskey; Jackie Cochran (who set a lightplane closed-course speed record of better than 173 mph/278 km/h with it in 1939) and, of course, Ruth Barron.

In about 1946, Bunch sold NC511 to Jose Acebo, the "Cuban Match King," and it was operated for several years in that country, until, in 1950, Acebo reportedly suffered a heart attack and could no longer fly. The Monocoupe, then pretty weary also, was sold to another Cuban, Florientine Sequire,

(Above) One of the few Monocoupe D-145s, least successful of the clan, and (below) the 110 Special N2064, which flies today as N606G after a complete rebuild.

who ran an aircraft sales business in Miami. There, it was picked up by Joe Marrs, a dealer in nearby Lake Placid, for $2,300 and was promptly sold at the same figure to his lifelong friend "Rusty" Heard, a retired senior Eastern Airlines captain. Re-registered N101H, Heard's brilliant red 'coupe was a familiar sight around South Florida for 15 years, until on 3 April 1965 he failed to recover from a low altitude hammerhead while stunting at a friend's private strip and went straight in. He was 52 years old.

The Washington commuter

Meanwhile, in 1941, the factory produced NC36Y, fifth in the series and the second built as a Clipwing (incorporating both the small wing and abbreviated tail). This example passed quickly through two owners and ended up in the hands of an aircraft dealer in Houston, Texas, who sold it to W W "Woody" Edmondson, then of Lynchburg, Virginia. Edmondson was looking for fast cross-country transportation. He had a pilot training contract with the Army Air Corps, a job demanding frequent trips to Washington and New York City. His 145-hp Baby Laird wasn't fast enough to suit him, so when he saw NC36Y advertised, he was immediately interested. Edmondson already knew a little about Clipwings, for he had watched Ron Kendall fly NC2347 in the Sportsman races at Miami in 1939, clocking a reported 211 mph (339 km/h).

Edmondson met dealer J D Reed in New Orleans and ended up paying $2,000 more for the Clipwing than the advertised price — and handing over the Laird as well! "He took a look at the Laird and the price went up! And I wanted the 'coupe, and he knew it. He was a good salesman, too, so I finally met the price that he wanted," says Edmondson. Over the next decade, Woodrow Wilson Edmondson put in more hours on a 110 Special than anyone before or since — nearly 1,100. Commuting to Washington, he soon found he had a handy aerobatic mount in the Clipwing, and shortly after the end of the war he began giving airshows with the little tiger.

Late in 1946, he removed the original 145 hp engine in favour of a 185 hp Warner with pressure carburettor for inverted work and an Aeromatic propeller — thus necessitating another STC. So equipped, Woody and '36Y won the world aerobatic championship in 1948 at Miami, after previously placing second to his friend Bevo Howard two years in a row. Howard had flown a clipped Piper Cub in 1946, then his famed Bücker Jungmeister, in which he was finally killed. To beat Howard in the three-day event, Edmondson

worked out a five-minute, 32-manoeuvre routine that went from the ground up, whereas Howard climbed to altitude and worked down. This almost lost Edmondson the competition on the first day, when he was penalized for what the judges called a "dangerous manoeuvre" — a snap roll on take-off. Actually, his routine called for a four-point roll on take-off, and he was inverted when a downdraught caught the ship. "I rolled out — fast. The wingtip just cleared the ground. It was so fast the judges concluded it was a snap manoeuvre", Edmondson recalls. Protesting at the judges' decision, he said they might as well penalize him for the next two days as well, since he intended to use the same manoeuvre. When they relented, it put him even with Howard for the first day and enabled him to draw ahead and win in succeeding days.

In 1962, Edmondson sold *Little Butch,* as he had named the aircraft, to Johnny Foyle, a young airshow pilot from nearby South Boston, Virginia. Foyle's enthusiasm for the Monocoupe dwindled rapidly when he flipped it on landing three times in two years. When Foyle was killed in another aircraft, the 'coupe passed into the hands of Eastern Airlines captain John McCulloch, who owns it still, the contemporary registration being N36Y.

Post-war Specials

Two Specials were built after World War II, in Monocoupe's last (Melbourne, Florida) factory. The first, N15E, went to Walt Jackson, then a Monocoupe test pilot. Rolled off the line in 1949, it was the first built with the definitive big engine and Aeromatic propeller, and it remained in Jackson's hands for more than 11 years, until he finally sold *Super Putt Putt* to Don Taylor, a diminutive United Airlines captain and aerobatic enthusiast then located in Denver.

Taylor wrecked the Clipwing and almost himself in a 1965 crash during an air show at Grand Junction, Colorado (elevation 4,857 ft/1 480 m) while trying to do a deck-level slow roll. He had N15E well on the way to rebuilding when he sold it to Dr Sid Stealey, a Fairbanks, Alaska, dentist who already had the aft fuselage remains from Heard's plane and the fuselage and some other oddments from NC546W, a "wildcat" Clipwing built up outside the factory in the early 'fifties, using a stock 110 and some bits and pieces purchased from Margaret Warren. Stealey subsequently sold the lot to Dick Austin, who finished reconstructing the aircraft, flew it for a year and then sold it to furniture magnate Leon Levitz of Phoenix, in May 1973 for $25,000.

Last of the line was N16E, built in 1950 for Edmondson's long-time friend Carl Poston. Poston, a crack engine specialist, had several times stored NC36Y in his shop at Portsmouth, Virginia, and says he flew it more than once. The more he saw of '36Y, the more he decided he needed a Clipwing, and he ordered one from the factory in 1949. The company first tried to use a standard 90A fuselage, but Poston, tipped off by Edmondson, went to Melbourne personally to assure that he was getting a new 110 fuselage. The company was dying and work progressed slowly, the aircraft being still far from finished when the firm finally went bankrupt.

Poston made a hurried trip to Melbourne, bought a truck, loaded the aircraft on it and hauled it back up the coast to Norfolk, Virginia, where he and two other men finished it themselves — including covering, heat treating of the landing gear and manufacture of various small fittings and fairings. Lacking enough paint of any one colour, Poston mixed the odds and ends around his shop, coming up with a peculiar near-lavender shade which N16E carried for many years. With eyesight dimmed by a double cataract operation, Poston finally sold his Clipwing to William T Hutchins, a Miami-based Pan American Airways pilot. A World War II ferry pilot who logged time on virtually every US combat aircraft used in that conflict, Hutchins calls the Clipwing "the most airplane" he's ever strapped on — as does Taylor, himself veteran of a

The 110 Special N36Y as it is today, owned and flown by Capt John McCulloch; as NC36Y, it was built in 1941 since when it has had five owners.

long military stint, including time on such aircraft as the P-51 Mustang.

Morton W Lester, of Martinsville, Virginia, built the last Special to date, converting a 1931 Model 110 which cracked up in 1955 at Greenville, South Carolina, and even going so far as to build up his own 185 hp engine. Now registered "N110SP", this Clipwing flew for the first time in June 1973, but has flown very little since. It was, in fact, initially a project begun by William C "Red" Nichols, Marion, South Carolina, but dropped when he bought a flat-engined Clipwing replica from an estate. This he registered as N10RN and installed a 180 fuel-injection Lycoming with a constant-speed propeller, making it

the most modern of the Monocoupes but, surprisingly, not the fastest. The only 'coupe registered in the "experimental" category, it has since been sold to Richard Montague of Spruce Pine, North Carolina.

The Special is a paradoxical aeroplane. Even Edmondson flatly refused to spin it from any altitude, nor would he do snap rolls anywhere near the ground. McCulloch recalls taking his hands off *Little Butch's* controls in smooth, stable air at 7,000 ft (2 135 m) over Florida; "It made a leeetle turn off to the left; levelled out . . . made a leeetle turn back to the right; levelled out . . . flew along just a little — then rolled right over on its back!" He says he doesn't know how the FAA ever approved

One of two Monocoupe 110 Specials built after the end of the war, N15E has the 185 hp Warner engine and after being crashed and rebuilt, is now owned by Leon Levitz of Phoenix.

the aeroplane; today, anyone coming in with a machine like that, "they'd throw you out on your ear."

Yet Ken Olson, a one-handed pilot, successfully raced NC2347 at Miami when Kendall owned it . . . and there was Jim Heim, flying with hand controls alone . . . and Woody Edmondson calls it "the nicest airplane Monocoupe ever built; the safest, the strongest and the easiest to handle," and relates how he used to fly it "with two fingers only," practiced his air show routine by keeping a pack of cigarettes perched on the rounded top of the instrument panel and regularly flew it in crosswinds that grounded other ships.

Relatives of the Clipwing

The 110 Special is not the only paradoxical aeroplane in the Monocoupe family. There was also the D-145, shady lady of the clan. Unlike all other Monocoupes, her wings were built separately, left and right, and joined by a hefty tubular steel carry-through structure just above the pilot's head. Few aeroplanes have been so universally condemned. Only 22 of the "Ds" were built and 15 of these went to the old Department of Commerce, forerunners of today's Federal Aviation Administration. Most were soon badly wrinkled and retired in short order; the last few were given away to college aeronautical departments for use as instructional airframes lest they, too, be wrinkled.

One D-145, specially built, of course (with flaps and coupled drooping ailerons), went to Lindbergh, who does not seem to have coped very well. He ground-looped NR211 shortly after claiming it at the factory, never flew it much, refused to sell it and finally gave it to a St Louis museum where it moulders quietly today. He once remarked he was unwilling to sell it because he feared it would kill the new owner. Edmondson (who also owned one) has nothing but unkind words of the "D", calling it "a dog" and "the lousiest airplane Monocoupe ever made". The late C B "Scotty" Burmood, ex-factory test-pilot, never had anything good to say about the D-145 and chief designer Folkerts — who, in truth, wasn't responsible (it was Ivan Driggs, abetted by Tom Towle) — never could put enough distance between him and the "D". Others were known even to suggest it wasn't a true Monocoupe.

At 129·7 sq ft (12,05 m²), the "D" had 2 sq ft (0,19 m²) less wing area than the 90A, although the span was the same at 32 ft (9,76 m) — a difference caused by the latter's wider cabin, It weighed 1,224 lb (555 kg) empty and grossed 1,860 lb (845 kg), (up 250 lb/113,5 kg from the 90A), had a VMAX of 167 mph (269 km/h), a 75 per cent cruise of 140 mph (225 km/h) and stalled at 55 mph (88,5 km/h). Initial climb was 1,500 ft/min (7,63 m/sec) — good in anyone's book — and range 560 mls (900 km). One D-145, N11733, was later uprated with a 185 hp Warner, proving it would cruise within 6-7 mph (9,5-11 km/h) of the Clipwing, was far more stable, a crack performer and a top cross-country aeroplane.

Don Luscombe, who left Monocoupe late in 1933, felt the future of light aircraft lay with all-metal construction, but he was so enamoured with the "D", which had been designed to his specification, that the lovely Luscombe Phantom, first production to bear his name, was essentially a metal version of that aeroplane. Only 25 Phantoms were turned out — laboriously, by hand, with the help of a power hammer — but, like the D-145, they were ultra-efficient, cruising at 144 mph (232 km/h) and delivering an initial climb of 1,400 ft/min) 7,1 m/sec) on a 145 hp engine. Also, like the "D", (in fact, like all Monocoupes) the Phantom was fully aerobatic.

The darling of the sports plane set has always been that curvaceous compromise, the Monocoupe 90A, which offers performance equal to or slightly better than the latest Cessna 150, combined with handling characteristics that are a great deal more challenging. With 10 fewer horses, the 90A has a gross weight 10 lb (4,5 kg) greater than the Cessna and a factory empty weight of 940 lb (427 kg), about what the Cessna

would be without radio and battery. It delivers an initial climb of 900 ft/min (4,6 m/sec) — better than the Cessna's 670 ft/min (3,4 m/sec) — and offers a maximum still-air range of 600 mls (965 km), burning 4·5 US gph (17,4 l/hr). It cruises at 110 mph (177 km/h), will hit an honest 125 mph (201 km/h) at full throttle and has a service ceiling of 15,000 ft (4 575 m), up a thousand from the Cessna's. Even without its little drag flaps extended, it will sink rapidly, somewhere between 1,100 and 1,300 ft/min (5,6-6,6 m/sec), depending on where you want to fly it.

The type was so reliable that Shell Oil used a fleet of them for pipeline patrol during the 'forties, and it, too, has set its share of records. In April 1939, Clare Bunch flew a stock 90A nonstop from Burbank, Calif, to Long Island, NY, in 23 hrs 27 min, setting a new lightplane record and averaging 30 mpg (182 km/h) along a route that ran via Needles, Winslow, Albuquerque, Amarillo, St Louis, Terre Haute, Columbus and Pittsburg. Even with a 690-lb (313-kg) overload, take-off from Burbank required only 1,600 ft (488 m) of runway.

Engine of the Monocoupe 90A was originally the little Lambert R-266 five-cylinder radial, which was a good engine but demanding its share of care: for example, the rocker arms required to be greased every five flight hours. And it was expensive to build compared to the new opposed engines cropping up in other lightplanes, whilst its service life was shorter by far. Thus, beginning in 1941, Monocoupe produced a series of 43 "90AFs", with the 90-hp four-cylinder Franklin opposed engine, following these with a single 90AF-100 and a series of 11 (so far as the author can determine) 90AL-115s, powered by the 115 hp Lycoming O-235C-1. These were the last of the 'coupes, save only Poston's N16E, although a successor company drastically revamped the old twin design a few years later and built one example. Even though modified as recently as 1960, it, too, failed to catch on and vanished from ken.

It's hard to be really accurate about specifications, equipment and even performance, for there probably never was a "standard" Monocoupe, in any model. There were literally hundreds of minor variations based on stocks of available components, on individual customer requests and on guesses about what would keep a financially shaky company afloat. The very last 90AL built (N87622, s/n 870) even sported wheel controls and side windows much like an Aeronca 7AC Champ, and the whole aeroplane was simplified and cheapened up as much as possible for economical production. The entire 90AL series had hydraulic toe brakes — a feature that never fails to surprise other 'coupe owners, who must make do with mechanical heel brakes.

On the other hand, basic construction never changed, from first to last — the one-piece wood wing with two spruce spars routed out to reduce weight, on which the steel-tube fuselage was slung by four bolts, the flat-wrap windshield, the "V" wing struts and the braced tailplane. Some minor items also never changed, such as the wood-and-wire over-centre latch for the pilot's window (an item adapted from a toilet paper holder) to give the pilot eight inches (20 cm) of open air and enable him to see for landing regardless of ice or engine oil on the windscreen. But almost everything else did.

Landing gear changed, became wider, more streamlined and efficient. Flaps appeared, on the 90A only. Wingtips were rounded, struts wrapped in fabric, tailplane shape changed, the fuselage made more rounded and better faired with the engine cowling. Small fairings appeared and disappeared, wheel size and pant shape varied. Most of the later aeroplanes showed evidence of careful streamlining, with fabric and aluminium strips over control surface gaps and a distinctive stabilizer-to-fin fairing of fabric snugged tight with elastic. All of this makes generalisations nearly impossible, and leaves only one flat statement true for all: The Monocoupes are unforgettable! □

capacity, improved navaids and communications equipment and underwing floodlighting for night refuelling operations. As already noted, the F.R.17 was designed primarily to refuel bombers or transports, with more than three times the refuelling rate of the wing pod units, but it could also be used, of course, to refuel fighter aircraft. The first three-point tanker conversion flew at Radlett on 2 November 1965 and a total of 24 was converted — 10 from B Mk 1 airframes to become K Mk 1s and 14 from B Mk 1As to become K Mk 1As.

The three-point tankers entered service with No 57 Squadron in January 1966, this squadron becoming fully operational on 1 June in that year, and No 214 Squadron (the RAF's first tanker unit) began to receive the new aircraft in October 1966, becoming operational in March 1967. At about the same time, No 55 Squadron relinquished the task of training tanker crews to a Tanker Training Flight (also at Marham) and itself became a fully operational unit on Victor K Mk 1As.

Although this fleet of Victor tankers gave excellent and reliable service for a number of years — the last few are still in service — the K Mk 1/1A proved to be weight-limited when operating in high ambient temperatures or from high elevation airfields. For example, take-offs could not be made from Bahrain, Gan or, in some cases, Cyprus, in high daytime temperatures with a full fuel load, and to meet some operational cases it was necessary to launch two part-loaded tankers together so that one could top up its tanks from the other immediately after take-off and before setting course for the RV.

Enhanced capabilities

With the reduction in Britain's overseas commitments that has now taken place, these limitations have become less important than they were in 1968, at which time plans began to be formulated for the development of a tanker version of the more powerful (Conway-engined) Victor B Mk 2, which would be less restricted in "hot and high" situations. A

damaged Victor SR Mk 2 (differences between the B Mk 2, SR Mk 2 and other variants are described later in this account) was earmarked for conversion at Radlett and plans were made for 21 Victor B Mk 2Rs to be converted to tankers in 1969/70, followed by eight SR Mk 2s in 1973. Handley Page completed the preliminary designs, which included provision for additional wing-tip tanks to supplement the internal fuel capacity, improved navaids and structural modifications to increase the wing fatigue life. The provision of ejection seats for all crew members in the Victor was studied concurrently, and the contract for the K Mk 2 conversion programme was technically approved in October 1969.

By this time, however, Handley Page was in deep financial trouble (primarily as a result of the soaring costs of the H.P.137 Jetstream programme). The original company had gone into voluntary liquidation in August 1969, being succeeded by Handley Page Aircraft Ltd, formed by a Receiver and backed for a time by K R Cravens Corporation, the North American distributor of the Jetstream. Late in 1969, the Ministry of Defence confirmed that a contract to convert 18 Victor K Mk 2s would be forthcoming, despite the American ownership of the new company, but Cravens was unable, in the event, to continue financing Handley Page Aircraft and in February 1970 this company also collapsed.

Moving rapidly to protect its own interests and those of the RAF, the MoD had begun discussions with Hawker Siddeley Aviation as the situation at Handley Page deteriorated, and immediately following upon the latter's collapse, concluded a contract providing for HSA to take over product support for all HP military aircraft (including the few examples of the Hastings still in service) and responsibility for the K Mk 2 tankers. Between March and June, 1970, every aspect of Handley Page Aircraft Ltd, insofar as it related to the MoD, was closely reviewed by HSA and all relevant jigs, tools, drawings, etc, were transferred to Manchester, where about 25-30 senior HP staff also joined HSA. The situation was not without its irony, for Handley Page and Avro (which had become Hawker Siddeley's Manchester Division) had been

Victor K Mk 2 XL233 bearing the markings of No 232 OCU, RAF Marham.

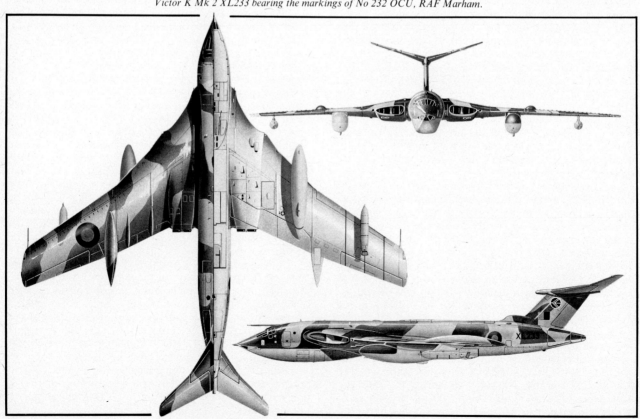

long-time rivals, as personified by Sir Frederick Handley Page himself and Sir Roy Dobson, and exemplified by the competition between the Halifax and the Lancaster, the Halton and the Lancastrian, the Hermes and the Tudor and, above all, the Victor and the Vulcan. Fate was, perhaps, kind to delay the arrival of the Victors at HSA's Woodford, Manchester, airfield until after both Sir Frederick and Sir Roy had gone to their graves!

At the time of Handley Page's final liquidation, 21 Victor B Mk 2Rs were parked on the airfield at Radlett, in preparation for conversion to tankers. A Hawker Siddeley field unit restored these, plus a single B Mk 1 trials aircraft, to minimum airworthy standards to permit each to make a single ferry flight, at low airspeed and with undercarriage down, from Radlett to Woodford, whither all 22 were safely delivered during July and August 1970. While this work was going on, HSA put in hand a revised design study for the K Mk 2, this work being completed by the end of July. The HP plan to fit tip tanks was dropped. To obtain some bending relief for the wing — with benefit to the fatigue life — the extended tip fitted to the B Mk 2 was reduced from 5 ft (1,53 m) to 3 ft 6 in (1,07 m), the ailerons were rigged up +2 deg from neutral and the F.R. Mk 20B refuelling pods were moved outboard by 2 ft (0,61 m). The last change had the effect of putting the refuelling pods in the same relationship to the wing tip as on the K Mk 1/1A aircraft, and uprigging the ailerons, which produced a slight increase in drag, caused the aircraft to fly at a greater angle of incidence.

Some structural modifications were also introduced by HSA, principally to safeguard the fatigue life: the RAF wanted a minimum service life of 14 years for its Victor K Mk 2s, the airframes for which had accumulated anything from 1,500 to 3,000 hrs each prior to modification. A full-scale fatigue test on a B Mk 2 airframe had been completed by Handley Page but the test specimen has been updated by HSA and testing is continuing to keep ahead of the airframe hours on the lead aircraft in the Victor K Mk 2 fleet. The avionics also incorporate some changes, with 18 of the original 25 systems removed, four modified and six added. Since the Mk 2 aircraft has AC electrics and the Mk 1 was DC, there are some differences in the electrical system equipment, and because the air bled from the Conway engines is hotter than that from the Sapphires, an intercooler has to be fitted between the engine and the turbine pump operating the F.R.17 HDU in the bomb-bay. An Ultra intercom system is fitted, as on the K Mk 1 but not previously used in the K Mk 2.

The original HP plan to fit six ejection seats has been abandoned and the K Mk 2, like the other Victors (and the Vulcans) has these seats only for the two pilots; the other crew members have swivel seats (including, in the K Mk 2, the supernumerary) to enhance the chances of escape in an emergency, although these chances are recognised to be slender and it is believed that non-ejecting crew members have escaped from Victors on only two occasions. Provision is made, in the K Mk 2, for freight to be carried under the front fuselage floor (in place of the bomber's HS radar scanner); in the nose of the crew compartment, in the window box forward of the nosewheel and in a rear compartment.

The fuel and fuel transfer systems of the Victor K Mk 2 are substantially the same as those in the K Mk 1, the principal additional tanks being two of 16,000-lb (7 264-kg) capacity each in the bomb bay. There is a seven tank group in the fuselage with a capacity of 36,000 lb (16 344 kg) and 10 wing tanks containing 32,000 lb (14 528 kg) of fuel. The fuel jettison point is relocated at the farthest extremity of the rear fuselage, a new position made possible by the deletion of *Red Steer* ECM previously carried in the rear radome.

Hawker Siddeley flew the first K Mk 2 conversion at Woodford on 1 March 1972 and the third conversion became the first to enter service, in May 1974, at No 232 OCU, the

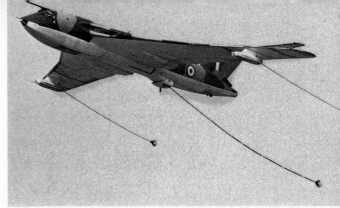

A Victor K Mk 1A trailing all three refuelling drogues. Normal practice is for fighter-type aircraft to use the wing tip drogues and larger aircraft to use the fuselage position.

Victor training unit at Marham. This was somewhat later than had originally been planned, and subsequent deliveries were also behind the initial schedule, because HSA discovered, upon close examination of the Victors in for conversion, very considerable variations in the MoD standards. This made progress up the learning curve slow and imposed an additional burden in refurbishing the aircraft to a common standard. By the end of 1976, all but a few of the 24 aircraft currently planned for conversion had been completed; originally, it had been intended to convert 29 of the 30 available airframes (including SR Mk 2s) but this figure was reduced in the defence cuts of April 1975.

Victor's origins

Although the Victor and the Vulcan were contemporaries in the V-force for most of their service life as bombers, and were produced to the same official specification (B.35/46), the Handley Page design team had turned its attention to the development of a jet bomber successor to the Lincoln somewhat earlier than its Avro counterpart. Indeed, the submissions of early design proposals made by Handley Page to the Ministry of Supply and the Air Ministry helped to crystallize official ideas on such an aircraft and the first drafts of the Air Staff requirements were largely written round the HP proposals.

Within a few weeks of the end of the war in Europe, Sir Frederick Handley Page had instructed his senior design staff (R S Stafford, Frank Radcliffe and Godfrey H Lee) to turn their attention to jet bomber designs in the general category of a Lincoln replacement: one project he suggested should be a four jet of about 100,000 lb (45 400 kg) gross weight, the other a twin-jet of 60,000 lb (27 240 kg). At this time, Handley Page was pre-occupied with the potential advantages that could be derived from a tailless configuration, with sweep-back on the wings to obtain lateral stability, and possibly a "riderplane" on the nose (instead of the canard's usual fore-plane and elevator) to provide longitudinal stability; a research aircraft, the H.P. 75, of such configuration had been flying intermittently (and with only limited success) since 1943. Consequently, Sir Frederick recommended that the bomber projects should have 40 deg of sweepback on the wings, and later in 1945 Godfrey Lee was able to learn at first hand of German work confirming the importance of sweepback in delaying the onset of compressibility effects at high subsonic speeds.

By the end of February 1946, with no guidance from official sources as to possible future RAF requirements, Lee had completed the project design of a 90,000-lb (40 860-kg) aeroplane which, with four Avon or similar engines, would have a 5,000 ml (8 045 km) range at 520 knots (963 km/h) TAS. The wing, with a span of 122 ft (37,21 m), ended in upturned tips incorporating rudders, and a swept-back tailplane, with elevators, was carried above the rear and relatively short fuselage on a short fin. The type number H.P.80 was allocated to the proposal, which formed the basis of Operational

The first Victor prototype, XB771, with rear-fuselage air brakes open. The dorsal fin, incorporating a cooling air intake, was deleted from production aircraft.

requirement OR 230. By the beginning of 1947, changes in this OR made it obvious that the H.P.80 as initially projected would not meet the requirement and specification B.35/46 was therefore issued to industry early in 1947 to obtain competitive tenders. The target first flight for prototypes was March 1952.

Revised to meet this specification, the H.P.80 emerged a little later in 1947 with a novel crescent wing plane form, but still with wing tip rudders and an all-moving tailplane carried on a miniscule fin. The tailplane was for trimming purposes only, large elevons on the wing outer panels being used for lateral and longitudinal manoeuvres. The crescent wing feature, much about which was said in HP publicity at the time, involved combining three different sweepback angles from root to tip, the actual angles being 48·5 deg inboard, 37·5 deg for the centre panels and 26·75 deg outboard. With a span of 100 ft (30,5 m), this project was to be powered by four 7,500 lb st (3 405 kgp) Metrovick F.9 engines and, as required by the specification, would have a range of 3,500 mls (5 632 km) at 575 mph (925 km/h), carrying a 10,000 lb (4 540 kg) nuclear bomb load.

The intention of the MoS to order two prototypes of the H.P.80 was notified to the company on 28 July 1947, subject to

One of the earliest project forms of the H.P.80, before the crescent wing layout had been evolved, and with the wing-tip fins that were a distinctive feature of the original design.

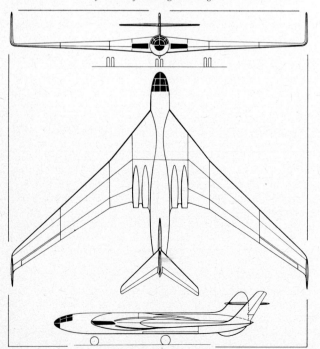

the satisfactory completion of wind tunnel tests; at the same time, it was learned that Avro was to receive similar support for its equally radical proposal, the delta-winged Type 698 Vulcan, design work on which had been triggered by the issue of OR 230.

In the remaining months of 1947, much consideration was given to crew accommodation and means of emergency escape; the company favoured separate ejection seats for the five crew members but the Air Staff was keen to have a jettisonable capsule, as it was believed that ejection at 50,000 ft (15 250 m) and 500 mph (805 km/h) would necessarily be fatal. Provision was in fact made in the prototype for the separation of the pressure cabin by explosive bolts, but the capsule concept was abandoned in 1950 after a series of model trials had been made.

The need for a flying scale model of the crescent wing and all-flying tailplane arrangement was recognised and early in 1948 it was decided to adapt a Supermarine Swift for this purpose*. At about the same time, the configuration of the H.P.80 received its final major change with the deletion of the wing tip rudders and the substitution of an orthodox central fin-and-rudder at the end of the fuselage, to which the tailplane was attached at the top to give a distinctive T-tail. A later change eliminated the elevons and substituted normal ailerons on the wing and elevators on the tailplane, but neither this change nor some amendments in the wing planform and the thickness/chord ratios of the various wing panels were reflected in the H.P.88. The definitive contract for the two H.P.80 prototypes was signed on 28 April 1948, at which time the target first flight dates were put at May and November 1952, respectively. The choice of the Metrovick F.9 engine was confirmed, although by this time its development had been taken over by Armstrong Siddeley and named the Sapphire; a thrust of 9,000 lb (4 086 kg) was now being promised for production versions, a similar output being offered by Rolls-Royce for its R.B.80 turbofan that was being evolved from initial Napier work on an engine known as the E.132 and would eventually emerge as the Conway for use in later Victors.

The name Victor was adopted for the Handley Page bomber in June 1952, at which time an initial production order was

*Specification E.6/48 was issued to cover this work. Handley Page assigned the designation H.P.88 to the modified Swift, which Supermarine identified as the Type 521. Detail design of the 0.4 scale wing was entrusted to General Aircraft Ltd at Feltham and after this company merged with Blackburn, the latter became responsible for both the design and conversion of the aircraft, which it designated Y.B.2. By the time the H.P.88 first flew, on 21 June 1951, its wing and tail unit both differed in some important details from the configuration finally adopted for the full-size H.P.80. Blackburn test pilots made 25 flights to clear the aircraft for delivery to HP in August 1951, but it crashed on the 26th of that month, apparently as a result of structural failure during a low-level airspeed calibration run at Stansted.

placed for 25 Victor B Mk 1s (a similar quantity of Avro Vulcan B Mk 1s being ordered at the same time). This was before either of the RAF's new V-bombers had flown, the Victor prototype (WB771) being taken into the air for the first time at the A & AEE Boscombe Down on 24 December 1952 by the company's chief test pilot, Hedley G Hazelden, accompanied by flight test observer Ian Bennett.

Public appearances were made by WB771 at the Queen's Coronation Preview fly-past at Odiham on 15 July 1953 and then at the annual SBAC Flying Display and Exhibition at Farnborough in September, but the year was taken up by the steady routine of test flying, which revealed a few inevitable snags as well as, overall, satisfactory performance and handling characteristics. The programme received a major set-back on 14 July 1954, however, when WB771 suffered a structural failure of the tailplane/fin junction and crashed while making a low-altitude airspeed calibration flight at Cranfield. Necessary changes were designed and the second prototype, WB775, flew for the first time on 11 September 1954, appearing later the same day in the flying display at Farnborough.

Official handling trials of the Victor began at the A & AEE on 14 March 1955, using WB775, and the first round of trials confirmed the impressions already gained by Handley Page pilots — that the Victor was easy and pleasant to fly, a good bombing platform and capable of being developed, in the production version, to comply with the specified performance. Production aircraft, as defined by Specification B.128P, were to be powered by the 11,050 lb st (5 020 kgp) Sapphire 202 (ASSa.7) engines and to have a normal take-off weight of 160,000 lb (72 640 kg), with an overload weight of 190,000 lb (86 260 kg). Carrying a 10,000 lb (4 540 kg) bomb load, it could cruise at 575 mph (925 km/h) and with a still air range of 5,000 mls (8 045 km) it could reach an altitude of 50,800 ft (15 500 m) over the mid-point target. If a reduced height over target was acceptable, the range could be increased to 5,580 mls (8 980 km), or with extra fuel in part of the bomb-bay and at the overload weight, to 7,100 mls (11 424 km). One of the Victor's special virtues was the size of its bomb bay, exceeding that of both the Valiant and the Vulcan by a substantial margin and making possible the carriage of a 22,000-lb (9 988-kg) Grand Slam, two 12,000-lb (5 448-kg) Tallboys, four 10,000-lb (4 540-kg) bombs, 35 1,000-lb (454-kg) bombs or 39 Type S 2,000-lb (908-kg) mines; plans were also made for the fitting of two underwing panniers, which would accommodate a further 14 1,000-lb (454-kg) bombs each, although these were never carried.

Production Victors differed from the prototypes in having a 40-in (1,02-m) forward fuselage extension to bring the CG within the desired limits, and the fin height reduced by 15 in (38 cm), with dorsal fin and equipment-cooling intake deleted. Like the prototypes, they made use of a sandwich double-skin wing structure, corrugated sheet being used for the core. Handley Page had conducted a lengthy development programme to arrive at the final honeycomb sandwich construction, which used Araldite adhesive and DTD 687 aluminium skins. The production fin also made use of a corrugated sandwich construction, this being part of the corrective action taken after the loss of WB771 and the reason for the reduction in fin height.

Bombers in service

The first production Victor B Mk 1, XA917, made its first flight at Radlett on 1 February 1956 and 10 had flown by the end of the year; three participated in the Queen's Review of RAF Bomber Command on 23 July that year and after four production aircraft had emerged in natural metal finish, a switch was made to the overall white anti-radiation flash scheme that distinguished the V-Force bombers for several years. Flying the first production aircraft, HP test pilot John

The Victor Family of Designs

H.P.72A	"Cover" designation for preliminary design investigation of unarmed high-speed bomber, early 1946. Four Avons; 90,000 lb (40 860 kg) gross, 45 deg sweep with wingtip rudders and small swept tailplane and elevators.
H.P.75A	"Cover" designation for preliminary design investigation, alternative to H.P.72A. Tailless configuration with front rider-plane.
H.P.80	Redesignation of H.P.72A in March 1946, progressively developed to meet the requirements of OR 230 and Specification B.35/46 and eventually finalised in the configuration built as Victor. Designation applies to all examples of the Victor built, all marks.
H.P.87	Proposed one-third scale towed glider test model of H.P.80.
H.P.88	Supermarine 521 (Swift fuselage) fitted with 0·4 scale wing and tail of H.P.80 to detail design by General Aircraft Ltd and built under MoS contract to Specification E.6/48 by Blackburn and General Aircraft Ltd as Y.B.2, serial number VX330.
H.P.96	Proposed military transport variant of H.P.80 with new fuselage of increased length and diameter and optional swing-tail for rear loading; Sapphire or Conway engines.
H.P.97	Proposed civil transport variant of H.P.80 with new double-bubble fuselage and wing-tip tanks.
H.P.98	Proposed target-marker (pathfinder) version of H.P.80 in November 1951, with remotely-controlled radar-sighted tail guns and Conway or Olympus engines.
H.P.101	Proposed military transport similar to H.P.97 (also known as H.P.97A) submitted to RAAF in 1956.
H.P.104	Proposed Victor Phase 3 with four Olympus or six Sapphire engines and other changes.
H.P.111	Proposed military or civil (H.P.111C) transport derivative of H.P.80/H.P.104 with increased span and new circular section single- or two-deck fuselage, May 1958. Four Conways and wing-tip tanks.
H.P.114	Proposed Victor Phase 6, with wider centre section, larger bomb bay, tip tanks and two or four Skybolt missiles carried externally.
H.P.123	Proposed military tactical freighter derived from H.P.111, for submission to GOR 351 in 1961.

(Above) An early production Victor B Mk 1 in the original silver finish and (below) a B Mk 1A (distinguished by the ECM radome in the rear fuselage) in anti-radiation white finish, dropping 35 1,000-lb (454-kg) bombs from five septuple carriers.

(Above) Victor B Mk 1 XA930 was used for a large number of special trials and is shown here with flight refuelling probe, underwing fuel tanks and Spectre rocket ATO packs. (Below left) The Victor B Mk 2 prototype and (lower) a production B Mk 2R carrying Blue Steel.

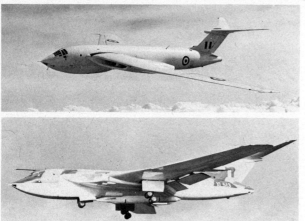

Allam inadvertently exceeded the speed of sound on 1 June 1957 in a shallow dive; no indications of the event were noted in the cockpit — other than on the instruments — confirming the excellence of the Victor's transonic characteristics. Evaluation, weapons dropping, handling and performance trials and other work occupied all of 1956 and much of 1957, during which year RAF ground and air crews began training on the type at Radlett as a preliminary to its service introduction on 28 November 1957 at RAF Gaydon, when 'A' Squadron of No 232 OCU received the first of five Victor B Mk 1s from the initial production batch. Between June and August 1958, this unit completed a 1,000-hr intensive flying trial, using seven Victors.

While the first bomber squadron was equipping on the type, three Victors (later joined by a fourth) were assigned to a special reconnaissance rôle, carrying "Yellow Aster" sensors and equipping the Radar Reconnaissance Flight at Wyton from April 1958 after first being used at Gaydon to convert crews from the Valiant-equipped No 543 Squadron. On April 9 1958, three Victor B Mk 1s arrived at RAF Cottesmore as the initial equipment for No 10 Squadron, which became operational six days later and in due course received a further nine aircraft from the initial batch. Production, meanwhile, was proceeding on a second batch of 25 B Mk 1s which had been ordered in May 1955*, and from this batch nine aircraft were assigned to equip No 15 Squadron at RAF Cottesmore in September 1958 and 10 went to No 57 Squadron at RAF Honington early in 1959.

While the three Bomber Command squadrons concentrated on a training routine to bring both aircraft and crews up to a

---

*The second production contract was in fact for 33 aircraft, specified in February 1956 as eight B Mk 1 with Sapphire ASSa 7 and 25 Phase 2 aircraft with uprated Sapphire ASSa 9s. However, work on the ASSa 9 was almost immediately discontinued and in November 1956 it was decided that 25 of this batch would be B Mk 1s and the final eight would be Phase 2A Victors with Conway engines, these appearing as Victor B Mk 2s, described later in the article.

high pitch of operational preparedness, several production aircraft were assigned to trials tasks at Radlett and elsewhere. One was used to develop a flight refuelling system (as a receiver, with Valiant tankers), a probe being added above the cockpit, plus flush-fitting underwing tanks to increase the range. To permit operation at the overload weight of 190,000 lb (86 260 kg), assisted take-off was required and this was achieved by fitting two DH Spectre liquid rockets under the inner wings, with the aid of which the fully-laden aircraft took off in 1,600 ft (488 m). Another Victor B Mk 1 was fitted with a photo-recce pack in the bomb-bay and a third had fixed droop incorporated on the wing leading edge in place of the usual Krueger flaps. Starting in April 1960, Handley Page began a programme to convert the final 24 production B Mk 1s (one other of the last batch having been written off) to B Mk 1A configuration with a range of ECM (electronic counter measures) equipment, some of which was installed in the forward lower fuselage behind the H_2S scanner, some in the aft bomb bay initially intended to carry flash-bombs (the requirement for which had been dropped) and some in a small new radome at the end of the fuselage — this last-mentioned providing the external distinguishing feature between the B Mk 1 and B Mk 1A. The subsequent conversion of these aircraft to tankers has already been described.

Possible developments of the Victor, especially with the object of improving the height over target, which was considered to be a critical factor in the performance of the V-bombers, had been under study since well before the production B Mk 1s began to come off the line. Mention has already been made of the Phase 2 proposal with Sapphire ASSa 9s, which did not proceed; simultaneously, early in 1955, with this proposal, the company suggested a Phase 3 H.P.104 with an enlarged centre section giving a span of 137 ft (41,79 m), using four Conways, four Olympus or possibly six Sapphires. This was thought to be promising but was too big a change to be introduced without a major interruption in production, and a somewhat less ambitious Phase 2A was then proposed, with the span extended to 120 ft (36,6 m), four Conways (with Olympus suitable for installation if the Conways failed to come up to expectation) and a normal gross weight of 170,000 lb (77 180 kg).

This Phase 2A proposal was accepted, and instructions were given for eight aircraft on the second production batch to be completed to this standard, with 18 more ordered in January 1956 (later increased to 24) and a final 27 in 1961, although later amendments cancelled 25, making the production total of this version, designated the B Mk 2, 34. The first Victor B Mk 2, with 17,250 lb st (7 832 kgp) Conway 200 (RCo 11) engines, flew on 20 February 1959, and flight testing proceeded routinely until 20 August that year, when this same aircraft, on a flight from Boscombe Down with an A & AEE flight crew and an HP flight engineer on board, disappeared off the SW Wales coast. After a six-month search by four trawlers and a salvage vessel, the wreckage was found on the sea bed at a depth of 400 ft (122 m) and using special trawls, some 75 per cent, by weight, was recovered by November 1960, comprising nearly 600,000 fragments. These were taken to the RAE, Farnborough and reassembled for what must rank as one of the most remarkable investigations ever conducted into an aircraft accident. This concluded that the accident resulted from an initial failure of the pitot static head on the port wing tip when a retaining collet came loose. This would have led to a spurious loss of airspeed being registered by the Mach trimmer, which would have tried to compensate by putting the nose down, whilst the stall detector, also linked to inputs from the port pitot-static, would have lowered the nose flaps, as it was no longer protected by a high-speed over-ride switch. The Mach trimmer would eventually have been stopped by a negative-g cutout switch, but not until the dive had become catastrophic, causing failure of the starboard pitot static and producing a situation beyond control by the crew.

The investigation served to settle any doubts about the structural integrity of the Victor, and strengthening of the pitot-static attachment was easily accomplished. While the investigation was going on, additional Victor B Mk 2s had been completed and were allocated to various phases of engine and systems trials, and the carriage and launching of Blue Steel supersonic nuclear guided missiles. The Blue Steel trials were conducted at Woodford (the missile being of Hawker Siddeley Manchester origin) and later at Woomera, Australia, and involved at least three aircraft. Another of the early trials batch of Mk 2s was fitted with 20,600 lb st (9 352 kgp) Conway 201s (RCo 17s), and after some early problems with engine surging had been overcome, this same aircraft was fitted with fixed wing leading-edge droop of the type adopted as standard for the B Mk 2 in service. High-level and low-level photographic reconnaissance systems were fitted and cleared for service use, the latter comprising sideways-locked H_2S in the nose bay, and an overload weight of 200,000 lb (90 800 kg) was approved for the new mark of Victor. Plans were also made for the Victor B Mk 2 to carry two Skybolt missiles, instead of the Blue Steel, on the standard wing strong points used to carry external tanks, but by the time Skybolt was cancelled in December 1962, no examples had been flown on the Victor. Earlier, Handley Page had proposed, as the H.P.114 or Victor B Phase 6, a much-developed version of the bomber with a wider centre section, wing-tip tanks, provision for four Skybolts and an endurance of 14 hours after taking off at a weight of 240,000 lb (108 960 kg). Neither this nor the B Phase 4 proposal, which was based on the B Mk 1 airframe with improvements in speed and ceiling but no provision for carrying Blue Steel, found official favour.

Deliveries of production Victor B Mk 2s to the RAF began in November 1961, with the first three aircraft going to the B.2 Trials Unit and No 139 (Jamaica) Squadron at Wittering equipping on the type on 1 February 1962. It was followed by No 100 Squadron at the same base in May 1962, where it was joined by the Trials Unit as the Victor Training Flight, and No 100 Squadron received the last production Victor at Wittering in May 1963. To help clear the aircraft for its service introduction, the Trials Unit completed 1,000 hrs of intensive flying on the B Mk 2 in 1961, one of the most successful trials of its type up to that time.

As delivered to the two Wittering squadrons, the B Mk 2s were powered by the 17,250 lb st (7 832 kgp) Conway 200 engines and were not equipped to launch Blue Steel, although a number of trials aircraft, as noted, were engaged in Blue Steel development. Associated with the Blue Steel installation and the uprated RCo 17 engines were several other modifications, the most eye-catching of which comprised the installation of fairings above each wing trailing edge, projecting some distance aft; developed from a concept by R T Whitcomb of NACA in the USA and Dr Kuchemann at the RAE Farnborough, these so-called "Kuchemann Carrots" served

to delay the appearance of shock-waves at high sub-sonic speeds and were especially helpful on the Victor when it was adopted for the low-altitude conventional bombing rôle previously fulfilled by the Valiant. They also served as containers for "Window" anti-radar strips.

With the wing fairing modification, uprated engines, Blue Steel, additional ECM and other internal changes, the Victor was designated B Mk 2R and a retrofit programme was started as soon as production of the B Mk 2 ended at Radlett. No 139 Squadron began to re-equip with B Mk 2Rs towards the end of 1963 and No 100 received its first retrofit aircraft in January 1964. In all, 30 Victors were converted to this final operational standard; of this total, the last nine were specially equipped to operate in the strategic photographic reconnaissance rôle with No 543 Squadron at Wyton, these being identified as SR Mk 2s and the first example flying at Radlett on 23 February 1965. In service from May 1965 onwards, these aircraft had a number of optional equipment fits in the bomb bay, including extra fuel tanks, day or night cameras and photo-flashes.

Progressively higher weights were approved for Victor operations, as the structural testing proceeded. By 1963, the B Mk 2R was cleared to 216,000 lb (98 064 kg) and the maximum possible limit for the tanker is now 244,000 lb (110 776 kg), although the highest weight permitted for RAF operations is currently 223,000 lb (101 242 kg) with an increase to 238,000 lb (108 052 kg) to come soon. The advent of the Victor K Mk 2 tanker has already been described; changing operational requirements of the RAF had curtailed the service life of the B Mk 2 and 2R to less than seven years, the last two bomber units flying their aircraft back to Radlett at the end of 1968 for storage and eventual conversion. The PR variants soldiered on with No 543 Squadron, however, until 1975, when they were superseded by modified Vulcans, allowing the tanker force of K Mk 2s to be brought up to strength.

As a tanker, the Victor is destined to continue in service at least until the end of the 'eighties, and as a bomber it made a distinctive contribution to the maintenance of Britain's nuclear deterrent during the 'sixties. Its design, started in 1945, was nothing less than inspired and its subsequent refinement for production was testimony to the talent of what was — at the time — one of Britain's oldest established and most independent aircraft companies. Last of a long line of large aeroplanes built by Handley Page for the Royal Air Force, it was — and is — a worthy successor to the "Bloody Paralyser" of 1916. □

H.P.80 Victor Production		
Prototypes	2	WB771, WB775
B Mk 1	50	XA917-XA941, XH587-XH594, XH613-XH621, XH645-XH651, XH667
B Mk 1A	(24*)	XH587-XH594, XH613-XH616, XH618-XH621, XH645-XH651, XH667
B(K) Mk 1A	(6)*	XH615, XH620 (first conversion) XH646-XH648, XH667
K Mk 1	(10)*	XA918, XA926-XA928, XA930, XA932, XA936-XA939 (first conversion, XA939), XA941
K Mk 1A	(14)*	XH587-XH591, XH614, XH616, XH618, XH619, XH621, XH645, XH649-XH651
B Mk 2	34	XH668-XH675, XL158-XL165, XL188-XL193, XL230-XL233, XL551-XL513, XM714-XM718 (28 ordered but later cancelled: XL250-XL255, XM745-XM756, XM785-XM794)
B Mk 2R	(21)*	XH669, XH671, XH673, XL158, XL160, XL162-XL164, XL188-XL231-XL233, XL511-XL513, XM717
SR Mk 2	(9)*	XH672, XH674, XL161, XL165 (prototype conversion) XL193, XL230, XM715-XM716, XM718
K Mk 2	(24)*	XH669, XH671-XH673, XH675, XL158, XL160-XL164, XL188-XL192, XL231-XL233 (first conversion, XL231), XL511-XL513, XM715, XM717
*Conversion programmes		

UNITED KINGDOM

BAC X-ELEVEN

CONTINUING its studies of possible derivatives of the One-Eleven shorthaul transport, in the context of the efforts of the "Group of Seven" European manufacturers to analyse the requirements of the (primarily European) airlines for new equipment, British Aircraft Corporation has evolved the X-Eleven proposal. Whereas the earlier One-Eleven 700 and 800 projects used lengthened versions of the basic fuselage with various combinations of wing refinements and uprated engine, the X-Eleven has an enlarged fuselage diameter to obtain a genuine six-abreast seating.

Commonality with the One-Eleven 500 is reduced to 40 per cent, a much lower figure than expected for the One Eleven 700/800, but the "wide body" feature would, it is believed, make the X-Eleven considerably more attractive to potential customers, and it is now being actively evaluated by a number of airlines and several potential industrial programme partners. The aircraft is based on using two of the forthcoming "ten tonne" engines.

The X-Eleven would make use of the nose and rear fuselage sections of the One-Eleven, plus the main wings, fin and tailplane, with appropriate root section extensions. The landing gear would be strengthened, and the fuselage would be structurally similar to that of the One-Eleven.

Power Plant: Two General Electric/SNECMA CFM-56 or Pratt & Whitney JT10D turbofans each in the 22,000-24,500 lb st (10000-11 123 kgp) power bracket.

Performance: Normal cruising speed, Mach = 0·73; full-load range, about 2,300 mls (3 700 km); airfield capability, 5,000-7,000 ft (1 525-2 135 m).

Weights: Max payload, 39,300 lb (17 826 kg); max take-off, 140,000 lb (63 504 kg).

Dimensions: Span, 106 ft 2 in (32,36 m); length, 132 ft 9 in (40,28 m); height, 28 ft 6 in (8,69 m); internal cabin width, 143 in (3,63 m).

Accommodation: Flight crew of two and 135-160 seats.

USA

CESSNA CITATION I

SINCE its introduction five years ago, the Cessna Citation has consistently proved to be the fastest-selling of the biz-jets, a total of some 340 having now been delivered. In that period, the type has been the subject of progressive refinement and improvement, with the gross weight being increased in a number of successive steps from 10,350 lb (4 695 kg) to the present figures of 12,000 lb (5 448 kg) but with no changes in the power plant or external

A three-view drawing and model photograph of the BAC X-Eleven short-range transport proposal.

dimensions. A further stage in the development of the type has now been reached with the introduction, effective in December, of improved engines and an extended-span wing.

The new model, which replaces the present Citation in production at the 350th airframe, is known as the Citation I and has a considerably improved performance in several respects, including about 100 mls (161 km) greater range, the ability to climb to 41,000 ft (12 505 m) in about half the time taken by early Citations and max cruising speeds that are 14 mph (22,5 km/h) greater at 35,000 ft (10 675 m) and 38 mph (61 km/h) greater at 41,000 ft (12 505 m). Price of the Citation I, complete with Collins/Sperry IFR avionics package and crew training courses, is $945,000 (£583,300). The specifications that follow are described by Cessna as "preliminary".

Power Plant: Two Pratt & Whitney Canada JT15D-1A turbofans each rated at 2,200 lb st (998 kgp) for take-off. Fuel capacity 564 US gal (2 135 l).

Performance: Max speed (VMO) 275 knots (509 km/h) CAS; max mach (MMO), 0·70; cruising speed at average weight, 404 mph (650 km/h); initial rate of climb, 2,680 ft/min (13,62 m/sec); single-engined climb rate, 800 ft/min (4,07 m/sec); max certificated altitude, 41,000 ft (12 505 m); single-engine ceiling, 21,000 ft (6 405 m); balanced take-off field length, 3,370 ft (1 028 m); take-off distance to 35 ft (10,1 m), 2,750 ft (839 m); landing distance at max landing weight, 2,300 ft (702 m); range with six passengers, 45 min reserve, 1,535 mls (2 470 km).

Weights: Typical licensed empty weight, 6,464 lb (2 935 kg); max fuel capacity, 3,807 lb (1 728 kg); max take-off weight, 12,850 lb (5 834 kg); max landing weight, 11,350 lb (5 153 kg); max zero fuel weight, 8,400 lb (3 814 kg) or (optionally), 9,500 lb (4 313 kg).

Dimensions: Span, 47 ft 1 in (14,36 m); length, 43 ft 6 in (13,27 m); height, 14 ft 4 in (4,37 m); wheelbase, 15 ft 7 in (4,75 m); undercarriage track, 12 ft 7 in (3,84 m); wing dihedral, 4 deg constant; tailplane dihedral, 9 deg constant.

Accommodation: Maximum of eight seats including crew; cabin (pressure vessel) length, 17 ft 6 in (5,34 m); max height over aisle, 4 ft 4 in (1,32 m); width, 4 ft 11 in (1,5 m). Pressure differential 8·5 psi (0,60 kg/cm²). Baggage capacity 66 cu ft (1,87 m³)/1,000 lb (454 kg).

CESSNA CITATION II

TO COMPLEMENT the new Citation I (see previous entry), Cessna has announced that it will introduce, in February 1978, the stretched model Citation II, with accommodation for up

An artist's impression of the Cessna Citation II, to be introduced in 1978.

to 10 passengers with a crew of two. Retaining the same overall configuration and structure as the Citation I, the Model II features uprated engines, a lengthened fuselage and a wing of greater span and increased aspect ratio. Fuel capacity is increased by 150 US gal (568 l) and the lengthened fuselage results in greater clearance being achieved between the engine nacelles and the wing, thus reducing drag.

The result of these changes, as well as an increase in the cabin headroom and maximum accommodation, is to improve the speed, climb and range performance of the Citation II, compared with the Citation I. With a 2,000 ft (610 m) increase in certificated cruising height, to maintain an 8,000-ft (2 440-m) cabin equivalent at the new max altitude of 43,000 ft (13 115 m). The new JT15D-4 engines offer 14 per cent more take-off thrust and an increase of 19 per cent in the cruising thrust at altitude, with a slight improvement in SFC.

Orders for the Citation II are now being accepted by Cessna at a price in 1978 dollars of $1,295,000 (£804,350) including a complete Collins/Sperry IFR avionics package, complete all-weather provision, anti-skid equipment and crew training. Preliminary data follow:

Power Plant: Two Pratt & Whitney Canada JT15D-4 turbofans each rated at 2,500 lb st (1 135 kgp) for take-off. Fuel capacity, 714 US gal (2 702 l).
Performance: Max speed (VMO), 275 knots (509 km/h) CAS; max mach (MMO) 0·70; max cruising speed at average weight, 420 mph (676 km/h); initial rate of climb, 3,500 ft/min (17,8 m/sec); single-engined climb rate, 1,020 ft/min (5,2 m/sec); max certificated altitude, 43,000 ft (13 115 m); single-engined ceiling, 26,500 ft (8 083 m); balanced take-off field length, 2,900 ft (885 m); take-off distance to 35 ft (10,1 m), 2,400 ft (732 m); landing distance at max landing weight, 2,290 ft (698 m); range with 45 min reserve 2,080 mls (3 347 km).
Weights: Typical licensed empty weight, 6,960 lb (3 160 kg); max fuel, 4,820 lb (2 188 kg); max take-off weight, 12,500 lb (5 675 kg); max landing weight, 12,000 lb (5 448 kg); max zero fuel weight, 10,500 lb (4 767 kg) or (optionally) 11,000 lb (4 994 kg).
Dimensions: Span, 51 ft 8 in (15,76 m); length, 47 ft 3 in (14,41 m); height, 14 ft 11 in (4,55 m); wheelbase, 18 ft 2 in (5,54 m); undercarriage track, 17 ft 7 in (5,36 m); wing dihedral 4 deg constant, tailplane dihedral 9 deg constant.
Accommodation: Maximum of ten seats including crew; cabin (pressure vessel) length, 20 ft 11 in (6,38 m); height over aisle, 4 ft 9 in (1,45 m); width, 4 ft 11 in (1,5 m). Pressure differential, 8·7 psi (0,61 kg/cm²). Baggage capacity, 78 cu ft (2,21 m³).

CESSNA CITATION III

THIRD in the trio of new Citations just announced by Cessna (see previous entries), the Citation III is, despite its name, virtually a totally new design for a 10-15 seat long-range biz-jet, available in either US-transcontinental or intercontinental versions. Definition of the Citation III in its present form was completed only a few months ago, concluding more than three years of effort to add a "big brother" to the Citation range. This effort was initially directed towards an enlarged version of the straight-wing Citation, known as the Citation 600, and followed by the straight-wing three-engined Cessna 700 Citation III project at the end of 1974.

In the form now launched, and scheduled to appear in 1980, the Citation III is intended to compete with the Dassault-Breguet Falcon 50 (which is on the point of embarking on its flight test programme) and — if it goes ahead — the

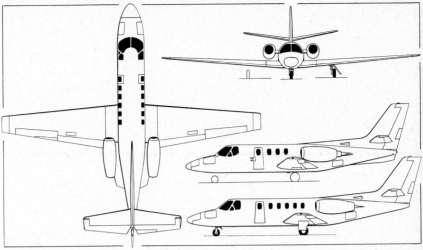

Three-view drawing of the Cessna Citation II, which has a lengthened fuselage and increased span, plus a side-view of the shorter Citation I.

Canadair Learstar 600. It has a new supercritical wing based on NASA research and a fuselage of greater cross section than the Citation I and II. After a lengthy search, Cessna has opted to use the Garrett AiResearch TFE 731 turbofan, which is proving to be one of the most popular of the power plants in this class for biz-jet use.

In its transcontinental version, the Citation III will seat up to 13 passengers, with a crew of two, although a more normal layout will be for nine. The intercontinental model has a reduced cabin length, eliminating two passenger seats,

to provide space for a supplementary fuel tank of 262 US gal (993 l) capacity; operating at increased gross weights, this version also has greater take-off distances.

Expected sales price of the Citation III will be $2·3m (£1·43m) at 1976 rates and deposits for delivery positions are now being expected. Preliminary data follow, 'T' indicating the transcontinental model and 'I' the intercontinental model.
Power Plant: Two Garrett AiResearch TFE 731-3 turbofans each rated at 3,700 lb st (1 680 kgp) for take-off. Fuel capacity (T), 990 US gal (3 746 l), (I), 1,250 US gal (4 738 l).
Performance: Max speed (VMO), 320 knots (593 km/h) CAS; max mach (MMO), 0·81; max cruising speed at average weight, 540 mph (869 km/h); initial rate of climb (T), 5,325 ft/min (27,1 m/sec), (I), 4,690 ft/min (23,8 m/sec); single-engine climb rate (T), 1,630 ft/min (8,3 m/sec), (I), 1,370 ft/min (6,9 m/sec); max certificated ceiling, 45,000 ft (13725 m); single-engine ceiling (T), 29,700 ft (9 060 m), (I), 27,000 ft (8 235 m); take-off FAA field-length (T), 3,990 ft (1 217 m), (I), 4,810 ft (1 467 m); landing distance at max landing weight, 3,400 ft (1 037 m); range with 45-min reserve (T), 2,760 mls (4 440 km), (I), 3,450 mls (5 550 km).

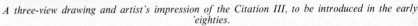

A three-view drawing and artist's impression of the Citation III, to be introduced in the early 'eighties.

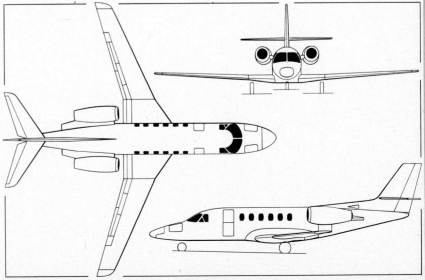

(Above) The Sabreliner 60 test aircraft fitted with early Raisbeck wing modifications and *(below)* an impression of the Sabreliner 80A.

Weights: Typical licensed empty weight (T), 9,441 lb (4 286 kg), (I), 9,621 lb (4 368 kg); max fuel load (T), 6,680 lb (3 033 kg), (I), 8,450 lb (3 836 kg); max take-off weight (T), 17,150 lb (7 786 kg), (I), 19,100 lb (8 671 kg); max landing weight, 15,700 lb (7 128 kg); max zero fuel weight, 13,000 lb (5 902 kg).

Dimensions: Span, 50 ft 7 in (15,43 m); length, 51 ft 7 in (15,73 m); height, 17 ft 0 in (5,19 m); wheelbase, 19 ft 9 in (6,02 m); undercarriage track, 13 ft 4 in (4,07 m); sweepback, 23 deg; aspect ratio, 9·1:1.

Accommodation: Flight crew of two and up to (T) 13 or (I) 11 passengers; cabin (pressure vessel) length (T), 23 ft 0 in (7,02 m), (I), 21 ft 2 in (6,46 m); max height over aisle, 5 ft 6 in (1,68 m); width, 5 ft 4 in (1,63 m). Pressure differential, 8·9 psi (0,63 kg/cm²). Baggage capacity, 80 cu ft (5,62 m³).

ROCKWELL SABRELINER
60A, 65A and 80A

ROCKWELL INTERNATIONAL has announced plans to introduce two new production models of the Sabreliner from 1978 onwards, and to make available aerodynamic and engine retrofit kits for three existing Sabreliner models. Both the new models, and the aerodynamic retrofit kits, feature modifications to the wing evolved by the Raisbeck Group of Seattle, in conjunction with Rockwell.

Known as the Raisbeck "Mark Five" system, the modifications comprise an increase in chord (at the leading edge) and span, with a fixed droop leading edge replacing the present leading edge slats; in addition, redesigned Fowler type flaps are introduced on the trailing edge from aileron to wing root, and small wing fences are added at about mid-span on each wing. The modifications have been under test on a Sabreliner 60 with successful results and a second modified aircraft is now at Seattle for detailed performance measurement.

Starting in the first quarter of 1978, Rockwell will replace its existing Sabreliner 75A with the new Sabreliner 80A incorporating these changes and retaining the same CF 700 engines. The wing modifications permit an increase of some 180 US gal (680 l) in fuel capacity which, combined with the structural changes (including strengthening of the undercarriage) puts up the gross weight by 1,920 lb (872 kg); nevertheless, the aerodynamic refinements allow the balanced field length to remain virtually unchanged without any increase in engine thrust.

Retrofit of the existing Sabreliner 75A to have the new wing and other changes will be possible, in a similar timescale, the modified aircraft also being known as Sabreliner 80A. Approximately a year after the introduction of the Model 80A, Rockwell will introduce a replacement for the existing Model 60 as the Sabreliner 65A, featuring the aerodynamic changes plus Garrett AiResearch TFE 731-3 turbofan in place of the Pratt & Whitney

JT12A-8 turbojets; this variant will also use the larger tailplane of the Model 75A/80A.

At the same time that the Sabreliner 65A appears, in the first quarter of 1979, AiResearch Aviation will offer existing Sabreliner 60 users a conversion package to introduce the aerodynamic changes and the new engines; these modified aircraft will be known as Sabreliner 65. In the second quarter of 1979,

similar modifications of Sabreliner 40s will be offered, to produce Sabreliner 45s.

Other retrofit options, to be offered by Raisbeck, will comprise the installation of the aerodynamic refinements only on the Sabreliner 40A, to produce the Sabreliner 40B from second quarter 1978, and the Sabreliner 60 to produce the Sabreliner 60A from the fourth quarter 1977.

Brief data for the new and converted models follow:

Sabreliner 60A
Power Plant: Two Pratt & Whitney JT12A-8 turbojets each rated at 3,300 lb st (1 498 kgp) for take-off. Fuel capacity, approx 1,055 US gal (3 993 l).
Performance: Balanced field length, sea level ISA, 4,600 ft (1 403 m); balanced field length, ISA + 27 deg F at 5,330 ft (1 626 m), 9,000 ft (2 745 m); max range with 45-min reserve, 2,400 mls (3 862 km).
Weights: Max take-off, 21,320 lb (9 680 kg).
Dimensions: Span, 50 ft 5 in (15,38 m); length, 46 ft 10¾ in (14,30 m); height, 15 ft 11¾ in (4,88 m); tailplane span, 17 ft 6½ in (5,35 m).

Sabreliner 65A
Power Plant: Two Garrett AiResearch TFE 731-3 turbofans each rated at 3,700 lb st (1 680 kgp) for take-off. Fuel capacity, approx 1,237 US gal (4 682 l).
Performance: Balanced field length, sea level ISA, 4,650 ft (1 418 m); balanced field length ISA + 27 deg F at 5,330 ft (1 626 m), 8,130 ft (2480 m); max range with 45-min reserve, 2,600 mls (4 183 km).
Weights: Max take-off, 22,420 lb (10 180 kg).
Dimensions: Span, 50 ft 5 in (15,38 m); length, 46 ft 10¾ in (14,30 m); height, 15 ft 11¾ in (4,88 m); tailplane span, 19 ft 4½ in (5,91 m).

Sabreliner 80A
Power Plant: Two General Electric CF700-2D-2 turbofans, each rated at 4,500 lb st (2 043 kgp) for take-off. Fuel capacity, approx 1,275 US gal (4 822 l).
Performance: Balanced field length, sea level ISA, 4,100 ft (1 250 m); balanced field length, ISA + 27 deg F at 5,330 ft (1 626 m), 7,600 ft (2 318 m); max range with 45-min reserve, 2,200 mls (3 540 km).
Weights: Max take-off, 23,570 lb (10 700 kg).
Dimensions: Span, 50 ft 5 in (15,38 m); length, 47 ft 2¼ in (14,39 m); height, 17 ft 3 in (5,26 m); tailplane span, 19 ft 4½ in (5,91 m).

(Below) A three-view drawing of the Sabreliner 65A and *(above left)* an artist's impression, showing the new wing and engine installation.

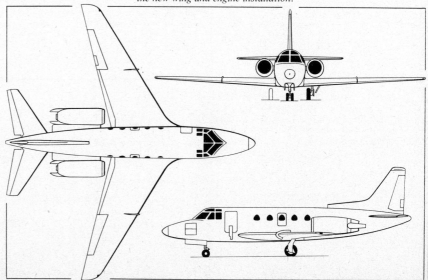